EDMUND BURKE

Memoirs of the

AMERICAN PHILOSOPHICAL SOCIETY

Held at Philadelphia

for Promoting Useful Knowledge

Volume 41

FIG. 1. EDMUND BURKE, *ae.* 45

Painted by James Barry in 1774, and reproduced with the permission of the owner, Professor Denis Gwynn of University college of Cork, and by the courtesy of the *Cork Examiner.*

EDMUND BURKE,
NEW YORK AGENT

with his letters to the New York Assembly

and

intimate correspondence

with

Charles O'Hara

1761-1776

ROSS J. S. HOFFMAN
Professor of History, Fordham University

THE AMERICAN PHILOSOPHICAL SOCIETY

INDEPENDENCE SQUARE • PHILADELPHIA

1956

To

WILLIAM EZRA LINGELBACH

with

affection and gratitude

Acknowledgments

I am most thankful to the late eighth Earl Fitzwilliam, the Fitzwilliam Estates Trustees, and Mr. J. P. Lamb, Sheffield City Librarian, for giving me permission to publish Burke's New York letter-book and to make free use of the Wentworth-Fitzwilliam Manuscripts. Mr. Lamb, in addition, has done numerous valuable favors for me that have helped much in preparing this volume. Similar kind acts of assistance have laid me under obligation to Miss Rosamund Meredith, of the Sheffield Central Library.

To Mr. Donal F. O'Hara I am grateful in the extreme for giving me permission to publish the letters of Edmund, William, and Richard Burke to Charles O'Hara, which have been a prized possession of his family at Annaghmore in County Sligo since they were received by his eighteenth-century ancestor. Mr. and Mrs. O'Hara also hospitably entertained me at Annaghmore in order that I might examine other historical documents pertaining to the Burke-O'Hara correspondence; and Mr. O'Hara generously provided me with a print of the portrait of Charles O'Hara, painted by Sir Joshua Reynolds in 1765, which hangs in the dining hall at Annaghmore.

To Dr. R. James Hayes, Director of the National Library of Ireland, I owe my discovery of Burke's letters to Charles O'Hara, the microfilm of them on which work could begin, and many other valuable favors.

It was Professor George R. Potter, of Sheffield University, who found Burke's New York letter-book among the Wentworth-Fitzwilliam Manuscripts and placed it in my hands. For this, and for the charming acts of hospitality shown by Professor and Mrs. Potter to my wife and to me during our visit to Sheffield, I am warmly grateful.

I owe much to Professor Thomas W. Copeland, of the University of Chicago, for giving excellent professional advice, lending me documents on microfilm, and even aiding me in editing the Burke-O'Hara letters.

vii

Professor F. W. Hilles, of Yale University, kindly allowed me to quote from an original Burke manuscript letter in his possession. The Rev. Aubrey Gwynn, S.J., of the University College of Dublin; Mr. Basil O'Connell, of Dublin; Mr. Gerard Slevin, of the Genealogical Office at Dublin Castle; Mr. Milton S. Smith, of Middletown, Connecticut, and Mr. Nicholas Varga, of Elizabeth, New Jersey, have supplied me with various points of information. Professor John J. Savage, of Fordham University, identified for me numerous recondite classical quotations in the Burke-O'Hara letters. Professor Denis Gwynn, of the University College of Cork, gave me not only good advice but the privilege of reproducing his prized portrait of Burke painted by James Barry in 1774. The following members of my historical seminar at Fordham University worked with me at the fundamental task of supplying dates for the Burke-O'Hara letters where no dates were given, and serially arranging and uniting both ends of that correspondence: Roger J. Bartman, Joseph Birri, James Bunce, Francis J. Dene, Herbert Gretsch, James Haggerty, Arthur Murphy, S.J., DeRoss O'Connor, S.J., Frederick G. Schmidt, Margaret Zack, and Albert C. Witterholt. To all I declare sincere gratitude.

I acknowledge with grateful appreciation the unnumbered courtesies shown to me by the library staffs of the New York Public Library, the New York State Library at Albany, the New York Historical Society, the Massachusetts Historical Society, the W. L. Clements Library at Ann Arbor, the New York Chamber of Commerce Library, the National Library of Ireland, the Royal Irish Academy, the British Museum, the Sheffield Central Library, and the Fordham University Library.

To the American Philosophical Society I am gratefully indebted for a generous grant made in 1949 to assist in carrying out the research.

To my former mentor, Professor William E. Lingelbach, now Librarian of the American Philosophical Society, and to Professor Robert L. Schuyler, of Columbia University, I express my thanks for excellent advice in the final stages of preparing the book for the press.

Finally, I must declare my gratitude to my superiors at Fordham University for granting me sabbatical leave to study in England and Ireland; and to my wife, who gave practical help and wise criticism from the beginning to the end.

Ross J. S. Hoffman

Rye, N.Y.

February, 1955

Contents

Illustrations

Introduction

WHEN Edmund Burke was only seventeen years old, he told his friend, Richard Shackleton: "We live in a world where everyone is on the catch, and the only way to be safe is to be silent—silent in any affair of consequence; and I think it would not be a bad rule for every man to keep within what he thinks of others, of himself, and of his own affairs." Burke made that rule a habit of his life, and it is one reason why he could achieve an immense fame without permitting the world to become very well acquainted with him. He wrote no memoirs and left no diaries. His published works yield little biographical information. He spoke and wrote copiously because, as Dr. Johnson said, his "stream of mind" was perpetual; but he was always full of discretion, cautious in uttering opinions of men, saying little about himself, and never allowing anyone to know what was no one's business but his own. Many of his letters have been published.[1] They are full of candor and strong emotion, but in them the veil rarely drops from an intensely reserved man. The most outspoken of men on the affairs of the public and on the greatest variety of literary, moral, esthetic, and historical topics, he was a clam about himself. Hence a curious obscurity has continued to surround him. The author of a recent volume of essays on Burke wrote in order to show "how much uncertainty" still hovers about him; and said that if his book contributed "little to our knowledge" it could at least provide "a rather full account of our ignorance." [2]

---

[1] Most of Burke's published letters for the period before 1776 are to be found in the following: Charles William, Earl Fitzwilliam and Sir Richard Bourke, eds., *The correspondence of the Right Honourable Edmund Burke*, 4 v., London, Rivington, 1844; Samuels, A.P.I. and A. W. Samuels, *Early life and writings of Edmund Burke*, Cambridge, the University Press, 1923; Prior, Sir James, *Memoir of the life and character of the Right Honourable Edmund Burke*, 2nd ed., London, Baldwin, Craddock, and Joy, 1826, and 5th ed., London, G. Bell, 1878. See also Copeland, T. W., Problems of Burke's letters, *Proc. Amer. Philos. Soc.* 94: 357-360, 1950.

[2] Copeland, T. W., *Our eminent friend, Edmund Burke*, 9, New Haven, Yale Univ. Press, 1949.

Another reason for the historical mist that has enveloped Burke is that his private papers, and those of his two most confidential political friends—the second Marquess of Rockingham and the fourth Earl Fitzwilliam—until recently were not available for study by historians and biographers. Burke's papers had indeed been carefully sifted more than a century ago by his literary executors, Dr. Walker King and William Elliot, and from those remains certain writings not published during his lifetime were selected for inclusion in the standard edition of his works.[3] The executors intended also to write an authoritative biography, but never did so; and the papers passed into the possession of the Fitzwilliam family. In 1844 the fifth Earl Fitzwilliam and Sir Richard Bourke brought out an edition of Burke's select correspondence, but they excluded from that work much more than they included. Hence only a small part of the large mass of Burke's papers ever found its way into print, and all of it continued to lie—bundled, unclassified, and disintegrating—in the muniment rooms of Wentworth Woodhouse, Yorkshire seat of the Fitzwilliam family. A few privileged scholars were permitted to explore in it some twenty-odd years ago, but a thorough inventory seems hardly to have been possible until 1949 when the papers of Burke, Rockingham, and Fitzwilliam were removed to the Sheffield Central Library and there made available to scholars.[4]

Among them was a folio-sized manuscript book in which Burke had kept drafts of the letters he wrote as agent for the General Assembly of the Province of New York from 1771 to 1775. Only a few of these letters had hitherto been known to be extant; for which reason, and also because Burke seemed never to have discussed his agency business with any persons other than his New York principals and those men with whom he transacted New York business at British government offices, little was known of his conduct as the assembly's agent. A few dry journal references to his appearances before the Board of Trade and Plantations; his defense of New York interests in the parliamentary proceedings on the Quebec Act of 1774;

---

[3] *Works of the Right Honourable Edmund Burke,* 16 v., London, Rivington, 1815-1827.

[4] See Wecter, Dixon, *Edmund Burke and his kinsmen,* Boulder, Univ. of Colo. Press, 1939; Magnus, Sir Philip, *Edmund Burke,* London, Murray, 1939; Hoffman, R. J. S., The Wentworth Papers of Burke, Rockingham, and Fitzwilliam, *Proc. Amer. Philos. Soc.* **94**: 352-356, 1950.

occasional colorless entries in the New York Assembly's journal, recording his election, authorizing his salary, noting that letters from him had been laid on the table for perusal by members; a brief parliamentary report of his presentation of the New York remonstrance to the House of Commons in May, 1775—that was about the sum of information available on this subject. Burke's New York letter-book, therefore, appeared as an interesting historical prize; and it also provided a solution to one of the minor mysteries of history.

Our earliest national historian, Jared Sparks, seems to have suspected that Burke's letters as New York agent existed but were purposefully concealed from the public eye. He wrote of this correspondence in 1832:

> Could the whole now be found and brought before the public, it would doubtless present in a full and luminous manner the views of that able statesman, on all the important topics agitated at that time between Great Britain and the Colonies, and prove a treasure of rare worth in the historical materials of this country. This correspondence has been studiously excluded from all the publications of his writings in England. Could it be ascertained what became of the papers of the old Colonial Assembly, before its career was terminated, the door of hope might not yet be closed against the possibility of these letters being discovered, but this is a subject on which the antiquaries of New York profess to be enveloped in as dark a mystery, as those of any other part of the globe.[5]

The suspicion of "studious" exclusion may have seemed further borne out when the Fitzwilliam-Bourke *Correspondence* was published in 1844. It contained no letter from the New York agent to his principals. Since the editors presumably had at their command the whole corpus of his papers, such a glaring omission appeared to indicate either that Burke had saved no drafts of his letters to New York or that these had been "studiously excluded," for it was most unlikely, if such letters did exist, that they would be regarded as having no historical value. The fact was, however, that the editors did not have Burke's New York letter-book in their hands until after they had finished their work. Among their editorial remains is a letter of May 15, 1844, from Sir Richard Bourke to his noble collaborator:

---

[5] *Life of Gouverneur Morris* 1: 51, Boston, Gray and Bowen, 1832.

I have looked thro' the letters of Burke to New York. If we had these Mss. in our hands at the time of the preparation of the first or second edition of the Correspondence I should have proposed the insertion of two or three letters which exhibit Burke's notions of the duty of an agent to the Colony which employs him and to the parent country to which he belongs, more particularly if the agent happens to be a member of Parliament. I might also have appended a note stating the fact of Burke's employment as part of his personal history, which, as well as I remember, is not referred to in any part of the Correspondence now in print.[6]

The oversight of the letter-book may perhaps be related to the circumstance that when it came to light in 1949, it was not among Burke's papers but with those of Lord Rockingham; although the latter, to be sure, were not less available to the editors of the *Correspondence* than were the Burke manuscripts. One further bit of evidence indicates that the editors were so far from "studiously excluding" Burke's New York letters as to have been indifferent or incurious about the subject of his connection with that colony. They had among their materials at least two letters from James Delancey, Burke's principal New York correspondent, who was leader of the dominant party in the Assembly and a prominent political figure in the province. Yet in publishing a letter from Burke to Rockingham, in which Delancey was referred to as a mutual friend, the editors appended a completely mistaken note of identification.[7]

Good internal evidence indicates that the drafts in the New York letter-book are not reserved copies of the official or "original" letters sent across the Atlantic, but are the dictated drafts from which the official letters were copied. They are in the hand of Burke's clerk and studded with abbreviations; they show occasional corrections, insertions, and excisions by Burke himself; so that as historical documents they are better than the official letters would be (if these could be found) because they tell some things that the lost documents could not tell. For example, there is in the library of the New York Historical Society a copy of Burke's letter of August 2, 1774, on the Quebec Act which was certified as a true copy of the original by H. Nicoll on the following February 16. One never could learn from it what the letter-book draft reveals, namely, that Burke wrote it on July 5, changed *June* to *July* in the second

---

[6] Wentworth-Fitzwilliam MSS.
[7] *Correspondence* 1: 430.

line, and dictated a few lines which on second thought he decided to strike out.

With the letter-book and a number of letters to Burke from correspondents in New York which were found among his papers at Sheffield, it became possible to write the history of his conduct as New York agent, thus adding a hitherto little known chapter to his political biography. In attempting this, I have thought it necessary to set the story within the general frame of Burke's whole conduct in American affairs before the outbreak of the American Revolution, because it turns out to be an integral part of that whole and in some important respects modifies prevalent concepts of Burke's American politics. I have therefore drawn upon many other documents in the Wentworth-Fitzwilliam Manuscripts, upon Burke's published writings, and a variety of other sources.

Among Burke's papers for the years before the American Revolution there appeared in 1949 a large number of letters from Charles O'Hara, a man whose name was not previously coupled with Burke's in any biography of the latter. So far as I have been able to notice, there are but two references to him in the whole of Burke's hitherto published letters, and these brief allusions were not accompanied by an identification of the man.[8] His letters showed that he was deeply interested in politics; that he was an Irishman and a member of the Irish House of Commons; that he was Burke's close, affectionate, and confidential friend, and stood in the same degree of intimacy with Burke's cousin, William Burke, his brother, Richard, and his father-in-law, Dr. Christopher Nugent. Between 1759 and 1776 he had written regularly and often to Burke and his family, and repeatedly visited them. From the nature of the letters, it was instantly evident that if Burke's end of the correspondence could be found there would be a rich new mine of fresh information about Burke's life. Very quickly Burke's letters to O'Hara were located for me by the diligent and industrious Director of the National Library of Ireland, Dr. R. James Hayes. The "find" was a hundred-odd letters, mostly from Edmund but some too from William, Richard, and Dr. Nugent—all from the Burke family "fireside." They are the property of Charles O'Hara's descendant, Mr. Donal F. O'Hara, proprietor of Annaghmore in County Sligo, who generously

---

[8] *Ibid.*, 75, 225.

granted a permission, long withheld by his family, to publish them. But in discovering these letters I was only learning what other scholars had previously found out. Mr. Arthur P. I. Samuels, more than forty years ago, knew of their existence and tried without success to get permission to study them. Mr. Valentine O'Hara in 1938 had made public mention of them in a book;[9] which probably caught the attention of the late Canon Robert Murray, a great collector of Burke's letters, who in 1947 obtained permission to copy those at Annaghmore. The transcripts are among Murray's literary remains in the Bodleian Library at Oxford.

The letters to Charles O'Hara are an astonishing mass of material of exactly the kind that previously had been missing from the records of Burke's life. Beginning in the summer of 1761 and continuing to January, 1776 (when O'Hara lay dying), they illuminate a period of that life for which sources of any kind have hitherto been very scarce, namely, the years just before and after he entered Parliament, when he was coming forward in public life against a strong current of prejudice and defamation and was, therefore, more silent than usual about himself and his affairs. The letters throw much new light also on Burke's part in the conciliation of America in 1766, on his always straitened financial circumstances, on his connection with Lord Rockingham, and his general behavior as a party man. But best of all, they open a record of the most intimate friendship he ever formed with a man not of his own family. For more than fifteen years Charles O'Hara was in the confidence of that tightly knit and clannish group, and when Burke wrote to him he cast off all his reserve and reticence. A quasi-avuncular figure, fourteen years older than Burke, O'Hara was often at the family fireside, and when he was not there some member of that assembly—usually Edmund, but sometimes Richard or the Doctor, and very often William— kept him posted on what was happening, in both the family and the state. And they told so much that Will Burke once said to him: "I don't know how, you are the repository of all our views, and hopes, and fears, of our passions and our feelings, of all that's good or evil in us, and a strange mass you hold; but whatever the contents may be, you are the casket, and valuable therefore, you will not dare deny."[10]

---

[9] *Anthony O'Hara, Knight of Malta*, 5, London, Secker-Martin, 1938.
[10] June 15, 1770.

O'Hara's social background and ancestral tradition were very different from that of the Burke family. He was the head— "the O'Hara"— of the O'Haras of Annaghmore, and master of a baronial estate of 28,000 acres spreading east and west of the Owenmore Valley in County Sligo. Of his family, the principal historian of Sligo has written: "The O'Haras are no aliens, but genuine scions of the old stock of Milesius, true sons of the soil; a family that produced saints and princes ages before Strongbow or Fitzempress set foot in Ireland."[11] They remained Catholic through the sixteenth century, but in the reign of James I "the O'Hara" of that generation, Kean, conformed to the Protestant Church of Ireland in order to avoid expropriation; so that afterwards the O'Haras were allied with the Anglo-Irish Protestant rulers of the country.[12] From Kean the great property was inherited first by his son, Adam, and then by a second son, Charles, who bequeathed it to a half-brother, Kean Oge O'Hara. The last married Eleanor Mathews of Tipperary and became, probably in 1715, the father of Charles, friend of Edmund Burke. Charles had two younger brothers, Kean, who became a playwright of some prominence, and Adam, of whom little appears to be known. Charles's letters tell nothing of his early education, but they show that he had a gentleman's smattering of the classics, that he knew some French, was an expert on horses, grasped political principles, saw through the shams and frauds of Irish politics in that age, and wished to do some good for his poor country if only that were possible. He possessed a charming sense of humor and a cultivated man's understanding of the world. His heart was warm, his head was witty, and his soul was full of honor and virtue. He wrote English in an Irish style, and his letters please most when read aloud by someone with a little brogue. In 1740 he was high sheriff of his county, and again in 1756. In 1742 he married Lady Mary Carmichael, a daughter of the Earl of Hyndford and a sister of William Carmichael, who became the Protestant Bishop of Dublin. Lady Mary bore her husband two sons and a daughter, Charles, William, and Mary, all of whom became warm friends of all the Burkes.

---

[11] O'Rorke, T., *History, antiquities, and present state of the parishes of Ballysadare and Kilwarnet in the county of Sligo, with notices of the O'Haras, the Coopers, the Percevals and other local families*, 364, Dublin, J. Duffy, 1878.

[12] O'Rorke, T., *History of Sligo* 2: 67-68, Dublin, J. Duffy, 1890.

If we are to rely on the gossip of the county, Charles, son of Kean Oge, won his wife and a fine fortune by skill and grace in horsemanship. The story runs that, being in England and after the hounds, Mr. O'Hara displayed such dash and gallantry in the presence of the Queen and the ladies of the Court . . . that one of the maids of honour, a Scotch lady, lost no time in offering him her hand and fortune. . . . Whether this story be true or apocryphal, and a hundred others like it that are told of him, and that turn, for the most part, on his wonderful horses, Arpinus and Sejanus, with their silvery shoes; his Irish servant, Johnny Cuffe, who was more than a match for all the English turfites and jockeys; his fabulous feats of horsemanship, such as the jump from the precipice of Knocknashee; and his successes but, still more, his losses by gambling; they at all events show the manner of man this Charles was in the minds of admiring neighbours.[13]

All this tradition is perfectly consistent with the character of the middle-aged gentleman whom we meet in his letters to Burke; and something of it lurks perhaps in the portrait of him by Sir Joshua Reynolds that hangs today in the dining hall at Annaghmore.

O'Hara entered the Irish House of Commons in 1761, the year Burke went back to his native country as a companion of studies and general political utility man for William Gerard Hamilton, Chief Secretary to the Lord Lieutenant. By this time O'Hara and Burke had become fast friends. O'Hara was a good friend too of Burke's chief, Hamilton, and continued the same even after the famous breach between those men. His letters show that he had a wide acquaintance among influential political people in England as well as Ireland, and suggest that by this means he helped Burke to get his start in British politics as private secretary to the First Lord of the Treasury, Lord Rockingham, in 1765. O'Hara was on terms of most intimate friendship with General Henry S. Conway, who became Secretary of State for the Southern Department in the Rockingham administration and made Will Burke his under-secretary. It is likely too that O'Hara had some influence with the powerful Cavendish family, and that he was a friend of William Fitzherbert, who sponsored both Burkes for public employment in 1765.

O'Hara watched with absorbing interest the British political scene and observed very astutely the crisis that steadily gener-

---

[13] O'Rorke, *History, antiquities* etc., 399.

ated in it as the years moved on to 1775; but he never sought
to play a part in British politics. Nothing in England concerned
him more than that his dear friends, Edmund and Will, should
get ahead in the world as rapidly as possible; and in the early
years of their careers he was ready with advice to both on how
to do this. But this was very pragmatic advice: he wished to
see them ascending from one good "place" to another, and
was unhappy when they went into opposition against the ministry. Soon Edmund was "expostulating" with him on some of
his ideas, and explaining the high and righteous principles of
the Rockingham party, which O'Hara feared would never lead
his impecunious friends to valuable offices and emoluments.
His politics were colored and conditioned inevitably by his
Irish political habitat, where the level of conduct among public
men could hardly have been lower. It was so easy for him to
see that, in Ireland, opposition to administration was usually
only an invitation to be bought; that support was often given
only for the purpose of embarrassing an administration that was
pretending to favor measures it really wished to have defeated;
that almost nothing was quite what it appeared to be. "Of all
the countries upon earth," O'Hara reflected, " 'tis hardest to
decide upon one's party in this. Men there are none to follow,
measures few. People are not enough blended together for a
common cause. A scheme for popularity is nonsense in Ireland;
for the people don't know their own interest. To feed their
faction is destruction to them."[14] O'Hara grew more and more
in admiration of the conduct of the Rockingham party in
England, but no such body could possibly exist in the Ireland
of his day. Hence a support of Dublin Castle, for what it had
to offer in return, was the sensible politician's best course.
O'Hara took that course and submitted with cynicism and
disgust (and for a government job which land-poor necessities
drove him to seek!) to a system that was in principle the exact
negation of the political ideals of Burke and the Rockingham
Whigs. Nor did Burke rebuke his friend for this conduct; for
he had himself become so disgusted with all things civil and
political in Ireland that he grew incapable of expecting anything virtuous in the narrow and oppressive oligarchy that
ruled the country of his birth.

In spite of the differing ways these two men took in public

---

[14] Feb. 7, 1767.

life, they saw eye to eye on every great political question of the age when the "king's friends" mismanaged two kingdoms and at length lost an empire in North America. Over the years O'Hara's admiration for the courage and steadiness of Burke's public conduct grew ever greater, and in the last year of his life he told him:

> Perhaps the rest of your friends are less acquainted with your real character than I am. Do they know that of all the busy men upon earth, you the busiest have the least ambition? Do they know that of all the opponents Government has, you are perhaps the only man who would not do evil that good may come of it? Do they know upon the whole that you are a much better man to bring honour and credit to a party than to conduct its intrigues? And yet these are the ruling features of your character.[15]

Those who are familiar with Burke's previously published letters and have admired many of them for the wonderful literary compositions that they are may be a little surprised or puzzled by many of his letters to Charles O'Hara, which certainly are not very polished pieces. The truth is that when Burke was writing what *he* considered to be an important letter or paper, pamphlet or book, he was most scrupulous, careful, and painstaking. His extant manuscripts show that he prepared rough drafts, then revised, corrected, amplified or abridged, polished and refined, until he was satisfied that he had said exactly what he meant with a measured degree of force. When he did not do that, when he dashed the thing right off, this literary artist whom John Morley held to be the greatest since Milton, could write very indifferent prose. When we meet him in his letters to Charles O'Hara, it is almost as if a sort of "candid camera" had sought him out in his nightcap and at his fireside. He is in his most natural and unaffected manner, without any little pretenses or affectations, weighing no words and practising no studied arts, but scrawling away in a hot haste or a relaxed ease to his most dear friend.

In my edition of Burke's correspondence with O'Hara I have omitted none of his letters that are extant, but of O'Hara's I have included only those which are either responsive to specific Burke letters or contain some historical value of their own. As a result, less than half of O'Hara's letters in the Wentworth-Fitzwilliam Manuscripts are reproduced in this volume.

---

[15] June 18, 1775.

There are a few of William Burke's and Dr. Nugent's letters to O'Hara among the Annaghmore Manuscripts which I decided to exclude as having insufficient interest. The reader will find that I have sown into the correspondence some letters to and from John Ridge, another intimate friend of the Burkes who became very close to O'Hara. He was a Dublin attorney. When he visited the Burkes during 1773-1774, he made one of that famous group of conversational gentlemen who met at St. James's Coffee House and were memoralized by Goldsmith in *Retaliation*. The Ridge-Edmund Burke letters are from the Wentworth-Fitzwilliam Manuscripts; the few from Will Burke to Ridge are in the Annaghmore collection.

Part I

EDMUND BURKE, NEW YORK AGENT

I. Colonial Agents and Agencies.

THE General Assembly of the Province of New York, in December, 1770, received official notification of the death of Robert Charles, who for fourteen years had served that body as agent at the Court of Great Britain. Promptly a successor was elected: Edmund Burke, a prominent member of the parliamentary opposition to King George III's ministers.

The choice of Burke was extraordinary because the American colonies had not usually employed as agents men who were totally disconnected from the royal administration. Most colonial agents during the few preceding decades had tended, in fact, to lose something of the character of spokesmen for the colonies that employed them and to take on the character of "placemen" attached to the Board of Trade and Plantations, which superintended colonial governments. Or at least it may be said that prolonged residence in England and a natural ambition to acquire place and influence affected their outlook by making them more "imperial" than "colonial." Some agents were never in their lives in the colonies, but were hired to transact colonial business because they already knew the ropes of administration in England. There was, for example, Richard ("Omniscient") Jackson, who in 1770 served as agent for both Pennsylvania and Connecticut; he was a member of Parliament and solicitor to the Board of Trade; for years he had been a well-known servant of the crown. Charles Garth, agent for Maryland and South Carolina, also was in Parliament; he sided with the crown when the American war broke out and became an excise commissioner in England in 1780. Edward Montagu, agent for both the Virginia Assembly and the King of Poland, was a member of Parliament and a master in chancery. Some time before 1760 New York's Robert Charles (during his agency) had been a lottery commissioner.[1]

---

[1] For what is known of Robert Charles see Lilly, E. P., *The colonial agents of New York and New Jersey*, Washington, Catholic Univ. Dissertation, 1936. On colonial agents and agencies: Appleton, Marguerite, The agents of the New England colonies in the revolutionary period, *New Eng. Quart.* **6**: 371-387, 1933: Bond, Beverly, The colonial agent as a popular representative, *Pol. Sci. Quart.* **35**: 372-392, 1930; Burns, James J., *The colonial agents of New England*, Washington, Catholic Univ. dissertation, 1935; Freiberg, Malcolm, William Bollan,

Some light is shed on the forces that could influence the choice of an agent by a little negotiation that took place in 1760-1761 between acting Governor Cadwallader Colden of New York and John Pownall, secretary of the Board of Trade. The former wished to be appointed governor and solicited the latter's influence for obtaining the commission. In return for this favor Dr. Colden was willing to sponsor the candidacy of Pownall for the New York agency, a job worth 500 pounds per annum. The Assembly, Colden said, was "not well satisfied with their agent Mr. Charles." So he proposed: "I shall be glad to know your inclination as to accepting of the trouble of the Agency for this Province. If it suit your inclinations it will give me the greatest pleasure to have you in the confidence of the people of this Province, as far as to be of use to yourself as well as to them."[2] Pownall sensed an impropriety in his becoming an agent whose principal duty would be to transact business with the government office that he himself administered, but he was not unwilling to suggest a candidate for the post.[3] He recommended a man who was "very desirous of serving the province in that station . . . and in point of ability and connection with persons in power his services would far exceed any poor endeavours or efforts of mine, or indeed of any other man I know." Pownall's man was Thomas Burke, a gentleman of "unwearied industry and application in whatever may contribute to the public good and felicity of mankind, a great character in the world of letters as the author of many ingenious essays on the best subjects, and who has particularly made the state and interests of our colonies his study."[4]

agent of Massachusetts, *More Books, Bull. of Boston Pub. Lib.* **23:** 43-54, 90-100, 135-146, 168-182, 212-220, 1948; Penson, Lillian M., *The colonial agents in the British West Indies,* London, Univ. of London Press, 1924; Tanner, E. P., Colonial agencies in England during the eighteenth century, *Pol. Sci. Quart.* **26:** 22-48, 1901; Van Doren, Carl, *Letters and papers of Benjamin Franklin and Richard Jackson,* Philadelphia, *Mem. Amer. Philos. Soc.* **24,** 1947; Wolff, Mabel W., *The colonial agency of Pennsylvania, 1712-1757,* Philadelphia, privately printed Bryn Mawr College dissertation, 1933.

[2] Colden to Pownall, Nov. 11, 1760. *Colden Letter Books* **1:** 38. *Collections of the New-York Historical Society for 1876.*

[3] It would probably have been contrary to Board of Trade regulations for Pownall to accept the agency. Clarke, M. P., The Board of Trade at work, *Amer. Hist. Rev.* **17:** 17-43, 1911.

[4] *Colden Papers* **5:** 307-308, *Coll. of N.Y. Hist. Soc. for 1922.* The date of the letter is given as Jan. 10, 1760, but the contents show the year was 1761. It has been suggested that Pownall's Thomas Burke was really Edmund Burke. See Stebbins, Calvin, Edmund Burke, his services as agent to the province of

Colden agreed to sponsor the election of this man as agent, but presently found that he could not succeed. The choice rested exclusively with the assembly, which voted the agent's salary, and in the newly chosen assembly of 1761 Colden lacked a controlling influence. A major obstacle, he told Pownall, was that Thomas Burke was "not so much as known by name to any person in this place."[5] Colden hoped that the "character" Pownall had given this man and his being Pownall's friend would be sufficient to remove all obstacles to his election, but in the end the acting Governor could not overcome the unwillingness of the assemblymen to have another London placeman foisted upon them as their agent. When Pownall understood the circumstances, he told Colden that Thomas Burke had been suggested only because it had been expected that there would be a vacancy, "which you, in your letter to me, supposed would happen." But since no vacancy had occurred, Pownall now thought that Robert Charles was "much better qualified to serve the Province of New York in that character than any other man."[6] Charles held his place through the next decade.

An interesting description of colonial agents in 1770 was written by a certain "A. S." in a letter from London, dated April 10, which was published in the *New York Journal*.[7] The writer believed "every Well-wisher to America" would be obliged to have the "plain facts," and left it "to the Clear-sighted Americans themselves to make the proper Comments thereon." Richard Cumberland, agent for Nova Scotia, was "a Placeman, holding posts under the Government at Pleasure, to the Amount of near eighteen hundred Pounds per Annum, some of which may be seen in the Court Calendar." William Bollan, agent for the Massachusetts Council, had "a monstrous and most unreasonable Account unsettled with his Constituents." He had served his employers so ill that they were holding up his salary. But Dennys de Berdt, agent for the Massachusetts Assembly, had a more creditable record; he was "a North American Merchant, who has suffered much in his commercial Concerns by adhering strictly to the true political interests of

---

New York, *Proc. Amer. Antiquar. Soc.* (n.s.) **9:** 89-101, 1903. But the fact that Pownall was an accurate and methodical man, and well acquainted with Edmund Burke, suggests that there was no mistake. Nothing among Burke's papers suggests his seeking the New York agency in 1761.

[5] *Colden Letter Books* **1:** 80-82.
[6] *Colden Papers* **6:** 83.
[7] June 7, 1770.

America, and has always discharged his Duty as an honest Man." Rhode Island's agent, Joseph Sherwood, was praised as "an honest Quaker—he refused his Assent to America's being taxed by the B——sh P——t, when the American Agents were applied to by the GENTLE SHEPHERD [George Grenville] to obtain their Approbation of the American Stamp-Act." Richard Jackson, agent for Pennsylvania and Connecticut, "was Private Secretary to George Grenville at the Time of passing the American Stamp-Act, worth about 2000 £ per Annum, in the great constitutional Contest between the Free-holders of England and an arbitrary Ministry, in the Case of the Middlesex Election in 1769 he voted for Colonel Luttrell, an avowed Ministerial Tool—he also seems inclinable still to become a dependent Placeman, by being a Candidate for the solicitorship to the Board of Trade." Jackson was so much the mere instrument of ministry that Connecticut had sent over an extraordinary agent, Dr. William Samuel Johnson, who was "a sensible and well-meaning American." Pennsylvania had done the same by sending Dr. Benjamin Franklin, who, how-ever, was "Deputy Post-Master in America during Pleasure," and his son, William, was Governor of New Jersey, "appointed during the Administration of LORD BUTE." But in spite of Franklin's "situation and Connections" it had to be "con-fessed he has on many occasions strenuously exerted himself in defence of the Rights of the British Colonies." Mr. Wilmot, agent for New Jersey, was "Private Secretary to the Lord Chan-cellor." Mr. Abercrombie, agent for the Virginia Council, had a pension of 200 pounds a year on the Virginia establish-ment; and Mr. Montagu, Virginia's assembly agent, was a master in chancery who had committed the offense of voting "for Colonel Luttrell, with the successful Minority, in the Middlesex Election in 1769." Charles Garth was described as "a concealed Placeman, by holding the Post of Warden of the Fleet-Prison during Pleasure, in the name of Jyles, the annual salary 200 £ and the perquisites supposed to be about 600 £ per Annum more." As for New York's agent, Robert Charles, he had been "appointed Comptroller of the Post-Office by George Grenville, but turned out by Lord Rockingham."

Some colonies had but one agent; others had two, each branch of the legislature employing its own man. Where there was only one agent, he was usually responsible to the colony as a corporate whole. But two agents did not always signify one for the assembly and the other for the council; sometimes this circumstance meant rather that the regular agent had lost his usefulness, or the confidence of his employers who instead of discharging him sent over or hired an additional extraordinary agent from whom more attentive and conscientious service was expected. Some agents made a sort of profession of their activity, gathering as many agencies as they could. In 1755, for example, John Sharpe, a London attorney, was agent for Jamaica, Barbados, Antigua, St. Christopher's, and Nevis; he declined an invitation to become agent for the Massachusetts council only because there were questions at dispute between the New England and West Indian colonies.[8]

The principal duties of colonial agents carried them frequently to the Board of Trade (which Burke usually called the Plantations Office) to explain and defend the enactments of colonial legislatures. All such measures were sent to that office for study and consideration before being recommended to the king in privy council for approval or disallowance. Occasionally an agent had business with the Treasury or the Admiralty, and sometimes even approached a secretary of state. An agent who was a member of Parliament might look out for the interests of his employers in imperial legislation: Burke did that, and without any instruction from New York, in the passage of the Quebec Act of 1774. It was not uncommon for agents to appear before parliamentary committees to give information on matters pertinent to preparing bills affecting the colonies. The agents were consulted by Grenville in 1764 when the Stamp Act was being prepared in the Treasury. A leading historian of the British Empire before the American Revolution has written that the influence of the agents was "so great, taken as a body, that no decision of importance affecting the colonies was ever arrived at without the most careful consideration of their informal testimony and arguments as well as their formal memorials and petitions."[9]

But their ability to serve their employers well was to a great extent dependent on the measure of influence and confidence they were able to establish in government circles, and this in turn was dependent largely on their disposition to accommodate themselves to high official points of view. Hence, the agent's facility in his business transactions was likely to be in inverse ratio to his careful concern for the local interests of those who

---

[8] Freiberg, *loc. cit.*, 141.

[9] Gipson, Lawrence H., *The British Empire in North America before the American Revolution* 1: 17, Caldwell, Caxton, 1936.

hired him. The best agent was he who combined a watchful care for the interests of his employers with a good deal of personal influence in government offices. Even a man connected with parliamentary opposition could extract favors from politicians in office who might hope to attach him by laying him under obligations. Burke was in this position.

It was not unnatural that the Board of Trade should attempt to place colonial agents under some degree of regulation. In order to be certain that properly authorized persons were being dealt with, the Board had ruled as early as 1705 that all persons appearing as agents for any of the plantations should register their credentials.[10] Although irregular agent-board relations continued, this registration order was often reaffirmed. A next step was to try to fix a uniform principle and procedure for colonial appointment of agents, and the official preference was that an agent should be the representative of the whole colonial body politic—of assembly, council, and governor, with each having a voice in his election—instead of being commissioned solely by the elective branch of the legislature. The latter was the status of several agents, notably of New York's, and that colony's assembly was jealous of its exclusive right of appointment. Under its rule the agent's salary was paid by annual appropriation and on an order signed by the speaker. Dr. Colden, as acting governor from 1760 to 1765, disliked this arrangement and wished to possess some part in the choice of the agent or some authority over him, since an agent who owed nothing to the governor might cause him some embarrassment with authorities in England. On one occasion Colden thought it "his duty" to inform the Board of Trade that Robert Charles had no authority to act for the government of New York: it was "no wonder" that the lords commissioners of trade and plantations "should not be well informed of His Majesty's interest in this Province, while they trusted to the information of a person no wise instructed thereon, or authorized by this Government."[11] But the assembly, though far from being satisfied with Charles's services in the ensuing critical years, remained unwilling to share its authority over him with the executive administration. And there was nothing Colden or any other governor could do to change the status of the agent

---

[10] Lilly, *op. cit.*, 15.

[11] O'Callaghan, E. B., ed., *Documents relative to the colonial history of the state of New York* 7: 607, Albany, Weed, Parsons & Co., 1853-1857. (Cited hereafter as *N. Y. documents*.)

because the agent's salary was authorized by an act which provided for all other officers of government. No single appropriation could be vetoed by the governor without stopping the other salaries.

The Board of Trade was unable to enforce its preferred uniformity in the choice of agents because it lacked authority. During the period from 1748 to 1761, when the Earl of Halifax presided over it, the board had a real direction over colonial affairs and the control of colonial patronage; but afterwards, although its superintending procedures underwent little change, it became only a board of report and recommendation to the Privy Council and the secretary of state for the southern department. Then in 1768 a very important change occurred. A secretary of state for the colonies was created and the Earl of Hillsborough was named to the office. He was given the colonial patronage and the Board of Trade became essentially his advisory council. He fused with his very high office the lower post of first lord commissioner of trade and plantations, attended and presided at the meetings of the board, and made it very much his own instrument.[12] He was energetic, conscientious, and officious, so that in his administration ministerial authority was united with the Board of Trade's rather bureaucratic spirit and a more forceful effort was made to eliminate irregularities. Hillsborough meant to enforce upon the colonies the officially preferred method of choosing agents. To Governor Harry Moore of New York he sent the following command on November 15, 1768:

The King having observed that the Assembly of New York has for some time fallen into a very irregular method of appointing an Agent to solicit the affairs of the Colony in England, & His Majesty being apprehensive that this Deviation from the mode of appointing an Agent approved of in other Colonies, which has usually been an act of Governor, Council & Assembly, especially passed for that purpose, may in future create difficulty, embarrassment and disappointment in transacting the affairs of New York. . . . I have His Majesty's commands . . . to desire you will recommend it to the Assembly as a Matter in which their interest is concerned. . . . I would not be understood by what I have said concerning the appointment of an Agent to insinuate disapprobation of Mr. Charles, who appears to have executed his Duty with

---

[12] Basye, Arthur H., *The lords commissioners of trade and plantations, 1748-1782*, 170-171, New Haven, Yale Univ. Press, 1925.

the utmost regard to and zeal for the Interest of the Colony, and with every mark of proper respect and deference to Government.[13]

When this command was sent, Anglo-American relations were in the crisis generated by the Townshend Acts of the previous year and British ministers were preparing stern measures against Massachusetts. When it was received, the New York Assembly was in such indignant reaction against Parliament that the Governor dissolved it for misconduct and ordered new elections. At the opening of the new assembly on April 4, 1769, Governor Moore presented Hillsborough's request, but met with a flat refusal from the assemblymen to alter their mode of electing their agent. The question was important and the full text of the refusal was made public.[14] Hillsborough was to persist in this effort, as in all other attempts to spin out a system of uniformity and heightened royal authority in the colonies. Two years later he would enforce his rule against Benjamin Franklin by refusing to recognize him as agent for the Massachusetts Assembly because the governor and council of that colony had no voice in choosing him.[15] But that rule was never imposed upon New York, and although Burke as the assembly's agent became apprehensive that it would embarrass him at the Board of Trade, it seems never to have done so. Had the assembly adopted the Hillsborough rule before Burke was chosen agent, he never would have accepted the office; had it been adopted afterwards, he would have resigned.

Why did he accept the agency? Why did he lay himself under the necessity of transacting business with a government office headed by a man whose politics were opposed directly to his own, and whose administration of American affairs he most severely criticized? And what had Burke to do with New York? To answer these questions it may be well to consider first the sort of public man he was and the nature of his American politics.

---

[13] N. Y. documents 8: 108.

[14] New York Gazette, April 24, 1769.

[15] Franklin wrote to Thomas Cushing, Feb. 5, 1771, that Hillsborough "insists that no agent ought to be received or attended to, by government here, who is not appointed by an act of the General Court, to which the Governor has given his assent. This doctrine, if he could establish it, would in a manner give to his Lordship the power of appointing, or at least negativing any choice of the House of Representatives . . . every agent that valued his post must consider himself as holding it by the favour of his Lordship, and of course too much obliged to him to oppose his measures, however contrary to the interest of the province." Smyth, Albert H., Writings of Benjamin Franklin 5: 294, N.Y., Macmillan, 1905-1907.

II. Burke and Colonial America

EDMUND BURKE was born in Dublin in 1729, and after taking a degree from Trinity College he went to England in 1750 to study law at the Middle Temple. But soon he gave up the ambition for a career at the bar, and turned to the study of literature and political economy, earning his living by writing for the book-sellers. In 1757 he confided to a friend in Ireland that his life had been "chequered with various designs; sometimes in London; sometimes in remote parts of the country; sometimes in France, and shortly, please God, to be in America."[1] He did not go to America, but the temptation persisted, or at least recurred, for to another Irish friend (in County Sligo) he wrote in 1761: "When you look at the Atlantic Ocean do you think of America? In our old fabulous history I think I have read that the Prophet Moses advised his ancient Scots to go as far westward as possible; is this good advice to their posterity?"[2]

The idea of going to America was perhaps related to the circumstance that Burke, his brother, Richard, and his cousin, William Burke, in the late 1750's got into the political entourage of George Montagu Dunk, second Earl of Halifax, an influential politician who was allied with Henry Fox and headed the Board of Trade. It is not unlikely that Halifax and his fellow commissioners were interested in a work that appeared in the bookshops in 1757 under the title, *An Account of European Settlements in America*. This was known generally to be the product of Edmund's or William Burke's pen, or the joint work of both; and it showed that these men were well informed about the great transatlantic world in which the British and French empires were struggling for supremacy.[3] In 1759 Burke became private secretary to William Gerard Hamilton, one of the lords commissioners of trade; and about

---

[1] Fitzwilliam, Earl, and Sir Richard Bourke, eds., *The correspondence of the Right Honourable Edmund Burke* 1: 30, London, Rivington, 1844. (Cited hereafter as *Correspondence*.)

[2] Annaghmore MSS, to Charles O'Hara, July 10, 1761.

[3] William wrote the book and Edmund revised it. Tinker, C. B., *The letters of James Boswell* 2: 285, Oxford, Clarendon Press, 1924.

the same time Richard and William Burke obtained employment in the administration of the West Indies.[4]

In the ministerial changes that followed the succession of King George III to the throne, Halifax in 1761 left the Board of Trade and became Lord lieutenant of Ireland. John Pownall, the board's secretary, took leave of absence from that post to accompany his old chief; and William Gerard Hamilton was named chief secretary to the Lord lieutenant. Burke accompanied Hamilton and spent the Irish parliamentary winter of 1761-1762 residing in Dublin Castle as an unofficial member of the royal administration. Juridically a separate kingdom rather than a colony or plantation within the British Empire, Ireland was nevertheless a British dependency. The main business of an Irish viceroy and chief secretary was to manage the Parliament of Ireland by conciliating an oligarchy of native politicians, to maintain the domination of English interests, and to hold the kingdom in strict subordination to Great Britain. The problems of the government of Ireland were not dissimilar to those which royal governors encountered in America. Dublin Castle was a good school in which to learn the evils of a political system formed by a native assembly and an executive administration created by powers far removed from the local scene. Burke was an apt pupil in this school.

From the spring of 1762 to the fall of 1763 Burke was back in England with Hamilton.[5] He watched all public events with close attention, recording them in the *Annual Register* which he had edited since its first number for 1758.[6] The main event of this period was the negotiation and ratification of the Treaty of Paris whereby the Seven Years War was ended. That settlement, which put French Canada under the British crown and handed back British-conquered French West India islands to the enemy, was more popular in North America than in England. Burke disliked it because it frustrated the hopes and

---

[4] Wecter, Dixon, *Edmund Burke and his Kinsmen*, 19, 52, Boulder, Univ. of Col. Studies, 1939.

[5] At that time the leading crown officials rarely were in the country when the Irish Parliament, which met biennially, was not in session.

[6] How long Burke continued to edit the *Annual Register* and write historical articles in it, is not certainly known, but students of the subject are agreed that he carried the work from 1758 at least through the 1766 number. See Copeland, T. W., *Our eminent friend, Edmund Burke*, 92-117, New Haven, Yale Univ. Press, 1949; also, Burke and Dodsley's Annual Register, *Pub. Mod. Lang. Assn.* 54: 223-245, 1939.

interests of Richard and William; but when the latter entered
the service of Henry Fox, who bribed and browbeat Parliament
to approve the peace, Edmund was not displeased. Will Burke's
conduct was motivated by the expectant hope of obtaining the
governorship of Grenada (which he did not get) and Edmund
naturally wished for his success. At this time these men were
more interested in getting on in the world than in the wisdom
or unwisdom of public measures over which they could not
exert the slightest influence. They "belonged" to Fox and
Halifax, leading members of the ministry headed by the unpopular royal "favorite," Lord Bute, and therefore were attached loosely to the administration. Halifax had become a
secretary of state in 1762 and Burke greatly admired him as
one whose character was "as high as ever almost any man's
was in this country, for unspotted honour, and for equal love
and confidence of all parties."[7]

In April, 1763, Bute gave way to George Grenville as first
lord of the Treasury. Fox lost power, but Halifax continued
as secretary of state in an administration that was presently
joined by the Duke of Bedford and his friends. The Grenville-
Bedford alliance was to rule the state until the summer of
1765. The Earl of Northumberland, a Bute man, was named
viceroy of Ireland at the same time Grenville became head of
the ministry, and William Gerard Hamilton was continued
as chief secretary, so that Burke returned to Ireland that fall
for another parliamentary winter in Dublin.

But in the spring of 1764 Hamilton was removed from
office, and so ended Burke's connection with Dublin Castle,
save for a pension that Hamilton had obtained for him on the
Irish establishment; nor did that long continue. Burke had
for some time been chafing under the servitude Hamilton imposed on him, and presently they came to a breach.[8] It probably was in anticipation of leaving Hamilton that Burke
began to look about for other employment. His brother had
been appointed collector of customs at Grenada, and Burke
tried to become agent for that colony.[9] He did not succeed,

[7] Annaghmore MSS, to Charles O'Hara, Nov. 23, 1762.

[8] For Burke-Hamilton relations, see Copeland, T. W., Burke's first patron,
History Today **6**: 394-399, 1952.

[9] "The conquered islands which compose General Melville's Government in
all likelihood must soon think of appointing an Agent for managing their
affairs here, upon the same footing of other colonies. . . . I am desirous of serving them as their Agent; if I obtain that honour I shall endeavour to act for

but early in February, 1765, he angrily broke with Hamilton and even gave up the Irish pension. Followed then a short-lived political connection with Charles Townshend, a rising brilliant public figure destined to leave his mark in the history of Anglo-American relations. How Burke linked himself with Townshend and exactly in what way, it is impossible to state; but it is certain that the connection had been established by May, when Townshend became Paymaster.[10] Nine years later Burke would say of Townshend that he could not remember him without "some degree of sensibility"; that he was "the delight and ornament" of the House of Commons and "the charm of every private society which he honoured with his presence."[11] In the early summer of 1765, when the King changed his ministers and brought back to office the "High Whigs" with Lord Rockingham as first lord of the Treasury, Burke was on fire for Townshend to accept one of the first places. He told Charles O'Hara that Townshend might have been secretary of state or chancellor of the exchequer with the leadership of the House of Commons but was held back by the perverse influence of his elder brother. This refusal drew "tears of indignation and grief" from Burke.[12]

Employment with Rockingham, 1765

Precisely what Burke's politics were at this time is not easy to say. He had been on the fringe of the outgoing administration, yet his new patron, Townshend, while refusing a leading place, remained in the Pay Office with the new administration. It is evident from the historical articles in the *Annual Register* that Burke had not been hostile to the Grenville administration.

them with care and fidelity."—Burke to an unidentified person, Dec. 31, 1764; quoted with permission of Professor F. W. Hilles, of Yale University.

[10] After his breach with Hamilton, Burke wrote to John Monck Mason: "Hamilton . . . has the impudence to pretend that my leaving him and going to Mr. T. is the cause of our rupture. This is, I assure you, an abominable falsehood. I never had more than a very slight acquaintance with Mr. T. till long after our rupture."—*Correspondence* 1: 74-75. The editors of the *Correspondence* were unable to identify "Mr. T." but were sure that he was not Charles Townshend. However, the Annaghmore MSS, the letters of Charles O'Hara to Burke and a letter from Henry Flood to Burke, May 30, 1765 (Wentworth-Fitzwilliam MSS) established beyond doubt that "Mr. T." was none other than Charles Townshend.

[11] *Works of the Right Honourable Edmund Burke* 2: 422, London, Rivington, 1815-1827.

[12] Annaghmore MSS, to O'Hara, July 9, 1765.

His articles were objective and dispassionate, but opinion sometimes broke through, and it is easy to see that the author's
sympathies were with the ministers when they resorted to
issuing the famous general warrant in the prosecution of John
Wilkes and other persons involved in publishing "number 45"
of the *North Briton*. "The libellous spirit," wrote Burke, "was
raised to the highest pitch of audacity and insolence"; and the
North Briton was marked by "boldness and indecency." General warrants were but "a loose office form, which had been
constantly practised from the Revolution." It was true that
they had now been used "upon a much greater number of
persons, and of a quality much lower, than was in any way
requisite for the purposes of prevention or punishment," but
"when the people began to cool, the fault appeared, almost
to all, to be nothing more than an irregularity." When Wilkes
was prosecuted for blasphemy, expelled from the House of
Commons, condemned as an outlaw and driven into exile,
Burke thought that just deserts had been meted out for
"offenses against decency and sober morals." Of the Parliament that expelled Wilkes and upheld general warrants Burke
wrote that "no body of men, in any state, had given at any
time, a stronger proof of its moderation, and its regard to
strict constitutional principles."[13] Even after Burke became
associated with Rockingham against Grenville's bitter opposition, he had words of praise for two leading members of the
ministries that governed the country from 1761 to 1765.[14]

Not yet had there come into existence a corps of men known
as the Rockingham Whigs; nor had Burke as yet formulated
the principles that would determine the character of that corps.
One of the leading principles of the Rockingham party would
be opposition to the politics and influence of Lord Bute. But
so far was Burke in 1765 from the views he would hold when
Rockingham became a real party leader, that he hoped for
a Rockingham-Townshend government broadly based with re-

[13] *Annual Register* (1764), 18-19, 24-25, 30.

[14] Burke praised Halifax as president of the Board of Trade and lord
lieutenant of Ireland, and Grenville for his strict economies at the Treasury.
Of both he wrote: "However mistaken, or even inconsiderate, these ministers
might have been, on some occasions, in the choice of measures to promote the
honour of the crown and the welfare of the subject, they ever had the interests
of both sincerely at heart."—*Annual Register* (1765), 45-46. This volume was
published in May, 1766, when Burke had been for ten months in Rockingham's
employ.

spect to parties. "It is certain," he confided to Charles O'Hara during the long ministerial crisis, "that if they act wisely, they cannot fail to make up a lasting administration. I call taking in Lord Bute, or at least not quarrelling with him, and enlarging their bottom by taking in the Tories, and all the men of business in the House of Commons not listed against them, acting wisely."[15]

The change of government in the summer of 1765 was the first great turning-point in Burke's political career. He was in eager search of a post in government, and it can hardly be doubted that his wish for Townshend to accept a leading place was connected with his own ambition; for he was not yet even personally acquainted with the Marquess of Rockingham.[16] He told O'Hara that the arrangement proposed on Townshend's declining was "Lord Rockingham the Treasury, the Duke of Grafton and Conway Secretaries of State, Dowdeswell Chancellor of the Exchequer. . . . So much for the ambitious. Now for the honest necessitous. Will and I are down on their lists and I hope and believe will be attended to." Two days later a hasty note was dashed off to the same friend: "I have got an employment of a kind humble enough; but which may be worked into some sort of consideration, or at least advantage; private secretary to Lord Rockingham, and with whom, they say it is not difficult to live."[17]

In taking the post under Rockingham, Burke had no rupture with Townshend. The latter continued at the Pay Office under the new ministers, and it is probable that Burke continued to urge him to come forward actively in support of the administration.[18] Time would bring a wide divergence between

---

[15] Annaghmore MSS, June 6, 1765.

[16] It has been said that Burke knew Rockingham as early as 1763.—Sutherland, L. S., Edmund Burke and the first Rockingham administration, *Eng. Hist. Rev.* 47: 46-72, 1932. The evidence offered was a letter from Burke to Lord Hardwicke of Oct. 20, "1763" (British Museum Add. MSS 35424). An examination of this letter shows that the year was 1769. Abundant evidence, including his own testimony, shows that Burke did not become personally acquainted with Rockingham until July, 1765.

[17] Annaghmore MSS, to O'Hara, July 9, 11, 1765. To David Garrick, Burke wrote of "this little gleam of prosperity which has at length fallen on my fortune. My situation is, for the present, very agreeable; and I do not at all despair of its becoming, in time, solidly advantageous."—Prior, Sir James, *Life of the Right Honourable Edmund Burke*, 5th ed., 86, London, G. Bell, 1878.

[18] Letters of Townshend to Dr. Richard Brocklesby and other persons not identified, in W. L. Clements Library, Ann Arbor, Mich. Some of these letters,

these men, but not yet. "I understand from yours," wrote
Charles O'Hara, "that you still go on with him, tho' you belong
to Lord Rockingham. This may be a nice card to play, and
the opinion people have of Charles will make it more so."[19]
Nobody then thought of Rockingham as a strong public man,
and the administration he nominally headed was considered
a makeshift not likely to last long. It came into being because
William Pitt had declined to form a different kind of administration, and because it was the King's only alternative to the
Grenville-Bedford combination. Contemporary opinion at the
start regarded the Rockingham ministry as a restoration to
power of the great Whig families whose political connection
had been managed by the Duke of Newcastle, and who had
been driven out of government by Bute and Henry Fox in
1762. It was believed too that Rockingham rather than Newcastle had taken the Treasury, lest Pitt's aversion to the aged
Duke (who took the privy seal) be extended to the whole
administration. The Marquess was a ministerial novice, only
thirty-five years old, and hitherto known to the public as a
rich man of good character who cut a prominent figure at the
Newmarket horse races; whereas Charles Townshend had held
several high government offices and was regarded as perhaps
the brightest star on the political horizon. Rockingham was
far from being a prime minister when he became first lord of
the Treasury, and he had no large part even in forming the
administration of 1765. That had been recruited by the Duke
of Cumberland, the King's uncle, who, as Burke said, undertook "to recommend to his majesty such other noblemen and
gentlemen, as, though new in office, and not far gone in years,
might, by joining to the rectitude of their intentions and the
greatness of their abilities, the confidence of both prince and
people, more than replace, under a patriot king, and a free
constitution, the veterans they succeeded." [20]

The connection with Rockingham signified for Burke the
end of opportunist adventuring for place and career. He found
in the Marquess not only a generous patron and friend, but a
man of courage, integrity, liberality of temper, and sagacity

particularly of Oct. 24, 27, 28, 30, 1765, contain evidence consistent with their
having been written to Burke; they show how hard Townshend was being urged
to take an active part in the administration.

[19] Wentworth-Fitzwilliam MSS, July 19, 1765.
[20] *Annual Register* (1765), 44.

in managing men. Rockingham succeeded in becoming the real as well as the nominal head of the cabinet council, and he desired to revive the vitality of the Whig party. But for this undertaking he needed experience and some one to help him interpret that experience. "You have pride to deal with," wrote O'Hara to Burke that summer, "but much softened by manner; and exceedingly good sense, but you must feed it, for it can't feed itself."[21] Burke was to feed that good sense for seventeen years. But in the association that now began each man was to supply deficiencies in the other. Rockingham, who had hardly less charm than moral excellence, naturally attracted the friendship of virtuous men, and he was able to open to Burke a circle of political friends in whom high moral character was combined with birth, breeding, and wealth. He gave Burke an opportunity to fertilize his genius with experience in the inner region of the state and in party politics. He provided too, in his own person, an object for Burke's admiration and love. Burke's principles and philosophy of politics were largely abstracted from Rockingham's political conduct.

The Grenville Measures and the Crisis in America

Since Burke was now at the right hand of the king's first minister, and soon afterwards came into the House of Commons and won his first laurels there by the part he took in repealing the Stamp Act, it is worth while to notice his views on the development of that immense crisis in imperial political and economic relations which came to a head in American resistance to the measures of the preceding administration.

The *Annual Register* historical article for 1765 shows that he took a severely critical view of the Treasury-Admiralty orders initiated by George Grenville in 1763 to enforce the trade laws strictly by suppressing the trade between the British and Spanish West Indies. That trade

did not clash with the spirit of any act of parliament made for the regulation of the British plantation trade . . . but was found to vary from the letter, enough to give the new revenue officers a plea for doing that from principles of duty, which there were not wanting the most powerful motives of conduct to make them do. Accordingly, they seized, indiscriminately, all the ships upon that trade, both of subjects and foreigners.

---

[21] Wentworth-Fitzwilliam MSS, July 30, 1765.

The result had been to shut off a Spanish market for British manufactures and British North-American produce, thus reducing North America's ability to buy goods from the mother country, so that "a want of employment" arose in England which "soon appeared to be positively owing to the ministry." Not less ill-conceived had been the setting of naval officers at the debasing tasks of revenue men, thus exciting in them a cupidity to make prizes of vessels belonging to their own countrymen. Harsh, irrational, and violent acts inevitably occurred which not only disgraced the naval service but further damaged the interests of trade and disappointed the revenue expectations of the Treasury. Besides the British-Spanish trade, so rudely broken up by enforcing the trade laws in a narrowly legalistic manner, there had been a long-subsisting profitable but illicit commercial intercourse between the North American colonies and the French West Indian sugar islands. Burke regarded this trade as of great advantage to both sides because it "united in the strictest sense, all those benefits which liberal minds include in the idea of a well-regulated trade, as tending, in the highest degree, to the mutual welfare of those who carry it on." Deprived of it, the North Americans and the British at home, who imported this French sugar from North America, were at the mercy of the British West Indian planters. So great was the need for this trade that not even the war with France had suppressed it completely, and as soon as the peace of 1763 "had taken the sting of treason from this trade, it returned to its pristine flourishing condition, and remained so, till it sunk under the same blow with the trade between us and the Spaniards." Burke attributed the suppression to the influence of the British West India interests who wished to raise prices by monopolizing the sugar market of the empire. To him it "savoured of oppression" to permit such a raising of the price of sugar, "considering the vast demand for it, and even by the poor, to whom from long habit it has become one of the chief necessaries of life."

The effect on North America of Grenville's regulations was not only to block access to the foreign sugar supplies, but to stop up those sources for acquiring bullion and specie which had always been needed for settling the unfavorable balance of trade with the mother country. Hence, it was "no way surprising, if the inhabitants of these colonies, immediately on a stop being put to this trade, came to a resolution not to buy any

cloathing they could possibly do without, that was not of their
own manufacture." So was depressed the North American
market for British manufacturers and exporters. It was true
that Grenville's Revenue Act (the so-called sugar act) of 1764
legalized the trade of the British colonies in North America
with other European colonies in the new world, but "loaded
the best part of it with duties so far above its strength to bear,
as to render it contraband to all intents and purposes. Besides,
it ordered the money arising from the duties to be paid, and in
specie too, into the British exchequer, to the entire drawing off
of the little money remaining in these colonies." And all was
made worse for them by Parliament's enacting at the same time
a law to prohibit the colonies from issuing bills of credit as
legal tender. It was true that the British government sought to
compensate the Americans by granting certain bounties to
stimulate their exports to the United Kingdom; but nature itself decreed that such compensation could not be adequate,
since Great Britain could not absorb enough North American
produce to sustain the American market for her manufactures.
Moreover, as Burke pointed out, "the effect of all these laws to
restrain the foreign trade of the colonies . . . was certain and
instantaneous; whereas the effect of the laws made for their
benefit . . . was, if not uncertain . . . so remote as to require,
perhaps many years after its coming to compensate the delay."
Burke thought the Americans "bore this stroke of the supreme
legislature of Great Britain with all that patience and submission, which the most indulgent parent could have expected
from the most dutiful children." But it was not to be expected
that "out of a compliment to the mother country, they should
perish for thirst, with water in their own wells." Unable to
buy from British merchants, they were intensifying their efforts
to manufacture for themselves; so that England was threatened
not only by the loss of a great market but by the rise of an in-
dustrial rival. The *Annual Register* articles do not show that
Burke had an insight into what was taking place in the inner
recesses of the American mind and spirit, but they indicate a
very intelligent grasp of the nature, principles, and dimensions
of the violence that had been done to the economic life of the
British nation and empire. Probably he understood as well as
any man then living the problem that Grenville had bequeathed
to the Rockingham administration.

It was "very surprising" to him that a ministry containing

such men as Halifax and Grenville should have approved what
was done, and "still more surprising" that some of their measures should have passed through Parliament and Privy Council.
"But that, after almost the worst idea that could be well formed
of them, had been in a great measure realized, another measure,
the bare proposal of which had given so much offense, should
be approved . . . argues such want of reflection, as can scarcely
be paralleled in the public councils of any country." Burke described how Grenville had cautiously delayed bringing forward
a stamp act in order to consult with colonial agents and invite
proposals from them "for any other tax that might be equivalent in its produce to the stamp tax." The Minister had even
suggested that his considerate procedure might well create a
precedent for the regular consultation of the colonies in all such
matters in future. "But the colonies seemed to consider it as an
affront rather than a compliment . . . and some went so far as
to send over petitions, to be presented to the king, lords and
commons, positively and directly questioning the authority and
jurisdiction of parliament over their properties." It was Burke's
opinion that this circumstance alone should have prevented
laying the tax. He summarized the arguments brought forward
in Parliament against the act and said they had great weight.
But he believed "little or nothing worth notice" had been
adduced in favor of the act, unless one were "to admit claims
for titles, assertions for proofs, fictions in law for substantial
arguments, the statutes of England for the dictates of nature
and the private opinions of the gentlemen of Westminster for
the general sense of mankind."

Some of the arguments advanced against the Stamp Act he
regarded as poor ones—for example, that the colonies ought not
to be taxed directly by Parliament unless they were represented
there. In later years he would repeatedly condemn both the
denial of Parliament's right to tax the colonies and the im-
practical scheme of establishing such right by creating parliamentary constituencies in the colonies.[22] But in the *Annual
Register* for 1765 he rejected that proposal for a different and
very interesting reason, namely, that slave-owners were not
morally fit to sit in a parliament of free men: "common sense,
nay self-preservation, seems to forbid, that those who allow
themselves unlimited right over the liberties and lives of others,

---

[22] e. g., *Works* 2: 137-143.

should have any share in making laws for those who have long renounced such unjust and cruel distinctions." It was impossible that such men should have "the proper feelings for such a task." Burke's feelings towards American slave-owners thus were not unlike his sentiments towards the "bashaws" who as a master class ruled the people of his native Ireland.

Not the grievances of slave-owning Americans, but the hardships of the people of England and the inconvenience in empire relations inspired Burke's condemnation of the Grenville system and the Stamp Act. Nor did he rejoice, as Pitt rejoiced, that the Americans resisted the enforcement of the act. To Burke it was one thing for people to protest against unwise or unjust trade and fiscal measures—they had the undeniable right. But it was something very different, and entirely without right, for them to break the law and call into question the authority of the imperial legislature.

Burke and the Repeal of the Stamp Act

By the fall of 1765 the economic consequences of the Grenville system had struck Great Britain with full force. American resort to non-importation and suspension of debt payments brought the Stamp Act crisis down to earth in the lives of thousands as a question of solvency or bankruptcy, bread or starvation. Burke described the country as being in "the most distressful circumstances that could well be imagined; our manufacturers at a stand, commerce almost totally annihilated, provisions extravagantly dear, and a numerous populace unemployed."[23] To this condition was added the ominous fact of general disobedience throughout America to a law of Parliament; hence a great political as well as economic crisis had struck the British Empire.

Parliament, which in normal circumstances would not have convened until January, was summoned for December 17. Well in advance of its opening, Lord Rockingham and his secretary were in close contact with the merchants engaged in the American trade. Those at London met early in December under the lead of Barlow Trecothick, a close friend of Rockingham, and sent a circular letter to some thirty trading and manufacturing towns urging them to support an application to Parliament for a redress of North American grievances: "We mean to take for

---

[23] *Annual Register* (1766), 31.

our sole Object the Interests of these Kingdoms—it being our Opinion, that Conclusive Arguments for granting every Ease or Advantage the North Americans can with a propriety desire, may be deduced from that principle only."[24] This appeal produced a stream of petitions to Parliament drafted in nearly uniform language; so that a great "outdoor" activity was generated to influence the legislature. Burke was in the thick of this, working as agent for ministers who preferred to reserve determination of policy until they had tested the parliamentary ground on which they would have to move.

That ground was not firm; nor was the ministry's support solid in court circles. Much depended on the line of conduct adopted by Pitt, whom the Americans considered a great friend; but he declined to speak his mind on American affairs except from his seat in the House of Commons, and not until the house re-convened after Christmas. His attitude made for great ministerial uncertainty because he was known to tolerate rather than support the administration. No hints of a ministerial plan were given in the King's speech on December 17, and it seems likely that Rockingham intended to make no proposals until a general opinion was aroused for conciliatory measures. As yet such an opinion was not very audible; rather did it appear that the dominant sentiment was an enormous indignation at American disobedience, which George Grenville went so far as to call rebellion.[25] Parliament recessed for Christmas after two days and did not meet again until January 14, but in the meantime ministers were busy and the atmosphere in official circles was charged with tension and uncertainty. There could be no thought of going against the near-unanimous opinion in Parliament that the American doctrine which denied the *right* of the imperial legislature to tax the colonies should be refuted. As

---

[24] Wentworth-Fitzwilliam MSS. The letter, dated Dec. 6, is endorsed in Burke's hand: "N.B. This letter concerted between the Marquess of R. and Mr. Trecothick, the principal instrument in the happy repeal of the Stamp Act, which without giving up British authority quieted the Empire." *Cf.* Albermarle, George Thomas, Earl of, *Memoirs of the Marquess of Rockingham* 1: 319, London, Richard Bentley, 1852.

[25] Burke characterized Grenville at this time: "He shows I think no talents of a leader; he wanted the stage of administration to give him his figure. He is eager, petulant, inaccurate, without dignity and quite the reverse of that character, which might be expected from a man just descended from great situations. Charles Townshend who handled him roughly described him accurately in two words of his speech—Quantity without force.—Annaghmore MSS, to O'Hara, Dec. 24, 1765.

Burke put it, "this was the only question that could be thought of, upon which the Ministry, and their antagonists in the opposition, would have gone together into a division."[26] And since to many it appeared inconsistent and weak to declare the right while giving up the exercise of it, repealing the Stamp Act on principles of commercial prudence and political equity would be difficult and would depend considerably on the degree of outdoor pressure brought to bear on Parliament. Even before Christmas an influential movement to prevent repeal was being organized in court-influenced circles by the former royal favorite, Bute.[27]

Tentative plans for conceding to the Americans while affirming the supremacy of the British legislature were drawn up at a cabinet meeting on December 27, but these were subject to further consideration and revision.[28] Burke confided to Charles O'Hara on December 31 that

in this narrow but dreadful interval, preparations are making upon all hands. There are wonderful materials of combustion at hand; and surely, since this monarchy, a more material point never came under the consideration of parliament. I mean the conduct which is to be held with regard to America. . . . Administration has not yet conclusively (I imagine) fixed upon their plan in this respect, as every day's information from abroad may necessitate some alteration.[29]

Burke was to have a voice in the determination of parliamentary action, since he had on December 23 been elected to the House of Commons from Wendover, a Buckinghamshire borough constituency in the patronage of Will Burke's friend, Lord Verney. He took his seat on January 14.

On that day Pitt opened the great Stamp Act debate by calling for the repeal of the law on the ground that it was unconstitutional, that Parliament had no right to lay a direct tax upon the Americans. So great an impression did his speech make on the House that Rockingham the next day advised the King to call Pitt to office. The King reluctantly agreeing, Pitt defined his terms: repeal of the Stamp Act, no declaration of Parliament's right to tax the colonies, and the exclusion of the

[26] *Annual Register* (1766), 44.
[27] Walpole, Horace, *Memoirs of the reign of King George the Third* 2: 183, New York Putnam, 1894.
[28] Wentworth-Fitzwilliam MSS, Newcastle to Rockingham, Jan. 1, 1766.
[29] Annaghmore MSS.

Duke of Newcastle from the cabinet council. Rockingham however, was not to be budged from his conviction that Parliament had the right to tax the colonies and that repeal could not be carried without first enacting a declaratory resolution affirming the right. Hence the negotiation with Pitt failed.[30]

Meanwhile, the many petitions that had been started over the country by the Trecothick committee of merchants were pouring into Parliament and generating there, independently of Pitt, the strength needed by the ministry to obtain repeal on Rockingham's principle of prudence and equity. The presentation of one of these petitions was the occasion, on January 17, for the new member for Wendover to make his first speech in the House of Commons.[31] He spoke again on January 27 when the House had before it the question of receiving the petition from the American Stamp Act congress which George Cooke, member for Middlesex, attempted to present. Although Pitt was present and spoke for receiving it, the ministerial leaders feared that the temper of the house was hostile to allowing a petition from an unconstitutional body that challenged the taxing authority of parliament, to be laid on the table. Conway and Dowdeswell succeeded in persuading Cooke to withdraw his motion, and Conway was able to report to the King that "the thing passed off almost unanimously without any ill humour on the part of Mr. Pitt." The moment was dangerous, for a breach with Pitt or defeat in a division might have brought a dismissal of the ministers. Of Burke's words no textual record survives, but the position he took may be known. Horace Walpole noted that he spoke for receiving the petition. Secretary of State Conway's list sent to the King gave the names of twenty-three speakers all shown as *pro* or *con* except Burke, who was marked "R[eceive] but ag[ains]t Division," indicating that he sided with Pitt in principle while agreeing with Conway and Dowdeswell in their tactic of avoiding a division which must have gone either against the petition or against the ministry.[32]

Conway on February 3 brought into the committee of the

---

[30] Fitzmaurice, Lord Edmond, *Life of William, Earl of Shelburne* 1: 375-376, London, Macmillan, 1875-1876; Albemarle, *op. cit.* 1: 269-271.

[31] Annaghmore MSS, Burke to O'Hara, Jan. 18, 1766; Wentworth-Fitzwilliam MSS, Garrick to Burke, Jan. 18, 1766.

[32] Fortescue, Sir John, ed., *The correspondence of King George the Third* 1: 216, London, Macmillan, 1927; Walpole, *Memoirs* 2: 193; Albemarle, *op. cit.* 1: 288-290.

whole House five ministerial resolutions, the first of which declared the right of crown and Parliament to bind the colonies
and peoples of America "in all cases whatsoever." On this
resolution was founded the famous Declaratory Act, and it was
approved almost unanimously, only Pitt and four or five others
dissenting. Conway reported to the King that "there was no
division or scarce anything that could properly be called a
debate," and cited Burke as one of three members who had
particularly distinguished themselves.[33] Another witness described Burke's speech as "far superior to that of every other
speaker on the subject of the colonies that night."[34] Two nights
later the other resolutions, all declarative of the existence of
disorders which had to be subdued, were carried; and Burke
spoke again. On February 7, Grenville, encouraged by a reverse which the ministry had suffered at the hands of Bute's
friends in the House of Lords, attempted a grand maneuver:
he moved for the enforcement of the Stamp Act. A great debate
took place in what was the first test of strength between the
forces who favored and those who opposed the conciliation of
America. Grenville was beaten by 274 to 134. Burke played a
leading part that night. No record survives of his speech, but
it pleased Pitt so much that the "Great Commoner" praised his
"ingenuity and eloquence" and congratulated his friends "on
the acquisition they had made." Writing to a friend on February 11, Richard Burke said that "Edmund has gained pro-
digious applause from the public" as well as a compliment from
Mr. Pitt, "who paid it to him in the House, in the most obliging manner, and in the strongest terms."[35] This was the time
when Burke began, as Dr. Johnson said, to fill the town with
wonder.

While Rockingham was standing his ground against hostility in court circles and stiff opposition in the Lords, Conway
on February 21 obtained leave from the Commons to bring in
a bill to repeal the Stamp Act. The division of 275 to 127 was
decisive for the ultimate act of repeal. That night the issue was
finely drawn when Charles Jenkinson moved an amendment
to substitute the words "amend and explain" for repeal, arguing
that outright repeal would spell the end of British authority in

---

[33] Fortescue, *op. cit.* 1: 254-255.

[34] *Correspondence* 1: 97-98.

[35] Wright, J., ed., *Sir Henry Cavendish's debates of the House of Commons*
1: 13, London, Longmans, 1841. (Cited hereafter as *Cavendish's debates*.)

America. Whether Jenkinson's motion reflected royal instability or duplicity, there could be no doubt of its meaning, since
Jenkinson was a close confidant of the King. Burke's speech
that night was in direct reply to Jenkinson. Three days later
the House of Commons approved a repeal resolution, and a
committee which included Burke was appointed to engross the
bill.[36] It passed final reading and was sent to the Lords on
March 4. Of the peers and the bill Burke wrote on the eve of
the vote: "Their courage will never carry them to those lengths
which their strength might enable them to go."[37] The bill
passed the upper house against a court-backed opposition so
stiff that a formal protest was signed by thirty-three peers. On
March 18 the royal assent was given.

The principal men toasted on both sides of the Atlantic for
their part in the repeal were Pitt, Lord Camden, Lord Shelburne, General Conway, Colonel Isaac Barré, and Burke. Much
less appreciated was the strong but unostentatious part played
by Rockingham, who was compelled to suffer the ill will of the
King and had trembled repeatedly on the brink of dismissal.
But Burke knew and later would testify:

> Everything, upon every side, was full of traps and mines. Earth
> shook below; heaven menaced above; all the elements of ministerial
> safety were dissolved . . . the firmness of that noble person was put
> to the proof. He never stirred from his ground; no, not an inch.
> He remained fixed and determined, in principle, in measure, and
> in conduct.[38]

That tribute to Rockingham signifies an important part of
Burke's history, closely related to his American politics. The
admiration Rockingham inspired in him during that critical
period cemented his attachment to the Marquess, who was
probably the most sympathetic friend the American colonies
had among the leading public men of England.

Reform of the North American Trade Laws

Repealing the Stamp Act was not the whole of the Rockingham ministry's effort to conciliate the American colonies and
serve the interests of the British mercantile community. Parlia-

---

[36] For the impression made by Burke's speech of Feb. 24, see *Correspondence*
1: 102-103.

[37] Annaghmore MSS, to O'Hara, March 1.

[38] *Works* 2: 406-407.

ment was called upon also to modify Grenville's Revenue Act of 1764, which had been a subject of great complaint in the colonies.[39] At the close of the debate on the Stamp Act repeal, Burke wrote:

We now prepare for a complete revision of all the commercial laws which regard our own or the foreign plantations, from the Act of Navigation downward. It is an extensive plan. The North Americans and West Indians are now in treaty upon it; and as soon as they have settled some preliminaries (and they are better disposed than any one could think, to practicability and concord) the whole arrangement will be ordered between them and some of the Board people and detached members. This you see will find me as much business as the evidence over the Stamp Act; but it is a business I like; and the spirit of those I act with is just what I could wish it in things of this kind.[40]

Accomplishment was to fall short of these expectations, but the history of what was done forms not only an important epilogue to the repeal of the Stamp Act, but a chapter, scantily noticed by his biographers, in the history of Burke's American politics. The administration attempted to promote commerce within the empire by enlarging the lawful commerce of the colonies with lands outside the empire. According to Burke,

many of the colonies, and those the most abounding in people, were so situated as to have very few means of traffic with the mother country. It became therefore our interest to let them into as much foreign trade as could be given without interfering with our own. . . . Without some such enlargement, it was obvious that any benefit we could expect from these colonies, must be extremely limited.[41]

In short, the idea was to enable North America to find the means of purchasing more goods from British manufacturers and merchants.

The Grenville measure of 1764, which in practice had

---

[39] Henry Cruger, Jr., wrote to his father in New York on Feb. 16, 1766: "Parliament have not yet done anything about the Sugar Act and other destructive restraints on your trade. It will come as soon as ever the Stamp Act is settled. I imagine they will rescind all the restrictive clauses and grant everything you ask . . . they seem convinced that vast benefit will accrue to this Kingdom by giving you almost unlimited trade, so far as doth not interfere with British manufactures. The West Indians are collecting all their force to oppose us; I have reason to say that they will at length be defeated."—*Commerce of Rhode Island, 1726-1800* 1: 139-143, Boston, *Coll. of Mass. Hist. Soc.*, 7th Ser., 1914.

[40] Annaghmore MSS, to O'Hara, March 1.

[41] *Works* 2: 177-178.

damaged the commerce of North America, had been designed largely for raising a revenue to relieve the British Treasury by levying duties on certain commodities imported by the colonies from foreign countries and the British West Indies. It was proposed in 1766 to modify this act in such a way that, without sacrificing revenue, commerce might be encouraged. But since a leading feature of the proposed amendment was to abolish the preferential tariff on foreign molasses imported by North America, to the damage of the British West Indian monopolists, a conflict of interests between the North American and West Indian merchants in England had to be resolved before a new law could be passed.

Early in March these interests were compromised, and Rockingham was able to inform the King that there was "the greatest prospect of an advantageous system of commerce being established for the mutual and general interest of this country."[42] Courtesy and political prudence moved Rockingham to send copies of the merchants' agreement to Pitt, who acknowledged "a very obliging attention" and said he trusted it would be "productive of the best consequences."[43] The House of Commons went into committee on the reform of the trade laws on March 17, and afterwards Secretary Conway felt warranted in writing to the American governors that Parliament intended to "give to the Trade & Interests of America every Relief which the true State of their Circumstances demands or admits."[44]

In addition to modifying the Revenue Act of 1764 it was proposed to establish one or more free ports in the West Indies.[45] Petitions for these had come from merchants in Bristol, Lancaster, and Liverpool, and to Burke's great satisfaction the administration was willing to adopt such a plan. He thought

---

[42] Fortescue, *op. cit.* 1: 282; *Manuscripts of the Earl of Dartmouth* 2: 38, London, Hist. Mss. Comm., 14th Rep., App., Pt. X, 1895.

[43] Wentworth-Fitzwilliam MSS, Pitt to Rockingham, March 21, 1766.

[44] Schlesinger, A. N., *The colonial merchants and the American Revolution,* 83, N. Y., Col. Univ. Press, 1918.

[45] Colonial ports in which foreign ships could deliver and take off cargo under strictly defined conditions. Under the Navigation Laws foreign ships were hitherto forbidden to enter the ports of the colonies. "I remember we used sometimes to talk on the advantage of a free port in that part of the world, when we were so angry with Grenville for stopping what he called a counterband trade in the West Indies. . . . Either you and I have talked of Dominica upon the same plan, or I have read of such a design. There, a preference given to the mother country, by moderate duties on exported goods for any other place, would do wonders, both as to revenue and wealth brought into commerce."— Wentworth-Fitzwilliam MSS, Charles O'Hara to Burke, March 10, 1766.

it would meet with no insuperable difficulties. He wrote on April 8:

> Last night we closed the examination of our witnesses to the propriety of opening Dominica as a Free Port, which concludes the inquiry previous to the Resolutions that are to be the foundation of the new North American Trade Act. . . . I do not look now for much opposition; the spirit of the adverse faction begins to evaporate; even Mr. Grenville begins to slacken in his attendance; his language is, I am told, that of despair of the Commonwealth. . . . So much popularity never was possessed by any set of people who possessed great offices. Yet all is in an odd way.[46]

Then suddenly Pitt turned an angry face upon the administration. His mouthpiece among the London merchants, the Jamaica-born William Beckford, raised an opposition to the free-port plan. Since it was believed that he voiced the views of the "Great Commoner," something like a ministerial crisis was brought on. Rockingham sent Burke to Pitt on a mission of explanation and conciliation, but that only made matters worse. Burke's account of the mission records his earliest known head-on encounter with the most famous Englishman of the age:

> I went down to Hayes with a very respectable merchant of Lancaster, to talk him, if possible, out of his peevish and perverse opposition to so salutary and unexceptionable a measure. But on this point I found so great a man utterly unprovided with any better arms than a few rusty prejudices. So we returned as we went, after some hours fruitless conference. But the truth is, he determined to be out of humour; and this was the first object he had to display it upon; for he had in a better temper approved of all the previous regulations.[47]

Burke was convinced that Pitt was jealous of the accomplishments and popularity of an administration that more and more appeared able to succeed without leaning on him. According to another account of this interview, Pitt had felt himself slighted because the plan for free ports had been sent to him only three days before it was to be brought before Parliament. And he was indignant when Burke informed him that Rockingham wished to know the terms on which he would consent to enter the government. A few months before, the Marquess had appealed to Pitt to come into office, and the latter had said he would not discuss such a subject with any one but the King; he

---

[46] Annaghmore MSS, to O'Hara.
[47] *Ibid.*, to the same, April 23.

had even complained to Shelburne of Rockingham's tone as being "that of a Minister master of the court and of the public."[48] To Burke he now said: "I wonder you should make that proposition when I have given it under my own hand in a letter to Lord Rockingham that I will open myself, upon that subject, to nobody but the King himself."[49] This day (April 11) was an important one for Burke, and for his American politics. After it few words of praise for the American idol Pitt ever would drop from his mouth.

The next day Rockingham held a cabinet and the result was a decision to postpone the free-port project until the next parliamentary session.[50] Thus, on the eve of the House's going into committee of the whole on the trade resolutions, Burke sorrowfully wrote:

When the Free Port came to be debated in full cabinet, the Old Stagers frittered it down to an address to the King for the opinion of the boards on the matter, etc. So we come hopping into the house with a half-measure; the most odious thing, I am sure, to my temper and opinion that can be conceived. However, even this miserable remnant is better than nothing. The Great Commoner sets his face against it.[51]

Burke added the next day:

This day Pitt came down, and made a fine flaming patriotic speech chiefly against any sort of personal connections; he means with any besides himself. It was a speech too virtuous to be honest. . . . The enemy plan seems to be to start object after object to keep off our doing any thing in American affairs and they have hitherto been but too successful. This day nothing is done. God knows when anything will.

Pitt, however, presently altered his attitude and by May 9 Rockingham was able to tell the King that all proposed resolutions for altering the trade and revenue laws, including the free-ports plan, had been moved and carried in the House of Commons without a division.[52] Engrossed as statutes, they passed without further debate and received the concurrence of the Lords. They abolished the preferential duties on the im-

[48] Fitzmaurice, *op. cit.* 1: 377-383; Albemarle, *op. cit.* 1: 311-312; Wentworth-Fitzwilliam MSS, Pitt to Rockingham, Feb. 28, 1766.

[49] An account of Mr. Thomas Walpole's conversation with Mr. Pitt, & afterwards with the Duke of Newcastle, British Museum Add. MSS 32974.

[50] *Ibid.*, Rockingham to Newcastle, April 13, 1766.

[51] Annaghmore MSS, April 23-24.

[52] Fortescue, *op. cit.* 1: 306-307.

portation of molasses into the North American colonies by laying a penny a gallon on both British and foreign molasses. Thus
the North American rum distillers were freed from the monopo-
listic British West Indian producers, although the latter were
protected in Great Britain against the competition of sugar re-
exported from America. A number of port duties hitherto laid
on goods coming into the American colonies for re-export were
extinguished. Several duties on foreign goods imported from
Great Britain were abolished, or lowered; others were trans-
formed into export duties paid by the British re-exporters. A
duty previously levied on the export of cotton from America
was abolished. Free ports were authorized in Jamaica and
Dominica, but with duties for revenue and a provision against
the re-export to North America of foreign goods imported by
those islands.

These measures formed an intricate work in economic statesmanship constructed largely by Chancellor of the Exchequer
William Dowdeswell, Sir George Savile (Rockingham's closest
political friend), and Burke. The revised tariff system for
North America rendered the Grenville Revenue Act of 1764
much more tolerable. Although it was generally recognized that
more legislation concerning the trade laws and colonies would
confront Parliament when it reconvened, it seemed to Burke
that more was accomplished than he had dared six weeks earlier
to believe possible. An address of thanks was tendered to him
by the merchants of Lancaster for the "great attention" he had
given to "the commercial interests of Great Britain and her
colonies . . . by removing obstructions that lay in the way of
commerce, and opening new sources of trade, unknown in
former times."[53] He had impressed himself deeply and favorably on the British mercantile community. In America the revision of the trade laws was received with general satisfaction.
Burke believed and never ceased to reiterate the opinion, that
the colonies had been wholly conciliated by the repeal of the
Stamp Act and the more liberal trade regulations. So much
importance did he attribute to the latter, that he devoted to it
a third of the space in his *Short Account of a Late Short Administration*.[54]

But in one respect the principle of the Navigation Acts,

---

[53] *Correspondence* 1: 104.
[54] *Works* 2: 2-6.

cement of the empire, was breached. The molasses duty which fell with equal charge on the produce of the British and foreign sugar islands was a duty for revenue, not an instrument for protecting the avenues of commerce within the empire.[55] It was more nakedly a revenue duty than any Grenville had laid. Moreover, it was to be paid "into the Receipt of His Majesty's Exchequer, and there reserved to be, from Time to Time, disposed of by Parliament, towards defraying the necessary Expences of defending, protecting, and securing, the said Colonies and Plantations." Thus the germ of the Townshend Revenue Act of 1767, which would raise a new crisis in America, may be seen in the 1766 revision of the trade and revenue laws. But no man desired more than Burke, to make American prosperity dependent on British dominion.

Opposing Lord Chatham's Administration

Since it had been Lord Rockingham's misfortune to incur the King's displeasure without winning a large support and confidence in Parliament or in the country, many signs were given, after Pitt had shown displeasure with the ministry, that there would be a new administration after parliament rose in the spring of 1766. It was Burke's opinion that the ministers had weakened themselves by too much deference to Pitt, instead of standing firm on the ground of their own achievement. To O'Hara he lamented at the end of April:

As to us here, with such real abilities as perhaps few men at the head of affairs have had in our time, by looking for a support exterior to themselves, and leaning on it, they have weakened themselves, rendered themselves trifling, and at length have had drawn away from them that prop upon which they leaned.[56]

Not Rockingham, who had hardly opened his mouth in the House of Lords, but Pitt, who had dazzled the House of Commons, and with whom the country was still infatuated, had gained the chief credit for resolving the American crisis. During his last two months in office, the Marquess suffered so many resignations and refusals of office that he had much difficulty even in filling up government positions. Burke at this time hoped

---

[55] "By no possible interpretation could it be construed in any other light than a tariff for revenue. It was an unvarnished contradiction of the colonial claim to 'no taxation without representation.' "—Schlesinger, *loc. cit.*, 85.

[56] Annaghmore MSS, April 29, 1766.

for some eminent place, but it was not given him.[57] Early in
June the King refused Rockingham's request to remove
Jeremiah Dyson from his seat on the Board of Trade because
of "the difference of opinion which Mr. Dyson professes even
in regard to the great Commercial Regulations & Improvements
which have been so much the Object of the Business this session."[58] Neither in this nor in any other way would the King
show pleasure in his Minister; hence Rockingham's credit and
authority sank. A little later a wide breach opened in the cabinet over legislative proposals for the new royal province of
Quebec, and the Lord Chancellor advised the King to summon
Pitt to remodel the administration. During July, Pitt was made
Earl of Chatham and Lord Privy Seal in place of the Duke of
Newcastle, with authority to weed out undesirable men and
bring in new ones without respect to party. Rockingham, who
had tried while in office to revive the vitality of the Whig
"connection" by accenting the principle of party, was now dismissed under circumstances that widened the abyss between
himself and Chatham. But since the Marquess had then no intention of heading a party in opposition, he advised those of
his friends to remain in office who were permitted to do so;
and many of them remained. Burke might have taken a post
under the Chatham ministry without offending Rockingham,
but nothing was offered him. "I consider myself as rather ill
with Pitt's whole party," he told O'Hara. "The situation and
conduct of my own friend is most unfavourable to me." Presumably, "my own friend" was Rockingham. Burke's few extant letters of this period show that he resented the cool treatment he received from the new administration: "If a house
had changed its master, some attention would have been paid
to the footmen of the former family."[59]

The Duke of Grafton, who had been a secretary of state
(until his resignation in April, which began the disintegration
of Rockingham's ministry), was now placed at the head of the
Treasury. The Earl of Camden, who owed his peerage to the
previous administration's desire to please Pitt in 1765, was now
Lord Chancellor. Conway, to whom Rockingham and Burke
were strongly attached, continued as a secretary of state. Nothing
happened at this time in any of the great offices of state to por-

[57] *Correspondence* 1: 308-309.
[58] Fortescue, *op. cit.* 1: 354-355; Albemarle, *op. cit.* 1: 347.
[59] Annaghmore MSS, to O'Hara, July 28, Aug. 19, 1766.

tend the slightest change in American policy; neither the Grenvilles nor the Bedfords had been brought into government as yet, and it was not until late in the year that Chatham was thrown into dependence on the friends of Lord Bute. Even Charles Townshend, who left the Pay Office to become Dowdeswell's successor at the Exchequer, was one of Rockingham's friends and had voted for the redress of American grievances. From the colonial point of view the renovated ministry looked more "American" than ever. Chatham considered creating a third secretary of state for American affairs and taking the office for himself;[60] and, although he did not carry out that plan, colonial patronage and policy were placed in the hands of Secretary of State Shelburne, who had the reputation of understanding and sympathizing with the North American colonies.

Nevertheless, Burke disliked the new administration from the start, and for three reasons: his own exclusion, his now inveterate hostility to Chatham, and the fact—as he wrote to Rockingham—that "nothing but weakness appears in the whole fabric of his ministry."[61] Soon after the opening of Parliament in November, Rockingham chose to resent certain official affronts to his friends still in office; a spate of resignations occurred and the "Rockingham Whigs" appeared as a corps in opposition. Shortly before this happened, Conway had sounded Burke on the possibility of an offer of place, but Rockingham's breach with administration ended that negotiation and Burke went with his party into opposition.[62] They defended the East India Company against government efforts to take control of it and levy heavily upon its resources. They tried to provoke Townshend and Conway, men of great weight with the public, to resign and unite with their party. Thus was opened the great breach in the ranks of those who had united to conciliate America. It never would be closed. When Chatham fell ill his administration went into a state of leaderless confusion and began the fateful crisis in government that eventuated in the dissolution of an empire.

The aim of Burke and his friends was to master this crisis by building a coherent and principled political party different in quality and purpose from the "jobbing" factions of the age

---

[60] Ritcheson, C. R., The elder Pitt and an American department, *Amer. Hist. Rev.* 57: 376-383, 1952.

[61] *Correspondence* 1: 107.

[62] Annaghmore MSS, Burke to O'Hara, post Nov. 11, 1766.

and entirely independent of court influence. He wished to weld
a body of men who trusted one another, held the confidence
of the people, and could give tranquillity to the king because
they would be "united for promoting by their joint endeavours
the national interest upon some particular principle in which
they are all agreed."[63] He had not yet written those words and
probably was not the first Rockingham man to apprehend and
define this principle of party government, but his actions
pointed toward that object. He saw no prospect of gaining
office in the near future, because he knew his chief would make
no unprincipled bargain with the Butes or Bedfords or Grenvilles.[64] How far this parliamentary strategy of neither supporting government nor uniting with other groups in opposition
may have contributed to the general enfeeblement of administration, it would be hard to say; but there can be no doubt that
Burke and his friends helped to alienate Conway and Townshend from Chatham, and inadvertently to encourage Townshend to start upon the rash course that revived the angry
temper of America.

The New York Restraining Act and the Townshend Revenue Act

The repeal of the Stamp Act having left unsolved the
problem of raising what was deemed to be an adequate and
necessary revenue in America, Townshend told the House of
Commons in January, 1767, that he knew how to obtain it; on
challenge from Grenville he pledged himself to devise the way
to get it. The boast was much applauded by men who were
ready to try any expedient that might lighten what was felt to
be an intolerable tax burden; and it became the more necessary for Townshend to make good his word when the House,
late in February, carried against him a reduction of the land
tax—a measure supported by most of the Rockinghams, but not
by Burke.[65]

Moreover, other circumstances conspired to provoke the
Chatham ministry to turn a stern face toward America. A
petition arrived from a body of New York merchants asking for
a relaxation of the 1764 prohibition of bills of credit as legal

---

[63] *Works* 2: 535.

[64] ". . . our leader is steady, and nothing will remove him from the clear
walk he has chosen."—Annaghmore MSS, Burke to O'Hara, March 31, 1767.

[65] Walpole, *Memoirs* 2: 298; Annaghmore Mss, Burke to O'Hara, Feb. 28.

tender and for freer trade in French West Indian sugar.[66] It both annoyed Chatham and embarrassed the Rockinghams, for Burke had boasted that the previous administration had "perfectly reconciled" the interests of the North American and West Indian colonies. The New York merchants even cited the trade and revenue act of the previous spring as having "increased the heavy burden" under which they were compelled to carry on their business. When the petition was brought before the House of Commons and tabled on February 16, it found no champions in Burke and his friends.[67]

This affair probably contributed to that souring of ministerial temper caused by the repeated refusals of the New York Assembly to obey the 1765 Mutiny Act, which obliged that body to provide for the support of the king's troops stationed there. By early 1767 this had become a grave imperial scandal, and Chatham, shortly before going into ministerial eclipse, directed that it "be laid before parliament, in order that his Majesty may be founded in, and strengthened by the sense of his grand council, with regard to whatever steps shall be found necessary to be taken in this most unfortunate business."[68] The Prime Minister evidently envisaged strong measures, but he was stricken before a cabinet decision was reached which reflected the more lenient views of Shelburne, Conway, and Townshend.[69]

But before any ministerial proposals touching American affairs were laid before Parliament, the Duke of Bedford on April 10 moved for an address to the throne to take into consideration the reprehensible conduct of Massachusetts, which had refused to comply with the will of Parliament that compensation be granted to persons who had suffered for attempting to enforce the Stamp Act. Bedford wished the peers to ask the King to act in support of his just rights in Massachusetts, but the ministerial peers were unwilling to be goaded into action by the opposition and rejected the Duke's motion by 63 to 36. Rockingham and his friends voted with the majority, but for reasons of party strategy rather than the merits of the question; for Bedford's motion had reflected discredit on Conway, whom

[66] *Journal of the House of Commons* 31: 158-160.

[67] *Ibid.*, 160; Fortescue, *op. cit.*, 1: 450.

[68] Taylor, W. S., and J. H. Pringle, *Correspondence of William Pitt, Earl of Chatham* 3: 209; London, Murray, 1838-1840.

[69] *Ibid.*, 231.

the Rockinghams still were trying to claim for their own. According to Burke, Rockingham was

of opinion that if the parties [in opposition] had carried on this measure in concert they would have had a majority of one. But the Bedfords and Temples [Grenvilles] chose to be politic, and did not communicate. A motion in which they would agree might easily have been settled. . . . Lord R. did right unquestionably; but an impression was given that weakened the whole body. I make no doubt that it hurt our division when we endeavoured again last Tuesday to hustle this villainous East India enquiry out of the House.[70]

Burke's words suggest that he might have been willing to concert with the other opposition groups against Massachusetts in return for their help in defending the East India Company against the aggressions of the government.

A month later (May 13) Charles Townshend brought before the House of Commons an extraordinary ministerial program of taxes and penalties for America. He proposed new port duties which he believed would approximately double the American customs revenue, and the creation of an American board of customs commissioners for the more effective enforcement of all the revenue laws. The new duties were to fall upon glass, paper, lead for paints, and tea, and Townshend hoped that with this additional revenue all governors and judges in the colonies might be rendered independent of the assemblies for their salaries. He surveyed various instances of colonial disobedience to parliamentary authority, especially refusals to comply with the Mutiny Act, and recommended that an example be made of one colony: New York, where the military headquarters for North America were situated and the defiance of Parliament had been flagrant. Hence, he moved a resolution that the Governor of New York should be restrained from approving any act of the assembly until it had met the requirements of the Mutiny Act. This he considered very moderate: some gentlemen had advised blocking up the harbor and using the military, but he would hear of no such measures. Horace Walpole observed, however, that his speech was "well calculated to inflame the passions of a legislature whose authority was called into question." Townshend's colleague, Conway, thought the proposed punishment of New York went too far:

---

[70] Annaghmore MSS, Burke to O'Hara, April 18.

and Grenville thought it did not go far enough. Burke imputed the plan to Chatham and denounced it as being at once harshly provocative and weakly ineffective.[71] Although attacked from all sides, Townshend's proposal made its way easily into a statute more severe than was perhaps at first intended, since it restrained the legislative functions of the New York governor, council, and assembly until the military forces were provided adequately with all that Parliament required. Burke played no conspicuous part in the debates on this punitive measure, and there is no evidence to indicate that he was New York's champion, although Horace Walpole recorded that

He arraigned the idea of dissolving their Assemblies, at the same time that the House seemed to allow them as a co-ordinate power, since the execution of the Act was to depend on their acquiescence. Yet the suspension of all their laws would fall heavier on the innocent, than the punishment could on the guilty; and what effect would the penalty have? Would not the turbulent be re-chosen? He advised a new model of their police.

Townshend's proposals for a new American revenue and customs board made their way no less easily though a Parliament impatient for prorogation and became laws simultaneously with the New York Restraining Act. It was provided in the Revenue Act "that the said Duties, to be raised in the said Colonies and Plantations, be applied, in the first place, in making a more certain and adequate provision for the Charge of the Administration of Justice, and the Support of Civil Government, in such of the said Colonies and Plantations, where it shall be found necessary. . . ." Thus the clear purpose of Parliament was spelled out: to provide for a colonial civil list, wholly independent of colonial assemblies.

Of Burke's conduct in the passage of the Townshend Revenue Act no more is known than what he said in the house a year and a half later when America was in angry agitation against parliamentary taxation. He declared on November 8, 1768:

With regard to my own conduct, when the proposition was made to the House, I expressed the little opinion I had; and I shall prove a true prophet. I said, that you would never see a single shilling from America. I reminded you, that it was not by votes and angry resolutions of this House, but by a slow and steady conduct that

---

[71] Walpole, *Memoirs* 3: 26.

the Americans were to be reconciled to us. . . . We resumed an act altogether similar to the Stamp Act.[72]

It seems unlikely, however, that Burke either foresaw the consequences of the 1767 Revenue Act and the creation of the American customs board at Boston, or took very great interest in these measures when they were passed.[73]

Parliament and the Crisis in America, 1768-1769

During the session of 1767-1768, no American affairs of consequence occupied the attention of Parliament or, so far as is known, of Edmund Burke. But events in North America were preparing a new storm in empire relations.

The Massachusetts Assembly in February sent to the other colonies its famous circular letter avowing that Parliament had no right to impose duties for revenue in America, claiming therefore that the Townshend Revenue Act was unconstitutional, and denouncing the principle of salaries independent of assembly authorization for governors and judges. These strong assertions exacerbated a long-standing quarrel between the assembly and Governor Bernard, alarmed the new customs commissioners at Boston, and produced an atmosphere of tension and alarm that spread through New England to the other colonies.

About the same time there took place a change in the British ministry which augured ill for improving that situation. The Duke of Bedford's friends in January were brought into the administration, and of all parties these had least sympathy for American points of view; yet they were now united with men who had supported the repeal of the Stamp Act. In the resulting shifts, Conway ceased to be a secretary of state, and although Shelburne remained as secretary for the southern department American affairs were taken out of his hands and entrusted to Hillsborough, who was made a third secretary of state (for the

---

[72] *Cavendish's debates* 1: 39.

[73] Significant, perhaps, of the slightness of his interest is the fact that no notice whatever was taken of the Townshend Revenue Act in the historical article in the *Annual Register* for 1767. Nor was the topic touched by Burke in any of his extant letters of this period. To O'Hara he wrote on June 4: "We have begun the session early; we have continued it long; and we have done nothing."—Annaghmore MSS. That Burke's relations with Townshend were no longer very friendly is suggested by his telling John Hely Hutchinson on Aug. 3, 1767, that Townshend "has no regard for me and I have no confidence in him."—Hist. Mss. Comm., 12th Rep., App., Pt. IX, 260.

colonies) while retaining the presidency of the Board of Trade. Chatham was still in office nominally, but kept by illness from all participation in state affairs. Camden was still Lord Chancellor, but without influence because distrusted by the King. Grafton was still First Lord of the Treasury, but a cipher as head of the cabinet. Charles Townshend was dead. In this administration there was no prime minister, although Lord Frederick North, who was at the Exchequer and led the House of Commons, was fast becoming the chief servant of the King. The new government was weak because it was composed of disparate and mutually distrustful men; moreover, a general election impended. Like all weak governments when faced by defiance, this one's disposition was first to threaten and then to retreat.

When the Massachusetts circular became known in England, Hillsborough commanded Governor Bernard in the King's name to request the assembly to "rescind the resolution which gave birth to the circular letter . . . and to declare their disapprobation of that rash and hasty proceeding." If the assembly refused to do this, it was to be dissolved. To the other governors Hillsborough denounced the circular as of "a most dangerous and factious tendency"; if any assembly gave countenance to such sedition, it would be the governor's duty "to prevent any proceedings upon it by an immediate prorogation or dissolution."[74] But these orders arrived too late to prevent a continental demonstration of support for the Massachusetts position. In June that assembly refused to rescind its resolution, and a Boston mob stoned the custom house, which frightened the commissioners into taking refuge aboard a warship. Military and naval forces were dispatched to Boston. An ugly situation was preparing and out of it arose during the summer a revival of the same kind of non-importation agreements and boycotts that had been started against the Stamp Act.

But in England no great attention was paid to this development for many months. A parliamentary election which touched off the "Wilkes and Liberty" riots in the spring, and the French appropriation of Corsica, dominated the minds of public men; and an early prorogation of the new House of Commons prevented any parliamentary consideration of American affairs until November.

---

[74] *N. Y. documents* 8: 57-58.

No record is known to exist showing that Burke was aware of a serious crisis arising as the news of Massachusetts' conduct reached England during the spring and early summer. His mind was on party affairs, the election and the riots, a projected trip to Italy (which he did not make), and the purchase of a manorial home at Beaconsfield in Buckinghamshire. It is certain that Rockingham by early August was greatly disturbed by the disorders in America, and solicited the opinion of Dowdeswell, who seems to have been the party's specialist on American affairs at this time.[75] The latter regarded the Townshend duties as too small to be a real grievance in America; it was the imprudent exercise of the parliamentary right of taxation that had given offense, and the denial of the right was a most grave matter. Dowdeswell did not believe the Rockingham party could ever support that denial. If the example of Boston was not followed at New York and other places, he saw no difficulty: a show of force would produce submission to the law, after which the Townshend duties might well be repealed on prudential grounds. But if the resistance became general, retreat and conciliation by the British government would be better than war, in which "this country possessed of everything has everything to lose and nothing to get. For a contest with the colonies supported as they will be by the enemies of this country, must be destruction to us in the first place." Dowdeswell, however, was not anticipating such a calamity, but rather believed that "we shall be soon trying who shall stand most forward in proposing terms of accommodation to end the struggle. . . ." In any event, moderate measures were "least dangerous, & if we come off at last with a loss those must answer for it who have wantonly & unnecessarily revived the question & I believe now profess that these duties were laid merely as a test to the Americans." Dowdeswell agreed with Rockingham that George Grenville would presently be recalled to office since his American ideas were apparently being adopted by the ministry. "Port duties laid for revenue only," said Dowdeswell, "are in their nature the same as qualified stamp acts." The Townshend Act

---

[75] Wentworth-Fitzwilliam MSS, Rockingham to Dowdeswell, Aug. 11, 1768; *Ibid*, Rockingham to Burke, Aug. 16, Sept. 27, in which there is no allusion to American affairs. Nor did Burke mention them in his only extant letter (July 18) to Rockingham that summer.—*Correspondence* 1: 158-163. For the importance of Dowdeswell in the party, see Boran, Mother M. Consilia, *William Dowdeswell and the Rockingham Whigs*, N. Y., Fordham U. dissertation, 1954.

could, therefore, be regarded as a revival of Grenvillism, although he acknowledged that the Americans opposed even the "reduced duty on the molasses meant now to be really collected & to say the truth for revenue not for commerce." If the Rockinghams chose to attack the Townshend Act, it would be convenient and bear the appearance of consistency if it could be painted as like the Stamp Act.[76]

Without doubt Dowdeswell's opinion had the greatest weight with Rockingham and strongly influenced Burke's view. The latter's earliest recorded remark on the new American disorders was a denunciation of the ministers. He told O'Hara on September 1 that

the affairs of America prosper ill in their hands. Lord Hillsborough has taken a step which has influenced and united all that country. In short, they proceed wildly, by fits and starts, without order or system. They are made up of a set of people of opposite opinions and no principles; and they are steady to nothing, but perpetual attempts to betray and disgrace one another.[77]

The most copious expression of Burke's mind at this period may be found in the book he published in January, 1769, but probably wrote during the late summer and early fall of the previous year.[78] It contains some passages that seem curiously irrelevant to the new dispute that had arisen with the colonies, and suggest that Burke had not fully apprehended what the real American grievance was. He seemed to regard the Townshend Revenue Act as a measure designed solely to relieve the British Exchequer. He said nothing of the act's declared purpose to establish a colonial civil list; he did not touch upon the controversial question of the right of Parliament to tax the colonies. Possibly his concept of the 1767 measure was colored by his intimate knowledge of its author, for there is little doubt that Townshend personally was more interested in raising money than in reorganizing the empire.[79]

---

[76] Dowdeswell MSS (W. L. Clements Library), Dowdeswell to Rockingham, Aug. 14, 1768.

[77] Annaghmore MSS.

[78] *Observations on a late Publication intituled "The State of the Nation,"* in *Works* 2: 2-213.

[79] "He [Townshend] was indifferent to imperial plans, although his actions had the deepest imperial ramifications. . . . Grenville had seen the vision of an orderly and steadily expanding commonwealth; Townshend saw only an imperial budget."—Ritcheson, C. R., *British politics and the American Revolution,* 100-101, Norman, Okla. Univ. Press, 1954.

Burke's 1769 tract was not directed primarily against the ministry of the day which had plunged into new troubles in America, but against the ideas of George Grenville, who, in spite of the accession of his Bedford friends to ministerial places—and the expectations of Dowdeswell and Rockingham— had remained in opposition, while continuing to utter lamentations over the undoing of his work by the Rockingham administration. Burke's book, therefore, rather memorializes the feud that split the opposition, than states an opposition case against the ministers of the day. He again defended the repeal of the Stamp Act and the passage of the Declaratory Act; and he poured scorn on the Grenvillian idea of obtaining a revenue from America and from Ireland to relieve British taxpayers of the costs of empire. Attempting that meant "calamities that outweighed tenfold the proposed benefit." No idea could be more contemptible "than that of proposing to get any revenue from the Americans but by their freest and most cheerful consent." There was something in the nature of commercial colonies that rendered them an "unfit object of taxation." They made their contribution to the support of empire by submitting to the regulation of their trade by the mother country. The idea of surmounting American objections to taxation without representation by adding American members to Parliament, Burke condemned as chimerical. It was "against the order of Providence;" geography forbade it; America was and ever would be without actual representation in the House of Commons. Nor would any minister be "wild enough even to propose such representation in parliament." America was an object "wholly new in the world," and all reasonings about it that were likely "to be at all solid" should be drawn from its actual circumstances." Under the Navigation Laws it formed a system in which

a principle of commerce, of artificial commerce, must predominate. This commerce must be secured by a multitude of restraints very alien to the spirit of liberty; and a powerful authority must reside in the principal state, in order to enforce them. But the people who are to be the subjects of such restraints are descendants of Englishmen; and of a high and free spirit. To hold over them a government made up of nothing but restraints and penalties, and taxes in the granting of which they can have no share, will neither be wise nor long practicable.

The colonies, in Burke's view, should be compensated by every indulgence that could be reconciled to British interest, not for their own sake but for the preservation of the British Empire; which was not the materialization of a great human plan or the raw material for designing legislators, but an intricate and complex growth of multiform organization that required the most careful study and the most artful and prudent management.

We have a great empire to rule, composed of a vast mass of heterogeneous governments, all more or less free and popular in their forms, all to be kept in peace, and kept out of conspiracy, with one another, all to be held in subordination to this country; while the spirit of an extensive and intricate trading interest pervades the whole, always qualifying, and often controlling, every general idea of constitution and government. It is a great and difficult object; and I wish we may possess wisdom and temper enough to manage it as we ought.

Burke touched very lightly on the new crisis in America, which he thought much less serious than that raised in 1765. It arose, he said, because ministers had returned to the Grenville system—"to measures of the very same nature with those which had been so solemnly condemned"; and he was sure that the nation and the colonies would never fall back "upon their true center of gravity, and natural point of repose," until the ideas of 1766 were resumed and steadily pursued. But one of the ideas of 1766 had been an undisguised tariff for revenue only, not differing in its object from Townshend's fateful duties. It seems to have been Rockingham party strategy to see a revival of Grenvillism in the Townshend Revenue Act, and to ignore that measure's relation to their own North American trade-revenue legislation.

In Parliament on November 8 Burke assailed the inconsistency of those who, after voting for the repeal of the Stamp Act, turned round and supported new measures of the same kind to oppress America. "How can Americans be sure," he asked, "that the persons who voted for them today, will vote for them tomorrow?" Nothing could tend more to estrange America from England than the opinion that all were unsteady. He made the charge that "these taxes or regulations—it is indifferent to me which they are called—were intended to distress the manufacturers of Great Britain." He rebuked the government for ordering the dissolution of the Massachusetts Assembly, and asked,

Was it wise, sir, to bring troops into that government? And with regard to quartering them, after the assembly was dissolved, who was to provide for them? . . . While you have your troops in one place, you will want them in another. There is no such thing as governing the whole body of a people, contrary to their inclinations.[80]

By this time Lord Hillsborough, instead of obtaining compliance to his commands from American assemblies, found himself with his hands full of their petitions denying the right of Parliament to tax the king's subjects in America. He and his colleagues now were, upon reflection, astonished that Parliament ever could have approved the Townshend Revenue Act— a measure so "uncommercial," so incompatible with the principle of the Navigation Act, so obstructive to the export of British wares to North America. Nevertheless, the administration intended to uphold the supreme authority and would not think of repealing the offensive duties until the colonies dropped their denial of the parliamentary right; nor could the conduct of the people of Boston pass without the sternest censure. Hence, on December 15, Hillsborough brought the subject before the House of Lords and moved a series of resolutions in condemnation of the behavior of Massachusetts. The Duke of Bedford followed with a motion for an address to the king promising the support of Parliament for whatever measures were needed to uphold royal authority, and requesting the application of a statute passed in Henry VIII's time for punishing treasons committed outside the realm. The resolutions and address were passed by the peers with little debate and against small opposition.

When they were brought into the lower house, a great debate took place on January 25-26. It began with a request by William Beckford to present a Massachusetts petition for the repeal of acts for raising a colonial revenue. Burke spoke for receiving it, and the House consented to its being read, but divided heavily against referring it to committee. Next an effort was made by William Bollan, the Massachusetts Council agent, to present a petition asking the House to refuse to concur with the resolutions passed by the Lords. The members would not receive so unusual a petition, although Burke urged that it be allowed on the ground that "in these times, and upon these

---

[80] *Cavendish's debates* 1: 38-39.

great occasions, when so many perilous questions are depending, we ought to let the Americans know that they are fully heard." On the main question of approving the Lords' resolutions, Burke made a strong and impassioned speech, charging that the conduct of the government had not been strong and wise, but full of threats and folly: "Without the slightest management, without at all consulting the temper of the people to be governed, they sent out a crowd of undigested orders to the American assemblies, to reject such and such propositions, and adopt others." The assemblies did not obey; they were dissolved; new assemblies were elected which would convene and maintain the same attitude—"you must dissolve them *toties quoties*." Government could only irritate, and never quiet the colonies by such measures. The Duke of Bedford's motion, which implied transporting for trial in England men accused of treason, meant that ministers could not trust a jury in America, a circumstance that "must convey horror to every feeling mind." It meant breaking through all principles of justice and unhinging human society:

Suppose a man brought over for high treason . . . he sends for his witnesses: but by what process can the witnesses be brought here? If they do not appear he cannot have a fair trial: and if he cannot have a fair trial, you fall into injustice, or the law is eluded. God and nature oppose your doing it justly; and whatever acts of injustice you commit in America will react upon ourselves. . . . You have drawn it out from the stores of Henry the Eighth; which are more dangerous than the arms of Boston. . . . The resolutions are the scaffolding, the address the building; all the traverses are in place. I see a bastille behind them.

The Commons finally, on February 8, concurred by large majorities with the Lords.[81]

But out of this ominous bluster the partisans of conciliation drew at least one advantage. The Townshend Revenue Act was subjected in the debate to its first careful parliamentary scrutiny, and as a result there arose a widespread opinion that the act had been wrong in principle; that it laid tariffs which were likely to stimulate the growth of competitive American manufacturers, and hence was incompatible with the purpose of the Navigation Laws.

In this opinion George Grenville and his friends were in

---

[81] *Ibid.*, 185-207.

agreement with Burke and the Rockinghams, although the minister of the Stamp Act still deplored its repeal, and the attitude of both corps towards the removal of the Townshend duties was to be governed by the exigencies of party strategy. Other issues too were meanwhile drawing these long-standing opponents into a tenuous concert.

American affairs came up in Commons again on March 14 when Barlow Trecothick moved for permission to lay before the House a petition from the New York Assembly against the imposition of "duties in the colonies for the declared purpose of raising a revenue," and against the Restraining Act of 1767. Ministerial members opposed receiving the petition because it questioned the parliamentary right of taxation. Colonel Isaac Barré and William Beckford supported Trecothick, and Grenville, exasperated and bitter, said that government must do one thing or another—execute the laws or give up the right. Burke arose to remark "that we had an undoubted right to tax them, but that the expediency of putting that right into execution should be very evident before anything of that sort passed." He favored receiving the petition, which however was not allowed.[82]

Another debate on America took place on April 19, when Thomas Pownall, former Massachusetts governor and an outstanding expert on colonial administration, moved for the House to go into committee to consider modifying or repealing the Revenue Act of 1767.[83] He said there was general agreement "that we should seize the first occasion that offers itself to get back again to that old safe ground of administration upon which American affairs were conducted until the last few years of experiment." Pownall, who was not connected with a party, made a strong and able speech that probably impressed and influenced the administration, but Lord North, its spokesman, was unwilling to go into the question then, not because he had anything to say in defense of existing revenue laws in America, but because of "the combinations going on in America against the mother country." Any new legislation so late in the session would "furnish a fresh instance of haste, impatience, levity, and fickleness unworthy of parliament."[84] Barré urged that the

---

82 Cobbet, William, and J. Wright, *Parliamentary history of England* 16: 603-605, London, Hansard, 1806-1820. (Cited hereafter as *Parliamentary history*).

83 *Cavendish's debates* 1: 391-401.

84 An implied censure on both the Rockinghams and Charles Townshend whose trade and revenues measures of 1766 and 1767 were introduced and passed

House at least adopt a resolution declaring its intention for the next session to enter upon a revision of "all the laws relating to America passed since the beginning of the reign." This was in line with a wide-spread opinion, especially among the Chatham-Shelburne and Grenville factions, that what was needed was a large, general, and comprehensive new plan for the empire in America. But North would not commit the ministerial side to any conciliatory gesture unless and until "America shall have behaved with duty and proper respect." Burke took part in this debate and stated an interesting and almost unique opinion, which showed again how cautious was his attitude toward the Townshend Revenue Act. Recognizing the impossibility of Parliament's doing anything immediately, he deplored agitating the question because that could only embitter feelings on both sides of the ocean:

The Americans have made a discovery, or think they have made one, that we mean to oppress them: we have made one, or think we have made one, that they intend to rise in rebellion against us. Our severity has increased their ill behaviour: we know not how to advance; they know not how to retreat. . . . If the question was, whether we should repeal the act in question, I have no hesitation in saying repeal. But we cannot, the gentlemen say, repeal it during the present session; it is part of a complicated commercial system. The question, therefore, is whether, when you cannot repeal it, you ought to agitate it. . . . The disposition of the administration, with regard to America, must have some change. Why go on with the parade of parliamentary debates, which is poison, gall, and bitterness to the Americans? The more eloquence we display, the further we deviate from wisdom. What is done must be done silently, and in the closet. . . . I would be to the Americans personally a friend; to their power an eternal enemy: but I would never agitate or stir that question. I hope that, when they see the unfortunate end of every measure, they will come to a better feeling.

Burke's argument thus ran as hard against Barré's proposal as against the administration. Repealing the Townshend duties or committing Parliament to any future course of conduct in the American crisis drew no support at this time from the Rockingham party. Those who spoke for the Pownall and

---

late in the session. "The inability of the country gentlemen to stay until the end of the session was so notorious that it was sometimes thought sharp practice to propose anything serious after the Easter recess."—Pares, Richard, *George III* and *the Politicians*, 10, London, Oxford, 1953.

Barré proposals were chiefly of the Chatham-Shelburne corps; and it was politically significant that George Grenville concluded a long and ambiguous speech by saying, "You ought to make no declaration, as to your future intention."

The advice offered by Burke was actually followed in a limited way that spring, when the administration began a conciliation policy towards America. The cabinet agreed to ask Parliament in the next session to repeal all the 1767 port duties except that on tea. Whereupon, Hillsborough sent a circular letter (May 13) to the colonial governors assuring them that the present administration not only entertained no design of proposing to lay further taxes on America, but intended to ask Parliament to take off the glass, paper, and paints duties, "upon consideration of such Duties having been laid contrary to the true principles of commerce."[85]

After the harsh threats of ministers and Parliament during the winter, this move bore the appearance of a capitulation to colonial malcontents, and it would draw severe criticism from Burke for that reason. Hillsborough also recalled the unpopular Governor Bernard from Massachusetts. But some months had to pass before this appeasement could produce mollifying effects in America, so that throughout 1769 ominous reports of defiance and association for boycott continued to arrive. Burke, however, seems to have been too much concerned with other great affairs, to pay much attention to those of America.

"Wilkes and Liberty"

It was not the championing of American grievances that caused Burke in 1769 to rise to fame and popularity among American as well as English Whigs. That was due to the part he took, or rather was believed to have taken, in a cause hardly less interesting to Americans than to Englishmen. This was the year the electors of Middlesex county were denied the right to be represented in Parliament by the man they had chosen—John Wilkes, and instead had forced upon them a court-backed minority candidate—Henry Lawes Luttrell. The issue went to the very sources of civil and political liberty, and the Whigs of America were at one with the Whigs of England in indignation at a constitutional outrage. American and English discontents seemed to blend in one reaction against a common

---

[85] *N. Y. documents* 8: 164-165.

oppressor, George III's ministry; and in America it seems to have been assumed generally that the partisans of Wilkes were *ipso facto* the partisans of America. It is important, therefore, to note exactly what were Burke's opinions and acts in this great question of the rights of electors in England.

We have already seen that he held Wilkes in low esteem at the time (1763-1764) that bold and prickly gentleman had been prosecuted for seditious libel and blasphemy, expelled from Parliament, and driven into exile. There is no reason to believe he had a better opinion of Wilkes when the latter returned to England in 1768 and stood for a seat in the new Parliament. On hearing of Wilkes's election for Middlesex (while illegally at large but undisturbed by crown authorities) Burke told O'Hara:

That Wilkes has been chosen for Middlesex is an event which, from the dull state of the public, and the oblivion into which he had fallen, I confess I did not at all expect. But at a time, when the people are unfastened from all their usual moorings, as they are at a general election, nothing ought to occur as a matter of surprise. Besides the crowd always want to draw themselves from abstract principles to personal attachments; and since the fall of Lord Chatham, there has been no hero of the mob but Wilkes. The surprise aided him; Government had not time to take measures; and they are indeed too disunited to take any that can be effectual.[86]

Burke had no more relish for mob heroes than for the licentious ministry whose too-ready resort to the use of military force against municipal disorder provoked what was popularly called the "massacre of St. George's Fields," in early May, when the new Parliament was convened. The occasion was a riotous demonstration against the imposition by the King's Bench court of a prison sentence on Wilkes (for his former crimes) after he had voluntarily surrendered to the authorities. At this moment and for some years thereafter, Burke and his friends stood completely aloof from Wilkes and his partisans. He confided to O'Hara:

The plan of our party was, I think, wise and proper; not to provoke Administration into any violent measures upon this subject; nor be the means of stirring questions, which we had not the strength to support, and which could not be lost, without leaving

---

[86] Annaghmore MSS, *ca.* March 28, 1768.

the constitution worse than we found it. It could be no service to Wilkes to take him out of the hands of the *law,* and to drive him under the talons of *power;* besides we had not the slightest desire of taking up that gentleman's cause. . . . He is a lively agreeable man, but of no prudence and no principles. Had they [ministers] attempted to attack him, we must have defended him, and were resolved to do it; but still as the cause, not the person.[87]

When Wilkes from his prison in November petitioned the House of Commons to order his release that he might take his seat as member for Middlesex, Burke advised that no notice be taken of the petition, since Wilkes's jail-term had still more than a year to run. That sagacious counsel might have been followed had Wilkes not published a new libel against the ministers, and behaved, when summoned to answer for it before the House of Commons, with such aggravating insolence that a motion was carried to expel him and declare his seat vacant. Against this motion a strong opposition formed which included the followers of Rockingham, Grenville, Chatham, and Shelburne. When the Middlesex voters re-elected Wilkes unanimously, the House of Commons passed a resolution declaring him disqualified from sitting in the Parliament of 1768.

Burke pleaded with the House not only against the doubtful legality of the disqualification, but against doing anything at all. Since Wilkes was still a prisoner of the state, why force the issue and inflame the voters? "The people will take fire," he said, "if they find the sense of the House going one way, and the sense of the public another." Instead of challenging repeatedly the Middlesex electors and sparking the angry passions of the metropolitan mob, Parliament ought to inquire into the causes of the strange and mysterious public discontent that underlay the "Wilkes and Liberty" turbulence. Believing that ministerial misgovernment lay at the root, Burke made a formal motion in the House (the first of his parliamentary career) on March 8, to inquire into the conduct of government in connection with the riots and tumults of St. George's Fields. In a long and eloquent speech, he warned that,

if ever the time should come, when this House shall be found prompt to execute and slow to inquire; ready to punish the excesses of the people and slow to listen to their grievances . . . ready to invest magistrates with large powers and slow to enquire into the

[87] *Ibid.,* June 9, 1768.

exercise of them; ready to entertain notions of military power as incorporated with the constitution—when you learn this is in the air of St. James's, then the business is done: then the House of Commons will change that character which it receives from the people only.

Burke's motion was deeply offensive to ministry, which had been libelled by Wilkes in connection with this affair; and the house too took offense because the Wilkite mob had defied its authority. Burke's motion was voted down heavily.

Shortly afterwards, Middlesex again re-elected Wilkes and the House declared the election null and void. Burke opposed both the writ for the election and the nullifying resolution, warning once more against a contest between the House of Commons and its constituency. He urged that the Middlesex seat be allowed to remain vacant until the electors cooled off:

We have not given quiet to the County, by urging a repetition of elections. Let us try if a little repose will not be the best mode of obtaining it. . . . Those persons are the friends of Wilkes and the enemies of their country, who keep his name constantly in the public eye.

But a writ for yet another election was issued by the House, and the final result was the seating of Luttrell, who had got but a small minority of votes. Burke fought this action to the end, not as a partisan of Wilkes, but as a defender of the right of lawful electors to choose their own member of Parliament instead of having a court-backed candidate foisted upon them.[88]

Although ominous reports from North America were arriving almost daily and Wilkite radicals likened their grievances to those suffered by the Americans, all colonial questions receded into the background before the issue of the violated right of electors. The seating of Luttrell brought the whole Commons minority into temporary union, and after the prorogation of Parliament on May 10, a great petitioning movement got under way in the cities and counties. It reached to the dimensions of a near-national appeal to the King to dissolve a House of Commons guilty of so grievous a breach of the constitution.[89] Burke

---

[88] *Cavendish's debates* 1: 46, 61-82, 93-105, 106-185, 226-237, 307-337, 345-356, 360-386, 404-413.

[89] But opposition members dispersed for the summer without uniting in a common plan. The tone of Burke's letter to O'Hara of May 31 suggests that he was tired of the Middlesex election crisis and skeptical of any further con-

and his political friends had no part in starting this movement,
which was Wilkite in origin, but once it was under way he
threw himself into it with great energy. He spurred Lord
Rockingham to activity, and their party, while trying to prevent the petitioning movement from being diverted to wild
extremes, exploited it for the purpose of consolidating all opposition groups and overturning the administration.[90] How
small the American question appeared to Burke at this time, in
comparison with his party business, may be measured by the
lengths he was prepared to go to sustain the concert with Grenville. Early in September he was visited by Grenville's political
agent, Thomas Whately, to whom he said very agreeable words
about the author of the Stamp Act and sought to expand their
area of agreement for the next session of Parliament. The subject of America inevitably came up and Whately said that if,
as was expected, ministry proposed repeal of the Townshend
duties, "we should certainly not agree to it." Burke answered
that "as for himself, he hardly thought he should oppose; most
probably he would absent himself; for his friends, many of them
agreed in his principles, and some of them did not go so far."[91]
Two days later Burke commented in a letter to Rockingham
that "America is more wild and absurd than ever." [92]

The Party Strategist and the American Question in 1770

When Parliament was opened in January, 1770, the royal
and ministerial strategy was to ignore the spate of petitions for
a dissolution and to direct the attention of the Houses to
America. There, said the King in the speech from the throne,
his efforts to bring back his subjects "to their duty, and to a
due sense of lawful authority," had not answered to his expectations. The House of Commons approved an address promising
to take into consideration the serious state of His Majesty's government in America. Burke took a leading part in the debate on

solidation of opposition groups.—Annaghmore MSS. It was not until after the
Wilkites in London and Middlesex began to meet and petition that Burke became active in the outdoor campaign.

[90] *Correspondence* 1: 168-220; Albemarle, *op. cit.* 2: 92-106; Wentworth-
Fitzwilliam MSS, Rockingham to Burke, June 29, July 17, Sept. 1, 3, Oct. 15,
1769, Burke to Rockingham, Sept. 8, 9; Annaghmore MSS, Burke to O'Hara,
Aug. 28. Rockingham's cautious disposition tried Burke's patience that summer.

[91] Smith, W. J., ed., *The Grenville Papers* 4: 440-452, London, Murray,
1852-1853; Wentworth-Fitzwilliam MSS, Whately to Burke, Aug. 30, 1769.

[92] Wentworth-Fitzwilliam MSS, Sept. 9, 1769.

the address. According to the most reliable account of what he said, he laid responsibility for the trouble in America on the backs of ministers who had found America "in the most perfect peace and harmony" and were "the first and only cause of destroying that harmony." They had begun by treating America harshly and afterwards spoke of her as disaffected, thus reversing "the rule of all wise and prudent governments, which try gentle measures first, and if those fail, have recourse to compulsive ones." He did not wish to justify all that the Americans had done, but in most things they had "reasoned better on the constitution than we do."[93]

But no effort was made by the ministers to lead Parliament to a fulfillment of the promise made in the address. They had nothing more to propose than the partial repeal of the Townshend duties, in accordance with the intention Hillsborough had stated to the colonies in his letter of the previous May 13. Lord North, who in January had succeeded Grafton as First Lord of the Treasury, on March 5 moved to bring in a bill to extinguish the American port duties on glass, paper, and paints. He explained that the proposed measure was not for the appeasement of rebellious Americans, whose conduct he censured severely, but for the benefit of London merchants who had petitioned against obstacles to British exportation. He grounded his argument on the "uncommercial" character of the duties. If it were argued that the same could be said of the duty on tea, his reply was that tea, unlike the other commodities taxed by the Townshend Act, was not a product of British industry; that the tax on it was an excellent port duty and would ultimately "go a great way towards effecting the purpose for which it was laid"; and finally, that it should be kept to vindicate Parliament's right to lay taxes for revenue in the colonies. Beckford, Pownall, Barré, Trecothick, General Conway, and even War Secretary Barrington spoke for making a clean sweep of the Townshend port duties. Burke seems not to have been present at this occasion, but much was heard from two men with whom he and the Rockinghams were now in a tactical alliance, Grenville and Alexander Wedderburn. They opposed North's motion on two main grounds: that it was not adequate for

---

[93] There is no authentic report of this speech, but the *London Magazine* version given in *Speeches of the Right Honourable Edmund Burke* 1: 14-27, London, 1816 (a poor collection of no great value) is fairly consonant with what appear to have been Burke's views at this time.

conciliating America, and that it implied a return to the practice of raising money in America by crown requisition instead
of parliamentary taxation. These men chose to regard the
American question in the light of the issue raised by the
Middlesex election—undue crown influence—which was the
cement of their concert with the Rockinghams. North, however, carried his motion without a division and the bill was
enacted.[94]

During the stormy session of 1770 there was scarcely a debate that did not relate in some way to the violated rights of
electors, ministerial mismanagements at home and abroad, and
the petitions and outdoor agitations for a dissolution of the
House of Commons. But as the King stood firm, and the
agitation took on a more and more radical tinge, Rockingham
and his friends gradually disassociated themselves from it; and
when news arrived in April of the Boston "Massacre" of March
5, it became the strategy of Burke's party to concentrate their
attack upon government misconduct in America. Barlow
Trecothick brought the Boston incident before the House on
April 25 with a motion for papers. Burke seized the occasion
to deplore Parliament's having done nothing to keep its promise
to take American affairs into serious consideration: "Having
finished your war against Mr. Wilkes—if finished it be—you have
broken your faith to the Crown." The motion for papers was
carried, and Burke said he would shortly "open a more ample
view of the government of America for three years past."[95]

He did this on May 9, which was one of the most important
days so far in his parliamentary career. Although prorogation
was imminent and many members had dispersed for the summer, the House was not as small as it usually was so late in the
session. According to Will Burke, although "all the world had
gone into the country, and business over," yet "the expectations
were very great, the house very full."[96] It was understood that
Burke intended a major party maneuver, and ministerial partisans took care to have the lobby and gallery cleared so that the
speech would not resound outdoors. He spoke for his party,
in concert with Grenville. He said (but not quite accurately)
that he and his party had been silent upon American affairs for

---

[94] *Cavendish's debates* 1: 483-500.

[95] *Ibid.*, 548-552.

[96] Annaghmore MSS, W. Burke to O'Hara, June 15, 1770.

three years; not that they had failed to give their assent or dissent when measures touching the colonies had been before Parliament, but "no vexatious proceedings, no enquiries, with a view to obstruct government in their plan of operations" had been started by them.

Our former silence, however, obliges us to speak now. I postponed my motion from day to day, in the hope that those who, on the first day of the session, involved the House in a promise to the throne, would have helped us a little at the last, and thrown some light upon the mode in which we could best perform it. That hope has passed away. . . . In this situation, even I, Sir, shall, I hope be excused for venturing to bring this great matter before the House. . . . I do it from a conviction that it involves the immediate salvation of the empire.

No doubt Burke wished to maintain the Empire (which certainly was not yet collapsing) but his immediate aim was to use America as a stick with which to beat the ministers, for his speech was a mixture of the fundamentally unfusable opinions of the Grenvilles and Rockinghams on America. Grenville, who had agreed in advance to support Burke's resolutions, had been continually calling for a comprehensive plan of government in America to solve the problem that had vexed and baffled every administration since his own. But Burke had no such plan, because he agreed with Rockingham that America could not be governed from England—"the profoundest deliberations of cabinet wisdom would shrivel into folly, if once blown upon by the rude breath of a popular assembly." But this most un-Grenvillian proposition was only an incidental remark, not the burden of his argument, which he kept as near as possible to Grenville's views. In recollecting the conciliation of America in 1766 he did not rub salt in old wounds, but referred to the debate in repealing the Stamp Act as if that fierce controversy had been only a small difference among gentlemen over the proper policy for subduing the ill temper of the colonists. After that Burke could inveigh as hard as he liked against the Townshend measures and all that followed without risking a murmur from Grenville. He condemned passing the Revenue Act of 1767 without taking any steps "to reconcile it to the minds of the Americans." How to have done that, he did not say! And after he had scored the ministers for their bullying coercion, he scolded them again for a cowardly appeasement. Never did an administration appear "so mean, so contemptible," as the British government in the fall and winter of 1768-1769:

Finding the no effect of some of their measures, and the small effect of others, they next came forward with an address to the throne, respecting the riots and disturbances in the Town of Boston; and, upon this plan, there was brought before you—I really know not what to call it—a proposition to revive an obsolete act of Henry VIII., passed in the dotage of his understanding and the last year of his reign. . . . They laid it upon your table, and you accepted it. One would have imagined . . . that they were about to annihilate these rebellious subjects; that they were proceeding forthwith to crush these disobedient people. They were going to do nothing of the kind. On the contrary, they were, at this very time, launching a measure of absolute, unconditional, entire submission to them.

As a result of conduct that was at once provocative and poltroonish, British government, Burke charged, had collapsed in America. "Sir, you have lost everything. You have not kept a single rag of your authority to cover you. . . . Every act of authority exercised by you has been treated with contempt, and attended with the disgrace of your forces." Grenville doubtless was delighted to hear Burke go on to assail Hillsborough's promise to the colonies to seek repeal of the Townshend duties, as an infringement upon the freedom of parliament:

Why was the word of the King, why was the word of his confidential servants, so pledged, but to influence Parliament? . . . They promulgate in America what it is intended we should do, before we are allowed to think of it. Surely, the least they could have done was to leave your judgment free. Suppose you should think proper to levy a tax upon America—would not the people have reason to look upon the King's word as forfeited? Parliament is not free: the Ministers are bound up: the King is bound: the Parliament is bound.

It must be evident that these words were extravagant and unfair. They were hardly consistent with what Burke had said in April, 1769, when Thomas Pownall moved for repeal of the Townshend duties. At that time he had deplored parliamentary discussion of the subject and called for a change in the disposition of the administration—for doing something "silently, and in the closet"; and that had been done. But now it appeared that conciliating America was not properly a ministerial but a parliamentary business. It was not becoming of Burke to talk the language of Grenville.

Not a word did Burke say in defense of American conduct; his heart was not melted with sympathy for oppressed colonists, but hard with hostility against the ministers of the day who by rashness, ignorance, imprudence, weakness and timidity, had bungled the management of America and thus discredited British authority there. The Americans had lost their faith in British government because of the servility of Parliament to a bad set of ministers. Here the argument went to that alleged court-subornation of Parliament which was at the bottom of the violation of the rights of Middlesex electors: "Restore Parliament to its native dignity, and you will then restore repose to America. When they see you have honour and dignity and power enough to put down their systems of fraud and violence, they will believe you can bring back tranquillity and happiness." Like the wisest of men, Burke could sometimes talk nonsense.

He concluded by offering eight resolutions. The first two declared the existence of disorders in America "prejudicial to the trade and commerce of this kingdom, and destructive to the peace and prosperity of the said colonies," and cited the "ill-judged and inconsistent instructions" of the administration as the principal cause of the disorders. The third and fourth condemned both the dissolution of colonial assemblies and permitting newly chosen ones to deliberate without complying with royal commands. This was a "proceeding full of inconsistency, and tending to lower, in the minds of his Majesty's subjects in America, all opinion of the wisdom and firmness of his Majesty's councils." The fifth branded Hillsborough's promise to seek repeal of certain duties as "a high breach of the privilege of this House." The sixth and seventh declared that conduct to be "highly derogatory from his Majesty's honour" and likely to "weaken the authority of lawful government." The eighth asserted "that to lay before this House suggestions of treason, or misprisions of treason, subsisting in America, when in reality no such treasons or misprisions of treason did subsist, or if they did subsist, no measures whatsoever have been taken, or appear to have been intended, for apprehending or punishing the persons concerned in the same, is an audacious insult on the dignity of Parliament. . . ."[97]

Grenville and Wedderburn were the principal speakers who

---

[97] *Cavendish's debates* 2: 14-37.

rose to support Burke's resolutions, but the combined attack caused no great embarrassment to Lord North. With wit and truth he said that since the gentlemen had no other plan for America than to remove the present ministers, they ought to determine what sort of government should succeed. Was it to be the government that proposed the Stamp Act, or the government that repealed it? Burke forced a division on only his second resolution, which was rejected by 199 to 79. When the same resolutions were offered by the Duke of Richmond in the Lords they were rejected by a comparably heavy majority.

This was the last business before Parliament was prorogued. Burke was of the opinion that "the session ended well for me, I thank God. . . . The American day did me no discredit."[98] Perhaps it did not; at least he had executed a party maneuver that brought a good many country gentlemen back to Westminster in response to his call of the House. Horace Walpole, who disliked and distrusted Burke, said he had made a "fine oration."[99] William Burke, no impartial judge, thought his gifted cousin had won a great personal triumph—"the utmost expectations were fully answered—and he certainly stands higher than ever he did in his life. I had almost said the highest of any man in the country."[100] Connecticut's agent, William Samuel Johnson, was less impressed. He reported:

> It is plain enough that these motions were not made for the sake of the Colonies, but merely to serve the purposes of the Opposition, to render the Ministry, if possible, more odious, so that they may themselves come into the conduct of affairs, while it remains very doubtful whether they would do much better, if at all, than their predecessors.[101]

By 1770 Burke had been four years in Parliament, and his contemporaries saw him still as an Irish newcomer of obscure origins who derived his political existence from the Marquess of Rockingham, chief of the strongest and most coherent body of Whigs. Although the most active and energetic of that noblemen's following, he was second to William Dowdeswell in managing the business of the Rockinghams in the House of Commons. The libellous gossip of the day, inspired by political

---

[98] Annaghmore MSS, to O'Hara, May 21.
[99] Walpole, *Memoirs* 4: 99.
[100] Annaghmore MSS, to O'Hara, June 15.
[101] *Trumbull Papers*, 437, *Mass. Hist. Soc. Coll.*, 5th ser., No. 9, 1885.

malice and fed by the "get-rich-quick" schemes and speculations of his brother and cousin, spread doubts about his honesty; and his gifted pen and long previous career as a writer for the book-sellers gave rise to the slander (or the compliment) that he was the author of the "Junius letters" which at this time were assailing the reputations of leading public men. But he was connected politically with men whose characters were un-blemished, and all marvelled at his talents of utterance in the House of Commons. The Rockingham party pamphlet, *Thoughts on the Cause of the Present Discontents*, which had been published in April, 1770, and which Burke was known to have written, not only displayed his genius as a political thinker but emphasized his complete separation from the demagogic radicalism of the age. His politics were the politics of aristoc-racy, so that he did not appear as a man who would burn him-self out in some momentary fire of political enthusiasm, but as one possessing the sobriety and sagacity to take part in a future administration.

Such was the Burke whose fame crossed the Atlantic, and who was solicited by the New York Assembly to become agent for its affairs in England. He was not a political friend of John Wilkes or Lord Chatham; he had never agreed that Parliament lacked constitutional authority to lay what taxes it pleased on America; nor had he ever defended American views and in-terests except on prudential grounds determined by the strategy of his party and the exigencies of the British mercantile com-munity. As yet he had not even identified himself as a man primarily interested in American affairs; certainly those of the East India Company had concerned him more. He was not well acquainted with the contemporary colonial scene and, so far as is known, had no regular correspondents in North America until after 1770. He envisaged the colonies as subordinate members of an empire in which the supreme senate was the British Parliament. He wished to maintain them in just that position, and to see them so managed that their good will was cultivated and no strain put upon their imperial loyalty. He was a thoroughly Briticized Irishman who had become an English country squire, a passionate patriot for his adopted country and an ardent upholder of its empire.

Why did a man so circumstanced and so connected politi-cally accept the New York agency? Even now a certain answer cannot be given to the question. Although the letters he wrote to his employers in New York have come to light, there are no surviving communications to show how they first approached him or how he first reacted to their offer. Nor can information about this be found in his other papers, since he seems never to have said anything about his agency business to anyone except his principals and the government officials with whom he transacted New York affairs. Several probable reasons for his accepting, may, however, be suggested. The first is negative and explains why he could except rather than why he did. The agency being solely for the assembly, it carried no taint of "place." An opposition man could hold it without compromising his independence of administration, and perhaps Burke's dislike of crown influence in the House of Commons made him a natural sympathizer with the resistance of colonial assemblies to subornation by royal governors. Undoubtedly he saw in the agency a modest opportunity to help in cultivating a spirit of mutual accommodation between the colonies and the mother country. He had for long stood on a friendly footing with John Pownall, secretary to the Board of Trade, and it is certain that he consulted with Richard Jackson, solicitor to that office, before he accepted the position.[102] With such men he could get along well. It is very likely that an important reason was the salary of 500 pounds per annum. He had very little money and seems to have pooled his small resources with his brother and cousin. When the Beaconsfield estate was acquired, Richard and Will, the fortune-hunters of the clan, were on the road to great prospective wealth through speculation in East India Company shares. But in 1769 they suffered a financial catastrophe in which all was lost. The blow fell before even the downpayment for the estate had been made or the heavy mortgages completely negotiated.[103] A regular income of five hundred a year must have been highly attractive to an impecunious politician lately turned farmer, whose party had no prospect of coming soon into office.

Perhaps his friend O'Hara answered the why-question asked here when he wrote to Burke of a piece of news he had heard

---

[102] Wentworth-Fitzwilliam MSS, Burke's New York letter-book, *infra,* Burke to Delancey, Aug. 20, 1772.

[103] Annaghmore MSS, Burke and Richard Burke to O'Hara, June 1, 1769; other letters in this collection throw new light on Burke's financial embarrassments. See also Wecter, *loc. cit.,* 28-29.

that pleased him: "I mean the American Agency which you have accepted of. It is a mark of approbation of a people, and therefore more welcome than any favour from a single man. It leaves you free to your own pursuits, both in politics and in farming."[104]

---

[104] Wentworth-Fitzwilliam MSS, O'Hara to Burke, July 11, 1771.

III. New York in the British Empire, 1760-1770

WILLIAM TRYON, Governor of New York during the period when Edmund Burke was the assembly's agent in London, described the constitution of that colony as a near-replica of the British constitution. The governor was in the place of the king. The Council, of which the members were named by the king to serve during royal pleasure, had some resemblance to the House of Lords as an upper legislative chamber, and in its advisory function could be compared with the Privy Council. Tryon likened the Assembly to the House of Commons, since it was elected by the freeholders and was convened, prorogued, and dissolved by royal authority acting through the governor. "All laws proposed to be made by this Provincial legislature," wrote Tryon, "pass thro' each of the Houses of Council and Assembly, as Bills do through the House of Commons and House of Lords in England, and the Governor has a negative voice in the making and passing of all laws."[1]

This comparison could be developed much further and extended beyond civil institutions to history and the structure of society, for New York had become a royal colony in 1685 by the accession of its proprietor, James, Duke of York, to the throne in England, and had acquired its elective organ of representation almost simultaneously with the parliamentary revolution that overturned King James. The ruling classes in both Great Britain and colonial New York were landed and mercantile aristocracies. Moreover, the colony with its large Dutch stock and non-English origin was, like the United Kingdom, more British than English. These and other similarities were striking and often remarked. Dr. Cadwallader Colden once observed invidiously that "the New England Governments are formed on republican principles & these principles are zealously inculcated in their youth, in opposition to the principles of the Constitution of Great Britain. The Government

---

[1]Report of Governor William Tryon on the state of the Province of New York, 1774, O'Callaghan, E. B., *Documentary history of the state of New York* 1: 753-754, Albany, Weed, Parsons, 1850-1851.

of New York, on the contrary is established, as nearly as may be, after the model of the English constitution."[2] If New England's political tradition was puritan, New York's was preeminently whiggish. Doubtless all this may help to explain why New York was less victimized than were other colonies by politicians in Great Britain whose passion it was to remodel colonial governments. It was so much what the British authorities desired all colonies to be: royal, not proprietary or chartered, and mirroring the institutions of the mother country. The similarities suggested here may help also to explain why New York was the stronghold of loyalism when the imperial civil war broke out in 1775; and why that colony's leaders, although quick enough to resist oppressive acts of Parliament, were very reluctant to rebel and secede from the empire. In a broad and general way they may help to explain also the curious connection that arose between New York and Edmund Burke.

Assembly vs. Governor and Province vs. Great Britain

But differences existed that were of equal or greater historical importance. The governor's council, for instance, in reality was not at all like the British House of Lords, that powerful assembly which was capable of buttressing both the freedom of the people and the authority of the king. The peers of England were not councillors serving at the royal pleasure, but members of a body wherein they sat in their own right. The king might remove a member from the New York Council, as he might strike the name of any man from his Privy Council, but he could not bar a peer of the realm from his place in the House of Lords. There was nothing in New York or in any other colony that resembled the House of Lords in its principle. Again, the royal legislative veto had fallen into obsolescent disuse in Great Britain, but the principle of colonial subordination to the mother country kept that veto a living reality in New York. It was often exercised by the governor, and not infrequently measures he approved were afterwards disallowed by the king in Privy Council.

All colonial enactments repugnant to the laws and statutes of Great Britain were certain to be disallowed, which meant a real and sometimes vexatious restraint on the natural tendency of the colonial legislature to adapt its legislation to local needs

---

[2] *N. Y. documents* 7: 565.

and circumstances. And the procedure of disallowance could be perfectly infuriating. Colonial laws were always referred to the Board of Trade for close scrutiny by officials who could not be well acquainted with the actuality of conditions three thousand miles away; nor could colonial agents always provide all the information needed for a fair and just consideration. Burke, for example, complained several times that his New York employers did not supply him with adequate explanations and instructions. When the laws emerged from the routine processes of the Board of Trade's secretary, solicitor, and clerks, they were brought before the lords commissioners (who were the board) and these often found it necessary to refer them to the law officers of the crown. The number of subjects and quantity of papers referred to these commissioners (often called the lords of trade) varied a great deal over the years, but the mass was always large and the commissioners would have been swamped with business had they attempted to give careful consideration to any but important subjects. One need but open their journal at random to see that this was so. The journal for April 21, 1774, for example, shows that the board attended to affairs of Jamaica, Antigua, New Jersey, Pennsylvania, Massachusetts, Virginia, and New York. The New York entry is as follows: "Their lordships read and considered sixty-seven laws passed in the Province of New York in 1773, together with Mr. Jackson's report thereupon, and some objections occurring to two of the said laws, it was ordered, that the draught of a representation to his Majesty thereupon should be prepared."[3] It is manifest that the commissioners could not have *read* these laws; it is unlikely even that they read Jackson's report of them. Only a few points could have been considered, the rest being left to determination by the lower officials.[4] It seems almost never to have happened that the lords commissioners overrode an opinion of Secretary Pownall or Solicitor Jackson, so that a colonial enactment that was great in the eyes of those who passed it, but small when viewed at the imperial center, might run aground among the permanent board officials and be disallowed

---

[3] *Journal of the Commissioners for Trade and Plantations from January, 1768, to December, 1775,* 393, London, H.M. Stationery Office, 1937. (Cited hereafter as Journal of Commissioners.)

[4] According to A. H. Basye, the lower officials performed "the greatest part of the business of the board, and it is very probable that many policies were carried out and many reports written of which the commissioners themselves had only perfunctory knowledge."—Basye, *op. cit.,* 36.

on their recommendation through the commissioners to the king in Privy Council—a year or several years after it had gone into effect in the colony. Much depended, therefore, on the wisdom and prudence of the secretary of state under whom the Board of Trade carried on its work.

It is then easy to see that the constitutional connection between New York and Great Britain provided causes and opportunities for conflicts not only between assembly and governor, but between legislators on one side of the ocean and a disallowing authority on the other. Given the growth of the colony in wealth and population, and the British parliamentary model of government before all eyes, contests were inevitable. Nor could it be in any way surprising that the new spirit in government inaugurated by George III and his ministers should tend to communicate itself to a body politic constructed so like Britain, and to provoke a corps of opposition comparable to that which sprang up in the parent country.

A lively source of quarrelling between the Assembly and the crown officials in the colony was the way in which public servants were paid. The governor received a salary from the king but depended also upon an additional annual grant from the assembly, which had jealous control of the colonial purse and believed itself to be the sole taxing authority. The king indeed owned vast property in the colony and the assembly neither taxed it nor pretended to any rights whatever over his revenues from it; he had too the disposal of the customs revenues, although the assembly reserved its right by making an annual grant of these to the crown. As for direct taxation, the assembly considered that domain to be exclusively its own, and not the governor but the assembly appointed the provincial treasurer. All other officials, save the assembly's clerk, doorkeeper, serjeant-at-arms, and agent in London, were appointed by the king directly or by the governor. The chief justice was named by the king, but three-fourths of his salary was provided by the assembly, which meant that a chief justice needed friends in that body. The puisne, or lower judges were appointed by the governor; they depended entirely upon the assembly for their salaries, and thus were beholden even more to the assembly than to the governor. The attorney-general, a direct crown appointee, received part of his pay from the king and part from the assembly; and this was the situation also of the secretary of the province. There were a number of other officials—of the customs, the king's woods, the Indian department, etc.—who were solely dependent on the crown; and still others, such as the clerk and messenger of the council, the printer, etc., who were appointed by the governor but paid by the assembly.[5] In this variety of arrangements lay abundant fuel for feeding an almost inextinguishable fire of dispute and contest between the appointing governor and the disbursing assembly, between local interests and the higher interests of imperial administration. The assembly had acquired the means, if not of obstructing and paralyzing, certainly of hampering and embarrassing the king's government in the colony; and for several decades before 1770 it had been using those means to obtain a controlling influence over the administration.[6]

A stimulus was given to this conflict by the rise in the 1750's of a Whig organization that was to a great extent Presbyterian, or Puritan, and antagonistic to the privileged position of the Church of England in the colony. Its members were mostly lawyers with a kind of natural jealousy of the mercantile aristocracy that dominated New York City.[7] Increasingly they pressed the Assembly into conflict with the governor and became valuable allies of some of the greatest territorial magnates in the colony—whiggish grandees jealous of their rights and suspicious of all power above them—who had frequent use for the kind of lawyers Burke would later describe as "acute, inquisitive, dexterous, prompt to attack, ready in defence, full of resources."[8]

The year 1760 was hardly less a turning point in provincial politics than in the larger politics of Great Britain, where a new reign was opened. Lieutenant-governor James Delancey, a popular man and head of one of the chief families in the province, died. Since he had been acting governor the administration passed provisionally into the hands of the senior member of the council, Dr. Colden, who was a staunch royalist with little popularity and less prudence. Very quickly the new acting governor was at odds with the newly elected assembly, and

---

[5] Tryon's report, loc. cit. 1: 770-771.

[6] Becker, Carl, History of political parties in the province of New York, 1760-1776, 5-8, 26-28, Madison, Bull. Univ. of Wis. No. 286, 1909.

[7] Jones, Thomas, History of New York during the Revolutionary era 1: 3-18, N.Y., N.Y. Hist. Soc., 1879.

[8] Works 3: 56.

with the lawyers in and out of it; and the situation was exacerbated by the circumstance that Colden was not only commissioned lieutenant-governor but permitted (during the absence of Governor Sir Richard Monckton) to conduct the government of the colony until 1765. His troubles began when the king in 1761 sent over an instruction that royal governors were no longer to issue commissions to judges during good behavior, but only during the sovereign's pleasure.[9] This was a direct blow at the assembly's influence over judges whose salaries it provided, and the issue was drawn by the royal appointment of Benjamin Pratt as chief justice during pleasure. Pratt was not even a resident of the colony. The assembly showed its disapproval of the appointment by refusing to vote the Chief Justice a salary. But Colden became his champion, seeing in "this obstinacy of the Assembly" an "evident proof of a formed design of undue influence." He told his superiors that the people could more safely "trust the Administration of Justice with a stranger, who has no private connections, than with an inhabitant." It seemed very perverse of the people to desire to be judged by men they knew. "Sure am I," wrote Colden, "men of greater abilities may be found out of the Province than in it;" but the assembly would "have no Chief Justice unless he be a gentleman of Estate in this Province." Colden suggested that the difficulty might be surmounted by paying the Chief Justice's full salary out of the king's quit rents from the province, but the king had other and better uses for his income than paying salaries to colonial judges. Parliament and the people of England thought Americans should pay their own judges. But if so, ought not the Americans to have a voice in selecting them? The assembly thought they should. Colden, who was jealous even of the assembly's naming its own clerk and agent, saw the greatest danger both to the cause of justice and the royal authority in a chief justice dependent in any way upon the assembly. Things had come to such a pass that few persons any longer had dependence on the governor, but a chief justice had an influence on every man, because none among these litigious people knew when he might have a dispute at law: "If then a Chief Justice for life, with a large family connection, form a party . . . the Governor must either become a tool of this party, or live in perpetual contention."[10] The

---

[9] *N. Y. documents* 7: 479.   [10] *Ibid.*, 483-484.

unpaid Chief Justice shared Colden's opinion and warned the Board of Trade that the laws of colonial assemblies were gradually varying from the common law, thus losing their harmonious connection with the laws of England. Judges dependent on assemblies encouraged that dangerous and divisive trend, which must continue "while the post is so provided for, that none but men of fortune, family, & connections in the Colony will accept." The king's lands would never be safe from intrusions and encroachments (especially when the acquisitive were men of large local influence) as long as the first judicial magistrate had to go to the assembly for an annual and precarious grant of his salary. And what perhaps was worse, "Law & the People's Rights & Properties" would be in jeopardy" where a judge "without peril to his subsistence cannot, sometimes, do his duty between Partys, as may be the Case where there is such an unequal Distribution of Property, & consequently of Power & Influence in the Assembly, as exists at New York."[11] Soon the move against judges' serving on good behavior was complicated and worsened by Colden's attempt to establish a right of appeal from the verdict of juries to the governor and council and thence to the crown. The reform era opened by the new reign may be said to have begun in New York by tampering with judges and juries.

The Stamp Act and the Restraining Act

While Colden was still quarrelling with "a set of lawyers as well skilled in all the chicaneries of the Law, as perhaps are to be found anywhere,"[12] the effects of the Grenville measures of 1763-1764 struck New York. The Revenue Act crippled the trade with the foreign West Indies, and the enlarged jurisdiction of admiralty courts, necessitated by stricter enforcement of the trade laws, accented what many New Yorkers felt to be a serious threat to the right of trial by jury. The colony was in some degree of economic distress and sensible of an ill-defined oppression even before the Stamp Act was passed. The assembly had named a committee of correspondence to communicate with other colonies about recent parliamentary enactments, and had directed Agent Charles to present a protest to Parliament against passing the Stamp Act. When news arrived of this viola-

---

[11] *Ibid.*, 501-502.
[12] *Ibid.*, 549.

tion of colonial autonomy in direct taxation, resentment ran high and wide. Suddenly the Sons of Liberty appeared in New York City, fused or allied with the older radical Whig organization, and capitalized upon the universal disapproval of the Stamp Act.

It was the more sober and cautious men who met with leaders from other colonies in the New York Stamp Act congress, which petitioned for repeal and asserted the ancient rights and liberties of the colonies. But it was the radicals who organized a non-importation boycott, paralyzed business transactions and civil procedures, and forcefully prevented the sale of the stamps. At the height of the crisis a new governor, Sir Henry Moore, arrived upon the scene. Bowing somewhat before the storm, he recognized *de facto* that the stamps could not be sold, that the law could not be enforced. By this tactic he managed to rally influential men of property to support the cause of order, so that the city was spared a reign of anarchy. In the spring came news of the act's repeal and rejoicing was great—not for a victory won over England, but for a reconciliation among the loyal subjects of the king.

The Stamp Act crisis showed that New York, especially the city, was riven by deeply antagonistic parties, but it is worth observing that at this time the assembly, organ of the dominant class, was in no way set against the feelings and wishes of the populace. Later it would seem to be a defective mirror of its constituents, like the House of Commons in the Middlesex election and the seating of Luttrell, but that was not the position of things in 1765-1766. But if the assembly reflected the opinions of the people, it cannot be said that its agent, Robert Charles, did the same. He had refused to present to Parliament the assembly's protest against the Stamp Act, because he thought the document "too warm and tedious." As a result the assembly, although not firing Charles, engaged John Sarjeant of London as a special agent and instructed him to employ the most capable means for effecting the repeal of the act.[13]

A letter survives which Charles wrote on September 25,

---

[13] Lilly, *op. cit.*, 131-132. The assembly on Oct. 18, 1764, approved a petition to the king and representations to both Lords and Commons. The last claimed "an Exemption from the Burthen of ungranted, involuntary taxes" as "the grand principle of every free State" without which there could be "no Liberty, no Happiness, no Security"; it was "the natural Right of Mankind."—*Journal of the votes and proceedings of the General Assembly of the Colony of New York from 1691 to 1765* 2: 769-780, N.Y., Hugh Gaines, 1764-1766.

1765, to Lord Dartmouth, President of the Board of Trade. It covered the transmission of an application for a grant of land in Florida.[14] A man seeking such a favor from the crown could hardly be relied on to represent very energetically the interests and claims of a colonial assembly that challenged the laws of the empire. After 1765 New Yorkers probably had no great confidence in Charles's zeal to serve them, but there is no record of a move to replace or supersede him again until 1769.

The trouble brewing in New York might subside temporarily, but in the nature of things it could not be wholly removed. The permanent sources of conflict between assembly and governor, and colony and imperial authority, continued to generate. If Governor Moore knew how to conciliate an assembly that Colden had been able only to antagonize, this did not save him from involvement in a new contest even before the rejoicing over the Stamp Act repeal had died down. It arose over the supplying of the king's troops.

Early in 1765 Parliament had extended the Mutiny Act to the colonies, whose assemblies were laid under statutory obligation to provide certain supplies for the soldiers. Because New York was the British military headquarters in America and therefore more troops were stationed there than in any other colony, the Mutiny Act laid the greatest burden upon New York. Hence it was resented, and the assembly was most reluctant to comply with a demand for supply originating in an act of Parliament. Not until June, 1766—after Governor Moore had sent two messages on the subject—did the assembly act, but in what seemed an uncompliant and niggardly manner. Although salt, vinegar, and beer or cyder were specified by the law, the assembly would not provide them because they were not required for barracks in England. Here was one instance in which the British government did not insist upon strict conformity of colonial laws to the laws of England! When the assembly's conduct was known in England, Moore was instructed to withhold assent from all bills until proper provision had been made for the troops. An impasse arose which was not without danger, since ill feeling was stirred between soldiers and civilians. When the assembly convened in November it refused to give way, and Moore informed Secretary of State

---

[14] *Manuscripts of the Earl of Dartmouth* 2: 19.

Shelburne: "The House was unanimous in their opinion, and I am fully persuaded that they not only have given their own sentiments, but those of their Constituents also."[15]

The result was Parliament's passing of Charles Townshend's bill to restrain the New York legislature until full compliance was given to the Mutiny Act. But even as that punitive enactment was being rushed through in the closing days of the 1767 session, the New York Assembly was displaying a more accommodating spirit by voting the funds needed for the troops. If they did not obey the Mutiny Act to the letter, they gave substantial compliance, which was enough for Governor Moore, who approved the bill. Therefore, the sole effect of the Restraining Act was to enrage loyal men and heighten their suspicion of everything Parliament might do to affect their affairs in the future. It was due to become operative on October 1, 1767, but by that time Governor Moore could assure Shelburne that "the troops are supplied with all the articles mentioned in the Act of Parliament in as full and ample a manner as if they had been particularly specified in the bill." [16] Therefore, he saw no legal impediment in the way of the assembly's functioning normally, and the next month the members convened and legislated as if they had never been restrained. In April, 1768, the new Secretary for the Colonies, Hillsborough, informed Governor Moore of the King's satisfaction with the conduct of the New York Assembly.[17]

But a harsh, unjust, and unnecessary act had been done, and its unfortunate results could not be extinguished. Indignant recollection would not be erased from New York minds. To Shelburne (still a minister) Moore had confided on March 5: "The suspension of the legislative powers here was a measure which very much alarmed the people. . . . They were made to believe that this was only the first step toward the total abolition of the civil power in order to introduce a military government."[18] This absurd and abortive measure rankled for

---

[15] *N. Y. documents* 7: 878.

[16] *Ibid.,* 948.

[17] *N. Y. documents* 8: 55. But not until May 7 did the Board of Trade submit to the King a report on the New York bill for supplying the troops. It was judged to be "a full and complete compliance," but how far that fact gave validity to acts and proceedings of the assembly after Oct. 1, 1767, was a question for crown law officers."—*ibid.,* 63-64.

[18] *Ibid.,* 18.

years in New York memories, and was cited as a grievance eight years later in the assembly's remonstrance to Parliament.

New York Party Politics: Livingstons vs. Delanceys

By 1768 the time had come for choosing a new assembly and elections were held in March. It will be well therefore at this point to consider the provincial parties, if such they may be called.

The men who dominated the assembly and often used it to oppose gubernatorial and crown influence had long tended to divide into two recognizable factions headed by rival family interests; for the principle of family was as powerful in New York politics as in England. Both parties naturally thought of themselves as Whigs, for an American Tory before 1774 was hardly to be conceived, and in their differences one may be tempted to liken them unto the rivalling Chatham-Shelburne and Rockingham Whigs in England. On the one hand were the Livingston Whigs who had much strength among the great manorial families yet tended to court the radicals and were in 1768 in some sort of alliance with Governor Moore. Philip Livingston (1716-1778), a New York City merchant, was speaker of the assembly, and his brother William was an influential city politician who managed the radical wing of the party. The latter, a graduate of Yale, had been one of the organizers in the early 1750's of the Whig Club, which brought something of the spirit of Puritan radicalism into New York politics. Another brother, Peter, sat in the assembly for Livingston Manor, and Philip Livingston's son was secretary to Governor Moore. The cousin of these brothers, Robert R. Livingston (1718-1775), was probably the most powerful politician in the province.[19] A puisne judge of the supreme court, who sat for Dutchess county in the assembly from 1758 to 1768, he had led the fight against Colden's judicial reforms and was the perfect embodiment of almost everything the Lieutenant-governor feared most—a territorial magnate on the bench with a large political following. In 1764-1765 he had been chairman of a committee of correspondence to concert with the other colonies in opposition to the Stamp Act, and a

[19] Father of the later statesman, diplomat, negotiator of the Louisiana Purchase, and Chancellor of New York, Robert R. Livingston (1746-1813).

leader in the New York congress that petitioned against it.[20]

Rivalling and sometimes directly opposing the Livingstons was another party, the Delanceys. They were more attached to the Church of England, more cautious in resisting the power of crown and parliament, more representative of the mercantile interest; and although their chief strength was in New York City, they were less disposed than the Livingstons to court the radicals. Politically they were close to Colden whose daughter was married to Peter Delancey, who sat for years in the assembly as a member for Westchester and was a brother of the late Lieutenant-governor James Delancey. Another brother was Oliver Delancey, a member of the council. Sons and other relatives of these three men were outstanding in the social and political life of the province, and represented a great part of its wealth.

In the late 1760's the leading Delancey in the political sense was the late Lieutenant-governor's eldest son and heir, Captain James (1732-1800), who entered the assembly from New York City in the 1768 election and rapidly became a party leader. Born in a house that became famous as Fraunces Tavern, he had been educated at Eton and Cambridge and had taken an army commission. He served with the British forces that captured Fort Niagara in 1759. While in England he had been fascinated by the sport at Newmarket and on his return he imported English thoroughbreds, becoming known as Dr. Colden said, as "the father of the New York turf." As we shall presently see, he became a correspondent of Edmund Burke and was acquainted with him even before he became the assembly's agent. Their letters reveal that Delancey was an admiring friend of that foremost figure at Newmarket, the Marquess of Rockingham. It seems not unlikely that Delancey saw both Burke and Rockingham in England when he visited there during 1767 and early 1768. During his absence his friend John Watts wrote from New York:

I hope he is improving his time seriously, a great deal of the future importance of his life depends upon it, with due attention his Father's character and memory will be a Rock he may build upon all his life—even now in his absence the people are proposing

---

[20] Livingston, E. B., *The Livingstons of Livingston Manor*, N. Y., Knickerbocker Press, 1910; also various relevant articles in *Dictionery of American Biography*.

him for a member at the ensuing Election and I have no doubt he
will be chosen unless some unforseen crossgrained turn of popular
humor should cast up.[21]

Surviving letters from James Delancey to Burke show that his
political opinions were very similar to those of Burke and the
Whig chief in England.[22]

The Delancey party had rather languished before 1768, but
now they scored a striking success in the city, where the main
contest was fought. Two forces seem discernible in the election:
the rising importance of the mercantile interest and the recoil
of conservative opinion from the violence and radicalism of
the Stamp Act crisis. Philip Livingston retained his seat, but
the other three city seats were won by Delancey and his two
friends, Jacob Walton and James Jauncey. One of the main
elements of strength in the Livingston party had been the
lawyers, but these were now regarded with suspicion. According to Carl Becker,

The conservative property owners charged them with having instigated the riotous proceedings that had troubled the city since the
passage of the Stamp Act. . . . The mercantile interests felt very
strongly that lawyers could not properly represent a commercial
city, while the Church was opposed to them because they were
identified with the Dissenters. . . . The result was that the Delancey-
mercantile-Church combination was easily successful.[23]

The event was eloquent of the strength which the forces of
political moderation had in New York City. Thirteen of the
twenty-seven members of the assembly were new, and a serious
reverse was suffered by Judge Robert R. Livingston who failed
to be returned for Dutchess county. Colden wrote to Lord
Hillsborough very exultantly about this. The great politician
"had so far lost the esteem of the Freeholders in that County,
that he gave up before the Freeholders then present had given

---

[21] John Watts to Gen. Richard Monckton, Jan. 23, 1768. George Chalmers
MSS (N. Y. Pub. Lib.) , papers relating to New York 2: 18.

[22] James Delancey has sometimes been confused with a cousin of the same
name who was sheriff of Westchester and later commanded a brigade of
loyalists. What is known of him may be found in the following: Story, D. A.,
The Delanceys, 18-19, London, T. Nelson, 1931; Delancey, E. F., Memoir on
Lieutenant-Governor James Delancey, *Documentary history of New York* 4:
627-639; Hamm, M. A., *Famous families of New York* 1: 95, N. Y., Putnam, 1902;
Jones, Thomas, *History of New York, op. cit.* 1: 658; Sabine, Lorenzo, *Biographical sketches of loyalists in the American Revolution* 1: 365-368, Boston, 1864;
Dictionary of American Biography.

[23] *Loc. cit.*, 59-60.

in their votes, tho' he had everything in his favour, which power could give him. The Members of the City of New York, generally have the direction of the House of Assembly."[24] When the new house met, however, Philip Livingston was again chosen speaker.

After the election Governor Moore made a move to strengthen the Livingstons and attach them more firmly to his administration by recommending Judge Livingston for a vacant seat on the council. Moore told the Board of Trade that Livingston's "great possessions here, Education and abilities will always give him great weight in this Province, and from his readiness to give his Assistance where I have stood in need of it during our late troubles, I am persuaded that he will endeavour by his services to merit what I have said of him." The recommendation was considered by the lords commissioners on June 10, but no decision in Livingston's favor was taken, probably because of Colden's blackening his reputation. Meanwhile, a second council seat having been vacated, Moore sent over a recommendation of Hugh Wallace, and the lords commissioners on November 1 agreed to propose to the king not only Wallace but James Delancey. Both were appointed.[25] How the latter's name was first proposed, available records do not reveal. But before the mandamuses for the appointments reached New York, momentous events had transpired there.

The Constitutional Resolves, the Dissolution of 1769, and the Delancey-controlled Assembly

When Hillsborough in April, 1768, ordered colonial governors to command their assemblies to ignore the Massachusetts circular denying Parliament's right to tax the colonies, the New York Assembly was not in session. The old house had been dissolved before the circular was received, and the new one did not meet until late October. By that time, even the most sober and conservative of New Yorkers were in no mood to hear affronts and threats from the British Secretary of State.

As early as April, soon after the election, a body of merchants in the city who agreed with the Massachusetts doctrine began to promote a non-importation agreement to force the repeal of the Townshend Revenue Act. The tactic resembled

---

[24] *N. Y. documents* **8**: 61.
[25] *Ibid.*, 59-61, 187; *Journal of Commissioners*, 32, 56.

that which had brought Parliament to its senses in 1766, but now it was much less spirited and widespread. Moore informed Hillsborough on July 2 that "the Apprehensions which every Person of Property was under during our late Commotions from the Licentiousness of the Populace are not yet forgotten, and I believe they would not willingly see those scenes of disorder renewed." He added on August 18 that there had not been "the least complaint from the behaviour of any persons here, on account of the late duties imposed." What distressed New Yorkers, said Moore, was a money shortage—"a scarcity not only of silver but of every other currency, even paper;" and this had been made worse by a late order from the customs commissioners (the new board created by Parliament in 1767) requiring the payment of duties in specie.[26]

The cause of the money shortage probably was, in part at least, the parliamentary act of 1764 prohibiting further emission of bills of credit as legal tender or the extension of bills then outstanding beyond the dates specified for calling and sinking them. By 1768 the effects of that anti-inflationary measure were being felt painfully in an acute scarcity of cash—a circumstance that rendered the new port duties and the demand for silver at the custom house very objectionable. In these conditions, which worsened as the year advanced, the non-importation movement made great headway, and when the assembly met at the end of October a wave of popular discontent was sweeping the city. Hence the assembly, on November 8, appointed a committee

to draw up a petition to his Majesty, a memorial to the lords, and a remonstrance to the commons . . . praying relief from the grievances his Majesty's subjects in this colony labor under, from the acts of parliament passed in the sixth session of the last parliament for raising a revenue, and of several other acts passed by that parliament relative to the colonies.

Political excitement was further intensified at this time by two local party quarrels. John Morin Scott, a leading city radical who had been defeated for a seat in the assembly, petitioned the house against the validity of James Jauncey's election; Lewis Morris similarly contested the right of John Delancey to sit for the Borough of Westchester. In these disputes the Delancey and Livingston parties were ranged against

---

[26] *N. Y. documents* **8**: 80, 96.

each other, with the Delanceys ultimately prevailing. But they were not strong enough to prevent an address to Governor Moore upholding his conduct in repressing popular disorders. In a curious reversal of the usual political attitudes, Captain Delancey and his friends were now trying to outbid their rivals for popularity as stout champions of New York's grievances against Parliament. They took the lead in preparing the addresses to king, lords, and commons, which were adopted on December 31 and accompanied by a daring declaration of "constitutional resolves."

The "resolves" showed that the assembly was less indignant at the Townshend Revenue Act (although this was denounced as unconstitutional) than at the Restraining Act. It was now avowed

that this colony lawfully and constitutionally has and enjoys an internal legislature of its own, in which the crown, and the people of this colony, are constitutionally represented; and that the power and authority of the said legislature, cannot lawfully or constitutionally be suspended, abridged, abrogated or annulled by any other power . . . the prerogative of the crown ordinarily exercised for prorogation and dissolution only excepted.

Captain Delancey wished to make these words even stronger by adding: "And therefore, that the act of parliament suspending the legislature of this colony, is a high infringment of the freedom of the inhabitants of this colony, and tends to deprive them of their natural and constitutional rights and privileges." This amendment was rejected only because the members believed that the sense of it was implicit in the resolution.

In answer to Hillsborough's attempt to suppress intercolonial communication on the Massachusetts circular, the assembly resolved

that this house has an undoubted right to correspond and consult with any of the neighboring colonies, as with any other of his Majesty's subjects out of this colony, or belonging to any part of his Majesty's realm or dominions, either individually or collectively, on any matter, subject or thing whatsoever, whereby they shall conceive the rights, liberties, interests or privileges of this house, or of its constituents, are, or may be affected.

The petition to the king and representations to the houses of Parliament spelled out in detail the grievances that lay back of the "resolves": the Townshend duties, the Restraining Act ("still more dangerous and alarming"), and the extension of admiralty court jurisdiction which deprived many of the king's subjects of the right of trial by jury. Curiously, nothing was said about provisioning the troops or bills of credit. The documents were sent to Agent Robert Charles and a committee of correspondence was named to communicate with him after the assembly rose, and with other colonies or persons in behalf of New York rights and interests.[27]

However deeply Governor Moore disapproved sending these addresses to king and Parliament, he could not prevent it. But he could and did take notice immediately of the resolves on the assembly's journal. On January 2 he sent an order of dissolution, saying: "The extraordinary nature of certain resolves lately entered upon your journals; some flatly repugnant to the laws of Great Britain, and others, with an apparent tendency to give offense, where common prudence would avoid it, have put it out of my power to continue this assembly any longer."[28] Both Moore and Colden wrote to Hillsborough about what had happened. The former rather apologized for the assembly's conduct by saying the members had been overawed by "the remains of that licentious Rabble who during the late disorders, called themselves the Sons of Liberty"; the assemblymen were well-meaning enough, but "their notions from their education" were "extremely confined," and "their fears of being . . . pointed out as enemies of their Country, engaged them in measures they never wished to see adopted." Moore considered the Delanceys to have been largely responsible for what had occurred. Colden, on the other hand, laid the blame on the Governor for his long appeasement and courting of the Livingston party, which Colden had thought it his duty to oppose. He described the city as

now divided into two parties, which violently oppose each other. One consisting of the new members chosen into the last Assembly [Captain Delancey and his principal friends] and the other supposed to be favored by the Governor; both sides had the preserving their popularity in view. It is supposed this opposition will continue at the ensuing election.[29]

---

[27] *Journal of Votes and Proceedings* (Oct. 27—Jan. 2, 1769), 16, 30-31, 70-71, 76.

[28] *Ibid.*, 76.

[29] *N. Y. documents* 8: 143, 146.

That contest was bitter and hard-fought. "Our people are in high spirits," wrote Peter R. Livingston to Philip Schuyler on January 16, "and if there is not fair play shewn there will be bloodshed, as we have by far the best part of the Bruisers on our side, who are determined to use force if they use any foul play."[30] In the midst of the canvassing Governor Moore received from Hillsborough the royal mandamus to appoint Captain Delancey to the council, and was much surprised when he declined to accept the honor. The Governor could not understand what extraordinary engagements Delancey could have entered into "which could be either incompatible with his duty to his Majesty, or inconsistent with his attendance on the service of his Country at the Council Board."[31] But there was nothing mysterious about his refusal: he was a party leader aspiring to control the assembly by winning an election. The historian and diarist, William Smith, recorded:

Nothing could be more fortunate than the arrival of the Mandamus to swear Capt. Delancey into the Council while he was canvassing for Votes, for tho' the game was a high one he rejected the King's grace & preferred the Honors of the people. And now the utmost efforts were made by the family to secure an assembly still more pliable than the last. They succeeded.[32]

They made a sweep of the city seats, turning out Philip Livingston in favor of their friend John Cruger, whom they elected speaker when the new assembly convened.[33] The outcome was not determined by "the Bruisers," if we may believe a Livingston partisan who described the city election as "a lasting monument to the power of the mercantile interest. It is impossible there ever could be a more decently conducted election."[34] In a total of twenty-six seats seven changed hands and the Delanceys commanded the majority.

---

[30] Lossing, B. J., *Life and times of Philip Schuyler* 1: 235-236, N. Y., Sheldon, 1873.

[31] *N. Y. documents* 8: 148.

[32] Diary of William Smith, N. Y. Public Library MS.

[33] John Cruger (1710-1791) was of a leading mercantile family connecting New York with Bristol and the West Indies, and founder and first president of the N. Y. Chamber of Commerce. His brother Henry had long been a member of the council; his nephew, Henry junior, became Burke's parliamentary colleague for Bristol in 1774.—Hamm, M.A., *op. cit.* 1: 69; Letter of Mr. John Austin Stevens, *Pamphlet publications*, N. Y. Chamber of Commerce, 1865; *Dictionary of American Biography*.

[34] Livingston, *op. cit.*, 182-183.

During all this period of the "resolves," the dissolution and election, news had been arriving of the critical state of affairs at Boston, and of the Hillsborough-Bedford motions and their approval by Parliament. In the storm that was gathering New York was threatened, if not by the vortex, certainly by the periphery. "Things are drawing to a crisis," wrote William Smith, Jr., to Philip Schuyler on February 11. "I suspect we should be obliged next to send Home special Agents as our last shift." Evidently a problem was envisaged that would be too much for Robert Charles. Smith thought Schuyler and Judge Livingston would be the right men for "this momentous Embassy."[35]

In England the news from New York of course added further details to the ominous American picture. Hillsborough was shocked in the extreme by the assembly's resolves, and informed Moore (March 24) that "the King saw with great concern, the violent and unwarrantable resolutions entered upon the Journal of the Assembly on the 31st December last." The Governor was ordered "to make inquiries, and to find out, if possible, whether any methods had been made use of, and by whom, to stir up such a spirit." If Moore could make any such discoveries, he was to communicate them to his lordship, "to the end that his Majesty's Servants may be put upon their guard with respect to men of so mischievous and treacherous a disposition." Hillsborough even took exception to the manner in which the assembly had sent its petition to the King. It had gone to Agent Charles, who submitted it to Hillsborough, who presented it to the King. But his Majesty had considered the assembly's sending a petition through any other channel than that of the governor "as irregular and disrespectful."[36] However, Hillsborough and his colleagues were already on the road of appeasement; they had only angry words and no intention of repeating Charles Townshend's folly of punishing the New York legislature.

The new assembly was opened on April 4 and at the beginning of the session appeared to manifest the same disposition held by its predecessor. Governor Moore on the first day requested, as Hillsborough had instructed him the previous November, that the assembly modify its procedure of choosing an agent. He said:

[35] Schuyler MSS (N. Y. Public Library) 1845.
[36] N. Y. documents 8: 155-156.

I have it in command to recommend to you the rule observed in the West India islands, Virginia, Carolina, and Georgia, as the only proper and constitutional mode by which any person can be sufficiently authorized to represent the province, and to act for it in all matters which concern its interests in general: this has been usually done by an act of the Governor, Council and Assembly, specially passed for the purpose . . . a regulation of this kind, so evidently appears to be calculated for the public benefit, as to require nothing further to be said in support of it, and a deviation from the mode approved of in other colonies, may, in future create great difficulty and disappointment in transacting the affairs of this Province, both in office and in Parliament.[37]

The Governor's recommendation was coldly rejected.

Captain Delancey on April 7 moved and obtained approval for publication of the petition to the king and addresses to parliament adopted the previous December. The next day, Philip Schuyler introduced the following motion:

As the repeated resolves and applications of the colonies, relative to Parliamentary taxations, and the embarrassed state of our commerce, and several other grievances, have not been attended with the success so ardently wished for, and so mutually conducive to the tranquillity of the British Empire; and as the growing distresses of our constituents loudly call for the most earnest attention to measures best calculated to preserve the union between Great Britain and her plantations, and restore a lasting harmony, founded in mutual affection and interest; I therefore move, that a day be appointed for taking the state of this colony into our most serious consideration, and for the appointment of special agents, of approved ability and integrity, to be sent home, instructed to exert their most strenuous abilities, in conjunction with such agents as the other colonies have sent, in soliciting the important affairs of this country, at the Court of Great Britain, and before the two houses of Parliament, during the course of the next session.[38]

A postponement of consideration of Schuyler's motion was ordered. Two days later, however, the house approved a motion by Philip Livingston (who had got back into the assembly for Livingston Manor) for a vote of thanks to the merchants for their "disinterested public spirited and patriotic conduct" in maintaining non-importation.

But when Livingston on April 12 moved for a declaration

---

[37] *Journal of Votes and Proceedings* (April 4—May 27, 1769) , 4.
[38] *Ibid.,* 18-19.

of concurrence with the views of the last assembly, meaning a re-affirmation of the "resolves," it was evident that the parties were engaged in a new contest for popularity. Instead of approving the motion, they broke into violent quarrelling over two disputed elections—curiously, at the very moment the House of Commons was in the throes of the Middlesex election crisis. John Delancey, who had been defeated by Lewis Morris in the Borough of Westchester, petitioned against him on the ground that he had no residence in that borough and his election, therefore, violated a law of 1698 requiring members to reside in their constituencies. The Delancey party supported the petition and presently Morris was unseated. More important was the contest involving Philip Livingston. On the very day he moved for a concurrence with the views of the previous assembly, a Delancey member moved his dismissal from the house because he had no residence at Livingston Manor. After bitter debate he was expelled. Whereupon Judge Robert R. Livingston, who had again failed to be returned from Dutchess county, had himself returned for the Manor, only to be met by an assembly resolution against the propriety of judges sitting in that body.[39] This move had the nature of a constitutional innovation, since Livingston had sat in the assembly for ten years while being first an admiralty court judge and then a judge of the supreme court. From this time to the Revolution his repeated elections and exclusions were a leading issue in provincial politics.

Thus did the Delanceys enlarge themselves and diminish their opponents in the assembly, but at considerable cost to their popularity, since their conduct was inevitably compared with those who had excluded the current hero, Wilkes, from the House of Commons. According to William Smith, "those who were best acquainted with the politics of the Delancey Family saw that . . . the Colony was duped to promote the interests of a few. They had so weeded the House as to be sure of a majority for the purpose of humbling the Governor, & yet as they dreaded the indignation of the Crown, it was necessary to make compliances to recover the Reputation they had lost to gain the Sons of Liberty on their side."[40] A complete change now came over their conduct. The proposal that the

---

[39] *Ibid., passim;* Livingston, *op. cit.,* 189-192; *New York Gazette,* Feb. 12, 1770.

[40] Diary, *loc. cit.*

new house concur with the views of the former house was never adopted, nor was Schuyler's motion to send special agents to Great Britain. In spite of strong popular feeling against granting a request from Moore for a deficiency bill for provisioning the troops, this was conceded in return for the Governor's promise to seek authority to approve a bill passed at this time for emitting 120,000 pounds in bills of credit in such fashion as to evade the parliamentary act of 1764. When the assembly was prorogued on May 27 relations between it and the Governor were somewhat improved, although non-importation agreements were still being maintained by the merchants. These would not dissolve until Parliament the next year repealed the Townshend duties. But as Hillsborough's virtual promise to obtain that repeal was on its way over the Atlantic, a spirit of conciliation was already beginning to creep into the dispositions of the New York Assembly.

In September, Moore died and Dr. Cadwallader Colden again became acting governor. When the assembly met in November he was more disposed to cooperate than to quarrel with it, since it was under the control of the party he preferred. Outdoors, however, bitter attacks were now made upon the assembly, which was charged with betraying the people, and this discontent was naturally exploited by the Livingston party to rebuild their broken political fences in the city. Such was the situation when Colonel Schuyler, who usually acted with the Livingstons, on December 20 brought forward a motion for obtaining a more vigorous and effective agency representation for the assembly in London. He proposed "that Mr. Edmund Burke may be appointed agent for this colony, in room of Mr. Charles." [41] Discussion of this motion was postponed repeatedly and never brought to a vote; presumably the party in control did not then approve it, and it died with the session.

The assembly acted determinedly on the question of bills of credit, passing another act like the one for which the late Governor had promised to seek approval but which still languished at the Board of Trade. Colden not only appealed anew for the allowance of the first act, but nervily signed the second and penned an appeal for allowance of it. Soon afterwards he notified the lords commissioners of the wonderful

---

[41] *Journal of Votes and Proceedings* (Nov. 21, 1769—Jan. 27, 1770), 44.

harmony subsisting between the different branches of the legislature.[42]

Exactly the opposite was the state of the rival political parties. Great bitterness was aroused when the assembly arrested and jailed the radical pamphleteer and later revolutionary general, Alexander McDougall, for publishing a libel against it. He was feted in prison as an American Wilkes, and the Livingston party made great capital of him. They were aroused too by the assembly's refusal again to seat Judge Livingston for the Manor, and by an act passed to give legal basis to the previous resolution to bar judges from sitting in the assembly. The council approved the act and Colden signed it with great satisfaction, although it was subsequently disallowed by the crown.[43] The intensified party strife wore an ominous aspect because the assembly now seemed to be less the organ of the people than the prop of order and authority, instrument of the merchants and the church against the lawyers and the dissenters, champion of oligarchy against the unenfranchised, compliant towards the British ministry and Parliament. The assembly was moving to the right while the populace moved to the left. The counter-movement of political forces was exemplified in the circumstance that a riotous clash between civilians and the king's troops—the "battle of Golden Hill"—occurred on January 18, 1770, while the non-importation pact among the merchants was beginning to break down. So far apart had the parties drifted that on March 18 not one but two banquets were held to celebrate the anniversary of the repeal of the Stamp Act. One set of gentlemen calling themselves the "Friends of Liberty and Trade" toasted "Trade and navigation and a speedy removal of their embarrassments." The other party called for "a continuation of the non-importation agreement" and sent a delegation to visit the martyred McDougall in jail.[44]

The party of order remained firmly in the ascendant, however, and the year 1770 marked the beginning of a period of healing in New York's relations with British authorities. With

---

[42] *N. Y. documents* 8: 200; *Journal of Commissioners,* 183.

[43] The act pretended to follow "the ancient Usage of Parliament."—*The Colonial Laws of New York* 5: 73-74, Albany, J. B. Lyons, State Printer, 1894; *N. Y. documents* 8: 192, 206-210; *New York Gazette,* Dec. 11, 1769, Feb. 12, 1770; Grant, W. L., and James Munro, eds., *Acts of the Privy Council of England, colonial series* 5: 244, London, Wyman & Sons, 1908-1912.

[44] Becker, *op. cit.,* 87.

the repeal of the Townshend duties in March, non-importation (except of tea) completely collapsed. A new governor, the Earl of Dunmore, arrived in October and was well received. During the late fall and winter the threat of renewed war between Great Britain and the Bourbon powers, arising out of an Anglo-Spanish clash over the Falkland Islands, sent a spasm of imperial patriotism through the colonies.

To the restoration of a better temper in New York the Board of Trade can hardly be said to have made any contribution. In November, 1769, the lords commissioners considered the bill for emitting bills of credit which Moore had sought permission to sign. Unable to make up their minds, they referred the measure to the law officers of the crown, who returned a doubtful opinion. Whereupon the commissioners on December 20 signed a report to the king setting forth their doubts along with the arguments for the bill offered by Robert Charles, and recommending royal allowance on the grounds of pragmatic necessity. But before the king in privy council had acted upon this report, the second bill—in the form of an act signed by acting Governor Colden—arrived and was laid before the Board of Trade. The lords commissioners were affronted at Colden's signing a bill so doubtfully legal, and immediately recommended disallowance of it. Both measures passed to amplify the media of exchange in New York were annulled by the Privy Council in February, 1770. The following June five other New York acts were reported by the Board of Trade for disallowance.[45]

These annulments of provincial legislation emphasized the importance of naming an energetic and influential agent, when news arrived that Robert Charles had died in May of that year.

The Election of Burke as the Assembly's Agent

Available sources throw no light upon the circumstances that then led to the election of Burke, although some evidence indicates that he was not the only man considered for the place. The provincial Treasurer, Abram Lott, on October 3 wrote to Sir William Johnson, the king's superintendent of Indian affairs and a man of large influence: "You have no doubt Sir been long ago informed of the Death of Robt. Charles

---

[45] *Journal of Commissioners*, 107-112, 114, 116, 154, 167, 169, 173, 191; *N. Y. documents* 8: 194-195, 202-203; *Acts of Privy Council* 5: 216, 244, 284-285.

Esqr. late Agent of this Colony at the Court of Great Britain; hence it will be necessary at the next meeting of our Assembly that they appoint another. Various are the opinions that I can find fixed on." Lott hoped that a certain Mr. Kelly might be chosen and solicited Sir William's influence in his behalf.[46] But when the assembly met in December, nothing, so far as has been learned, was heard of Mr. Kelly or any other candidate. Speaker Cruger announced on December 21 that he had received certain accounts, by letters from London, of Charles's death, and the house thereupon "Resolved, *nemine contradicente,* that Edmund Burke Esqr., of London, be and hereby is appointed agent for this colony to the Court of Great Britain. . . . and that for his services as such, there be allowed to him the said Edmund Burke Esqr., at the rate of five hundred pounds per annum." [47] The *Journal* records no motion leading to the resolution, and yields no evidence whatsoever about the origin of Burke's nomination, although it will be recalled that Philip Schuyler had proposed his name the previous year.

That overtures had been made to Burke before he was elected is suggested by a letter which James Rivington wrote from London on January 14, 1771, when intelligence of the election could hardly yet have been known in England. Rivington said: "Mr. Burke will not accept the agency."[48] But he did accept, perhaps because Captain James Delancey, a friend of Lord Rockingham, persuaded him to change his mind. It is evident from his New York letter-book that a confidential exchange took place between Burke and Delancey in the winter or early spring of 1771. That his acceptance was known or assumed in New York as early as April 2 is shown by the fact that Judge Robert R. Livingston wrote on that date to solicit Burke's help in making good his claim to the seat which the assembly denied him. It is evident too that at least a month before June 9 (when Burke replied) Delancey had written to him on the topic of Judge Livingston's claim and the assembly's exclusion of judges.[49] On May 9 the *New York Journal* published an announcement that "Mr. Burke hath accepted the Agency for New York." His first letter to New York of

---

[46] *Sir William Johnson Papers* 7: 925-926, Albany, Division of Archives and History, 1931.

[47] *Journal of Votes and Proceedings* (Dec. 11, 1770—March 4, 1771), 17-18.

[48] *Johnson Papers* 7: 1077-1079.

[49] *Infra,* letter-book, Burke to Delancey, June 9, 1771.

which Burke preserved a draft is dated June 9 and has something of the character of a formal acceptance after a previous negotiation.

During the two preceding years New Yorkers could have read a good deal about Burke in their newspapers, especially in those of a strong Whiggish tendency. In the winter of 1768-1769 notices began to appear which marked him as a prominent opponent of the administration, and his part in the repeal of the Stamp Act became well known. A report was published late in February to the effect that a change of administration was imminent in England: Chatham was to become secretary of state in room of Hillsborough, and Rockingham would take the Treasury again with Edmund Burke "his secretary as before." On March 18 "a company of gentlemen" met to celebrate the third anniversary of the repeal of the Stamp Act, and thirty-three toasts were drunk—the first to the King and the twelfth to Burke, who thus was bracketed with such figures as Chatham, Rockingham, Conway, Camden, and Barré, as "an asserter of American rights." [50] The leading part he took in defending the rights of freeholders and opposing the ministerial persecution of Wilkes was copiously noted in the New York press. A typical instance was an account in the *Gazette* of the meeting of Buckinghamshire freeholders at Aylesbury in early September, 1769, to adopt a petition for dissolution of the House of Commons that had seated Luttrell: "Mr. Edmund Burke, member for Wendover . . . spoke for near an hour, in a pure, eloquent, and rhetorical manner, truly Ciceronian, which he is well known to be a master of." [51] The same paper was to spread over its first page "The celebrated Speech of Edmund B—ke, Esq." on January 9, 1770, in the House of Commons. He was quoted as saying:

the Americans are contending only for an inalienable right; the right of taxing themselves, which is inseparable from every country that boasts the least degree of freedom. When they crossed the Atlantic, they did not give up the rights of Englishmen. . . . On the contrary, they shifted their abode in order to breathe a freer air, and to give full scope to that independent, that unconquerable spirit, with which they are still animated.[52]

Since no reliable report of Burke's speech on that day

---

[50] *New York Gazette*, Feb. 27, March 20, 27, 1769.
[51] *Ibid.*, Nov. 27, 1769.   [52] *Ibid.*, April 30, 1770.

exists, and newspaper accounts of speeches were notoriously inaccurate, there is no good reason to accept these words as Burke's. Certainly they resemble rather the language of Lord Chatham or Colonel Isaac Barré, than that of Burke; but a newspaper put them into Burke's mouth and thus helped to create New York's concept of him. Many other notices of Burke appeared, and the general impression given was of an outspoken champion of the right of the colonists to tax themselves, and an opponent of the parliamentary corruption and ministerial tyranny under which the English people suffered not less than the Americans.

According to Hugh Wallace, member of the council, the election of Burke as agent was "ill-judged" and had "chagrinned our Governor greatly." [53] The *New York Journal*, organ of radical Whiggism, commented: "This gentleman's distinguished abilities and firm attachment to the American cause will, no doubt, render his appointment very disagreeable to our enemies at home." [54] It is perfectly evident that this newspaper regarded Burke as an exponent of its political ideas and preferences.

About the same time Burke was chosen agent, Hillsborough recommended to the King that Lord Dunmore be shifted to Virginia and William Tryon, hitherto Governor of North Carolina, be named Governor of New York.[55] This change, even more than the election of Burke, was to be auspicious for continuing the period of greater ease and calm in New York's relations with the imperial government.

---

[53] *Johnson Papers* 7: 1072-1073, Hugh Wallace to Sir W. Johnson, Jan. 7, 1771.

[54] Feb. 21, 1771. The same paper on March 14 spread over its first page a spirited "radical" version of Burke's speech of the previous Nov. 27 against the attorney-general's power to file information in libel suits.

[55] *Journal of Commissioners*, 218.

IV. The Agent at Work, 1771-1773

IT probably was sometime in May, 1771, when Burke was first called upon to perform services for his New York employers. James Delancey, who with the other City members—Speaker Cruger, Walton, and Jauncey—formed the assembly's committee of correspondence, wrote to him on two matters of business. The letter is lost, but Burke's reply on June 9 indicates that the affairs were an act determining the New York-New Jersey boundary and the question of disqualifying judges from sitting in the assembly. It will be recalled that the latter had been a great issue in New York provincial politics because Judge Livingston had been barred from the seat to which he had been elected. A disqualifying act passed early in 1770 had been rather quickly disallowed by the crown, but the Judge still had not been seated. He too sent some kind of address to Burke on the subject.

It is interesting to contrast Burke's replies to Livingston and Delancey. He told the former with cool civility that he scarcely knew what New York parties were and did not desire to become involved in any controversy between them. Hence he begged leave to decline giving "any opinion upon a matter so interesting to yourself and so delicate to the public." But to Delancey whose position entitled him to receive Burke's opinion, the latter opened his mind fully on the question. He explained why judges in England did not sit in the House of Commons, the reason lying in ancient practice rather than in any legislative act of exclusion. They were not disabled because of their judicial character, but from "their supposed attendance of the House of Lords." As for punitive disqualification in particular cases, Burke doubted that ministers who had burnt their fingers in the Wilkes case would wish to see their example imitated in the colonies. He did not presume to offer advice, since New Yorkers alone were in a position to judge whether it was to their interest "to push on that affair to the utmost," but he did not hesitate to say that such a course was "not likely to be supported by any body of people here,—as being contrary to the principles of some, and perhaps to the politics of all." Such thoughts were for Delancey's "private use only." Living-

ston, Burke said, had sent him "a state of his case" and expressed the hope that he would not consider himself "as the
agent of a party." Probably Burke had considered that an
offensive suggestion; in any event, he gave to Delancey an
opinion he had refused to give to Livingston, although the
opinion ran counter to a measure that Delancey had strongly
favored.

This is the first of the extant letters exchanged by Burke
and Delancey and it throws some light not only on the curiously
confidential nature of their correspondence, but on Burke's
conception of the nature and proprieties of his office as agent.
It was not an official letter written to the assembly's committee
of correspondence, but a private personal letter to a member
of that committee. Yet it was also the agent's communication
to a principal, and it illustrated something characteristic of
Burke, namely, the value that he placed upon friendly, confidential personal relations in affairs of public interest. He told
Delancey he took it for granted that he was entitled to open his
mind "fully and confidentially to you on the subject of our
correspondence." Plainly "our correspondence" meant the
correspondence of the assembly agent with his employers, but
the whole tone of the letter suggests that one of those employers
stood in a relation of special intimacy with the agent. Burke
said that in this way only could he be of service to the Province:
"I am near to the scene where your business is finally transacted; I have an opportunity of knowing something of the
temper, the disposition, and the politics of people here; and
not being so deeply and warmly engaged as yourselves, I may
be able sometimes to give you hints, on which your maturer
sense may build something useful to you in your affairs." If
he were not allowed such liberty, "any merchant in the City,
or any active clerk that can rummage public offices and wait
in the anti-chambers of Ministers" might be more serviceable.

Early in the summer Burke received from the committee
of correspondence what must have been a sizable packet of
business papers. His attention was drawn particularly to an
act for establishing New York's boundary against New Jersey
between the Hudson and Delaware rivers. Four years previously the crown had named commissioners to settle disputes
between the two colonies in this region and determine a boundary line. That line (which has remained unchanged) was
decided by the commissioners, but not to the perfect satisfac-

tion of all settlers in the region. Hence local disputes continued, and the New York Assembly sought to give quiet to the region by passing a boundary act declaring the line to be exactly where the commissioners had drawn it, and guaranteeing the security of property to all owners whether their titles originated from New Jersey or New York.[1] But the assembly acted before all legal phases of the commission's work had been completed. Burke's employers evidently wished him to accelerate royal allowance of the act. He went at once to Westminster, discovered that Lord Hillsborough was absent, conversed with the subordinate officials of the Board of Trade, and then sent to New York a detailed statement of legal obstacles that were likely to impede approval of the act. These were not simple and his letter on the subject shows that he had mastered a complex problem. After four months, during which he received no further instructions from New York, he reported that he had seen Hillsborough, who was "in a very proper disposition towards this business." But nothing could be done until the Board of Trade met, when Burke would press "the immediate allowance of the act." The Board, in recess since August, did not meet again until December 10, and it was not until April 29, 1772, that the boundary act was brought up for consideration, only to have the decision on it postponed. Not until May of the following year was the act recommended to the crown for approval.[2] Such were the ways of the Board of Trade.

Burke's Concept of What a Colonial Agent Should Be

Burke had not been agent for a year before a question was brought forward that might have forced him to resign. He learned from Delancey that the assembly might be forced to make the change which Hillsborough in 1769 had demanded in the method of choosing New York's agent, namely, to admit the governor and council to a voice in the election. A little later John Pownall, secretary of the Board of Trade, called on Burke to discuss the matter and said that although the point had not been determined, it was under deliberation. Replying to Delancey, Burke said Pownall was "of opinion that the Governor and Council ought to have their part in the nomination

---

[1] *Laws of Col. N. Y.* 5: 185-193.
[2] *Journal of Commissioners,* 298-299, 358.

of the Provincial Agents, or at least a negative on the choice of the Representative Assembly. . . . He thinks such a joint concurrence in the nomination would be very serviceable to the Colony, as the Agent appearing in the fullness of his character would act with greater weight in all his transactions with office." Burke, however, rejected Pownall's conception of an agent as the representative of a colony as a corporate whole.

His own view was that an agent from the very nature of things should be the creature of the elective assembly only, "that is, a person appointed by them to take care of the interests of the people of the province as contradistinguished from its executive government." The agent was in no way intermediary between the colonial executive and the crown authorities. His business was "always separate from that of the Governor, and might in many cases be opposite to his interests and wishes. The Agent might even be employed to make complaints against him for maladministration in his office." Giving to the governor a voice or veto in the choice of an agent would make the latter "to all intents and purposes an officer of the Crown," so that if the proposed change were adopted Burke said he "could not honourably think of continuing to take charge of your business." In an official letter to the committee of correspondence, he declared:

if you admit the plan . . . and that by such means your agency should become, in part at least, an appointment by Ministry, it will not be in my power consistently with my notions of honour to be officially charged with your business. I cannot act in my present situation except under the clearest and most satisfactory evidence that my employment is a matter wholly detached from Administration.

This idea of the nature and function of a colonial agency derived necessarily from Burke's concept of the nature of the British empire as a community of free peoples under one supreme authority, the crown and Parliament of Great Britain. Later, when the crisis of 1774-1775 had arisen, Burke's enemies were to accuse him of being a "paid American agent"—as if the New Yorkers who employed him were not British subjects whom any Englishmen might honorably serve—and to allege that his stand for conciliation was inspired by a private interest.[3]

---

[3] Macknight, Thomas, *Life and times of Edmund Burke* 1: 479-480, London, Chapman and Hall, 1858.

But in 1771 Burke's only apprehension was for his political honor as a man uncompromised by an administration which he opposed on the high ground of principle.

In due course he learned from his employers that the assembly would not submit to an invasion of its exclusive right to choose and direct the agent. He so informed the Board of Trade and afterwards wrote to his employers:

I was told that in time their principle will be found necessary in case the Agent is to give his consent to any agreement or other public act terminated here in the name of the Province; that then the validity of his power must necessarily come into question. I do not imagine, however, that they mean at present to proceed any further in this business.[4]

There was, as has already been pointed out, a long-standing rule of the Board of Trade that no colonial agent could be recognized and have his name officially registered unless he was chosen in the way Hillsborough desired. This rule was invoked against Franklin as the Massachusetts Assembly's agent in 1771, but it seems never to have embarrassed Burke, whose name was never registered officially at the plantations office. It does not appear that he ever found any impediments, arising from defective credentials, in his transactions as agent, although it is true that he was never called upon to give official consent to a "public act terminated here in the name of the Province."

It is difficult to see why the Secretary of State for the Colonies and the Board of Trade should have attempted to effect such an alteration as must have converted Burke, unless he resigned, into a quasi-diplomatic representative of the Province of New York. There was no principle in the British Empire that admitted the making of conventional treaties or agreements between a colony and the mother country. On the contrary, the British government had been trying for some years to tighten the bonds of empire and fortify crown-appointed executive administration in the colonies. It was moving in a direction exactly opposite to a federalistic organization in which colonial agents could serve as delegates from autonomous provincial governments. Probably the real reason why Hillsborough and the Board of Trade desired the change was nothing more than the wish to reduce the power of colonial assemblies and to obtain jobs for placemen.

---

[4] Letter-book, *infra*, Burke to committee, June 30, 1772.

During the winter of 1772 it must have seemed to Burke that his duties as agent were anything but burdensome. The Board of Trade's journal contains no record of his appearing there before the fall of that year, and his New York letter-book does not show that he so much as received a communication from his employers from the fall of 1771 to the spring of 1772. But if his duties were few, he was not inattentive to them. The Board of Trade on April 29 "read and considered" forty-four acts passed by the New York legislature in the years 1770-1771. Three of these were recommended for disallowance and two others were ordered to lie for further consideration.[5] Barely a week later Burke sent to New York a report of what had been done, along with a copy of the board's minutes.

His alertness to the interests of New York was demonstrated at this time by his taking an independent initiative in a matter of considerable importance. He learned that a certain M. Lotbiniére (whose name he spelled phonetically but incorrectly) and eighteen other Frenchmen were seeking royal confirmation of titles to more than a million acres of land in the region of Lake Champlain which was part of the Province of New York. The claims were founded on an article in the 1763 Treaty of Paris confirming all grants of land made by the French government of Canada prior to the British conquest and annexation. Burke reported to the committee of correspondence that Lotbiniére claimed about 115,000 acres southwest of the lake and comprehending Ticonderoga, and that he wished not only to validate his title but to hold the lands in question as a part of the Province of Quebec. Burke feared that the French claims "if admitted might be an infringement of the right and jurisdiction of the Province of New York, and affect the properties of several who may have taken lands and made settlements in virtue of grants passed under the seal of your Colony." Perhaps Burke did not know that the crown in 1768 had accepted and confirmed the Moore-Carleton boundary line between Quebec and New York (along the forty-fifth parallel from the head of Lake Champlain to the Connecticut River). His fears for the jurisdictional rights of New York were, therefore, unfounded, but it was entirely possible that the French claimants might obtain recognition of their titles as owners in New York and thus force the cancelation of grants

---

[5] *Journal of Commissioners*, 298.

made by the New York government since 1763. Burke said
that John Pownall had promised to apprise him of every step
taken in the matter, and he did not think anything decisive
would be done before he received instructions from New York.[6]
If this question was new to Burke, it was not so to his employers, who would presently brief him on it.

In the meantime, he was given other business to transact.
Speaker Cruger had written on April 14 to ask for a special
effort on Burke's part to obtain royal allowance of two bills:
An Act more effectually to prevent private lotteries, and *An
Act to prevent infectious distempers in the Counties therein
mentioned.* One can scarcely conceive why such measures
should not have received routine approval, but one never could
tell what catch might be found by Board of Trade officials or
crown lawyers. Two months later Burke replied stating that
he had sent the bills immediately to Richard Jackson and
"pressed him to make his report as soon as possible." If the report proved favorable, Burke said the business would be dispatched and the bills would receive royal allowance "in a short
time." But these enactments were not brought before the lords
commissioners until one year later and then were reported for
disallowance![7]

This letter to Cruger is of unusual interest because Burke
gave in it a general sketch of the British political scene. Something like a dead calm had set in after the "Wilkes and Liberty"
disorders. Burke dwelt especially on the inactivity of the opposition parties, saying of his own that "it has been thought
advisable to be less active than formerly." The reason for that
strategy was that "a determined, systematical, and considerable
majority in both houses in favour of the Court scheme" had
put the party into a position in which persistent opposition
would rather betray its weakness than augment its strength.
He touched on the Royal Marriage Act passed that spring at
the behest of a king who was determined to tighten his control
over all members of the royal family. Burke considered the act
"bad as a regulation and worse as a precedent," since the crown
would gain from it "an improper addition of not the best kind
of strength." He alluded also to two questions pertaining to
religion that had recently been debated in Parliament. One had

[6] Letter-book, *infra*, Burke to committee, May 6, 1772.
[7] *Ibid.*, Burke to Cruger, June 30, 1772; *Journal of Commissioners,* 365;
Acts of the Privy Council 5: 381-382.

been raised by a petition from certain clergymen of the Church
of England for relief from the obligation to subscribe to the
Thirty-nine Articles. The petition was denied, Burke voting
with the majority; he told Cruger "it was thought unreasonable
that the public should contribute to the maintenance of a
clergy without knowing anything of their doctrine." Another
petition for enlarging the toleration accorded to Dissenters
had led to a bill which Burke supported and which passed the
House of Commons but was rejected by the Lords. Burke told
Cruger he had "no doubt but that in time it will be carried,
and that this spirit of intolerance will vanish away by degrees
both on our side of the water and on yours." He added that
the refusal of Americans to receive a bishop of the Church of
England had been "urged in the House of Lords as a strong
example against the spirit of the Dissenters and to show the
danger of setting them too much at large."

It is evident that Burke expected Cruger to show his letter
to Captain Delancey and the other gentlemen of the committee
of correspondence, since although private and confidential it
concerned public business. But under the same date he wrote
also to Delancey. Having learned of the latter's marriage, he
wished him joy of it, and then told of a long and serious illness
suffered by Lord Rockingham, and of a banking crisis in England. The letter suggests that Burke had arranged for his
salary as agent to be paid to him through Delancey, and that
he had decided to spend some of it for American horses. He
asked Delancey to ship him "two good pacers not above five
years old," and to "retain the money or draw on me as you
choose."

By an odd coincidence Delancey at New York was writing
a letter of the same date to Burke. It is lost but a main part
of its contents may be inferred from Burke's reply later in the
summer.[8] Delancey had told him that the members of the
assembly were not satisfied with the letters Burke had been
sending to them. Probably he did not mean the private letters
but those which were official and which the journal of the assembly records as having been laid upon the table for members to peruse. One glance at these is enough to see that there
was indeed little of interest in them. The assemblymen wished
for more copious and frequent communications, more news of

---

[8] Letter-book, *infra*, Burke to Delancey, Aug. 20, 1772.

what was going on in England. Burke was displeased at learning of these wishes. It was very natural, he told Delancey, that
they should prefer a correspondent "who might contribute to
their entertainment by the frequency and agreeableness of his
letters," but he did not intend to accommodate them. There
was no need to report what gentlemen could read in their newspapers, and whatever news he "might chance to hear, which
had not got abroad in so public a manner . . . might be either
so insufficiently authenticated or so confidentially communicated, that it would be against all prudence and decency to
make it the subject of a correspondence of office." Did his
employers imagine that he would serve them as a purveyor of
news and political gossip? Nothing could be "so contrary to
all decorum" and all attention to his own character, as to commit himself for "opinions of men," except where the discharge
of his business transactions essentially required it. His letters
to the committee of correspondence, therefore, would "continue to be merely official, though such letters must be dry
and unpleasant enough by their own nature even in better
hands than mine." Nor would his sense of propriety permit
him to write more often than business required. If this did
not come up to the expectations of the gentlemen at New York,
he could only wish them "to employ a person more pleasing
to them."

Burke then alluded to an expense account he had sent to
his employers. He could not prevail upon himself to send a
closely itemized statement: "In my situation I cannot think it
right for me to make out such accounts." He wrote of his
salary as if in accepting it he were rather conferring than receiving an obligation: "If I accept the salary, which I am
informed is not the most considerable advantage of the employment, and which you know is a small object to me, it is solely
lest I should hurt the delicacy of any gentleman who might
succeed to the office, by putting him under difficulties in accepting of that emolument which another had declined." In
those days five hundred pounds was a very large sum, a good
annual income for a man in moderate circumstances. So that
it was not worthy of Burke, who was always in need of money,
to pretend to such condescension, since he concluded by saying
he would like eighty pounds a year more to pay his clerk.

It seems certain that about this time Burke did seriously
consider giving up the agency, for he was invited in mid-

summer by the East India Company to go to India at the head of a commission to inquire into and reform the abuses there. Late in July, William Burke wrote to Charles O'Hara about this offer: "The profit will be very great, the credit, if they really do any good, will be considerable to those concerned; yet I rather think on the whole he will decline it." [9] It was in early August that the decision to decline was made. Had Burke accepted the offer he necessarily would have given up the New York agency, which was a petty business as compared with a commission to reorganize an empire in India.

About this time an event happened which was auspicious for improved relations between Great Britain and the American colonies and for Burke's work as agent. Lord Hillsborough was forced out of office and the Earl of Dartmouth became Secretary of State for the Colonies. The latter had presided at the Board of Trade during the administration of Lord Rockingham and thereafter had been counted as a Rockingham Whig. Although his taking office under Lord North (to whom he was step-brother) meant a breach with that party, Dartmouth's personal friendships were not impaired. Of him Burke told Delancey: "When he had the first place at the Board of Trade he acted with those who were real well-wishers to the Colonies. He did not then differ with his colleagues, and I hope he still perseveres in sentiments so proper for his situation." Burke was to find Dartmouth very responsive to his solicitations.

Defending the Rights and Claims of New York Land Grantees

It would be unrewarding work to describe all the business placed in Burke's hands by the New York Assembly. Much of it concerned small matters of no historical significance. But there were several major questions which affected the whole position of New York in the empire and were relevant parts of the history of the background of the American Revolution.

One of these has already been touched upon lightly—the French land grants in the Champlain region. The origin of this affair went back to 1763 when Michel Lotbiniére, a former

---

[9] Annaghmore MSS, W. Burke to O'Hara, Aug., 1772; Wentworth-Fitz-william MSS, O'Hara to Burke, Sept. 11, 1772. See also Burke to the Duke of Richmond, Oct. 1772, *Correspondence* 1: 339-340.

officer in French Canada, went to London after the peace to seek confirmation, under the treaty, of his titles to lands granted him by the king of France. Although the British government had never recognized the Champlain region as French but viewed it as within the territory of the Five Nations, allies of England, the Board of Trade took a favorable view of Lotbiniére's claim and instructed acting Governor Colden (July, 1764) that no grants should be made "under the authority of the Government of New York of any part of the lands comprehended within the limits of these concessions." [10] But the government of New York had already begun to make grants, which thus collided with the claims of Lotbiniére. In succeeding years a tangle of claims and counter-claims arose, partly because the Quebec-New York boundary remained undetermined until 1768, and partly because the two provincial governments either ignored or misunderstood crown orders that were sometimes ambiguous or inconsistent. Powerful private interests in New York were involved, notably those of the wealthy and influential James Duane of Albany, who was son-in-law to Judge Robert R. Livingston and had many friends also in the Delancey party. Both the assembly and the governor were opposed to recognizing grants originating under a government that had been overthrown and, as New Yorkers believed, had never at any time possessed the right to dispose of land in the region around Lake Champlain. The British government, on the other hand, could not disregard its treaty obligation to protect the property rights of lawfully-holding French subjects in the conquered territory.[11] The Privy Council on June 17, 1772, referred the petitions from the French claimants to the Board of Trade for an opinion as to the validity of their pretensions.[12] Well in advance of this, Burke, as we have seen, alerted his employers to what he feared might be a danger to their interests.

In August the New York committee of correspondence drafted a long letter to Burke outlining the official views of

[10] O'Callaghan, *Documentary history* 1: 538-541.

[11] Crown authorities did not recognize the validity of French grants where French sovereignty had never been recognized, but were unwilling to deny prescriptive rights arising from settlement or improvement. See Hillsborough to Moore, Feb. 25, 1768; minute of Privy Council, Aug. 12, 1768, and order of the king in council to Governor Moore, July 5, 1769.—*Ibid.*, 312-317.

[12] *Journal of Commissioners*, 312-317.

the province on this question and on all boundary disputes yet unsettled. Only a rough draft of this document is known to exist and perhaps no finished draft ever was made and sent to Burke, since there is no indication in his letter-book that he ever received it, but it shows well the New York point of view.[13] The argument was that the French grants could have no validity because they were located in what was, at the time of the grants, the country of the Five Nations, who had submitted themselves in 1683 to the sovereignty and protection of the king of England; and by the Treaty of Utrecht France had recognized these Indians as British subjects. It was true that the French had built Fort Frederick at Crown Point in 1731, but that had been an act of hostile encroachment, and Britain had never recognized any French territorial rights south of the St. Lawrence River. It was "very surprising then that such Grants should meet with the least Favour, especially as they were unattended with Possession or Improvement; and there were many Considerations of Policy and Prudence which militate strongly against them." This position was fully supported by Governor Tryon, who believed the case of the French claimants could rest only on the king's generosity, which he hoped would "operate as powerfully in behalf of those Officers & Soldiers who now hold a great part of those disputed lands under grants from this Province."[14]

A memorandum on the question was sent to Burke by James Duane.[15] Burke acknowledged receipt of this in October, 1772, and praised it for "extraordinary accuracy and diligence." He trusted that "the strong reasons" which it set forth would be "prevalent with the Council" and promised to support "the rights of the Province" and those who derived under its authority with all his power. Such support would be needed, because Lord Dartmouth took an unfavorable view of the New York argument, thinking it would strip many of the king's new French subjects "of their ancient possessions, and must spread an alarm that may have very fatal consequences to the

---

[13] The document is in the Library of the N. Y. Hist. Society.

[14] *N. Y. documents* 8: 342, Tryon to Dartmouth, Jan. 5, 1773.

[15] Duane's memorandum is known only from Burke's acknowledgment of it. Duane, who became a leading figure in New York during the Revolution, was a lawyer and land-speculator on a large scale, especially in the region between the Hudson and Connecticut rivers. *Cf.* Alexander, E. P., *A revolutionary conservative, James Duane of New York,* N. Y., Columbia Univ. Press, 1939.

King's interest." [16] Therein one may perhaps detect that curious preference for Canadian interests over those of the older colonies that would find expression in the Quebec Act of 1774 which was so offensive to the latter.

Burke was present when the Board of Trade first took the question into consideration on November 12, 1772, and he asked the right to be heard by counsel.[17] Although nothing was decided at that time and the subject was not before the lords commissioners again until the following summer, Burke thought he had gained some advantage. He reported to New York that he "had a good deal of discourse with Lord Dartmouth and Mr. Pownall on the subject" and had found them reasonable and "well disposed in the matter." He had argued that "the honour and interests of the Kingdom" required that "our ancient limits should be settled according to the rights of Great Britain and not according to the pretensions of France." He thought it not unlikely that some compromise would be proposed whereby the French grantees might be persuaded to give up the claims they were pressing in return for a suitable compensation "either by grants in Canada or by such in New York as would not stir dangerous objections on territorial limits or affect the property of meritorious individuals." But he feared that there were English purchasers of land from the French grantees, and that these enjoyed some support with which he was "not so well acquainted."

When the lords commissioners resumed consideration of the business in the early summer of 1773, they invited Burke to attend their proceedings on July 1.[18] He did so and the next day wrote to New York an account of how matters stood. It appeared that any act on the part of the crown to confirm the French grants would operate only to secure the grantees against disturbance by government, and would not prevent New York claimants from defending themselves at law, "which defence their lordships did not imagine could be precluded by anything the Board meant to do on this occasion." Burke could not form an idea of what the Board of Trade and crown would do, but he was "very sure that no steps could be taken towards giving the French titles any sort of effect without manifest prejudice to

[16] *N. Y. documents* 8: 317-318, Dartmouth to Tryon, Nov. 4, 1772.
[17] *Journal of Commissioners,* 322-323.
[18] *Ibid.,* 362. For Burke's letter in reply, June 15, see *N. Y. documents* 8: 378.

those persons who claim under New York." He felt he had gained as much success as could be expected in the circumstances. To Delancey he confided that "we have so far prevailed that nothing adverse has been as yet determined . . . which in our situation, where we are on the defensive, is all that we can desire." It was true that he had observed that the lords commissioners were "strongly inclined to the French claimants," but they would find difficulty in attempting to do anything decisive in their favor. The question thereafter was in the hands of opposing lawyers until it came again before the Board of Trade on the eve of the outbreak of war in America.

Burke's energetic and forceful conduct in this contest was very pleasing to the New Yorkers and the committee of correspondence on November 2 told him so: "Your attention to the interests of the Colony in regard to the territorial rights, and to the private property of the Grantees under New York against the Canadian claims merits our warmest thanks." [19] Soon the assembly testified in a material way to the sincerity of this expression of gratitude. Heretofore, no attention seems to have been paid to Burke's requests for expense money, but in the next session he was voted an additional annual grant of 140 pounds per annum, although he had asked for only eighty.[20]

The question of the French grants in the Champlain region was closely connected and intertwined with the famous contest between New York and New Hampshire over the lands lying between the Hudson and Connecticut rivers, the country later formed into the state of Vermont. When Charles II in 1664 conferred the former Dutch colony, New Netherlands, upon James, Duke of York, its eastern boundary had been designated at the Connecticut River. Subsequently the expansion of the New England colonies had led to serious quarrels with New York, but it was not until after 1742, when New Hampshire became a royal colony, that its governor, Benning Wentworth, involved that colony in a dispute with New York over claims to land north of Massachusetts and west of the Connecticut River. In their draft of a letter to Burke in 1772 setting forth the details of New York's several boundary dis-

---

[19] Wentworth-Fitzwilliam MSS., committee of correspondence to Burke, Nov. 2, 1773.

[20] *Journal of Votes and Proceedings* (Jan. 6, 1774—March 19, 1774), 50-51.

putes, the committee of correspondence so described the rise of what had now become a most dangerous situation:

> In the Course of a Correspondence between the Governours of this and that Colony in the years 1749 and 1750, in which our Title was explained and Enforced, both agreed to refer the point of Right to his Majesty's decision, and their respective claims were accordingly transmitted. But the Governour of New Hamshire thought proper to break his Engagement and upon the Conclusion of the peace proceeded to grant away, with unexampled Rapidity, a great part of the Country between Hudson's River Wood Creek and Lake Champlain on the West and Connecticut River on the East; which is clearly within the ancient Boundaries of this Colony. When a so unfriendly and iliberal Measure was detected, this Government pressed for the Crown's adjudication; and on the 20th July 1764 His Majesty in Privy Council confirmed Connecticut River to be the Boundary between New York and New Hamshire, agreeable to our ancient Right and Jurisdiction.[21]

But in confirming anew the New York boundary at the Connecticut River, the crown had no intention of invalidating the property rights of settlers from New Hampshire west of the river, and an order in council was issued in 1767 forbidding the governor of New York to grant land already settled by persons from New Hampshire.[22] But Colden and Moore had already made grants of such land, chiefly to officers who had served in the war and were discharged at the peace. These petitioned the crown for recognition of their titles, and the Privy Council referred the petition to the Board of Trade for an advisory opinion. It came before the lords commissioners on July 13, 1770, but determination upon it was delayed in expectation of a statement in opposition from the governor of New Hampshire. Almost a year later (June, 1771) the Board of Trade prepared a report recommending an indulgent consideration of the New York petitioners' requests, but with due regard for the prescriptive rights of actual settlers from New Hampshire. The Board recommended also the validation of titles of New York grantees who held patents antedating "any pretence set up by the Government of New Hampshire to exercise the power of granting Lands to the westward of the Connecticut River and before any such grants were

---

[21] Courtesy of the New-York Historical Society.
[22] *Journal of Commissioners,* 4.

made." [23] But this effort to harmonize the principles of prescriptive right deriving from settlement with an abstract legality
based on priority of grant could not end a conflict which by
this time had become an armed struggle of rough and hardy
settlers defending their hands and homes against forces attempting to drive them away. Many of the original New York
grantees had by this time sold their titles to large speculators,
among whom was James Duane, described by his biographer
as "adept at buying up grants made to officers and soldiers as
a reward for their services in the late war." [24]

A new attempt was made by the Board of Trade in 1772
to reconcile prescriptive right and priority of grant, but to no
avail. The men in "the Grants" would not acknowledge the
authority of the government of New York, lest their enemies
drive them out, and New Hampshire persisted in attempting
to obtain a new boundary adjudication. In their draft of a
letter to Burke that summer, the committee of correspondence
said:

> The New Hamshire Claimants still unsatisfied are pursuing
> Measures to obtain a more favourable Determination; and having
> repeatedly been defeated in a Course of law, to disturb the peace of
> the Country by many Acts of Violence; declaring their resolution
> not to submit 'till they receive his Majesty's order on their late
> Application. The Proprietors under New York who are very numer-
> ous, fearing their Titles may be incumbered and obstructed by a
> hasty ex-parte order of the Crown, have entreated our assistance
> in maintaining the ancient Right and Jurisdiction of this Colony
> to the lands in question, which we think it would be unjust to
> refuse. We have desired them to prepare their case which should
> be transmitted to you by the next opportunity.

Time passed, however, and the crown authorities neither
acted on the recommendations of the Board of Trade, nor
permitted Governor Tryon to employ armed forces in "the
Grants." So that Ethan Allen's "Green Mountain boys" continued to hold James Duane and his friends at bay.

A petition from the frustrated and aggrieved New York
grantees was presented in the assembly on February 16, 1773,
"praying that this house will adopt such measures as to them
shall seem expedient . . . to prevent the success of the solicita-

---

[23] *Ibid.*, 199-200; *N. Y. documents* 8: 272-277.

[24] Duane acquired claims to 67,000 acres in the territory of the Hampshire
grants.—Alexander, *op. cit.*, 71-85.

tion and interposition of the government of New Hampshire, in prejudice of the ancient limits of this province, and of the rights of the petitioners and those claiming under them." The next day the assembly adopted a resolution asserting the jurisdiction of New York over "the Grants" and ordered "that a state of the just rights of this colony be prepared by a committee appointed for this purpose; and that the same, when agreed to by this house, be transmitted to the agent of this colony, that he may be enabled to maintain the just rights thereof at the court of Great Britain." A lengthy declaration of these "just rights" was heard and adopted by the assembly on March 8.[25] In due course this was sent to Burke, along with "proofs" to support it. James Duane appears to have been the moving spirit behind the assembly's action. He too wrote a long letter to Burke on the subject, expressing "the earnest entreaty of all the gentlemen concerned, that you will be pleased to be their advocate, and exert yourself in defending their just rights, against so many importunate adversaries." [26]

Upon receiving the several documents pertaining to the dispute, Burke consulted with John Pownall and received assurance that the Board of Trade in its recommendations to the crown would adhere strictly to the Connecticut River boundary. "But their lordships are of opinion," so Burke informed his principals, "that in consideration of the improvements that are made, these settlers ought to be confirmed in their possession notwithstanding the invalidity of their original titles." How far such equitable indulgence (or respect for prescriptive right) might be carried, Burke was unable to say, since nothing had yet been determined; but the lords commissioners "conceived that the Province could not consider itself injured, if they [the Hampshire settlers] were allowed lands to any extent which the King might think reasonable, as his Majesty is as much at liberty to grant within one province as within the other." This was Pownall's opinion as given to Burke. Whether it was also Burke's does not appear, nor would it have been proper for the agent to inject his personal views. But since nothing was more characteristic of Burke than his reverence for prescription, it is likely that he had much sympathy with the lot of men who had earned a right to possess land by clearing, cultivating, and

---

[25] *Journal of Votes and Proceedings* (Jan. 5—March 8, 1773), 62, 64, 90-118.
[26] Wentworth-Fitzwilliam MSS, Duane to Burke, April 7, 1773.

building homes on it. However, he promised not to be negligent in the matter and said he expected to receive early information of any action by the Board of Trade.[27] This report could have given small comfort to the interested New Yorkers. Replying to him, the committee of correspondence agreed that the New Hampshire settlers who had not invaded lands for which New Yorkers held patents might properly be confirmed in their holdings, but held that the king could not "recall those grants which have already been given under this government."[28]

No further instructions, so far as has been discovered, were sent to Burke on this subject by the committee of correspondence, although the strife in "the Grants" continued and the crown authorities merely marked time. Probably one reason why Burke was not asked to press the matter further was that Governor Tryon was going to England in 1774 and would take the New York case into his own hands. Another reason was that the whole affair was too big to be managed by an assembly agent. In the spring of 1774, as Tryon was on the ocean, and when much larger questions were at issue in America, Burke had another conversation with Pownall on this subject. He thought it his duty to tell the committee of correspondence that Pownall believed the dispute might be resolved by a committee of impartial persons nominated by the assembly and including "some of the most eminent of the judges or crown lawyers." But this proposal was not acceptable to the New York claimants.[29] No decision on conflicting land claims was reached by the crown until the spring of 1775, and then all was engulfed by war.

Such were the principal affairs in which the New York Assembly employed Burke prior to the great crisis of 1774. In handling them he showed himself to be industrious and conscientious, eager to promote good will between the colony and mother country. But in some lesser assignments he may have been a little negligent. Sometimes in his communications he did not even mention certain New York acts to which the committee had drawn his attention for the purpose of assuring or accelerating their allowance by the crown. For example, in March 1773 the New York legislature passed an act to make

---

[27] Letter-book, *infra*, Burke to committee of correspondence, July 2, 1773.
[28] Wentworth-Fitzwilliam MSS, committee of correspondence to Burke, Nov. 2, 1773.
[29] *Colden Papers* 2: 342, Colden to Tryon, May 31, 1774.

promissory notes, when assigned, recoverable by the holder against the endorser, and therefore to strengthen such notes as a supplement to the currency. Writing to Burke, the committee of correspondence laid great stress on the importance of this measure—its allowance was most urgently required. "The Credit of Notes of Hand and that they should be suable and Assignable," they said, "is of such moment to Trade, that without it a Commercial Country must be exposed to the greatest Difficulties and Inconveniences." [30] Burke never said one word about this act in his letters to his employers.

Burke, the Crugers, and James Delancey in 1773

Burke's duties as agent certainly were not large and could not have occupied more than a minute fraction of his time. No serious difficulties arose between the province and the imperial government at London; nor did any American questions come before Parliament from 1771 to 1774 to pose the issue of the compatibility of his activities as a colonial agent with his duties as a member of Parliament. His party carried on little active opposition to the ministry and he did not hesitate to ask favors from government in behalf of his friends in New York. One of these, granted by Lord Dartmouth, was especially pleasing to Burke and the more influential of his employers.

Early in 1773 John Cruger asked him to exert himself to have the council seat hitherto occupied by the Speaker's brother, Henry, who wished to resign, given to the latter's son, John Harris Cruger. Two years before, Governor Dunmore had made this recommendation to Hillsborough and it had been repeated by Tryon in 1772. But to Hillsborough and the Board of Trade it had appeared "inconsistent with the rule of their proceeding to advise his Majesty to accept of Mr. Cruger's resignation, upon the condition he proposes." [31] According to the Speaker, Hillsborough had seen an impropriety in such a father-son succession, but now that Burke's friend, Dartmouth, had replaced Hillsborough official views might be altered. Wrote Cruger:

As the present Secretary of State may probably be less tenacious of these punctilios,—I should Esteem it a Singular favour if you would

---

[30] Wentworth-Fitzwilliam MSS, committee of correspondence to Burke, April 8, 1773; *Laws of Col. N. Y.* 5: 544-545.

[31] *Journal of Commissioners*, 299.

be so kind as to Endeavour to Prevail on Lord Dartmouth to Gratify my Brother, my Nephew & My Self, in our present Requested Change at the Council Board where a Seat is Realy not Lucrative but merely honorary & Expensive.

Cruger added that formerly the influence of Lord Adam Gordon, Sir William Draper, and Moses Franks had been enlisted in support of this request. He thought these might again try to help, "and my Nephew Mr. Henry Cruger Junior Mercht. in Bristol will have directions from his father to pay the Expenses of the Mandamus should you Succeed in my Sanguine Wishes, to which Your friendly attention Will lay me under the most Lasting Obligations and Confirm me with Perfect Gratitude & great Respect." [32]

For this kind of business Burke had a special liking. Exerting influence with one man while laying another under obligation was pleasant to the politician; it was done easily, or not at all. Burke replied promptly that this request was "particularly interesting" to him because it related to "the arrangement and satisfaction" of Cruger's family; hence he had put the matter before Dartmouth and received "the most favourable answer." With remarkable celerity the Board of Trade, at Dartmouth's initiative, recommended John Harris Cruger to the council, and in due course he was appointed by the King to replace his father.[33] Speaker Cruger was most grateful and presently told Burke, "you'l permit me to assure you that it will make me verily Happy to have it in my Power to render you any acceptable Services on this side the Water."[34] Captain Delancey too wrote that "we are all much obliged." Evidently Burke had performed a service for the party that dominated provincial politics. The next year he would stand for the Bristol seat in Parliament in political alliance with the Speaker's nephew, Henry Cruger junior, and he would owe his success to that alliance. But there is not the slightest evidence to indicate a connection between his favor to the Crugers in New York and the advantage he drew from Cruger support at Bristol.

Apart from his agency duties, Burke probably paid little attention to American affairs during the year 1773. The prin-

---

[32] Wentworth-Fitzwilliam MSS, Cruger to Burke, Feb. 2, 1773.
[33] *Journal of Commissioners*, 353-354.
[34] Wentworth-Fitzwilliam MSS, Cruger to Burke, Aug. 3, 1773.

cipal parliamentary business of the year had to do with the East India Company (always a prime interest of Burke's) and the main legislative product was the Regulating Act by which the company was brought under a large degree of crown control. For reasons similar to those which had governed his conduct six years earlier when he opposed Chatham's designs upon the company, Burke fought against the 1773 act. He did not believe it would cure the real evils which he knew to be afflicting the company, but was convinced it would aggravate them, and he was as much alarmed by the attack on the company's charter as he would be in 1774 by the attack on the charter of Massachusetts. On the East India question he had an interesting exchange with James Delancey which shows how similar their politics were. He told the New Yorker in December, 1772, that the government meant nothing more "than to vest the immense patronage of office, now in the hands of the Company, in those of the Crown." Replying in April, Delancey said the proceedings against the company only strengthened him in the opinion he had long entertained of "the Reality of that System which has been uniformly pursued during the Present Reign, to render every Person immediately dependent on the Crown for the offices that are held under Government." Delancey sensed what he called "a total disregard of Public Faith or the just rights of individuals," and raised the question of what confidence the subject could have in the royal grants when even those confirmed by law and bought of the Crown in a solemn manner, may be by a majority in both Houses of Parliament revocable at the pleasure of the King or his Ministers." [35] This was the pure doctrine of the Rockingham Whigs.

Unable to rally more than a tiny minority against the ministry's measure, Burke gave up the fight and went to France in January, returning in March to witness the passage of the Regulating Act and another bill to allow the East India Company to export tea in its own ships to America with a drawback of the duty paid on importation first into England. The latter act led straight to the 1774 crisis, but Burke seems not to have

---

[35] *Ibid.*, Delancey to Burke, April 7, 1773. Delancey on July 7 wrote again: "I am astonished at the infatuation of the people on your side of the Atlantic relative to the affairs of the India Company and think they seem determined to punish the Directors to give an Influence to the Crown that must in the end be fatal to the liberties of the Nation."

had the slightest apprehension of its fateful consequences. He did nothing to oppose it. Perhaps he thought it futile to go against a proposition that passed routine through the House of Commons without a division.[36] But it is much more likely that he saw in it a benefit to the company whose interests he had championed. At the end of the session he wrote to his New York employers a brief but caustic comment on the Regulating Act. Of the Tea Act he made no mention. If that was a dark design to ensnare Americans into acceptance of Parliament's right to tax them, Burke either did not know it or preferred not to tell the colonials. Not even in private letters to Delancey and Cruger did he say one word on the subject in 1773.

In the whole of his New York correspondence prior to 1774 there is but one reference to ominous happenings in North America. It concerned two events of 1772: the burning of the king's revenue ship *Gaspee* in Narragansett bay, and the dispute that broke out in Massachusetts between Governor Hutchinson and the assembly when it was announced that crown officials would no longer depend on the assembly for their salaries. The *Gaspee* affair provoked the British government to attempt bringing guilty persons to England for trial, and the new dispute in Massachusetts exacerbated the long-standing dangerous situation at Boston. Burke naturally viewed the violence done to the king's ship as criminal, but he told John Cruger of his regret that the ministers had been "so ill advised as to order the persons guilty of the outrage . . . to England for trial." He was sorry too that "a certain carelessness (that looked like a countenance to such acts) in bringing delinquents to punishment in the ordinary and proper way" had furnished "anything like a plausible pretext for such a very improper mode of proceeding." As for Massachusetts, Burke thought it was regrettable that "the indiscretions of both sides in one of your neighboring colonies" had raised discussions that "ought forever to be buried in silence."

Something of the spirit in which Burke could consider such

---

[36] The act originated as a resolution presented by Lord North in committee and approved by the House of Commons on April 27. As a bill it passed the Commons on May 6 and was approved by the Lords the following day.— *Commons Journal* 34: 286, 293, 301, 304, 307. The purpose of the bill was to relieve the company financially by enabling it to dispose of a vast surplus of its teas at prices so advantageous to American purchasers as to tempt them to submit to the tea tax laid in 1767.

incidents in America comes out in a letter he wrote to Rockingham on July 19, 1773, in support of a request from Delancey that the Marquess send him an English jockey. Burke made an elaborate joke of the matter, saying:

If poor George Grenville was alive, he would not suffer English jockeys to be entered outwards without bond and certificate; or at least he would have had them stamped, or excised, or circumcised, or something should be done to them, to bear the burdens of this poor country, and to relieve the landed interest.

Burke hoped the Marquess could send a jockey because it was "better that they should be contesting about their horses than our acts of trade, and importing our jockeys than turning out our governors." [37] Burke enjoyed this vein of humor so well that he continued it six months later in a letter to Delancey. He cautioned the New Yorker with mock solemnity that "whenever we shall be able to send you out a boy" it would be "a part of your original contract, a solemn charter, a standing instruction, that the *Jockey Club at Old New Market* shall have all authority, jurisdiction, and preeminence, and a full, perfect, and entire legislative authority in all cases whatsoever over all the *New Markets* and all other *provincial sporting assemblies* in America." Were any jockey "to trespass against this supreme jurisdiction," he might be brought back to England "under an old act of Harry the 8th" and dragged through "an horse pond on any race course in England."

But such ironical pleasantry would not appear again in Burke's communications to his New York principals. As those words were being penned on January 5, 1774, news of the Boston Tea Party was crossing the ocean to England. The grand crisis was at hand.

---

[37] *Correspondence* 1: 420.

V. The Agent and the Crisis, 1774-1775

I T was an unfortunate coincidence, and a crushing blow
to the hopes of all men on both sides of the ocean who
desired to preserve the British Empire in peace, that intelligence of the violent affair in Boston harbor on the night of
December 16, 1773, arrived in England just two days before
the Privy Council hearing (January 29) of the Massachusetts
petition for the removal of Governor Hutchinson and Lieutenant Governor Oliver. That petition had been started because of the indignation aroused by the untoward publication
of certain private letters written by these officials in favor of
royalist reforms in the government of Massachusetts. To the
crown authorities the petition was highly offensive and their
sense of outrage was sharpened by the news of the Boston "Tea
party." Angry passions were stirred against America and vented
upon the nearest object: the most distinguished American of
the age—Dr. Benjamin Franklin, a well-known public figure
in England and the king's deputy postmaster general for
America. He was agent for the Massachusetts Assembly; he
had himself delivered that body's petition into the hands of
Lord Dartmouth; he had publicly acknowledged himself to
be the person who obtained the Hutchinson-Oliver letters and
sent them to Massachusetts; and he attended before the Privy
Council to promote the petition. High official indignation at
the conduct of the petitioners was concentrated for the moment
upon the man who acted for them, and the hearing was used
by Solicitor General Wedderburn as an opportunity for the
public excoriation of Franklin, with the applauding approval
of the assembled lords. Never before had this great man, who
was for years a sort of unofficial ambassador for all British
North America, so perfectly represented his country.

Burke was present as a spectator at this historic scene and
recorded his impressions in at least three letters. He told
General Charles Lee that Wedderburn "uttered a furious
philippic against poor Dr. Franklin. It required all his philosophy, natural and acquired, to support him against it." [1] To

---

[1] *Letters and papers of General Charles Lee* 1: 119-121. *N. Y. Hist. Soc. Coll.*,
1874.

Lord Rockingham, Burke described Wedderburn as "laying on most heavily, indeed beyond all bounds and measure, on Dr. Franklin. I am told the Doctor is to be dismissed from whatever employments he holds under the crown." [2] Burke's most detailed account of the occasion was that which he sent to the New York committee of correspondence. There he gave an outline of the arguments presented by the counsel for the petitioners, and of the opposing case developed by Wedderburn, "who ended by falling severely upon the means of obtaining and communicating these obnoxious papers, and on the evil effects that such proceedings . . . had upon the public peace." The Privy Council meeting was the fullest Burke had ever seen. He did not think from the nature of the case that a public trial had been necessary, but "it was obviously intended to give all possible weight and solemnity to the decision. The petition was rejected." Of Dr. Franklin, central figure in the drama, Burke wrote not a word, did not mention his name. He did not choose to say in what was not a private letter, that the first of all Americans had been intentionally insulted and humiliated before the highest court in England. He reported all facts except the most important fact, which was certain to excite ill temper in America. Why was this omitted? Probably because Burke was already trying to conciliate by the arts of doing little and saying less, of smoothing tempers and letting fires die from want of fuel. In conclusion he said that he did not think the question of American treatment of the tea ships would be "altogether kept out of Parliament," and added that he would "be glad of your instructions relative to my conduct with regard to office, if you should think any to be necessary." Followed then some words that sounded a soft warning: "I shall as religiously obey your orders in this respect, as in my parliamentary capacity I shall always steadily retain my own freedom and deliver my opinion only in what I shall think the good of the people." Circumstances now were forming in which Burke would not find it easy to harmonize the duties of his two offices.

The Boston Port Act

With massive support in both Parliament and the country, the king's ministers early in February determined to take

---

[2] *Correspondence* 1: 454.

severe reprisals against Massachusetts; other colonial governments were so informed, well before the first of the coercian
acts was brought forward. "I have it in command from the
King," wrote Lord Dartmouth to Governor Tryon on February 5, "to acquaint you, that it is his Majesty's firm Resolution
upon the unanimous advice of his confidential Servants to
pursue such Measures as shall be effectual for securing the
Dependence of the Colonies upon this Kingdom." [3] On this
high ground of professed justification the punitive course was
to proceed: on the allegation that disloyal and disobedient
Americans intended to separate from the British crown and
set up independent states. With the case so presented, it was
not easy for British patriots who wished to preserve the empire
to raise an effective opposition.

Lord North on March 14 brought into the House of Commons a bill to close the port of Boston: to interdict the offending city's commerce by sea until adequate compensation was
paid for the tea that had been destroyed, and until the crown
was satisfied that suitable conditions existed to warrant a re-
opening of the harbor. The bill passed rapidly through both
houses without a division in either. Burke's corps of friends
made no stand as a party against the measure, but on the final
reading (March 25) he and William Dowdeswell spoke a protest. Nothing, said Burke, had ever given him "a more heart-
felt sorrow than the present measure." He knew that to oppose
it was to draw public indignation upon himself, yet he would
voice a dissent and a warning:

Observe, [said he,] that the disturbances are general; shew me
one port in all America where the goods have been landed and
vended; the distemper is general, but the punishment is local. . . .
Whether it will be effectual or not, I do not know; but, Sir, let me
paint to this House the impropriety of a measure like this; it is a
remedy of the most uncertain operation; view but the consequence,
and you will repent the measure. . . . One town in proscription, the
rest in rebellion, can never be a remedial measure for general disturbances. Have you considered whether you have troops and ships
sufficient to enforce an universal proscription to the trade of the
whole continent of America? If you have not, the attempt is
childish, and the operation fruitless.

Passing from the question of feasibility to that of justice,

_____
[3] N. Y. documents 8: 409.

Burke condemned the bill for indiscriminately punishing the innocent along with the guilty. He entirely approved singling out and punishing the particular persons who had committed the crime, and he charged the king's officials in Massachusetts with negligence and irresolution: "How came they to be so feeble and inactive?" He warned against being drawn into "blocking up one port after another," for the consequence would be that "you will draw a foreign force upon you." He ended by declaring that there were only two ways to govern America: "either to make it subservient to all your laws, or to let it govern itself by its own internal policy." Parliament was now going to make it "obedient to all the laws of this country," but he desired a new legislative arrangement for America "not founded upon your laws and statutes here, but grounded upon the vital principles of English liberty." [4]

Ministry took the next parliamentary step on its road to war on March 28 when North obtained leave to bring in a bill to abolish the Massachusetts charter and create a new government in its place. This bill did not come up for first reading, however, until after the Easter recess, during which Burke found time to write to his New York employers an account of the momentous proceedings so far under way in Parliament. He said that Lord North had opened the subject of America in "a languid and moderate manner," but that air had then worn off, and the Boston Port Act had been "proposed and supported quite through, with expressions of the utmost firmness and resolution." The current of opinion both in Parliament and outdoors ran strongly against America, although there were some persons "who disapproved of the bill and who expressed their disapprobation in the strongest and most explicit terms," but they did this "more for the acquittal of their own honour and discharge of their own consciences . . . than from any sort of hope they entertained of bringing any considerable number to their opinion." Doubtless Burke was thinking particularly of himself and Dowdeswell. But he made it clear that these men who had stood up against ministers, majorities, and popularity entertained no thought of "giving up the constitutional superiority of this country."

---

[4] *Parliamentary history* 17: 1182-1186. Only summary and perhaps not wholly reliable reports survive of this speech, which Horace Walpole described as one of Burke's "painted orations."—Walpole, Horace, *Last journals* 1: 337, London.

Had they accepted the ministerial view that this was the issue at stake, they would have sided with the majority, because

all the true friends to the Colonies—the only true friends they have had or ever can have in England—have laid and will lay down the proper subordination of America as a fundamentally incontrovertible maxim in the government of this Empire. This idea, to which they tenaciously adhere in the full extent of the proposition, they are of opinion is nothing derogatory to the real essential rights of mankind . . . without the enjoyment of which no honest man can wish the dependence of one country on another. Very unfortunately, in my poor thoughts, the advice of that sort of temperate men has been little attended to on this side of the Atlantic, and rather less on the other.

There was one detail of the proceedings in Parliament which Burke thought should command the close attention of his employers. The Massachusetts council agent, William Bollan, had made application to Parliament to be heard in opposition to the Boston Port Act, but this privilege had been withheld because of the old Board of Trade regulation that denied official recognition to an agent who was not authorized to act as the representative of the whole colony. Thus the question that had troubled Burke in 1771 came up again: his own credentials might be similarly challenged. "To what consequences this will lead," he said, "you are, gentlemen, to consider."

"Such, Sir, Is My Idea of the Constitution of the British Empire"

It must have been during the Easter recess that Burke prepared the first of his most famous parliamentary efforts to introduce the principle of conciliation into the imperial crisis. This was the speech on *American Taxation,* delivered on April 19 in support of a motion to repeal the American port duty on tea. No epitome of this wonderful utterance can be given here, but something of its character may be observed. It was not "American" but "imperial"; not the New York assembly agent but the philosopher of prudence in imperial relations spoke the words.[5]

Burke urged the repeal of the tea tax not only as a means for improving the temper of Americans, but for the sake of

---

[5] *Works* **2:** 338-440.

the East India Company itself whose ships had been violated in American ports. An injurious tax of three pence a pound on tea imported into America had since 1768 locked up millions of pounds of that commodity to rot in English warehouses. Its sale would have prevented the bankruptcy that had put the company at the mercy of the crown.

America would have furnished that vent, which no other part of the world can furnish but America; where tea is next to a necessary of life; and where the demand grows upon the supply. . . . It is through the American trade of tea that your East India conquests are to be prevented from crushing you with their burden. They are ponderous indeed; and they must have that great country to lean upon or they tumble upon your head. It is the same folly that has lost you at once the benefit of the west and of the east.

The whole speech moved on the level of high and practical imperial considerations. He called for a restoration of "the corner stone of the policy of this country with regard to its colonies"—the Navigation Laws, which were not designed to raise colonial revenue but to promote and protect trade and the prosperity of the empire. After reviewing the history of the American taxation question since the administration of Grenville, he appealed for a return to the wise practices of the days when parliaments were not rash enough to vote tax levies in America:

Let the memory of all actions, in contradiction to that good old mode, on both sides, be extinguished forever. Be content to bind America by laws of trade; you have always done it. Let this be your reason for binding their trade. Do not burthen them with taxes; you were not used to do so from the beginning. Let this be your reason for not taxing. . . . But if, intemperately, unwisely, fatally, you sophisticate and poison the very source of government, by urging subtle deductions, and consequences odious to those you govern, from the unlimited and illimitable nature of supreme sovereignty, you will teach them by these lessons to call that sovereignty into question. When you drive him hard, the boar will surely turn upon the hunters. If that sovereignty and their freedom cannot be reconciled, which will they take? They will cast your sovereignty in your face. Nobody will be argued into slavery.

He could not agree with such men as Chatham and Franklin who held that Parliament had no *right* to tax the colonies for revenue and that colonial contributions for imperial defense ought to be in the form of royal requisitions. He rejected their view because it tended to sunder the British legislature by separating the king from Parliament. Burke never thought of Parliament as a two-chamber legislature facing a royal executive, but as the supreme legislature, the king *in* Parliament: a legislative trinity of king, lords, and commons. Thus when Burke argued that raising money in the colonies was not the business of the crown but of Parliament, he was thinking constitutionally according to the Declaratory Act of 1766, which he again defended in this speech. That act had not declared the unlimited authority of "Parliament" over the colonies, but had stated "that the King's majesty, by and with the advice and consent of the lords spiritual and temporal, and commons of Great Britain, in parliament assembled, had, hath, and of a right ought to have, full power and authority . . . to bind the colonies and people of America, subjects of the crown of Great Britain, in all cases whatsoever." This was the law of the constitution. The Americans could not pick and choose what parts of the supreme legislature they would obey; they could not keep the king and disavow the Lords and Commons without whom the king could not lawfully legislate and govern.

To those who argued that the abandonment by the British legislature of the practice of taxing the colonies would undermine the Declaratory Act, he replied:

For my part I look upon the rights stated in that act, exactly in the manner in which I viewed them on its first proposition. . . . I look, I say, on the imperial rights of Great Britain, and the privileges which the colonies ought to enjoy under those rights, to be just the most reconcileable things in the world. The parliament of Great Britain sits at the head of her extensive empire in two capacities: one as the local legislature of this island, providing for all things at home, immediately, and by no other instrument than the executive power.—The other, and I think her nobler capacity, is what I call her *imperial character;* in which, as from the throne of heaven, she superintends all the several inferior legislatures, and guides, and controls them all without annihilating any.

If in time of war one of these inferior legislatures were to refuse to contribute to the common defense of the empire, a reserved power of taxation in the British Parliament—deriving from the very nature of the empire—might properly be called into operation, but as an emergency instrument, not an ordinary means of supply.

Such, Sir, is my idea of the constitution of the British empire, as distinguished from the constitution of Britain; and on these grounds I think subordination and liberty may be sufficiently reconciled through the whole; whether to serve a refining speculatist, or a factious demagogue, I know not; but enough surely for the ease and happiness of man.

But instead of ascending to march upon this high ground of imperial prudence, Parliament not only refused to repeal the tea tax but proceeded forthwith to pass by decisive majorities two ministerial bills for remodelling the constitution of Massachusetts along royalist lines and altering the colony's administration of justice. These harsh measures were debated simultaneously in the House of Commons on May 2. The opposition, although overwhelmed by more than three to one, was stronger than against the Boston Port Act. Burke, who was ill from cold and fatigue, closed the debate with a brief but futile plea for abolishing the tea tax instead of passing laws likely to result in bloodshed. Only the briefest record of his remarks, and that unauthenticated, has survived.[6] But among his literary remains which the editors of his correspondence published as an appendix is the sketch of a speech for this occasion which undoubtedly shows his real attitude. He denounced the action of Parliament as "a proscription of whole cities and provinces," and was "beyond measure surprised" that men felt no terror at what they were doing.

A whole people culprit! Nations under accusation! A tribunal erected for commonwealths! This is no vulgar idea, and no trivial undertaking; it makes me shudder. I confess, that, in comparison of the magnitude of the situation, I feel myself shrunk to nothing. . . . If we lose our dominions, I am not surprised at it. We do not seem, by our virtues or our faults, to be a people qualified for empire.[7]

Many of the ideas in this sketch anticipate passages in the classic speech of the following year on *Conciliation with the Colonies*.

On May 4 Burke wrote to New York a long account of these ominous new developments. Pessimism pervaded it. Not a word suggested that if Americans stood firm and united, ministry and Parliament would again resort to appeasement. The letter reflected a sombre view of the crisis in which, from its nature, New York and all America must soon be involved. He

[6] *Parliamentary history* 17: 1314-1315.
[7] *Correspondence* 4: 488-489.

apologized for not reviewing the substance of what was said in the debate, but thought this hardly necessary "as the arguments of those who opposed the measure had little or no effect." He did give an explanation why the minority against the latest coercion acts was larger than in the case of the Boston Port Act: many had voted to punish the city of Boston because they believed that the ministry would afterwards show the good sense and lenity to support the repeal of the tea tax. But that hope had been dashed, and it would be an illusion to imagine that any signs had appeared of a disposition to soften the ministerial and parliamentary attitude: "That you may not be deceived by any idle or flattering report, be assured that the determination to enforce obedience from the colonies to the laws of revenue, by the most powerful means, seems as firm as possible, and that the Ministry appear stronger than ever I have known them."

Once again the Massachusetts Council agent had been refused the privilege of sending a petition to Parliament because of the defect in his credentials. Hence Burke cautioned his employers that "few colonies have and that you in particular have no agent properly authorized to communicate your desires in that character to Parliament"; he therefore recommended, if they thought it advisable, that they "conform to the ideas of the King's servants and qualify . . . for that official communication which all the subjects of this Empire ought to hold with the sovereign legislature." But he reminded the New Yorkers that they already had his sentiments on this matter and by implication reiterated his intention to resign if the change were made in the mode of authorizing their agent.

Not yet had New York become a target for punitive measures, but her involvement now lay in the logic of events, however much Burke wished to keep her clear of it. Probably he would not have been displeased to disencumber himself of the agency. He said he was "full of trouble on account of the late most unfortunate transactions." His advice had "little weight anywhere," but his wishes ever had been and ever would be "equally for the good and the freedom (without which hardly any good can be) of the whole."

The Arousal of New York

At New York an agitation against the Tea Act and the anticipated arrival of East India Company tea ships had begun early in the fall of 1773. "A new flame is apparently kindling in America," wrote William Smith on October 13. "We have intelligence that the East India Company resolved to send tea to America to be sold, they paying the duty on importation." Ever since the duty was laid in Charles Townshend's time, Smith noted, all the tea consumed in New York had been smuggled from Holland; now the Sons of Liberty and the smugglers would raise a cry and all the confusion of 1765-1766 would be repeated. "Time will shew the event. Our domestic parties will probably die, & be swallowed up in the general opposition to the Parliamentary project of raising the arm of Government by Revenue Laws." [8]

During October-November the *New York Journal* printed a series of bitter attacks on the East India Company, charging that the projected sale of its tea surplus in America was a scheme to corrupt Americans and undermine their liberty. Governor Tryon wrote to Lord Dartmouth on November 3 of "a ferment" in the minds of the people, and sent to the minister a number of local publications that appeared to be "calculated to sew sedition in the minds of the people, and to support and make popular the cause of those who are deepest concerned in the illicit trade to Foreign Countries." The Governor thus attributed the agitation to smugglers, and although he said he could form no judgment of what would happen when a tea ship arrived, he flattered himself "that the peace of the Government will be preserved." [9] That the assembly's committee of correspondence were not greatly alarmed is perhaps suggested by the fact that at this time they wrote a general business letter to Burke, covering many topics but saying nothing whatever on the subject of tea and the East India Company.[10]

By December, however, an association pledge against buying, selling, or drinking tea, in the event of East India Company shipments, was circulating in the city. Conservative New Yorkers may have disliked the numerous threats of disorder and riot, but they seemed at one with everybody else in opposing the tea tax and the company's plan to dispose of its surplus. Then came the news of what happened at Boston on the night of December 16. Agitation quickened, and although

---

[8] Diary.

[9] *N. Y. documents* 8: 400-401.

[10] Wentworth-Fitzwilliam MSS., committee to Burke, Nov. 2, 1773.

no untoward event occurred, General Haldimand, who commanded the king's troops at New York, advised Dartmouth on December 28 that such a ferment had been stirred up that the tea ship expected would probably have to go back without unloading.[11] A week later Governor Tryon wrote to the Secretary of State for the Colonies:

> From the general appearance of the united opposition to the principle of Monopoly, and the Importation Duty in America, I can form no Other Opinion than that the landing, storing, and safe keeping of the Tea, when stored, could be accomplished, but only under the protection of the point of the Bayonet, and Muzle of the Cannon, and even then I do not see how the consumption could be effected.[12]

When the assembly convened in January the members recognized that a serious new crisis had arisen. Their journal records nothing on the subject of tea, but they did agree unanimously (January 20) to appoint a standing committee of correspondence

> to obtain the most early and authentic intelligence of all such acts and resolutions of the British Parliament, or proceedings of Administration, as do or may relate to or affect the liberties and privileges of his Majesty's subjects . . . in America, and to keep up and maintain a correspondence and communication with our sister colonies respecting these important considerations.[13]

The creation of this committee was in no sense a protest against the Tea Act or the East India Company, but a precautionary tactic against measures that it seemed likely the British government would take because of the violence against the tea ships. Nor was this a wholly new committee. It was an expansion of the committee of correspondence which had for the previous few years communicated regularly with the assembly's agent in London. It included the four city members (Cruger, Walton, Jauncey, Delancey, with whom Burke corresponded) and nine other members. Any seven were authorized to act for the whole committee. After the appointment of this body the assembly occupied itself wholly with local affairs until the end of the session on March 19. And since no tea

---

[11] *Manuscripts of the Earl of Dartmouth* 1: 347, Hist. Mss. Comm., 11th Rep., App., Pt. V, 1887.

[12] *N. Y. documents* 8: 407-408.

[13] *Journal of Votes and Proceedings* (Jan. 6—March 19, 1774), 16.

ship arrived at New York until April, the city remained out-wardly quiet through the winter.

It was almost exactly the moment Burke was making his great speech on American taxation that the tea crisis came to a head in New York. A ship, the *Nancy,* arrived at Sandy Hook on April 19 with a cargo of tea. The captain came up to the city, there discovered himself to be the most unpopular man in it, and was relieved to learn that the merchants to whom the tea was consigned thought it imprudent for him to attempt to land it.

Only a few days before, Governor Tryon had sailed for England, so that once again it was fated that Lieutenant-governor Colden, now eighty-seven, should face a situation he could not control. He desired that the cargo be safely landed, but he could not protect such an operation against an angry populace without requesting the aid of troops, which he was loath to do; hence the tea remained aboard the *Nancy.*[14] But in the midst of the excitement another ship, the *London,* commanded by a Captain Chambers, came all the way up to its wharf in the East River. It belonged to the Cruger family of Bristol and New York, so that presumably the Speaker of the assembly and a member of the governor's council had an interest in it. Captain Chambers professed to be carrying no tea, but word got about that this was not the fact and suspicious citizens went aboard to investigate. He then admitted there was tea in the hold; whereupon a band calling themselves the "Mohawks" went into action. John Cruger wrote an account of this event to Burke, saying "thus are the minds of the people agitated against the importation of tea subject to duty."[15] This was New York's "tea party."

On May 12 news reached New York by ship of the passage of the Boston Port Act, and a new wave of consternation and anger moved over the citizens. The assembly not being in session, organized activity for manifesting sympathy and sup-port for Massachusetts arose spontaneously among the people. There now came into being the historic Committee of Fifty-one in New York City, wherein Sons of Liberty radicals were fused with conservative mercantile gentlemen. The latter seized the initiative in order to prevent the radicals from cap-

---

[14] Wertenbaker, T. J., *Father Knickerbocker rebels,* 33, N. Y., Scribners, 1948.

[15] Wentworth-Fitzwilliam MSS., Cruger to Burke, May 1, 1774.

turing the leadership of a thoroughly popular movement to unite New York with the other colonies in common defense of their rights and liberties. According to Colden, some of the principal men of New York, fearing that "hot-headed men might run the City into dangerous measures," were induced to appear in what they knew to be illegal proceedings, from a consideration that if they did not, the business would be left in "rash hands."[16] William Smith recorded on May 18: "The Delanceys urged their friends to attend, and pushed them in, to mix with the Liberty Boys, as well to drown the latter as to gain their confidence."[17] Conservatives formed at the outset a majority in the Committee of Fifty-one, and the fact was reflected in that body's refusal to approve a proposal for reviving a general boycott of British manufactures. The Committee, however, did approve the calling of an intercolonial congress.[18]

Little seems to be known of the part played in these May days by the assembly's expanded committee of correspondence. Four of its members (Cruger, Jauncey, Walton, and Simon Boerum) signed a letter to Burke on May 31 which is a perfect mirror of conservative opinion. They acknowledged receiving his letter of April 6 and thanked him for "early and circumstantial information of the proceedings in Parliament respecting the Town of Boston." That had been a thoroughly candid and unvarnished report of Parliament's determination and of the views of those who opposed the punitive act. Burke had urged his correspondents not to be deceived about the intentions of the British government, and had stated that even those in opposition firmly upheld the supremacy of the mother country over the colonies. The men who received his letter did not keep it privy to themselves until it could be laid on the assembly's table, but spread it about the city. They now told Burke:

In a matter of such general importance, we thought proper to communicate your sentiments to many of our friends, and as we did not enjoin them secrecy, the contents of your letter are pretty generally known in this City. We have the pleasure to assure you, that

---

[16] *N. Y. documents* 8: 433.

[17] Diary.

[18] Abbott, W. C., *New York in the American Revolution*, 104-111, N. Y., Scribners, 1929; Becker, *op. cit.*, 112-113, 117.

they are highly approved of, and that your attention to the affairs of the Colonies has impressed the inhabitants of this City with the most favorable ideas of your character.

But the only "sentiments" expressed in Burke's letter of April 6 were an affirmation, by implication, of the principle of the Declaratory Act of 1766, a disapproval of intemperate conduct, and a regret that "misunderstandings and heats" had been generated "where nothing should exist but harmony and good correspondence, which ought naturally to arise from the entire agreement of their [British and American] real interests." It is likely that New Yorkers were much more impressed by the sober realism of Burke's information, than by his "sentiments."

They went on to tell him that the conduct of administration and Parliament had excited "great uneasiness throughout the Colonies," and to express their regret that any one in England could believe the question of the dependence of America on the mother country was involved in the current disputes: "A desire of dissolving our connection with the Parent Country, is an idea to which every good American is a stranger, however difficult it may be with precision to state the true extent of their dependence." Burke's correspondents made no reference whatever to the subject of tea and the tea tax. What alarmed them most was "a Bill said to be before the House of Commons, to make persons accused of certain offences liable to be sent to Great Britain for their trial, and to subject even witnesses to the same hardship." They were referring to a provision of the act remodelling the administration of justice in Massachusetts, and they added:

An Act of this kind cannot but be considered with abhorrence by a people bred up under an idea that they had a right to the blessings of the British Constitution, and its admirable system of laws, of which they look upon this act as one of the most flagrant violations.

All the men who signed this letter to Burke were soon to be stigmatized as "tories"; all were loyalist when the war came.

They concluded by asking Burke to make contact with Henry Cruger junior, of Bristol, a New Yorker by birth and then visiting in America, but about to return to England. He was very well informed, and it was hoped that Burke might obtain for him "an interview with Lord Dartmouth, or such other noble personage as you may conceive would like to have

a full, precise & faithful communication of the general sentiments & wishes of the people of this Colony." [19] Henry Cruger
probably carried this letter to Burke.

The political attitude of these assembly committeemen was
well shown also in the reply which they sent to the Connecticut
Assembly's proposal, early in June, for a colonial congress of
correspondence committees or other representatives of the
elected legislative bodies in America. The New Yorkers wrote:

We agree with you, that at this alarming juncture, a general
Congress of deputies from the several Colonies, would be a very
expedient and salutary measure; such a Congress, consisting of men
of coolness, prudence and understanding, would, we conceive, be
the best means under providence, of restoring that peace and harmony between Great Britain and her colonies, which is the surest
foundation of happiness to both, and which every good man, every
well wisher to his country, ought to labour strenuously to establish.

But the committeemen felt unable to assume the authority
to commit their legislature, which had not been called into
session, to such a course of action, so that if a congress along
the lines of the Connecticut proposal were assembled, they
could only "most gladly and willingly assist" with their advice.
In the meantime they desired to know what steps might be
taken by other colonies situated like New York "by not having
an opportunity of knowing the sentiments of their houses of
representatives." When this was known, the New York committee would be better able to judge what would be "most
likely to procure a redress of our present grievances, and promote the union and prosperity, of the mother country and
the colonies." The letter was signed by ten of the eleven members of the committee; among them was Captain James Delancey, and all of them belonged to the assembly majority of
which he was the leader.[20]

They desired to form a united colonial front against the
overweening pretensions of the British Parliament, but they
believed it should be done through lawfully constituted bodies.
They could not call the assembly into session; that was the
prerogative of the governor. They did not believe that by

[19] Wentworth-Fitzwilliam MSS.

[20] The Connecticut Assembly's letter of June 3 and the New York committee's reply of June 24 were first printed in the *New York Journal* for March 9,
1775.

an act of self-constitution they could assume a representative capacity not conferred by the assembly; nor did it occur to them that self-appointed or casually elected popular committees formed to demonstrate public feeling could act in the name of the Province of New York with either authority or propriety. Moreover, they had a sober and well-informed view of the nature and gravity of the crisis; if this knowledge did not make them less zealous against oppression, it undoubtedly made them more circumspect in the choice of means. They did not share the widespread belief, founded partly on recollections of 1766 and partly on current rumor, that a spirited display of defiance would again result in a British backdown; that presently the North ministry would go out and new ministers come in to conciliate the colonies; that the opposition in England was strong and wholly sympathetic with American resistance. Burke had told them the ministry was strongly supported both in Parliament and in the country, and was determined to carry through its measures; and this was the truth.

Burke probably exercised much influence in New York. We have seen that the contents of his letter of April 6 were spread wide over the city, and it may have been the policy of the Delancey-Cruger party to attempt to moderate the populace by showing that Burke, although an opponent of ministry, yet upheld, as he had said, "the proper subordination of America as a fundamental maxim in the government of this Empire." His credit with the radicals was high, and he could be quoted to good advantage by the party that desired to prevent the dispute with England from being carried to the point of rebellion.[21]

---

[21] Prior to 1774 Burke's credit with the New York radicals had probably sunk somewhat. In March, 1772, his name had been omitted from the toasts drunk by the radicals at the annual commemoration of the Stamp Act's repeal, and during that year the *New York Journal* printed a number of small slurs on him. But in March, 1774, when the same gentlemen met again for the same purpose, the same paper reported that "our worthy agent, Mr. Burke" was toasted immediately after that greatest (in American eyes) of all Englishmen, Chatham. Other favorable notices of Burke studded the radical Whig organ at this time. On May 26, for example, a dispatch from London appeared, stating that of "five flaming patriots" of 1770 "Cornwall and Meredith have fallen, Germain and Barré are tottering, and Burke alone keeps his former position." Perhaps Burke's speech in support of the 1773 bill to relieve the Dissenters, which was much publicized in New York, helped to restore his credit with the radicals.—*Rivington's Gazetteer*, Jan. 6, 1774. Early in June it became known that he had attempted without success to obtain repeal of the tea tax, and on June 30 the *Gazetteer* published a summary of his speech of April 19, describing

Since that party formed a majority in the assembly, one is tempted to speculate on what might have been the course of events if acting Governor Colden in the spring or early summer of 1774 had convoked the assembly, and if that body had attempted then—as it would attempt in 1775, when the hour was too late—to formulate principles of Anglo-American conciliation and accord. It is at least possible that the constitutional legislature of New York might not have surrendered the political initiative to the unconstitutional Committee of Fifty-one, which the Delancey party failed to harness, and which chose the New York delegates to the first American continental congress.

Agent Burke and the Quebec Act

Meanwhile, another measure affecting New York's interests much more directly than the coercion acts passed to discipline Massachusetts, was making its way through the imperial legislature. Originating in the House of Lords and reflecting the views of Lord Dartmouth, a bill for establishing a new civil government in Quebec and determining the hitherto undefined territorial limits of that province, came down to the House of Commons on May 18. Since the subject of this bill had been before the British government since 1763, the time chosen for the legislation not less than the nature of it made it a consistent part of the effort to prop and fortify the imperial power in North America. The act was certain to become a new American grievance.

More than two months before the bill was introduced, Solicitor General Wedderburn had sought Burke's opinion on a draft of it, saying: "I trust to your public spirit that you will rather consider how it is to be corrected, than how it is to be opposed."[22] What views Burke may then have expressed have not been discovered, but it is certain that when the bill reached the House of Commons he took alarm. He disliked the royalist character of the proposed constitution for Quebec, which did not provide for an elective assembly, and he disliked still more a provision for maintaining the old French customary civil law, instead of giving the king's new French-speaking subjects

it as "the most masterly speech that has perhaps been ever uttered in a public assembly."

[22] Wentworth-Fitzwilliam MSS., Wedderburn to Burke, March 9, 1774.

the English civil law with the right of trial by jury. Further-more, he feared the territorial clauses might prove injurious to New York because the bill assigned to Quebec all the western lands not included in any other colony, as far south as the Ohio River.

On May 31 two petitions against the bill were brought into the House: one from London merchants asking for the estab-lishment of English law in Quebec, and the other from the proprietors of Pennsylvania alleging an infringement of their territorial rights. Burke chose the occasion to say that the bill appeared to violate also the territorial rights of New York. Lord North replied that it was never intended Quebec should entrench on other colonies, and that he had no objection to their being heard by counsel in committee. The merchants' petition provoked some debate, in the course of which Burke said the House was being asked to legislate hastily and with very small information: it was not proper to pass so late in the session so important a bill about which so little was known. Did the Canadian French desire to retain their own civil law, or had they learned to prefer the law of England? And just what was the French law which the bill proposed to recognize? Burke said:

I stand for the necessity of information, without which—without great, cogent, luminous information—I, for one, will never give my vote for establishing the French law in that country. I should be sorry to see his Majesty a despotic governor. And am I sure that this despotism is not meant to lead to universal despotism? When that country cannot be governed as a free country, I question whether this can . . . it is evident that this constitution is meant to be an instrument of tyranny to the Canadians, and an example to others of what they have to expect; at some time or other it will come home to England.[23]

The House voted to summon certain high Quebec officials to attend and give testimony before committee, but rejected two motions, supported by Burke, to order the reports of Governor Guy Carleton of Quebec and the king's law officers laid before it. Filled with apprehension, Burke wrote a letter to his New York employers on June 1, stating that the Quebec

[23] Wright, John, ed., *Sir Henry Cavendish's debates of the House of Commons in the year 1774 on the bill for making more effectual provision for the government of the province of Quebec*, 89, London, Longmans, 1839.

bill was "injurious to the territorial rights as well as to the property of many innocent and even meritorious individuals." At this moment he held the mistaken view that the bill had been so drawn as to validate the French grants in the Lake Champlain region which were still an undecided business before the Board of Trade. Although he had little hope of success, he promised to oppose that part of the bill with all his might, and he intended to enlist the aid of Governor Tryon, who had recently arrived in England.

By June 6, when the territorial clauses were considered in parliamentary committee, Burke had consulted with Board of Trade officials and learned that his fears for the security of the New York boundary at the head of Lake Champlain were groundless. But on the west there was real danger to New York because the bill assigned to Quebec a constructive rather than a precisely determined boundary. That is to say, the bill stated that all territories not hitherto adjudged to another colony were to be included in Quebec; and New York had no western boundary except against New Jersey. Burke proposed to define the Quebec line exactly, and told the house:

When I heard that this bill was to be brought in on the principle that parliament were to draw a line of circumvallation about our colonies, and to establish a siege of arbitrary power . . . I thought it of the highest importance that we should endeavour to make this boundary as clear as possible.

He pointed out that although the New York-Quebec boundary had been fixed by the crown in 1768 at the forty-fifth parallel (on this point the Board of Trade had refreshed his recollections) that line had been actually drawn only in the eastern Champlain region, so that the provision to extend Quebec south to the Ohio and include all territories "not within the limits of some other British colony as allowed and confirmed by the crown" was a real threat to New York on both its west and northwest. Burke said the reason he felt so anxious about it was that the line would be not merely of geographic distinction, not merely a line between one British colony and another, but "a line to separate a man from the right of an Englishman"; and if it were not determined precisely by Parliament the crown would have the power of "carrying the greatest portion of the actually settled part of the Province of New York into Canada." He therefore moved to fix the boundary of Quebec

by a line drawn from a point on the east side of Lake Champlain in 45° north latitude, and by a line drawn in that parallel west to the river St. Lawrence, and up that river to Lake Ontario, and across that lake to the river Niagara, and from Niagara across Lake Erie to the north-west point of the boundary of Pennsylvania, and down the west boundary of that Province, by a line drawn from thence till it strikes the Ohio.

Lord North suggested mildly that he doubted a clear boundary line could be drawn by Parliament, but Burke insisted it was perfectly practical and said he would take the sense of the committee on it: "I am as much in earnest as ever I was in my life. I have produced a practical idea—I can produce practical words." He put his proposal into the form of an amendment, and it was inserted in the bill to become law.[24] The Quebec boundary thus defined, at the insistence of Edmund Burke and by his words, was to become the permanent New York-Canada line. His success in guarding New York against the threatened encroachment on its west was the more extraordinary from the circumstance that just at this time news had arrived of New York's "tea party."[25]

Burke spoke again on June 7 against the bill's failure to give Quebec an assembly and the English jury. "I would have English liberty carried into French colonies," he said, "but I would not have French slavery brought into English colonies."[26] He did not join in the anti-popery cries against the bill, but he did attack a provision permitting the king to dispose of the Catholic tithes at his pleasure. The architects of the Quebec Act, although recognizing Catholicism as the established religion of the province, nevertheless placed that Church under royal supremacy and made the crown custodian of its revenues. They did not intend to allow papal interference in the Church of Quebec,[27] nor did they assume that the Catholic establishment would not ultimately be succeeded by a Protes-

[24] *Ibid.*, 189-197.
[25] Walpole, *Last journals* 1: 373.
[26] Wright, *Cavendish's debates* (Quebec bill), 213.
[27] North told the house on May 26 that "no bishop will be there under papal authority, because he will see that Great Britain will not permit any papal authority whatever in the country. It is expressly forbidden by the Act of Supremacy."—*Ibid.*, 12.

tant establishment when Protestants came to form a majority, which was expected ultimately. Under the act a Catholic could escape paying tithes by ceasing to be a Catholic. Burke regarded this as holding out a bribe for Catholics to abandon their religion, so that in this respect he did not think the bill provided for an "establishment of popery"—as some of its opponents charged—but rather envisaged an "establishment of atheism." Had his views been followed, there would have been immediately a Protestant establishment with perfect toleration for Catholicism.[28] He did not succeed in carrying any other amendments and at length gave up the effort. But when the committee reported the amended bill on June 10 he made a great speech against it, charging that the only difference it made for the Canadian French was that they would have George III instead of Louis XIV for their king.

> Give them English liberty, give them an English constitution—and then, whether they speak French or English, whether they go to mass or attend our own communion, you will render them valuable and useful subjects of Great Britain. If you refuse to do this the consequence will be most injurious: Canada will become a dangerous instrument in the hands of those who wish to destroy English liberty in every part of our possessions.[29]

The bill was passed on June 13 in a small house by a division of only fifty-six to twenty. Once again a measure of major importance in Anglo-American relations had been rushed through a thin Parliament eager to rise for the summer. Had it been brought forward earlier in the session it might never have been passed, for in spite of ministerial assurances against papal power reaching to Quebec there were powerful anti-Catholic prejudices against parliamentary recognition of an established Catholic Church within the British Empire. When the bill was returned to the Lords for concurrence, Chatham denounced it as a breach of the Reformation, of the Revolution, and of the king's coronation oath. And Horace Walpole recorded: "What may not be attempted when in one bill Parliament abrogates juries and establishes Popery! James II lost his crown for such enormities; the Prince that wears it to the prejudice of that family is authorized by a free parliament to do what James was expelled for doing."[30] The Quebec Act

---

[28] *Ibid.*, 222-224.　　　　　[29] *Ibid.*, 290.
[30] *Last journals* 1: 373-374, 378-379.

certainly commanded far less public approval than any other act of 1774 affecting America.

Burke wrote to his New York employers a somewhat curious account of his conduct in connection with the Quebec Act. It is the only one of his letters to New York of which the complete text was known and in print prior to the discovery of his letter-book, and the true date of its composition has hitherto been assumed to have been August 2. But the letter-book shows that the original date was July 5 and that the letter was afterwards slightly revised and re-dated almost a month later. The reason for this does not appear. Even early July was rather late for reporting to his employers on an act of such great interest to them which had been for more than two weeks on the statute book. He said that pressing business and "not the best of health" were his reasons for delay. Another odd feature was that he either forgot or ignored the hasty warning he had written on June 1 (if indeed he had sent that previous letter), for he said that at that time he had not believed the bill could materially affect the rights of New York; only later had he discovered that "you might be very much affected by it."

Before relating how he had acted to safeguard the territorial interests of New York, he explained what he conceived to be the general purposes of the act. There existed, he said, a "predominant and declared opinion" that the ability of the English colonies in North America to resist the authority of Great Britain ought to be reduced: "that any growth of the colonies which might make them grow out of the reach of the authority of this kingdom ought to be accounted rather a morbid fulness than a sound and proper habit." And not only ought growth to be restrained, but the prerogative of imperial power should be strengthened. Hence, "it was thought expedient to find in the tractable disposition of some provinces a check upon the turbulent manners, and a balance to the less manageable plan in the others." That was to say, the French habit of submission to despotism should be exploited by the British government as a means for curbing English colonists who were over-zealous for freedom. Such opinions were especially prevalent in the House of Lords, although it was true that

a few lords, and Lord Rockingham in particular, objected to the idea of restraining the colonies from spreading into the back country, even if such restraint were practicable; for by stopping the extent of agriculture, they necessitated manufactures, contrary to the standing policy of colonization. The general sentiments were, however, as I have stated them.

This was the reason, Burke said, why he had become uneasy over the "lax and indeterminate" boundary clause in the bill as it came down from the upper house. But he took care to say that even if such a restrictive plan and policy never had existed or were to pass away—as he hoped and thought it had in some degree, "with the first heats"—it would have been wise and right "to define with clearness." Since the ministers confessed that the clause had been hastily drawn, and "professed great candor in admitting alterations," he had gone to the Board of Trade for the information necessary to formulate and propose an amendment. There he had learned that "for a great part of the northern frontier and for the whole of the western until you met the line of New Jersey, you had no defined boundary at all. Your claims were indeed extensive and I am persuaded just, but they had never been regularly allowed." He sought to ascertain also what would be the principles on which the Board of Trade would in the future "determine what belonged to you and what to Canada." What he learned had made him uneasy. He painted the danger to New York (which had been averted by his amendment) in the boldest terms:

On your side a mere *constructive* boundary was established, and the construction, when examined, amounted to nothing more than the King's pleasure. No part of your Province . . . quite to the river Hudson was secured from the possible operation of such a principle. Besides, there was the possibility (at least) that in the settlement of the boundary Ministers would naturally lean to extend those limits the most where royal prerogative was most extensive and consequently their power the highest.

Burke qualified this by stating that he did not mean to charge the king and ministers with such intentions. He meant only that "no laws stood in the way of such an inclination, if it ever did exist or should happen to exist hereafter." His words suggest that he was in something of a dilemma in reporting to his employers on the Quebec Act. He naturally wished to augment his credit for having warded off a great danger, but since he wished also to minimize the ill temper he feared the act would generate in America, he preferred that the peril should be considered rather potential than actual. Apprehending that the New Yorkers might be more disposed to reflect unhappily on the fencing in of their undefined claims, than to rejoice over the limits he had managed to set for Quebec, Burke suggested that "well secured and tolerably extensive boundaries are better than the amplest claims which are neither defined nor allowed." To be sure, the line drawn in the act was not the boundary of New York, but of Quebec, so that there remained a theoretical possibility of the crown's erecting a new colonial government in New York's unsettled and undetermined western regions; but Burke thought that very improbable. "I think the line to all intents and purposes as much your boundary as if it were ever so expressly set down."

Burke considered that he had served his employers well and told them that those who were present during the deliberations had congratulated him "as on a great advantage." [31] The whole tone of his letter breathed a hope that New York might find cause for satisfaction rather than for grievance in the Quebec Act. On the subject of the French Catholic establishment—politically the most imflammatory feature of the law—he said not a word.

It is not possible to say what effect Burke's report may have produced upon his correspondents and public opinion in New York, but there is no doubt about that act's unpopularity in the province. The recognition of Catholicism, the territorial clauses, and the royalist character of the Quebec government were all offensive to provincial sensibilities. The *New York Journal* in September published several dispatches from London suggesting that "popery" was now in the ascendant in Great Britain. One of these averred that "since the Quebec bill passed our two august houses . . . there are not less than 7000 Jesuits arrived in this Kingdom." [32] Young Alexander Hamilton wrote that "a superstitious, bigoted Canadian Papist,

---

[31] Perhaps Burke took more credit than he deserved. So thought William Baker, who presented the Pennsylvania petition and stated that he had drawn the line protecting Pennsylvania and New York, "tho' I have since been told that Burke takes the merit to himself, but upon what grounds I know not as I proposed the line without communication with him."—Baker to Charles Lee, Sept. 3, 1774, in *Letters and papers of General Charles Lee* 1: 132. The parliamentary record, however, accords exactly with what Burke told the New Yorkers.

[32] Sept. 15, 1774.

though ever so profligate, is now esteemed a better subject by our Gracious Sovereign George the Third, than a liberal, enlightened New England Dissenter, though ever so virtuous."[33] Even the loyalist *Rivington's Gazetteer* ran two long articles entitled "Remarks on the Quebec Bill." These, however, criticised the act less for its alleged favor to Catholicism than for its territorial and constitutional clauses.[34] Said the author:

> While our ears are stunned with the dismal sounds of New England's republicanism, bigotry, and intolerance, it behooves us to be upon our guard against the deceitful wiles of those, who would persuade us, that we have nothing to fear from the operation of the Quebec Act. We should consider it as being replete with danger, to ourselves, and as threatening ruin to our posterity.

There is no doubt that the act was a hard blow and embarrassment to those advocates of conciliation who were Burke's friends in New York.

The Continental Congress and the New York Assembly

As intelligence of the passing of the Quebec Act was crossing the Atlantic, Lord Dartmouth wrote to acting Governor Colden on July 6 to express the wish "that His Majesty's subjects of New York may not be led into any further rash and hasty proceedings, that may expose them to the just Resentment of Parliament." [35] It was evident that ministers had one tone for New England and another and much milder for New York. Of course Dartmouth could not know that on the day he signed his dispatch, Colden was writing to him about a development far more ominous than the little affair of throwing tea into the East River, which was the occasion for his lordship's admonition. The people of New York under the lead of the Committee of Fifty-one had chosen delegates to an intercolonial Congress, which would meet at Philadelphia in September.

Colden wished that he could have prevented what was taking place, but he did not know how. There was no state of civil disorder to warrant the use of troops: no revolution had broken out. Had he convoked the assembly, much might have been different from what happened, but it seemed then

---

[33] Miller, J. C., *Origins of the American Revolution*, 373-374, Boston, Little, Brown & Co., 1943.
[34] June 12, 22, 1775.
[35] *N. Y. documents* 8: 468.

to be British policy to repress and bulldoze assemblies instead of inviting them to function constructively. Hence Colden could only lament:

> These transactions are dangerous my Lord, and illegal; but by what means shall Government prevent them? An attempt by the power of the Civil Magistrate, would only shew their weakness, and it is not easy to say upon what foundation a Military Aid should be called in. Such a Measure would involve us in Trouble, which it is thought much more prudent to avoid.

The delegates chosen were weighty and respectable men: two lawyers—James Duane and John Jay; and three merchants —Philip Livingston, Isaac Low, and John Alsop. None of these was a radical and one, Isaac Low, would be a loyalist when the final issue was drawn. Taken together they may be said to have exemplified the politics of the Livingston Whigs, who now led the people while the Delanceys preponderated in the assembly, which was not convoked until the following January. Efforts by the radicals to include the extremist, John Scott, and Alexander McDougall, whom Colden called "the Wilkes of America," had been defeated, and zeal for the Congress was confined almost completely to New York city.[36]

A month later Colden was able to report that a state of comparative tranquillity prevailed in the city, and to congratulate himself for having made no effort to prevent New York participation in the Congress, as otherwise "the most violent men would have gained great Advantage, and would have prevented the acquiesence in the nomination of moderate men." He dared even to hope that some good might come of the Congress. No longer did it appear likely that the populace would terrorize supporters of government into silence:

> Men now speak and publish Sentiments, in favour of Government, and argue upon the political subjects of the Times, with much greater freedom and security than has been known for some years past, which I hope is a sign, that the licentious spirit which has governed the People to their great Disgrace, is check'd.

This condition lasted right down to the publication, late in October, of the resolutions of the Congress, and it enabled conservatives to carry on a large-scale press campaign against

---

[36] *Ibid.*, 469-470.

the rebellious spirit.[37] So that, to the acting Governor at least, it seemed unlikely that New York would support any strong measures recommended by the Congress; indeed when the temper of the people was put to the test it required a great deal of bullying by a violent minority to whip them into line.

The strong and decisive action of the Philadelphia assembly of patriots was the call for forming a popular association to enforce continental non-importation until all acts of Parliament passed since 1763 in violation of traditional American rights, liberties and privileges, were repealed. The purpose of the association, as stated, was conservative, even in a sense reactionary since the declared ideal was restoration of the pre-1763 relations with Great Britain, but the means elected to achieve this end were radical. To give added force to them, non-consumption of imported goods was adopted; and the association rapidly manifested itself in an inter-connecting system of committees which served as the vehicle of the American Revolution. The association was directed not only against Great Britain, Ireland, India, and the West Indian plantations, but against any colony or province in North America that failed to adhere to the great boycott. Hence the party of the association in any one colony had the support and alliance of a party in every other colony. Non-importation was to begin December 1; if Parliament did not capitulate before the following September 1, non-exportation was to follow.

In New York there was no great enthusiasm for this mode of persuading Parliament to beat a retreat. Merchants envisaged ruin and provincial farmers were alarmed at the very suggestion of shutting off exports. But the Livingston party in general were prepared to cooperate with the association, and the radicals took heart in the expectation of bringing outside force from New England to bear upon New York conservatism. A combination of Livingston Whigs and radicals forced the dissolution of the moderate-controlled Committee of Fifty-one in order to choose a new committee to enforce the association, and by the end of November a Committee of Sixty with mob support was at work terrorizing the merchants into signing and observing the association pledge. Those who refused were from this time stigmatized as "tories." On December 7 Colden wrote to Dartmouth of "a dreadful situation. If we are not rescued from it, by the wisdom and firmness

---

[37] *Ibid.*, 485-486, 488, 492-494, Colden to Dartmouth, Aug. 2, Sept. 7, Oct. 5.

of Parliament, the Colonies must soon fall into distraction and every Calamity annexed to a total annihilation of Government." All conservatives were hoping earnestly that some great measure of conciliation to rally credit and strength for those who opposed the association would come from the new Parliament that had just been elected in England. They looked also to their own assembly which Colden decided to convene in January, thinking that the representatives might "propose something that may be countenanced by administration." The event was uncertain, but he said every means ought to be tried and he did not "apprehend that there is any danger that the Assembly will make Matters worse than they are." [38]

It was certain that great pressure would be brought to bear on the assembly to persuade the members to put their approval upon the work of the congress and the association. Colden opened the session with this appeal:

It is to you, Gentlemen, in this anxious moment, that your Country looks up for Council; And on you it, in a great Measure, depends to Rescue her from Evils of the most ruinous tendency. Exert yourselves with the Firmness becoming your important Office. If your Constituents are discontented and apprehensive, examine their Complaints with Calmness and Deliberation, and determine upon them with an Honest Impartiality. If you find them to be well grounded, pursue the Means of Redress which the Constitution has pointed out.[39]

In the event that there appeared no majority for keeping the means of redress within constitutional limits, Colden intended to prorogue the assembly until the plan of the new Parliament, which he hoped would prove conciliatory, was known. But he feared that such action on his part might provoke the rise of a provincial convention.

Colden's hope for a constitutional course proved well founded. The first business of the assembly was to name a committee, headed by Captain Delancey, to draft the address in reply to the acting Governor. This was so moderate in tone and responsive to Colden's wishes that he at once wrote to Lord Dartmouth of his "strong expectations that the conduct

---

[38] *Ibid.*, 510-514. For other conservative estimates of the situation after the publication of the Congress decisions, see abstracts of letters from Henry White, William Smith, Chief Justice Horsmanden, and Oliver Delancey, in *Manuscripts of the Earl of Dartmouth* 2: 38.

[39] *Journal of Votes and Proceedings* (Jan. 10—April 3, 1775), 4.

of this Province will every day more evidently shew the loyalty and affection of the People for their gracious Sovereign, and their earnest desire for a Reconciliation with Great Britain." [40] The assembly on January 26 rejected by a majority of one a motion "that this house take into consideration the proceedings of the continental congress held in the city of Philadelphia." Five days later the members approved, *nemine contradicente,* a motion by Peter Van Brugh Livingston to appoint a day for taking into consideration the state of the colony, "to enter such resolutions as the house may agree to, on their journals, and in consequence of such resolutions to prepare a humble, firm, dutiful and loyal petition to our most gracious Sovereign." Captain Delancey then moved for the preparation also of a memorial to the House of Lords and a remonstrance to the House of Commons. The motion was an implied recognition of the authority of Parliament, yet it passed without opposition, after which a committee was named to draft a statement of New York's grievances and report the same to the assembly.[41]

More than a month passed before the resultant resolutions were brought before the House, and in the meantime the influence of the association "patriots" on the assembly was shown in a series of hotly debated questions on which the divisions showed the strength of the rival parties. Colonel Philip Schuyler on February 17 moved to enter on the journal and publish the correspondence of the previous June between the assembly's committee of correspondence and the Connecticut Assembly, and also a letter allegedly written by that committee on September 5, 1774, to Agent Burke.[42] The Delancey party defeated the motion by sixteen to nine. The next day the same forces rejected by a similar majority a motion to extend the thanks of the House to the New York delegates to the Philadelphia Congress "for their faithful and judicious discharge of the trust reposed in them by the good people of this colony." On February 21 the same majority refused a motion to thank the merchants and others for adhering firmly to non-importation, and on February 23 a motion to take the sense of the house on the question of appointing delegates to the second Congress due to meet in May, was beaten by seventeen to nine. Thus

---

[40] *N. Y. documents* **8:** 531-532.

[41] *Journal of Votes and Proceedings,* 23-24.

[42] No such letter has been found among Burke's papers, nor does his N. Y. letter-book contain evidence of his having received the alleged letter.

did a consistently-acting majority led by Captain Delancey hold the assembly in disapproving aloofness from the patriot movement.[43]

The majority were less successful, however, in maintaining their cohesion when the grievance resolutions were brought up from committee on March 3. The first of these complained against the Declaratory Act of 1766 and appears to have been carried without debate. But when Delancey offered a resolution acknowledging Parliament's right to regulate the trade of the colonies and to lay duties for that purpose, Colonel Schuyler carried by fourteen to eleven an amendment "excluding every idea of taxation, internal or external, for the purpose of raising a revenue on the subjects in America without their consent." And Delancey was overwhelmingly voted down when he opposed the citation of the coercion acts against Massachusetts as grievances in New York.

Fifteen resolutions were adopted declaring the grievances of New York to be the following: certain provisions of the 1764 Sugar Act; admiralty court trials which infringed the right of trial by jury; the prohibition of bills of credit as legal tender; the molasses duty of 1766 on British and foreign West Indian produce, and all other duties on products imported from a British colony; the Townshend duties; the Restraining Act of 1767; an act of 12th George III. c. 24 under which crown authorities had attempted to transport Americans to England for trial; the 1769 parliamentary construction of 35th Henry VIII, c. 2; the coercion acts for Massachusetts, and the Quebec Act.[44] Manifestly, some of these grievances were of a sort that Agent Burke, however he might transmit them, could not as member of Parliament and Rockingham party man, give them his support.

On the basis of these resolutions a petition to the King, a memorial to the Lords, and a remonstrance to the Commons were drafted.[45] The assembly debated these on March 24; a number of amendments to make the language bolder were offered, but the Delancey majority voted all of them down. The next day they were signed by Speaker Cruger and on April 3 Colden prorogued the assembly to the same day of the following month. But by that time New Yorkers knew

[43] *Journal of Votes and Proceedings,* 37-38, 40, 44-45.
[44] *Ibid.,* 52-57, 63-64.
[45] *Ibid.,* 109-117.

that war had started in Massachusetts, and the populace and the legislative minority in New York had taken matters into their own hands. The assemblymen could not know it, but in fact their body was dead—an institutional casualty of the American Revolution.

During that fateful session of 1775 the men of the assembly must have read with interest several compositions by their agent, Burke. Their journal records that several letters from him were laid on the table on January 13. Probably these were Burke's accounts of the parliamentary proceedings the previous year against Massachusetts and his long letter on the Quebec Act. On March 11 his letter of January 3 was given to the assembly. Therein the members could read that ministers had promised to bring before Parliament "a plan of proceedings with relation to America," but what it would be no one could guess, probably "because as yet no settled plan has been arranged." If this letter had any influence in the assembly, it must have been on the side of moderation and restraint. In the last days of the session assemblymen could read in *Rivington's Gazetteer* serialized installments of Burke's speech of April 19, 1774, on American taxation, which he had brought out as a pamphlet in England.[46]

Another letter from abroad probably aroused some interest and speculation. The journal records that on March 13:

Mr. Speaker laid before the House a letter from William Bollan, Benjamin Franklin and Arthur Lee Esqrs. agents for some of the North American colonies, dated Dec. 24, 1774, directed to the Speaker of the General Assembly of this Colony, acquainting him that they have presented the petition of the Continental Congress, to Lord Dartmouth, who had laid it before his Majesty.

It must have been well known that Burke was one of the agents to whom the Congress had entrusted their petition. The absence of his name from this letter must have suggested that he, like his employers, would have nothing to do with the Congress.

It was to Burke that the assembly sent its appeals to King, Lords, and Commons. The first was a dutiful, loyal, and respectful appeal which made no pretense of justifying all American measures of resistance to the acts of Parliament. Some forms of American conduct had been admittedly wrong,

---

[46] The serializing began March 16.

but "we entreat you, as the indulgent father of your people, to view them in the most favorable light, and to consider them as the honest though disorderly struggles for liberty, not the licentious efforts for independence." The boldest of the documents was the remonstrance which Burke was personally to bring before the House of Commons.[47] Perhaps nothing mirrors better than this the opinions of the party that resisted but would not revolt. It began with a warm profession of loyalty to the crown and an avowal that "the Grandeur and Strength of the British Empire, the Protection and Opulence of his Majestys American Dominions, and the Happiness and Welfare of both, depend essentially on a Restoration of Harmony and Affection between them. . . ." But to achieve this great purpose it was necessary to ascertain "the line of Parliamentary Authority and American Freedom on just equitable and constitutional Grounds." Of recent years the British parliament had enacted certain laws tending to subvert

that Constitution under which the good People of this Colony have always enjoyed the same Rights and Privileges so highly and deservedly prized by their fellow Subjects in Great Britain, a Constitution in its Infancy modelled after that of the Parent State, in its Growth more nearly assimilated to it, and tacitly implied and undeniably recognized in the Requisitions made by the Crown with the Consent and Approbation of Parliament.

New York had ever been and ever would be ready to bear her "full proportion of Aids to the Crown for the Public Service," but "An Exemption from internal Taxation and the exclusive Right of providing for the Support of our own Civil Government and the administration of Justice in this Colony, we esteem our undoubted and unalienable Rights as Englishmen."

In complaining against the Declaratory Act the remonstrance did not avow the radical doctrine of its unconstitutionality. It did not directly repudiate the right of the British legislature "to bind the Colonies in all cases whatsoever," but expressed "distressing apprehensions" of this act because its principle had been "actually exercised by the Statutes made for the Sole and express Purpose of raising a Revenue in America, especially for the support of Government and the other usual and ordinary Services of the Colonies."

---

[47] The original document is among the Wentworth-Fitzwilliam MSS.

In stating more specific grievances, the remonstrators first protested against encroachment upon the right of trial by jury. The proposed revival of an obsolete act of Henry VIII's reign was viewed "with horror." Equal alarm was felt "at the late Act impowering his Majesty to send Persons guilty of Offences in one Colony to be tried in another, or within the Realm of England." Objectionable features of the Mutiny Act as extended to the colonies were described as implying "a Distrust of our readiness to contribute to the Public Service," and the 1767 Restraining Act of bitter memory was recalled. It was acknowledged that Parliament was "necessarily entitled to a Supreme Direction and Government over the whole Empire for a wise, powerful, and lasting Preservation of the great Bond of Union and Safety among all its Branches." With this went an authority to regulate the trade of the colonies, but the New Yorkers claimed an exemption "from Duties on all Articles of Commerce which we import from Great Britain, Ireland and the British Plantations or on Commodities which do not interfere with their Products or Manufactures," and they humbly conceived "that the Money arising from all Duties raised in this Colony should be paid into the Colony Treasury, to be drawn by Requisitions of the Crown to the General Assembly, for the Security and Defense of the whole Empire."

Parliamentary prohibition of the assembly's passing any law for the emission of a paper currency as legal tender in the colony, was described as "a violation of our legislative rights" and "an abridgement of the royal prerogative." The Quebec Act was scored for its territorial provisions: "a great Extent of Country is cut off from this Colony, in which hitherto the most lucrative Branches of the Indian Trade were pursued." Nor, said the remonstrators, could they forbear mentioning the jealousies that had been excited by extending so widely the limits of Quebec, "in which the Roman Catholic Religion has received such ample Supports." That bigotry was not with the majority in the assembly was indicated, however, by their voting down George Clinton's proposed amendment to insert after "Roman Catholic Religion" the words: "a sanguinary religion repugnant to the genuine simplicity of Christianity, and the maxims of sound philosophy."

Sympathy was expressed for the distresses of Massachusetts, but also disapprobation of the violent measures which had been pursued in some of the colonies and could only tend to multiply misfortunes and prevent obtaining redress. In conclusion it was said:

We claim but a Restoration of those Rights which we enjoyed by general Consent before the Close of the last War. We desire no more than a Continuation of that ancient Government to which we are entitled by the Principles of the British Constitution, and by which alone can be secured to us the Rights of Englishmen.

The remonstrance was thoroughly in the English political tradition, its appeal going not to rights arising from the eighteenth-century concept of the "law of nature," but to prescriptive rights embedded in an historic constitution. It was one of the last expressions of whig loyalism in the New York province of the British Empire: a last gasp of the old free colonial order which Grenville, Townshend, Hillsborough, and North had unsettled, and Burke tried to conciliate and preserve. It was now to be swept away in a storm of war and revolution.

VI. Last Efforts for Conciliation

AS the first Congress was deliberating at Philadelphia and political agitation was subsiding momentarily at New York in the latter part of the summer of 1774, Burke had little suspicion that a new and more dangerous turn in Anglo-American relations was in the offing. He told Lord Rockingham on September 16: "I agree with your lordship entirely; the American and foreign affairs will not come to any crisis sufficient to arouse the public from its present stupefaction, during the course of the next session. I have my doubts whether those at least of America will do it for some years to come." To this extent his intimations were correct: the American war that was soon to break out did *not* arouse the British public from stupefaction until it became an unsuccessful war. But for all his warnings and alarming prophecies in the previous session of Parliament, that the measures adopted would lead to bloodshed, Burke did not now believe that war was likely. He thought he knew the temper of New York, and he read in the newspapers the cautious and moderate instructions given to the Pennsylvania delegates to the Congress, which led him to believe "that the affair will draw out into great length." If so, he looked upon it as next to impossible for "the present temper and unanimity of America" to be kept up, since popular remedies unless quick and sharp were ineffectual. His vision of what lay in store was neither armed strife nor a statesman-like solution of the problem, but "the sight of half-a-dozen gentlemen from America, dangling at the levées of Lord Dartmouth and Lord North, or negotiating with Mr. Pownall." [1] Even a revival of American non-importation would mean only that "we should be in as much haste to negotiate ourselves out of our commercial, as they out of their constitutional difficulties." [2] Evidently, he had changed his views on the determination of ministers to pursue harsh measures to the limit. In any event, his seismic sense failed him in the fall of 1774.

Election politics were Burke's primary interest at this time,

---

[1] John Pownall was now under-secretary to Lord Dartmouth.
[2] *Correspondence* 1: 473-474.

and he felt more exasperated by the Rockingham party's inability to exploit the American question to advantage, than by the failure of ministers to propound a solution of that question. He was sure that only his political friends could manage America, yet there was not the slightest likelihood of their being given the chance. He had his own problem of getting into the new parliament elected that fall. Unable to afford the costs of standing again for Wendover he had to fall back on Rockingham's bringing him in for the Wentworth family borough of Malton. But hardly had he been chosen there than an influential body of citizens at Bristol invited him to stand for their city with a fair prospect of success. A victory at the polls in the second city of the kingdom would be of the greatest credit to himself and to his party, and he accepted the challenge.

Burke, Henry Cruger, and Bristol

Since the election at Bristol had some connection with Burke's New York agency and is part of the history of his American politics, it deserves here something more than passing reference. The first approach made to him by Bristol electors had come in June, 1774, when the Reverend Dr. Thomas Wilson addressed himself to Burke by letter. While visiting at Bristol, Dr. Wilson had conversed with many "merchants of fortune and character, and warm well wishers to the liberties and constitution of this *once* free nation." To these he had mentioned Burke "as having so ably stood forth in opposition to many odious measures carried on, *especially the affairs of America,* in the event of which they are so nearly interested." Several gentlemen had desired him to write secretly and confidentially to Burke, "to know whether, if they find themselves strong enough, you will be ready to serve them, if they put you up as a candidate to represent them." They were prepared to furnish Burke "with a proper colleague of their own town, who certainly has a very great influence and a large family connexion, and a man of spirit and understanding in commercial affairs, and is expected to arrive from New York." Unless Burke had by this time received the letter the New York committee of correspondence had written to him on May 31, he could hardly have known or suspected that the gentleman thus alluded to but not named was Henry Cruger, Jr., for whose father and uncle he had performed an important service during the previous year. Dr. Wilson supplied no concrete information about the Bristol political scene other than that the Quebec Act with its partiality to popery had given "an amazing turn within these last three weeks to the tame dispositions of the Quakers and Dissenters, who before that time were fast asleep."[3]

Burke returned a grateful and appreciative answer to Dr. Wilson's flattering letter. He said he was desirous of continuing to serve his country "in the situation, upon the principles, and with the friends" he had acted with during his previous eight years in Parliament. "If I have the honour of a choice which is upon all accounts so respectable as you propose, I shall be enabled without question to perform my duty with more satisfaction and greater authority." But he begged that the gentlemen who had shown such partiality to him "would not take any step of this importance but upon the most clear and solid grounds." A contest in a maritime town where court candidates necessarily had great advantage would be very costly, and he was in no position to assist in paying the expenses of the election.[4]

A fortnight later (July 11) Dr. Wilson again addressed Burke, reporting that the gentlemen at Bristol were sensible of the difficulties Burke had mentioned but did not despair of success. One of Bristol's two members in the expiring Parliament could surely be defeated, possibly both. Dr. Wilson then said:

> Mr. Cruger (just arrived from New York, and brought over some papers and letters for you) is intended for a candidate at the ensuing election, and supported by the gentlemen who desired me to write to you; and I make no question of his carrying it. . . . I have desired him to wait upon you . . . you may trust him as a person that may be perfectly confided in, and very knowing in American affairs, as he has resided so long at New York.[5]

Soon afterwards Burke and Henry Cruger became personally acquainted, but there appears no record of what passed between them. It is likely that among the letters Cruger carried to Burke was the New York committee's of May 31 in which they had requested their agent to obtain for Cruger an interview with Lord Dartmouth to explain the wishes and sentiments of the people of New York. The present writer has not

[3] *Ibid.*, 465-467.
[4] Wentworth-Fitzwilliam MSS., Burke to Dr. Wilson, July 1, 1774.
[5] *Correspondence* 1: 468-469.

been able to discover whether Burke in this instance complied with the wishes of his employers. The sum of what he said in reply to them was: "I have had the honour of seeing Mr. Cruger at my house on his return to Bristol. I endeavored to attend him in the manner to which his merit and connections entitled him." [6] These words have the ring of displeasure. Did Burke refuse to do what the New Yorkers and Cruger asked? Did mutual dislike spring up at once between the two men? All that can be said for certain is that we hear no more about Burke as a candidate at Bristol until October, and that when his candidacy was revived Cruger and his friends at first opposed it. In later years Burke would regard Henry Cruger as being infected with the doctrinaire radicalism which the Rockingham party held to be the bane of Whiggism, and Cruger would regard Burke as a deceitful "Jesuit." Such men were not formed to be friends. Moreover, Dr. Wilson was hardly a man in whom Burke was likely to place much confidence. He was an ecclesiastical eccentric with an almost worshipful devotion to Mrs. Catherine Graham Macaulay, the literary champion of metropolitan radicalism, who had once written a pamphlet against Burke, charging him with "corruptness of the heart" and "deception of the head." [7] As a practical politician, Burke was capable of making temporary alliances of expediency, but he could have had little taste for association with Dr. Wilson or Henry Cruger.

When new proposals were made to Burke from Bristol, they came from different people. Richard Champion, the ceramics manufacturer, who was not yet personally acquainted with Burke although destined to become one of his best friends, addressed him on October 1. Apologizing for the "impropriety" that attended "the address of a stranger," he said he would not "run the risque of bias, by desiring an introduction from Cruger." He wished to lay before Burke "the exact state of parties in this place" in order to persuade him to contest for one of the city's seats. He described how the old "joint interest" of Whigs and Tories who had for many years made collusive bargains to divide Bristol's two seats and thus avoided the tumult and expense of election contests, was losing control. Two main causes were weakening it: a rising disapproval

---

[6] *Infra,* letter-book, Burke to committee, Aug. 2, 1774.
[7] *Observations on a Pamphlet, entitled, Thoughts of the Cause of the Present Discontents,* London, Dilly, 1770.

among the merchants of the government's conduct towards America, which was harmful to trade; and the eagerness of ale-house owners and their customers for a flow of the taps at the expense of candidates. It appeared that Robert Nugent (now Lord Clare), a Chathamite Whig who had sat for Bristol since 1761, could probably be defeated because he had virtually become a Tory; his union in the joint interest with Sir Mathew Brickdale, a genuine old-style Tory, had weakened the latter's hitherto large popularity. Thus two Whig seats might be won. Henry Cruger had an immense ale-house popularity and would probably win, but Champion thought ill of him; moreover, Cruger was of merely local stature and had no other cause than that of disrupting the joint interest. A man of great public estimation was needed to run with Cruger, and that man was Burke. Champion said that "such a man of interest and abilities is necessary to a commercial town—but yet there is a higher view—the public good. I know that in this age of corruption such a doctrine will be laughed at, but all the contempt in the world cannot set aside a matter of fact." [8]

Soon after Champion first addressed Burke, he and his friends sent messengers to plead with their favorite and assure him that prospects for success were bright. The polling had begun and Lord Clare, sensing defeat, had withdrawn. The joint interest was broken, and Burke by capitalizing on the revolt Cruger was leading might win the city's second seat. He rose to the challenge and dashed post-haste to Bristol. Although Cruger's principal friends were interested solely in their own candidate and had been urging single votes for him, Burke's friends virtually forced their alliance on Cruger by raising the cry of "Cruger and Burke" and gathered enough second votes from Cruger's supporters to enable their lately-entered candidate to nose out Brickdale. [9]

Burke's success was unquestionably due to exploitation of the Cruger party's popularity. [10] But that is not to say he had incurred any obligation to his new colleague. The alliance was very reluctant on Cruger's part, and to Burke it had been pure election expediency. Differences between the two men were manifest to all. Cruger promised his constituents that he would

---

[8] Wentworth-Fitzwilliam MSS, Champion to Burke, Oct. 1, 1774.

[9] Weare, G. E., *Edmund Burke's connection with Bristol*, 26-96, Bristol, William Bennet, 1894.

[10] Cruger polled 3565 votes, but Burke defeated Brickdale by 2707 to 2456.

be guided by their instructions, but Burke (after he was elected) told them he would act publicly according to the dictates of his conscience and best judgment. Cruger's eye was on the local interest, Burke's on the national. Cruger, born in New York, was well known for pro-American sentiments. Burke talked the language of high imperial statesmanship. In his opening address to the voters he alluded to "our unhappy contest with America," which was difficult in itself and had been rendered more so by a great variety of plans of conduct. He did not suspect "a want of good intention" in these plans, but "however pure the intentions of their authors may have been," there was no doubt that the event had been unfortunate. On this subject he could promise nothing but the most honest and impartial consideration of which he was capable. He had held, and ever would maintain, "the just, wise, and necessary constitutional superiority of Great Britain," which was "necessary for America, as well as for us." That superiority was consistent with "all the liberties a sober and spirited American ought to desire," and his great object would be to reconcile British superiority with American liberty. He was "far from thinking that both, even yet, may not be preserved." [11]

The Member for Bristol and New York Agent in the Parliament of 1774

Burke's political stature was greatly heightened by his success at Bristol, which also gave an elixir to his party. He was still most faithfully attached to Lord Rockingham, but now he carried greater weight in the councils of the Marquess's corps, for he had won at Bristol on the strength of his own reputation. Instead of drawing strength from the party he was able to communicate it. Moreover, William Dowdeswell was dying, which opened the way to Burke's becoming leader of the Rockinghams in the House of Commons. So that he was certain to cut a large figure in the new Parliament.

It was opened on November 29. The King's speech dwelt upon the disobedient conduct of Massachusetts and declared His Majesty's firm resolution to withstand every effort to weaken or impair the authority of the supreme legislature over the colonies. Addresses approving the steps the government had taken since the last session of Parliament to carry into

---

[11] *Works* 2: 6-7.

execution the laws at that time enacted were passed overwhelmingly in both houses. Lord Dartmouth on December 10 dispatched copies of these addresses to all the governors in America, hoping thereby to remove "false impressions" and "to put an end to those Expectations of support, in their unwarrantable Pretensions, which have been held forth, by artful and designing Men." [12] The new Parliament would stand by the work of its predecessor. Burke, however, could see no evidence that ministers intended to bring any new anti-American measures before the Houses, and certainly no official decisions would be made until the resolves and petition of the American Congress arrived. His principal activity in the meantime was to attempt to rally his party for a strong stand against further rash and ill-considered policies.[13]

As for New York, one could hardly have suspected in London that any trouble was brewing in that so excellent and well-behaved colony, which appeared to be the object of studied ministerial preference and favor. On the same day Dartmouth circularized the governors to evince the firm resolution of government, he wrote to Dr. Colden of his expectation of an early settlement of the dispute over the "Hampshire grants" and a most favorable consideration of New York claims. He concluded by saying that the conduct of New York "in general & more especially in the present Moment" justly entitled "its well-disposed and peaceable Inhabitants to His Majesty's particular Favor and Indulgence." The Secretary of State had

the Satisfaction to assure you that their Conduct is seen in a very favorable light, and the Wishes they have in general expressed that all Violence might be avoided, & the Sovereign Authority of the Supreme Legislature might be supported, are graciously considered by the King as Evidences of their Respect & Affection for His Majesty & the just sense they entertain of the Rights of the British Empire.[14]

Dartmouth could not know, of course, that as he wrote, the Committee of Sixty and the Association were brow-beating New York merchants to sign the non-importation pledge.

About mid-December the petition of the Congress to the

---

[12] N. Y. documents 8: 516.

[13] See especially his letter of Dec. 5 to Rockingham, Correspondence 1: 503-508.

[14] N. Y. documents 8: 514.

King reached London. The Americans had sent it to five colonial agents—Benjamin Franklin, Arthur Lee, Charles Garth, Paul Wentworth, and Burke. Franklin sent a note to Burke on December 19:

Having just received a Petition from the American Congress with a letter directed to the North American Agents among whom you are named; this is to request you would be pleased to meet the other Agents, tomorrow at noon, at Waghorn's Coffee House, Westminster, in order to consider the said letter, and agree upon the time and manner of presenting the Petition.[15]

Burke did not attend the meeting. According to Franklin, he declined on the ground that he had no instructions from his New York principals. Garth and Wentworth also declined to join in the presentation, so that only Franklin and Lee accepted the commission.[16] It was hardly surprising that Burke should refuse to associate himself with a petition that challenged the Declaratory Act of 1766. But it was odd that on the morning Franklin desired his presence with the other agents Burke wrote at length to Rockingham about a London merchants' petition to Parliament for alleviating the distresses in the American trade, but did not even mention Franklin's request or the American petition.[17] Nor did he, when writing to his New York employers on January 3, consider it necessary to explain his declining to act for the Congress.

By that time, Burke knew that some new plan of proceeding in America was to be laid before Parliament, although he could not guess what it would be. He did what he could to exert a moderating and conciliatory influence. He took a leading part in instigating merchants' petitions for healing measures, but was disheartened to find that there was less life and spirit in this activity than at the time of the Stamp Act crisis. Certainly the merchants in London "had nothing like the sentiments of honest, free, and constitutional resentment, which Englishmen used formerly to feel against the authors of public mischief." [18] Perhaps his most important effort to stir public opinion was the publication (January 10) in pamphlet form of his speech on *American Taxation*. The preface explained

---

[15] Wentworth-Fitzwilliam MSS.

[16] Smyth, *Writings of Franklin* 6: 303, Franklin to Charles Thomson, Feb. 5, 1775.

[17] *Correspondence* 1: 516-518.

[18] *Correspondence* 2: 2.

that the speech had been reconstructed from notes furnished by certain members of Parliament who had heard it spoken on the previous April 19. For some months it had been ready for the press, but "a delicacy, possibly over-scrupulous" had delayed the publication. Burke said the reason for delaying it had been a desire to avoid giving any grounds to the charge, so often made by supporters of the administration, that American opposition to their measures was inspired by writings published in England. But now all the measures of government had had their full operation and could "no longer be affected, if ever they could have been affected, by any publication." These words must had seemed a little disingenuous. If Burke did not wish the speech-pamphlet to affect the measures of government, why did he publish it now, at the very moment new ministerial plans were forming? Some persons regarded it as a party maneuver of the Rockinghams aimed at discrediting all in opposition save themselves. Thus Horace Walpole: "His concealed objects were to misrepresent Lord Chatham as debilitated by age, to misrepresent Conway as corrupted and swerved from his patronage of the Americans, and thence, if the Ministry should be overturned, to hold out Lord Rockingham as the sole tutelary saint of America." If this could not be read *in* the pamphlet, there was no doubt it could easily be read *into* it. Walpole interpreted Burke's words on the legislative supremacy of Great Britain over the colonies as a statement of "high and despotic principles" put forth as "a subterfuge for acceding even to the views of the Court." [19]

But that criticism had validity only in so far as it was true that Burke believed his party alone knew how to manage the Americans and resolve the crisis. That he published his speech in the interests of his party was undoubtedly a fact, and it seems hardly less certain, despite his rhetorical disavowal, that he so timed the publication as to produce an effect on public and parliamentary opinion before the ministers came forward with new proposals concerning America.

Their first reply to the Congress was to authorize Lord Dartmouth to circularize the governors with a command in the king's name to do their utmost to prevent the re-assembling of the Congress, which was scheduled to take place in May.[20]

---

[19] *Last Journals* 1: 442.
[20] *N. Y. documents* 8: 527-528.

But before any further decisions had been made, Lord Chatham took a rash and impetuous step that revealed not only the weakness but the fatal division which not even the American crisis could heal in the ranks of the opposition. Without any previous concerting with Rockingham, Chatham on January 20 asked the House of Lords to address the crown for the removal of the troops from Boston as a convincing gesture of conciliation. The impracticality of the proposal was matched by his imprudence in angering Rockingham's friends by attacking again the Declaratory Act, as if that were the root of the American problem. It was a great victory for the anti-Americans when the peers voted sixty-eight to eighteen against Chatham's motion. According to Burke, "more would have been in the minority, if Lord Chatham had thought proper to give notice of his motion to the proper people." [21] The next day the ministers came to their fateful determination upon a two-fold plan: to offer peace, and to make war.

First, Parliament would be asked to address the throne with the proposal that any colony willing to make sufficient and permanent provision for the support of its own civil government, defense, and administration of justice, and in time of war contribute extraordinary supplies in reasonable proportion to what was raised in England, should be exempted from parliamentary taxation except for regulating the commerce of the empire. That was to say, immunity from parliamentary taxation could be purchased by a colony's establishment of a permanent civil list, which was a prime object of imperial policy since the days of Grenville and Townshend.

Secondly, and for the meantime, Parliament would be asked "to entreat his Majesty to take effectual methods to enforce due obedience to the laws and authority of the supreme legislature of Great Britain." The meaning of this was that Parliament should approve and associate itself with an authorization to General Gage to employ military sanctions in Massachusetts.

In line with this ministerial policy, Lord North moved on February 2 for an address to the crown proclaiming a rebellion in Massachusetts and avowing that "it is our fixed resolution, at the hazard of our lives and properties, to stand by his Majesty against all rebellious attempts, in the maintenance of the just rights of his Majesty and the two Houses of Parliament." The

[21] *Correspondence* 2: 14.

only record of what Burke said on this day states that he was "much indisposed," but nevertheless

laid forth the numerous ill consequences that must follow—called the present moment the true crisis of Britain's fate, painted the dreadful abyss into which the nation was going to be plunged; called upon the commercial part of the house to rouse themselves at the open declaration of their approaching ruin, and pathetically described to the landed interest the fatal effects that must inevitably reach them.

Debating North's motion four days later, Burke spoke again, asserting that the proposal meant nothing less than war. He denied the ministerial pretense that Americans were repudiating British sovereignty and listed numerous acts of tyranny that justified resistance. He struck at the official assumption that resistance to Parliament was localized in New England, and said that "from one end of the continent to the other, the like resistance had been found." If people would only realize the wide extent of the mischief and the magnitude of the undertaking to repress it, "they would think a little more seriously of what might have been the cause of so general a discontent, and might wish to apply other remedies than fire and sword." [22] But opposition was perfectly vain. North's motion was carried by 288 to 105.

North brought forward the "conciliatory" part of the ministerial plan on February 20. Burke called it mean and oppressive "because it was never the complaint of the Americans that the mode of taxation was not left to themselves." Since the scheme left "neither the amount and quantum of the grant, nor the application" to their free choice, it never could redress their real grievance. It amounted to holding the colonies prisoners of war until they consented to a ransom.[23] North's proposal was carried by 274 to 88 and approved overwhelmingly by the Lords. Dartmouth on March 3 communicated it to the colonies in a dispatch to the governors.[24]

Burke made another impassioned but no less futile effort on March 6 to arrest the descent into war. For several weeks a bill of the utmost severity—to restrain the trade and fisheries of New England—had been making its way through the House

[22] *Parliamentary history* 18: 224, 232, 262-264.
[23] *Ibid.*, 335-338.
[24] *N. Y. documents* 8: 545-547; *Manuscripts of the Earl of Dartmouth* 2: 277.

of Commons, and when it reached final reading Burke attacked. We can know with unusual certainty what he said because the notes he made for his speech are extant. He called the bill a scheme to preserve British authority by destroying British dominions. The proceedings against the colonies were not those of a sovereign whose subjects were in rebellion, but of "one independent nation against *another*." It was possible that such a conduct, between such nations, and in such a case, might be proper, but

a sovereign who, instead of fighting the rebels in a province, lays a dead hand on the trade of his subjects, is no better than a madman; he acts himself in the spirit of the rebel and the robber whom he persecutes. The great principle in subduing such disorders, is to strike at the individual criminals, and to beat down the armed resistance; but religiously to preserve the objects of trade, of revenue, of agriculture, and every part of the *public* strength, because it is the strength of the sovereign himself.

Burke thought it "a thousand times" better to send a regular army and large naval force to conquer and subjugate rebellious America, "than to waste the national vigour in a protracted, lingering hostility, which has neither the energy of war, nor the comforts and advantages of peace." It was absurd to suppress the trade of people whose major offense was their refusal to trade. Any form of war was an immense evil, but the worst was a war of prolonged half-measures that came to no decisive determination either in conquest or negotiated reconciliation.[25]

But the severe bill was passed into law, and on March 9 North carried three additional resolutions to extend the restraints to Virginia, Pennsylvania, New Jersey, and South Carolina—but not to the apparently well-behaved and strategically pivotal New York.

Legislative acts of such imbecility and inhumanity seem to have shocked Burke into a reconsideration of a hitherto fundamental principle in his American politics. He confided to Richard Champion on March 9: "I have been a strenuous advocate of the superiority of this country, but I confess I grow less zealous when I see the use which is made of it." [26]

Five days later he completed a long business letter to his

---

[25] *Correspondence* 4: 470-474. See also *Parliamentary history* 18: 389-392.
[26] *Correspondence* 2: 26.

New York employers in which he gave a coldly factual and
candid account of the new measures enacted for America and
of the reasoning that lay back of them. The declaration of a
rebellion was thought expedient "in order that the troops might
find themselves justified in those forcible operations which
the state of things in Massachusetts has rendered necessary."
With regard to the "taxing proposition," Lord North had not
expected that it would be generally acceptable, but "if only
a single colony complied the chain of opposition would be
broken." The restraint of trade and fisheries was a severe
measure but in the end lenient, as it would drive offenders
to "a more speedy submission" and lead more quickly to peace
and reconciliation. Such had been the leading arguments for
the several new coercive measures: "I give you, Gentlemen,
not my opinion but their reasons. In what manner these arguments were combatted by those who disliked the plan, it is
not necessary to lay before you." He said nothing of his own
opposition to the ministerial course and expressed no personal
opinion upon it:

> In a situation like yours and mine, I am very scrupulous in in-
> termixing any judgement which in any particular light might have
> a tendency to mislead yours. I ought undoubtedly to represent to
> you everything which may enable you to see your true situation,
> but I am very unwilling to speculate upon it. Your interests are
> concerned, and your wisdom will decide.

Were his letter to be intercepted by crown authorities, as
was now the fate of many transatlantic communications, not a
compromising word would be found in it. He explained why
New York had not been included in the restraining act. It
was "on account of your refusal to authenticate by any act of
yours, the non-importation agreement." He reported that the
merchants who disapproved the proceedings of Parliament
had "not been much regarded," and that efforts were being
made to persuade them "that the reduction by force of the disobedient spirit in the Colonies is their sole security for trading
in future with America." Parliamentary opposition was extremely weak, and although it was true that the numbers against
some of the severe measures had been larger than against the
coercion acts of 1774, the majorities too were larger. Once
again Burke gave to New Yorkers the stark unvarnished truth
about the disposition of official Britain.

On the same day, Burke wrote privately to James Delancey in reply to a letter which the latter had sent to him under date of February 1. Unfortunately, Delancey's letter has not been found. Doubtless it contained an account of the assembly majority's success in resisting the partisans of the Congress and the Association, since Burke congratulated him on the success of his endeavors and hoped that they would have "the desired effect in leading to that conciliation for which they were so honestly intended and so earnestly pursued." Burke regretted that an equally conciliatory spirit had not been shown in England, and confided:

I find that Ministry place their best hopes of dissolving the Union of the Colonies and breaking the present spirit of resistance, wholly in your Province. I wish that the bills which I transmit may be found well adapted to cooperate with your pacific system.

Probably Burke was not less desirous than was Lord North, for the New York Assembly to hold aloof from the congressional union. He told Delancey that his parliamentary efforts had caused his health to suffer, "partly by attendance, partly by vexation." He had acted with fairness towards the Mother Country and the Colonies, but a despair of success would abate his efforts and preserve, he hoped, his "little remains of strength."

And yet, eight days later, on March 22, he made his supreme utterance of the American crisis.

From "Management" to Conciliation

The words of Burke's wonderful and often-quoted speech on *Conciliation with the Colonies* are too familiar to warrant extensive quotation here, but the political strategy of them requires some notice. The speech contained nothing to mark it as a Rockingham party maneuver. Heretofore, Burke had always conceived the American problem as one of "management," that is, of prudent and artful conduct directed toward persuasion, avoidance of irritation, smoothing of tempers, and cultivation of America's natural affection for the mother country. But now he was thinking in terms of conciliation, of preserving a union rather than maintaining a superiority. He avoided topics that could annoy Chatham and his friends, and thus said nothing in defense of the Declaratory Act. Chatham indeed was to pronounce the speech "very seasonable, very reasonable, and very eloquent," and Horace Walpole was to contrast it with the speech-pamphlet on *American Taxation* and find it "more sober, judicious, and chaste from flights than the former." [27] It is even likely that Burke drew part of it from conversations with Franklin, whose connections had always been with the Chatham-Shelburne Whigs.[28] Nor did Burke inveigh against the ministers, but took as the first link in his chain of argument the implicit admission in North's resolution on taxation in the colonies, of the principle of conciliation. This having been allowed, how far in prudence ought it to be carried? He answered, as far as the nature of America and her circumstances required, because "after all our struggle, whether we will or not, we must govern America, according to that nature, and to those circumstances; and not according to our imagination." He dwelt upon the immense and rapidly growing population and commerce of America and doubted whether it was possible to subjugate so great a country more than temporarily. Certainly the attempt would mean Britain's spending her own blood and fortune to ruin her own empire, all the while she risked a foreign intervention in the contest.

There were only three ways of proceeding against "the stubborn spirit" of the American colonists: to change it by removing its causes, to prosecute it as criminal, or to comply with it—unless the colonies were to be abandoned, and to that Burke believed few would agree. Certainly he would not. He was sure that the temper and character of the Americans was unalterable by any human art. As for prosecuting them as criminal, he did not "know the method of drawing up an indictment against a whole people"; for wise men that was "not judicious; for sober men, not decent; for minds tinctured with humanity, not mild and merciful." Hence there was no prudent course but "to comply with the American spirit as necessary; or, if you please to submit to it, as a necessary evil"—in short, to grant to the Americans all they desired to have. Putting aside all questions of abstract right and theory, all disputes over sovereignty and the supremacy of the British legislature,

---

[27] *Last journals* 1: 490.

[28] Sixteen years later Burke would recall his conversations with Franklin at this time, the day before Franklin departed for America.—*Works* 6: 121-122. For relations between these men, see Dixon Wecter, Burke, Franklin, and Samuel Petrie, *Hunt. Lib. Quart.* 3: 315-338, 1939-1940.

he advocated a pragmatic sanction for American independence within the British Empire: recognition of all rights claimed by Americans, as privileges in the concord of imperial community. To this end he moved a series of resolutions of which the net effect would be a restoration of Anglo-American relations as they had been before 1763. The resolutions were rejected by 270 to 78.

Afterwards, Burke despaired of altering the temper of the House of Commons, but he was far from giving up all effort to stir the public. William Burke wrote to Charles O'Hara on April 7: "Edmund's plan of conciliation put him I think on a higher form than I believe any man has ever stood. He immediately withdrew, and has never once debated the American questions since; he is pressed by friends and foes I almost said, to print it. I took such notes; and some remembered such parts that he may do it, and I think will." [29] Late in the spring the speech appeared as a political pamphlet in the bookstalls.[30]

Last Efforts to Hold New York

As the king's ministers were laying the parliamentary ground for military coercion in America, their policy of soft words and indulgence for New York had continued.

In February, 1775, the Board of Trade, with Lord Dartmouth presiding and Governor Tryon in attendance, resumed consideration of the long-neglected disputes and disorders arising from New York land claims, especially in the region of the Hampshire grants. The Board's proceedings were unusually expeditious, and by March 2 a proposal offered by Tryon was accepted. Grants by New Hampshire authorities of land between the Hudson and Connecticut rivers which did not clash with those made by New York were to be confirmed, subject to payment of New York quit-rents. But where

---

[29] Annaghmore MSS.

[30] When Charles O'Hara, on reading the speech, suggested that Burke had adopted Chatham's view that taxation was not comprised within the meaning of legislative supremacy, Burke flared back: "How could you imagine that I had in my thoughts anything of the theoretical separation of a power of taxing from legislation? I have no opinion about it. . . . I never ask what government may do in *theory*, except *theory* be the *object;* when one talks of practice they must act according to the circumstances. If you think it worth while to read that speech again you will find that principle to be the key of it."—Annaghmore MSS.

New Hampshire grants did cross those made by New York (or
Canada before the conquest) conflicting claims should be
adjudicated in the supreme court of New York, with a right
of appeal to the governor in council and thence to the king in
Privy Council. This arrangement was probably as favorable
to New York as could reasonably have been expected. On the
same day, the Board of Trade considered three acts of the
New York Assembly, and although objections were raised that
normally would have been considered grounds for disallowance,
the acts were recommended for approval.[31]

Burke conferred with Tryon on the business of the Hampshire grants, but did not attend the sessions that produced
acceptance of the Governor's proposals. On March 9, however,
he did appear before the Board of Trade with a certain Colonel
John Reid who had just arrived from New York. Reid represented a group of influential land claimants in the "grants"
and around Lake Champlain who evidently suspected Burke
had not been very energetic in their business. Reid considered
the Tryon formula adopted by the lords commissioners to
be unfair and asked permission to present additional evidence.
The request was granted. Burke was displeased, naturally, by
the re-opening of the subject and the complaint against his
conduct. He told his employers that Colonel Reid's principals
were "very much mistaken in what they assert—that their business has not hitherto succeeded from want of solicitation. It
has been solicited, I must say vigorously." It was the Board of
Trade that had been unwilling to take any step in the matter,
and "if things remained in their former state their former
resolution would have continued." Burke's opinion was that
only some sort of compromise such as Tryon had proposed,
with his [Burke's] "entire approbation and hearty support,"
could have been gained, and that Colonel Reid would discover
this to be the fact.[32]

If in Reid's view Tryon had given up too much, he had
gained too much in the opinion of Paul Wentworth, the New
Hampshire agent. When the question was re-opened by the
Board of Trade on April 11, Burke, Tryon, Wentworth, and
Reid were present. Both sides were heard, and heard again
on April 24, after which the subject remained *sub judice*

---

[31] *Journal of Commissioners,* 411-415.
[32] *Infra,* letter-book, Burke to committee, March 14, 1775.

with the lords commissioners until it was lost in the war.[33]

But a real effort had been made by them, before the marplot Reid appeared, to accommodate Tryon and Burke in their solicitations, and this was a part of the high strategy of conciliating New York. Tryon was soon to be ordered back to his post, equipped by Dartmouth with authority to issue grants to a number of important New Yorkers of lands purchased very irregularly by them from the Indians in 1772. The American Secretary was "fully sensible of how much importance it is in the present moment that His Majesty's faithfull and well disposed subjects in New York should be gratified in every reasonable request." Provided, of course, that their political behavior was correct. The grants Tryon was authorized to make were conditioned upon the grantees' making "a disavowal of all association to obstruct the Importation or Exportation of goods to and from New York." [34]

About the same time, James Rivington, publisher of the *Gazetteer,* organ of New York conservatism, was appointed His Majesty's printer within the province, with an allowance of 100 pounds per annum. Rivington's paper had just serialized Burke's speech-pamphlet on *American Taxation.* If the British ministers were unwilling to adopt Burke's advice at Westminster, they seemed ready enough to recommend it at New York.[35]

Another indication of official zeal for conciliating New York was the Board of Trade's resumption on March 16 of the long-standing question of the validity of the French grants in the Lake Champlain region. Repeated postponements, due to Burke's inability to attend the Board with his counsel, kept off a full hearing of all parties concerned until April 27. But if prospects were then bright for a decision favorable to New York interests, they were soon darkened by the arrival of news indicating that the New York Assembly, up to this time regarded as a model of good colonial behavior, held reprehensible opinions on the subject of Parliament's rights over the colonies.

The assembly's petition to the King, and memorial and remonstrance to the Lords and Commons, reached Burke on May 4. He handed the petition to Lord Dartmouth who laid it before the King. The Duke of Manchester agreed to present

---

[33] *Journal of Commissioners,* 416, 420-422.
[34] *Manuscripts of the Earl of Dartmouth* 2: 292; *N. Y. documents* 8: 569-574.
[35] *N. Y. documents* 8: 568.

the memorial to the peers. Burke brought the remonstrance before the House of Commons on May 15. According to Dartmouth, King George received the petition "with the most gracious expressions of Regard and attention to the humble requests of His faithful subjects in New York." [36] But very different receptions were accorded to the memorial and remonstrance. Burke's account to his employers about this affair throws light upon what has heretofore been very obscure.[37] When Dartmouth first saw the petition, he "expressed great regard for the Colony," but upon glancing at the other two documents "wished that some part of the subject matter had been omitted, as it might tend to procure to your representation a very different reception from that which he heartily desired." Burke did not specify the part which Dartmouth feared would be objectionable, but it is hardly to be doubted that it was the complaint against the Declaratory Act. When Burke presented the remonstrance in the Commons he admitted that it protested against Parliament's right to tax the colonies for revenue purposes, but he argued "as that opinion, however erroneous, was employed in terms proper and decent— as it was accompanied with the most precise and full acknowledgment of our legislative authority in many, if not the most essential particulars—it could form no objection to the admission of the paper." The House ought not to "make a mistaken allegation of one grievance a reason for not attending to others . . . in which the authority of legislature is not disputed but the exercise only complained of." Burke read the remonstrance in a very full house and moved for its acceptance. Charles Fox, Henry Cruger, and several others supported his motion, but North mobilized ministerial forces against receiving it on the ground that it "called into question the supreme and unlimited authority of the British legislature over the colonies." Probably it took the heart out of Burke to hear North, in his ever pleasant and moderate language, reject the New York appeal on the ground that it challenged Lord Rockingham's act of 1766. Burke told the New Yorkers North admitted "that the conduct of the Colony of New York had his hearty approbation; that it had been moderate, dutiful, and prudent, and as such he thought it merited particular marks of the favour and

---

[36] *Ibid.*, 574-575.
[37] *Infra*, letter-book, to committee, June 7, 1775.

indulgence of Parliament," but he felt obliged to put a negative on a motion to receive its remonstrance, and the House supported that view. "Several who debated on the side of Ministry assigned the very title of 'remonstrance' as among the reasons for refusing to admit it into the House." The Duke of Manchester's effort to obtain acceptance of the memorial in the Lords provoked a long debate, but the memorial "had the same fate with the Remonstrance." Afterwards Burke gave both documents to the newspapers, but not the petition to the King. John Pownall had advised against publishing a paper addressed to the throne. The agent informed his employers that he "did not think it right to do anything against office, without absolute necessity." Whatever might be his opinion of the conduct of ministers he took care never to let his sentiments mingle with the business of New York, which he sought to "carry on solely with a view to your particular interest and entirely unconnected with everything else."

Nothing could have been more eloquent of the uncompromising spirit of ministers and Parliament than the rejection of the New York remonstrance. That document, as we have seen, was phrased in a language of reverent loyalty and was as much a profession of devotion to the empire as it was a declaration of grievances. It came from men who were striving to prevent New York from being carried along in a continental movement of physical resistance to parliamentary enactments. Its rejection seemed convincing proof that Parliament desired not peace but unconditional submission on the part of America. Ears that would not hearken to Burke and Fox, Rockingham and Chatham, were not less deaf to John Cruger and James Delancey.

The contents and tone of Burke's report of this affair to his employers, and the fact that it was not written (or completed) until more than three weeks after May 15, suggest perhaps that Burke did not make a great effort to obtain parliamentary consideration for the remonstrance. If so, there were probably at least two reasons for his less spirited conduct. First, it was not a happy conjunction of his duties as New York agent and member of Parliament: he could not but feel, as a member of the House of Commons, that it was hardly proper for him to appear there in the role of an agent for a special interest. Secondly, he may well have felt some lingering remains of hope that the King would make some change in the ministry in order to stop the drift to war, and that his own friends might be called to office. According to Horace Walpole, when North summoned his chief supporters to unite against Burke's presentation of the remonstrance, several disagreed, and among them was the War Secretary, Lord Barrington, who although a "king's friend" had always favored conciliation of America. This, wrote Walpole, "was noticed, as his Lordship was not subject to conscientious scruples, and therefore it was suspected that the King was meditating some change." [38]

Even before Burke brought up the remonstrance, it was Henry Cruger's opinion that he had little concern for the interests of New York, that he was "cursed crafty and selfish." Cruger wrote to Peter Van Schaak at New York on May 3:

> I think that every agent that preferred the interests of his constituents should hazard a little. Did Mr. Burke ever, in this grand dispute, assist the Assembly (or individuals) with any friendly advice or useful intelligence? No, No, he is too *cunning*. He will always be *at liberty* to take whichever side best serves his *immediate interest*. Today he will be the *first* great Promoter of a *Declaratory Bill*. Tomorrow, he shall *insinuate* the Parliament have not a right to bind the Americans in all causes—and yet, put *him in power*, and the third day you shall find him asserting the supremacy of this country with a vengeance. . . . May such deep Jesuits soon die. [39]

The criticism was unjust in the extreme. Burke had not only discharged with fair promptness most of the business assignments put on him by the assembly's committee of correspondence but shown great solicitude for the just demands of individual New Yorkers, and he had performed the very valuable service of sending to New York candid and truthful reports of the disposition of Parliament throughout the crisis. If he offered no advice to guide the conduct of New York, that was because he neither had any to give nor conceived it proper for him to attempt to influence the acts of his principals. Circumstances were such that any man in Burke's position was bound to become a target of unfriendly criticism from persons who expected from him more than he could possibly give. It

[38] *Last journals* 1: 488.

[39] Van Schaak, H. C., *Henry Cruger, the colleague of Edmund Burke,* 19-20, N. Y., C. Benjamin Richardson, 1859. An abstract of the letter may be found in *Manuscripts of the Earl of Dartmouth* 2: 296.

had never occurred to him when he undertook the agency for the New York Assembly that he was identifying himself with local provincial interests. He was a Buckinghamshire squire, a member of Parliament, and an imperial patriot. It had been one thing for him to advocate the merits of a New York legislative act before the Board of Trade, or to perform favors for his fellow British subjects across the ocean, or to champion the interests of New York in a colonial boundary question. But it was something very different to become the advocate or partisan of a colony at dispute with the imperial authority. He had no natural partiality for New York, which he had never so much as seen—there was not in him a trace of sentimental pro-Americanism—and his indignation at ministerial misman-agement of the colonies had always been a great deal warmer than his sympathy for their grievances. Conciliation of the colonies was to Burke a means rather than an end—a means of preserving the British Empire in North America. The tranquillity and prosperity of the empire formed the object of his American politics, not the vindication of natural justice. America was not India: never did Burke imagine that British officials in America were guilty of monstrous tyranny and crimes against the moral law: America was not afflicted by a Warren Hastings. As Burke envisaged the Anglo-American crisis, it was a quarrel brought on by ministerial and parlia-mentary ignorance and imprudence, inconsistency and imbecile feebleness, which had alienated the natural loyalty of the king's subjects on the other side of the Atlantic. He had always conceived his agency as a minor means for promoting good will between the colony and the mother country, and so he had ever tried to use it. But he was only an agent, not a representa-tive; he had employers at New York, not constituents. It was undoubtedly his duty to present and explain New York griev-ances before those to whom they were addressed, but it never could be his duty to champion them against what he conceived to be the supreme authority in the empire, for he was himself a part of that supreme authority. Had Henry Cruger fully understood Burke's politics and conception of the agency, he could hardly have written of him so unjustly—to which one may be tempted to add that if the New York Assembly had really understood him, they might never have engaged him as agent.

That New York was no longer an object of studied official favor was indicated plainly on May 25 when the Board of Trade came to a decision on the question of the French grants around Lake Champlain. The lords commissioners recommended to the crown that purchasers of land who had trusted in the validity of French Canadian titles be quieted in their possession. New York grants going counter to those titles were condemned as "unjust and unwarrantable," and the Governor of New York "should receive the most positive orders not to make any further Grants whatever of any part of the lands within the limits of these Seigneuries." [40] When Burke wrote to his employers on June 7, detailing the fate of the remonstrance, he neglected, for some reason that does not appear, to pass on this additional piece of bad news. And never again did he write to the New York Assembly's committee of correspondence.

Late in May arrived the news of Concord and Lexington, and Burke wrote to his friend, O'Hara: "All our prospects of American reconciliation are, I fear, over. Blood has been shed. The sluice is opened. Where, when, or how it will be stopped God only knows." [41]

Revolution Begins at New York

During the spring of 1775, the men who had given instructions to Burke as agent, lost all control of events in New York. The assembly's refusal to approve the program of the first Congress or to authorize delegates to the second, provoked the Committee of Sixty and the partisans of the association to act independently, on the principle that if the legislature would not act for the people, the people would act for themselves. A provincial convention met in the city on April 20 under the presidency of Philip Livingston. Crown officials made no serious effort to prevent it. As Colden explained to Lord Dartmouth, it was not in the power of government "to prevent such measures" since they were supported "by individuals in their private character" and did not come "within the energy of our laws." [42] A revolution was taking place but nobody seemed to realize the fact. Nine counties, or slightly more

---

[40] *Journal of Commissioners*, 422-426; *N. Y. documents* 8: 577-579.
[41] Annaghmore MSS.
[42] *N. Y. documents* 8: 566.

than half the province, were represented—in the sense that the convention accepted credentials from men of nine counties. About one third of the members of the assembly—the minority that had voted to approve the Congress—took part in the convention, which was not conceived as a new legislature, but only as an *ad hoc* gathering of leaders to choose delegates to the forthcoming second Congress. In three days that purpose was accomplished and the convention dissolved. This was not the action of all the people, but only of a party and probably a minority party. Colden at any rate was still convinced that a majority of the people were opposed to participating in the Congress, and that New Yorkers were succumbing to pressure exerted by other colonies which threatened them with "every species of public and private resentment." [43]

The day after the provincial convention dissolved, news of the British march on Concord and retreat to Boston reached New York. As if a signal had been given, the violent party rose. The king's government was prostrated and the association committees ruled the city. The custom house was closed; ships were forbidden to sail for Boston or Halifax, in order to prevent the provisioning of General Gage's troops; the arsenal was captured and arms were seized. All this was possible because the New York military headquarters had been nearly stripped of soldiers in order to reinforce Gage at Boston; only a hundred (of the Royal Irish Regiment) were on hand. The Committee of Sixty was now expanded to become the yet more radical Committee of One Hundred, which ruled the city like a revolutionary provisional government. The assembly had been due to meet again on May 3, but Colden and the council were compelled to recognize the necessity of a new prorogation. A provincial congress came into being on May 22. New York was out of constitutional control.

John Cruger wrote to Burke on May 4 that "the melancholy situation" of the city and province was "beyond expression." [44] The next day he and twelve other members of the defunct assembly addressed an appeal to General Gage for a cessation of hostilities "until his Majesty can be apprized of the Situation of his American Colonies." And to prevent New York from becoming a scene of carnage these men of peace begged Gage

---

[43] *Ibid.*, 571.
[44] *Manuscripts of Earl of Dartmouth* 2: 298.

not to send additional troops to New York.[45] Presently the old Speaker would retire to Kinderhook and complete political inactivity. Many members of the assembly would join the "loyalists" for protection against the "patriots." Delancey at some time this spring sailed for England, never to return.[46]

But New York in May-June, 1775, was far from being a city prostrate before revolutionary violence. Among Burke's papers is an unsigned letter, written at New York on May 4, which depicts the scene:

Before the irritating blow of the 19th April, there were many who tho' they were staggered at the open avowal of the House of Commons respecting the Taxation of America still flattered themselves that some sort of Compromise would take place. . . . But from a Persuasion, that the General has Orders to make the last Appeal to the Sword, they consider the Proposal of Peace as a Cheat, & fly to their Arms. The News of the Attack at Boston reached us on Sunday the 23, & that very day the Populace seized the City Arms; unladed two Vessels bound with Provisions to the Troops at Boston. In the course of the Week they formed themselves into Companies, under Officers of their own chusing; demanded the Keyes to the Custom House, & shut up the Port, trained their Men publicly, convened the Citizens by beat of Drum, drew the Cannon into the interior Country, & formed an Association of Defence in perfect

---

[45] *Colden Papers* 7: 291-293.

[46] No evidence has been found by the present writer to throw any light on Delancey's relations with Burke after going to England, although the following passage in Burke's letter to Rockingham of Aug. 23, 1775, may refer to him: "I have seen J. D. and Penn. The former, I believe, has suffered himself to be made a tool; your lordship will soon see him."—*Correspondence* 2: 56. Delancey was attainted by the revolutionary government of New York in 1779, and all his property was confiscated. His estate in the city, which extended from Bayard to Houston Street and from the Bowery to the East River, was sold by forfeiture commissioners for 69,306 pounds in 1784, and passed into the hands of the Livingston, Gouverneur, Beekman, and Roosevelt families. His properties confiscated and sold in other parts of the province brought almost as large a sum when liquidated. Delancey took a leading part in obtaining compensation from the British government for the American loyalists; he represented New York exiles on the board of agents created to treat with commissioners appointed by Parliament to adjudicate loyalist claims. His own compensation was but a fraction of the value of the property he had lost. With his wife and five children (three daughters and two sons) Delancey settled at Bath where he died on April 8, 1800. Three of his letters, written to a nephew in 1792, may be found among the W. H. Delancey Papers in the Museum of the City of New York. His son, Charles, became a British naval officer and lived until 1840; the other son, James, entered the army and survived to 1857.—W. H. Delancey Papers, 42.315: 324, 327, 328, 482, 584; Jones, *op. cit.* 1: 658; Yoshipe, Harry, The Delancey estate, *New York History* 7: 167-179, 1936.

League with the rest of the Continent, which is signing by all Ranks, Professions, & Orders of Men.

No social revolution was being unleashed, no rising of the poor against the rich. Some "friends of government" fled the city, but conservative loyalist newspapers continued to appear. The provincial congress did not yet usurp the authority of the old assembly, but pretended to be only an emergency body to act for the province in standing with the other colonies against British military and political aggression. It sought to maintain peaceful relations with civil and military officers of the crown, even while reducing these to impotence. Another unsigned and unidentified letter from New York found among Burke's papers describes the scene on June 4:

Barring the first Ferments, which inspired Terror and occasioned the Flight of a Few, who had been suspected by the Populace, nothing has happened to excite the least Apprehension of Violence to any Man's person or Property. . . . If a Stranger was to land here, he would be at a loss whether to pronounce this City immersed in Commerce, or a great garrisoned Town, the same Men who at one time crowd the Wharfs, appearing at another in uniforms well appointed and parading the Fields with as much adroitness, as they transact the Business of their Traffick in another part of the Day. . . . We live under the Protection of the Laws, and with such Confidence in our Rulers, that the Tranquillity enjoyed since the change of your Power for the present republican System, greatly increases the Risk you run of never regaining the Government you lost. . . . You know my political creed, and how early I predicted the Consequences of that System of Conduct, which the Nation is adopting, and by which means a Union might have been established friendly to the Empire, and salutary to your Supremacy. I flatter myself still with some hopes, that it may yet be effected.

But hopes of that kind were weakened by the arrival early in July of the news that Parliament had refused to receive the assembly's moderately phrased and loyal memorial and remonstrance. The London dispatch printed in the *Gazetteer* on July 6, and reprinted verbatim in the *New York Journal* a week later, reflected no credit on Agent Burke, who "introduced the Business in a short and pathetic Speech, and was answered by Lord North in a very plausible Manner; to which Mr. Cruger replied with Spirit and Eloquence." According to John Harris Cruger, this news "irritated and vexed many of the moderate and well disposed people," and he predicted it would "hasten

on the scene of confusion, ruin and anarchy." [47] By this time
Governor Tryon had returned to New York, only to find himself without control or influence. And yet, even in mid-summer
—after Washington had passed through New York on his way
to Cambridge—Governor Tryon believed that New York could
be won back to obedience if Parliament would but renounce
taxing the colonies.[48]

About this time, James Rivington, who was hated as a
"Tory" by the patriot party, attempted to cultivate loyalism
by publicizing the views of Burke. The *Gazetteer* began on
July 27 to serialize the speech-pamphlet on *Conciliation with
the Colonies*. Weekly installments spread over the first page of
the paper continued until September 7. The issue for August 10
carried also that part of the *American Taxation* speech in which
Burke had drawn his classic portraits of Chatham and Townshend. In view of the former's immense popularity in America,
this probably was not very good propaganda. In September
Rivington brought out New York editions of both the taxation
and conciliation speech-pamphlets, which were simultaneously
published in Philadelphia by Benjamin Towne. These were the
first of Burke's works to be published in book form in
America.[49] Doubtless their influence on New York political
opinion was much handicapped by the prejudice against Rivington and all his works. It was a characteristic detail of the chaos
into which the British Empire had drifted, that the king's
printer at New York should propagate Burke's ideas in order
to soften American resistance to a ministry that Burke so
bitterly opposed.

Burke and the "Olive Branch" Petition

By the summer of 1775 Burke's tenuous connection with
New York had all but dissolved. He was an impotent and
uninstructed agent of an assembly that in effect had ceased
to exist. After June 7 he never wrote again to his official employers. Nor did he expect a return of the old order in Anglo-
American relations. To his friend, O'Hara, he wrote on July 26:
"You see we are actually engaged in a civil war, and with little,
very little hopes of any peace; and in my poor opinion with full

---

[47] *Manuscripts of the Earl of Dartmouth* 2: 326-327.
[48] *Ibid.*, 328.
[49] Evans, Charles, *American Bibliography* 5: 167.

The SPEECH of EDMUND BURKE, Efq; on moving his Refolutions for Concili-ation with the Colonies, March 22, 1775.

I HOPE, Sir, that, notwithftanding the aufterity of the chair, your good-nature will incline you to fome degree of indulgence towards human frailty. You will not think it unnatural, that thofe who have an object depend-ing, which ftrongly engages their hopes and fears, fhould be fomewhat inclined to fuperftition. As I came into the houfe full of anxiety about the event of my motion, I found to my infinite furprize, that the grand Penal Bill, by which we had paffed fentence on the trade and fuftenance of Ame-rica, is to be returned to us from the other houfe*. I do confefs, I could not help looking on this event as a fortu-nate omen. I look upon it as a fort of providential favour; by which we are put once more in poffeffion of our deli-berative capacity, upon a bufinefs fo very queftionable in its nature, fo very uncertain in its iffue. By the return of this Bill, which feemed to have taken its flight for ever, we are at this very inftant nearly ⬤ free to choofe a plan for our American government, as we were on the firft day of the feffion. If, Sir, we incline to the fide of conciliati-on, we are not at all embarraffed (unlefs we pleafe to make ourfelves fo) by any incongruous mixture of coercion and reftraint. We are therefore called upon, as it were by a fuperior warning voice, again to attend to America; to attend to the whole of it together; and to review the fub-ject with an unufual degree of care and calmnefs.

Surely it is an awful fubject; or there is none fo on this fide of the grave. When I firft had the honour of a feat in this houfe, the affairs of that continent preffed them-felves upon us, as the moft important and moft delicate object of parliamentary attention. My little fhare in this great deliberation oppreffed me. I found myfelf a partaker in a very high truft; and having no fort of reafon to rely on the ftrength of my natural abilities for the proper execution of that truft, I was obliged to take more than common pains, to inftruct myfelf in every thing which relates to our colonies. I was not lefs under the neceffity of forming fome fixed ideas, concerning the general policy of the Britifh empire. Something of this fort feemed to be indifpenfible; in order, amidft fo vaft a fluctuation of paffions and opini-ons, to concenter my thoughts; to ballaft my conduct; to preferve me from being blown about by every wind of fafhionable doctrine. I really did not think it fafe, or manly, to have frefh principles to feek upon every frefh mail which fhould arrive from America.

FIG. 2. The beginning of the first installment of the first publica-tion in America of Burke's speech of March 22, 1775, on Con-ciliation with the Colonies.—Rivington's Gazetteer, July 27, 1775.

cause to despair of any that shall restore the ancient confidence and harmony of the parts of this empire." [50]

In mid-August, Richard Penn arrived in England with the "olive branch" petition to the King from the second Continental Congress. Like the New York appeals for conciliation and restored harmony, this petition (which had disgusted American extremists) was modestly phrased. It beseeched the King "to direct some mode by which the united applications of your faithful colonists to the throne . . . may be improved into a happy and permanent reconciliation; and that in the meantime . . . such statutes as more immediately distress any of your Majesty's colonies may be repealed." The dominant temper of the Congress was better reflected, however, in its simultaneous adoption of a declaration of the causes and necessity of taking up arms. Nothing now could have been plainer than that the fundamental American grievance was the principle of the Declaratory Act of 1766, and to Burke, however far he may have gone toward a willingness to surrender up that principle, the fact was exasperating. If the Rockinghams had once been right in contending that this act was not an American grievance, they could no longer maintain that position. If Lord Chatham's view had not been correct in the past, events had made it correct in 1775, and the old Rockingham-Burke prescriptions for the "management" of America had been rendered obsolete. This was not pleasant to admit and Burke was very vexed. After seeing Richard Penn he wrote to the Marquess:

He brings a very decent and manly petition from the congress. It mentions no specific conditions, but, in general, it is for peace. Lord Chatham is the idol, as usual. I find by Penn that, in America, they have scarce any idea of the state of men and parties here, nor who are their friends or foes. To this he attributes much of their nonsense about the declaratory act. [51]

To O'Hara, Burke let himself go more freely on the perversity of the Americans in failing to see who their real friends had all along been:

Our madness passes all conception. Theirs too in some particulars is extraordinary. They have attempted to discredit and disable the only friends they have in this country; and they place all their reliance on a man, who refused to put himself into a responsible position to serve them; and when he came to power him-

---

[50] Annaghmore MSS.   [51] *Correspondence* 2: 57.

self, if he did not actually produce at least made one of the Administration who laid the tax which is the fatal cause of all this
mischief; and indeed never did them a single service, that I can
recollect, in the whole course of his life.[52]

Burke was one of the men to whom the Americans had
sent their petition, in the hope that he would take part with
others in presenting it to the King. Arthur Lee on August 21
invited him to attend a meeting to wait on Lord Dartmouth
with the petition. Burke declined on the ground that he had
not been authorized by his New York principals to act in the
matter: since the New York Assembly had refused to send
deputies to the Congress, it would be improper for their agent
to participate in presenting the petition. But he was willing
to declare his wish for success in "this laudable undertaking
for the restoration of peace." On learning of Burke's declina-
tion, the ardently pro-American William Baker addressed a
somewhat spirited appeal to him, arguing that the Congress
had not asked him to perform a service in his capacity as a
colonial agent. It was to Mr. Burke, "a name that carries with
it terror to tyrannous ministers, and comfort to insulted free-
men," that Americans had appealed: "America, defended by
your eloquence, and deriving credit to her cause from your
worth, looks up to you, and in these her last months of peace,
to mediate with those who will be content with nothing less
than her ruin." [53]

But Burke was unmoved by this rhetoric and did not budge
from his position, which was not grounded on a narrow official
scrupulosity, or on fear, or on party pique at the Chathamite
character of the petition. It was grounded in political prudence.
He wished to stop the war, and the only way to do that was
to disintegrate public support of it in England. He knew the
petition would be rejected, and that a royal proclamation was
about to be issued declaring the existence of a rebellion in
North America. It was not consistent with prudent strategy
for a man who hoped to arouse the British public against the
war, to appear as an agent for petitioning "rebels." Of the
great task of stirring the people, he wrote to Rockingham on
August 23:

I see, indeed, many, many difficulties in the way; but we have
known as great, or greater, give way to a regular series of judicious

---

[52] Annaghmore MSS, Aug. 17.   [53] *Correspondence* 2: 42-46.

and active exertions. This is no time for taking public business in their course and order, and only as a part in the scheme of life which comes and goes at its proper periods. . . . It calls for the whole of the best of us.[54]

But that "whole"—even if it had been given—would not have been enough to reverse the tide of catastrophe. When Parliament convened in November, opposition efforts to prevent more fuel from being fed into the fire were perfectly vain, and overwhelming support was given to new ministerial war measures. Still Burke hoped that the Parliament of Ireland might resist British pressure and come forth as mediator of the quarrel in the empire. When that hope failed and the government of Ireland authorized the king to employ Irish military forces in America, Burke was finally convinced that arms alone would decide the issue. It was the end. Of America, he told O'Hara: "I look on that people as alienated forever—let the event of the war be what it may." [55]

Conclusion

In bringing this study to an end, it seems worth while to take a brief backward glance over it and to set down a few summary observations and reflections on Burke as New York agent.

His employment by the New York Assembly was to him strictly a side-line activity that had little connection with his main interests, purposes, and conduct in public life. In no significant way did it influence him as a party politician and member of Parliament, unless perhaps it caused him to increase his knowledge of colonial affairs by keeping in close contact with the Board of Trade and Plantations. It may not even be said that the New York connection produced any particular effect on his attitude towards American questions, because his American politics remained unchanged from the time he argued for the repeal of the Stamp Act until he opposed the ministerial and parliamentary measures of 1774-1775 that plunged the empire into a civil war. Throughout the period of his service to New York the key to his conduct in all American questions confronting Great Britain is to be found in the

---

[54] *Ibid.*, 53.
[55] Annaghmore MSS, Jan. 7, 1776.

principles and exigencies of his party, not in the demands of the agency office, and when the great crisis came, his conduct as agent was limited and controlled by his higher duty as a member of Parliament. Never did he allow the interests of New York to draw him into a compromise of the primary and main interests of his party and country. On only one occasion, when he offered the New York remonstrance on the floor of the House of Commons, did he discharge an agency assignment in Parliament, and then his behavior was half-hearted and perfunctory—unusual for such a man as he.

But there was no inconsistency in his conduct, or incompatibility between his agency, as he conceived it, and his membership in the supreme legislature of Great Britain. Ready and willing to transact business for his principals with the crown officers in London and Westminster, or to do personal favors for leading persons in New York, he refused absolutely to become a kind of colonial diplomat to negotiate with his own government. He was always resolved to give up the employment if the Board of Trade forced the New York Assembly to admit the governor and council to a voice in naming and instructing the agent, since that would inevitably have converted him into a "placeman" with obligations to the North administration. Moreover, his concept of an agent as properly the creation of the assembly alone, was the only idea of this office that was consistent with his conviction that the British legislature had supreme and unlimited authority over the colonies. He wished to maintain in all its fullness and integrity the supremacy of that legislative trinity of king, Lords and Commons, because he saw it as a grand part of the providential order which he had found on coming into the world and never was willing to disturb. Passionately did he desire to preserve American dependence upon and subordination to Great Britain, and if the colonists were properly "managed" he was sure that such a relation did not militate against any freedoms that Americans could rightly cherish or desire. Such "management" was the high virtue of prudence in government, and it was a practice of that prudence that colonial assemblies—parts of Burke's providential order—should have direct access, through agents of their own choosing, to the supreme authority in the empire. He did not believe there was much wisdom in such assemblies, but thought of them as mirroring public sentiments which rulers ought to take account of if they intended to rule with justice and prudence. Since the ideal of liberty was connected in his mind with the British constitution and empire, he was sure that British legislative supremacy, sagaciously self-restrained, was perfectly consistent with allowing the Americans to manage their own affairs very much as they pleased. That was why he could sympathize with American protests against British government measures, without in any way abandoning his belief in the unlimited authority of crown and Parliament over the colonies.

Burke was never an "American" agent, but the New York Assembly's only. He never acted with the body of American colonial agents. None of their names—not even the great Franklin—was mentioned in his letters to New York. He flatly refused to allow himself to be used by either the first or second American Congress, and it cannot be doubted that in 1775 he wished success to the Delancey party in their effort to keep New York from being swept into the rebellion. Burke had no natural sympathy for America except as a part of the British Empire, and if, when the war came, he did not wish success to British arms, neither did he desire the Americans to triumph. Peace and Anglo-American reconciliation within the empire were his objects. After the Americans won their independence, he seems to have lost all interest in their country.

Granting all this, may it not be said, nevertheless, that Burke's lively activity against the ministers of the day and his often-expressed hostility to the clique called the "king's friends," contributed to stirring up a rebellion in America? Perhaps so—but only in the few years before he became an agent, and then only because American patriots, misled by inaccurate newspaper reports and their own preconceived ideas, built up in their minds an idea of Burke's sentiments and conduct that did not correspond perfectly with reality. They bracketed him with Wilkes and Barré, with Conway and Chatham, and did not know how far aloof he stood from such men, or understand his aristocratic conservatism. After he became connected with New York, and prior to 1774, he and his party were comparatively inactive in opposing the ministry; he neither produced in writing nor spoke in Parliament any attacks on the administration that reverberated in American ears; from the summer of 1772 he was on excellent terms with the Secretary of State for the Colonies.

Nevertheless, an able historical writer who made use of Burke's letters to New York in preparing a work that has but recently appeared, charges that these letters "added fuel to a fire soon to be grown beyond control" because they were studded with sharp thrusts at court politics, and because Burke permitted his correspondents to circulate them in the province. His letter of August 2, 1774, wherein he gave an account of the Quebec Act's passage and of his successful effort to determine a boundary that would not damage New York interests, has been cited as a particularly flagrant example of "violent misinterpretation of ministerial policy" that was of "vast importance in swinging New York into line with the other colonies." [56]

These interpretations do not appear to take account of the following facts: (1) Burke's occasional barbs (there were not many) against court and ministry—common coins of Whig political exchanges—do not appear in his public letters to the assembly committee of correspondence, but in his private letters to James Delancey and John Cruger, and there is no ground for believing that he expected such communications to be circulated for public information. (2) He did not give permission to circulate his letters until he wrote the one of August 2, 1774, and he did so then in answering a letter from the committee informing him that they had taken the liberty of allowing the contents of his letter of the previous April 6 to be circulated in the city. Those who spread what Burke had written were all conservatives who wished their fellow-subjects to know the gravity of the parliamentary proceedings which he had described with perfect candor and truth. (3) If Burke, in his account of the Quebec Act, reported the existence of a strong opinion favoring the hemming in of the English colonies by expanding Quebec against their western rear, he also did his best to persuade New Yorkers that their interests had been adequately safeguarded by his territorial amendment. What effect, if any, Burke's letter on this subject may have had on New York opinion, the present writer has not been

---

[56] Ritcheson, Charles R., *British politics and the American Revolution*, 150-151, 167-168, Norman, Okla. Univ. Press, 1954.

able to discover. New Yorkers without doubt discerned very objectionable features in the Quebec Act, but Burke's letter was rather designed to soften those features than to throw them into bold relief.

These facts, which appear consistent with his whole course of conduct in American affairs, enforce in the mind of the present writer this belief: to the extent that Burke, as New York's Assembly agent, exercised an influence on colony opinions and sentiments, that influence worked for moderation, loyalism, and acknowledgment of the supreme authority of the British legislature. Such a spirit appears to animate his letters to New York, now to be presented to the reader.

VII. Burke's New York Letter-Book [1]

To [John Cruger] [2]

Sir,

I am very happy in the unanimous testimony of the gentlemen of the Assembly of New York in favour of my endeavours to serve the public. Such a testimony from so large and respectable a part of my fellow subjects persuades me that I have not been mistaken in the line of conduct I have pursued, and it will be a strong motive with me for persevering in the same course. How long it may be consistent with the duties of my situation to continue my little offices to the Province, I know not. But the obligation you have conferred upon me by this mark of your good opinion is such that I think myself entitled to claim the honour of some relation with New York, and that you will therefore have a right to call upon me for all the attention I can show, in whatever situation I may be. I have the honour to be with great regard and esteem, Sir,

Your most obedient and most humble servant

E. B.

Beaconsfield June 9th 1771

To Mr. Livingston [3] in answer to his dated 2d. April 1771

Sir,

I am honoured with your letter of 2d. April last and with the three papers enclosed. [4]

I am obliged to you for the kind opinion you entertain of my intentions. I hope you will have no reason to alter it. In accepting the care of the business of New York, I wished to be as serviceable as I could to the whole Province. It is impossible I should have any party views or party sentiments on your side of the water. I scarcely know what your parties are,

[1] The letters are not in Burke's hand but in that of his clerk. In reproducing the letter-book the editor has preserved the original grammar, syntax, and paragraphing, but the punctuation has been a little modernized; all contractions have been spelled out, and capitalization and spelling have been occasionally made to conform to modern usage.

[2] *Infra*, to Delancey, June 9.

[3] Judge Robert R. Livingston (1718-1775).

[4] Letter and papers not found.

and I am sure that when I become better acquainted with them, I shall be as little disposed, as I am now qualified, to enter into the passions of any of them.

My duty to the gentlemen who have thought of me with so much partiality, makes me rather wish to conciliate these differences if it were in my power, than to aggravate by attempting to decide upon them. I therefore must beg leave to decline any opinion upon a matter so interesting to yourself and so delicate to the public, as that which makes the subject of your letter. But of this you may be assured, that I never shall be found assisting in any measure which may be injurious to the rights of individuals or prejudicial to the legal constitution of any part of the British dominions.

I am with great esteem

E. B.

To James Delanc[e]y Esqr.
Dear Sir,

I trust that by this time you have received my answer to your first letter.[5] This opportunity takes my answer to the Speaker. It is a letter merely general and ostensible; nor have I the honour of so much acquaintance with him as to make it as yet proper to enter into any details, especially when I write to him in his public capacity. But I take it for granted that I am entitled to open my mind fully and confidentially to you on the subject of our correspondence. In doing so, I shall certainly take great, but I hope not improper liberties; in this way, and in this way only I may be of some service to the Province. I am near to the scene where your business is finally transacted; I have an opportunity of knowing something of the temper, the disposition, and the politics of the people here; and not being so deeply and warmly engaged as yourselves, I may be able sometimes to give you hints, on which your own maturer sense may build something that may be useful to you in your affairs. If I am not allowed this liberty, any merchant in the City, or any active clerk that can rummage public offices and wait in the anti-chambers of Ministers, may be more serviceable to you than ten such people as I am.

I can do nothing as yet about the Boundary Line.[6] I have

---

[5] Neither letter has been found.

[6] Reference is to an act fixing the New York-New Jersey boundary, passed Feb. 16, 1771.—*Colonial Laws of New York* 5: 185-193.

got some papers that set forth the title of your Province, but nothing which can give me sufficient light into the present posture of the controversy, nor indeed into anything which may enable me to speak with weight and authority in the business. No gentleman has hitherto been with me upon it; and I think it better to have no conference at all with the Ministers than to confer with them on the disadvantageous ground on which I must stand for want of information. The business is of importance and as such I shall attend to it, with just as much assiduity as if I could entertain any hopes from those who now direct your affairs and ours.

The other matter of the disqualifying vote is of greater difficulty.[7] I do not imagine that Ministry here are so much pleased with the consequences of their own measure of a similar nature that they will wish to see it adopted in the Colonies; and perhaps they are not so confident of the influence which they may have in the Assemblies of America, as to make them desirous of vesting in those Assemblies the powers they have been so earnest in establishing here, where they flatter themselves they may be better able to direct them to their own purposes. As for those in the opposition, it is impossible that we can concur in establishing a principle of that extent in the Colony Representatives which upon such solid reasons we have denied legally to exist in the Commons of Great Britain. We never can admit that the House of Commons has any right to make, whether by declaration under pretence of judgment or by voluntary vote and resolution, any incapacity whatsoever. They are restricted to those which have been uniformly recognized in all ages by the practice of Parliament. The incapacity of the Judges is of that sort grounded not upon the opinion of the House on the propriety or policy of their sitting in it, but on the mere usage; as it never has been known in any period of our constitutional history that the Judges of the four great Courts have been eligible into the House of Commons; nor has a controversy ever existed in favour of such eligibility.

Upon this principle and upon this only, and not at all in

---

[7] The assembly, in January, 1770, professing to follow the principle of the British constitution, had passed an act to disqualify judges of the supreme court from sitting as elected legislators; the target of the measure was Judge Livingston. Although the law was disallowed by the crown in June, 1770, the question remained alive.—*Ibid.*, 73-77.

virtue of any vote or resolution of the House of Commons, we admit that the Judges are excluded from a seat in Parliament. It is possible enough that the Judges might have been disqualified by some early statute. A great part of our statute law is lost, and much if not the whole of what we receive as common law at this day was undoubtedly at first the result of positive constitution by the legislative authority; though the record being lost by the injury of time, the practice remains as the only evidence as well as the best interpreter of the law. Such have been invariably our sentiments on this question so far as it regards the Parliament of Great Britain. When the question comes to be applied to the Colony legislation, the same rule must hold for the same limitation of the Representative Assembly in creating disqualifications either unknown in the original constitution of these Assemblies or not made by subsequent legislative acts. With regards to the arguments drawn from the similitude of the Colony Assemblies to the House of Commons, I wish it to be considered, whether *disqualifications* which are in the nature of *penalties* can be extended merely by construction and analogy? Whether all the reasonings taken from the analogy of correspondent parts of legislature and judicature here will hold exactly and in all cases in America? And whether it be in effect desirable to the Colonies that such analogical reasoning should be established in such an extent, even supposing that the law admitted that mode of argument as a ground for abridging the general rights of the subject. We do not reason in the House of Commons by analogies taken from the disabilities of some Judges. The Master of the Rolls (a judge) sits. The Chancellor of the Exchequer, the Chancellor of the Duchy [of Lancaster], the Chief Justice of Chester, the Welsh Judges, many other judicial officers, sit. It certainly is not the judicial character which creates the disability. I make no doubt that the sole reason was their supposed necessary attendance of the House of Lords. This I take to be the reason; but the practice and not the theory becomes our rule in judging on this point.

These, my dear Sir, are my thoughts on that part of your business. I lay them before you for your own consideration, and that of your friends, that you may judge who are best able to judge, whether it will be your interest to push on that affair to the utmost which on the whole is not likely to be supported

by any body of people here,—as being contrary to the principles
of some, and perhaps to the politics of all. These thoughts
are, however, for your private use only. If you should think
fit not to pursue this vote you will consider how you may most
handsomely and most advantageously give it up or compromise
it. Mr. Livingston has sent me a state of his case, and hopes
I shall not consider myself as the agent of a party. To his
letter which is civil, I have sent a civil answer, and have declined to give my opinion upon the subject.

Poor Lady Rockingham has been extremely ill of a painful
and dangerous disorder for several months past, but I hope she
is now quite out of danger. Lest you should imagine by the
strong controversy in the papers that we have got into some
sort of quarrel amongst ourselves, I must just let you know that
R[ockingham]'s friends have nothing to do in it. It is a battle
in that City faction with which we never had any close connection.[8] I am with great esteem and regard,

Dear Sir,

Your most obedient and humble servant

E. B.

Beaconsfield June 9th 1771

To the Committee of Correspondence for the General Assembly
of the Colony of New York

Gentlemen,

I received your letter of the first of June by Captain Lawrence, together with the acts and votes of the last sessions of
the Assembly.[9]

I went immediately to town, but found that nothing conclusive can be done at present. Lord Hillsborough is now in
Ireland, and will probably continue there for some weeks. I
thought it, however, expedient to converse with Mr. Pownall,
Secretary, and Mr. Jackson, Council [sic] to the Board of
Trade, upon the subject of your instructions. I stated to them
your earnest wishes for the speedy confirmation of the Boundary

---

[8] A quarrel between Wilkes and some of his friends which came to a head
in electing a sheriff at London in June, 1771.

[9] Committee's letter not found.

Act, arising from your uneasiness at the distracted state of that part of the country to which the law relates.

They seemed not insensible to the propriety of putting a speedy end to the controversy between the two Colonies. Some objections were indeed started; they grew out of the arguments formerly used on the part of your Province to justify your dissent from the Commissioners. In the petition against that determination it was affirmed that the interests of the *Crown* as well as those of the Province of New York had been injured. Mr. Pownall seemed therefore to think it might be proper for the King's servants to inquire more minutely into the particulars of that allegation, before the royal sanction was given to the act. It was objected also, that one of the acts contained a clause confirming certain possessions without any reservation in favour of the rights of the Crown.

To these objections I made such answer as seemed at the time to give satisfaction. But it is not improper to acquaint you with every sort of difficulty, that you may furnish me with a sufficient answer in case the former objections should be revived and enforced by any new facts or new applications in the further progress of this business. The capital objection on which they relied, and which I was not able totally to remove, arose from *the want of a return to the Commission.* This was not properly an objection on the merits; and may be a reason for postponing the establishment of the act, but can be none for rejecting it entirely.

I told them that the litigant parties having withdrawn the appeal, the determination of the Commissioners now stood as if no exceptions had ever been taken to it; that therefore it waited for the only thing necessary to make it conclusive,—his Majesty's approbation; that the act of Assembly adopting that determination and yet containing a suspending clause until the King's pleasure should be known, was virtually such a return to the Commission as in effect and substance satisfied all its objects, not only in relation to the settlement proposed to be obtained by it, but with regard to the decorum which ought to be observed towards the Crown. They admitted that in this particular case there might possibly be no great difference between the formal return and the act of Assembly; but they were strongly of opinion that it would be a precedent dangerous in office if any collateral matter, however respectable, were suffered to supply the place of a direct return which had been actually prescribed by the authority under which the Commission acted; that if they should do so, they would allow an act of Assembly confirming a supposed determination, without so much as knowing, regularly and officially, that any determination whatsoever had been made,—for that this act of Assembly was only evidence of a return and not the return itself. I do not think that this objection can be any otherwise overcome than by getting an immediate regular return of the determination which the act is made to ratify. When this is done I have little doubt that the act will be passed. The waiting for the return can cause no great additional delay, as Lord Hillsborough's absence would at any rate prevent the conclusion of the business.

When an application is made to me, I shall assist the passing of Mr. Van Cortland's acts.[10] I have the honour to be,

Gentlemen,

Your most obedient and humble servant

E. B.

Beaconsfield
6th August 1771

To James Delanc[e]y Esqr. at New York

Dear Sir,

I have not delayed my answer to your last letter from any want of a due sense of its importance.[11] The appointment of their agents cannot be a matter of indifference to the Colonies. But Lord Hillsborough continued until lately in Ireland. Mr. Pownall for some time said nothing to me upon the subject. It was no business of mine to be forward in entering upon so delicate a topic. I was sure if the ideas you mentioned to me were seriously entertained by Ministry I should hear of it in a reasonable time.

At length Mr. Pownall called upon me and opened the matter from himself. He speaks of it rather as a scheme under

---

10 Not identified.
11 Letter not found.

deliberation than as a point actually determined. He is of opinion that the Governor and Council ought to have their part in the nomination of the provincial Agents, or at least a negative on the choice of the Representative Assembly. He thinks as the Agent is called, not the agent of the Assembly but of the Province, the consent of all the parts which compose the legislature is proper, in order to invest him with the complete authority of the body he is intended to represent. He thinks such a joint concurrence in the nomination would be very serviceable to the Colony, as the Agent appearing in the fullness of his character would act with greater weight in all his transactions with office. Lastly, he rests upon the equity of admitting the consent of the Governor and Council to the appointment of the Agent as their concurrence is necessary to charge the Province with his salary and expenses. This is the substance of what Mr. Pownall urged in favour of the proposed alteration.

As he seemed desirous of hearing my sentiments, I gave them to him freely. I told him that I looked upon the Agent for a Colony under whatever name he might be described, as *in effect agent for the House of Representatives only;* that is, a person appointed by them to take care of the interests of *the people* of the province *as contradistinguished from its executive government.*

In this light, his business was always separate from that of the governor, and might in many cases be opposite to his interests and wishes. The Agent might even be employed to make complaints against him for maladministration in his office. I thought it ridiculous to expect that such a charge should be pushed with vigor and effect by a person who was, in substance, the representative rather of the governor complained of, than the Colony complaining. By the new plan, the Governor by his own vote and that of the Council would have two parts, to one of the people, in this nomination. If his conduct became never so unacceptable to the Province, it would be totally out of their power to remove the Agent. Perhaps the very circumstance of his being unpleasing to them might become a reason for refusing the Governor's consent to an act for displacing him.

I have always been and shall ever be earnest to preserve the constitutional dependence of the Colonies on the Crown and legislature of this kingdom, and a friend to every just and honourable measure that tends to secure it. But this I consider in effect as a destruction of one of the most necessary mediums of communication between the Colonies and the parent country. The provinces ought in my opinion to have a direct intercourse with Ministry and Parliament here by some person who might be freely confidential with them who appoint him; who might be entrusted with the strength and weakness of their cause in all controverted points; and who might represent their own sentiments in their own way. The intervention of the governor in the nomination would totally frustrate their purposes. If the Colony differed from the Governor one can conceive nothing more improper than an agent confidential between two contending and perhaps very hostile parties.

I confess I could not see what the Governor had to do with this appointment. No part of his correspondence, as I apprehend, passes through the provincial agent. With regard to the arguments drawn from the concurrence of the Governor and Council in granting the supply for the salary and charges of the Agent, I thought it one of those arguments which by proving too much proves nothing at all. For if concurrence in the grant of salary implies the propriety of a similar concurrence in the appointment of the officer to whom salary is paid, then the Assembly, who have a part and the most essential part in the granting a salary to the Governor, ought to have a part in the nomination. But as this is against all usage, and against all reason, in most of the Colonies, the argument is full as little valid in the case of the Agent as the Governor. If your Agent does not depend totally on the Colony for his election and for his continuance, he must be something more than useless to you. He will be to all intents and purposes an officer of the Crown. However, this business rests upon your own judgment. Only I must add, if this new plan should take place, I consider it as so much a ministerial affair that in my present situation I could not honourably think of continuing to take care of the charge of your business.

I have seen Lord Hillsborough and stated to him your difficulties from the unsettled state of your boundary. He showed very obliging dispositions, but could do nothing until a board could be got together. The moment it meets I will urge your business with all the expedition in my power.

I have called on Mr. Izard, but he is out of town.[12] I will call again. I shall be very happy to hear of your health, as I feel very sincerely for anything that can impair any of the satisfactions of a man whom I greatly love and esteem.

I am etc.

E. B.

P. S. I have written by this post to the Committee of Correspondence. I have had no answer to my last; indeed as things stood it was not very necessary, except in relation to the return.

I direct simple to the Committee of Correspondence and am not sure whether I am right, but the mistake is not considerable. If there be any particular manner, let me know.

Decr. 4: 1771

To the Committee of Correspondence at New York

Gentlemen,

I had the honour of writing to you soon after the receipt of your instructions relative to the Boundary Act. I then informed you of the difficulties which were likely to be opposed to the allowance of that law. These were, however, suggested to me only argumentatively and in ordinary conversation: nothing was then, or has been since, officially resolved upon the subject. I have seen Lord Hillsborough, and I must do him the justice to tell you that he seems in a very proper disposition towards this business, but that he can say nothing approaching to positive until the Board of Plantations can be got together. This is expected very shortly. When that Board meets I shall press the immediate allowance of the Act. If the return to the Commissioners could be had (which I heartily wish), I apprehend there would be no further difficulty. If this should be out of your power, I am not altogether destitute of hopes that we shall succeed without it.[13]

Mr. Pownall, Secretary to the Board of Trade, is desirous

---

[12] Ralph Izard (1742-1804) of South Carolina, in 1767, married Alice Delancey, a sister of Burke's correspondent; he became a member of the Continental Congress and the United States Senate.

[13] The act was not considered by the lords commissioners until April 29, 1772, and then decision was postponed.—*Journal of Commissioners*, 299.

that I should communicate to you a plan relative to the Colonies (yours included) which the Ministers have at present under deliberation, but which they have not, so far as I am able to learn, taken any steps to carry into execution.

The plan is, that you should admit the votes of the Governor and Council in the appointment of your Agent in Great Britain, or at least their negative upon your choice. This mode of appointment, they are of opinion, will add to the weight and authority of your Agent in his negotiations with office, as he will thereby become a person more fully and perfectly representing the whole of that body politic for which he acts. They conceive also that principles of equity and reason render such an arrangement highly proper, as all the parts of provincial legislature concur in the supply for the payment of the salary and contingent expenses of that office.

It is for your consideration whether it will be more for your advantage to remain in your ancient situation with an Agent appointed solely by yourselves and removable at your pleasure, as your immediate and appropriate means of communicating with the mother country, or to admit the reasons and coincide with the views of administration.

I must only beg leave to inform you that if you admit the plan, the outlines of which I have the honour to communicate to you, and that by such means your agency should become, in part at least, an appointment by Ministry, it will not be in my power consistently with my notions of honour to be officially charged with your business. I cannot act in my present situation except under the clearest and most satisfactory evidence that my employment is a matter wholly detached from administration. But you may be assured that if your opinion of your own advantage in this respect should not fall in with my ideas of the propriety of my particular conduct, I shall still preserve the highest and most grateful sense of your confidence in me, and shall during my life continue most sincerely attached to the interests of the Colony.

I am with greatest esteem,

Gentlemen,

Your most humble and most obedient servant

E. B.

4 December 1771

To the Gentlemen of the Committee of Correspondence at New York

Gentlemen,

I have the honour to transmit to you a copy of the minutes of the Board of Trade on several acts of your Assembly passed in the years 1770 and 1771. Three of these acts have been disallowed. The reason assigned for disallowing the two first is, that they were founded on acts which his Majesty thought fit to be repealed last year, and that, as *consequential* laws, they were already virtually repealed.[14]

As to the act entitled an Act for Preventing Abuses Committed by Tenants, etc., they thought it too great an invasion of the jurisdiction of the Supreme Court, the extent of which they think it of the highest importance to both the Mother Country and the Colony to preserve.[15] They were further of opinion that it must frequently happen, in the jurisdiction given by this act, that titles will come in question before those who cannot be competent for that purpose. Had the object of that act been to restore *possession* only (though as they affirm, not similar to any in England), it might have been free from this last objection. But a plaintiff, under the last clause of the act, is to support his *ownership* as well as his former *possession*, and must therefore produce a title for the opinion of three justices.

I thought it necessary to state these objections for your consideration, that if you should think it proper to renew these acts, you may model them so as to be free from those difficulties.

The determination on the Boundary Act has been suspended for the reasons I have formerly stated to you. The Act for [emitting] Bills of credit lies by for further consideration because it is said to have a clause creating a crime triable within your Colony though committed outside its bounds. But as they think this may be expedient for supporting the credit of bills [emitted] under the sanction of an act of Parliament, they could not determine yet to disallow, nor could they at the same time countenance the Act. It has at present its full operation.[16]

---

[14] *Colonial Laws of New York* 5: 120-126, 250-254; *Journal of Commissioners,* 298-299; *Acts of Privy Council* 5: 342-343.

[15] *Colonial Laws of New York* 5: 204-206.

[16] *Ibid.,* 149-170. This act, passed in Feb., 1771, was so drawn as to evade the parliamentary prohibition of bills of credit as legal tender. The Board of

Another business has lately appeared upon which I reques.
your instructions. By an article of the last Treaty of Peace
with France all grants of land made by the Government of
Canada previous to the conquest of that Province are confirmed.
In consequence of that article, a Monsieur L'Aubiniére [17] and
eighteen other claimants have demanded one million-twenty-
three thousand-five hundred and forty acres including a tract
of country which extends from Fort George to 45 degrees north
latitude on both sides of the water. It takes in the whole of
Lake Champlain. Of this tract, M. L'Aubiniére claims for
himself about 115 thousand acres which lie on the south west
extremity and comprehend Ticonderoga. He desires that those
lands should be for him as a grantee under the French Government and as a part of the Province of Quebec. It appeared
to me that these claims if admitted might be an infringement
of the territorial right and jurisdiction of the Province of New
York, and affect the properties of several who may have taken
lands and made settlements in virtue of grants passed under
the seal of your Colony. I need not state to you the boundary
which was settled by the Governors Moore and Carleton for
ascertaining the limits of the two provinces, and which seem
to determine in your favor the whole object of the French
grants.

Mr. Pownall indeed thinks that the line settled by Sir H.
Moore and Col. Carleton was not a line ascertaining a right
which had a prior existence, but only a line of conveniency
made for the future ascertainment of jurisdiction without determining anything of private property.[18]

Though I had no instructions from you upon this subject,
I thought it necessary to object to the allowance of the grants
until I could know from yourselves how far you considered
yourselves affected or not affected by them.

Mr. Pownall promised me that I shall be apprised of every
step that is taken in this matter. He does not think that anything decisive can be done before I receive your instructions.

Trade on April 29, 1772, ordered that the act "do lye by for further consideration."—*Journal of Commissioners,* 299. Never again did New York bills of credit
legislation come before the Board of Trade or Privy Council, but the prohibition
of these as legal tender continued to be resented.

[17] Michel Lotbiniére.

[18] A copy in an unknown hand of the preceding two paragraphs is among
the James Duane MSS in the Library of the New York Historical Society.

I have the honour to be with the most perfect esteem and regard,

Gentlemen,

[E. B.]

London. May 6. 1772.
By the Packet

To John Cruger Esquire. New York. June 30. 1772

Dear Sir,

I received your letter of the 14th of April last recommending to my particular attention two bills that have passed in the last session of your Assembly.[19] Independent of my duty to the Colony, which will not permit me to delay any of its business, I have a particular pleasure in obeying your commands. The two bills, together with that for the recovery of small debts, were immediately sent to Mr. Jackson, Council to the Board of Trade. I have pressed him to make his report as soon as possible. I have no doubt but that it will be ready in a few days; I have solicited at the office, and I am persuaded that if his report should be favorable, the business will be dispatched and the bills will receive the royal allowance in a short time.

Our session has ended with great tranquility, though during the course of it we had some subjects for warmth. The Royal Marriage Bill did indeed produce no small ferment. It is an act little conformable to the spirit of our laws and the genius of the English constitution. It seemed to me bad as a regulation and worse as a precedent. The Crown will have from it an improper addition of not the best kind of strength, by creating an entire and slavish dependance upon the head of a family that may become very numerous unless prevented by the exertion of a power that is very unjust.[20] The Opposition did not seem stronger in any instance since the Middlesex election. To those who consider things but superficially, op-

[19] Cruger's letter has not been found, but the bills can be identified as acts to prevent private lotteries, and "infectious distempers" in certain counties.— *Colonial Laws of New York* 5: 351-354, 398-399.

[20] The Royal Marriage Act forbade members of the royal family to contract marriage before the age of twenty-five without the assent of the king. Burke and the Rockingham party had opposed the bill as giving additional power to the sovereign.

position seems to be at an end, but I think they are mistaken. Very few have been changed in their opinions or principles. The strength of Opposition remains nearly the same as ever— unexerted indeed, but unimpaired. You know that everything in political conduct depends upon occasions and opportunities. In the present state of things it has been thought advisable to be less active than formerly. Since it has appeared upon a multitude of trials and upon a great variety of matters that there is a determined, systematical, and considerable majority in both houses in favor of the Court scheme, an unremitted fight would only serve to exhibit a longer series of defeats. It was therefore thought advisable to attend to circumstances and to pitch only upon those where the advantage of situation might supply the want of numbers, or where, though without hope of victory, you could not decline the combat without disgrace. This was, during the last session, the measure of our conduct. We had religion thrown in among us, but we were too con- scientious to be very zealous; the matter was treated in general with great temper. The petition of the Church of England clergy was disallowed, not from any adherence in the majority of the House to some part of the Thirty-nine Articles, but because the petition desired that (in effect) they should be freed from any subscription. But it was thought unreasonable that the public should contribute to the maintenance of a clergy without knowing anything of their doctrine.[21] The bill to relieve the Dissenters stood upon a different ground, and therefore passed the Commons with little difficulty. It met another fate in the House of Lords.[22] But I have no doubt that in time it will be carried, and that this spirit of intolerance will vanish away by degrees both on our side of the water and on yours. The reluctance of many on your side of the water to receive a person in an episcopal character, though wholly con- fined to ecclesiastical functions, was urged in the House of Lords as a strong argument against the spirit of the Dissenters and to show the danger of setting them too much at large. We

---

[21] A petition from certain Church of England clergymen for relief from the obligation of subscribing to the Thirty-nine Articles, was presented Feb. 6, 1772, and rejected, with Burke voting in the majority. His speech may be found in *Works* 10: 3-21.

[22] Sir Henry Houghton's bill to extend the toleration provided for Dissenters in the Toleration Act of 1689; Burke supported it; the Commons approved and the Lords rejected it.

have little news stirring since the prorogation of Parliament. That which engages the people most at this time is the steps the King of Prussia is taking to make himself master of a considerable part of Poland and particularly of the free City of Danzig. Such a measure must affect us in time, in some degree as a naval, in no small degree as a commercial power. Any accession to the power of Prussia in its present disposition towards our Court and nation, cannot be indifferent to us; yet I do not hear that we make any movements upon our side to prevent it.[23]

You will easily perceive that this letter is not public (to the Speaker of the Assembly) but particular to Mr. Cruger, a gentleman for whose conduct and character I have a very high regard, and whose wishes upon every occasion must have the greatest weight with me. I am with the greatest esteem and respect,

Sir, your most obedient and most humble servant

E. B.

Broad Sanctuary   June 30. 1772.

———————

To James Delanc[e]y Esqr. New York June 30. 1772

My dear Sir,

I shall say less to you at present, because I have wrote somewhat at large to the Speaker. I had wrote likewise to the Committee of Correspondence by the last packet upon the French grants, wishing their instructions, which I hope shortly to receive.

I am extremely glad to hear of your recovery and wish you much happiness, (it is too late to wish you joy) in your marriage.[24] An ague at such a moment is an ugly *contretemps,* but I am glad to find it did not affect the main business and that you were soon rid of it.

Lord Rockingham has had a long and severe illness, and though he is now much recovered he has still disagreeable returns of pain in his stomach and bowels, and regains strength very slowly. As soon as he gathers a little more vigor he pro-

---

[23] The first partition of Poland was executed in August, 1772.

[24] Delancey married Margaret Allen of Philadelphia, daughter of the Chief Justice of Pennsylvania, on Aug. 19, 1771.—Jones, Thomas, *History of New York* 1: 658. If he wrote of this to Burke, his letter has not been found.

poses to set off for Yorkshire, which I hope will reestablish him.

We have very little news except the conversation which arises from the shock to the credit of Scotland which arose from the failure of Fordyce's bank. This shock has in some degree affected English houses as well as Scotch, and may touch every part of the world with which the banks of that part of the kingdom have had connections. However, it is to be hoped that any further ill consequences in the City of London are now not so much to be apprehended. There was a run upon several bankers, but it showed the solidity of their foundations, as none have given way after the first failure but that of Glynn and Halifax. The terror of the beginning was indeed great, and the worst was dreaded for some time.[25]

I send you a letter of attorney. It is to yourself. I beg pardon for the trouble I give you, as I have not the honor of any other acquaintance at New York. With regard to the contingent demands I have already given you my sentiments. Whether the way I pointed out is practicable I know not, but I can think of no other.[26]

I am with great esteem and affection,

Dear Sir,

Your most humble and most obedient friend

[E. B.]

Broad Sanctuary June 30 1772

P. S. You will oblige me much if you will send me as soon as you can two good New England pacers not above five years old. You will either retain the money or draw on me as you please. I may trust to your judgment and friendship to get the best as well as to send them by a careful captain. On recollection I am not able now to find the person to authenticate the letter of attorney, nor have I the leisure to go into the City at present. So I must defer sending it to you until some other opportunity.

---

[25] A grave credit crisis was precipitated by the failure in June, 1772, of the Scottish banker, Alexander Fordyce. "Twenty important houses fell within three weeks; others were only saved by the intervention of the Bank . . . stagnation of credit and trade depression continued until well into 1773."—Sutherland, L. S., *The East India Company in eighteenth-century politics*, 223, Oxford, Clarendon Press, 1952.

[26] Burke probably had authorized Delancey to receive the 500 pounds which the assembly had voted to him as his salary, in March, 1772.

(By the packet)

To James Delanc[e]y Esqr.

To the Committee of Correspondence at New York June 30.
  1772

Gentlemen,

I am honoured with your letter of the 13th of April last
and lost no time in getting the acts which you recommend
referred to Mr. Jackson, and have since applied to him to
hasten his report. If any objections are made to these acts or
to any others of the same transmiss I shall not fail to desire a
final proceeding on them to be postponed until your reasons
are heard and considered.

The objection which lies in general to laws for establishing
a summary process is on the magnitude of the debt, an objection which I apprehend is no ways applicable to yours, as you
have confined it to a very low object. I acquainted the office
with your resolution relative to the scheme for a new mode
of appointing an agent. I was told that in time their principle
will be found necessary in case the Agent is to give his consent
to any agreement or other public act terminated here in the
name of the Province; that then the validity of his power must
necessarily come in question. I do not imagine, however, that
they mean at present to proceed any further in that business.

I am with great esteem and regard,

Gentlemen,

[E. B.]

June 30. 1772

By the *Lady Gage Palmer*

To William Wickham Esqr., at New York

August 19. 1772
Sir,

I received the favour of your letter of the 6th of July in
relation to the Wawayenda Patent Act.[27] The day before I

---

[27] An act for dividing and setting apart lands in the patent of Wawayenda
in Orange County.—*Colonial Laws of New York* 5: 438-440.

received your letter, Mr. Pownall acquainted me that Dr. Smith had signified his intention of presenting a memorial to the Board of Trade praying to be heard against the confirmation of that act.[28]

I beg leave to remind you that no instructions have been sent which may enable counsel on your part to answer the objections which will be made by Dr. Smith's counsel. Nobody has attended to give me any lights upon the subject; and proper instructions to counsel are no less necessary to them than their fees. In this situation the consideration of your act comes before the Board of Trade under great disadvantages. But as that board will not do any material business until winter, you have still time sufficient to send over the materials necessary for the support of your act.

Nobody has been as yet with me upon the part of the gentlemen whom you have directed to supply me with the cash requisite for the charges of the act. When I incur any expense I will apply to them.

I am, Sir,

Your most humble and obedient servant,

E. B.

To William Wickham Esqr.   Duplicate by the
Beaconsfield August 19. 1772   October packet

By the *Lady Gage Palmer*
To James Delanc[e]y Esqr. New York

London, August 20. 1772

Dear Sir,

I received yours of the 30th of June, and had an opportunity soon after to acquaint Lord Rockingham with your obliging and friendly wishes for him and his interests.[29] He desired me to inform you that he is extremely sensible of the value of your friendship and returns it, as he has always done, by reciprocal and very real regards. He is recovered surprisingly, considering the length and heaviness of his disorder. He now thinks of going into Yorkshire within a few days.

---

[28] Dr. James Smith filed a memorial against confirmation of this act.— *Journal of Commissioners*, 369-370.

[29] Delancey's letter not found.

The Colony business, as you see, is to be transacted by a new Secretary of State. Lord Dartmouth has thought fit to accept that office. He has certainly talents for it. When he had the first place at the Board of Trade he acted with those who were real well wishers to the Colonies. He did not then differ with his colleagues, and I hope he still perseveres in sentiments so proper for his situation.

Very extraordinary circumstances attended the resignation of Lord Hillsborough. He went out of office on an idea of his having been over-ruled in a matter immediately and entirely within his department; and he was so over-ruled by some in Council who cannot be considered as holding any station properly ministerial. Such a want of official support seemed at first view to indicate proportionable want of favour in the Closet. However, the moment of his humiliation is made the period of his honour; and while he goes out on account of an official affront in his office, he is advanced to the dignity of an earl.[30]

As to the matter of the contest, I have looked too little into the state of the Ohio grant to risque any judgment upon the merits of it. With regard to the *politics* of the proceeding, if we are to consider the principal actors, one might be inclined to think what was at first generally conjectured: that this opposition to Lord Hillsborough on the grant had been a maneuver of the friends of the late Duke of Bedford, in hopes of getting Lord Weymouth into some office acceptable to him in the jumble and confusion created by such a controversy.[31] If this were their design, they are extremely mistaken in the event, and if any strength is acquired to any of the ministerial factions by this remove, it is to Lord North, who in Lord Dartmouth has acquired the support of a very close family connection of his own;[32] and I am far from sure that the influence which governs everything and, in order to do so, takes care to keep up a balance of power in the Ministry, did not think that the Bed-

---

[30] Hillsborough was overruled in his effort to prevent a group of speculators from acquiring a grant of 2,400,000 acres in the Ohio country. Hitherto an earl in the Irish peerage, Hillsborough was at this time created an earl in the English peerage.

[31] Weymouth at this time was offered the place that Dartmouth accepted, but declined on the ground that he had always opposed the existence of a third secretary of state.—Walpole, *Last journals*, 1: 127.

[32] Dartmouth's mother had become the second wife of North's father, the Earl of Guilford.

ford people were already so strong and that Lord North, who had not a man in the Cabinet he could call his own, was rather too naked for that ostensible load they had given him in public business. Now two capital departments both for figure and patronage are on that side, and consequently so much is detracted from the consequence of those other factions, which are to be preserved in a state of humble existence in the Ministry.

The troops which have been sent from North America are gone upon a different errand from that you supposed. By this I presume you know they have been ordered to the island of St. Vincent's, on that short way of all weak and sinister policy, for the extirpation of that part of the Caribbees called Black Caribbees, who had been for some time established there. They who act in that part were not possessed of the skill of governing them, or perhaps the desire of it; and having found or rather made them troublesome neighbors, they could think of no other method to free themselves from than uneasiness but by removing them by force from their habitations. They are to offer to carry them to some other part of the world. On their refusing to quit their settlements, the troops are ordered to proceed to extremities with those unhappy savages.[33]

I am extremely sorry that my correspondence has not been so pleasing as I could wish to the gentlemen of the Committee. It is very natural that they should desire a correspondent who might contribute to their entertainment by the frequency and agreeableness of his letters. Nobody I am sure can exceed me in regard for those gentlemen to whose good opinion of me I am so very much indebted. It is, however, impossible that I should gratify them in the particulars you mention; and I am persuaded that on a little consideration you will think with me upon the subject. Almost all matters of public concern get immediately into the newspapers. It would not be very respectful to myself, perhaps it would not be very respectful to them, to transcribe what had before appeared fully in print;

---

[33] For several years British authorities in St. Vincent's (acquired from France in 1763) had been negotiating with the natives for a re-allocation of lands for the benefit of white settlers and speculators. The Black Caribs resisting, British forces, including two regiments sent from North America, in April, 1772, compelled the natives to submit. Afterwards some territory of the Red Caribs was assigned to the defeated Black Caribs. Richard Burke, who had bought a large tract of land from the Red Caribs, was to lose a prospective fortune as a result of these events.—Wecter, *Edmund Burke and his kinsmen*, 57-66.

and whatsoever news I might chance to hear, which had not got abroad in so public a manner, it might be either so insufficiently authenticated or so confidentially communicated, that it would be against all prudence and decency to make it the subject of a correspondence of office. In my situation nothing can be so contrary to all decorum and all attention to my own character, as to commit myself in such letters for opinions of men, except where the discharge of my duty did not [sic] essentially require it. My letters, therefore, to the Committee of Correspondence must continue to be merely official, though such letters must be dry and unpleasant enough by their own nature even in better hands than mine. Neither will the same sense of propriety suffer me to write more frequently than business requires; and business, I assure you, shall never be either neglected or over-done by me. That I might not be mistaken in my ideas of propriety in this matter, when I did myself the honour of accepting the trust your Colony was so very obliging as to repose in me, I took the opinion of my friend Mr. Jackson, a very sensible and informed man as any we have and who had been engaged for several years in affairs of this nature. I did not find from him that more than I have mentioned was at all expected. However, as it is in all delegated powers the sense of the principal which ought to prevail, if my notion on this subject should be different from theirs, and that they think this mode of acting does not come up to what they look for from the person they honour with their confidence here, I shall wish them to employ a person more pleasing to them and more capable of rendering them the service that is acceptable to them; having great pleasure in obeying their orders as long as I am entirely agreeable to them, but not a moment longer. You will therefore be so good as to inform me whether the gentlemen do require letters of political facts and speculations as a part of the official correspondence; for if they do, it is with great pain to myself that I shall be obliged to acquaint them with my inability to comply with anything they desire. I make, as you see by the course of this letter, as well as by that of others I have wrote to you, a great difference between what I write to a friend (which I do with all freedom and confidence), and what must pass through the course of office. But I have troubled you enough on that subject.

I am obliged to you for accepting the power of attorney.

I send it to you by this conveyance. With regard to the bill of contingent and extra expenses, I cannot prevail upon myself to make them out further than my actual expenditure. If the plan I mentioned to you formerly be impracticable, the Province will be exonerated of that part of the expense.[34] In my situation I cannot think it right for me to make out such accounts, and therefore shall not trouble Mr. Charles upon that occasion.[35] If I accept the salary, which I am informed is not the most considerable advantage of the employment, and which you know is a small object to me, it is solely lest I should hurt the delicacy of any gentleman who might succeed to the office, by putting him under difficulties in accepting of that emolument which another had declined.

I forgot to mention when I spoke of correspondence that I had written to the Speaker. I did write by the pacquet, and I believe my letter to him was as long as the letter I now trouble you with. I should be extremely concerned if I could appear but for a moment guilty of the least apparent disregard of a gentleman for whom I have so very sincere a respect; indeed, I esteem his character extremely upon every account. Shall I flatter myself with the hope of seeing you and Mrs. Delancey in England? It would give me very real pleasure as I am with the greatest truth and affection, My Dear Sir,

Your most obedient and faithful humble servant

E. B.

I find no opposition as yet made to the Harlem Township Act.[36] That of Wawayenda is like to meet with difficulties. Dr. Smith has given Mr. Pownall notice that a caveat will be entered against it; possibly the other may also be opposed. I have received a letter from Mr. Wickham informing me that orders have been given relative to the expenses. I have not however yet received the money. What is more material, I have not received a line of instructions concerning the defense of either these bills or the objections which may be made to them; nor has anybody attended me with the least idea on the subject. This is indeed of the less importance, as I am told at the Board

---

[34] Refers to a communication that has not been found.
[35] Mr. Charles not identified.
[36] An Act to settle and establish the line . . . between the City of New York and the Township of Harlem.—*Colonial Laws of New York* 5: 532-537.

of Trade that it is so difficult if not impossible to get the officers of state and the placemen to attend, that there is no hope of doing business in the summer.

As this is a letter relative (too much so) to charges and expenses, permit me to suggest to you that I have employed a gentleman as my clerk, who is very useful to me in your business. He has hitherto stood me in about four score pounds a year. If the Province think fit to allow for that expense, I shall be obliged to them. If not I shall continue him at my own.

By the *Lady Gage Palmer*

To the Gentlemen of the Committee of Correspondence at New York

August 20. 1772

Gentlemen,

The King having appointed Lord Dartmouth to be Secretary of State for the Colonies and first Commissioner of Trade and Plantations, in the room of Lord Hillsborough who has resigned, I waited on his Lordship officially, but not having met him at home, I will take an early opportunity of repeating my visit and recommending to his particular care and attention the business of your Colony.

The cause of Lord Hillsborough's resignation [it] is said was the preference given to the opinion of others in Council over his in a matter within his particular department,—the new Patent for a settlement on the Ohio. However, I understand that his Lordship has not resigned in discontent, but will continue earnestly to support that system in which he has not chosen to act, and in consequence of his practicability and good humour has received distinguished marks of the King's favour.

This change and the difficulty of getting an attendance of the officers of the Crown during the summer will prevent any decision of the matters now under consideration of the Board of Trade. As soon as the Board enters upon business I shall take particular care of the acts which you have more particularly recommended. I must entreat that you may add to my zeal for your service the ability of serving you with effect, by sending me such materials of fact and argument as may enable me in all disputed cases to answer objections and instruct council. Without this I can proceed only in a general way, and consequently fall very short of the true merits of the case. In cases where the acts are private and therefore more the concern of individuals, it appears to me that it might facilitate business if the parties in whose favour such bills are, should of course transmit an abstract of the grounds and principles on which the bill went, together with a solution of the objections against it.

I take the liberty of reminding you again of the return to the Commission for the Boundary Line. I believe this business will proceed very dully without it. I hope the gentlemen of New Jersey will make no unnecessary delay. I am with the greatest respect and esteem,

Gentlemen etc.

E. B.

20 August 1772
To the Gentlemen of the Committee of Correspondence at New York

Duplicate by the October Packet.

By the October [1772] packet
To James Duane Esqr. New York

Sir,

I have duly received your letter of the 2nd of August, and am much flattered by the obliging sentiments you are so kind to entertain of me and of the endeavours to serve the public.

So able and satisfactory a performance as the Memorial on the Canadian Grants stands in no need of an apology for its length.[37] I can discern no other works of the profession in it but what appears in the extraordinary accuracy and diligence with which it is drawn up. I trust that the strong reasons which it contains will be prevalent with the Council. Instructed as I now am, I shall certainly support the rights of the Province and of those who derive under its authority with all my power. The Board of Trade have not for some time done any business, nor do I think any material will be done for the month to come, or even before Christmas. However, as I am acquainted with the [   ][38] in which the Board will give its affairs, I shall

---

[37] Duane's letter and memorial not found.
[38] Space left blank in original.

take care to lose no opportunity. When you have further commands I shall be very happy in being honoured with them, and of taking every occasion of showing the attention and regard which are due to a character in all respects as valuable as yours.

I have the honour to be etc.

E. B.

P. S.

The maps have not yet come to my hands. I suppose on further inquiry I may receive them. I have sometime since procured a map which will answer our purposes tolerably well.

To James Duane Esqr. New York
   (By the October 1772 packet)

———————

By the January 1773 packet
To the Gentlemen of the Committee of Correspondence at New York

Gentlemen,

As soon as the Board of Trade met, I attended Lord Dartmouth upon the Wawayenda and Harlem affairs, as well as on the French claims. With regard to the former, all I could do was to postpone any adverse proceeding on them; because I have not been furnished with any matter in defense of either of them, and a caveat is entered against one. I did not choose to suffer a decisive hearing on a matter so affecting to the rights of individuals as well as to the public without being able to instruct council in a manner sufficient to give the defense to your acts its full weight. I have already suggested my wishes, that along with every bill likely to be contested, the principal matters of fact and the leading arguments of justice or policy which were the grounds of that bill, should be transmitted to me. The same caution I hope will be used with regard to every attempt likely to be made against your interests. This has been done in a very ample and very satisfactory manner with regard to the Canadian Grants.[39]

———————

[39] The minutes of the Board of Trade for Nov. 12, 1772, contain the following: "Mr. Edmund Burke attended, and moved their lordships, that he might be heard by his counsel, as well in behalf of the province of New York, as of sundry persons, proprietors of lands within the said province under grants from the Governor and Council thereof, against the confirmation by the Crown of any grants made by the French King, or the Government of Canada within the limits of the said province of New York."—*Journal of Commissioners,* 323.

I had a good deal of discourse both with Lord Dartmouth and with Mr. Pownall on the subject. My point was to satisfy them of the prudence of not pushing these Canadian demands in the Province of New York to the detriment of grantees who had on all accounts a prior claim of merit, as well as to the prejudice of the honour and interest of this Kingdom, which requires that our ancient limits should be settled according to the rights of Great Britain and not according to the pretensions of France. I found them very reasonable and, as I imagined, well disposed in the matter. They thought that the case of some of these grantees might be deserving of compassion and that it would be most advisable to compensate them, either by new grants in Canada or by such in New York as would not stir dangerous objections on territorial limits or affect the property of meritorious individuals. I believe they very greatly inclined to some compromise of this sort. But it seems the French grantees (or rather I suppose the English who have purchased their titles) are very urgent for their confirmation and press for an immediate hearing, in confidence of some support with which I am not so well acquainted; for I can hardly imagine that they would otherwise choose to stake their all upon the mere legal limits of the question, without leaving themselves any claim upon the equity and compassion of Government which they might ensure by a conciliatory and graceful concession.

I postponed this hearing because I would if possible save the half-pay officers the charge, and because Sir George Younge,[40] who has a claim which is swallowed up in these grants, may bear his part of the charge if it should become necessary. He is not yet come to town.

We have had some business in Parliament. Two things were recommended in the King's speech: the rendering of provisions cheap, in which it is not in our power to do anything; and the India affairs, in which it is both in our power and, I am afraid, in our will to do too much. We have as yet taken no steps to redress disorder in the Company's settlements. We have only aimed at taking their affairs out of their own hands, in order to vest them where I doubt the management may not be the better but where the danger to the remaining independence of Parliament will be very great and serious. After the recess the House will proceed upon their accounts. The

---

[40] Probably Sir George Yonge, member of Parliament and later secretary at war.

short result for them is this: their trade is much greater than it ever has been, and it is continually increasing; but the money which Government under various pretexts has taken and still demands from them amounts to such sums as neither this nor probably any increase in trade can bear.

Their servants in India have also made great waste of their revenue. This has been one cause of their distress, but the least considerable, because even though their proceedings had been as honest and as careful as they ought to have been, bullion which is an article of export from Europe to India can hardly in its own species be remitted from India into Europe. Besides, this would exhaust and indeed ruin Bengal, from whence the supply of this very treasure is to arise. The method of transmitting it to Europe in goods has gone to all the extents which the demands of trade (regulated as trade is at present) can possibly bear. They have already the supply of three years' sales of tea in their warehouses. The subject before Parliament is nice and critical, as well as extremely important. But I fear the temper of the public is not quite as proper upon this subject as upon others. The great fortunes made by persons in the Company's service has raised a great envy; the effects of which fall on the Company, who is the sufferer by the method in which their fortunes are made; and dangerous precedents are established with regard to that body in this ill temper of the public, that are applicable to the subjects at large.

Several dealers in corn complain of our method of settling the assize of bread; which is so ill constituted that when we import foreign flour it does not come within the description of the sorts prescribed in the act. This mistake will be set to right with some advantage to the trade, and possibly with some relief to the poor, as long as the importation of flour is admitted.

As to foreign affairs, they are little thought of. I have the honour to be,

Gentlemen,
Your most obedient humble servant

E. B.

Beaconsfield
31 December 1772
To the Gentlemen of the Committee of Correspondence at New York

By the January 1773 packet
To James Delanc[e]y Esqr. New York

Dear Sir,

I have written two letters to you, one to the Committee of Correspondence besides that which I send by this packet, and one to the Speaker, since I had the pleasure of hearing from you. It was indeed of the less consequence both on one side and on the other, as the late change in the department of the Colonies rendered it impossible that anything material should be done for some time. However, I always wish—I shall trouble you to have it done as a matter of advantage to the Colony—that a little abstract of the merits of the question should be sent with every act likely to be opposed here, either on the part of private people or of the Crown; and if the business may grow into a serious controversy, that you will arm me with the fullest instructions and proofs. Unless I am so supplied I cannot serve you as I ought.

The Parliament met earlier than usual this year. When Ministry have a point to carry this early meeting is of consequence to them. The spirited but undisciplined troops of an independent opposition will never make such a figure in an early muster, as the well formed and well paid bands of the Court. They have at length compassed what they have long intended. They have taken so much money from the East India Company by the composition for the dewanees and by the tea agreement (more than three millions) that they have fairly run the Company aground for cash. The Ministry have taken advantage of this difficulty to bring the matter in Parliament, and there their first act was to appoint a secret committee,—the first that ever was attempted without a charge of delinquency. By this means no opposition could be made to the leading steps of their attacks on the rights of charters. The people have been amused for several sessions with the hopes of some useful regulations in India, but nothing further is meant than to vest the immense patronage of office, now in the hands of the Company, in those of the Crown. It has been proposed entirely to suspend the Company's dividend in order that the proprietors may become the more tractable and submissive to Government in this attempt on their charter privileges. I find no other business of much consequence as yet proposed in Parliament. There was an intention last summer of paying about 300,000 pounds of the Civil List debt. But the difficulties into which they have brought the East India Company's cash, by which 400,000 pounds a year is for some time lost to the Exchequer, disable them from the attempt.[41] Under these circumstances no one thing would go so far in making them unpopular. Our friend Lord Rockingham is not yet come to town. Though his health has been improving for the greatest part of the summer, it was necessary that he should keep for some time out of the bustle of business in order to restore him to his original strength. This has in great measure happened; so that I flatter myself he will be in town after the holidays at least as well as he has been for some years—a matter of importance to the public as well as to his friends. I am etc.

E. B.

You will be so obliging as to remember the horses which I formerly mentioned to you.

(Private)

To John Cruger Esqr. Speaker of the Assembly New York

16 April 1773

Dear Sir,

I am honoured with your letter of the 2nd of February in which you express a wish that Mr. Henry Cruger may have leave to resign his place in Council in favor of his son.[42] As this business relates to the arrangement and satisfaction of your family, it became particularly interesting to me. I directly applied, and it is with pleasure I inform you that I received the most favorable answer; so that I have little doubt but that

---

[41] The East India Company in 1767 had been obligated to pay 400,000 pounds annually to the government in order to retain the territorial revenues of Bengal. Subsequently Lord North had forced an arrangement for payment of tea duties in England which worked badly for the Company. Cf. Sutherland, L. S., *The East India Company in eighteenth-century politics*, 216, 227.

[42] The original and a duplicate of Cruger's letter are among the Wentworth-Fitzwilliam MSS.

I shall be able to send you a proper authority for the appointment by next pacquet. Though as the thing is not yet done, it will be prudent to take no step until the order arrives. I hope the same pacquet will also carry the confirmation of some of the bills which you are most anxious for. I have hastened Mr. Jackson's report; it will soon be made, and it will be favourable.

Our recess for Easter is but short. Before the adjournment Lord North moved a call of the house which will be strictly enforced. We are to be kept sitting the greatest part of the summer. It is very unusual for a minister to move a call of the house. This therefore has given rise to many and various conjectures. Some think a payment of the King's debts is intended. In the present state of the finances, though I know that the Civil List is distressed, I cannot persuade myself that they intend to make application for such a payment. Others imagine that this solemnity is intended for the communication of the project of a French alliance against the three partitioning Powers. The partition of Poland is certainly mischievous to us in the immediate act, and may in future be prejudicial to the balance of power in Europe. The mistaken politics and the supine neglect of our Court with regard to all the affairs of the continent have brought us to this pass, that we must be tame spectators of this act of violence, or join in an alliance with those whom we have most reason to fear, without much probability of success even by that measure, considering the situation of the theatre of war. The consequence either of victory or defeat in such a conjunction must be almost equally mischievous.

For my own part, I do not believe that such an alliance is at all resolved on, notwithstanding the positive assertions that are so generally current. The Ministry is so strangely composed that they hardly can take any step of a *decided* nature, even though it were less contrary to the general inclinations of our people, and less dangerous to those who undertook to manage it, upon the least possible failure. If anything could bring our Court to a determination of joining with France, it must be the King of Prussia's menacing Hanover. It is not very probable that Austria could be so overseen as to countenance him in such a scheme. At his time of life, I should think he would rather wish to establish and to improve a conquest which he has achieved without any expense of blood or treasure, than want only to draw a war upon himself from those who are otherwise disposed or necessitated to let him enjoy his usurpation in peace.

I take the call of the House to mean no more than the desire the Ministry have of securing the sanction of a full house for the completion of the measures by which they have brought the East India Company, even for their dividend, into an entire dependence upon the Crown. The opposition to their schemes in violation to that company was so weak that we did not venture to divide upon them. The popular madness coincides with the Court politics; and so blind and undistinguishing are the public prejudices, and so bitter are the dispositions in the Company itself, that if the Court uses any apparent moderation, it arises rather from difficulties in the object than from any fear of resistance to their designs.

In all other respects things continue as they have been: the same balance among the Ministers, the same influence in the Closet as far as may be collected from every appearance. I am sorry that the Ministers could be so ill advised as to order the persons guilty of the outrage on the King's vessel in America to England for trial. I am really sorry too that a certain carelessness (that looks almost like a countenance to such acts) in bringing delinquents to punishment in the ordinary and proper way, furnishes the enemies of America with anything like a plausible pretext for such a very improper mode of proceeding. In the first instance, no principle can justify the use of it, nor until every other method has failed.[43] I see with sorrow too that the indiscretions of both sides in one of your neighboring colonies has introduced discussions that ought forever to be buried in silence.[44] I am with the greatest truth and regard,

Dear Sir,

---

[43] H. M. S. *Gaspee*, operating against smugglers, had been attacked and burned in Narragansett Bay on June 9, 1772. No culprits were apprehended and taken to England for trial.

[44] The dispute raised in Massachusetts between Governor Hutchinson and the assembly when announcement was made that the governor and crown officials would in future be paid by the crown instead of having their salaries appropriated by the colony legislature. Samuel Adams provoked a debate between Hutchinson and the assembly on constitutional questions.

Your most obedient and obliged humble servant

E. B.

Beaconsfield 16 April 1773
To John Cruger Esqr. Speaker of the Assembly New York.

To the Gentlemen of the Committee of Correspondence at New York

16 April 1773

Gentlemen,

I am honoured with your information and your command by your letter dated the 1st of March.[45]

I am particularly pleased with the transmiss of the Commission and the proceedings thereon with the copy of the New Jersey Act, as I am persuaded from my conversations with Mr. Jackson, as well as with the acting persons of the Board of Trade, that very little further delay will be given to laws so necessary to the repose and settlement of the two Colonies, and now so happily brought to a conclusion by the amicable dispositions of the parties interested.

The acts have not yet been referred to Council. I applied to the Board of Trade that no time might be lost in making the reference; and I requested of Mr. Jackson, as soon as he should receive it, to expedite his report. I received very satisfactory and obliging answers upon both points. You may depend upon it that I shall omit no means of securing and hastening the success of this useful measure.[46]

Mr. Jackson's report is ready upon the act for the recovery of small debts. I found that doubts had been entertained upon the policy of such acts, as tending rather to increase litigation than to support a proper credit, or to further justice. Besides the powers given in the acts were generally esteemed too great for the little solemnity in the process, the rapidity of the determination, and the quality and number of the magistrates. But as the object is not new, and the sum determinable in this

---

[45] Letter not found.

[46] The Board of Trade on May 27 reported favorably on the acts passed in New York and New Jersey fixing the boundary of the two colonies.—*Journal of Commissioners*, 360.

summary method not great, after discussing the matter we at length agreed in opinion. A favorable report will be made, and I flatter myself the paquet will convey to you the King's approbation of that act.[47]

As to the Wawayenda and Harlem Acts, I have endeavored to bring them to a hearing. But as there are other parties, this has not been so much in my powers; but before the recess of the Board of Trade I have no doubt of doing it. As the proceeding in this case is similar to a law suit, it is impossible for me to do more than superintend it. I have therefore put the affair into the hands of my attorney, Mr. Hickey, an eminent solicitor, to be conducted under my direction.[48] I have not called upon the gentleman to whom I am authorized to apply for the charges of the Wawayenda suit, nor shall I trouble him until Mr. Hickey's bill of costs shall be made out. The Harlem Act is put into the same hands; the money I have received shall be employed to defray whatever charges may happen.[49]

I have some expense for a clerk who is necessary to me in your business. He has hitherto been at my own charges. I suggested this to a member of your Assembly, leaving it to your choice whether you will let him continue so, or allow him the sum I mentioned; that is, £ 80 a year.[50] This I do by no means press. Your house will act in the manner they think most advisable for the Province, and I shall be perfectly satisfied with their determination. I am with the highest esteem and regard,

Gentlemen,

Your most obedient humble servant

E. B.

Beaconsfield. 16. April. 1773.

---

[47] *Supra*, to Cruger, June 30, 1772; *infra*, to committee of correspondence, July 2, 1773.

[48] Joseph Hickey, one of Burke's close friends. The Board of Trade minutes for June 14, 1773, contain the following: "Read a memorial of Joseph Hickey to the Board, praying that he may be heard by Counsel in support of an Act passed in New York in 1772, *for dividing and setting apart such land in the Patent of Wawayenda* etc., if it shall be judged necessary."—*Journal of Commissioners*, 363.

[49] The Harlem Act was recommended for confirmation on July 16, 1773.

[50] *Supra*, to Delancey, Aug. 20, 1772.

By the July 1773 packet

To the Gentlemen of the Committee of Correspondence at
New York

2nd July 1773

Gentlemen,

You will receive confirmation of the act for adjusting your
boundaries on the side of New Jersey, and I congratulate you
on the happy termination of that controversy.

I earnestly wish and do indeed hope that your other limitary
disputes may be adjusted in a manner so satisfactory.[51] With
regard to what relates to New Hampshire, Mr. Pownall told
me that the Board will adhere strictly to the boundary formerly
established in your favour. I mean that of the River Connecticut. But so far as the settlers upon your side of that river are
concerned, their lordships are of opinion that in consideration
of the improvements that are made, these settlers ought to be
confirmed in their possession notwithstanding the invalidity
of their original title. On asking to what extent, or in what
proportion to their claims that equitable indulgence in consequence of settlement was to go, I found that the Lords of
Trade had not come to any precise determination on that part
of the subject; but they conceived that the Province could not
consider itself as injured, if they were allowed lands to any
extent which the King might think reasonable, as his Majesty
is as much at liberty to grant within the one province as within
the other.

These are the present sentiments of the Board which I
thought necessary to state to you in order to receive your
further instructions. In the meantime, I do not apprehend
that any step will be taken which can finally affect your rights
without my having an early information of it; and in that case
I shall not be negligent of your interests.

Some days since I received a letter from the Secretary of
the Board of Trade wishing to know on whose behalf and on

---

[51] He had received a number of communications from New York which
survive among the Wentworth-Fitzwilliam MSS: a short letter from Cruger,
April 6; a letter from Duane about the Canadian and Hampshire grants, April 7;
a letter from Delancey, April 7, and one from the committee of correspondence,
April 8. The last concerned assembly legislation and the dispute over the
Hampshire grants.

what question I desired that counsel should be heard against the Canadian grants on Lake Champlain.[52] I returned for answer, that I would have counsel heard on behalf of the grantees under New York Government, who are in a great measure composed of half-pay officers; and that I was instructed by you to take care of the interests of these grantees, not only so far as they are concerned, but so far as the territorial rights of the Province may be affected by the admission of the French claims; that with regard to the question on which I desired to be heard, I requested that counsel might not be restrained, but might be admitted to speak to all such matters as the parties should advise as proper for invalidating the French grants and establishing those under New York. This letter was written on the 15th June.[53]

I have since had a long conference with Mr. Pownall, and yesterday had an audience at the Board of Trade upon the same subject. Lord Dartmouth told me, that the question between the claimants under Canada and New York being a matter of law which might come judicially by an appeal before the Council, it was not proper for the Board to determine prematurely and extrajudicially upon it; that all that they should do, and this they thought themselves bound to do, would be merely as the King's Council, who were obliged, by the faith of treaties, to see that those who derived under that of Paris, had justice done to them; that whatever shall be done in their favour will be passed with an express reservation that it should not be in prejudice to any of the ancient rights or claims of the Crown. As therefore such act of confirmation will only respect the possession, and only operated to secure the Canada grantees against any disturbance on the part of Government, the New York grantees who have other claims are free to defend themselves at law; which defense their lordships did not imagine could be precluded by anything the Board meant to do on the occasion. He was of opinion that on the state of the matter it would be unnecessary to hear counsel.

I could by no means form a distinct idea, either from what I heard at the Board or from my private conversations with Mr. Pownall, of the plan which they meant to pursue. But I was very sure, that no step could be taken towards giving the

---

[52] *Cf. Journal of Commissioners,* 362.
[53] Printed in *N. Y. documents* 8: 378.

French titles any sort of effect, without manifest prejudice to those persons who claim under New York. I was the more confirmed in this opinion, because I found that the Canadian claimants refused to take out new grants by which they might be fully reprised in value (even in the same Province) without prejudice to the rights of others, or giving rise to political discussion of the most delicate nature. And I must add that I saw no disposition in the Board to drive them to the expedient of a new grant.

With these ideas, I told my Lord Dartmouth that if the Council left the affair to the course of law without the intervention of any act of theirs, I had nothing more to desire. The claimants on both sides would then be upon an exact equality. But that if any act of ratification of what kind so ever was to pass from authority in favor of the Canadian grants, I must oppose that act in the first instance; because although it might be conceived in such terms as not directly to attack the rights of the New York grantees, yet if it did directly affect them by furnishing matter of inference and argument against those rights, it must be highly injurious to the grantees who derive under you. This early opposition I conceive to be the more necessary, because any act giving a previous sanction to the Canada claims by that very Council who were to decide ultimately on the appeal, would be if not absolute prejudication, yet would furnish upon any future trial a strong presumption against the rights you wish to support.

On this representation, the Board, with that fairness which I must say I have always observed in them, agreed that it was proper counsel should be heard. They find it difficult to get a sufficient number of their colleagues together at this time of the year for that purpose. But Lord Dartmouth said he would endeavor to have the matter ready for an hearing in the course of this month, and desired that counsel should be prepared on their part. Accordingly, two eminent barristers, Mr. Skinner and Mr. Lee, are retained.

Mr. Jackson has not yet reported on the Wawayenda and Harlem Acts. As soon as he can be got to report and the Board to sit, no time shall be lost in bringing them to an hearing. I know their importance, but there is no getting them forward with that expedition which we wish.

The bill for recovery of small debts I have the pleasure to

tell you is allowed.[54] But as it is in force and that no disallow-ance is to be apprehended, Mr. Pownall does not think that you need be at the expense of the fees for a final confirmation.

The bill against lotteries is rejected, the powers given by that bill to the justice of peace being thought unreasonable and above the competence of a magistrate of that degree.[55]

The session is ended. The East India Company's political and financial affairs are put into the hands of the Crown, but I am much afraid with little benefit either to the Crown or to the public, if the mere increase of Court influence is not to be reckoned a national advantage. The framers of the new bill of regulation do not seem to be perfectly satisfied with their work. Undoubtedly it is very crude and confused, and leaves to the Company too much or too little authority. Changes are to be made in the plan, but I apprehend they will all be further infractions of the charter and further additions to the power of the Crown. I have the honour to be,

Gentlemen,

Your most obedient humble servant

E. B.

Westminster 2d. July 1773

By the August packet
To James Delancey Esqr.

Beaconsfield. August 2d. 1773

Dear Sir,

It is now a good while since I had any matter worth trou-bling you with. Nothing occurred which required a private and confidential explanation, or you should have heard from me upon it, and largely as well as freely. The public business has gone on its own train, not so rapidly as we could wish, but as successfully as we had reason to expect. Most of the material acts which had been in arrear are allowed; and I trust the same good event will in its own time attend those which are still

---

[54] *Colonial Laws of New York* 5: 304-314; *supra*, to Cruger, June 30, 1772.

[55] At the same time *An Act to prevent Infectious distempers etc* also was reported for disallowance. It is curious that Burke neither mentioned this nor so much as alluded to a series of other acts to which the committee of cor-respondence had asked that he give special attention.—Wentworth-Fitzwilliam MSS, committee to Burke, April 8, 1773.

under consideration. Your Province is invested on every side.
You have quieted your New Jersey controversy, but others remain. With regard to what relates to the Canada controversy,
we have so far prevailed that nothing adverse has been as yet
determined by the Board; which in our situation, where we
are on the defensive, is all that we can desire. It is true that
I observed in the audience I had of the Lords of Trade they
are strongly inclined to the French claimants; but they will
find difficulties of no small magnitude in the attempt to do
anything decisive in their favor. I fancy that these claimants
are not so strong upon their merits as upon the interest of some
old British subjects who have become purchasers of the titles
of many of them, as I am told. I have given a particular account
of that transaction to the Committee of Correspondence.

You see that the Harlem Act has passed.[56]   Mr. Jackson
has reported favourably for that of Wawayenda. I had concluded that the Board had approved it, and Mr. Pownall told
me so; mistaking it, I suppose, for the Harlem Act. Under
this opinion, I told Col. Skene, who interests himself for the
gentlemen concerned in that patent, that it has actually past
[sic]; but I was misinformed in the manner I have told you,
and you will be so good as to let Mr. Wickham know how this
error arose, if Col. Skene should communicate to him my information.[57] I find by the Colonel's conversation that the
gentlemen concerned are apprehensive that I have neglected
their business. I am sorry that they should entertain so groundless a notion. They must know by very long experience that
the Board which has the business of so many Colonies on its
hands can scarcely be other than slow, especially as the only
time in which the Lords can be got to attend is that in which
the business of Parliament is also going on. It is no wonder
that those who are deeply interested in any particular business
before them should think it lingers. But I must observe to you
that it is my constant maxim in any affair entrusted to me
rather to look to its final success than to its speedy decision.
If I had hurried Mr. Jackson's report, which was not made till
the 22nd of July, I had run the risque of one that might be

---

[56] Recommended for allowance on July 16.

[57] Col. Philip Skene, who served under Sir Jeffrey Amherst and acquired in
1765 a large property in the region just south of Lake Champlain where he
settled a number of families and founded Skenesborough.—*N. Y. documents* **8:**
415-416.

neutral, or perhaps not favorable. I have always observed that his report has, as it ought to have, great weight with the Board; and indeed in most cases is decisive. I transmit to you a copy of that report, not to be publicly used or put out of your hands, but for the satisfaction of the gentlemen who are anxious about an affair of importance. I took care that the first steps should be favorable, which in all these matters is a considerable point, and that Mr. Jackson's mind should receive, when it was at leisure to receive it, a proper impression of the business. Consistently with this plan, I could not proceed with more rapidity, nor, I am persuaded, agreeably to any other rational plan. It is impossible to get these matters through more expeditiously. I hope the Province has no reason to be dissatisfied, as most of their bills have been allowed.

I flatter myself that the Speaker has no reason to think I delayed in his brother's business. Not a single moment's time has been lost. My Lord Dartmouth and Mr. Pownall used me with much personal kindness on the occasion. I hope Mr. Cruger has received my letters on the occasion, and that his mandamus has got safe to you.

Lord Rockingham is perfectly well; he has written to you lately. I am with the greatest truth and affection,

> My Dear Sir,
>
> Your most obedient and humble servant
>
> E. B.

Beaconsfield August 2. 1773
Can you do anything for me relative to the pacers? [59]
To James Delancey Esqr. New York

To the Gentlemen of the Committee of Correspondence at New York
By the August packet

Gentlemen,   Beaconsfield. August 2. 1773

I have the honour of transmitting to you a copy of the

[59] "I have been most of the Winter looking out for Horses and I have not yet been able to meet with such as would answer your purpose but expect to get them as soon as the New England men will be down whenever our European vessels arrive and we expect them every day when I make no doubt of purchasing them time enough to have them sent next month."—Delancey to Burke, April 7, 1773.

representation of the Board of Trade to the King approving the Harlem Act.

That for the division of lands in the Wawayenda Patent is not yet passed the Board; neither will anything, I presume, be done in that or any business until the Board of Trade, which has now a recess for some time, shall meet again. I was in a manner certain that this business would be happily concluded before this. I omitted nothing in my power to expedite it which was consistent with the proper means for securing its final success. I have the satisfaction to inform you that Mr. Jackson has at length made his report as favorably to that act as can be desired; I am prepared to resist Dr. Smith's attack, if he should think it advisable to persist in his resolution of making one.[60] I am in no small hopes that this act will be represented for allowance immediately on the meeting of the Board.

With regard to the affair of the French grants and the Hampshire Boundary, nothing has been done since my last, when I had the honour of transmitting to you a full account of that affair. I shall be as vigilant as the weight of these matters requires, and I shall carefully transmit to you accounts of what is done, when anything is done that has any relation to them. I am with the greatest esteem,

     Gentlemen,

        Your most obedient and humble servant

               E. B.

Beaconsfield August 2. 1773
To the Gentlemen of the Committee of Correspondence at
   New York.

To the Gentlemen of the Committee of Correspondence.
   New York.

                 December 7. 1773

Gentlemen,

As soon as the Lords of Trade had met I endeavored to bring forward the business of the Wawayenda Patent Act.[61] Doctor Smith had taken no steps during the recess of the Board

---

[60] *Supra*, to W. Wickham, July 2, 1773.
[61] Cf. *Journal of Commissioners*, 369-370.

towards a serious opposition to it. So that as his petition appeared rather a vexatious and dilatory measure, than a matter of weighty objection to that act, I gave notice that I would desire an hearing on it immediately. Their lordships have allowed him until Thursday the 9th instant to appear to make good his allegations. If he does not appear that day, they will report the bill as proper to be passed. If he should appear, a day will be appointed for an hearing and counsel will be properly instructed. I know the importance of the act to the property of many individuals, and shall omit nothing in my power to procure it the royal allowance. A copy of Dr. Smith's petition has been sent to Mr. Wickham through Col. Skene during the last summer.

I hope you have received the act for the boundary with New Jersey, and that for Harlem Township.

The Parliament is to meet on the 13th January. The Ministers give out that we are to have no material business before us during this session. They say that the East India Company is resolved to obtain the favour of Government by humility and submission. Indeed, the privileges left to that body are so very few, that it is little able, if it were never so much disposed, to give any effectual opposition.

In the Parliament of Ireland there has been a great deal of agitation. The finances of that kingdom were much deranged, and it afforded the Ministers an occasion for suggesting themselves, or for approving some private suggestion, of a project which seemed to strike directly at the principle of the unity and order of this Empire. It was a tax on the landed property in Ireland of those resident here. There was something plausible in this idea in a narrow view and upon superficial consideration. But though Government there supported it as much underhand as they could, and in public as much as they dared, it was rejected by the Parliament there.[62]

Endeavors have been used here to raise mercantile credit, but though it is something recovered it is as yet by no means restored to its former height and vigour.

Your business which remains with me not yet dispatched

[62] Rockingham and those of his political friends who were large proprietors in Ireland energetically opposed a tax on the revenues of absentee landlords that was brought forward in the Irish Parliament with the connivance of the English government. Burke's opinion that the measure would tend to dismember the Anglo-Irish community was set forth in his Letter to Sir Charles Bingham, Works 9: 134-147.

shall be prosecuted with as much expedition as circumstances will admit. I have the honour to be, with the greatest esteem and regard,

　　　　Gentlemen,

　　　　　　Your most obedient and very humble servant,

　　　　　　　　　　　　　　　　　　　　　E. B.

London December 7. 1773

P. S. When I wrote above, the temper of the Company since its late constitution had not been tried. This day the first experiment was attempted on the new modelled body. A set of instructions had been prepared for the Parliament Commissioners who are to govern India; these instructions were calculated to surrender to the Commissioners the few powers reserved to the Company. They passed the Directors, but the General Court which met this day, animated (which I confess I did not expect) with the full spirit of their predecessors, rejected these instructions, and appointed a committee of their own to draw new ones. The Duke of Richmond is at the head of the committee.[63]

　　　　　　　　　　　　　　　　　　　　　E. B.

10 at night
To the Committee of Correspondence at New York
Duplicate by the January 1774 packet.

————————

To William Wickham Esqr. New York
5. January. 1774

Sir,

I am honoured with your letter of the 7th of November.[64] Your business has been attended with all the diligence in my power. A very able and active solicitor has been employed; counsels were retained and instructed and we were prepared to meet Dr. Smith in such a manner as [we] had reason to believe would have rendered his opposition fruitless. I trans-

————————

63 Charles Lennox, 3rd Duke of Richmond, usually acted in alliance with Rockingham, and for more than a year had led a body of East India Company proprietors in resistance to domination by the crown. He was defeated in the effort to which Burke here alludes.—Sutherland, L. S., *The East India Company*, 266-267.

64 Preserved among the Wentworth-Fitzwilliam MSS.

mitted to Mr. Delancey the report of Mr. Jackson's counsel to the Board of Trade for your perusal, in order to remove any uneasiness you might have conceived at the delay. My letters to him which accompanied that paper stated my mode of proceeding, with my reasons first.[65]

When Dr. Smith was called upon and a day assigned to him, which was the 9th of last month, to be heard by counsel in support of the allegations in his petition, he chose to decline it, and thereby did, I think, in effect but not nominally withdraw the petition. As therefore no opponent, or what ought to be considered as none, appears, I have reason to be satisfied that your acts will be among the first reported for the royal allowance after the Christmas recess. And it is not unlikely that the next pacquet at furthest will convey to you this intelligence.

Dr. Smith's petition was sent to you through Col. Skene.

The memorial which you transmitted with your letter of the 7th November was very able and satisfactory. But I trust we shall have no occasion to present it. However, a copy has been put into Mr. Pownall's hands. I am with the greatest regard and esteem, Sir,

Your most obedient and humble servant

E. B.

London 5. January. 1774
To William Wickham Esqr.

New York by the January 1774 packet

To the Gentlemen of the Committee of Correspondence at
New York
January 5. 1774

Gentlemen,

Since my last, the duplicate of which I have the honour to transmit to you by this pacquet, very little new has occurred in your affairs, or in those of this kingdom. What may appear on the opening of the session is not yet known. The Ministry are either very reserved, or have found no plan. Their own internal arrangement has received no alteration. Of foreign

---

[65] *Supra,* to Delancey, Aug. 2, 1773.

politics, if there be not a total disregard, there is a deep silence. In Ireland they are successful in the general matter of supply, but very unsettled and very indifferent about everything else. It is understood (but the authority is not very certain) that in this session they mean to resume the consideration of the East India Company, but less as a subject of regulation than of patronage. Their plan will be, if they have any plan, to add something new to the powers of the King's Commissioners and Judges; and particularly to the whole of the military power in the former, out of the control or interference of the Company. They will probably name a Commander in chief by act of Parliament, if the Company should not save the appearance of their privilege by surrendering the substance of it. One of the military commissioners will probably be forced upon them. Whether the affairs of the American Colonies at large or of any part of them will be brought before us, or upon what plan, is as yet uncertain. Something however of this kind is talked of on account of the proceedings in Boston and South Carolina.[66]

I was in hopes to give you an account of the allowance of the two acts relative to the Wawayenda Patent before this.[67] But that business cannot be concluded until the meeting of the Board after the holidays. As Dr. Smith had a day allowed to be heard by his counsel, and as that day has passed and as he has declined to be so heard, I considered the petition as virtually withdrawn; and so represented it. The Board seemed to fall in with my ideas, and as Mr. Jackson, Counsel to that Board, has reported in favor of the acts, his reasons by the retreat of Dr. Smith stood in their full force; and I have no sort of doubt that the first ships which sail after the Christmas recess will carry you an account of the allowance of these acts. I do assure you, Gentlemen, that I omitted nothing which could accelerate or render favourable the issue of a business recommended to

---

[66] Probably refers to refusal of Bostoners to permit unloading tea from the *Dartmouth* which had arrived Nov. 28. Charleston had been in agitation over the arrest of the publisher, Thomas Powell, and was preparing to resist the landing of East India Company tea.

[67] William Wickham's letter of Nov. 7, 1773, suggests that there were legal inter-connections between the Wawayenda Patent Act and another act passed in March, 1772, entitled *An Act for defraying a moiety of the expences accrued on settling the contested boundaries between the patented lands commonly called Cheescocks and Kakiate.—Colonial Laws of New York* 5: 424-428; cf. *Journal of Commissioners*, 381-382.

me by you. I have the honour to be with the highest regard and esteem, Gentlemen,

Your most obedient and humble servant,

E. B.

London January 5. 1774

To the Gentlemen of the Committee of Correspondence New York by the January 5 packet

---

To James Delanc[e]y Esqr. New York

January 5. 1774

Dear Sir,

I am very sorry to find that Lord Rockingham after all his enquiries has not been able to engage for you a jockey, such as you wanted.[68] Boys of a right weight, sober, honest, and clever at their business, are very hard to be procured. They are treasures here; otherwise I should think the good establishment which has been procured for the lad you have already had, would prove a great encouragement to adventurers from the English turf; and that New Market might send out its sporting, with as much success as the other parts of England have their commercial colonies. Only sir, take care to observe that I make a reservation whenever we shall be able to send you out a boy: it shall be a part of your original contract, a solemn charter, a standing instruction, that the *Jockey Club at Old New Market* shall have all authority, jurisdiction, and preeminence, and a full, perfect, and entire legislative authority in all cases whatsoever over all the *New Markets* and all other *provincial sporting assemblies* in America. If any jockeys shall dare to trespass against this supreme jurisdiction, we have found an old act of Harry the 8th under a certain implement in the Tower, which authorizes us to send for the said jockies and without mercy to drag them through an horse pond on any race course in England. This I think necessary for the dignity of the mother country and lest my American agency should be thought to make me forget what I owe to the sovereign turf of Great Britain. We shall be very moderate in taxing you; the only mode we mean to pursue is now and

---

[68] Delancey had made this request in his letter of July 7, 1773.

then to send a knowing one to take you in a little. As this can only be done by real knowing ones, you will enjoy an happiness, which few countries in the world do—that of being taxed only by such as understand their business.

This pacquet takes my letter to the Assembly, together with one to Mr. Wickham, about the Wawayenda business. I think we are in a fair way to get speedily and happily through it. I do not wonder that those who were so materially interested felt uneasy at what they thought a delay.[69] But these things must take their course, and our duty is to secure, not the most rapid, but the most favourable decision. In order to make this time easy, I took the liberty of sending you Mr. Jackson's report, which was as favourable as we could wish. Since then, Dr. Smith though he very strenuously insisted on the matter of the petition, yet not receiving the offer of being heard by counsel when we were in readiness with ours, this will be considered as a dereliction of cause. I hope to send an account of the allowance of these acts by the next pacquet at the furthest.

In the course of the summer Lord Rockingham wrote to you pretty much at large. He is still in Yorkshire where indeed he had little time to stay. The business of the proposed Irish Absentee Tax took up a great deal of his time. It was a dangerous and an insidious attempt; and he resisted it much more upon its unconstitutional tendency than on account of its effect on his own property. It was rejected in Ireland. His early opposition here had a great effect in that rejection, and he had much credit for the prudent and firm conduct which he held on that, as he generally does upon every public occasion.

I received the Speaker's letter acknowledging in terms much higher than the matter deserved his kind acceptance of my endeavours to serve his friend in the business of a seat at the Council Board.[70] Be so good as to make my compliments to him, and assure him of my very earnest desire at all times of

---

[69] *Ibid.*, "I could wish you would bring the Wawayenda Business to a hearing with all possible dispatch. I had with me yesterday one of the Members from that County [Orange] who desired I should mention to you the uneasiness of his Constituents on that head and the fatal consequences that must come by the Repeal of it, particularly that of having their possessions by a new division taken from them and losing the labour and money they have expended in improvement of their farms by having their Lotts drawn by other persons."

[70] Wentworth-Fitzwilliam MSS, Cruger to Burke, Oct. 6, 1773; *supra,* Burke to Cruger, April 16, 1773.

receiving his commands, and of doing, so far as in me lies, everything that can give him pleasure.

I received about this time twelvemonth £ 461 which you remitted to me on account of salary. The rest you retained for the horses. I am sure I am much obliged to you for your friendly attention to this matter. But as the friend for whom I wanted these pacers is become indifferent about them, if you have not already bought them I shall discharge you from the commission which you were so good to undertake; and you may remit that reserved money with that which shall accrue.

I took the liberty of making a request to the Committee of Correspondence, after mentioning it in a private letter to you; which was that the Assembly would allow a small salary to my clerk, Mr. Zouch. This I thought (though I left the matter entirely to themselves) they would hardly refuse, as on looking over the former Agent's bill several matters which I do not charge them with would amount very nearly to what I wished for him. I have charged the Province with nothing but the money which I am actually out of pocket at the Boards—nothing of stationery, postage, etc. However, if they do not think it reasonable, I shall continue at my own charges. It is some time since I was favoured with a letter from you. It will always give me much pleasure to hear of yours and your lady's health and happiness. Adieu, and believe me with great truth and affection, my Dear Sir,

Your most obedient and humble servant,

E. B.

January 5. 1774
To James Delanc[e]y Esqr. New York by the January 1774 packet

---

To the Gentlemen of the Committee etc. New York

February 2. 1774 by the packet

Gentlemen,

I have the satisfaction to inform you that the Wawayenda Act has been reported for the royal allowance. I have endeavored to procure the same approbation for that which relates to the Patent of Cheescocks, but without success.[71] All I could obtain was, that it should *not be disallowed;* and as the act is in force while it continues without any report against it, I hope no very material inconvenience can arise to the proprietors from the refusance of a formal allowance. If however the parties concerned, for private reasons, or the Assembly, for such as are of a public nature, should think this not sufficient, the only remedy seems to be by another bill to explain and amend the present act, or to make one in the place of it entirely new and that shall be free from the objections which have proved prejudicial to this. Such a proceeding may appear the more necessary, as the objections made to the act are not made to the general principle and equity of the law, but to the mode of executing the intention of your legislature in several particulars. The first and principal objection made to the Board is that the money arising from the lands to be sold under the authority of this act is ordered to be paid not only to persons *sui juris* but to infants and feme coverts who by law are incapable of receiving it. And they held that no guardian or husband can be authorized by any construction to give a proper acquittance for such money or to make any disposition of it that shall bind those whom they represent.

It is further objected to the act, that the time limited for the parties to consent is too short, as they may be absent in other colonies or even in Great Britain.

A third objection is, that no appeal is provided but the decision of the Commissioners appointed by the act is absolute and final—a power which, in all cases where property is concerned, they are of opinion is too great to be put into the hands of the Commissioners in the first instance without any check or control whatsoever.

These seem to me the only material objections. Some others

---

[71] The Board of Trade on Jan. 13 recommended confirmation of the Wawayenda Patent Act, but ordered the Cheescocks Act "should be laid aside for the present, and that Mr. Jackson and Mr. Burke should be desired to attend the Board on this day se'nnight." On Jan. 20, "Mr. Jackson, and Mr. Burke, agent for New York, attending as desired, their lordships resumed the consideration of the Act of Assembly at New York . . . and the said Act appearing upon discussion to be, and being admitted by Mr. Burke to be liable to many material objections, their lordships did not think fit to lay it before his Majesty for his royal confirmation; but ordered a letter to the Governor to be prepared, stating the objections, to the end that, if it should not have been carried into compleat execution, another Act for amending it may be passed."—*Journal of Commissioners,* 381-383.

of less moment were started but they were not strongly insisted upon. I thought it necessary to state them not for the interests which are particularly affected by the act, but in order to acquaint you as fully as I am able with the rules and principles which govern the Board on all occasions of this nature. By conforming your private acts to this standard, a great deal of delay, uncertainty, trouble and expence may possibly be saved to parties.

I have received information that the proprietors of Pennsylvania intend to run the lines of their patent on the side of Virginia and on yours, and that they have instructed the Governor of that Province to take the proper preliminary steps towards it. I am assured that they mean nothing but that certainty which is the mutual interest of all borderers; and that they wish to proceed not only fairly but in all respects amicably with your Colony. I shall be glad to receive your further instructions relative to this object, as I shall carefully transmit to you all the intelligence that regards it which may be material for you to be acquainted with.

On Saturday last, the Lords of the Council took into consideration the petition of the Colony of Massachusetts Bay for the removal of their Governor and Deputy Governor. The counsel for the petition were Mr. Dunning and Mr. Lee;[72] for the Governor, Mr. Wedderburn. The counsel for the Province contended that *no cause* was instituted; that they did not think advocates necessary, nor were they demanded on the *part of the Colony;* that the petition of the Colony was not in the nature of accusation, but of advice and request; that it was an address to the King's wisdom, not an application for strict criminal justice; that when referred to the Council [it] was a matter for political prudence, not for judicial determination. Therefore, as such the matter rested wholly on their lordships' opinion of the propriety or impropriety of continuing persons in authority who are represented by legal bodies, competent to such representation, as having (whether on sufficient or insufficient grounds) entirely forfeited the confidence of those assembles with whom they were to act, and of that people whom they were to govern. That the resolutions, on which

[72] John Dunning and John Lee were leading lawyers connected with the rival opposition parties. The former, close to Chatham and Camden, had been solicitor-general, 1768-1770. The latter was of the inner corps of the Rockinghams and became solicitor-general in 1782.

that representation is founded, lay before their lordships, together with the letters from whence those resolutions arose. That these were the materials, and the only materials, on which the prudence of the Council was to operate. They were fully sufficient as grounds for that prudential consideration, however inadequate they might prove for the support of a criminal charge—a charge they were by no means authorized to make, nor furnished with legal evidence to support. If their lordships should think that these actions, which appeared to the Colony Representative to be faulty, ought in other places to appear meritorious, the petition has not desired that the parties should be punished as criminals for these actions of supposed merit. It does not even desire that they may not be rewarded; it only humbly requests that these gentlemen might be removed to places where such merits are better understood, and where such rewards might be more approved.

The ground was taken with skill. It was attacked too with no small ability. Mr. Wedderburn stated the determination on this petition as what must decide whether the King should ever be faithfully or resolutely served in any part of his dominions. He considered the petition as a criminal accusation and expatiated largely on the insufficiency of the *matter* charged as well as the invalidity of the evidence. He extenuated the supposed offense in the content of the letters. He asserted that they were private letters written to a private person, and (in the usual freedom and confidence of such intercourse) starting [*sic*] sentiments and running into discussions wholly remote from any view to practice, as a mere exercise of fancy like the politics of *Utopia* or *Oceana*. He dwelt on the merits of the Governor, to his Province and to Government, and the confidence which, it was admitted, he had long possessed; which from his constant affection to his countrymen he still merited, and which he had by no means generally forfeited. That this confidence so justly acquired was only affected partially and for a time by the management of a faction that had got into momentary power. He expatiated on the disorders which had prevailed in town meetings, and on the temperate and manly conduct of the Governor in the midst of such trials. He ended by falling severely upon the means of obtaining and communicating these obnoxious papers, and on the evil effects that such proceedings (which he contended could not possibly be fair ones) had upon the public peace, and the fatal ones they were very near producing to the quiet, fame and lives of individuals.

The Council was the fullest I have ever known. It did not seem absolutely necessary from the nature of the case that there should be any public trial whatsoever.[73] But it was obviously intended to give all possible weight and solemnity to the decision. The petition was rejected.

News has arrived of several ships loaded with teas having been forced to return from different parts of America. As yet I do not find any measures have been taken in consequence, though I do not think the matter will be altogether kept out of Parliament. I should be glad of your instructions relative to my conduct with regards to office, if you think any to be necessary. I shall as religiously obey your orders in this respect, as in my parliamentary capacity I shall always steadily retain my own freedom and deliver my own opinion only in what I shall think the good of the public. I am with all possible regard, attention and esteem,

> Gentlemen,
>
> Your most obedient and most humble servant,
>
> E. B.

London. February 2. 1774
To the Gentlemen of the Committee etc. New York
(Duplicate)

To the Gentlemen of the Committee etc. New York

April 6. 1774

Gentlemen,

Since I had the honour of writing you last, nothing new has occurred relative to the affairs of the Province. The Lords of Trade have been almost wholly occupied on the papers and letters received from the Colonies, and on the measures which have been proposed in Parliament in consequence of the materials laid before the two houses.

The subject was ample and serious. Lord North's speech, on the first opening of the matter, turned on the absolute

---

[73] Burke witnessed the scene.—Macknight, T., *Life and times of Edmund Burke* 2: 45-46.

necessity of doing something immediate and effectual. For things were come to such a pass, by the evil disposition, the turbulent conduct, and the dark designs of many in the Colonies, that the deliberation was no longer upon the degrees of freedom or restraint in which they were to be held, but whether they should be totally separated from their connexion with and dependence on the parent country of Great Britain; and that according to the part which gentlemen should take for or against the measures to be prepared, a judgment would be formed of their disposition to or against that connexion and dependence. This topic was strongly insisted upon and stated in the same invidious light by other persons in office, and in general by most of those who declared themselves in favor of the ministerial proceedings. On the first day appointed for the consideration of the papers, Lord North spoke of the indispensable necessity of vigorous measures, but in a tone more languid and moderate than is usual in the expression of such ideas. The outline of what has since appeared, though faintly and imperfectly, was chalked out from the beginning.

The air of languor, however, wore off in the progress of the business. The Ministry seems to be better arranged than they appeared to be at first. Lord North has assumed a style of more authority and more decision; and the bill laying Boston under a commercial interdict during the King's pleasure has been proposed and supported quite through, with expressions of the utmost firmness and resolution. The house was not so much animated as I have seen it upon other occasions of a similar nature; it did, however, readily concur in the proposition that was moved; not so much from any predilection, that I could observe, to the particular measure which was adopted, as from a general notion that *some act* of power was become necessary, and that the hands of the Government ought to be strengthened by affording an entire credit to the opinions of Ministry in the *choice of that act;* as the best pledge of the future support the house was to give in the effectual execution of any coercive proceeding.

The popular current, both within doors and without, at present sets strongly against America. There were indeed not wanting some persons in the House of Commons who disapproved of the bill and who expressed their disapprobation in the strongest and most explicit terms. But their arguments upon this point made so little impression that it was not thought advisable to divide the house. Those who spoke in opposition did it more for the acquittal of their own honour and discharge of their own consciences, by delivering their free sentiments on so critical an occasion, than from any sort of hope they entertained of bringing any considerable number to their opinion, or even of keeping in that opinion several of those who had formerly concurred in the same general line of policy with regard to the Colonies.

The gentlemen who spoke against the bill rejected that state of the question by which it was invidiously presumed that those who opposed the bill were for giving up the constitutional superiority of this country. That imputation will always be cast off with disdain by every Englishman. Every good Englishman, as such, must be a friend to the Colonies; and all the true friends to the Colonies—the only true friends they have had or ever can have in England—have laid and will lay down the proper subordination of America as a fundamentally incontrovertible maxim in the government of this Empire. This idea, to which they tenaciously adhere in the full extent of the proposition, they are of opinion is nothing derogatory to the real essential rights of mankind, which tend to their peace and prosperity and without the enjoyment of which no honest man can wish the dependence of one country on another. Very unfortunately, in my poor thoughts, the advice of that sort of temperate men has been little attended to on this side of the Atlantic, and rather less on the other. This has brought on misunderstandings and heats where nothing should exist but harmony and good correspondence, which ought naturally to arise from the entire agreement of their real interests.

I ought not to omit acquainting you with one circumstance that happened a little before the third reading of the Boston Bill. Mr. Bollan, Agent for the Council of the Massachusetts Bay, desired to be heard against it. His petition was not received by the House of Commons, on the idea that no agent could be authorized but by the act of the whole provincial legislature. To what consequences this will lead you are, gentlemen, to consider.

In the House of Peers the business was carried in nearly the same manner in which it passed through the House of

Commons. The question for the second reading produced a long and interesting debate, but for the same reasons which prevailed in the House of Commons no division was attempted.

Several alterations have been proposed in the Charter Government of Massachusetts Bay, but the plan of the alterations is not yet so distinctly settled with regard to their nature or to their extent, as to afford sufficient means of forming any judgment concerning them. I do not find that the Ministers intend anything further relative to America in this session.

Such is, as well as I am able to discern it, the temper of Parliament and of the nation at the moment; which I thought it my duty to lay before you without heightening or without palliation. Nobody can long more earnestly than I do to see an end put to those unfortunate differences.

I thought to have been able to transmit the royal allowance of the Wawayenda and Cheescocks acts, but I find they will not be ready until the middle of next week. At this time it was impossible to get them more forward, but I apprehend that no great inconvenience can have happened from the delay, as the account of a favorable report from the Board of Trade has been already transmitted, and the parties concerned might make their arrangements very much with certainty.

I had some conversation a few days ago with Mr. Pownall on the subject of the New Hampshire settlers. He is of opinion that nothing can tend to the speedy and happy adjustment of that troublesome matter so much as to settle it by a commission composed of impartial persons nominated by act of assembly; among which he thinks it would be proper to have some of the most eminent of the judges or crown lawyers; and that if an act for that purpose was framed agreeably to the general instructions it would receive countenance here.

I have the honour to be with all possible regard and esteem,

 Gentlemen,

  Your most obedient and humble servant,

         E. B.

(April 6. 1774 The Wawayenda and Cheescocks acts sent by the packet of this month)
To the Gentlemen of the Committee of Correspondence
        New York

To the Gentlemen of the Committee etc.

Westminster. May 4. 1774

Gentlemen,

Since my letter of the 6th April the affairs of America have engaged almost entirely the attention of Parliament.

I had the honour of representing to you what I conceived the temper then was with which the King's Ministers and both houses entered into that delicate and important business. I informed you of the passing the act for shutting up the harbor of Boston, and of the very slight opposition which it met with in either of the deliberative branches of legislature.

Two bills relative to the same general objects have been since introduced into the House of Commons. One is now with the Lords; the other is reported from committee and will probably be read the third time and passed the House of Commons before the end of this week. The plan of the first is to alter the constitution of the Charter Government of Massachusetts Bay, and to invest the Crown or rather the Governor of that Province with extraordinary powers. As you will very soon receive this act, it is not necessary to make any remarks upon its spirit and tendency. The second bill, which is still before us, proceeds upon a supposed disposition to resistance grown general in that country (if not in others) which it is apprehended will necessitate strong measures on the part of Government. This sort of unhappy conflict may bring on effusion of blood, and it is presumed in such a case that no magistrate or person acting in support of magistracy, whether in a civil or a military capacity, or in the capacity of a revenue officer, can receive the legal protection of a fair and impartial trial. The right of ascertaining the existence of such a case is vested in the governor, who according to his discretion is empowered to send any person indicted under the above description to another colony or to Great Britain for trial.

As these two bills, though separate in form, compose but one system, it was thought advisable by those who disapproved their principles to debate them together. Accordingly, by an implied consent on both sides, they were debated in that manner upon the third reading of the bill for regulations.

In the course of the previous proceeding Mr. Dowdeswell first, and then Col. Barré, had very strongly and fully expressed their disapprobation of the scheme. It was not however until the period I have mentioned that the point was regularly and solemnly debated. The debate began Monday near four o'clock in the afternoon and continued until two in the morning of Tuesday.[74] Mr. Dunning opened the opposition to the measure in a very long and very masterly speech. The other speakers on the same side were Mr. Byng, Mr. Stephen Fox, Mr. Charles Fox, Sir George Savile, General Conway, Col. Barré, and Mr. Edmund Burke, who closed the debate against the third reading of the bill. The speakers for the question were many more in number: Lord George Germain, the Attorney-General, Mr. Rigby, the Paymaster General; Sir William Meredith, lately made Controller of the Household; Mr. Rice, Treasurer of the Chamber; Mr. Jenkinson, Vice Treasurer of Ireland; Mr. St. John, Lord Caermarthen, Mr. Thomas Townshend, Lord North and several others. Lord North spoke last.

I have not yet sufficiently recovered from the fatigue of that day and the uneasiness of a cold caught in consequence of it, to give a satisfactory account of the principal topics urged upon both sides of this great question. Besides, other public business presses very much. Your loss of this account is the less material, as the arguments of those who opposed the measure of the Court had little or no effect; and the minority, though in a very full house, did not exceed fifty-six.

On mentioning this debate, I take the liberty of cautioning you against giving credit to the speeches printed in the newspapers. They are rarely genuine; they are for the most part extremely misrepresented, often through ignorance, often through design; and very frequently the whole is a mere matter of invention.

It was remarked in the course of the debate that far more opposition was made to these latter bills than to the first, which shut up the port of Boston; although it was said that the rendering the means of the subsistence of a whole city dependent upon the King's private pleasure, even after the payment of a fine and satisfaction made, was without precedent, and of a most dangerous example.

The case of Boston certainly to me seemed as strong or stronger than that of the regulating and protecting bills, but many gentlemen who at first supported the bill against that town asserted that they had been some way led to imagine that

---

[74] May 2-3.

Ministry would propose the repeal of the tea duty; and they gave way in that instance in hopes that a measure of lenity would be adopted, to qualify the harshness of the interdict under which the act had laid the unhappy town of Boston. I do not know upon what grounds the gentlemen, who do not frequently act with Ministry, presumed on their dispositions towards a repeal; but I do believe that this opinion (however taken up) had great weight in procuring the countenance which was given in the beginning to proceedings so contrary to the whole tenour of the former conduct of many of the opposition. It is but fair to attribute their concurrence with the Court to this cause, as they opposed the subsequent parts of the system with the greatest vigor,—after Mr. Fuller's motion for the repeal of the tea duty had been rejected.[75]

I am to inform you that Mr. Bollan, agent to the Council of Massachusetts Bay, offered another petition. The house refused to receive it from him in that character. It was asserted that no temporary assembly could give general powers of agency; that this Council changed every year, and that an agent properly authorised to act for a part of any body corporate, must be named by the whole corporation. I may have misunderstood the arguments. I confess I did not perfectly comprehend them. However, if they be of the sort which I imagine, I am persuaded that few colonies have and that you in particular have no agent properly authorised to communicate your desires in that character to Parliament. I therefore wish that when you think proper you may advert to this circumstance, and if you find it advisable, that you will conform to the ideas of the King's servants and qualify yourselves for that official communication which all the subjects of this Empire ought to hold with the sovereign legislature. But on this you have already my sentiments, at least as far as I am personally concerned.[76]

That you may not be deceived by any idle or flattering report, be assured that the determination to enforce obedience from the colonies to laws of revenue, by the most powerful means, seems as firm as possible, and that the Ministry appear stronger than ever I have known them.

---

[75] The occasion for Burke's historic speech on American Taxation, April 19.

[76] *Supra,* Burke to committee of correspondence, Dec. 4, 1771. For Burke's critical opinion of the house's refusal to recognise Bollan, see *Correspondence* 4: 475-476.

I am full of trouble on account of the late most unfortunate transactions. My advice has little weight anywhere. My wishes are, and my endeavors ever have been and ever shall be equally for the good and the freedom (without which hardly any good can be) of the whole.

I have the honour to be with greatest esteem and regard,

Gentlemen,

Your most obedient and humble servant,

E. B.

Westminster 4 May 1774

(Duplicate sent)

To the Gentlemen of the Committee of Correspondence. New York.

To the Gentlemen of the Committee etc. New York

June pacquet, 1774

[June 1, 1774] [77]

Gentlemen,

I am this day honoured with your letter of the 4th of April and am made very happy by your approbation of my endeavors to serve you.[78] I find that Governor Tryon is arrived. I have not yet seen him, but propose to wait upon him immediately. I think the subject of our conversation must be interesting. I mean that he should join me in endeavoring to defeat, or at least to postpone a part of the Quebec bill by which I imagine your rights may be affected. It stands committed for tomorrow and then in regularity we are to debate the clauses and particular provisions.

This bill, not satisfied with establishing a new mode of government for that new colony, has given it limits, as I apprehend, injurious to your territorial rights as well as to the property of many innocent and even meritorious individuals. These boundaries on the side of the ancient settlements are determined by the words of not being 'within the limits of

---

[77] Date established by internal evidence.

[78] Letter not found.

some other British Colony *as allowed and confirmed by the Crown,'* by which words I conceive that all the territorial limits which at present are under litigation, are hereby adjudged to the Colony of Quebec.

It appears to me a very extraordinary decision of property and jurisdiction. I shall certainly oppose this part of the bill with all my might, but I apprehend with very little prospect of success. This limitary clause was contrived to establish the French claims within your Province, and to save the Council the odium of deciding against the officers who have contributed so largely to the conquest of that very Province, in favor of which they are now to be deprived of what they have so much reason to think their undoubted right. Their claims and the national honour are upon the same bottom.

The business you have recommended to me, I shall take care to attend to very exactly. I am quite of your opinion of the use of an authorized lottery as a diversion of that species of gaming to public purposes, and as an easy method of providing for the erection of expensive works.

I have already laid before you an account of the bills which passed the House of Commons and which are now acts of Parliament, relative to the Colony of Massachusetts Bay. As they are now laws, they are no longer subjects for my speculation.

The death of the King of France will bring about in all probability a change in the Administration of that country; but that change, I rather imagine, will not be a return of the persons or politics of the Choiseul Ministry. If that should be the case, this Ministry may be as peaceable as the last of Louis the 15th. At any rate, I think no sudden change relative to *foreign arrangements* can be produced until the new French Cabinet has acquired a greater degree of consistency than it can arrive at for some time.

I am to thank you for the provision for contingent expences, and am with the greatest truth and esteem,

Gentlemen,

Your most obedient and humble servant,

E. B.

Westminster 1774

To the Gentlemen of the Committee etc. at New York [79]

August 2. 1774

Gentlemen,

I was prevented by pressing business and by not the best of health from sending you a letter by the June pacquet.[80]

When I had last the honour of writing to you on your affairs, I entertained no strong apprehensions that the clause in the Quebec Bill concerning the boundary of that new Province could materially affect the rights of your Colony. It was couched in general and saving terms; it reserved all rights and confirmed all adjudications; it was in all appearance sufficiently equitable; but upon a close consideration and subsequent inquiry, I found that you might be very much affected by it. I take the liberty of stating to you the light in which it appeared to me, and the conduct which I held in consequence of that view of your interests.

I must first observe to you that the proceedings with regard to the Town of Boston and the Province of Massachusetts Bay had been from the beginning defended on their absolute necessity, not only for the purpose of bringing that refractory town and province into proper order, but for holding out an example of terror to the other colonies, in some of which (as it was said) a disposition to the same or similar excesses had been marked very strongly. This unhappy disposition in the colonies was, by the friends of the coercive measures, attributed to the pride and presumption arising from the rapid population of these colonies, and from their lax form and more lax exercise of government. I found it in general discourses and even in public debates, the predominant and declared opinion, that the cause of this resistance to legal power ought to be weakened, since it was impossible to be removed; that any growth of the colonies which might make them grow out of the reach of the authority of this kingdom ought to be accounted rather a morbid fulness than a sound and proper habit. All increase of

---

[79] Two contemporary copies, neither in Burke's hand, are in the Library of the New York Historical Society. One bears the following certification: "The above is a true copy of the original Letter to the Committee of Correspondence for the General Assembly of New York examined and compared with the said original the 16th Feby. 1775. By H. Nicoll." This copy was published in *Colden Papers* 7: 232-239. Between it and the letter-book text there are some significant discrepancies.

[80] In the certified copy mentioned in the preceding note, the month named is not June but July. Burke unquestionably completed his letter early in July; the fact is proved by the crossed-out "July 5. 1774" appended to the letter-book text.

the Colonies which tended to decrease their advantage to this country they considered as useless and even mischievous.

From this predominant way of thinking, the enormous extent of the colonies was censured. It was not thought wise to make new grants of land but upon the weightiest considerations, if at all. Prerogative was to be strengthened as much as possible; and it was thought expedient to find in the tractable disposition of some provinces a check upon the turbulent manners, and a balance to the less manageable plan of government in the others.

These principles (whatever their merit may be) became very fashionable. During the agitation of the Massachusetts bills in the House of Commons, a peer, who I think does not always vote in the majority, made a sort of proposition for an address to the King, that no more lands should be located in America. This was the substance of the proposition, although it proceeded no further, from reasons of decorum. The ministerial side in that house fell in very directly with those sentiments and, as I am told, plainly shewed a resolution to act in conformity with them, so far as the power of the Crown in that particular extended. It is true that a few lords, and Lord Rockingham in particular, objected to the idea of restraining the colonies from spreading into the back country, even if such restraint were practicable; for by stopping the extent of agriculture, they necessitated manufactures, contrary to the standing policy of colonization. The general sentiments were, however, as I have stated them.

I mention this disposition of the House of Peers particularly (though it prevailed almost equally elsewhere) because the Quebec Bill originated in that house. Very many thought, on a careful perusal, that the lines of the plan of policy I have just mentioned were very distinguishable in that bill as it came down to us. It was for that reason I became more uneasy than at first, about the lax and indeterminate form in which the boundary clause of this new colony was worded in the original bill. The idea which (whether seriously adopted by Ministry or not) was very prevalent, that the British Colonies ought to be restrained, made it necessary that this restraint should not be arbitrary. It was the main ground of the amendments which I proposed and carried; with regard to the boundary clause, however, as a mere unconnected arrangement it was right to define with clearness, although such a plan of policy never had existed or should pass away, as I hope and think in some degree it has, with the first heats. The bill passed through the House of Lords with some opposition, but no amendments; but when it came into the House of Commons the Ministers confessed that it was hastily drawn, and they professed great candour in admitting alterations. The part by which your Province would be directly affected was only the boundary clause.

As the boundary was in the most material parts in the original bill only *constructive* and, in words of reference to the boundary lines of the other provinces, as judged and allowed by the Crown, I thought it necessary to know with regard to you, what lines had been actually drawn and allowed, and next, what principles were to guide in adjudging your real boundaries in future.

With regard to the first point, I found that a line of division between your Colony and that of Quebec had been allowed by the King in Council to be run from a point on Lake Champlain in 45 degrees of north latitude. So far had been agreed between the governors of the two provinces, and allowed. But no line had been actually run in consequence of this agreement, except from the River Connecticutt to the Lake. Even this line had not been formally allowed; and none at all had been run to the westward of Lake Champlain. So that your boundary on the north had never been perfectly delineated, though the principle upon which it should be drawn had been laid down. For a great part of the northern frontier and for the whole of the western until you met the line of New Jersey, you had no defined boundary at all. Your claims were indeed extensive and I am persuaded just, but they had never been regularly allowed.

My next object of inquiry, therefore, was upon what principles the Board of Trade would in the future discussion, which must inevitably and speedily arise, determine what belonged to you and what to Canada.

I was told that the settled uniform doctrine and practice of the Board of Trade was this: that in questions of boundary, where the jurisdiction and soil in both the litigating provinces belonged to the Crown, there was no rule but the King's will, and that he might allot as he pleased, to the one or to the other. They said also that under these circumstances, even where the King had actually adjudged a territory to one province, he might afterwards change the boundary, or, if he thought fit, erect the parts into separate and new governments at his discretion. They alleged the example of Carolina, first one province, then divided into two separate governments; and which afterwards had a third, that of Georgia, taken from the southern division of it. They urged besides the example of the neutral and conquered islands. These after the Peace of Paris were placed under one government. Since then, they were totally separated and had distinct governors and assemblies.

Although I had the greatest reason to question the soundness of some of these principles, at least in the extent in which they were laid down (and whether the precedents alleged did fully justify them in that latitude), I certainly had no cause to doubt but that the matter would always be determined upon these maxims at the Board by which they were adopted. The more clearly their strict legality was proved, the more uneasy I became at their consequences. By this bill a new province under an old name was in fact erected; the bounds of the proclamation of 1763 were cancelled. On your side a mere *constructive* boundary was established, and the construction, when examined, amounted to nothing more than the King's pleasure. No part of your Province (not even of the settled quarters of the country) quite to the River Hudson was secured from the possible operation of such a principle. Besides, there was a possibility (at least) that in the settlement of the boundary Ministers would naturally lean to extend those limits the most where the royal prerogative was most extensive and consequently their power the highest. I do not mean to charge them with that intention; but no laws stood in the way of such an inclination, if it ever did exist or should happen to exist hereafter. It was not (as it might be between two ancient British colonies) a mere question of geographical distinction, or of economical distribution, where the inhabitants on the one side of the line and on the other lived under the same law and enjoyed the same privileges of Englishmen; but this was a boundary discriminating different principles of jurisdiction and legislation, where in one part the subject lived under law and, in the other, under prerogative.

From these impressions I proposed my objections on the second reading, reserving a more regular opposition to the committee. In the interval I conferred with Lord Dartmouth and Mr. Pownall, and afterwards with Lord North, upon the subject; but first I formed my plan for an amendment to the clause as it stood in the bill before it was committed. I could have wished for a more perfect and authorized information, but I was obliged to act at the instant. The bill came in late in the session, and if I had let it pass for want of being instructed, the occasion could in all human probability never be recovered.

I saw you had claims founded on these grounds: the old Dutch settlement; the placing of the Five Nations within your government; the boundary line of Governors Moore and Carleton; and the maintenance of the Fort of Oswego during the late war, which carried you to Lake Ontario.

These claims had no fault but the want of definition. To define is to abridge; something then must be given up. I was persuaded that when one negotiates with power it is policy to give up handsomely what cannot be retained; and to gain that strength which will always more or less attend the reasonableness of a proposition, even when it is opposed by power. I thought that well secured and tolerably extensive boundaries were better than the amplest claims which are neither defined nor allowed. My idea was to get the limits of Quebec (which appeared to many as well as myself, intended to straiten the British colonies) removed from construction to certainty, and that certainty grounded on natural, indisputable, and immovable barriers—rivers and lakes where I could have them; lines where lines could be drawn; and, where reference and description became necessary, to have them towards an *old British colony* and not towards this *new* and, as was thought, favourite establishment.

I assured Ministry that if they refused this reasonable offer I must be heard by counsel. As they found some opposition growing within and without doors, and as they were in haste to carry through their bill (brought in so late in the session) after some discussion and debate, they gave way to the amending clause as you see it.

The work was far more troublesome than those who were not present can well believe. It cost us near two whole days in the committee. The grand difficulty arose from the very unsettled state of the boundaries of Pennsylvania. We could not determine whether it advanced northward beyond Lake Erie, or ran within that lake, or fell to the south of it. And this uncertainty made the whole matter beyond expression perplexing. Objections on the part of Quebec were raised to the last moment and particularly to the post of Niagara, which Mr. Carleton, I am told, was very earnest to have within his government; but by the act it is excluded and is on your side. I believe some imagined that these difficulties would make me give up the point; but it is carried, and if not a perfect arrangement it prevents a very bad one, and may form a basis for a much better in times more favourable to the old colonies.

After the affair was over, it was suggested to me that I ought to have expressly defined this line *to be the limit of New York,* as well as of Canada. To this I answer that I was aware of the inconveniences which might arise from the whole of this clear specification; supposing the Board of Trade to act invidiously, unfairly, and captiously, which I have no reason to imagine they will do, from anything I have observed in them, or in other parts of Ministry. But I confess, when I consider that Canada is put on the other side of the waters, its bounds being expressly so marked out, it appears to me absolutely impossible to say to whom the land on this side belongs, except to you; unless His Majesty should choose to erect a new government, a thing no way likely or convenient for any good purpose. The Quebec line was constantly stated and argued in the House as the boundary line between the provinces, in that public discourse (rather than debate) which latterly we had on this subject. I think the line to all intents and purposes as much your boundary as if it were ever so expressly set down. Canada at least cannot say, "This belongs to me."

I did not press to have the line called the boundary between New York and Canada, because we should again fall into discussion about the bounds of other colonies, as we had about those of Pennsylvania; which discussion alone had very near defeated me. It would be asked why the line along Nova Scotia, New Hampshire, and the northern Massachusetts claim, was not called the boundary of these provinces as well as of New York? It would be said that this act was to settle a constitution for Quebec and not for adjusting the limits of the colonies; and in the midst of this wrangle the whole object would have infallibly escaped. The House as it was grew quite tired of it. All business stood still whilst we were wording the clause and on our difficulties Lord North proposed to revert to the old words, which, he said, to him were the best, and that he only gave way to the sentiments of other people who, on his concession, found a difficulty in effectuating their own purposes. *Perhaps those who were disposed to risque all, might have gained more, as sometimes happens to fortunate rashness. But for you I could risque nothing. I had no instructions from you. I had no confidence in my strength in the House.*[81]

I must therefore accept what I could get. And the true method of estimating the matter is to take together the time, what we escaped, what we have obtained, and then to judge whether we have not had a tolerable bargain. Those who were present congratulated me, as on a great advantage. I am sure I acted for the best, with great rectitude of intention and a good deal of assiduity. I send you the bill with the amendments marked. As to the other parts of the bill, they are matters of more general policy, on which, as I have already given you a great deal of trouble, I do not mean to detain you any longer upon foreign matters.

I received your obliging letter of the 31st of May whilst I was writing this, and am extremely happy in the honour of your approbation. You undoubtedly may dispose of my letters as you judge proper. I must in this respect confide entirely to your prudence, being fully satisfied that the matter will always direct you sufficiently in what you ought to conceal and what to reveal.

I have sent off long ago the Wawayenda and Cheescocks Acts.

I have had the honour of seeing Mr. Cruger at my house on his return from Bristol. I endeavored to attend him in the manner to which his merit and connections entitle him.

I have the honour to be with the highest esteem and regard,
    Gentlemen,
       Your most obedient and humble servant   E. B.

Beaconsfield August 2d. 1774
July 5. 1774 [crossed out in MS.]
To the Committee of Correspondence for the General Assembly
   at New York

---

[81] Italicized passage marked for excision; it does not appear in the *N. Y. Hist. Soc.* copy.

To the Committee of Correspondence etc. and to John Cruger
Esqr. by the January packet

Gentlemen,

It is now some time since I had the honour of writing to
you or receiving your commands. The general recess from all
Parliamentary and official business left me nothing worthy of
being communicated to you; and the interesting scene in
America did very naturally, I suppose, attract the whole of your
attention.

Since the meeting of the new Parliament nothing remarkable has happened relative to your Continent. The Court seems
to have as great a strength in this as in the last Parliament,
but I do not look upon anything which has happened yet as
a real trial of its disposition towards the Colonies. The King's
speech was far from being clear or decisive. If anything is to
be gathered from that speech it is this, that at the time of
making it the Ministers seemed resolved to persevere in carrying into execution the measures of the last session, without any
addition of rigor or any step towards conciliation. They trusted
there was so much intrinsic efficacy in the three American acts,
that they could not fail of quieting all the disturbances in
North America and executing themselves. The general tenor
of conversation amongst those who are the most likely to
express, if not what the Ministers meant, at least [what] they
wished to have understood as their meaning, gave great
countenance to that opinion. This, however, is to be understood of Ministry previous to the arrival of the Resolves of the
Congress and the Petition to the King. The arrival of these
will probably make some change in their disposition. At first
Lord North, possibly from the resolution of confiding in the
operation of the acts of the last Parliament without any further
efforts, seemed resolved to lay no papers before us. But since
the publication of the proceeding of the Congress there seems
some alteration. The house is promised not only papers for
information, but also a plan of proceedings with relation to
America. Of what nature that plan is, nobody that I know of
pretends so much as to guess. It is, I suppose, because as yet
no settled plan has been arranged.

A meeting of the North American merchants is to be on

the fourth. I shall inform you of their proceedings as soon as I hear of them.[82]

I am exceedingly concerned about the Cheescocks Act. How the mistake could have happened, I cannot conceive, for Mr. Pownall is generally very exact and he certainly always acts a part remarkably kind and obliging in your affairs. However it has happened you may be assured it shall be set to right immediately.[83] Your other business shall be expedited with all possible diligence. I have the honour to be with the greatest esteem and regard,

     Gentlemen,

         Your most obedient and very humble servant,

                     [E. B.]

Beaconsfield 3rd January 1775
To the Gentlemen of the Committee of Correspondence for the General Assembly New York. (By the packet January 1775)

To James Delanc[e]y Esqr. New York

                   14 March 1775

Dear Sir,

I have heard nothing from you since you informed me in a short letter that you were setting out for Annapolis, until your letter from New York of the 1st of February.[84]

I congratulate you on the success of your endeavours and hope they will have the desired effect of leading to that conciliation for which they were so honestly intended and so earnestly pursued. I wish that we on our side had been as earnest to meet you with conciliatory measures. But whatever different measures may be pursued by you on your side, or by Government here, provided they lead to a happy settlement, I shall be perfectly satisfied. I find that Ministry place their

---

     [82] A promise Burke seems to have forgotten to keep.

     [83] The difficulty is obscure, but see *infra*, Burke to committee of correspondence, March 14.

     [84] Neither letter has been found.

best hopes of dissolving the Union of the Colonies and breaking the present spirit of resistance, wholly in your Province. I wish that the bills which I transmit may be found well adapted to cooperate with your pacific system.

I have been busy in these matters so as to have for some short time an ill effect on my health, partly by attendance, partly by vexation. I have acted to the best of my judgment, with fair intentions towards the Mother Country and the Colonies. I am now better in health. Despair of success will abate my efforts, and preserve I hope my little remains of strength.

In my public letter I have stated the proceedings in Parliament as clearly and as shortly as I was able, not as I saw them, but as the leaders in them represented their own measures.[85] I may therefore save you the trouble of hearing anything further on the subject.

In your short letter, which I received in the summer, you mentioned your not being able to procure bills for the amount of my arrears. I fancy they now amount to 540 sterling or thereabouts, besides the Assembly's last allowance for clerk and contingencies.

I have not had hitherto an opportunity of congratulating you on Mr. Cruger's seat for Bristol being confirmed by the election committee. I wrote to Mr. Cruger the Speaker to congratulate him upon the original election. I am with the best respects to your lady,

 Dear Sir,

  Your most obedient and humble servant,

        [E. B.]

Westminster March 14th 1775
To James Delanc[e]y Esquire

To the Committee of Correspondence at New York
        (14 March 1775)
Gentlemen,

I had been a long time without the honour of any commands from you, until I received the Speaker's letter of the 1st of

---

[85] See next letter.

February, which, I take it for granted, I must consider as public and official.[86]

On my part, I have been much occupied in business which surely is most interesting to the British Empire, and in this I have taken that part which in my judgment appeared to be most conducive to the benefit of the whole. I was afraid, in a conjuncture which in all accounts is so very critical and delicate, to hazard anything whatsoever by way of information to you that had been collected from report or conjecture, however probable. In the beginning of the session Ministry appeared to me so undetermined in their plan of conduct that I could not furnish you, even if I were better acquainted with their designs than I can pretend to be, with any intelligence which the next day's information might not contradict.

I now transmit to you three papers, in order that, considering them together, you may yourselves form the better judgment of the plan of Ministry, as far at least as it has hitherto been opened. The first is the Address of both houses declaring a rebellion in Massachusetts Bay. The second a resolution of the House of Commons declaring their expectations from the Colonies as a condition of peace, and the manner in which the House thinks it most advisable to carry into execution the right of taxing those Colonies. The third is a bill for restraining the trade and fishery of the four provinces of New England.

With regard to the first, the declaration of rebellion, it was thought expedient in order that the troops might find themselves justified in those forcible operations which the state of things in Massachusetts Bay has rendered necessary.

With regard to the second, the taxing proposition, Lord North declared his opinion that it would probably not suit the *taste* of several of the Colonies, but that if only a single colony complied the chain of opposition to our rights would be broken. He thought, however, that in reason it ought to be accepted by *all* the Provinces; for whilst by declaring that Parliament will in future assess the amount of the taxes which the Colonies are to pay as well as determine the purposes to which that payment shall be applied, the resolution supports in the fullest manner the contested right of the British legislature, it provides at the same time equally for the ease and

[86] Not found.

happiness of the Colonies by having the mode entirely to themselves.

As to the third, the bill for restraining the commerce and fishery of New England—it was defended on the principle of retaliating on these Provinces their combination not to trade with this country. It was also supported on the principles of the preamble of the Act of Navigation, which preamble supposes no right in Colonies to trade at all except with the parent country; all relaxations of that principle being only matter of mere favor and indulgence. The penalties of the bill were considered as a mode rather merciful of treating a people in rebellion. But whatever severity might be in these penalties, a sharp course, it was urged, is in the end the most lenient; as it drives the offenders to a more speedy submission and of course leads the sooner to peace and conciliation.

These are, I believe, exactly the leading arguments upon which the three parts that have hitherto appeared of the plan of Ministry are defended. I give you, Gentlemen, not my opinion but their reasons. In what manner these arguments were combatted by those who disliked the plan, it is not necessary to lay before you. In a situation like yours and mine, I am very scrupulous in intermixing any judgment which in any particular might have a tendency to mislead yours. I ought undoubtedly to represent to you everything which may enable you to see your true situation, but I am very unwilling to speculate upon it. Your interests are concerned, and your wisdom will decide.

Since I began this letter, Lord North has moved in the American Committee some resolutions as a ground for a bill to restrain the trade of the Colonies of New Jersey, Pennsylvania, Maryland, Virginia, and South Carolina, in a manner similar to the restrictions of New England.[87] North Carolina is not included as Ministry has not received intelligence, at least not official intelligence, of the state of that Province; and New York is not included on account of your refusal to authenticate, by any act of yours, the non-importation agreement.

I am not able to form any opinion to what further objects, or of what kind, the penal spirit of the ministerial plan is to extend. That plan has never been laid before us all together.

[87] It is evident that Burke began this letter before March 9, since North moved the resolutions on that day.

Matters were opened to us separately, some at one time, and some at another. Possibly no fixed plan at all is formed, but that each detached article of intelligence, just as it arrives from America, alters, extends, or modifies the measures which are taken. But in this too I would be supposed to speak with uncertainty.

The merchants have taken steps to oppose these proceedings, but they have not been much regarded; and no small pains are used in all the manufacturing parts of the kingdom to persuade the people concerned that the reduction by force of the disobedient spirit in the Colonies is their sole security for trading in future with America.

There are certainly some Members in both houses who earnestly desire that measures of another complexion and tendency might be adopted. But these men (whom I should call moderate) are not apparently much more numerous, or much more considerable, in this Parliament than in the last. It is true that the numbers which divided in the minority against some of the strong measures are somewhat higher than those which divided on similar questions in the last Parliament. But the majority also is greater. The numbers against the proceedings never exceeded in this session one hundred and six, whereas those for enforcing them have been raised to near three hundred. Such is the state of Parliament.

On looking carefully over my correspondence, I find that in my letter of 6th April 1774 by mistake I have mentioned the Cheescocks Act being transmitted with the other. How it happened, unless through hurry or inadvertence, I know not—I am sorry for it. But by referring to my letter of 2d February 1774 you will see that I informed you of my failure in my endeavors to obtain the royal allowance for the Cheescocks Act (which however is only suspended) together with the plan proposed upon that subject by the Lords of Trade. The enclosed office copy of the letter from the Board to the Governor will explain the matter more fully.

I have been twice at the Plantation Office since the arrival of Col. Read on the business of the New Hampshire patents.[88]

---

[88] Col. John Reid, an officer under Sir Jeffrey Amherst, who in 1771 obtained a grant of land between the Hudson and Connecticut rivers, only to have his tenants expelled by the men of "the Grants." He was associated with James Duane and acted for a group of New York claimants against New Hampshire settlers.—*N. Y. documents* **8:** 312.

The gentlemen who signed his instructions are very much mistaken in what they assert—that their business has not hitherto succeeded for want of solicitations. It has been solicited, I must say vigorously. But the Board constantly declared that they would not take any step whatsoever on that matter, and if things had remained in their former state their former resolution would have continued. My opinion was and is that nothing but a compromise could settle it. But no person was authorized either to propose or to agree to such a treaty until the arrival of Col. Read. Governor Tryon is strongly of the same opinion, and Col. Read by his conversation with the Board and its officers must plainly discern their resolution on this subject. The plan proposed by Governor Tryon had my entire approbation and hearty support before their lordships. He knew better than I could the state of the several parties, and his plan (much better and more particularly adjusted) was in effect much the same as my own. I refer to the above-mentioned letter from me of the 2d of February 1774, to which I received no answer with regard to that particular.

I have the honour to be with the greatest regard and esteem, and best wishes for the restoration of your tranquillity, freedom and prosperity,

Gentlemen,

Your most obedient and humble servant,

[E. B.]

Westminster 14 March 1775

(Duplicate)

To the Committee of Correspondence for the General Assembly

To the Gentlemen of the Committee of Correspondence New York [89]

7 June 1775

Gentlemen,

On the 4th May I received the important papers which you did me the honour to transmit by the packet, with your letter of the 5th of April. I received also the duplicate which arrived

[89] This letter was officially intercepted; see *Dartmouth Mss.* 2: 309.

soon after.[90] I had reason to believe that your memorials would be as favourably received as the system adopted by the Ministry could possibly permit. The Ministers had entirely approved of the conduct of the Representatives of New York in declining to send deputies to the Congress or to thank those who had formerly been deputed to that Assembly. Confiding in these dispositions, which seemed to me very real, I waited on Lord Dartmouth and presented to him the Petition to his Majesty, requesting that it might be delivered as soon as possible. At the same time I shewed him the Remonstrance to the Commons and the Memorial to the Lords. His Lordship expressed great regard to the Colony; acknowledged that the papers were written in a style of great decency and moderation; but added that he wished that some part of the subject matter had been omitted, as it might tend to procure to your representation a very different reception from that which he heartily desired.

On the 15th of May I offered your Remonstrance in my place. Although I found myself in no very good state of health and spirits, I did not fail to urge the policy as well as justice of the house's receiving and taking into consideration the complaint you had made in behalf of yourselves and the other Colonies, and upon grievances of a general as well of a local nature. I showed that although your opinion concerning the universality of the legislative power of Great Britain might not meet with the approbation of the house, yet as that opinion, however erroneous, was employed in terms proper and decent—as it was accompanied with the most precise and full acknowledgment of our legislative authority in many, if not the most essential particulars—it could form no objection to the admission of the paper. This admission did not, as I conceived, prevent the House from marking its dissent from the obnoxious parts by future resolutions; that the suffering a petition to be brought up did not imply an approbation of all its contents, nor indeed of any of them. I conceived that this matter stood unconnected with several other articles of

---

90 The papers were the petition, memorial, and remonstrance to King, Lords, and Commons. The letter has not been found, but an abstract showing that it had been intercepted and copied before being sent on to Burke, is given in *Dartmouth Mss.* 2: 287. The signers of the letter—Cruger, Walton, Jauncey, and Delancey—asked Burke to use his best efforts to obtain allowance for two recent New York acts, and expressed the hope that he would communicate by the first opportunity any measures likely to be pursued in regard to the colonies.

grievance which it would be proper for us at least to hear, and not to make a mistaken allegation of one grievance a reason for not attending to others which might be real, and in which the authority of legislature was not disputed but the exercise only complained of. I added that I conceived the house had pledged itself (by our address to the Crown on declaring a rebellion in Massachusetts) that we should attend to the grievances of the Colonies whenever they should be dutifully presented to us. I then, under the idea of stating its contents, read, as is usual, the whole of your Remonstrance, and after again pressing for a consideration of the matter, concluded with a motion for leave to bring it up.

I was strongly supported by several gentlemen and particularly by Mr. Fox, Governor Johnston, Mr. Cruger, Mr. Aubrey, and Mr. Sawbridge. Lord North was of opinion that the house could not so much as receive any paper which tended to call in question the right of Parliament to make laws to bind the subjects of this Empire in all cases whatsoever; that in this point the Declaratory Act had only stated the ancient constitution; that if this Remonstrance were admitted, it would be tacitly to abandon legislative authority in its most essential part and that which was most immediately connected with the particular privileges and dignity of the House of Commons. Otherwise, he said, he should be for receiving and even for entering into some consideration of the other complaints, whatever their foundation might be. He declared that the conduct of the Colony of New York had his hearty approbation; that it had been moderate, dutiful, and prudent, and as such he thought merited particular marks of the favour and indulgence of Parliament. And as that Colony had merited, so had it received those marks of favor, by being left out in the general act for restraining the trade of the Colonies. He said he was willing to give further proofs of his regard to that Colony by entering immediately into their particular grievances with regard to the Quebec duties, to which he would instantly propose redress.[91] He was very sorry he was obliged to oppose the bringing up the paper, but he would propose an amendment

---

[91] The remonstrance stated: "We are at a loss to account why Articles imported from the Continental Colonies, and imported into the Province of Quebec, should be loaded with heavier Duties than those brought from the West India Islands, by which we are deprived of a most Lucrative Branch of Commerce. . . ."

that should mark his reason. After this the proceeding was as you see in the votes, which I herewith transmit to you. The Remonstrance was not suffered to be brought up. Several who debated on the side of Ministry assigned the very title of 'remonstrance' as amongst the reasons for refusing to admit it into the house, considering that title as well as the matter to be highly and studiously disrespectful to the house, as they said it made a marked distinction in your addresses between the House of Commons and the other branches of legislature.

The Duke of Manchester was so obliging as to take upon himself the presenting the Memorial to the Lords. The order of the House of Peers does not require a particular leave to bring in a petition (as it does with us) but every lord has been always understood to have the privilege of presenting a petition and of having it read by the clerk. It was thought, therefore, that the House of Lords could not have the same pretext to refuse a formal reading of the Memorial that the House of Commons had. The Duke of Manchester only stated the general purport of the Memorial, and desired it might be read. A long debate ensued, partly on the merits (which were presumed from a private knowledge of the contents) and partly on the matter of order. You were much obliged on that occasion to the good offices of several peers, and particularly to the Duke of Manchester, the Duke of Richmond, the Marquess of Rockingham, Lord Camden, and the Earl of Effingham. The latter had just resigned his company in order to avoid serving against his declared public principles. He spoke in a very noble and very affecting manner. The Memorial had the same fate with the Remonstrance. As soon as they were rejected I followed your directions and gave them to my clerk to convey to the newspapers, *the managers of which made such comments on the transactions as thought fit without my knowledge.*[92]

Concerning the petition to the King I have as yet received no answer. I have not printed it, as Mr. Pownall, Under-Secretary of State for the Colonies, seemed to wish (though he did not directly desire) that I should not. The substance was already conveyed to the public by the printing of the Memorial and Remonstrance; and I did not think it right to do anything to displease office, without absolute necessity. Mr. Pownall is very obliging in facilitating your business; and whatever I

---

[92] Italicized words marked for excision.

may think of the conduct of Ministers, I take care never to let my sentiments mingle with your business; which I endeavor to carry on solely with a view to your particular interest and entirely unconnected with everything else.

Governor Tryon has, I suppose, communicated to you every particular which passed at the Board of Trade relative to the business of the French grants and the New Hampshire intruders. I had the satisfaction to concur with him in the temperaments which he purposed for accomodating the latter affair. The plan which he formed seemed to me judicious, and he knows that I supported it with all the vigor I could, without entering into details for which the affair was not then in ripeness, or without hazarding the great general ground of the adjudication in favor of the Province,—on which I stood, and which gave us all advantages which attend a possession in law. Mr. Dunning exerted great abilities in defence of the provincial rights, as well as those of individuals, against the French grants. You are happy too in having a Governor who has omitted nothing towards the support of your claims and the advantage, quiet, and good order of your Province.

I shall take the best care I can of the two acts which you have recommended to me. I have the honour to be with the highest regard and esteem,

> Gentlemen,
>
> > Your most obedient and humble servant

[E. B.]

Westminster
June 7. 1775
To the Committee of Correspondence for the General Assembly
    at New York

To Philip Livingston and Barnard Lagrange Esquires [93]

> October 3. 1775
> (by the packet of October 75)

Gentlemen,

I am extremely sorry that I have not yet been able to obtain

---

[93] Philip Livingston and Bernardus La Grange, of New Brunswick, N. J. were materially interested in *An Act to confirm a submission to referees of a controversy concerning the bounds of the Patent of Jan Hendrickse Van Baal.—Colonial Laws of New York* 5: 753-766.

the royal confirmation of the act which you recommended to me. I suppose the unhappy confusions which prevail at present have delayed it. But I hope I shall be able to send it to you by the earliest opportunity. We have had public notice that no packet after this will regularly sail for America. Nobody can more deeply and sincerely regret than I do the unfortunate differences which have thus cut off the intercourse of countries which ought to be united by the strongest and dearest of all ties.

I think it necessary to inform you that I declined presenting the Petition of the Congress to the King. I certainly should think myself much honoured by the office of conveying to the Crown the dutiful representations of any of his Majesty's subjects. But the Assembly of New York, by whom alone I have been authorized to act for any public body in America, not having thought it expedient to send new deputies to the Congress, or to approve the conduct of the deputies before sent thither, and having transmitted their resolutions to me on that subject, I could not *as Agent to that Assembly* present the acts of the Congress to the King or his Ministers. This was my sole reason for declining to present the Petition. You are already acquainted with the reception it has met with. I have in my letter to the Committee of Correspondence stated the proceedings in both houses upon the Remonstrance and Memorial of your Assembly. I laid before the Committee of Correspondence reasons for not printing it.[94]

I have the honour to be with the warmest wishes for the reestablishment of our former correspondence,

> Gentlemen,

> Your most obedient and humble servant

> > > > E. B.

Westminster
October 3rd. 1775

---

[94] The petition to the king.

Part II

EDMUND BURKE AND CHARLES O'HARA
AN INTIMATE CORRESPONDENCE
1761-1776

I. Mr. Hamilton's Secretary

[At an undisclosed time before 1759, Burke made the acquaintance of Charles O'Hara. Since their letters contain evidence to show that O'Hara knew Burke's father-in-law, Dr. Christopher Nugent, before he knew Burke, it seems likely that the doctor brought them together; this must have been before March, 1759, when Lady Mary, O'Hara's wife, died. The letters indicate that Burke had been acquainted with her.

O'Hara's earliest extant letter to Burke was written from Dublin on November 20, 1759, which was about the time Burke entered into his secretarial employment with William Gerard Hamilton. O'Hara sent some small local news and gossip, and thanked Burke "for an account of your own welfare and that of your family which will always be most welcome to me." It is evident from another letter of April 10, 1760 that a regular correspondence had sprung up between these men (although nothing of Burke's before July of the next year has been found) and that O'Hara had placed his sons, Charles, aged thirteen, and William, aged ten, in an English school conducted by a Mr. Cleaver. Burke was keeping a watchful and interested eye on them, and O'Hara wrote: "I am much obliged to you for your goodness to my boys; and as owning one's weakness is the strongest proof of confidence in a friend, I will confess that I believe most of what you say of them." O'Hara's sons appear frequently in the scenes depicted in the letters that follow, and were great favorites with all the Burkes.

In 1761 a new chapter opened in the lives of both Burke and O'Hara. The Earl of Halifax was appointed Lord Lieutenant of Ireland and William Gerard Hamilton was made Chief Secretary. As a result, Burke returned, in service to Hamilton, to his native city, there to live in Dublin Castle and assist his employer in managing the Irish Parliament. A new Irish House of Commons had just been elected, because a new king, George III, had just succeeded to the throne. O'Hara, who had never before been in Parliament, would sit in the new House as member for Ballynakil in Queens.

It was on the eve of his return to Dublin, and when the new Irish administration was still in the preparatory stage, that Burke wrote the first of his extant letters to O'Hara.]

BURKE TO O'HARA, July 3, 1761 [1]

Dear Sir,

I did not believe it possible that a letter from you could give me uneasiness. But I own I was sorry, and most heartily ashamed, to see a second letter from you before I had answered your first; especially as it was written in a time of so much hurry, and attended with all those obliging circumstances with which you know so well how to grace every thing you do.[2] My excuse is that I waited to get to town, to discover if possible into what posture things had fallen since you left us, in order to fill my paper with something that might entertain you. But my most diligent enquiry was without much effect; either there is great secrecy, or there is nothing done; however people speak as confidently of peace as if they knew more; the stocks rise, and we expect in a very short time to hear of a cessation.[3] As to domestic affairs my Lord Talbot's reformations make the greatest noise, who has made great sweepings of the Kitchen.[4] Most of the officers have either resigned or been turned out, and those that remain, abridged of their profits and obliged to a small certain salary, lament the bountiful times of an avaricious King. In the meantime I don't find the reformation is very popular; we are so degenerate that we cannot bear the redress of these evils we complained of.

As to the Irish politics, except what I have had from you, I hear very little, and understand still less. I took the liberty of communicating to our friend[5] what you said of the difficulties which arose concerning the commissions. He desired me to tell you that he did every thing he could to remove these difficulties, but at the same time begged leave to laugh a little at the fears they occasioned, the true spirit and character of

---

[1] The original grammar, syntax, and paragraphing of all letters have been preserved, but not obsolete spelling and capitalization. Slight modernizing alterations have been given to the original punctuation. All contractions have been spelled out without bracket enclosure, but where persons are mentioned only by initials, identification is shown by spelling out the names in square brackets. Words that appear to have been omitted by oversight in the original also are printed within square brackets.

[2] These letters have not been found.

[3] Negotiations for peace with France had been going on since March, 1761.

[4] William, first Earl Talbot (1710-1782) was appointed Lord Steward of the Household earlier in the year. For a later comment by Burke on Talbot's attempted economical reform, see *Works* 3: 281-284.

[5] William Gerard Hamilton (1729-1796), as appears from a later passage.

which he entered into perfectly. I heartily wish that things may go on quietly and that my Lord Lieutenant may find his government as successful as the means I dare say he intends to employ in it are fair and disinterested.[6] As for the Secretary, every thing is with him, as you know, manly and honest; he is one of the few men of business whose honour, I am satisfied, is entirely to be relied on, and can neither deceive nor betray; and as to being deceived, you know that is not over easy. If there be a party in Ireland that goes into opposition because the country has been misrepresented, I am afraid it is not the right way.[7] It may perhaps be rather a means by which they may be truly represented as much to their disadvantage as by their former representation; however, I exclude the honest men you mention, who I suppose are some of the most respectable persons you have. I own I am somewhat out of humour with patriotism; and can think but meanly of such public spirit as, like the fanatical spirit, banishes common sense. I do not understand that spirit which could raise such hackneyed pretences, and such contemptible talents as those of Dr. Lucas to so great consideration, not only among the mob, but, as I hear on all hands, among very many of rank and figure.[8] If any of them do it through policy, one may predict without rashness that he will give them room to repent it. I do not know how it is, but I feel myself hurt at this, and the rather as I shall be obliged from decency and other considerations to hold my tongue. I find I run on at a vast rate; but you are kind and will be indulgent to me, as when we met over a little stirabout at St. James street. As to the figure he makes in a medical way, I do not at all wonder at it; that profession is the proper sphere of pretenders; and it is not odd that people should be imposed upon in what they do not under-

---

[6] George Montagu Dunk, second Earl of Halifax (1716-1771) had been named Lord Lieutenant of Ireland in March, 1761.

[7] In the new Irish House of Commons there were a large number of "patriots" who manifested an Irish national spirit.

[8] Dr. Charles Lucas (1713-1771), a Dublin apothecary and political pamphleteer who in 1749 had been driven into exile for attacking the ruling oligarchy. He practised medicine in London for some years, and with the opening of the new reign and the dissolution of the Parliament that had banished him, he was allowed to return to Ireland. A "patriot," he was elected to Parliament from a Dublin constituency. For Burke's attitude to Lucas, see Vincitorio, Gaetano, Edmund Burke and Charles Lucas, *Pub. Mod. Lang. Assn.* **48:** 1047-1055, 1953.

stand, and indeed well cannot, when they cannot distinguish nonsense and absurdity in a common advertiser.

Willy left us more to his satisfaction than ours in about a week after you had quitted London.[9] Mr. Cleaver tells me that the place seems well to be liked and that the person most concerned seems to be pleased with his situation; but the Doctor [10] and I thought, if you approve, that in about a month or so Mr. Cleaver would do well to pay him a visit, and see how all goes on. I am much obliged to you for your kind visits to my father; you spoke of my going over quite in the proper way, enough to try the ground and no more.[11] I am obliged both to your friendship and your prudence in this point, as indeed in what am I not? I expect Will every week from the West Indies.[12] The Doctor is I think better than when you saw him, as I must tell you if he does not, and he will forgive this kind of remark on looks. Adieu my dear sir, and believe me

your ever obliged and faithful humble servant,

E. Burke

July 3d 1761.

BURKE TO O'HARA, July 10, 1761

Dear Sir,

Every time I hear from you gives me occasion of thanks for some new instance of your friendly attention. I am much better since I came into the country, though by [no] means free from pain, nor perfectly restored to my natural rest.[13] However, I find myself getting forward in strength and spirits; for I ride some miles every day, which does me almost as much service as if I had taken Dr. Hill's five medicines, or Dr. Lucas's one. If the latter mountebank should now descend from his

---

[9] O'Hara's second son, William (1749-1790), who was at school under the tutelage of Mr. Cleaver, possibly the Rev. W. Cleaver, master of a private school at Wyford in Buckinghamshire.

[10] Dr. Christopher Nugent (1697-1775), Burke's father-in-law.

[11] Burke had displeased his father, Richard Burke, a Dublin attorney, by abandoning his studies for the bar, and for some years their relations were strained. The elder Burke died in November, 1761.

[12] William Burke (1730-1798) had been appointed secretary and register of Guadeloupe after the British captured it from the French in 1759.

[13] Since boyhood Burke had suffered a chronic ailment of which one symptom was a recurring pain in his side.

stage, it would be of great service to his character; which, if he returns to the usual unhealthy soundness of his intellects, will infallibly come to be known by the dullest of his admirers; and thus his medical quackery will cover the blunders of his political. According to all reports from your side of the water, you will of all losses hardly miss a patriot; we are told that they abound, and that the mob act the part of those troops that are placed to the rear of soldiers of suspected courage to push them forward with their pikes. This I assure you fills me with a real and sensible concern. The disposition which you observed so general here with regard to Ireland still continues, and seems growing into something like a principle of government. There is but one voice about these matters, unless we except Mr. Pitt's; who will however not probably consider them of importance enough to put his whole strength to them, especially as he would probably stand alone in the attempt.[14] As to those most immediately concerned, I am desired to tell you that they have no notion of dividing in order to govern; they only propose not to be absolutely *governed,* and to effect that by whatever means shall be presented.[15] To speak my own opinion, any dryness, slowness, or *sang froid* in the proceedings in that quarter, probably comes from an intention to try new expedients; and if possible to do business on an independent footing and at any hazard; but this is only my own conjecture; for, as you see, what I have said from authority is general enough. However, in putting together what you have hinted in your last[16] with what I have been able to observe, I am more and more confirmed in my opinion; if this be the plan, you see it puts the whole to a short issue, and on a single point; I apprehend they will be supported in this method of proceeding.

If I had answered your letter immediately, I should have told you that the report of the delay on account of the coronation had nothing in it; neither had it at that time; but as the marriage is now settled and declared, I imagine my Lord Lieutenant will wait to assist and to pay his duty to the new

---

[14] William Pitt (1708-1778) , Secretary of State for the Northern Department, whose dominance in cabinet council had now begun to decline.

[15] The Halifax administration in Ireland was to initiate a policy of strengthening the influence of the crown.

[16] Not found.

Queen.[17] Part of her establishment is already fixed: Lord Harcourt is Master of the Horse, and is to go for her immediately.[18] Duke of Manchester is Chamberlain;[19] and Mr. Stone Treasurer.[20]

This letter will probably find you in your rural amusements at Nymphsfield. When you look at the Atlantic Ocean do you think of America?[21] In our old fabulous history I think I have read that the prophet Moses advised the ancient Scots to go as far westward as possible; is this good advice to their posterity? I have been a day in town lately and saw the Doctor and your friends in Wimpole Street, who are well and as usual entirely yours *a vertice usque ad talum;*[22] from the Doctor down to Dick.[23] I am dear sir,

> your ever obliged and obedient servant,
>
> E. Burke

July 10th 1761

I hope you have got my last. Excuse the blots. I can scarce ever write without mistakes and I have as seldom time to copy.

[Burke arrived in Ireland in August, 1761, and spent the ensuing fall and winter in residence at Dublin Castle. He must have seen a great deal of O'Hara, who belonged to the "country gentlemen party" and supported the Halifax-Hamilton administration in which Burke had an unofficial but not unimportant part. Hence the Irish politics of Burke and O'Hara were probably very similar. Both were zealous for the economic improvement of Ireland, and both regarded the "patriotism" of Charles Lucas and his allies with a disapproval bordering on contempt. When the parliamentary session ended, Burke returned to England sometime in the spring of 1762. There he watched the public events of the Earl of Bute's

[17] The marriage of King George III to Princess Charlotte of Mecklenburg-Strelitz took place in September.

[18] Simon, first Earl Harcourt (1714-1777), lieutenant-general, went as ambassador extraordinary to Mecklenburg-Strelitz, there married the Queen by proxy, and escorted her to England.

[19] Robert Montagu, third Duke of Manchester (d. 1762).

[20] Andrew Stone (1703-1773) from 1751 had been sub-governor of the new king and is said to have inspired him with the idea of "the patriot king."

[21] Certain elevations on O'Hara's estate commanded extensive views of Sligo bay and the ocean beyond.

[22] Horace, *Epistles* 2.2.4.

[23] Burke's son, Richard, born in 1758.

administration, which began in May and continued through the making of peace with France and Spain to the spring of 1763, and he reported from time to time to O'Hara. Their extant exchanges begin anew in August, 1762.]

O'HARA TO BURKE, August 10, 1762

Nymphsfield,[24] 10 August, 1762

Dear Sir,

I was as lucky in the receipt of your favour last night so much sooner than answers generally come from London, as I have been ever since I saw you in uninterrupted good health. You may figure to yourself what you please of the happiness of retiring into a place of one's own, but it's by no means such as not to receive an immense increase from your letters. 'Tis however pleasant; not perhaps what you think it, who from the relish you have had for places not your own, are left at liberty to suppose that every void you feel would be agreeably filled up by *property*. 'Tis very well when mixed with a good deal of the world; when one brings from thence a stock of materials for reflection and speculation. The dispositions and habits acquired in one state are corrected by the other; and philosophy has fair play. But one's mind relaxes too much in constant retirement: it is at last *made weak with musing*. If one is religious, one falls into meditation, which is the indolence of religion; if one is prudent, the heart contracts and grows stingy; and if one had any natural address, it turns to cunning and one looks out for a contiguity from a neighbour. This all my knowledge of people who live constantly in the country leads me to think. Then, ambition in retirement is the devil: bashaw over the poor, an intriguer for injustice and oppression on grand juries, and a false neighbour. 'Tis a shocking caricature of *manliness*. I must in addition to all this tell you a discovery that I have made of myself; that too much of the pleasure one has in improving a place of one's own is from vanity. I am never so fond of walks as when I find strangers in them, that think them worth seeing. Nay, it even descended to servants, till they tore all my flowering shrubs, and obliged me to retrench this gratification of my vanity. No, a mixture always does best. I shall go to my solitude on

---

[24] The manor house at Annaghmore.

the Curragh [25] the last day of this month; stay there the meeting, spend a fortnight about Dublin, then to Celbridge races; then home for a month to plant, till November ensures me a new gale, and enables me to see you, Mrs. Burke, the Doctor, my boys, and some other friends. And here I congratulate my two friends with great sincerity on their success in negotiating their several points.[26] Your brother's arm I suppose almost well as no fever followed it. But pray my good friend, give me leave to ask how you came to show my letter to Mr. Hamilton? Wives I have heard should keep no secrets from their husbands, but I never knew that this was a rule in friendship. What I said of him I don't remember; but I am sure it was of a sort I would not say to him. I don't believe he'll ever answer my letter, and I suppose I must pay the King's plate out of my own pocket. This in addition to the multiplicity of business in the new Department, leaves me no sort of chance. However, if rightly informed, I have the *solamen miseris* that nobody on this side of the water has been taken much more notice of than myself.[27] I think his Grace of Bed[ford] will do well at Paris, for a resident minister would not do.[28] But at this time I think him the properest man in England to bring the French to speak with precision. But if Spain and Portugal be not included, they'll only change ours into a land war; and the scene from Westphalia to the confines of Portugal.[29]

I shall write presently to Mr. Jack Burke, who I hope is by this well.[30] He tells me Will's father has brought over some books for me, I suppose from you; I guess what they are, and

---

[25] Race course in County Kildare, thirty miles from Dublin; O'Hara had stables there.

[26] What these "points" were, does not appear.

[27] O'Hara may refer to a pension of 200 pounds per annum that he had been receiving for about twenty years, in compensation for a property claim to the ground on which the custom house at Dublin was built. Among the Annaghmore MSS are: an application from O'Hara to Lord Halifax, Oct. 16, 1761, for an official clarification of the grounds on which the pension had been granted; a copy of a letter from O'Hara to Halifax in the spring of 1762 to remind the Viceroy of some requested favor that had not yet been granted; and a letter from Halifax, April 14, 1763, informing O'Hara that the King had confirmed his pension for thirty-one years.

[28] John Russell, fourth Duke of Bedford (1710-1771), Lord Privy Seal, was sent to Paris to complete negotiations for peace; he sailed from Dover on September 8. Bedford had been Lord Lieutenant of Ireland from 1757-1761.

[29] Portugal, as Britain's ally, was at war with Spain, and a British expeditionary force had been sent there.

[30] Not certainly identified.

FIG. 3. CHARLES O'HARA, *ae.* 50

Painted by Sir Joshua Reynolds in 1765, and reproduced with the permission of the owner, Mr. Donal F. O'Hara.

am much obliged to you. Whether Jack will come here before I set out, or come back with me, is as yet doubtful. When I get into the world again I'll write to you, without waiting for an answer. This phrase of *going into the world* puts me in mind of an island about six leagues from Sligo, which I have but lately known any thing of, called Inish Murray.[31] The race of inhabitants now there are by their tradition of many hundred years standing. If ever they come over to our continent, they call it going into the great world. They are an unmixed people, their Irish purer than our people speak and many of their stories I am told have all the natural beauty so well counterfeited in *Fingal*. They have ruins very singular and of great antiquity. But the innocent simplicity of their lives is extraordinary: extremely hospitable to any stranger that goes among them, and miraculously chaste. Whatever disputes may arise are settled among themselves; they were never known to carry a complaint into *the great world*. 'Tis a part of our County, and yet few of our gentlemen had ever heard of it. When I go to London, I shall try to get this Island. I think you'd pay me a visit there, tho' you won't here. I went yesterday to divide a large mountain farm among its inhabitants, who according to their own tradition have lived under me here for five hundred years; 'tis their phrase. With great difficulty I divided them into four villages, for 'twas an innovation; but I told them they must be modernized. They were sufficiently so as to vice, and I have a desire to make them industrious, and to preserve them. You'd hardly expect this from a man you used to accuse last winter of being as bad as any Cromwellian. I therefore tell it to retrieve your favour. My eyes won't admit of much longer letters; well for you that some defect obliges me to conclude, for I should otherwise gratify myself without mercy to you. A conclusion in form, I have no room for. Yours most truly,

Charles O'Hara

BURKE TO O'HARA, *ca.* August 20, 1762.

Dear Sir,

I returned from London yesterday; I there received your

---

[31] In 1779 there were five houses and forty-six persons on this island; in 1948 all inhabitants departed for the mainland.—Casey, M. T., The story of an island, *Summerhill Annual* (St. Mary's, Sligo) 5: 124-126, 1950.

obliging letter from Nymphsfield. I need not say how agreeable it was to two or three people whose satisfactions you have always been kind enough to think worth your attention. I shall say no more in favour of retirement, lest I should hear still stronger arguments against it; but I shall *feel* as much as ever in its favour, notwithstanding the very philosophical, that is to say, the very solid and ingenious reasons you have given on the other side. As I allowed Celsus's maxim, that a change from city to country, and so reciprocally, is best for the health of the body, I must yield as much to you, that a change of the same nature is most conducive to the health and soundness of the mind. What a pity it is that there should be so much reason and experience against one of the most agreeable delusions with which the human mind has been ever entertained. To settle my thoughts I must enter into a course of Cowley; I shall appeal from the philosophers to the poets, because (as a servant of Mr. Hamilton's said the other day) *I know well enough* they will determine on my side. Thus far you must admit, that while you reasoned against this way of life, you have given a very agreeable picture of it. You charm me with this account of your little new world, which you have discovered so near home. Of what size is this island, or is it described in the map? I wish you may get it with all my heart, for I know that you will be no Cortez, Pizarro, Cromwell, or Boyle to the natives. Happy and wise are these poor natives in avoiding your great world; that they are yet unacquainted with the unfeeling tyranny of a mungril Irish landlord, or with the horrors of a Munster circuit.[32] I have avoided this subject whenever I wrote to you; and I shall now say no more of it, because it is impossible to preserve one's temper on the view of so detestable a scene. God save me from the power, (I shall take care to keep myself from the society) of such monsters of inhumanity. An old acquaintance of mine at the Temple, a man formerly of integrity and good nature, had by living some years in Cork contracted such horrible habits that I think whilst he talked on these late disturbances, none but hangmen could have found any pleasure in his company. Can you get drawings of any of the ruins on Inish Murray?

---

[32] In the province of Munster some of the most cruel excesses had been committed by grand juries and magistrates in repressing the agrarian crimes of the Whiteboys. For Burke's studied opinion of these, see his memorandum in *Correspondence* 1: 41-45.

We expect hourly an account of the conclusion of a peace. This will entirely destroy the hopes of our two friends, upon which you founded your last kind congratulations. They have certainly agreed to give up all their conquests in the West Indies; with them go down a great part of the views both of Will and Dick, who are in great measure at sea again. Will had got almost ready, before this determination of our Ministry, a piece, not to prove, but to demonstrate the superior value of one of those islands only, to every thing else we should have acquired by the last treaty or by the present, which is on the plan of that which we read together in Dublin. It is mortifying that he suffers so deeply by this, and yet dares not tell the public that they suffer too.[33]

The Duke of Bedford continues in his resolution of going to Paris; it is thought he will set out in a fortnight. Before he goes the marriage between his daughter and the Duke of Marlborough will be concluded.[34] This alliance is you see a vast accession of strength to Lord Bute.[35]

Nothing has been done about Irish affairs in general—but the Curragh business Mr. Ham[ilton] tells me has been settled long ago.

Mrs. Burke and my brother are both come to town. They met with Charles and Mr. Cleaver on the road to Luton; both well. I do not hold it right, very much otherwise, mutually to communicate to each other the secrets of one's friends. But there is nothing I knew ill meant, ill wrote, or ill taken in your letter. Mr. H[amilton], if I do not mistake, is as much as any man almost in your interests. I am a little heavy and I take the liberty of scribbling something to you in all humours, as in all humours I am most truly, my dear Sir,

Your most affectionate and obliged humble servant,
Hampton

E. Burke

---

[33] But William Burke did publish his "piece," which was entitled *Considerations on the Approaching Peace*. He was a leading advocate of West Indian annexations, as preferable to the British retention of Canada, and had written two or three earlier pamphlets on this subject.

[34] The marriage of Lady Caroline Russell to George Spencer, fourth Duke of Marlborough, took place on August 23. Later in the year Marlborough was made Lord Chamberlain to the King.

[35] John Stuart, third Earl of Bute (1713-1792), the royal favorite, who had been tutor to the King before his accession to the throne; he had become First Lord of the Treasury in May, 1762, succeeding the Duke of Newcastle.

William Burke, Edmund Burke, and Dr. Nugent to O'Hara,
   October 9, 1762

Dear Sir,

You may imagine that I was a little disappointed yesterday when I came to the borough to wish my friend William a good journey, and found that Mr. Cleaver had taken him out, so that I was not likely to see him before we both go to sea; but this disappointment like many others turned out to my satisfaction in the end, for I had a conversation with the Master which could not so well have passed before Will's face. It gave me so much pleasure that I could wish I had every word of it. He assured me that within a few weeks Will had done more than almost any boy he ever instructed had done in so many months. He showed me his book, and assured me seriously that it was all his own work. He said indeed that Will had cheated him, for that he might make the most use of his time, he had confined him entirely to the necessary branch of the mathematics, and not permitted him to go to the drawing master or music master; but that Will in spite of his teeth had picked up, as he phrased it, his drawing, and had made some proficiency upon the German flute. These are thefts against which there is no process in *foro conscientia,* and I own I think no man will make what he steals more thoroughly his own than William will what he picks up in this way. On the whole the Master ended with saying that he was very cautious of giving characters, as in reality his own character depended upon it, so that upon the whole I do not regret my having missed the sight of my friend; as I think this is much more material than telling he is fat, tall, and handsome; tho' if I had come in here half an hour sooner than I did last night I might have told you that too, for he came to pay a visit to the Doctor, who as well as the women (who to be sure are the best judges in this point) declares him a fine fellow.

I inclose my last effort to *save my country,* and I think it comes in good time; when the balance is even, a grain in either scale will make it preponderate; and I think Guadeloupe, which you may guess is my country, has begun to have a little weight.[36] Charles is quite well, but the rogue gives one none of that joy that is said to be in repentance.[37] Farewell, Ned

---

[36] *Supra,* n. 33.
[37] O'Hara's eldest son, Charles (1746-1822)

has a story of a cock and bull-y to tell you. I am most sincerely, dear Sir,

>   yours,

>> W. Burke

Will has taken all the friendly part, and has only left me that of a newsmonger. However I submit to the condition, and am ready to assume any shape in which it may be in my power to divert you. You remember where the correspondence between Lord Talbot and Wilkes ended in my last letter.[38] Every thing then wore, as you must have observed, a very pacific appearance. After a proper time for recollection, my Lord renewed the negotiation by sending Wilkes a challenge to meet him the next day about five miles from town. Wilkes said he was engaged on a very jolly good humoured party for that day, whom he would be very sorry to disappoint; especially as Sir Francis Dashwood [39] made one of the company, and if he missed him would not fail to guess the occasion and probably might disappoint his Lordship's intentions. At the same time he agreed with my Lord's friend for another day at Bagshot Heath. My Lord consented to the delay, and to the other appointment; and had not been long at the inn at Bagshot before Mr. Wilkes arrived. Norborne Berkeley was my Lord Talbot's second.[40] It was late in the evening and Wilkes proposed with an air of levity that they might pass the evening together and do their business cooly and at leisure in the morning, adding that their *partie carré* that night would not spoil the duet which was to be the entertainment of the following day. The proposal was rejected with great disdain and much abuse; Mr. Berkeley was commissioned to tell Mr. W[ilkes] that he was a great scoundrel, and that my Lord looked upon him as the most impious and profligate of all men, who could

---

[38] The "last letter" has not been found. John Wilkes (1727-1797), member for Aylesbury, in his paper, the *North Briton,* had offended Lord Talbot, by ridiculing his clumsy horsemanship when he officiated as Lord High Constable at the royal coronation. Talbot challenged Wilkes to defend his honor.

[39] Sir Francis Dashwood (1708-1781), at this time was Chancellor of the Exchequer.

[40] Norborne Berkeley (d. 1770), later Baron of Botetourt and Governor of Virginia, at this time was Groom of the Bed Chamber.

think of jesting in an affair of that nature. This message was literally and with a true Homerian fidelity delivered by the serene and gentle Norborne; a situation which I think must make you laugh. Wilkes observed that the abuse in their circumstances was a matter of no consideration; that if my Lord considered the business they came upon as any way criminal, he was himself alone to blame who brought him from London to engage in it. That he valued his life as much as my Lord and thought it as valuable as his Lordship's, and though he expressed himself with levity, he really would be glad of time to write a letter or two, his affairs being in the utmost confusion (which is but too true). The decision, on these reasons, was put off to the next morning.[41] They came to the ground; ten paces were measured; while this ceremony was performed my Lord vented a torrent of billingsgate against Wilkes of which he took no sort of notice. But when they had taken their ground he addressed himself to my Lord and told him that if his Lordship should happen to fall he must expect to be prosecuted with all the rancour backed with all the power which an enraged administration could employ against him; he therefore desired that before these gentlemen who were present he would declare that it was at his Lordship's desire he came to that meeting. My Lord could not refuse this acknowledgment. Their pistols were mutually discharged without any execution; the seconds interposed to prevent a recharging and thought enough had been done. Wilkes took the word again. "My Lord, I have given you one of the kinds of satisfaction you desired; I will now give you the other; I *am* the author of the paper which you thought reflected upon you. I am likewise the author of such and such offensive paragraphs in other papers, which may be thought to reflect upon your friends. I give this explanation once for all and cannot be expected to be ready to answer every call, whenever your Lordship shall think fit. I desire that we may finish every thing here with a perfect reconciliation, or a perfect satisfaction." The former part of the alternative was accepted, I suppose by the interposition of the seconds. The public, always malevolent to great men, think this business ended to the advantage of Wilkes, who they think behaved more firmly, consistently, and coolly than Lord T[albot] from the beginning to the end. I have not

---

[41] The duel took place Oct. 5.

seen H[amilton] since I saw your letter to the Doctor.[42] I think I shall speak to him about the affair of Charles's commission. The negotiation for peace is at a dead stand. No Council has been lately held. Coalitions among the great are talked of, but nothing else. In short, so far as can be discovered all things are in an entire confusion. Compare Lord Bute's situation with yours on the ocean shore. Adieu and believe me dear Sir,

      ever yours,

                          E. Burke

October 9th 1762   I rejoice that we shall soon talk over these things together. Dr. Crane is Bishop of Exeter by our all powerful Lord. F. Keppel had the promise.[43]

Though I come in last, I shall probably be first read.[44] It is somewhere in the Gospels that the last shall be first and the first last. You see by Ned's that I received yours about Charles's affair. I am to have the pleasure of two or three hours with Willy here tomorrow. I talked to him a little of plain and Mercator sailing, and I find he has made the use of his time that Will tells you of in his part. Lord Tyrawley is at Margate taking a warm bath of salt water for his rheumatism, as he calls it. I encouraged the scheme. It were cruel to deprive one of the pleasure, at least, of hoping.[45]

                          C. N.

BURKE TO O'HARA, October 30, 1762

My dear Sir,

I suppose you found large pacquets at Nymphsfield from the Doctor, from Will Burke, and from me. Some of them will entertain, and others at least occupy a good part of your time; **and** prevent something of that *ennui* which otherwise might

---

[42] Letter not found.

[43] Burke was mistaken; Frederick Keppel on Oct. 16 was appointed to the see of Exeter.

[44] Dr. Nugent wrote his postscript across the top of Will Burke's first page.

[45] James O'Hara, second Baron Tyrawley (1690-1773), a relative of Charles O'Hara; he commanded the British army in Portugal, returning to England broken in health in August, 1762.

prey upon you a little, in spite of farming, hunting, and country squires. I assure you I am not the only person who is pleased with the approach of November, and the hopes of seeing you shortly in London. The gentlemen from whose house I write has very many good wishes for you.[46] We shall go to town tomorrow for the winter. I have at last got an house, pretty dear, very good, and extremely remote. I know you play cards sometimes near Cavendish Square, and we may expect to see you (when you happen to break up early) about twelve; and whenever you have ill luck, you need not fear a robbery. If you had not the management to bear that ill luck tolerably, we should have the misfortune of never seeing you, but in an ill humour; for when you were winner you could not be rash enough to attempt Queen Anne Street—so it will be called— *nunc sunt sine nomine terrae.*[47]   As the session approaches things come nearer to a decision. The Duke of Devonshire resigned or rather was turned out last Thursday.[48] Lord Besborough resigned yesterday.[49] This may make pretty sport in Ireland and may provide matter for a very *manly* opposition.[50] I am heartily sorry for the Primate. All the accounts of him which I have seen correspond with yours. I think, take him all in all, he would be a real loss to the country.[51] You have by this read Will's pamphlet, which with regard to public approbation has the success it deserves; with regard to its ultimate object it will I fear have none. Our virtuous Ministry intend to make a clear evacuation of all the French islands. His hand cannot save his *Pergamus.*[52] Nothing has however been omitted. My brother went to Liverpool and excited their sluggish traders to a sense of the danger they were in of losing so vast a trade. They addressed; and their address has been presented by their Member. *Atlas* [53] was "surprised at the greatness of the trade"—

---

[46] W. G. Hamilton.

[47] Virgil, *Aeneid* 6: 776.

[48] William Cavendish, fourth Duke of Devonshire (1720-1764); former first lord of the treasury and lord lieutenant of Ireland; Lord Chamberlain since 1759, he resigned his office and was affronted by the King, thus opening a wide breach between the great Whig leaders and the court.

[49] William Ponsonby, second Earl of Besborough (1704-1793), brother-in-law to the Duke of Devonshire, had been Postmaster General.

[50] Devonshire and Besborough had great property and influence in Ireland.

[51] George Stone (1708?-1764), Archbishop of Armagh since 1747 and one of the most influential men in Ireland; brother of Andrew Stone.

[52] Guadeloupe was restored to France by the Treaty of Paris.

[53] Probably Henry Fox. See next letter.

"knew it not before; obliged by the information"—"but it was now too late." This was his answer. I own I think it hard to form an idea of a shameful peace, if this is not the most shameful that ever was made, and with the least possibility of an excuse. Our friends in London are well. I am sure you will be concerned to hear that my poor mother is in a very declining way under a very cruel nervous disorder. There will I fear one of my strongest links to Ireland be snapped off.[54] I think I have told you every thing. I need not tell you with what truth I am, dear Sir,

your ever affectionate humble servant,

Ed. Burke

Hampton, Oct. 30th.

---

[54] Mary Nagle Burke lived on for some years and is known to have been alive in 1766.

II. Parliament and the Peace of Paris

[Edmund, William, and Richard Burke were together in London in November when Parliament was opened, and the letters that went from their fireside in a house on Queen Anne Street to Charles O'Hara reveal almost all that is known of them during the fall and winter of 1762-1763. They all disliked the treaty which the Duke of Bedford had brought back from Paris, but that did not prevent them from hoping that the ministers responsible for the peace would obtain the necessary support in Parliament. Will Burke had entered into the service of Henry Fox, the Paymaster General, who undertook for Lord Bute to persuade the House of Commons, by whatever means might prove necessary, to vote approval of the treaty. The great point for the Burke clan at this point was, that Will should succeed in laying Fox under an obligation and thus obtain the reward at which he aimed—the governorship of Grenada. On the eve of the debate on the peace, Will sent to O'Hara an account of the situation.]

WILLIAM BURKE TO O'HARA, November 20, 1762

It were not at all surprising that such a fellow as Ned should love to hear from you, but the truth is he loves even to write to you; and but that his Jane carried him off this morning, to bring up their little boy, you would have had a very good account of all our factions and parties, with their pretended and their real intentions; and to make you thoroughly sensible of what you lose by his not writing, he has had the assurance to insist that I should inform you of the views and aims of all our great ones; and if I should in the whole sheet chance to furnish your sagacity with a single hint that may lead you to guess what any one of our numerous factions would be at, I shall not only let you know more than I know myself, but more too I verily believe than they themselves know. There are certainly seeds of discontent in quantity enough to overthrow any ministry, and a sun of prejudice warm enough to ripen them, but they are fallen on rocky bad soil. In one word, the opposition is made up of men whose nature and habit are not simply unfit, they are repugnant to all opposition. The

Duke of Cumberland,[1] affronted, mortified, and so sensible of it as to be resolved upon revenge, is still so full of the old notions of passive obedience and non-resistance as to decline all connections with the creature of the people;[2] but he is close with the old Duke,[3] who has great levées, and in his raven-like voice talks of friendships. The day before yesterday he asked almost every man in the room if they had seen the Dukes of Devonshire and Rutland,[4] "both my very good friends" (his own words). The former stays still in the country; the other goes every day to court. This for the principals, and for the followers Lord Ashburnham [5] desires leave to keep the Park and resign the Bedchamber; Lord Mansfield [6] professes public regard for the old, and sets in council with the new minister, and adds the sanction of his approbation to the terms of the peace. His brother lawyer Lord Hardwicke [7] in any *material question* will divide with Newcastle, thinks that way to pay the debt of obligation so burthensome; one son [8] continues an ambassador, the other Attorney General;[9] that office, it is said must be in hands of trust. But will they [not] fear to leave it with one who professes that if the seals are to be disposed of he hopes to be preferred to Pratt,[10] should Mansfield decline them, to whose merit he submits but who certainly will not take them?

---

[1] William Augustus, Duke of Cumberland (1726-1765), third son of George II and uncle of George III. His political friendships lay with the leaders of the Whig connection whose control of the state was being broken by the King and Lord Bute. These leaders, long accustomed to rule the country, had been thrown into confusion by the resignations of the Duke of Newcastle and the Duke of Devonshire, chiefs of the connection; and a disposition towards parliamentary opposition was beginning to grow among them.

[2] Pitt.

[3] Thomas Pelham Holles, first Duke of Newcastle (1693-1768), long the political manager of the Whig connection; First Lord of the Treasury, 1757-1762.

[4] John Manners, third Duke of Rutland (1697-1779), was Master of the Horse; he deserted the connection for the court.

[5] John, second Earl Ashburnham (d. 1812), was a lord of the Bedchamber and Ranger of St. James's and Hyde Park.

[6] William Murray, Baron Mansfield (1705-1793), Chief Justice of the King's Bench, an unofficial member of the cabinet council.

[7] Philip Yorke, first Earl of Hardwicke (1690-1764) had been Lord Chancellor from 1737 to 1756, after which he had sat as an unofficial member of the cabinet council.

[8] Joseph Yorke (1724-1792), Ambassador to The Hague.

[9] Charles Yorke (1722-1770), Attorney General, who was ambitious to become lord chancellor.

[10] Sir Charles Pratt (1714-1794), Chief Justice of the Court of Common Pleas.

And Pratt is certainly the abomination of the present administration. And when the father has *honourably* discharged his obligations, I should think they would not be jealous or suspicious of his old connections or attachments. Surely this is a conduct worthy of a man whose wisdom has thrived in the world; *ultra spem* should the old people return—he stood by them in the day of disgrace. Should the present people stand their ground, he did but what his honour demanded, nought in malice. His honour once satisfied to his old friends, he and his family are ready to embrace new ones and to enter into new offices. These are the Duke of Newcastle's followers, Devon's are not numerous; Lord Besborough resigns to serve his friend, and for fear it should serve him he writes, as possibly you know, to the Speaker,[11] that he does it not from resentment or dislike, but simply to avoid the unfitness of voting in the same house on a different side from the Duke of Devonshire. This is very pretty, and in a schoolboy's declamation the propriety of weighing out his duties, public and private, with such exactness, will not be omitted, if the lad is ingenious. But in life and in action sure it is absurd. He has strengthened the opposite party by furnishing them with his office, to acquire a new or settle a wavering friend. Devonshire too wisely disclaims any connection with Pitt, who in his turn rejected all offers of Newcastle. Pitt certainly trusts to the chapter of accidents, which to use a friend's phrase will be voluminous. Pitt will probably raise and direct the storm if there is any. One Nuthall[12] of the City certainly told him, that it was reported that the peace was made with his participation and approbation; to which he answered, and begged Nuthall to divulge it, that he knew nothing of the terms but from the public papers, and if the public papers were right, he thought the terms inadequate to our successes, injurious to our allies, and disgraceful to ourselves. I have some mistrust that the Ministry are a little divided, or rather that Bute is a little weary of or afraid of Bedford, who, however he has managed the peace, has certainly strengthened and fortified himself; and they accuse him of having exceeded his instructions, in leaving the fishery open and inserting only that upon the word of the French King there should not be many vessels employed; whereas he should

---

[11] Sir John Cust (1718-1770), Speaker of the House of Commons since 1761.
[12] Thomas Nuthall (d. 1775), friend and legal counsel to Pitt.

by his instructions have restrained the number expressly to I think 20. Which certainly was a fine scheme, a trap to catch moles, who have no eyes, for who that had any would not see that it was directly the same thing, and mere words to name a number of vessels to be employed in a part of the world almost uninhabited and almost perpetually in a fog.

It is said to be almost incredible, the flattery that is thrown upon Bedford at Paris, but it may easily be believed that a great man will receive it all.

The King of Prussia [13] is among the discontented. Some-time since, a kind of half-letter, half-memorial, half-manifesto, or rather in old Tyrawley's words neither letter, memorial, nor manifesto, *mais le Roi de Prusse qui parle* (for it was in that style which none but a mad man or the King of Prussia could be capable of) gave great offence at court. It is now said that his Minister stays only to deliver a memorial to the Parliament. This is so strange that you are not readily to give faith.

For the trouble you have of coming so far, blame Ned. For what you take in going on, I will thank you, for I must not omit answering or thanking you for your last.[14] You very elegantly bid me employ another hand in telling you of the success of my pamphlet. After what you are so kind to say, I will not say that my vanity is unconcerned, for your approbation is not an indifferent thing to me. It was in vain to deny it; it was laid at my door. Some said it was like me, and that whore the public swore I had an interest in it. It was therefore time to see what was thought of it where I hoped it to be well thought of. I waited upon Fox,[15] who began with saying he was much displeased with my having wrote it, why did it not come out sooner, why did I not send a copy, etc. etc. etc. I have always observed that a justification is of more weight than an excuse; in short, you give your money sooner to a robber who demands it, than to a beggar who sues for it. As to sending it, I said that he must know that it would have been thrown under the table. Not to trouble you with all I said, the most material was, that when I wrote he was not in the Ministry, that my dependence was on him and him alone, and

---

[13] Frederick II ("the Great"), who had been allied with Britain and now felt himself abandoned.

[14] Letter not found.

[15] Henry Fox (1705-1774), Paymaster since 1757; long-standing political enemy of Pitt, and now allied with Bute; created first Baron Holland in 1763.

consequently I was to consult the pleasure of none other, but to pursue the likeliest measure to me, for my own interest. And I conceived that if I could draw the public attention, I hoped that of the Minister would follow. He did not, he said, suppose I meant to hurt my friends—owned that he was not then the Minister. I thank God he now is. A day or two after, I went to let him know that I hoped I had some weight with Lord Verney, who had more than one voice.[16] It happened to be the very man he knew not how to come round, and from whom he had received no answer to a letter he had wrote. I had before applied for the government of the Grenades; he now renewed his promises of services; and I left town that moment, found my friend had wrote to him, but pretty much as I could have wished, not warm, and no offer of service. I got his leave to write to Fox that he and his friends would be with him; upon my return I waited on Fox; he said he had already mentioned me as one who might and would serve them, was answered that so I ought for that I had hurt them damnably. I smiled and said that if I had meant to hurt them, it was the *present* not the late treaty which I should have examined—at which he grinned and said it was all one. He is however a man to be depended upon, and I have good hopes that something will be done. If I get the Grenades (and I hope nobody is yet applying) tho' I lose the bet, I have made a good hedge. We are all, even to little Dick if he is father or mother's child, all yours.

Most affectionately,

W. B.

London. Nov. 20, 1762

I am seriously almost ashamed of the length.

BURKE TO O'HARA, November 23, 1762

Dear Sir,

If you are in Dublin you can have no loss in missing this letter; if you are still at Nymphsfield, to which I direct, you

---

[16] Ralph, second Earl Verney in the Irish peerage (1712?-1791). Fox in a letter to Lord Sandwich on Nov. 12, 1763, described Will Burke as "a very clever fellow, and I believe a very honest one. He has as great a sway with Lord Verney, as ever I knew one man to have with another. Lord Verney has another vote besides his own. I owed both to Mr. Burke last session, and they were never absent."—Jucker, N. S., ed., *The Jenkinson Papers*, 413, London, Macmillan, 1949.

may possibly not receive the intelligence it conveys so early by another way. That campaign is at the point of opening and is likely to be fought with more acrimony and with a more balanced strength than any one has for a good while past imagined.[17] Some time ago Mr. Walpole,[18] the great remitter in the City, was sent by the Duke of Newcastle to Mr. Pitt to renew the proposals of accomodation he had formerly made to him; which Pitt rejected as before with disdain; though he had, about that time, made very express declarations, which were carefully spread about the City by his friends, that he would take a warm part against the peace, which he called a *felonious* one, inglorious, and inadequate to our successes. Last Wednesday the Duke of Cumberland went to him, and by pledging himself and Lord Hardwicke for the Duke of Newcastle's fidelity, prevailed upon him to enter the coalition; which is now perfect in all its parts and of such strength, that it threatens to all appearances a more powerful and determined opposition, than has perhaps ever been known before in the commencement of any combination of that kind, and in the outset of the administration they would oppose. It was expected we should have no less than 25 resignations yesterday; but as this has not happened, I suppose they choose rather to wait to be turned out. Lord Mansfield I believe now suffers inwardly for the part he has taken. Lord Halifax is to take the lead in the House of Lords. His character is, without any jest, as high as ever almost any man's was in this country, for ability, for unspotted honour, and for the equal love and confidence of all parties.[19] This is the fact, let the learned reason on the cause. This combination is supposed will be very fortunate to Lord George Sackville and may very probably terminate in some thing to his advantage.[20] You know, that he is said to have refused to take a part if he is not restored to his rank in the army. This however is not yet done. Charles Townshend is thought not yet to be quite fixed.[21]

[17] The King was to open Parliament two days later.

[18] Thomas Walpole (1728?-1803).

[19] Halifax in March had been made First Lord of the Admiralty, and in October replaced George Grenville as Secretary of State for the Northern Department, Grenville taking the Admiralty.

[20] Lord George Sackville (1716-1785) had been courtmartialed and dismissed from the army in 1760, for disobedience to orders at the battle of Minden; his name had been struck from the Privy Council. He now gave energetic support to Fox, but was not recalled to office until 1765.

[21] Charles Townshend (1725-1767) had been Secretary at War since 1761.

There is no more news. We are all well, thank God. Will has
wrote by the last post. His object is the government of the
Grenades. What will become of my brother I know not.
Adieu dear Sir, and believe me most truly and faithfully yours,

E. Burke

23 November. We expect daily to see you.

[The King informed Parliament on November 25 that the preliminary articles of peace had been signed with France and Spain,
and that these would in due time be laid before both houses. The
King stated that the articles not only added an immense territory
to the British Empire, but laid a solid foundation for the increase
of commerce, and that the utmost care had been taken "to remove
all occasions of future disputes between my subjects, and those of
France and Spain, and thereby to add security and permanency
to the blessings of peace." In spite of a wide-spread suspicion that
too much had been sacrificed to obtain the peace, both Lords and
Commons adopted addresses of gratitude and congratulations.
Burke immediately sent an account of the day to O'Hara.]

BURKE TO O'HARA, November 25, 1762

Dear Sir,

I wrote to you by last post, and directed to Nymphsfield.
A body of opposition was then regularly formed; and great
expectations were entertained of their proceedings today. But
if their army is not in disguise, their operations are. This
day of so much expectation has ended in nothing but a very
fine coach, a very long speech, and a very unanimous, dutiful
and loyal address from both houses of Parliament. The administration had so contrived the speech and the address, that
the one did not state the preliminaries as finished, nor the
particulars to which they related, but kept aloof in pompous
and general (though very ill conceived) terms; and the other
did not of course contain any particular approbation, but many
general expressions of satisfaction and confidence. This it
seems satisfied the gentlemen of the opposition. You will
think I conceive no great idea of the opposition by their falling
into so common and so poor a *piege;* and not contriving one
of the many very obvious methods for bringing on a debate,
which would have given the people an idea of their activity,

if not of their strength, and spread about an early discontent. All the plans which I hear they intend to pursue seem to me incomprehensible. It is said Mr. Pitt in his agreement with the Duke of Newcastle made some reserves; what they are I do not hear. He was not in the house today; he has the gout in both his hands, and is besides ill of a fever. Fox was also absent on account of the reversion of the clerkship of the pells which is fallen to him.[22] Lord Carysfort [23] opened the address and Lord Charles Spencer seconded.[24] Lord Carysfort began his speech—"In the splendor of Athens etc."—you may judge how it was from the outset. Calvert, a mad member, after saying some rambling things about the peace, promised the house that he would make them laugh before he had done; and notwithstanding the boldness of this declaration, he succeeded very happily.[25] He observed that his reading had taken the same turn [as] that noble Lord's who made the motion; and that he found all he said in the preface to the Bishop of St. Asaph's sermon upon the peace of Utrecht, which he repeated; and which was very near word for word the same with my Lord's speech.[26] He observed that my Lord had stopped short and not gone so far as the Bishop; for that part of the preface which my Lord had borrowed only mentioned the hopes of the nation, when a treaty was carried on by a virtuous Whig ministry; and then repeated from the same preface an invective against that which was afterward made by the Tories. It was every way well and applicable; the house was pleased, and my Lord infinitely disconcerted. I think one must have suffered for him. This, with a little grumbling by Beckford,[27] and a little defence by Townshend, who took the lead in Fox's absence, formed the whole of this day's work among the Commons.

---

[22] Fox's accepting the valuable sinecure of "writer of the tallies and counter tallies, and of clerk of the pells, in the receipt of the exchequer of the Kingdom of Ireland," necessitated his standing for re-election.

[23] John Proby (1720-1772), first Baron Carysfort in the Irish peerage.

[24] Lord Charles Spencer (1740-1820), second son of the third Duke of Marlborough; he was made Surveyor of the King's Gardens and Waters in December, and Comptroller of the Household the following April.

[25] Nicholson Calvert (1724?-1793).

[26] William Fleetwood (1656-1723), latitudinarian Bishop of St. Asaph, preached a sermon in the House of Lords, Jan. 16, 1712, denouncing the Treaty of Utrecht.

[27] William Beckford (1709-1770), Jamaica-born London merchant and frequent spokesman for Pitt among the merchants.

Lord Egmont moved the address in the House of Lords.[28] He spoke a good while; and ill enough, as I thought. The general drift of his discourse was to show we were a reduced, beggared, depopulated, undone nation, who were notwithstanding very victorious glorious etc. etc. in the style which you will find in the *bon ton* among us at present. Lord Weymouth seconded.[29] There were but 240 at the Cockpit last night, though most of the members were in town.[30] Of these, five were not friends, and one of the five a capital enemy, Wilkes. It was rather impudent of him to appear there. Lord Temple it is said will not be in town till Christmas.[31] Do you know what to make of all this? Pray come hither as soon as you can, and try to decipher us; if you can, you will deserve Bath and Wells at the next vacancy. I saw Charles today. He is grown a very fine fellow; he is certainly much handsomer than when you saw him. The fireside here, for which you are so kind to entertain such good wishes, are your very humble servants, and believe me dear Sir,

Your most affectionate and obliged friend and servant,

E. Burke

November 25. 1762.

BURKE TO O'HARA, December 9, 1762

Dear Sir,

At this instant both houses are sitting on the Preliminaries; they are on a work in which they do not require a great number of spectators, and have accordingly, to my great mortification, issued such orders as have excluded me and the rest of the mob from hearing their debate; before this goes off I shall tell you some particulars; the issue in general we know before-

---

28 John Perceval (1711-1770), second Earl of Egmont in the Irish peerage, and Baron Lovel and Holland in the English peerage since May, 1762; succeeded Lord Besborough as joint Postmaster General in November.

29 Thomas Thynne (1734-1796), third Viscount Weymouth; named Master of the Horse for the Queen early in 1763.

30 Privy Council chambers where government supporters met to hear preliminary reading of the speech and address.

31 Richard Grenville-Temple, Earl Temple (1711-1779), head of the influential Grenville family; brother of George Grenville and brother-in-law to William Pitt; Lord Privy Seal from 1757 to 1761, when he followed Pitt into resignation.

hand. It was a long time in doubt among many gentlemen of the discontented party whether they should oppose the address of thanks intended on this happy occasion; but they began at last to perceive that if they concurred universally in applauding the Administration for a transaction of this importance, their opposition afterwards would not prove so graceful, nor perhaps quite so effectual. They have therefore resolved to draw out their forces on this day, and reckon that they may divide, the moderate people say 110, the sanguine, 170. Not that they imagine this contains their whole strength; but many who will infallibly join in the general opposition, will not concur in opposing this measure; as some of them, before their party was regularly formed, had pledged themselves to support the peace;[32] and many others had been the avowed abettors or makers of terms as bad, or if possible, of worse. They threaten to commence their great game after Christmas. They certainly have derived no small strength from the desertion of Charles Townshend.[33] He resigned last Tuesday. He wanted the Board of Trade with all the plantation patronage which it possessed in Lord Halifax's time, and the cabinet which in the same office had been formerly refused to Lord Halifax.[34] The Administration never loved him; and they trusted him no more than he is commonly trusted; and it was thought too hard a measure to strip Lord Egremont, who had just set his hand to the peace, of so material an appendage of his office as the plantation patronage.[35] I think the opposite party want him more than the Administration, and that they ought to receive him with open arms. They will this day chiefly oppose on the articles of the fishery and the East Indies; the parties are all concerned one way or another in overlooking the West India concerns. Would you believe that the French

---

[32] The Duke of Devonshire, titular head of the Whig connection, was bound by such a commitment. "I am afraid my dear Marquis there will be some difficulties. I shall not be able to go so far as some may wish upon the point of the peace, as I must take care to act consistently with what I have said to the King."—Devonshire to Rockingham, Nov. 18, 1762, Wentworth-Fitzwilliam MSS.

[33] Townshend's knowledge that Pitt was going to attack the peace inspired his desertion of the ministry.

[34] Halifax headed the Board of Trade from 1748 to 1761, and was admitted to the cabinet in 1757. In February, 1763, Townshend deserted the opposition and accepted the presidency of the Board of Trade, with nominal cabinet rank.

[35] Charles Wyndham (1710-1763), second Earl of Egremont, had succeeded Pitt as Secretary of State in October, 1761; although Lord Sandys was then at the head of the Board of Trade, the patronage was controlled by Egremont.

Ministry is charmed with the Duke of Bedford—so reasonable, so moderate, so polite; whenever any difficulties arose, they always left it to himself, and he always put it on the most conciliatory footing imaginable. The air of Paris makes people practicable. You could not learn this secret in Dublin. The merchants have taken great offence at the article which surrenders the conquered islands in 3 months from the definitive treaty. They petitioned Lord Egremont; it is said he ordered himself to be denied; they gave the address to Beckford, and I hear he was to lay it before the House of Commons this day. I have stayed until the post is ready to go out. (I mean the bellman.) The debate still continues, however, the address of thanks will pass; which from a very extravagant, has been lowered to a very modest approbation in order to fit it to the narrow swallow of some squeamish people. I am told you are in love with the peace in Ireland. Adieu dear Sir, and believe me

your very affectionate and obliged humble servant,

E. Burke

9 December. Thursday
Queen Anne Street, Cavendish Square.

BURKE TO O'HARA, December 12, 1762

Dear Sir,

I wrote to you directed at Frederick Street last post. I mentioned the debate and expectation of that day. You know the blustering of the opposition. The Court divided 319 against 65.[36] In the House of Lords there was no division. Lord Hardwicke spoke very nonsensically, and in every respect both of manner and matter, wretchedly; confounded as he was between his attachments to the Duke of Newcastle, his attention to his family interest, and the natural love he has for a bad peace, and any thing low and pusillanimous. Lord Mansfield with his usual dexterity; Lord Bute for two hours—the

---

[36] On Fox's move for an address to the throne thanking the King for "his gracious condescension in ordering to be laid before us the Preliminary Articles of Peace," and stating that the Commons "were impatient to express to his Majesty their approbation of the advantageous terms upon which his Majesty hath concluded Preliminary Articles of Peace."—Cobbet, W., and J. Wright, *Parliamentary history of England* 15: 1258-1259, London, Hansard, 1806-1820.

ministerial people say admirably; Lord Halifax above par. In the House of Commons Pitt spoke for three hours and twenty-five minutes; an apology for himself rather than attack on the peace; very tedious, unconvincing, heavy, and un-methodical.[37] He only spoke some paltry things about St. Pierre and Miquelon. They would not hear Beckford. Charles Townshend said little. Hamilton, Elliot [38] etc. nothing. They did something towards resuming the debate next day but it went very little further than a matter of order, though they sat long on it. In short, all parties are involved in the wrong system, and while they stick to that they will bungle forever. The Duke of Newcastle was quite ridiculous. Pray when shall we see you at our new fireside, which is as cheerful as the old one? I really long for your coming, and am with great truth your very affectionate and obliged friend and servant,

Edm. Burke

Queen Anne Street 12 December 1762

I forgot to tell you that though Lord Hardwicke opposed, his two sons voted in the House of Commons for the address. Will tells me that I am wrong and that they went out of the house before the division.

---

[37] An abstract of this speech is extant. *loc. cit.*, 1259-1271.
[38] Gilbert Elliot (1722-1777), Treasurer of the Chamber since May.

III. Irish Affairs, 1762-1764

[The aftermath of Fox's success in winning parliamentary approval of the preliminaries of the peace was the wholesale expulsion of leaders of the Whig connection and all their dependents from government offices high and low. Political vengeance was carried even to the point of stripping the Duke of Newcastle, the Duke of Grafton, and the Marquis of Rockingham of their lord lieutenancies. Burke seems to have witnessed this "general rout" of the Whigs with cool indifference, while his thoughts turned again to Ireland.]

BURKE TO O'HARA, December 30, 1762

My dear Sir,

We received your last letter with less satisfaction than usual because we expected your own arrival, and your letter was a sort of disappointment;[1] it would indeed be a very heavy one, if the winter should pass over without our seeing you here. Indeed the world is dull enough; even faction is languid; but still you may find more entertainment than in one of the intermediate winters in Dublin. Your next will be sufficiently animated, if I am not mistaken.[2] Though you love peace in Ireland, it seems you have no objection to an army. A scheme for maintaining 18,000 effective men on the Irish establishment has been lately sent over here, warmly supported and recommended by my Lord Lieutenant.[3] Last Tuesday it was agreed to in council, and that number for Ireland will be in the next Mutiny bill. Here it will certainly meet little or no opposition;[4] and we are assured that no measure can be more universally agreeable to, or more ardently desired by the whole people of Ireland. For my part, this same people of Ireland, their notions and their inclinations, have always been a riddle to me. Why they should love heavy taxation; why they should

---

[1] Letter not found.

[2] Presumably, the winter of 1763-1764.

[3] Still Lord Halifax, although he was now Secretary of State.

[4] The plan, which would have meant a fifty per cent increase in the Irish army, was withdrawn; not until 1768 was an augmentation of the Irish forces carried out.

abhor a civil and covet a military establishment, I cannot, I
confess, in the least conceive. As to the latter point, I believe
it is really true. I observed that the least pension or raised
employment was far more odious and unpopular than ten
times that military expence. The truth is this military servitude
is what they have grown up under; and like all licentious and
wild, but corrupt people, they love a job better than a salary;
it looks more like plunder. After all I cannot from any state
of the revenue which I could collect last winter among you,
conceive where you can discover funds for this amazing augmentation. A land tax would not displease me, who have no land,
if I did not see that this tax would terminate in some measure
on the wretched poor; whose burthens are already so lamenta-
bly heavy. It may look whimsical but I am really of opinion
that the last stroke (if something is not done towards enlarging your trading advantages in some little proportion to your
new expences) is given to Ireland. You had none but a landed
interest which had any strength or body in Ireland; and if this
is broke and crumbled to pieces, you are gone without redemp-
tion. Good God, what can these men mean who carried through
this serious measure in mere *gayété de cœur*, and did not take
half the time to think of it, that a man of sense would who was
going to add a single jobman to his family? But I hate to think
of Ireland, though my thoughts involuntarily take that turn,
and whenever they do meet only with objects of grief or indignation. They speak of Lord Hertford [5] or Lord Waldegrave [6] for you; Lord Granby [7] has declined it; Lord Waldegrave, if it were not for the General,[8] would not be very fond
of it; and as it is, I believe will not pursue it with great earnestness. Lord Hertford inclines that way very strongly, but it is
not certain that they will give him what he desires. Our Ministry is thought to have some internal uneasiness. All the
friends of Lord Bute are to the last degree jealous of the progress of Fox. On the other hand, their common enemies charge

---

[5] Francis Seymour Conway (1719-1794), first Earl of Hertford; not until
1765 did he obtain the viceroyalty.

[6] James, second Earl Waldegrave (1715-1763) had been governor of George
III during his minority; he was presently offered the lord lieutenancy, but declined it, and died soon afterwards.

[7] John Manners, Marquis of Granby (1721-1770), eldest son of the Duke
of Rutland; lieutenant general; accepted office of Master General of the Ordnance
in 1763.

[8] Reference not clear; probably Lord Granby.

upon Fox all the late violent measures and he is far from dis-
avowing them. He seems growing fast into a Minister; and
in a short time we shall see whether Caesar and Pompey can
divide power between them. The Duke of Devonshire was not
turned out in the last disposition of lieutenancies; I believe
they choose to leave a door open for him—with a little stooping
he may enter into it, and I imagine he will stoop.[9] He is
thought to be narrow and proud, and that character is to be
wrought upon by being treated with the proper contempt.
You can send no news so agreeable as that of your speedy
arrival. Adieu my dear Sir,

> most affectionately yours,
>
>   E. Burke

Thursday, 30 December 1762

They have got into a new scrape about the great fishery.
It may delay the definitive treaty for some time.

[If Burke's expectation of O'Hara's visit was realized, that may
explain in part why there is no correspondence between these
friends in the first six months of 1763. Little is known of Burke
in this period other than that he received a pension of 300 pounds
per annum from the Irish government, through the influence of
Hamilton and the retiring Lord Lieutenant Halifax.[10]

Among the few surviving letters written by Burke during these
months is one to John Ridge, of Dublin, who was an intimate of
the Burke family and became a close friend of O'Hara. Dr. Nugent
had written to O'Hara on September 28, 1762:

"There left us this day on his way to Ireland where he intends
for the bar, Mr. Ridge. You saw him either at my house or Ned
Burke's; and a better man is not easily met with; uncommonly
sensible and knowing, delicately honest, very friendly, and highly
humourous. I really do not exaggerate. He intends to wait upon
you as soon as he gets to Dublin. You may one time be possibly of
use to him, and if such occasion should arise, I make no doubt
but you will, more on his account than ours, though he is particularly attached to us all."

John Ridge's name crops up frequently in the Burke-O'Hara

---

[9] Burke misjudged Devonshire, who in a few days resigned as Lord Lieutenant of Derbyshire in protest against the dismissal of his friends, Rockingham
and Newcastle.

[10] *Correspondence* 1: 46

exchanges, so that Burke's letter to him of April 23, 1763, which carries on the stream of political commentary and throws some light on the circumstances that led to Burke's return to Ireland, is well worth inserting here.]

BURKE TO JOHN RIDGE, April 23, 1763 [11]

Dear Ridge,

I hope, though you have not answered, you have received my last; it gave you a short account of our change of ministers;[12] everything still remains in a state of the utmost uncertainty. The Duke of Rutland is disgusted, and Lord Granby of course, not well pleased; Charles Townshend is in the greatest and most merited disgrace for his unsteady behavior; he was offered the Admiralty; deliberated on it; accepted it; and on the very day and at the very moment, when his fellow commissioners were kissing hands, refused it, because two of his friends (who never had any promise) were not brought in with him. The King ordered Lord Halifax to send him word the next morning, that he had no occasion for his service in any capacity. What is not a little extraordinary, Lord G[eorge] Sackville, who has long been in favour, is now coming into place. Some speak of Treasurer of the Household, others of the Navy; but that he is coming in is not to be doubted.[13] He will not be a ballast for the loss of Townshend; and he seems to bring only an additional reinforcement of unpopularity to the Administration without a full, though with some, proportion of ability. The Irish arrangement is at length fixed: Lord N[orthumberland] [14] and H[amilton], Lieutenant and Secretary. This will be I dare say a thing advantageous to the country; and it is to me particularly agreeable, as I may hope to see you this winter. Be so good as to give me a very full account of all the speculations on this subject which you have on your side of the water. I see by Williamson's last paper that they are reviving the rebellion stories; and have produced a second story, indeed more plausible as to the manner than the former; they assert it was

[11] Wentworth-Fitzwilliam MSS.

[12] Bute resigned on April 8, and the administration was reconstituted with George Grenville as First Lord of the Treasury.

[13] Sackville received no office until 1765.

[14] Hugh Smithson Percy (1715-1786), second Earl of Northumberland; closely allied with Bute, he had been made Lord Chamberlain to the Queen and Lord Lieutenant of Middlesex (in succession to the dismissed Newcastle).

proved on the trial of Dweyr at Clonmel; for God's sake let
me know a little of this matter, and of the history of these new
levellers. I see that you have but one way of relieving the
poor in Ireland. They call for bread, and you give them not a
stone, but the gallows.[15] Adieu my dear Ridge; we have no
news; we are all thank God well and wish to hear as soon as
possible that you are so. God bless you, Kitty and your little
ones, and believe me with great truth yours.

E. Burke

April 23

Though Lord B[ute] is out it is universally believed that
he governs every thing and indeed appearances are favourable
to that supposition.

[No letters from Burke to O'Hara of the years 1763 and 1764
have been preserved by the O'Hara family, but two that O'Hara
wrote to Burke in July, 1763, are worth inserting because of the
light they cast upon a particularly obscure period of the latter's
life.]

O'HARA TO BURKE, July 4, 1763

Ardbraccon, 4 July

My dear Sir,

At my return to Dublin from the Curragh, I found most
of my acquaintances engaged in a jolly round of dinners to
welcome Rigby; [16] who was more caressed than ever man was in
a country where people thought he would not be well received.
Hamilton came time enough to be at many of the dinners, took
kindly to his claret, and grew fat upon it. Rigby pronounced
he would do but expressed apprehensions that seeing the many
friends his jollity had made, Ham might run into excesses next
winter, and hurt his constitution. I found the gentleman with
a complexion unusually florid the night I came to town, and
sat with him half an hour. I happened to find him once more

---

[15] Burke was undoubtedly alarmed for the safety of his numerous Catholic
relatives on his mother's side in County Cork.

[16] Richard Rigby (1722-1788), political agent for the Duke of Bedford,
whose party was soon to be strongly represented in the Grenville administration.
Rigby had been Chief Secretary in Ireland during Bedford's viceroyal administration, 1758-1761, and was made Master of the Rolls for Ireland; he was also one
of the vice-treasurers of Ireland.

at home, but so hurried that I did not stay ten minutes. And he had so much to do, and so much to negotiate, that I doubt whether I could have seen him for ten minutes more without breaking in upon his manœuvre. So I left town before he was to sail. You'll have his story from himself before you receive this. I followed him in some places *sur ses brisées;* could just discover that he had been busy, and that he will still have a good deal more to do at his return. I found he had expressed great attachment to Lord North[umberland] and was told so in a way which demanded my opinion; I said I believed it very sincere, and that the affection was mutual; that it must be so if the report in London was founded, that each had a share in the other's appointment; but that I could answer for it, from what I myself had observed, that it was with the most visible satisfaction on both sides. Since I left town I have heard that there is some sketch of the present state of Ireland in hands for the press.[17] I said I hoped that nothing would be published to foment the discontent and suspicion of people at this time, etc. etc. etc., that if ever we were to be served it must be by an humbler address than could be founded upon angry and disrespectful resolutions. What I said was agreed to, and I was given to understand that this piece was to recommend a spirit of that kind, but yet to let the people know how they were used. Should this be the case, we may wish to see you on more accounts than one. My vow, never to abuse Lord Halifax, sits very easy upon my mind at present, for go where I will, I hear it done for me, and very often in this singular tack, "I am sure I have no reason to complain of a breach of promise, for he did what I asked for but—"

I have not heard from Cleaver since my arrival in Ireland, tho' when I saw him at Oxford, he left me in doubt whether he should be able to stay with Charles much longer. But as he seemed resolved to consult you before he took a resolution, I am pretty safe as to knowing it long enough before hand.

Mr. Dennis paid me two or three visits at the Curragh at race time, and between the heats we had a little conversation.[18]

---

[17] O'Hara may refer to something Burke was writing. Among the Wentworth-Fitzwilliam MSS is a short paper in Burke's hand which appears to be a plan, or rough draft of an introduction for an analysis of "The Public Debt and the State of Ireland." No such work was ever published by Burke.

[18] William Dennis had been Burke's friend when they were together at Trinity College; he took holy orders, and by 1763 had obtained a parish in the diocese of Kildare.—Samuels, *op. cit.,* 209-214.

I stopped at Naas in returning to town; and he was good enough to dine with me. He told me he was the author of a letter about the Levellers printed in *Wilson's Magazine* which the Doctor lent me in London, and which we liked so much. He also showed me an answer to it in the *Cork Gazette* which licks him handsomely for a mistake in his computation of the number of houses in Munster, which he was led into by Wilson, but which Wilson after corrected, tho' Dennis had not observed it. He told me he had not done with the subject, but was preparing something more upon it, for the next magazine. I hope he'll give full employment to the Cork writers. By the papers I find the Rev. Mr. Ellis is returned from England, which puts me in mind to tell you his piece of good fortune, extremely singular in its kind. The late Lord Meath had a natural daughter for whom he intended all his personal estate, the rest being settled; and having explained his designs to his parson, made his will and left it all to him in trust for her. The daughter died some time ago, and my Lord very lately without having made any other will, so that Ellis becomes now entitled for his own to about £60,000, a pretty circumstance for a poor parson. The night before I left town, I saw old John Burke at the play; he looked well, but I found him in conversation a good deal moped.

I am now on my way home to spend two quiet months at Nymphsfield, before the hurry of town life begins. I have wrote and got others to write to different parts of the sea coast about the fishery,[19] and shall expect my answers there. I wish we may have people left over for this business; for besides the daily reports of people's going to North America from other parts, there are at this very time in (I think) the *Belfast Gazette* fourteen ships advertised to sail in some short time from that coast with passengers to different parts of North America. A detachment of the army being ordered to quell the Blue Stone Boys, a set of northern Levellers will fill these ships immediately. These Blue Stone Boys object to the barony cesses appointed by a late act of Parliament. Dr. Young has been

---

19 Burke and O'Hara were interested in promoting fisheries off the west coast of Ireland. It is not improbable that they helped to prepare An Act for the Encouragement of the Fisheries of this Kingdom. 3 George III c. XXIV, *Statutes at Large passed in the Parliaments held in Ireland* 9: 132-137, G. Grierson, Dublin, 1786.

extremely lucky in a bishopric's being so soon vacant;[20] but I doubt whether my Lord North[umberland] be so. It might as well have happened next spring. Present my compliments to Mrs. Burke, the Doctor, and the two Americans.[21] Before I conclude give me leave to give you the trouble of calling at Dodsley's in your walks. I sent some books to him which I had bought, and intended to have called upon him to have added to the number to fill a box to be sent to me by long sea to Dublin. If you should meet with any other books there worth my having, lay them by for me. I owe Mr. Dodsley [22] a little bill; he will add these others to it, that I may desire Mr. Cleaver to pay him. If the box should be small it may be directed to Mr. Kenna at Chester to be forwarded to me. I am

> my dear Sir, yours most truly,
>
> Charles O'Hara

O'HARA TO BURKE, July 26, 1763

Nymphsfield, 26 July 1763

Dear Sir,

I had not only the pleasure of being relieved from some apprehension about you last night, for the silence of a cholicky man is unpleasant, but also of reading a whole page in the spirit I expected, relative to our Northern bustle.[23] What it is, I neither know nor care, tho' five or six clergymen from the North have taken refuge in my neighbourhood, and tho' some of the Hearts of Oak are within a few miles of me.[24] It has hurt our market, and so far I'm concerned. The various speculations which come forth upon it are extremely entertaining. But as they are all mixed with political reports, I could not help observing that not one of them has been in favour of our

---

[20] Edward Young was created Bishop of Dromore in 1763.

[21] Presumably, Richard and William Burke.

[22] Robert Dodsley (1703-1764), author and bookseller, or his brother James (1724-1797), also a bookseller.

[23] An insurrection that broke out in Armagh and spread through several other northern counties. Viscount Charlemont, chief patron of the Irish patriots and the man who introduced Burke to Hamilton, took the lead in suppressing it; for which service he was made an earl.—*Manuscripts and Correspondence of James, first Earl of Charlemont* 1: 22, 136-137. Hist. MSS Comm. 12th Rep., Appendix, Part X, London, H. M. Stat. Office, 1891.

[24] An insurgent organization.

Lord Lieutenant. At best, he's a poor weak man, means no harm himself, but is entirely under the government of his Secretary. I was in hopes that the tide of lies would have flowed in his favour by this time, but of this I am certain, that it has not yet flowed thus far.

I did myself perceive less warmth in the Bishop of Kildare [25] towards Dennis than there had been. But we'll blow up the embers. He's a very agreeable fellow. But I left him on a wrong scent for remedying the evil he so well accounts for, and he was not at Naas as I came through. My enquiries about our fishery have as yet procured me but little satisfaction, from the ignorance of the people concerned in it. But I am pleased to find that they can dry them very well upon our coast and cure them well with salt made on the shore of our own ocean. They have killed but two whales on this coast this season, through the unskilfulness of the people employed. I don't apprehend that the spirit of Patriotism will be the least obstructive to us next winter. And I am very sure our house would be a quieter scene if the attention of *Gentlemen* was a little diverted to the public good. This is true, but Ham[ilton] will call us a pair of fools for all this. But go on, prepare your materials, and I am very apt to believe that before the end of the session he will allow we have done no harm.

I grieve at what you say of Will Burke. Reversions will never do for his impetuosity.[26] But as the Ministry in general don't promise a long duration, I hope his refusers will take the lead in retiring. I have had a long letter from Cleaver since I wrote to you in which he desired my opinion, and seemed desirous of the Christ Church scheme. I hope he'll show you my answer. I would not hinder his preferment, and my conformity to this new scheme will but send Charles three months sooner to Oxford than he otherwise would have gone. I had a letter from him last night wherein he asks me how he shall get passports for France. My scheme is only that he should spend his vacation in French Flanders, to talk French. And the passports won't be wanted. I wish a letter was procured for him to the Governor of Calais or St. Omer just to say what sort of people they are to prevent Cleaver's being taken up for a spy. If Lord Hertford were in London I would write to him

---

25 Richard Robinson (1709-1794), translated to Armagh in 1765.

26 Will Burke had been disappointed in his hope for employment, probably because of the change of administration.

for one,[27] but if you would take the trouble to get whoever is chargé d'affaires spoke to about it, the end would be equally answered. If any difficulty should occur, they need not go. The French are not *apprivoisé* yet; their giddiness in going about the ramparts of a fortified town might occasion their being taken up. Last night's post brought me a letter from Will wrote in high spirits and dated at Havannah.[28] I shall say nothing of my obligations to you and Mrs. Burke for the trouble taken on this account, but that I am dear Sir,

most truly yours,

Charles O'Hara

[Burke spent the parliamentary winter of 1763-1764 in Dublin. Little more is known of his life at this time than that he was to some extent involved in the sharp political disagreements that arose between Chief Secretary Hamilton and Primate Stone. Northumberland, the Lord Lieutenant, sided with Stone and Hamilton early in 1764 was removed from his office. Since Burke had no official place in the Irish administration but was attached solely to Hamilton, this event marked the end of his duties at Dublin Castle. Hence he returned to England.

Soon afterwards, the Burke fireside on Queen Anne Street suffered the departure of Richard Burke for the West Indies, where he received an appointment in the customs administration on the island of Grenada.]

---

[27] Hertford had been recently named ambassador to King Louis XV.
[28] O'Hara's son.

IV. Secretary to Lord Rockingham, 1765

[It is evident that all was not smooth in Burke's relations with William Gerard Hamilton, even before he became, through his employer's influence, a pensioner of the Irish government in 1763.[1] These relations seem to have deteriorated greatly after the men returned to England. Against Burke's wishes, Hamilton asserted a right to monopolize all his time and energies. In a letter to O'Hara (July, 1764), which unfortunately has not been found, Burke seems to have hinted his discontent and wish for some different employment. Replying on July 24, O'Hara commented: "What has happened within your own circle, not satisfactory, you don't say. . . . I learned from Will Burke that the employment offered to you would have taken up your whole time. This was certainly one reason, and I can imagine some others against your accepting it. I should fancy it however of use to have the sort of thing you would like known to people."

Early in 1765 Burke and Hamilton came to a parting of their ways, with great bitterness of feeling on both sides. Burke even gave up his pension in order to be free of all obligations to Hamilton, and in private letters denounced him in bitter terms.[2] O'Hara, a friend to both men, went to England and attempted to bring them to reconciliation, but Hamilton appears to have been as implacable as Burke.[3] The differences that broke their connection were political as well as personal, for Burke testified that Hamilton's conduct in public affairs had become "directly contrary to my opinion, very reproachful to himself, and extremely disgustful to me." [4] Perhaps the personal differences would have been resolved if Hamilton had been willing to go over to the parliamentary opposition, for in that direction Burke's preferences now lay. Hence he formed some sort of connection with Charles Townshend, a leader among the younger and more energetic opposition Whigs.

The hopes of these Whigs rose high during May, 1765, when the King sought to rid himself of the ministry led by George Grenville and to place William Pitt at the head of a new administration. The royal effort failed because Pitt declined the offer made to him, and Burke's new "patron," Townshend, then accepted the Pay

---

[1] *Correspondence* 1: 46-51.

[2] *Correspondence* 1: 65-81.

[3] Annaghmore MSS, Hamilton to O'Hara, March 18, 1765.

[4] *Ibid.*, 77.

Office, although without wholly disconnecting himself from the opposition forces.[5] The ministerial crisis continued, and, early in June, Edmund and William Burke sent to O'Hara, now back in Ireland, an account of the political situation.]

EDMUND AND WILLIAM BURKE TO O'HARA, June 6, 1765

My dear Sir,

I never received a letter from you which gave me more joy than your last;[6] for having calculated that I ought to have heard from you a good deal earlier, I began to apprehend something for your health; and my fears were confirmed by your appearing not [to] be quite so well as usual when you left us. I do declare, I do not think there is a man living for whose welfare I should be more heartily solicitous than yours. We were making a sort of scale of our affections yesterday, and we were unanimous in that opinion. For God's sake attend a little to yourself, and remember, that though fifty is a good age for business, it will not bear the kind of riotous life that you lead. Things here are still in confusion. You know, that by the defection of Lord Temple to his brother George, the minority is divided;[7] Pitt will not part from his family, but declares much obligation and gratitude to the King, and a resolution in consequence not to oppose. Mr. Pitt having declined all share in the negotiation, the Whigs are resolved to try whether they cannot make up an administration by themselves. The King has left the terms and the men entirely to themselves and protests himself willing to acquiesce in any thing but the present administration. They proposed last night, that the King should send for Townshend, who is in the country, and not in the best state of health, to desire him immediately to come to town. They intend to offer him the Chancellorship of the Exchequer with an addition of salary, and a proper measure of power, suitable to the place. This scheme was yesterday sent to Richmond to the K[ing], and I suppose a messenger went that night to Atterbury. So that unless it met some remora

---

[5] Townshend professed the conviction that Pitt alone could form a durable and strong administration. Wentworth-Fitzwilliam MSS, Townshend to Burke, June 23.

[6] Not found.

[7] Temple, hitherto at odds with his brother, was reconciled to him, and advised Pitt not to accept the task of forming a new administration.

at the first suggestion at Court, Townshend will be up tonight.[8]
You will hear that Lord Temple flew off on account of Lord
Bute; but do not believe a syllable of it.

[here William Burke writes]

Your letter was indeed equally grateful to us all. Ned
could not on your own account wish more to see you just now
than I do, but I, with whom our interests weigh more than
with him, for their sakes can wish more ardently than he, that
some chance had detained you here until now.[9] If that had
been the case, I verily believe some good would have turned
up to us both; but for want of such a friend as you to forward,
to ripen the little budding hopes that arrive, get birth today
and die tomorrow, nothing will be. Lord John Cavendish,[10]
possibly from some things dropped by yourself, has mentioned
us both as fit men to be employed to Lord Rockingham,[11] who
received it well—but what then? We have not a friend in
the world to keep the impression alive. Some thing will, I hope
however, turn up. Adieu, you shall have your act and the
customs.

[here Edmund resumes]

We ought not to forget how much we are obliged to Fitzherbert [12] for his most friendly and zealous, and indeed well
managed and elegant recommendations of us to all this batch of
people. I cannot express to you, how much and how well he
has done. Lord Rockingham went down to Townshend; but
as neither are yet returned, though it is now near ten at night,
we know the effect of that negotiation. It is certain, that if
they act wisely, they cannot fail to make up a lasting administration. I call taking in Lord Bute, or at least not quarrelling
with him, and enlarging their bottom by taking in the Tories

---

[8] Townshend declined.

[9] Probably because of O'Hara's friendship with General Conway, who seemed
certain to come soon into high office.

[10] Lord John Cavendish (1732-1796), brother of the late fourth Duke of
Devonshire, became one of the treasury lords in the new administration.

[11] Charles Watson Wentworth (1730-1782), second Marquess of Rockingham, who was now coming to the front as leader of the Whig connection.

[12] William Fitzherbert (d. 1772) was to occupy a seat on the Board of
Trade in the new administration. He has been described as "a great friend to
authors and to letters."—Prior, Sir James, *Life of the Right Hon. Edmund
Burke*, 80, 5th ed., London, G. Bell, 1878.

and all the men of business of the House of Commons not listed against them, acting wisely. As to the Lord Lieutenant, that totally depends on the other arrangements; this only I can say for certain, that let the arrangement be what it will, Lord Weymouth [13] may go if he thinks proper (by news of the Duke of Portland) .[14] I am much hurried and it is late; next Saturday I shall enlarge on all the points you mention in your letter. My humble respects to the Primate.[15] You see I am little affected by Hamilton. However I should not have been sorry had you called on the parties we first mentioned. Adieu my dear Sir,

> your ever affectionate friend,
>
> E. B.

Thursday 6th June

[By the time another month had passed, the King, negotiating through the Duke of Cumberland, was able to transfer ministerial power from Grenville and his associates, to the leaders of the Whig connection. But this did not take place until after new efforts had been made to coax Pitt to return to office. Some Whig leaders did not believe they could succeed without Pitt, but a majority decided to attempt it. At their head was the young Marquess of Rockingham, on whom the mantle of the aged Newcastle and the titular leadership of the deceased Devonshire now fell. Among those who doubted the durability of an administration without Pitt, and who therefore refused to take an active part, was Charles Townshend.]

BURKE TO O'HARA, July 9, 1765

My dear Sir,

In this immense stir and uncertainty of affairs, I know you cannot be unconcerned even at Nymphsfield; though you, whose mind gaming and politics cannot disturb in Almack's and Arthur's, will hardly be driven out of your course on the shore of the Atlantic Ocean. But if politics do not find the way to you, to disturb your domestic and rural happiness, your

---

[13] Weymouth's appointment to the Irish viceroyalty had been forced upon the King by Grenville and Bedford; he never assumed the duties of the office.

[14] William Henry Cavendish Bentinck (1738-1809), third Duke of Portland, who became Chamberlain of the Household in the new administration.

[15] Richard Robinson, Lord Rokeby, succeeded George Stone as Primate in 1765.

friendships will still engage you to think a little of those whose ambition or necessities oblige them to live in the storm; you have friends high enough to be actuated by the one, and low enough to be impelled by the other; and if the latter are the least considerable, they are the most innocent, and, I am sure, as much therefore in your thoughts and wishes as the former.

After several consultations and much irresolution, the principal people who are to compose the new administration kiss hands tomorrow. The delay was chiefly owing to Charles Townshend; who in this affair acts a part which time, and circumstances concealed at present, may show to have been a proper one; but which as far as I can look into the motives, conduct, and consequences of it, gives me no satisfaction. His actions, which seem never to have been influenced by his most wonderful abilities, are grown of a much worse complexion, (because they are much less his own), since his reconciliation and close connexion with Lord Townshend.[16] This connection, which ought in the order of nature and common justice to be for the advantage of the younger brother, has been totally carried on for the interest, and been governed by the spirit of the elder. It has drawn tears of indignation and grief from me, to see the manner in which they proceed. The party coming in, who would have derived from and given dignity to Charles Townshend, by his management has been hurt very considerably; and they in turn have put him backward in the estimation of a great part, at least, of the world. His situation and abilities gave him great importance; he might have, and was solicited to choose his place; and he might have had it with much importance, and much honour; and *there* (but not where he is)[17] might be in a capacity of correcting the errors, which certainly exist in the system. But his brother, hating and hated by the Duke of Cumberland; and probably held down besides by some concealed engagements with Mr. Grenville, and wishing, as I know he did, for the Lieutenancy of Ireland, (which it is not clear that he could get) has kept Charles from taking the seals or the Chancellorship of the Exchequer, or standing forward in this new administration. He proposes indeed, and engages to support, but, *I am told,* will not come forward into any of the active situations. I say

---

[16] George, Viscount Townshend (1724-1807), major general; Lieutenant General of the Ordnance since 1763.

[17] The Pay Office.

I am told; because I saw the two brothers this morning, just as they were going to Court; they talked in a dissatisfied manner, but I imagined, knowing Lord T[ownshend]'s object and the necessity of pleasing Charles at this time, that they would have settled every thing at the Queen's house. I proposed to see them on the return but missed them; I tell you what I heard. However, the arrangement proposed on his declining is, Lord Rockingham the Treasury, Duke of Grafton [18] and Conway [19] Secretaries of State, Dowdeswell [20] Chancellor of the Exchequer. The other lines are not at present worth knowing; these are the principal. Conway had engaged to become Chancellor of the Exchequer, but is got off of it at his own desire. I am not clear whether he will even stick to the seals. But the next Gazette will settle all. So much for the ambitious; now for the honest necessitous. Will and I are down on their lists, and I hope and believe will be attended to. Words cannot paint to you the indefatigable, unconquerable zeal and friendship of Fitzherbert to serve us: I shall give you an history of his good or ill success by the next post. In the meantime thank God, appearances are tolerable.

The young gentlemen [21] will learn classical elegance and honest agriculture with you; in both which I envy them; whilst we are tagging at the heels of factions. But they too will be so engaged; but with better abilities and, in more honourable stations, with better success; but not with more honest intentions. Pray continue to love us, who value you as much as any man ought to be valued. O! what a loss to us, that you are not here for a few hours! I never felt the loss of you more than now; no, not the day you left me. Your Lord Lieutenant is not fixed. I fancy Lord Hertford. [22]

Tuesday 9th July 1765

You go to Richhill. [23] Pray present my most affectionate duty to my Lord Primate. You will tell Sir Septimus [24] that I

---

[18] Augustus Henry Fitzroy (1735-1811), third Duke of Grafton, became Secretary of State for the northern department.

[19] General Henry Seymour Conway (1721-1795), younger brother of the Earl of Hertford, became Secretary of State for the southern department.

[20] William Dowdeswell (1721-1775), a Worcestershire county member who had taken a leading part in protesting Bute's Cider Act of 1763.

[21] Charles and William O'Hara.

[22] Hertford was named Lord Lieutenant.   [23] Village near Armagh.

[24] Sir Septimus Robinson, brother of the Primate.

am most sensible of his kind partiality to me. My respects to Mr. Robinson. I remember a saying of my Lord Primate's that we had not in Ireland the materials of a nation. Assure his Grace that we are not in a condition to supply that deficiency from England. Shall we ever see men? You are narrow in Ireland; but you know what you would be at. If you find my friend Dean Barrington say I am a sad dog, for to him I am so, and he will be goodnatured enough to contradict you.

Burke to O'Hara, July 11, 1765

My dear Sir,

My letter by last post was a long one. This will be very short. The papers show you the ministerial changes, in which you will be pleased to see your friend Conway in possession of the seals. I have got an employment of a kind humble enough; but which may be worked into some sort of consideration, or at least advantage: Private Secretary to Lord Rockingham; who has the reputation of a man of honour and integrity; and with whom, they say, it is not difficult to live. Will is strongly talked of for a better thing.[25] All my speculations are in my last letter. Adieu my dear Sir,

       affectionately yours,

                             E. Burke

July 11th 1765

O'Hara to Burke, July 19, 1765

                          July 19th, 1765

My dear Sir,

Your letter has not given me information only, but infinite satisfaction also. You could have nothing more to my mind, than what you now set out with. Lord Rockingham is the properest man for you in the world: extreme good sense, of very gentle manners; and what pride there may be is of a sort never to offend. I like the thing so well, that I could not help saying a good deal about it to Conway, to whom I have just wrote. You will naturally come in his way. Don't be kept off by a dryness of manner; you'll find both the head and heart sound and good. I stayed a week with him in my way to Ireland,

---

    25 He presently became secretary to General Conway.

where much was going on; part of which has now taken place.
Ch[arles] Townshend risks a good deal to please his brother.
It will be natural I think to let somebody loose upon a man
they can't gain; to destroy that character they can't avail themselves of; for he is less in their esteem than in the opinions of
those people who have lately made him offers. I understand
from yours that you still go on with him tho' you belong to
Lord Rockingham. This may prove a nice card to play; and
the opinion people have of Ch[arles] will make it more so. I
like their going on slowly, it promises more certainty than
sudden changes have. I hear Conway will make room for Pitt.
What now becomes of my respectable friend! [26] Amongst these
men he'll never do. And I don't believe he'll come over with
Lord Hertford. I am now at Hazlewood, and was called upon
last night by Col. Wynne to tell him the whole story of your
separation. 'Tis certain that while he was expected to come
over with Lord Weymouth, Lucius O'Brien [27] and one or two
more received his account more favourably than I believe they
now would. I did not think it worth while to set them right.
All people of consequence were so clear on your side. But at
Conway's I took a little more pains. I found O'Brien talked
of for the Chair of Privileges and Elections. Pery [28] has talked
the Speaker [29] into it. Whether I have talked him out of it or
not, I can't say; but he had my opinion freely, and shall have
it again. The Primate knows the story very well; we were upon
it at different *reprises*. I shall transcribe a passage from your
letter for him presently, for I can't go to Richhill. My agent
has kept me too much employed. I closed accounts with him
the day before yesterday about £1100 out of pocket, for which
I have taken back a lease he has from me that will bring in
about £80 a year additional rent. But money's more to me
than income. You do Ireland honour in saying we know what
we would be at. Perhaps we might find it out if we dared look
towards it. But this we are deterred from by the insufficiency
of our means. We feel we are injured, but we know too that
we are extremely ignorant. Lord Hertford however will find
us in good humour with him. But we are split into such a

---

[26] William Gerard Hamilton, who was eager to return to office in Ireland.
[27] Sir Lucius O'Brien (d. 1795), a patriot member of the Irish House of
Commons.
[28] Edmund S. Pery (1719-1806), member of the Irish Parliament.
[29] John Ponsonby (1713-1787), brother of the Earl of Besborough.

variety of parties that it will require some management to collect us.

I long to know something about Will Burke. In the meantime present him my congratulation upon his being at liberty to abuse George Grenville as much as he pleases. I find you had not got my letter [30] when you wrote and upon my word I want your help. The merchants of Sligo are building some busses.[31] And think of me left to myself to draw heads of a bill in my own most *illegal* style for giving leave to papists employed in the linnen manufactury or fishery to take long leases. Besides you have my fish bill. I still propose to see you next Christmas, and nobody but one of your new secretaries,[32] and your own fireside. The boys and I fagg a little, but shall do more. Charles's leg grows better, by the application of Lady Shelburne's plaister. Is her son thought of? I do love you and shall continue to love you. Adieu my dear Sir,

Chs. O'Hara

O'HARA TO BURKE, July 30, 1765

Nymphsfield, 30 July

I greet you both with sincere congratulation. Will, with all thy noise, *etourderie* and abuse, thou art now connected with the gentlest manners, and the best heart that ever approached the ministerial rank. I hope you'll neither of you catch from the other: your noise would make a strange riot in Conway's character, and you don't want either his honesty or his good nature. Edmund, you are a little less lucky than Will. You have pride to deal with, but much softened by manner; and exceeding good sense; but you must feed it, for it can't feed itself. I dare say Conway has long since talked you over with him.[33] I shall always join you in most sincere regard and esteem for Mr. Fitzherbert; I feel a share in the obligation, and in the gratitude which should accompany that feel. Lord Holland, whom you quote in favour of the present administration, talks differently to different people; I had some account of him along with two letters from you last night.[34] To animadvert upon what I hear at this distance would be idle: so much

---

[30] Not found.
[32] Conway.
[34] Letters not found.

[31] Fishing vessels of fifty to seventy tons.
[33] Rockingham.

will the circumstances have changed before the receipt of my letter. It would be making use of the dark language of prophecy in relating its accomplishment. Contempt is never so deeply rooted in the mind of man as to prevent all use of the despised object where he can be serviceable. Therefore Lord Bute may be called in; but I doubt it, and fear it. You two have of late carried me along with you; but now, I am ministerial from loving the Ministers. But however I may pique myself upon this state of independency, I do confess that I still feel enough of my old frailty to love them better, if they use you well. I think the only man among them likely to stand in the Ministerial class is the Duke of Grafton; and the man amongst them with whom the Great Commoner would join by choice. Conway will return to his profession.

You must remember there were some enquiries making in London about the validity of *my friend's* patent, while I was there.[35] I have learned more of that matter since. What would you think of the Provost of Dublin College in that office along with his own? [36] But this in confidence. It will not take place under this administration. But *my friend* will have a brush, let who will be lord lieutenant or whoever may be thought of to succeed.

If any of you should go by Dodsley's pray put him in mind to send my books. I left him the direction. As for the [accounts] of Parliament I fear new business will defeat my hopes, tho' you promised them, Will—I conclude the promise yours because it was scarcely legible. As for health, thank God mine is as good as ever it was. This is a very healthy place, and we all find the benefit of it. But the boys have too many amusements here; I wish Charles again at Oxford, and Will at sea. As for myself, I ought never to come, or to spend more time here. My residence is just long enough to set things a-going; and my absence, to let all go to confusion. Between a broken agent and disorderly servants and workmen, my leisure has been so totally broke in upon, that I shall probably bid adieu to this place.

Yours,

C. O'H.

---

[35] Probably W. G. Hamilton's patent for the office of chancellor of the exchequer in Ireland, a sinecure acquired in 1764 and kept until 1784.

[36] The Provost from 1758 to 1774 was Francis Andrews.

V. American and Irish Affairs, 1766

[No letters written by Burke to O'Hara during the months from July to December, 1765, have been found. Possibly he did not write many because he was too busy, or because his duties imposed on him an unusual measure of discretion.

Sometime before October 15 Burke must have told O'Hara of his expectation to go into Parliament. For this reason, O'Hara, writing on that date, "thought it more necessary than ever to have it ascertained in Parliament that you have no pension upon our establishment." The previous April, Burke had assigned the pension to a person nominated by W. G. Hamilton, but the wheels of administration moved slowly at Dublin, and Burke's name probably remained for many months on the pension list. But if he was now to go into Parliament his name had to be struck off that list, because it was unlawful for a member of the British House of Commons to hold a pension at pleasure or for a term of years on the Irish establishment. O'Hara moved to make the official record clear, lest it embarrass Burke in any way.

Meanwhile, Parliament was opened on December 17 to consider the grave crisis raised by the resistance of the American colonies against the Stamp Act. A writ was issued for an election to fill a vacancy for the borough of Wendover in Buckinghamshire. The borough was dominated by the influence of Will Burke's friend, Lord Verney, and through this influence Edmund was elected member for Wendover on December 23. The next day he reported the news to O'Hara and John Ridge.]

BURKE TO O'HARA, December 24, 1765

My dear Sir,

I am to thank you though I have neither time nor spirits to do it as I ought for your most affectionate letter, and for that very gracious and polite letter from my Lord Lieutenant, that attended it.[1] I shall say more to it in the next post, please God. This is only to tell you in a few words that yesterday I was elected for Wendover, got very drunk, and this day have an heavy cold. This news would all together give you pleasure so I have not delayed it one post. George Grenville debated

---

[1] O'Hara's letter of Dec. 17 indicates that Burke had addressed some communication to Lord Hertford concerning the pension he had given up.

every day about America, taking care *to call whore* first. On the rebellion there he moved for amendment to the address the first day; seconded the motion for papers the second day, and opposed the adjournment the third. The two last days he divided the house; his best 35 to 70, the last day the same number to 78. He was kind to show his personal insufficiency and his party weakness at the very opening of the campaign; his uncandid and ungentlemanly opposition contrary to his public declarations to men who were not present to answer him, has done infinite service.[2] He shows I think no talents of a leader; he wanted the stage of administration to give him figure. He is eager, petulant, inaccurate, without dignity, and quite the reverse of that character which might be expected from a man just descended from such great situations. Charles Townshend who handled him very roughly, described him admirably in two words of his speech: "Quantity without force." They tell a mighty good thing of Rigby; when somebody said to him, "Rigby you made but a poor figure on the division, but you had the advantage of being in the right in point of argument"—"In the right: No! Damme a minority never was in the right from the beginning of the world to this day; a minority is always absurd." I never saw opposition carried to such a length as in Rigby laughing aloud in the house at George Grenville's dull jokes. Calcraft is routed at Rochester.[3] All their manœuvres have been unsuccessful, and this Administration, that could not live for an hour, seems to have pretty strong stamina.[4] I wish you would be as good as your word and see our fireside here this winter; but you talk of Christmas just on the eve of the day.[5] Wherever you are may you pass it to your heart's wish. God bless you. The Doctor, Will, Jenny,[6] etc. are sincerely yours.

December 24

[2] Some ministerial members could not attend because of their having to be returned anew from their constituencies.

[3] John Calcraft (1726-1772) had unsuccessfully contested this seat against Grey Cooper, Secretary of the Treasury.

[4] General opinion held that the Rockingham ministry without Pitt was too weak to manage Parliament or control the court.

[5] O'Hara had said on Dec. 17: "I have not yet said to myself that I shall not see you this Christmas." But he did not go over.

[6] Jane Nugent, Mrs. Edmund Burke.

Burke to John Ridge, December 24, 1765

My dear Ridge,

I know you are too much interested in every thing which relates to us, not to be very angry with me, if I should omit for a single post giving you an account of any thing advantageous that happened in our affairs. The cover, before you read this, will let you know that I am returned for Wendover. I was elected yesterday. Lord Verney, whose kindness was without bounds, went down with us. I feel the effects of the drinking and exposure to a very misting air, this day.[7] Will was with us, and has a sufficient headache also. I shall when I am better and a little clearer tell you some of our news; but in one word, hitherto the unstable Administration stands firm; and never did an adversary show more fury and impotence than George Grenville and his set did in their three days' opposition. Their best division, when they thought they had surprised Government, and so in truth they had by a stolen march, was but 35 to 70. The Grand Financier behaved like a rash hot-headed boy. Remember me affectionately to Leland,[8] Reddy,[9] and all my friends—adieu. Jenny desires her love to Kate and the little ones—we all embrace you. Pray let us hear from you soon; in the meantime we wish you a merry Christmas. Pray give my most sincere regards to Mr. Lyster.[10] I have been so hurried that I have not yet been able to attend to his business, but as it is his, I cannot easily forget it, Pray my affectionate compliments to Mr. Harward.[11] Let my Mother and Juliana [12] know this piece of news.

(in Dr. Nugent's hand)

Though the Doctor never writes to dear Mr. Ridge, he assures him he pays it off in thinking very often and very affectionately of him and all his dear family, to whom he desires to be remember in the warmest manner possible.

Christmas eve

---

[7] The start of a malady that afflicted Burke all winter.

[8] Dr. Thomas Leland (1722-1785), fellow of Trinity College; classical scholar and historian.

[9] Not identified.   [10] Not identified.

[11] An Irish attorney described by Burke as "a man of great honour and spirit, perfectly well acquainted with everything which relates to the criminal law."—Burke to Garret Nagle, Nov. 6, 1766, *New Monthly Mag.* 24: 384, 1824

[12] Juliana Burke, Mrs. Patrick French.

[Parliament had adjourned for the Christmas holiday on December 19, before Burke's election, and did not meet again until January 14. But ministers were busy at preparing measures to meet the crisis in America. Burke was near to the center of this business when he wrote to O'Hara on the last day of the year.]

BURKE TO O'HARA, December 31, 1765

My dear Sir,

I do not know how to thank you sufficiently for having remembered me so often and so kindly in the midst of that hurry of business you must have been in. It is but a poor return I can make to you. I am myself as much occupied as you have been; and I am sure I am far less able to fill up the vacant moments by furnishing entertaining accounts of any public *occurrences* (if I may venture to use a word which our great statesman G. Grenville has proscribed).[13] At present there is a sort of cessation from the exterior operations of politics; and it will continue during the recess. However, in this narrow but dreadful interval, preparations are making upon all hands. There are wonderful materials of combustion at hand; and surely, since this monarchy, a more material point never came under the consideration of Parliament. I mean the conduct which is to be held with regard to America. And there are difficulties in plenty interior and exterior. Administration has not yet conclusively (I imagine) fixed upon their plan in this respect, as every day's information from abroad may necessitate some alteration.[14] In the mean time the Grenvillians rejoice and triumph as if they had obtained some capital advantage, by the confusions into which they have thrown every thing. With regard to myself and my own private opinion, my resolution is taken; and if the point is put in any way in which the affirmative or negative become a test of my [notions] I shall certainly vote according to them; though some of my very best friends should determine to the contrary. You will think me ridiculous; but I do not look upon this as a common question. One thing

---

[13] The address to the throne on Dec. 17 promised "the utmost Diligence and Attention to those most important Occurrences in America." For the last words Grenville's amendment would have substituted "Tumults and Insurrections etc." *Journal of House of Commons* 30: 437-438, London, 1803.

[14] Tentative plans to declare the supremacy of Parliament and to repeal the Stamp Act were laid at a cabinet meeting on Dec. 27.—Wentworth-Fitzwilliam MSS, Newcastle to Rockingham, Jan. 1, 1766.

however is fortunate to you, though without any merits of your own, that the liberties (or what shadows of liberty there are) of Ireland have been saved in America. I do not know how I come to concern myself about Ireland, where sure I have been latterly treated in a most unhandsome manner.[15]

I received your letter yesterday; and I waited on General Conway about it this day.[16] As soon as he was apprised of the present state of your bill, for he had formerly had an account of its progress at large from my Lord Lieutenant, he wrote to Mr. Yorke,[17] that it might pass without alteration. And I believe it will pass accordingly. At every instant you feel the want of an agent; I heard that my friend Fitzgerald was to be appointed. I hope nothing has defeated his pretensions. I shall be glad to give him every little assistance in my power.

I have not the most astonishing good opinion of the firmness of the House of *Commons*.[18] Will the *Lords* show a little attention to their personal honour, and to their dignity as a body? Here has Joe Hickey [19] become security in a sum of more than 3,000 pounds for the shabby rascal Lord Lisle. His Lordship last year ran away from his security, and Hickey has been obliged within these few days to pay the money. Can you get a peer to present his petition, desiring that Lord Lisle's privilege may be withdrawn, and that he may have liberty to sue him? A more infamous affair was never heard of. If you have any friend who regards justice and the honour of the peerage and of our country, sure he cannot refuse this most reasonable request. I heard lately from Paris. Dick is very well.[20] Will you entreat Charles sometime or other to come to town, and to let me have a moment's conversation with him.[21] Indeed I may do this myself. Adieu my dear friend. What has the Archbishop done?

31st December

---

[15] Replying Jan. 10, O'Hara said: "Don't understand what you mean by saying you have been latterly treated here in an unhandsome fashion. I am a stranger to it; I don't know the facts. I am sure it has not been among my friends."

[16] O'Hara on Dec. 24 had said the Irish Parliament was "sending over heads of a bill to ascertain the duties to be paid on imported spirits under the excise act."

[17] Attorney General Charles Yorke.

[18] In Ireland.

[19] A London attorney often employed by Burke.

[20] Richard Burke returned from the West Indies on sick leave, in October, 1765; he spent the winter in Paris.

[21] O'Hara's eldest son, now at Oxford.

[Doubtful of their ability to surmount the American crisis without the aid of Pitt's influence both in the House of Commons and in America, Rockingham and his colleagues during the Christmas recess attempted to bring the "Great Commoner" into the administration. Grafton and Conway feared that the ministry could not go on without Pitt, but his terms proved to be such that neither the King nor Rockingham thought them acceptable. Pitt refused to give ministers any opinion on the American question except from his seat in the House of Commons. This he delivered on the floor of the house on January 14, when Parliament reassembled. Burke took his seat on that day, and four days later wrote an account to O'Hara, which included some information about his own first speech in Parliament.]

BURKE TO O'HARA, January 18, 1766

My dear Sir,

Last Tuesday we drew up the curtain, and discovered the Great Commoner, attended by his train, *solus*. From better correspondents you have heard of that most extraordinary day; of Mr. Pitt's disclaimer of the late Ministry and all their works;[22] his good opinion and his doubts of the present; and his strongly reiterated declaration of our having no right to impose an interior tax on the Colonies. This proposition and some others similar to it, brought on an altercation of several hours between him and G[eorge] Grenville. They were both heated to a great degree—Pitt as much as contempt, very strongly marked, would suffer him. The Ministers Messres. Conway and Dowdeswell did just what was necessary and no more, leaving Pitt to do Grenville's business. Conway went perhaps too far in his compliments to Pitt, and his declared resolution to yield his place to him. The day ended a little awkwardly; for the address being carried without any dissent, the friends of Government went off, and Rigby finding a thin house carried a motion for printing the papers. This had been the same day refused by the Lords on a motion of the Duke of Bedford. You see this was getting into a scrape, and the worse scrape, as the lives of some in America would be endangered by such a publication. Yesterday it was set to rights; in the intervening time between that and the first day it had been

---

[22] Pitt called for repeal of the Stamp Act because he held it to be unconstitutional.

carried to refer the dangerous papers to the Speaker, that he
might cut out the parts which might expose those who communicated intelligence to Government, to the resentment of
the populace in America; yesterday the Speaker was of opinion
that no precaution of that kind would be sufficient for the
purpose and Mr. Dowdeswell moved, on the Speaker's report,
to discharge the order for printing. This brought on a debate
which lasted till near ten. Mr. Conway never shone so much;
he was attacked on every side and supported himself with so
much spirit, energy, and good humour as to draw more and
sincerer applause from the house than ever I knew a man to
receive. He made an apology on being attacked for adulation
to Pitt. He made his apology with so much dignity as not only
fully to bring back what he might have lost by his first declarations on the subject, but to get him new credit. Rigby said
some good things; that he had heard of a doctor *malgré lui*,
but never before of a minister *malgré lui;* and that on such
compulsion he never could expect a good physician or a good
statesmen. That day I took my first trial. Sir William Meredith[23]
desired me to present the Manchester petition;[24] I know not
what struck me, but I took a sudden resolution to say something about it, though I had got it but that moment, and had
scarcely time to read it, short as it was; I did say something;
what it was, I know not upon my honour; I felt like a man
drunk. Lord Frederick Campbell [25] made me some answer to
which I replied; ill enough too; but I was by this time got
pretty well on my legs; Mr. Grenville answered. I was now
heated, and could have been much better, but Sir G[eorge]
Savile [26] caught the Speaker's eye before me; and it was then
thought better not to proceed further, as it would keep off the
business of the day. However I had grown a little stouter,
though still giddy and affected by a swimming in the head;
so that I ventured up again on the motion, and spoke some
minutes, poorly, but not quite so ill as before. All I hoped was
to plunge in and get off the first horrors; I had no hope of
making a figure. I find my voice not strong enough to fill the

---

[23] Sir William Meredith (d. 1790), member for Liverpool and a member
of the Admiralty board.
[24] To redress American grievances for the sake of British merchants.
[25] Lord Frederick Campbell (1729-1816), son of the fourth Duke of Argyle.
[26] Sir George Savile (1727-1784), member for York County; a leading man
in the house and Rockingham's earliest political friend.

house; but I shall endeavour to raise it as high as it will bear. This is probably like a child to a father. Whenever I enter into such minutiae about myself I beg you throw my letter into the fire. All here are yours. The last bell rings. We are in an odd posture. Adieu.

[From January to March, Burke was in the thick of the parliamentary battle for repeal of the Stamp Act, speaking often and acquiring rapidly a parliamentary reputation. We have none of his letters to O'Hara until March, but several of the latter's indicate that Burke kept his friend continually informed of what was transpiring. O'Hara watched with affection and fascination the beginnings of what he was sure would be a brilliant public career, and he was ready with helpful bits of advice and information. To Burke's account of his first speech in the house, O'Hara replied on January 25: "Give me leave to know you, tho' I know nothing else so well, better than you know yourself; your voice will form from practice, your manner will improve, the great point you are to attend to is temper. Was it not Jephson that used to tell you that in some circumstances you had an air of anger? Get rid of this air." On February 20, O'Hara told Burke he was "mentioned in almost every letter from England. . . . Some people say you are too abstracted; others that you take in too great a compass for debate, that your turn is rather for writing, than speaking in public, all commend you. I can only collect from the whole that the swimming in your head is gone off, and a pleasant thing it is to have got so far." On March 4, O'Hara sent what proved to be a well founded warning: "Rest your spirits now and then: take care of your health, for I am interested in your outliving me."]

BURKE TO O'HARA, March 1, 3, 1766

My dear Sir,

I catch a moment of very interrupted leisure and of very precarious health to write to you. I have been extremely ill of a flux, which was relieved by violent sweats; both these causes, together with the heavy cold with which the session began, and which this session was ill calculated to relieve, have so reduced me, that I am scarcely the shadow of what I was when you saw me. However, weak as I am, I thank God my spirits have not wholly deserted me; and I am now once more

able to apply a little to business.[27] We have just got the resolutions (I mean those which were intended for laws) reduced
in the Committee into acts (repeal and all) and we shall have
a third reading please God on Monday, so that they may go
without delay to the Lords. There an opposition will certainly
be raised; but I am convinced their courage will never carry
them to those lengths which their strength might enable them
to go. The repeal will be carried there. Lord Chesterfield [28]
went down to the house of peers a day or two ago to qualify;
he said he could not die in peace if he did not send his proxy
to be used for the repeal; nothing can be more sanguine than
he is for the present measures. They are honest ones. We now
prepare for a complete revision of all the commercial laws which
regard our own or the foreign plantations, from the Act of Navigation downwards; it is an extensive plan. The N[orth] Americans and West Indians are now in treaty upon it; and as soon as
they have settled some preliminaries, (and they are better disposed, than any one could think, to practicability and concord)
the whole arrangement will be ordered between them and some
of the Board people and detached members, and will be
brought into the House, a regular and digested scheme.[29] This
you see will find me at least as much business as the evidence
on the Stamp Act; but it is a business I like; and the spirit of
those I act with is just what I could wish it, in things of this
kind. Could not Ireland be somehow *hooked* into this system? [30]
Send me some arguments from those who are most intelligent
relative to the direct import of English W[est] India sugars
into Ireland; and that as soon as you possibly can. The late
regulations here were to shut out in a civil way the Portuguese;
but I think they have hurt the whole trade. Cannot the good
be kept and the bad part rejected? The principle I remember,
the details have passed away from my memory. If good men
were as practicable for the sake of their good purposes as the

---

[27] Since Burke had taken a prominent part in the debate, Feb. 21, when
Conway asked leave to bring in a repeal bill, it is evident that his illness had
not long incapacitated him. Yet he never forgot it, and thirty years later said
he had thought himself very near death.—*A Letter to a Noble Lord, Works* 8: 26.

[28] Philip Dormer Stanhope (1694-1773), Earl of Chesterfield.

[29] This agreement was reached March 10. *Manuscripts of the Earl of
Dartmouth* 2: 38, Hist. Mss. Comm., 14th Rep., App., Part X, London, H. M.
Stat. Off., 1895. See also Sutherland, L. S., Edmund Burke and the first Rock-
ingham administration, *Eng. Hist. Rev.* 47: 65-67, 1932.

[30] Ireland, prior to 1775, was excluded from all trade directly with the
colonies.

people of the world are for theirs, this Administration would be on a rock. What it *will* be I know not; indeed I scarcely ask; I mind my business to the best of my power, and leave the rest to Providence; so little have I profited by my long connections with the arch-politician, *your friend*.[31] This same *friend* of *yours*, and *man* of *Pitt's*, (and whose will he be in Heaven!) to manifest his thorough consistency of *character* by a thorough inconsistency of *conduct*, voted on the question of repeal against this very Pitt, notwithstanding his contrary professions these three months past. All parties, as far as they descend to think of him, think of him just alike. As to myself, I work on, and I thank God not without some encouragement. Mr. Pitt has been very kind and generous in protecting me by very strong and favourable expressions, twice or thrice in public, and often in private conversations. Those who don't wish me well, say I am abstracted and subtile; perhaps it is true; I myself don't know it; but I think, if I had not been known to be the author of a book somewhat metaphysical,[32] the objections against my mode of argument would be of another nature, and possibly more just. However until I know better, I intend to follow my own way. Observe when I say so much of myself it is for your private ear. You would perhaps think me full as affected, if I did not speak to you of whatever touches myself nearly. Adieu. Pray let us hear often from you. You have many thanks from us all for your last letter. Adieu, God bless you.

March 1, 1766

You don't wholly forget Dennis and Sisson.[33] Pray give my most humble respects to my Lord Primate, whose excellent conduct in his high station is not unknown here, as I hope it is not unfelt in Ireland. I wrote this last Saturday and foolishly forgot to send it. No alteration since. I am only to tell you that Rigby made an able stand for Ireland (foolishly brought into the debate on the bill for ascertaining the right of taxing the Colonies) with spirit and sense. I spoke too on the same subject, to the purpose I think in some degree; but my weakness of body made me long and diffused. Rigby really

[31] W. G. Hamilton.

[32] *A philosophical enquiry into the origin of our idea of the sublime and the beautiful*, London, Dodsley, 1757.

[33] Richard Sisson (d. 1767), a boyhood friend of Burke's, and an Irish portrait painter.

spoke like a man of business and of spirit. This night the repeal will be got through; but the previous debate will make it long and tedious. We shall sit I fear till morning. I here write in one of the Committee rooms. The commissionership you mention in your last was intended for Milbank and I think he will still get it.[34] We are in an odd way, too much so for this letter to explain: in the road of being the strongest ministry ever known in England, are our superiors now; in the probability of being none at all.[35] My disease is (thank God) gone but a weakness remains—I tell you every thing. My argument tonight has I think hurt me. Not for the matter but the propriety. The house was teezed to death and heard nobody willingly.

O'HARA TO BURKE, March 10, 1766

Monday 10 March

My dear Sir,

I write on Monday in order either to add tomorrow, or to have time for other business. But I have leisure now, and believe me, I mean not to pay court to you, I never enjoy it so much as when I write to you. I apprehended your illness when I wrote last, and still fear your not giving yourself sufficient rest. Your mind is too busy for your constitution. I speak from late experience; I worked myself too much, for small as the objects were they were yet too many. But I am thank God well again. A mind somewhat harrassed, a heavy cold, and long sittings in the House took away my appetite, and broke my rest. Such a sitting as that on the 5th was, and to such purpose. I enclose the votes, to which I am only to add that the Speaker from the chair declared he had put the question as reported, and ordered it upon the votes. Yet it was voted a mistake of the Clerk's, and he was afterwards moved to correct them according to the truth. It has hurt him greatly, and yet was his own measure, his own choice. We are in a strange state, hot and disorderly, and ready for a *caning out*.[36] Nothing keeps

---

[34] About this time Mr. Milbank, a close friend and relative of Lord Rockingham, was named Commissioner of the Revenue in Ireland; Lord Hertford had wished to appoint one of his own friends.

[35] Burke feared a court move against the ministers, because the King had not approved the outright repeal of the Stamp Act.

[36] O'Hara alludes to a typical mix-up which occurred on March 4 when a motion was made to correct the clerk's record of the previous day. The motion

us quiet but the universal persuasion of my Lord Lieutenant's having nothing more at heart than the good of this country. I had like to have done mischief; the disorders committed by Revenue Officers wantonly taking out the army were such as I could not bear. I begged of the Board that this might not be done without previous authority from the civil magistrate. They all treated my proposal lightly; I moved that the Revenue Committee should be empowered to receive a clause to that purpose. They all opposed it; I stood my ground, and under pretence of being called upon answered each. The clause was [not] ordered to be received. But I made some impression; the alarm spread; and I was this morning much solicited to come to terms. In the conversation I desired them to modify it, and turning to Lord Beauchamp [37] said, all I desire is to be saved from slavery on one hand or opposition on the other. So I stand.

I think I understand all you say much beyond the letter. Your part is desirable, 'tis large. And I know the execution will do you honour. 'Tis making noble ground for your superiors. God forbid that the spirit of resignation should get amongst them. I fear nothing else. Upon reading your plan of a revision of all the commercial laws etc. I went to my Lord Lieutenant and communicated that part, desirous that whatever may be done should turn to his honour. He caught at it greedily. But the subject was new to him. I first talked of the article of sugar, because Pery to please the sugar bakers here has got a resolution in the Committee of Trade to take off the whole duty on imported muscavado sugars; which Government is now to get rescinded, under the disadvantage of disobliging a body of merchants. The duty is 3s. 8d. upon 112 [pounds] weight. I desired him to consult the Commissioners, tho' they were all together incapable of suggesting any plan to him. I promised to give him such information as should enable him to state matters to them. I happened to have some merchants at dinner with me yesterday; you will believe the trade of this country had its share in the conversation. This morning I went to breakfast with a friend of mine, consul for the K[ing] of Denmark. He is himself in trade, but his

offended the Speaker, but the motion was carried against him. *Journal of Irish House of Commons* 14: 197.

[37] Francis Seymour Conway (1743-1822), son of Lord Hertford and Chief Secretary.

theoretical knowledge goes far beyond his practice. We first fell upon the article of sugar imported directly from the Islands. We soon agreed that a permission to import sugar and other produce from the plantations into Ireland, would save a heavy and an useless expence, and afford material advantages to both countries. That under the present regulation plantation sugar must first be landed in Great Britain, before it is admissable here, tho' the whole duty there paid is drawn back upon exportation and no part remains in aid of the British revenue. I got him to compute the extraordinary expence of landing and reloading sugar in Great Britain, which is as follows:

Freight of 112 pounds of sugar at a medium while the ship lies by	1d 2f.
Risk at sea and cost of insurance on said quantity	1d
Landing and reloading in Great Britain and advances of duty	1d
Loss of time, risk of market, and waste by leakage	1/6d
	1/9d 2f

The 112 pounds of sugar [is] on an average worth about £1.9/, of which this 1/9.2f. is a loss. About 1d of this being for landing and reloading is spent among the quay porters at Holyhead, and so far is a gain; all the rest total loss, without resting in either country. The planters or West India merchants connected with them will benefit greatly by taking off this load; they will get more quickly to market, free from the extraordinary advance, and the ship return timely with provisions to feed the negroes. They may send their ship loaded to Europe as may best suit their convenience, with part sugar, and part other produce, which under the present regulations can't be done, as any part sugar subjects the whole to detention. One thing occurs to me relative to this subject, which may be worthy your consideration. I think the Guinea trade is open to us, at least I am sure it was, for I remember a ship's going from Cork thither. And I remember also that they quitted the trade, because they could have no freight home. Now this want of freight home arises from a most extraordinary policy. There are such quantities of W[est] Indian and N[orth]

American produce which pay no duty in England, and can consequently leave no benefit in their passage through, which yet cannot be directly imported hither. Some also which pay a small duty, drawn back upon exportation. The advantage of bringing these directly would be such as to allow a duty in the Islands upon being shipped for Ireland; which at the same time that it would serve us, would raise a revenue towards the support of the several establishments, and preserve a preference to the subjects of Great Britain. On these articles I shall send you my thoughts more at large by Thursday's post.[38]

I remember we used sometimes to talk on the advantages of a free port in that part of the world, when we were angry with Grenville for stopping what he called a counterband trade in the W[est] Indies. *My friend* [39] was the projector of opening St. Cruce for a free trade. The advantages reaped by Holland from St. Eustatia gave him the hint, and it is thriving apace. G[eorge] Gr[enville] created the necessity for the exertion of his ingenuity. Either you and I have talked of Dominica upon the same plan or I have read of such a design. There, a preference given to the mother country by moderate duties on exported goods for any other place, would do wonders, both as to revenue and wealth brought into commerce. How would the other islands like this? But this occurs to me, in preparing to answer your question about Portuguese sugar, that they took that trade from us is certain, and hurt us by so doing; that it might be restored, and a preference still preserved for the produce of our own islands, is equally certain. But I am talking wildly, as if all men were reasonable. 'Tis however right to lay all things before you. Lumber you remember, I took care of when in London. May not all the woods of this country be considered as such? They pay no duty in Great Britain and yet we are laid under the disadvantage of their detention here.

To descend from this large plan of commercial disquisition, to a more private sort of traffic, I must tell you in confidence that I am about marrying both my niece and my daughter. Terms are verbally settled, and I think the conclusion will soon happen. The terms for the first are moderate and safe;

---

[38] O'Hara did this on March 13, stating: "It is not necessary that I should remark to you, that everything in the enclosed keeps clear of the trade and revenue of Great Britain." The "enclosed" has not been found.

[39] W. G. Hamilton.

for the latter considerable. As soon as these take place, I shall
send the people away and run over to see you all. And if I
were to wish for a happy incident in my journey it should be
to catch General Conway at Park Place. The General there is
a different thing from the Secretary in London.

The disposal of the Commissioner's place has given us
disturbance here. Colonel Nash's getting a regiment before
Pomeroy rather more. Yet neither could be helped, and so
'tis understood. But yet, want of power is a crime. Adieu my
dear Sir.

[While O'Hara's suggestions, that could only mean the admission of Ireland to the privileges and advantages of the British
mercantile system, were on their way to Burke, he was witnessing
the concluding phase of the repeal of the Stamp Act.]

BURKE TO O'HARA, March 11, 1766

The House of Lords has not yet come to a division on the
committment of the Repeal Bill. But it will be carried, and
by a sufficient majority reckoning the proxies. Lord Chancellor,[40] though in most things adverse, spoke for the repeal;
and spoke extremely well. The ground he took was the in-
conveniency of putting the King into that extremely difficult
and distressing situation, that he should have a law upon his
hands which by his oath he was to execute, disavowed by that
part of the constitution from which alone he could derive
support and supply. Lord Mansfield took the ground of the
consequences which must arise from yielding, by raising the
presumption of the Americans to the attack on other laws; he
was in some parts very ingenious, but in general unequal to
his usual performances. Lord Camden replied and I never heard
him or any man more able. It was a long speech supported with
much spirit and much argument quite through. The Duke of
Grafton spoke in a manner extremely beautiful, and had a
vast deal of matter. The Duke of Richmond showed much
shrewdness; I think he will become a considerable man.[41] I
thought Lord Lyttleton well on the other side.[42] Last Friday

---

[40] Robert Henley (1708-1772), first Earl of Northington, had been Lord
Chancellor since 1761.

[41] Charles Lennox (1735-1806), third Duke of Richmond, who presently
became a secretary of state.

[42] George, Baron Lyttleton, cousin to Temple and Grenville; poet and
author.

the motion for the repeal of the Cider Act was carried without difficulty or division; the enemy breaks fast. I spoke about half an hour on that subject. Dowdeswell made the motion, Pitt seconded. I wrote in low spirits on what I said about Ireland. I have had since some compliment on it, through another, from Lord Hardwicke [43] and others. Oh! What are you doing? The reins are thrown over the neck of your House of Commons. Sure the expunging was most shameful to Government. How comes all this? [44] You love a *bon mot*: on that accidental mention of Ireland, most of those who had been secretaries of Ireland spoke; somebody asked Sir Charles Bunbury why he did not.[45] He said he waited for *your friend* to speak first.[46] It is late, and I snatch this from business at Sir A. Gilmour's. How good you are to write, continue that goodness.

11th March

O'HARA TO BURKE, March 18, 1766

My dear Sir,

I find by yours of the 11th that all things go well, but not without anxiety and management. The Provost is arrived, and we shall have things from him, but this on t'other side. I always thought of the Duke of Richmond as you describe him. But great art is either so much above, or so much below our rank of being that it never weaves well into human systems. My friend has intrigued himself out of his talents. He cannot tell whose to be even in *this world*. The Primate communicated to me a letter of intelligence last night. His friend says, Burke is equal to Lord Mansfield in parts and knowledge, but not in judgment. We both agreed that he should have said in experience. A good heart beats all plan. You know that, my Lord does not.

You ask *what are we doing*. Are you now at a loss for it? You have known its progress from the beginning: *vide* Ridge for the rest. But carelessness does so well, that I think it but another name for Philosophy, and more immediately derived

<hr/>

[43] Philip Yorke, second Earl of Hardwicke.
[44] Previous letter, n. 36.
[45] Sir Thomas Charles Bunbury (1741-1821) had been secretary to the embassy at Paris, 1763-1765, when Hertford, now Irish viceroy, was ambassador to France.
[46] W. G. Hamilton, whose sobriquet was "Single speech." He seldom spoke.

from the root. In this perhaps they may differ: the first loves
narrow means, the last a more comprehensive plan. Since the
receipt of your first letter on the subject, I have stuck close
to such articles as may find a place in the new commercial
system. I told you that the Commissioners would give my
Lord Lieutenant no help without orders from the Treasury.
I went on however; the service of the whole was my first object;
the service of my Lord Lieutenant was second. In the course
of my enquiries however it appeared that he had ordered Mr.
Scott,[47] a member and a merchant, to inform himself of what
would be proper to solicit for. He wrote to me, and a collection of such hints is preparing as may be useful, for Scott
showed me this day what they are about; and I am to meet
some people of trade at his house tomorrow morning. I shall
go from him to my Lord Lieutenant and as far as I can prevail,
he shall write in general, while you are informed of all particulars. But I think he should go so far as to express a desire
that something may be done.

I think our recess will begin next Saturday, and a hurried
piece of business it will be. My Lord Lieutenant goes to the
North; how we shall be governed in his absence, I don't know.
Nothing has transpired about Lords Justices, after his departure
for 18 months. Do you know anything of them? [48] You know
how the Primate and I converse. He has at last been prevailed
upon to speak his opinion, and great good it has done. Were
it not for him, many bills would have gone over which will
now be stopped. People grow sanguinary in Munster. But an
opinion prevails that Sheehy the priest was guilty of murther,
for which he suffered.[49] Suspend your opinion till you hear

---

[47] Robert Scott, a Sligo member.

[48] Lords justices ruled the country in the absence of the lord lieutenant.

[49] Nicholas Sheehy, a Catholic priest of Clogheen in Tipperary, was arrested
in 1765 on a charge of inciting to riot and rebellion. Acquitted by a Dublin
jury on Feb. 10, 1766, he was immediately rearrested on a charge of instigating
the murder of a "Whiteboy" informer. O'Hara wrote Burke on Feb. 11: "Sheehy
the priest was acquitted yesterday of treason, but I think will be hanged for
murther. . . . His escape yesterday was of the narrowest, saved only by the infamy
of the witnesses. But yet the circumstances hung so well together that court,
bar and jury think there was more in the affair than we imagined." Taken to
Clonmel in Munster, Father Sheehy was convicted in a trial that the historian,
Lecky, called "one of the most scandalous ever known in Ireland." Protesting
his innocence to the end, the priest was hanged, disembowelled and quartered.
On March 20, O'Hara wrote to Burke: "Sheehy the priest is hanged, and we
now expect proofs of a rebellion. Whether we shall have any such or not is
doubtful, but if they should not come out at this time, all suspicion of treason
must cease."

from me again, for this business will go much further. Lord Drogheda [50] is much in favour and in confidence. Adieu.

There is one Robert Williams a merchant in London who knows (as I am told) much of Irish affairs. He is the man our people would instruct.

[By the time Burke wrote again, he had discovered that the grand plan for a revision of the commercial laws "from the Act of Navigation downwards" had been reduced by the administration to something much more modest. He had discovered too that there was no disposition in parliament to "hook" Ireland into the new system.]

BURKE TO O'HARA, March 27, 1766

My dear Sir,

I write this late in the House, whilst one of our witnesses is examining. Many thanks for your letters. Your proposition about camblets and cotton will not do. They cross British manufactures, at least in prejudice, and things are not ripe for it. As to the sugar, it shall be tried. So shall soap. But none of your hints obviated my difficulty upon foreign sugars. The revision to be made of the Trade Laws was not proposed to be total; but only so far as they regarded America. Adieu my dear Sir; I have not a minute. How can many of the particulars you mention be squeezed into the American act? We have no evidence here that I know of to examine to a single point.

BURKE TO O'HARA, March 29, 1766

My dear Sir,

By the last post I wrote you a short and hurrying letter. This I fear will scarcely be more long or more leisurely. I have considered all the proposals you have made concerning trade, and am sorry (I think you may believe me) to say that they seem, at this time, every one of them impracticable; because they all stand directly in the way of some predominant prejudice, and some real interest or supposed, of this country; and therefore they require time and leisure to make their way by

---

[50] Charles Moore (1730-1822), sixth Earl of Drogheda, succeeded W. G. Hamilton as chief secretary in 1764; married daughter of Lord Hertford in early 1766.

the slow progression of reason into the minds of people here, who just now seem shut against them. Sure you don't think *camblets* will not be thought to interfere with the British manufactures? And will they be fond of encouraging any thing like a fabric of cottons in Ireland? You remember cotton is the basis of one of the most extensive and most favourite manufactures in England, that of Manchester. Are not printed linens directly in the same predicament? As to sugars, you have not said a word to my difficulty with regard to the foreign. But this however I do not think of so much weight as another which I found on conferring with Mr. Benson on this subject. The great quantities of sugars both raw and refined sent hence to England this very year will make the difficulties in giving some indulgence to Ireland at this time peculiarly great. Indeed our hands are so full of America, that I do not see how it is possible to attend with effect to any thing else this session. The Irish affairs are a system by themselves, and will I hope one day or another undergo a thorough scrutiny, but in my opinion it would only hurt them to attempt crowding them into the train of an act relating wholly to America. Do you know that we sat to ten on Thursday? Yet we did not get through half our evidence; nor shall we be able to propose our first resolution until Thursday fortnight. The only thing I have any chance for is the soap. You see I take these difficulties or rather impossibilities in a right point of view. As to the other matters, I shall call on Yorke about them. Oh, how I long for an hour with you to give you the whole of the private history of this family since I saw you. Your friend Mrs. Burke is just now slowly recovering from a complaint in her bowels. Dick is far from well, and the Doctor has got the gout. You see we are an infirmary. Yet we can all, from the bottom of our hearts, rejoice in the pleasing prospect of an establishment to your satisfaction for your young ladies. Let us hear something further. You say nothing of the parties. Cleaver is by me and desires his respect to you. Adieu.
29th March

BURKE TO O'HARA, April 8, 1766
My dear Sir,

I am ashamed of talking any longer of business as an apology for the small number and small value of my letters. No business I believe could employ my time better, and I am very sure none could employ it half so pleasantly; although in general I find the things which I have most at heart going on very much as I could wish them; I mean the transactions in Parliament, which find my thoughts some employment both in and out of the House, and which I stick to exclusively of every thing else, not only as a satisfaction, but as a refuge. There I go on, in my own imprudent way, speaking my mind without fear or wit, as the old proverb says; and doing my party what service I can, without asking in what light they will consider or attend to it. Last night we closed the examination of our witnesses to the propriety of opening Dominica as a free port; which concludes the enquiry previous to the resolutions that are to be the foundations of the new American Trade Act. These resolutions will be proposed in the Committee for America, next Monday. I do not look for much opposition; the spirit of the adverse faction begins to evaporate; even Mr. Grenville begins to slacken his attendance; his language is, I am told, that of despair of the commonwealth, prophecies, omens, ruins, etc. etc. In short, if some foolish measure of those at the head does not precipitate them from their situation, or if some court earthquake (the thing most to be dreaded in this climate) does not shake the ground under them, I see nothing in the union, the ability, or the spirit of opposition, which is able to move them. So much popularity never was possessed by any set of people who possessed great offices. Yet all is in an odd way, which nothing less than a long conversation can explain; if even that were capable of explaining so odd a situation of things. General Conway's illness redoubles the perplexity; he went to the country in a tolerable state of convalescency, but making too free with himself he was again struck down; he is said to be quite out of danger; I wish he may; but he gets on slowly. His loss would be inexpressible. I do believe he is the most virtuous man in every particular public and private, and he has ability for any thing. If he could stick a little more steadily to his points he would be by far the best leader of an House of Commons I ever saw.

I find you go on in Ireland plotting; alarming; informing; seizing and imprisoning as usual; what surprises me is to find by one or two of your letters, that you are a little giving way to the ingenious *bon ton* of our country. I see it is impossible

totally to avoid it. You seem to think, that if they do not discover the cause of their distempers by the *dissection* of Sheehy,
they will leave off their villainous theories of rebellions and
massacres. *Sic notus Ulysses?* [51] I hear they intend to poke in
the bowels of a few more for further discoveries. Why had I
a connection of feeling or even of knowledge with such a
country! I am not sorry that our schemes for it, for the present
at least, will not do. On this we will talk more in the summer.
I tried last night the free exportation of soap to the West Indies.
The evidence turned out as well as we could wish. I had some
little weight with some of the merchants of the outports; and
they will not oppose. It will be indeed no great matter; but a
beginning is somewhat. Adieu. We are all well. Are all yours
so? God bless you.

8th April 1766

O'HARA TO BURKE, April 15, 1766

April 15th

My dear Sir,

Yours of the 8th I began answer to, as soon as I had received
it. I meant at that time to have sent it by Sir Robert Dean.
I changed my mind as to the messenger, and the letter went
of course into the fire. I long for a packet. Conway's life at
Park Place will not do for his convalescence; his favourite walks
till dark I used to think would hurt him even in his best health.
He is as you say virtuous to a degree that I have always admired,
and sometimes wondered at. Rigby writes us word that the
present Ministers are solely employed in undoing what their
predecessors had done. It was certainly the right half for him
to take notice of. The other which has been, and is, your work,
would not by any means answer his purpose. The undertaking
is great, such as head alone without your spirits would never
have undertaken, and 'tis much for the honour of a Treasury
Minister [52] to have enterprise enough in his composition to
adopt yours. If you have made no mistake, you build for him
upon a rock, and a building so constructed as no man after
you will dare to attack. My idea of the plan must be imperfect,
but from your making Dominica a free port I can conceive

---

[51] Virgil, *Aeneid* **2**: 44; *supra*, n. 49.
[52] Rockingham.

in general, tho' ignorant of particulars. The advantages will be vast, while the French and Spaniards suffer you to enjoy them. There never was a business upon the *tapis* in England which was so much the object of my curiosity as this will be when digested into a law. The system involves such a mixture of commercial and political interests as will do infinite honour to the compilers, if successful. I only dread that something may be left undone, as all cannot be justly conceived at once, which may make a declaratory law in another session necessary. And the court earthquake intervening may leave vantage ground for a successor. If I am right in my idea, the very forming this plan in the British Parliament, in treaty with the Americans, is of itself a point of some magnitude in the political system of Great Britain; for tho' no man has a doubt in speculation of her power to make commercial laws for her Colonies, yet it has been a power subject to cavil, even as to its right, when disagreeably exercised. This must hereafter cease; for America now regenerate as to commerce will derive its existence wholly from the British legislature. And this idea pursued, would probably suggest to us that of more certain security for the British dominion, than enforcing the Stamp Act could possibly have done. The establishment of dominion upon general principles never will be objected to; even an Irishman says so. They are partial interests and partial considerations which we murmur at. Go on and prosper, my dear fellow. I long to talk these matters over. As to us, when you hint at a revision of our commercial system, as a thing sometime to happen, you will consider that our political stands still more in need of it. As to the first, you have been the cause of my looking more narrowly into it than I should otherwise have done. Much may be done for its improvement, and at the same time, for the increase of the revenue. But in the hands which now govern it, the object never is either one or the other, but on the contrary, multiplying the expense of management in order thereby to multiply employments; this serves to strengthen one department of administration which a ch[ief] gov[ernor] often finds too strong for him, as in our house we always find it above redress. Our political system is still in greater disorder, I may almost say approaching dissolution. I cannot give you an idea of us by letter: not from caution, for I care not who sees my letter, but from want of room. My former letters have gradually touched upon the causes in their progression. Pray return us the bill for a bounty on exported corn, or you undo us; it was Lord B[eauchamp]'s preparation upon the failure of his idle granary scheme. We want all the helps you can give us.

You do me wrong by saying that I am a little giving way to the ingenious *bon ton* of our country. Can't you conceive that you are the man in the world to whom I would last communicate the worst side of my opinion upon certain proceedings? To you I have always tempered it, and still think I ought to do so. When a cry of treason becomes general, a sudden check does but inflame it to enthusiasm, and moderate men are drawn into its vortex. When left to its own pursuits, it wastes itself and dies. Till at last, no foundation for it being discovered, it turns upon the people who first raised it. The turn of the tide is now not far off. But one could not answer [for] it to one's country to attempt to withstand a most thorough searching. Trials for treason have been instituted, none found guilty. Trials for murther have indeed been prosecuted to conviction; yet in some of these instances the infamy of the evidence has made deep impressions on the minds of many people. Let the torrent *work itself clear* and as it runs *refine*. It has some times appeared to me in reverie that the corruption of the election spirit and management is too great a price even for liberty; but poor England has all the first, and not the last.

Thus far I have wrote in a grave mood, thrown into it I believe by a long conversation with my daughter on the state she is soon to enter into; betraying my sex to her, by laying open all our *bizarrerie* and caprice. In the first week of May I shall take my leave of her, and between this and then the Curragh-meeting will hardly allow me to see her. I congratulate you all upon very sudden recoveries; for there was not above two packets difference between your account of illness, and all well. May you remain in the last state for many years. Adieu.

[Meanwhile, Burke's high hopes for reform of the trade laws had been struck a heavy blow by an obstruction thrown up from unexpected quarters, and by a loss of heart in the cabinet.]

BURKE TO O'HARA, April 23, 24, 1766

My dear friend,

I fly to your correspondence as a refuge from solitude, at a time when I do not find it pleasant to be alone. On my return from a City feast, where the majority (on the Stamp Act) of both houses dined with the North American merchants, I found the Doctor gone to Hampton. Jenny has been there for some time for the recovery of her health. Dick is with her; and Will remains with General Conway in the country. I was driven home, almost immediately after dinner, by the accident of a fish bone sticking in my throat. It gives me some pain, but much more uneasiness; it will look as if I shrunk from duty at a time of danger. God knows that kind of fear and management is far from my heart, and the appearance or suspicion of it would make me half distracted. Since I wrote the above, Gataker has been with me; he gives me great comfort; he thinks the bone is got down, and sees no sign of inflamation; and assures me, please God, I shall be able to go out without danger tomorrow. Tomorrow our American resolutions come on. In how over-sanguine a light friendship sees things! Of twenty good projects, it is well if two can be brought to bear; and it is well too, if one at least of these two be not maimed, mutilated, and deprived of its vital spirit and efficacy. When the free port came to be debated in a full cabinet, the old stagers frittered it down to an address to the King for the opinion of the boards on the matter etc.—so we come hopping into the House with half a measure: the most odious thing, I am sure to my temper and opinion, that can be conceived. However, even this miserable remnant is better than nothing. The Great Commoner sets his face against it. I went down to Hayes with a very respectable merchant of Lancaster to talk him, if possible, out of his peevish and perverse opposition to so salutary and unexceptionable a measure. But on this point, I found so great a man utterly unprovided with any better arms than a few rusty prejudices. So we returned as we went, after some hours fruitless conference. But the truth is, he determined to be out of humour; and this was the first object he had to display it upon; for he had in a better temper approved of all the previous regulations. We are, it is true, demolishing the whole Grenvillian fabric. Rigby is right. But we must clear the ground. After all but too much will remain in spite of all our labours. Don't be surprised if you should hear of some strange alteration in a week. Adieu. We are in a most unaccountable way.

23d.

This day (24th) Pitt came down, and made a fine flaming patriotic speech chiefly against any sort of personal connection; he meant with any besides himself. It was a speech too virtuous to be honest. I am quite well. The enemy's plan seems to be to start object after object to keep off our doing any thing in the American affairs, and they have hitherto been but too successfull. This day nothing is done. God knows when any thing will.

BURKE TO O'HARA, April 29, 1766

My dear Sir,

I thank you for your letters, enclosures etc. etc.[53] They give me light into your affairs, and into the spirit and temper of your time and country. I see that weak unsystematic government will be more odious, as well as more contemptible, than wicked government. As to us here, with such real abilities as perhaps few men at the head of affairs have had in our time, by looking for a support exterior to themselves and leaning on it, they have weakened themselves, rendered themselves trifling, and at length have had drawn away from them that prop upon which they leaned.[54] Pitt, because Administration (at least a part of it) would not submit to such terms as no man with a drop of blood in his veins would hearken to, came down to the House some two days ago, when Conway and Dowdeswell were both of them ill and absent, and abused Administration in the grossest and most unprovoked manner. This will, I hope, open their eyes and bring them to themselves, to union, self-dependence, consistency and firmness. They opposed Dowdeswell's regulation of the window tax for the supply of the year, in the Committee, and opposed it with great rancour. They oppose it this day on the report; we divided but

---

[53] The allusion is not only to O'Hara's of April 15, but to several others not of sufficient interest for reproducing.
[54] The prop was Pitt.

162 to 112. I suppose this day will be no better. Conway's long illness is a dreadful loss to us. I am in haste. I rejoice in the happy establishment of my friend your daughter. We rejoice in every instance of your felicity. Adieu. We live in a strange time.

[During the first two weeks in May, Pitt withdrew his opposition to the projected alteration of the trade and revenue laws of the empire, and all other difficulties were overcome, so that the House of Commons passed two bills embodying the reforms Burke had worked so hard to obtain. To the end he tried to do something for the trade of Ireland, by urging allowance for the exportation of Irish soap to the West Indies; but not even this small favor was conceded to that country.]

BURKE TO O'HARA, May 24, 1766

My dear Sir,

I am sure I receive nothing agreeable to my mind from Ireland, but your letters; I am truly obliged to you for remembering me so often. I am rejoiced at the account you give me of the settlement of my fair friend; and that there is such a prospect of the mutual happiness of the young people, from the good character I hear of one of them, and from the good disposition I know of the other.[55] To them I cordially wish many happy years; and as to you, who are almost an old beau, I wish you the humiliating satisfaction of being speedily a grandfather; and I have my reasons for this; for in order to fly from that respectable and mortifying character, you will come over to us; and then I shall have one tie the less with Ireland and its concerns. Indeed while you stay there, I shall be glad to hear even of their politics; for in passing through your mind they will lose something of their original nature and will soften from faction into philosophy. The last thing I did in the House was to make a battle, and a strenuous though an unsuccessful one, for the Irish soap bill. The season was far advanced, the House thin, the proposition (as they said) new and serious. The Treasury Bench gave way under me; I debated *alone* for near an hour, with some sharp antagonists; I grew warm, and had a mind to divide the House on it; but as I saw myself unsupported, and that a negative might affect

---

[55] Mary O'Hara (b. 1748) married James Ponsonby of Crotto in Kerry.

the proposition essentially, I escaped over a bridge which Oswald [56] laid for me; who pressed me, in very flattering terms, to withdraw my motion and to make it early in the next session. This I pledged myself to do. I was mortified to the last degree, having had all the reason in the world to be certain that the motion would not meet with the slightest opposition. You see all the trading arrangements and the free port are carried.[57] They talk of some opposition to them in the Committee, and on the report, but I believe it will be trivial, at least in the House of Commons. I attended your Corn Bill with assiduity and warmth. I think it a right bill; and it has so far had fair play that the Council have not rejected it; they resume the consideration of that bill next Tuesday.[58] General Conway is for it, at least for the principle; but the truth is, the corn system of Ireland is so ill contrived that its greatest embarrassments arise from its own confusion. For instance, they began with a bounty bill, in the Duke of Bedford's time, so low that it did no sort of service. In 1762 they passed a corn bill allowing *half* the English bounties; which was rejected, I suppose, as too high; and now they send over one near *four fifths* of ours. It makes that bounty cease at £ 1 6s (I don't know when it has been at that price) the quarter, which seems to infer, (if this be thought an *high* price and equivalent to the £ 2 5s at which our bounty stops here) that the ordinary price of corn is excessively low in Ireland, and that they want no bounty at all. However, no endeavour shall be wanting to get it through. As to the grand constitutional bills, I leave them to those who understand them; I am sure the people ought to eat, whether they have septennial parliaments or not.[59] We are all in a blaze here with your plots, assassinations, massacres, rebellions, moonlight armies, French officers and French money. Are you not ashamed? You who told me, that if they could

---

[56] James Oswald (1715-1769), financial expert, adherent to Bute; had held one of the Irish vice-treasuries under Grenville.

[57] Two acts: 6 George III, c. 49, c. 52, *Public General Statutes* (1765-1766) 800-811, 831-846. The first opened free ports for certain goods in Dominica and Jamaica; the second extinguished or reduced many import duties in America, and abolished the preference previously given British West Indian molasses in North America. For Burke's estimate of the value of these measures, see his *Short account of a late short administration*, *Works* 2: 2-6.

[58] In the Privy Council.

[59] The Irish Parliament had sent over heads of bills to limit the duration of a House of Commons, to determine the qualifications of lords justices, and to give judges tenure on good behavior instead of royal pleasure.

get no discovery from Sheehy they would cool and leave off their detestable plot mongering? You think well of Ireland; but I think rightly of it; and know, that their unmeaning senseless malice is insatiable—*cedamus patria!* I am told that these miserable wretches whom they have hanged died with one voice declaring their innocence. But truly for my part, I want no man dying, or risen from the dead, to tell me that lies are lies, and nonsense is nonsense. I wish your absurdity was less mischievous, and less bloody. Are there not a thousand other ways in which fools may make themselves important? I assure you, I look on these things with horror; and cannot talk of such proceedings as the effects of an innocent credulity. If there be an army paid, and armed, and disciplined, and sworn to foreign powers in your country, cannot Government know it by some better means than the evidence of whores and horse-stealers? If these things be so, why is not the public security provided for by a good body of troops and a strong military establishment? If not, why is the public alarmed by such senseless tales? But I know not why I reiterate such stuff to you; every company here is tormented with it. Adieu, it is late; and I am vexed and ashamed, that the Government we live in should not know those who endanger it, or disturb it by false alarms; to furnish the one with knowledge and vigour; and to silence the other with firmness. Adieu. Yours ever

E. Burke

Saturday 24

VI. An Unemployed Politician on an Irish Holiday

["It looks like the conclusion of the session and the return of leisure," wrote O'Hara to Burke on May 31. "You have nothing now to do, but to change Ministers; toss them about like bobins, and weave a new political system. I shall soon have the pleasure of seeing you all, so that my prospect of pleasure and satisfaction is as secure, as the changes and chances of this mortal life will allow; I wish to find you safely landed, and Conway at the head of a regiment of Guards."

A few weeks later, O'Hara was in England with the Burkes, and remained until the ministerial reconstruction began that had been generally expected for several months by all who knew of the King's dislike and William Pitt's jealousy of the Marquess of Rockingham and his friends. O'Hara's wish for Burke to be "safely landed" meant that he longed to see his friend acquire a good place in the new administration. In July the King summoned Pitt and commissioned him to reorganize the ministry. Rockingham, Newcastle, Richmond, Dowdeswell and others were removed from office. Conway, who as Secretary of State had before this shifted from the southern to the northern department, continued in the latter office, and, on the advice of their leader, many of Rockingham's friends stayed on in lower positions. Thus William Burke remained in office, but Edmund went out with his chief. Pitt was made Earl of Chatham and Lord Privy Seal; Grafton, on Temple's refusal, was placed at the head of the Treasury, and Charles Townshend was brought forward from the Pay Office to be Chancellor of the Exchequer. Pratt (Earl of Camden since 1765) became Lord Chancellor. The Earl of Shelburne was made Secretary of State for the southern department, which supervised all business connected with the colonies.

Had Burke been offered a place in the new administration, he might have accepted it without disconnecting himself politically from Rockingham, for he was no longer the Marquess's private secretary and the deposed first Minister at this time had no intention of going into opposition. But nothing was offered to Burke, and it is evident that he resented the slight.

While the ministerial changes were but beginning, O'Hara started back to Ireland. A letter from Burke followed him.]

BURKE TO O'HARA, July 29, 1766

My dear Sir,

I take the chance that my letter shall find you in Dublin. At the same hazard I directed a little article of intelligence to you at Plymouth. All that I was then able to communicate went no further than to let you know the event of Lord Temple's interview with Pitt, which broke off in great ill humour between them.[1] Lord Temple's demands at first included the bringing in of G. Grenville, but he soon gave up that point. Those at which he stuck were Lord Gower[2] for Secretary of State, and Lord Lyttleton for President of the Council. These were his demands; his objections, which were kept in reserve, and only to be produced in case the demands were not complied with, went to Lord North[umberland][3] and Mackenzie.[4] On the whole, it appeared very clearly that his madness took the turn to which it has been long inclining; that he ought to have the lead of Pitt. Whatever may [be] the ill effect of his frenzy on his own affairs, on those of our party it has produced none that are good for much. It is divided; and with circumstances that will alienate, I fear, the minds of people as much from one another as their situations are separated. The plan was originally that all should be wished to keep their places, who were suffered to remain in them; and that those who were put out should smother their resentments, and concur in the support of a system, which if they could not destroy, they could not replace with a better. But in such a plan, temper must have its place as well as policy. When it was once seen, that so great removes were effected, when Lord Rockingham, Newcastle,

---

[1] Pitt wished Temple to head the Treasury while he (Pitt) superintended and guided the administration; Temple at first seems to have accepted, but then quarrelled violently with Pitt (July 16) over questions of place and power. Temple presumed to an equality with his brother-in-law, and desired to establish the new administration as a Grenville family possession.

[2] Granville Leveson, second Earl Gower (1721-1803), brother-in-law to the Duke of Bedford, had been Lord Chamberlain during the Grenville-Bedford administration.

[3] The King had exacted from Pitt a promise to bring the former viceroy of Ireland back into government.

[4] James Stuart Mackenzie (1719-1800), brother of Lord Bute, had been made Lord Privy Seal for Scotland (with the Scotch patronage) in 1763, and was forced out by Grenville and Bedford, much against the King's will, in 1765; he was now to be restored, and to this Temple objected.

Richmond, Winchelsea,[5] and Dowdeswell were swept off at a
stroke, and without any softening circumstances to them, or
any sort of declaration how far the proscription was to proceed
with regard to the party, an ill humour very contrary to the
spirit of support, and yet not vigourous enough for the spirit
of opposition, got up and grows every day. The Southern
Department with the American patronage is for Lord Shelburne.[6] Dartmouth, who has firmness and feeling enough, will
never endure the cutting off his American pretensions by the
new people, when he contended for that point with his old
friends. It was indeed by them conceded to him without
difficulty.[7] Lord John Cavendish has sent word to the Duke
of Grafton that he will not be in the new commission.[8] Can
the Duke of Portland stand after this? What with the removes,
and the resignations which will be the inevitable consequence
of them, the party has none who may properly be called theirs
(except perhaps Conway) that remains in any situation of
importance. What can they do? Join in opposition with G.
Grenville? I can never be. Oppose without that party, and
not with a third of your own forces? Ridiculous and ineffective.
Well! Events must be trusted to. Charles Townshend took
twenty turns and played twenty tricks before he was finally
kicked up into Chancellor of the Exchequer. How like you
Pitt's new title—Earl of Chatham and Viscount Pitt of Pynsent
Burton? As to the step itself, I think it not a good one. He
ought to have kept the power of superintendency, if not of
direct management of the House of Commons, in his own
hands, for some time at least. But imprudent as it is, I do not
see any thing so fatal in it, as is commonly imagined. His
popularity may suffer something, but he stands on Closet
ground; I mean the Bute ground, which is better; he will indeed become rather the more dependent on that interest, which
will be attended with some unpleasant circumstances. He
omitted the great line of policy so plain before him, of joining
the present people and running jointly with them,—the Cabal
to the wall. Perhaps he thought this not so honourable, know-

---

[5] Daniel Finch (1688-1769), Earl of Winchelsea and Nottingham, had been
Lord President of the Council; he was an uncle of Rockingham.

[6] William Petty (1737-1805), Earl of Shelburne, had headed the Board of
Trade in 1763, until he deserted Bute to ally himself with Pitt.

[7] William Legge (1731-1801), second Earl of Dartmouth, president of the
Board of Trade, resigned on July 30.

[8] Cavendish had been a Treasury Commissioner.

ing upon what principles he was sent for.[9] Terms I am told were made for three of those who are in, and three only, Talbot, Litchfield,[10] and Egmont.[11] I believe among those who are to be brought in, Lord Despenser [12] is thought of. As to myself, I hear nothing. I consider myself as rather ill with Pitt's whole party. The situation and conduct of my own friends is most unfavourable to me. But my way, though unpleasant, is thank God plain. And nothing is truly miserable but a puzzle. I prepare God willing to set out for you in a very few days. Adieu my dear friend.

E. B.

29th July

They kiss hands tomorrow.

[Soon after the changes in the ministry, Burke went with his wife and brother to visit his native land, arriving in Ireland on August 19. They lodged themselves in O'Hara's house in Merion Square, but their host was absent. Five days earlier O'Hara had written a very interesting letter to Will Burke, who was still in employment with General Conway.]

O'HARA TO WILLIAM BURKE, August 14, 1766

Dublin 14th August

My dear Sir,

My journey from Plymouth to the Head was so tedious that I did not arrive here till yesterday, and found to my confusion that a packet which I received in London (I believe from you to be delivered to Admiral Parry) still remained among my papers. I had put it up too safe, and the hurry I was in about various things which my son wanted, put it out of my head. This has given me most hearty vexation. I send it either by a ship for Jamaica if it sails tomorrow, weather permitting, or if she does not, by a Mr. Wilson a merchant of London, to be returned to you. I have a long letter from Ned, in which he talks of setting out for Ireland so soon that I may consider him on the road, and Harward and a Mr. Taaffe from London told me this morning that he might be here tonight. I shall stay the utmost time I can in hopes of him,

---

[9] The principle of destroying all party distinctions.
[10] Solicitor to the crown.
[11] First Lord of the Admiralty.
[12] Sir Francis Dashwood, now fifteenth Baron Despenser.

which however can't be three days, for my agent was dead when I left London, and he had such a variety of transactions upon his hands, on my account, that I am under a necessity of getting home as fast as I can. If they should come while I am out of town, I have left orders to a trusty man of the name to find him out, as my house may be of use to him.

I have told you how far my expectations of his immediate arrival are founded. On the other hand, I have no comprehension of their letting him come away without some overtures: an administration so poorly supported, however divided their opponents may be, will not be guilty of such an oversight. If any thing reputable be offered, I should wish his acceptance of it. You and I sometimes differ in the means, tho' our object is always the same. I am for a gradual rise. Times and circumstances are always to be considered. If I am rightly informed as to Lord Rockingham's disposition, he does not think of opposition, and therefore our friend's honour cannot be affected by his acceptance of any thing which may be offered to him. You'll see by what I say that I think he is still with you; if so, I beg you will suffer a little of my phlegm to mix in the family councils.

I find Lord Hertford goes on in getting for his own family. He has made a bargain with old Hatten for the place of Constable of the Castle of Dublin, which he designs for one of his sons. I have had a hint that the little reversion which I asked him for Charles is also to be augmented for another son. I wish you would enquire how many sons he has, that we may be able to compute when we of this country may hope to get any thing. I know his Excellency has thirteen children; but the sons only as yet interfere with us. He is also about to appoint an agent to attend to Irish affairs in England, and this in favour of one Allen, a northern merchant resident in London, for we have not only the younger sons but some country interests to take care of. Adieu my dear Sir,

     most faithfully yours,

                               Chs. O'Hara

BURKE TO O'HARA, August 19, 1766

My dear Sir,

I was exceedingly mortified, at my arrival in Dublin, to find you just gone. The quick turn by which we missed you aggravated our vexation. But here however we are, thank God, well after our voyage, situated by your kindness in an admirable house and in a fine air. By the way, being well lodged is a mighty convenient thing, and I think you did wisely, even with some little difficulties, to get into so good an house. There is none better; I wish indeed your ink was as good as your study. If you find the writing white, pray accuse yourself. I had no civility from any of the new people, except a fine speech Lord Shelburne made to Will about me. He wished of all things to embrace me before I left town. I told Lord R[ockingham] of it, and said I would call on him. I did call on him. He was not at home, and I had no message to wish me a good journey or any thing. As to Conway, I called twice on him, to inform him of my going. I received from him no civil message, even by Will; as to the others, it is natural and I don't mind it. But in Mr. Conway it was not over kind. As to the policy of this conduct, with regard to me it signifies little or nothing; but it has done great hurt in regard to others. I know the whole of our party that has stayed in has taken great offence at it. Not a word has been said to one of them. If an house had changed its master, more attention would have been paid to the footmen of the former family. I say this with regard to the placemen. I just hear that there is a great resignation in the Board of Admiralty. Lord Egmont, I am told, chooses to go out. His dispositions towards Pitt are well known; but his devotion to Lord Bute is known too. If it be true that S[tuart] Mackenzie declines the Privy Seal of Scotland, which I know was offered to him, it will, combined with the affair of Lord Egmont, demonstrate that Lord Bute is not satisfied with the proceedings of his new Earl. Much of Egmont's conduct is to be always attributed to his failings and his humours. Perhaps Pitt treated him with the same high hand he has done others. That would be sufficient. But I fancy the truth is, Lord Bute requires much more to be done than the restitution of Mackenzie. I know it was hinted to our people from very sufficient authority, that a good deal more would be expected of them if they hoped to continue; and less will not satisfy him from Pitt. News we have no more. Direct me to Dr. Leland's, who will forward my letters to me wherever I am. You have given me no idea of your route, but I beg you will be so good to let us know exactly how and where we may contrive to meet; I should wish the county of Kerry. Jane, whom you have lodged so pleasantly, is much yours, and desires to be most affectionately remembered to you and to those with you. Dick is truly yours, adieu my dear friend.

19 August

O'HARA TO BURKE, August 25, 1766

Nymphsfield near Boyle August 25th

My dear Sir,

I was sincerely rejoiced to hear from you, and yet disappointed in finding your letter dated from Dublin. However animated Mr. Pitt's confidence may be, I should have thought you would have been talked to. Conway's coldness is his only insupportable quality. I have felt it at some times, and been astonished at it at others. I find it has surprised you, and I don't wonder at it. To say there was no more than this, will save him but from very little of its worst effects; for most people will look upon it as a desertion of his old friends. And yet it is not that; he is incapable of it. And of you he has a very high opinion. But I must at the same time declare some degree of apprehension from the influence of his brother and nephew.[13] I find Lord Egmont has resigned, so the breach widens between the two Earls. What this strange system will end in God knows, but I fear in no good. You told me in a former letter your part was clear, yet to me it was not at that time. I now understand it by your consulting Lord R[ockingham] previous to your going to Lord Sh[elburne]. I think you are well out of the way, and am equally certain that they should not have let you come. I was in a hurry, or I certainly should have waited for you; I wished, and now wish, earnestly to see you. My agent died some time ago, and besides the uncertainty necessarily attendant on such a circumstance, I had another business in his hands of more moment than my rent. He was an extreme honest man, and in very good circumstances, so that I have nothing but his having left accounts in disorder to apprehend. But as yet, I have been able to do nothing, for I found his widow so much afflicted and so little capable of business that I did not say one word of my own business to her. She expects a lawyer, and for him I wait; and this only

---

13 Lord Hertford and Lord Beauchamp.

it is which could keep me here while you are in Dublin. Charles is gone to see his sister, and I expect will bring the Kerry people [14] to meet me at my return from the Curragh. Thither I must go, having many things depending. They will be with me on or about the 20th of September. What chance of you about that time? How long shall you stay in Dublin? Your answer to this will overtake me here. I am very glad to hear that Mrs. Burke is so well, and am now persuaded the jaunt will do you both service. My own distress here puts me in mind of some of my own blunders when leaving town, for my daughter locked up things so carefully that I have been forced to borrow spoons, and to break open my cellar door. I think I left you neither spoons nor candlesticks. Adieu my dear Sir,

Chs. O'Hara

[After some days in Dublin, Burke paid a visit to his old friend, Richard Shackleton, who was now headmaster of the school at Ballitore in County Kildare, where they had studied together more than twenty years earlier. He then went south to Cork and Kerry, visiting for some days with his Uncle Garret Nagle at Ballyduff (near Mallow and Castletown Roche) where he had spent a number of years of his boyhood. He saw numerous relatives of the Nagle (his mother's) side of his family, and attended to the affairs of a small property at Cloghir which had come into his hands the year before when his elder brother Garret died. It is probable that he also did what he could to safeguard his Catholic relatives in Munster against the danger of involvement in the agrarian disorders which were being severely prosecuted by Protestant magistrates and grand juries.[15]

In the meantime, O'Hara had returned to Dublin, only to miss Burke again.]

O'HARA TO BURKE, September 18, 1766

Dublin 18th September

My dear Sir,

I am an unlucky fellow; I arrived at the Curragh intending to come from thence to see you, two days before your departure. This my neighbour Pomeroy told me, and prevented

---

[14] James and Mary O'Hara Ponsonby.
[15] See Burke to Garret Nagle, Nov. 6, 1766, *New Monthly Mag.* **24**: 384-385, 1824.

my coming to town at that time; and since my arrival Dr. Leland has told me how to direct to you. I am not at liberty to go in search of you, being under an absolute necessity of setting out tomorrow for Nymphsfield. Your vicinity to the County of Kerry where I have not yet been, would have been, to mention no other, a strong inducement. But this is not a season in which I am allowed to please myself. My maid Bell tells me an improbable story, that she heard amongst you something of a design to come to Nymphsfield. But I fancy the wench had only a mind to please me. It can't well be in your power, and particularly if our report of the Parliament's being to meet in November be founded. However, I wrote my daughter an account of it, knowing that it will be a very strong inducement to her to come to meet you and Mrs. Burke. Perhaps you may be tempted to go to Killarney, meet them there, for there they are, and make a party to come together. What of this sort will happen I know not, but I long most exceedingly to see you. I breakfasted this morning with Vesey,[16] and drove Madame about the grounds in her cabriolet. You were our subject for most part of our time; she'll take you in if Mrs. Burke don't watch you at your return. I have aired the house well for you, and if I had thought of it sooner, would have left you some blacker ink. My post town is Boyle where I shall expect to hear of all your movements. Be as exact as you can, for possibly I may be at liberty to come to you to town, tho' I can't stay for you. Present my compliments to Mrs. Burke and Dick, and believe me my dear Sir

> most truly yours,
>
> Chs. O'Hara

[During early October, Burke and his party were at Loughrea in Galway, visiting his sister, Mrs. Patrick French. At this time William Burke sent to O'Hara from England a letter containing news that would importantly affect his own and Edmund's career in public life.]

WILLIAM BURKE TO O'HARA, October 4, 1766

My dear Sir,

I have much to reproach myself for a too long silence, and that too when I ought to have acknowledged your letter, and

---

[16] Agmondisham Vesey, member of the Irish Parliament, was an old college friend of Burke's; his wife, Elizabeth Vesey, was a well-known "blue stocking" and a great admirer of Burke.

the no consequence of one that I think you happened to have at leaving on board of ship.[17] What you mention of it in your last to the Doctor makes me vexed that I did not at the time tell you that the thing did not signify, and what will convince you that it could not is that I have really and entirely forgot what it was about. I have just some faint remembrance of having given you a letter to deliver to Parry, I believe, or to some one on board, but have totally forgot the purport and portent of it. But let it have been what it would, you could hardly think me so idle as to imagine myself as entitled to take huff, or at all capable of doing so to you. I deserve a reprimand for not answering you, but I won't allow you from any folly of mine to lessen the prejudice and partiality which I flatter myself you entertain for me. I ought too to have told you that a dozen waistcoats (for I thought 6 were too few) and the quadrant mended and in perfect order, were long since sent by a friend of mine to my friend Will.[18] I am the more sure of their being safe delivered as I think the carrier would be glad to show some attention to me. It is a Mr. Bourke who is gone to Jamaica, and if at any time it should be necessary for Will to be on shore I am much mistaken if Bourke will not make his house agreeable to him.

The meeting of Parliament so soon will make it proper for Ned to be here by the end of this month at the farthest. For, although there is not to appearance any resolution of applying to him, I think still possible that before the campaign opens, it may be thought necessary to make the force as strong as possible. Whether it may or may not be proper for Ned to join them, I think is not without its doubt, but that, as indeed our whole conduct upon either supposition of his being or not being engaged, must depend on circumstance and the resolution taken *a re nata;* only one thing [is] to be resolved upon, to act upon principle, unbiassed by any view of personal advantage. It is the only road of comfort and satisfaction, and when it is understood to be the walk a man has chosen, the world is not so bad as not to smooth the way.

If Ned gets to you, which I doubt whether he will be able to do, he will tell you that our fortunes are in a condition to second our views of independency, and our resolution of acting

[17] *Supra,* O'Hara's letter of Aug. 14.
[18] William O'Hara.

in our public capacity with the same correctness as we have had the good fortune to observe in private life. You will be glad to know that in this we have no division of our obligation; all this, like as the all before, we owe to Lord Verney's wonderful goodness and friendship. In one word, the necessary rise of value of East India stock was foreseen, before the price rose or an increased dividend was talked of, but as that increase might possibly not be determined on in 3 or 6, or 9 or even 12 months, those who bought on what they call speculation, that is, who agreed to pay such a price for such a quantity at a particular day, ran the risk of losing if the price at that particular day happened not to answer his speculation; so that no one could with safety venture on buying with safety, but those who could actually pay down their money and keep their stock in their possession quietly till the dividend was increased. This Lord Verney could you know easily do and he had chosen to lay out a million that way. No one could have objected to his taking the consequential benefit of all the money he employed in that way, but he considered this an opportunity of making us independent, and actually paid down of his own above 9,000 and engaged for above forty more for me. The dividend is come sooner than I expected, and though the accounts are not yet settled, I may within compass say that I have made £ 12,000 at least.[19] It would be idle to use words to express what we owe to this man's disinterested unaffected worth and goodness to us. The season too is so critical, that surely we may think it providential, and without any superstitious vanity too, if the thought of it reminds us to endeavour to grow better men as we grow richer. It is our good fortune you see to have this advantage without even the imputation of stock jobbing, or the term of bull or bear being applicable to us.

As to public news, though I believe there is a great deal of business in agitation, there is so little apparent that I believe our London letters to you country gentle folk must be satisfied to tell that the pavement is gone all through Bond Street, and that they are working very hard in Berkeley Square— except indeed the one event of the creation of Lord Northum-

---

[19] Robert Olive's return to India, in 1765, to reorganize the affairs of the East India Company in Asia, aroused great expectations of increasing the wealth of the company. Hence the value of the stock rose from 164, in April 1766, to 273 a year later.—Sutherland, L. S., *The East India Company in eighteenth-century politics*, 138-141, London, Oxford Univ. Press, 1952.

berland Duke of Northumberland, and this was scarcely suspected when he went to Court yesterday to kiss hands. Some affect to say that it was done *invita* the Ministerial Minerva,[20] but that is not likely; it was however delayed you see till Chatham was gone to Bath, and is an event that may have consequences. This door being opened may let in other claims of other families who wish for *Grace;* suppose Lady Bute to attain that honour, will that be relished? Or does it signify whether it be relished or not? Will not our Marquess more than any other feel this new granted dignity as stepping over *his* head alone.[21] If it was done by the royal *sic volo, sic jubeo,* may not the Marquess, without obligation to Chatham, obtain the like? Or may Chatham himself use it as the means of quieting him? The Marquess is to be in town tomorrow and shall certainly see him; possibly some guess may be made from his temper, what the temper of the ensuing session may be.

I am ashamed to get to another sheet, and the rather as I do not prognosticate to myself to find any excuse from the matter for the quantity. But politics draws one on, and I can't, at this distance you are from the great scene, help attempting to tell you a little of what passes. You know enough of my situation and of my intentions to be aware that it will be impossible for me to give you any great insight. Thus much however is certain, that there was and perhaps still exists a negotiation with the Bedfords. It is known that the Admiralty and believed that the seals were offered to Lord Gower, and it seems pretty clear that the satisfaction proposed to that party was not confined to the person of Lord Gower. Lord Weymouth and Rigby were, it is thought, comprehended in the terms offered, and yet upon what principle they should have declined, is hard to say, if the offers were really so high; certain however it is that the language of Thurlow[22] does not imply pacific dispositions at Woburn.[23] It is as certain too that Lord Bute's language of a few days past manifested at least dissatisfaction; how far the ducal creation may operate, or in what way, I am not aware; or whether it is to be considered as the proof of

---

[20] That is, *not* inspired by the King's mother, Princess Augusta, alleged patron of Lord Bute's followers. Horace, *Ars Poetica,* 385.

[21] Rockingham was the only Marquess in the peerage of Great Britain.

[22] Edward Thurlow (1731-1806), an eminent lawyer attached to the Bedford party.

[23] Woburn Abbey, seat of the Duke of Bedford.

his independent power or as the terms of coalition, is I think doubtful; and as to Lord Rockingham's intentions, I doubt if he has formed any plan. Displeased and disgusted with Lord Chatham, still he feels a respect for his old colleagues whom he could not oppose with much propriety, and perhaps with less hopes of effect; then too he is still, I believe, a sort of self-dupe to the Closet; all this is a vast chaos from whence a world of mischief may arise. I think you give us a hope of your being here; our satisfactions and even our interests are deeply concerned that you should so, for our little council is very incomplete without you, and you see that there is likely to be food for consultation. I should mention, for it will give you satisfaction, that we have great encouragement to act well; for Ned's conduct to Lord Rockingham the whole world does justice to, and to do him justice he does not fail in any expression of regard and esteem to Ned; and I am sure Ned will not fail to deserve it by every return of esteem and affection, and if he would take a part Ned would be happy to coincide with him; but wherever we light now must and in reason ought to be in the style of cooperation, not of personal attachment to any man or set of men. Ned's ability and Lord Verney's weight may justly entitle us to our opinions; I think they will never be mean or base, and being what they ought to be, are to be pursued in a style of conduct suitable to them.

As to Irish politics, a resident Lord Lieutenant and I know not what is talked of on what foundation I cannot at all say. I rather suspect on none. I am not sorry at the resolution you have taken, and yet I know not enough of Irish politics to judge what is best there. I have wearied, but you're to consider this as 3 or 4 letters and then at an average there is no unpardonable length.

Charles is I think still with you. I beg you to make my assurances of very strong regard to him, and that I wish him some of his father's weaknesses. He won't find many of them; that of thinking very partially of me I wish he may inherit—farewell and believe me very truly and warmly yours

W. Burke

Oct. 4—1766

Our good friend has wrote to you, and promised a well told story which you will not find. What he says of himself however is, thank God, better founded—He is in very good health.[24]

---

[24] Doctor Nugent.

[By October 21, Burke had returned to Dublin, only to continue the charming comedy of missing O'Hara again.]

Burke to O'Hara, October 21, 1766

My dear Sir,

I thought to have found your house properly occupied; but I am sorry to feel that we have but too much room in it. Vexed as I am on this occasion, the cause of your absence is certainly right; I must confess it. Arrange yourself well at home, and then you will come abroad, and stay abroad with more satisfaction to yourself, and because to yourself, to us too, than ever. I do indeed most heartily feel your not being here; an hour's chat would be a great deal in this crisis; yet the business at Nymphsfield is more important; and I should be grieved yet more, to snatch a premature hour of satisfaction, which would debar me of, I hope, so much longer and so much greater. Will's news is indeed marvellous in the success, marvellous in the conduct, marvellous in the motive of action. It is really a joint stroke of Providence and friendship which is not easily equalled. His manner of telling it is quite (as the painters say) in his own manner, as indeed the action itself in all its parts. This certainly leaves one with some freedom of conduct, but the time holds nothing to guide that freedom. For my part, I see nothing on either side of the water but thick darkness and utter confusion. What light and what order may be brought out of them, is hardly, I believe, known to the great Anarchs themselves who rule in the midst of these discordant elements. The offers you mention were unquestionably made, or at least something like them was made, to the Bedford clan. They as certainly declined for that time to accept; but I hear today that the Duke and Duchess are, both of them, in a very bad state of health, and gone to Bath. This will drive the corps to accept any thing, as they are buying by inch of candle; and that they will be bid for, there is no doubt. I hear that Lord Chatham says it is very possible he may, from his ill state of health, never more be able to take part in any public assembly, or even in the King's councils; but that he will leave an administration so nobly composed, and on so broad a bottom as has never before been seen in England. In such an administration must not Rigby, Sandwich,[25] and Vernon [26] have places? The contempt and odium of your late Lord Lieutenant is not easily to be expressed. Never did I hear from a single person a single good word of him. Great apprehensions are entertained of the new. He promises to tread very nearly in the steps of his predecessor as far as I can judge, though in a more affected and effeminate pace, something between an effeminate foppery and a stiff Spanish stateliness; a good portion of hypocritical cant for the public, and numerous family to be made snug and warm.[27] Well! Well!—I don't look on the affair of the resident Lord Lieutenant as a question of right or wrong; but of practicable or impracticable.[28] It never can hold five years. Adieu my dear friend. Please God when we get on the other side of the water, you shall hear more from us.

Tuesday, Oct. 21st 1766

Jane and Richard are sincerely yours. Remember us all to Charles. I hear Pomeroy has got a regiment. I wish you joy of it.

---

[25] John Montagu (1718-1792), fourth Earl of Sandwich, had headed the Admiralty during the Grenville-Bedford administration.

[26] Richard Vernon (1726-1800), brother-in-law to Lord Gower and the Duchess of Bedford; Board of Green Cloth, 1763-1765.

[27] George William Hervey (1722-1775), second Earl of Bristol; Ambassador to Spain, 1758-1761.

[28] A plan was being considered for the lord lieutenant to reside all the year round in Dublin.

VII. The Rockinghams Go into Opposition

[At the end of October Burke and his party left Ireland and were back in London by November 6, five days before the opening of Parliament. A letter from O'Hara written at Nymphsfield on October 31 followed Burke home: "Whether this will find you in Dublin, or follow you to England is uncertain, but somewhere it will find you, and if well and happy, I shall be satisfied. I would have wrote sooner, but that it can be of no entertainment to you to know how I pass my time here; and more I had not to say. Charles is with me; and spends a great deal of time with books. 'Tis rather this than reading hard. But he gets on. You have been of great service to him, and in a way that you can't conceive. You may naturally suppose that we talk of you now and then. He has adopted my opinion of you; and seems a little ambitious of proving that sort of character. His disappointment was great when I told him we were not to expect you."

Soon after November 11 Burke replied with an extensive account of the political scene, and of the interesting approaches made to him by the Chatham administration.]

BURKE TO O'HARA, post November 11, 1766

My dear Sir,

It pleased God that we got safe through the storm to Holyhead;[1] and by easy and pleasant journeys arrived thither time enough to see how the land lay and to consult with our friends about the spirit and tendency of our future operations. In this consultation, resentment (as it was right it should) had but little share. The consideration that a large majority of our friends were in place, and none but our worst enemies in opposition;[2] that every thing would go to pieces if we fell out with the one, or joined with the other, and that Lord Bute's game could not be more effectually played than by distressing even the administration which he made; these considerations altogether determined Lord Rockingham to go himself to the meeting of the peers at the Duke of Grafton's and to wish all his friends in the House of Commons to go to the Cockpit,

---

[1] "Our passage was extremely rough. We never had been in any storm like it. All of us very ill."—Burke to Garret Nagle, Nov. 6.

[2] The Grenvilles and Bedfords.

and such as were asked to the previous private meeting at
Conway's to attend there.[3] I was at both. However this support
is entirely voluntary, and neither expresses nor implies any
contract, but will I suppose be more or less vigorous, as my
Lord Chatham shows himself better or worse inclined to the
party. If I could lay open to you fully the solid grounds upon
which this plan of moderation and at the same time of freedom,
is built, I am sure you would highly approve it. At first I
thought otherwise;[4] but every day convinces me of the rectitude
of the measure. The first day of the session was as curious to
a man of speculation as any that ever parliament met upon.
There was a kind of torpor in the House of Commons almost
without example. No joy, no grief, no love, no hatred; no
hope or fear, no anxiety or desire whatsoever; opposition was
without spirit, and support without firmness. G. Grenville indeed
stood out with his usual stubborn resolution. He inveighed
against the illegality of the Embargo;[5] agreed that had he been
in the Council he would have advised it; but laid a heavy hand
on that supineness and neglect which had rendered that illegal
remedy a necessary one. He fell, as usual, into some contradictions; but in the main pushed his points with force and dexterity enough; and in short showed that he was willing to lead
any opposition if he could find followers. But he scarcely found
any. The Bedford people held off. Their bargain, though not
concluded, is I believe in treaty. G. Grenville did not divide
on the amendment which his former Secretary made, and which
he supported whilst he could.[6] In the House of Commons the
proclamation was not defended on the legality, (if it had, I
for one would have opposed the address) but on the necessity,
which has been made very evident, and is a plea sufficient.
Grenville tried another amendment, (by way of a little, and
indeed a very little bait for popularity) containing a proposal
for supplying the poor out of the sinking fund. I found the
Treasury bench, though resolved to put a negative on his

[3] Traditional meetings of government supporters.

[4] "Nothing but weakness appears in the whole fabric of his (Chatham's)
ministry; yet I do not see what strength the party is likely to derive from
thence."—Burke to Rockingham, August 21, *Correspondence* 1: 107.

[5] A deficient harvest was the reason for issuing, in September, a royal
proclamation laying an embargo on the export of grain: an act not allowed
by the law.

[6] Thomas Whately (d. 1772), had been Secretary of the Treasury under
Grenville; his amendment lamented that Parliament had not been called earlier.

amendment, so little *sui juris* that they did not venture to decide directly on his proposal, not knowing how it may have chimed with the great Director;[7] and only spoke to the impropriety of mixing it with the address. Conway was very well for a man in such a situation; but good God! what a situation for him! I had not any such reasons for caution, and therefore went roundly to work on the proposition itself, and I am told made some impression.[8] It was a lucky point for my situation; I was not unwilling to show early that I had not changed my opinion of the Grenville knot; that where the interests of the administration *as a body* were not concerned, I was willing to go with them, and that I had particular regards for Conway, but would go no further. I think I made a shift to mark out this; and our friends thought it was as it should be. The House of Peers was the great scene. Lord Chatham played all his House of Commons pranks there with as good success as ever in the former scene. He has taken formal possession of his new freehold and I think will be at least as despotic there as ever he was with us. Lord Temple opposed, but did not dare to strike home. Lord Mansfield all for Liberty, Lord Camden for prerogative—public necessity made law—that this Embargo was a power Junius Brutus would have given to Nero—that at worst, it was but 40 days slavery etc. etc. It was a most curious scene. You will have more satisfactory accounts of it.[9]

As to my own peculiar, Conway sent for me soon after my coming to town, and with many obliging expressions of his own opinion and of that of his colleagues, spoke of my supporting, and their intentions and hopes of making me offers that would be pleasing to me. The conversation was long; the substance of my resolution was, and I explained it to him in terms strong and precise, that I had begun with this party, that it was now divided in situation, though I hoped not in opinions or inclinations; that the point of honour lay with that division which was out of power; and that if the place which should be offered should prove in itself never so acceptable, I could take it only on condition that, in accepting it and in holding it, I must be understood to belong not to the administration, but to those who were out; and that therefore if ever they should

---

[7] Chatham.

[8] His speech has not survived.

[9] Camden's speech was printed and reproduced in *Parliamentary history* 16: 251-311. The statement there that it was given on December 10 is mistaken.

set up a standard, though spread for direct and personal opposition, I must be revocable into their party, and join it. But
would act fairly and give due notice.[10] He told me he feared
that this condition might frustrate the whole—the last bell
rings. Adieu. You lose nothing for nothing is yet done. But
I have acted right and will tell you the rest next post. Choice
Augustus! *Nil oriturum alias.*[11] He moved the address and
took occasion to commend the peace and abuse the repeal of
the Stamp Act.[12] Happy effect of coalition and broad bottom.
Will has taken his seat.[13]

[If there had been any likelihood that Burke's terms for accepting office would prove acceptable to the administration, that small
chance was destroyed before many days had passed by two developments: (1) an unprovoked attack by Chatham on Lord Rockingham's friends remaining in office, and (2) the launching of a
legislative effort to limit the freedom of the East India Company.
From conditional support, Burke went with his party into active
opposition. The first account of this new development to go from
"the fireside" to O'Hara was from the pen of Richard Burke.]

RICHARD BURKE TO O'HARA, *ca.* November 25, 1766

My dear Sir,

It is once more my lot to write to you accounts of things
which you would wish to know, and which I am but ill qualified to inform you of.[14] However perhaps a confused and imperfect account is better than none. Ned cannot sit down to
write, neither can Will, and therefore I undertake the task.
Ned broke off his last letter to you with his answer to General
Conway's proposal. That affair slept for some time; we heard
nothing more of it, except that we might understand from some

---

[10] Grafton on Oct. 17 had recommended Burke to Chatham as "the readiest
man upon all points perhaps in the whole house."—Taylor, W. S. and J. H.
Pringle, *Correspondence of William Pitt, Earl of Chatham* 3: 110, London,
J. Murray, 1840.

[11] Horace, *Epistles*, 2. 1. 17.

[12] Lord Augustus Hervey, R. N., brother of the Earl of Bristol; he had just
been appointed Chief Secretary for his brother's projected administration in
Ireland; yet he praised what Chatham condemned, and condemned what
Chatham had played a great part in accomplishing.

[13] Will Burke came into the house for the borough of Great Bedwin, which
was in the patronage of the second Baron Bruce.

[14] No earlier letters from Richard Burke to O'Hara have been found.

unconcerned people, and indeed from the public voice, that Ned was to come in, and that in a tolerably high station. Before anything could be determined, or at least determined in this affair, some events, or rather an event happened, which in all probability will make a determination unnecessary. You do already know that those of the party who are out had determined upon a fair tho' independent support of the present Administration; they showed all possible marks of such determination; they went to the reading of the King's speech, Lord Rockingham and the peers to the Duke of G[rafton]'s, the Cavendishes and the commoners to General Conway's. They went further and actually supported on the matter of the address; or rather matters that arose out of the address. This conduct, which tho' perhaps they thought it not imprudent in regard to their own interests, they imagined so far meritorious in regard to Lord C[hatham] as to insure good treatment from him to such of their friends as remained in office. But men may mistake when they judge of great characters; Lord Chatham who does not go in a beaten track, has thought fit to take (to them a most mortifying) and to the world a most extraordinary step. Lord Edgecumbe,[15] Treasurer of the Household, who has always been of the same party both in support and opposition with Mr. Pitt, was about three days ago by Lord Chatham dismissed from that employment, without any the least offence alleged or intended. Now do not suppose that this is in consequence of some grand arrangement with the Duke of Bedford or any other very leading man; it is from a motive neither greater nor less than to introduce John Shelley Esq. into that place, for which he this day kissed hands.[16] This did alarm the party a good deal and they thought it high time to show that with all their moderation they could feel the extremity of ill usage and act from that feeling. They did therefore go down in a body and on the bringing in the bill for indemnity they fully showed their disposition, hostile but not inveterate; they would watch its wording and its operation; they would take care that whilst it provided for the safety of the officers who acted under the authority which the crown had assumed, and which they approved from the necessity of the acts, that it should effectually damn the doctrine which had

---

[15] George, third Baron Edgecumbe (1721-1795).

[16] Sir John Shelley (d. 1783) whose devotion to Chatham earned him the sobriquet, "the little Commoner."

been broached (by Lord Camden) that the crown had such
a power; that the indemnity should not be confined to the
officer who acted under, but to the officers who advised the
exertion of that authority; lest it might be concluded, if no
notice was taken of the latter, that what they had done was
justifiable from some other reason than the necessity approved
and allowed as necessity by Parliament.[17] That while the safety
of the officers was attended to, the property of the subject should
not be neglected, but a compensation be given to those who
suffered. This you will allow to be all just and could not be
opposition in any other sense, than that the bill proposed from
the Treasury Bench did not go so far. It went only to the
indemnity of the acting officer. It had however this effect, that
the bill is to be framed exactly on their plan as I have related
it, only that I am not totally sure (on my memory) of the
indemnity extending to the Council; the compensation may
not be in the same bill, but it is to be made. Thus this Ministry begins with a pardon about their necks; how they may
end, God knows. And there ends all that I can say on this
subject. Next post will probably carry to you the resignation
of the Duke of Portland and Lord Besborough; you will then
or very soon after hear of Lords Scarborough [18] and Monson [19]
with others having resigned, and probably the rear will be
brought up by General Conway; and it is not impossible that
the total disarrangement of the present system may follow;
whether a better, worse, or what system will be established, is,
I fancy, hard to say. Your friend (not Hamilton but Edmund)
took an immediate and unequivocal and no inconsiderable
part, indeed took the lead in this something like opposition;
as he had before, whilst such was the resolution of his friends,
in the independent support. I have told you now all that I
know of this matter, and if you understand it, I am not sure
but that you are wiser than I am, for I am somewhat confused
in my own notions. I am however set prating and I will not
end without telling you a little anecdote to make you laugh,
as what I have already said will make you speculate. In the

---

[17] Conway brought in the indemnity bill (necessitated by the embargo) on
Nov. 24; it was debated that day and the next.

[18] Richard Lumley Saunderson, Earl of Scarborough, had been Cofferer to
the Household since July, 1765; brother-in-law to Sir George Savile.

[19] John, second Baron Monson (1727-1774), was Chief Justice in Eyre;
head of an influential Lincolnshire family.

House of Lords, Lord Camden chose to stand up for the prerogative and for the King's having a legal power to lay embargoes; in this he was not clearly supported by any of the Ministers except Lord Northington; but was opposed by Lord Hillsborough [20] very warmly, and was also opposed by Lord Mansfield. Now how dexterously these great lawyers might have managed this sharp tool I can't tell, but poor Alderman Beckford chose to handle it in the House of Commons and cut his fingers most damnably. "I say that in all cases of necessity the King has a dispensing power." Here he was stopped by G[eorge] G[renville] who insisted on the words being taken down; they were taken down and Beckford complained that he was stopped before he could explain himself, and then— "whenever the *salus populi* required it and with the advice of the Privy Council." Grenville charged the explanation to be a great aggravation of his guilt as showing the deliberate opinion, and insisted on these words also being wrote down; they were so. Beckford blundered more and more, called himself (I do not mean this to be a blunder) poor culprit, *homo indoctus* etc. and etc. Nugent [21] undertook to excuse him as being what he called himself, and owned that he was grossly ignorant, and very fond of talking on subjects of which he was ignorant etc. and etc. Some people got about Beckford and framed in writing what they and he called, and the house accepted, as an explanation; but this was no other than a denial of the doctrine and thus it ended; Beckford standing on the journals as a favourer of the dispensing power.[22] I should have told you that he prefaced this ingenious and happy performance, by declaring that he understood common law as well as any lawyer in the house. Adieu, my dear Sir, accept of all our best and heartiest wishes; the last bell calls for the letter, and believe your most obedient and affectionate

    humble servant

                            Richd. Burke

---

[20] Wills Hill (1718-1793), Earl of Hillsborough in the Irish peerage, Baron of Harwich in the English peerage; president of the Board of Trade.

[21] Robert Nugent (1702-1788), member for Bristol.

[22] Beckford explained his real meaning in this way: "That on great and urgent occasions, when the Safety of the People called for an Exertion of a Power contrary to the written Law of these Kingdoms, such Exertion of Power is excusable only by necessity, and justifiable by Act of Parliament." *Journal of House of Commons* 31: 315.

BURKE TO O'HARA, November 27, 1766

My dear Sir,

I have only time just to tell you that affairs are come to a crisis. The Duke of Portland, Lord Besborough, Lord Scarborough, and Lord Monson resigned this morning. Their resignation was most graciously received; and nothing could be more kind than the expressions of the King on the occasion. Nothing like the least displeasure or resentment. More resignations will follow. The ill humour is incredible. The E[ast] India Company is a great resource; but requires great management to make it subservient to the national advantage. Lord Chatham chooses to act on this occasion, not by his nominal ministry, but by Beckford.[23] They supported the general motion for a committee of the whole house to examine into the affairs of that Company; but they gave up all his grounds; amended his motion, and rejected that part of it which required the laying their charters, accounts etc. and etc. before the houses. The motion was made in direct contradiction to the opinion of the second rate ministers, on the express order of the supreme directors. Never ministry made a more shameful figure. They were beat about like footballs. We divided but 76 to 129 on the main question; we should have had about 10 more had we put the previous. We got into odd company,— Bedfords, Grenvilles, etc., but we did not go in their train. To avoid an appearance of this, I jumped up instantly on Beckford's making his motion and took my own ground, I think very cautiously, lest they should give us a ground on which we should not be able to act. When you shall have heard distinctly what has been doing, you will approve it, and I flatter myself, see that we do not act on the principles of factious opposition. Lord Hertford is Lord Chamberlain. Oh Conway! Oh Conway! my heart bleeds for thee.[24] Adieu, adieu.

27, Thursday   November.

BURKE TO O'HARA, November 29, 1766

My dear Sir,

Our confusions still continue; but they are drawing to an end.

---

[23] Beckford on Nov. 25 moved for the House to take into consideration the state of the East India Company's affairs.

[24] Conway had separated from the Rockinghams on the East India vote, and now was more heavily compromised with the court by his brother's becoming Lord Chamberlain.

A settlement is coming on, but different only from the present state of things, as tyranny differs from anarchy. Yesterday the Admiralty tumbled down. Sir C[harles] Saunders,[25] Keppel,[26] and Sir W[illiam] Meredith resigned their places. Lord Gower was immediately sent for; and that night he and Rigby went together to Woburn. They are not yet returned, that I can hear. But nobody doubts the result of that consultation. They must be mad to refuse the offers that are now made them. Lord Chatham has in a manner surrendered prisoner at discretion to that party; by which he has purchased a momentary support, at the expence of a little more remote but certain ruin.[27] You may depend upon it, that he is not cordially supported by Lord Bute. Speculate on that disposition, and this negotiation. The grand difficulty made by the Bedfords is about G. Grenville; but they will abandon him, at least for a time; not that they will wholly do it, for they have nobody to lead the House of Commons who is so near their party, or their principles; at least as far as their bad principles are any motives to their bad conduct. You had, I take it for granted, my letter of Thursday's post. But I am not sure that I gave you an account of the [steps] that led to this great change. Take them in a few words. Lord Edgecumbe, Treasurer of the Household, was ordered to walk into the Bedchamber, to make room for Jack Shelley. His Lordship had, to oblige the late administration, and General Conway in particular, brought Lord Beauchamp into Parliament last year; though he did not take his seat until this session. He demurred a little at the arbitrary order which proposed the exchange to him; and he was instantly turned out. The party took fire, and General Conway seemed to be mortally offended; and several meetings were held, in which, upon full consideration of all circumstances, it appeared to everybody that Lord Chatham had resolved the ruin of the party, and that staying in office exposed to such ill designs and shameful indignities, would break every part of the yet remaining strength of the body and could be attended with no sort of good

[25] Admiral Sir Charles Saunders (1713-1775) had been on the Admiralty board during Rockingham's administration, resigned after Chatham succeeded to power, and then in September accepted the post of First Lord of the Admiralty.

[26] Admiral Augustus Keppel (1725-1786), brother of the Earl of Albemarle, had gone to the Admiralty board in July, 1765.

[27] Burke's expectations were not now borne out; the Bedfords did not go into administration until another year had passed.

consequences to the public. Yet such is the pacific disposition of our party, that Lord Besborough, if possible to accomodate Lord Chatham, offered to give up his Post Office to Lord Edgecumbe and take the Bedchamber. Judge of the humility of that offer! Judge of the insolence that refused it! Judge of the patience that bears that refusal. Lord Hertford has every thing!!!! [28]

As to me, I hope you will always find my little skiff out in the fair open sea—far away from the rocks, shelves, and quicksands of politics. I jumped in first; and plunged over head and ears. You cannot think with what spirit and system our little corps went on last Tuesday without the least previous consultation or concert between ourselves, or any of the casual auxiliaries. I have broke off all negotiations with the powers that be. So leave off flattering yourself with reading any thing about me in the red book, for some years. I suspect you will soon see W[ill] Burke's name also effaced from that book of life. Adieu, adieu. Prepare to congratulate Rigby—perhaps even your *friend*.[29] *fortunam ex aliis*.[30]

Saturday, Nov. 29.

BURKE TO O'HARA, December 2, 1766

My dear Sir,

I mean just to give you a minute, *de die in diem*, of what is going on. Lord Chatham is in for it; and he plunges deeper and deeper, with a glorious alacrity in sinking, every day. On Keppel's *resignation* of the Admiralty, without waiting until he gave a vote in opposition, he was *turned out* of the Bedchamber. Sir Ed[ward] Hawke has got to the head of the Board of Admiralty.[31] Sir Piercy Brett has got one of the vacant places at it. [32] The final determination of the Bedfords is yet uncertain. I believe they have agreed to the gross of the proposition; but there are some difficulties as to the detail. Some people more conversant than I am, about their particular dispositions and general situation, still affect to think they will not come in; but I stand firm, that they will; that they ought, upon every

---

[28] Hertford had now acquired also the place of Master of the Horse.
[29] W. G. Hamilton.   [30] *Aeneid*, 12. 436.
[31] Admiral Sir Edward Hawke (1705-1781), member for Portsmouth; later Baron Hawke.
[32] Admiral Sir Piercy Brett (1709-1781), member for Queensborough.

one of *their* principles; and that they must. As to our set, we must fairly content ourselves with cooling our heels in the lobby of power for a couple of years longer. Lord Chatham sent for Ch[arles] Townshend a day or two ago, as I am told, and read him a severe lecture on his conduct and told him he expected not an official, but a determined, manly, and earnest support.[33] Oswald and Elliot had likewise, I am informed, a rap over the knuckles. To say the truth the whole Bute party have been playing fast and loose. I know not what will be the end of it. Adieu. All here are yours. Salute for me those who are with you.

Tuesday, December 2.

O'HARA TO BURKE, December 6, 1766

Nymphsfield 6th December

My dear Sir,

I am infinitely obliged to you all three; to Will for his solid good news;[34] to Dick for the exertion of that peculiar talent of laughing on paper, for I have laughed at Beckford ever since I read it; and to you for carrying me along with you in your career, wherein I accompany you with all the warmth of friendship: this is not said at random, but from the bottom of my heart. I like your original plan, your answer to Conway, your taking the lead, and standing apart from the people you cooperated with. Your part in the House is not singly you, but Lord Rockingham—also, 'tis of a man also well supported by his own batch. I wish I knew whether Will was of the 76.[35] I rather think not, but doubt. You call this a crisis; and 'tis one indeed. Nothing answers my idea of the great Director better than his preferring his own tool [36] to all the ministerial *vulgus*. 'Tis high, 'tis vast, 'tis Pompey stamping the ground, Caligula's horse, and a hundred other things. He has probably by this time made a damned bustle, or certainly will. And all the resignations were graciously received; pretty! Are things so, and will they answer the purpose? The vast scene which is now opened; the East India Company, nice, complicated, and

---

[33] Townshend had failed to conduct himself as Chatham desired, on the East India Company question.

[34] There is nothing to show what was the "solid good news."

[35] The minority against Beckford's motion to take into consideration the affairs of the East India Company.

[36] Beckford.

of a tender nature; the landed interest so deeply concerned in every step which can be taken towards regulating the price of provisions; the liberties of the people in such close neighbourhood with their riots, tho' distinct in theory; the growing wealth of the nation, which must raise the wages of the manufacturers too high to live by the coarser kinds of manufactures; and when they cannot live, the certainty of disturbance! You will believe that when such thoughts occur, I wish myself in London. However inexplicable to me, they all make for you. The times are such as will make you attended to.

I am sorry to find Lord Hertford in such a moving style; he may return to us at this rate. If he does, he shall have my poss, tho' Conway's brother. As for him, his diffidence of himself will ever subject him to a brother or a wife. His situation is strange, and will daily grow more so.

'Tis actually so cold that I can't hold my pen. Adieu my dear Sir,

C OH

I have a good account from William.

[O'Hara wrote again on December 9, offering Burke some advice which showed little comprehension of the party principle which now governed the latter's conduct: "You are to look forward, and without knowing what set you may hereafter be joined with. Let your opposition then be to things, not men, and independency the *parole*. Excuse my reasons for saying this, you grow warm in argument. Let no man mark you out as personally averse to him but give them a thorough sense of your power, whatever measure it may cost them. I never will pay you a compliment while I live, and yet I will now tell you, keep your temper, give no individual marked offences, and they can't do without you."]

BURKE TO O'HARA, December 23, 1766

My dear Sir,

We received last night your letters of the 6th and 12th.[37] We are not surprised to find you take an interest in our affairs. I know not how, but our little concerns grow important in

---

[37] O'Hara's of the twelfth was to Richard Burke and contains nothing of interest save this request: "I beg you will suffer yourself now and then to be made to write me; If Ned speaks, you will tell me a little more of it than he will. You can look about too, and observe how people are affected. He can't see."

our eyes, when we find others anxious about them; and our conduct grows more firm and assured, when judicious friends go along with us in our notions. I think we are very, very far from port; but we keep the open sea; far likewise from rocks and sands and shelves, and all the mischiefs of an unfaithful coast. I see that an union of the corps in opposition (I mean the Grenvilles, Bedfords and ourselves) is an affair of infinite difficulty; and without such an union our opposition may be respectable, but never can be effective. In the mean time, I should conceive that Lord Chatham gathers strength; not from our total disunion, but from the immense services he has done the Bute party. Lord Bute, to be sure, is uncertain and unquiet in his nature; but who *will* do more, who *can* do more to satisfy him, than the present Minister? I therefore take it for granted, that he will continue his year at least. But if he should fall then, or even before that time, I cannot conceive that *we* shall rise by his fall. The Bedfords and Grenvilles, as a set of people at once more bold and more tractable than our party, will be preferred to us, and will run their course as others have done theirs. It may possibly, in the revolution of this political platonic year, come again to our turn. But I see this event, (if I see it all) at the end of a very long visto. The view is dim and remote; and we do nothing in the world to bring it nearer, or to make it more certain. This disposition, which is become the principle of our party, I confess, from constitution and opinion, I like. Not that I am enamoured of adversity, or that I like opposition. On the contrary, it would be convenient enough to get into office; and opposition never was to me a desirable thing, because I like to see some effect of what I am doing, and this method however pleasant is barren and unproductive, and at best, but preventive of mischief; but then the walk is certain; there are no contradictions to reconcile; no cross points of honour or interest to adjust; all is clear and open; and the wear and tear of mind, which is saved by keeping aloof from crooked politics, is a consideration absolutely inestimable. Believe me, I who lived with *your friend* so many years feel it so; and bless Providence every day and every hour to find myself delivered from thoughts and from characters of that kind. Will feels exactly as I do, that if C[onway] does not go out in a very short time indeed, he will get away from a situation of nicety, and fix himself upon more decided ground.

He has stayed so long in Babylon, merely in compliance with the desires of his friends. We have not been inactive in Parliament. The indemnity has been carried to the House of Lords with a preamble stoutly declaratory of the illegality. There we had a curious debate in which Northington and Camden fought, the one stoutly, the other insidiously, for the dispensing power in cases of necessity. Lord Chatham trimmed between legality and illegality with more skill than success or applause. Lord Mansfield stood for the constitution with his usual ability, and with an intrepidity that surprised friends and foes. They all felt his superiority. We fought the best battle we could, on a question of adjournment upon Beckford's motion of Tuesday sennight for the E[ast] I[ndia] papers.[38] We however divided but 56 for the question. Our friends were out of town. But the fight was as spirited as you could wish. We held it until near twelve. You desire to know something in particular of my conduct. I spoke a long time, upwards of an hour I believe. But I had not the good fortune to please your Secretary Aug[ustus] Hervey, who called me to order while I was pouring out some humble and warm supplications to Lord Chatham, to implore him not to destroy that national credit to which he owed the glories of the late war. The marine Secretary had however no reason to pride himself on the reception his point of order met with from the house; and he did not in the least embarrass me. It rather gave me an opportunity for some explanations, that I was not sorry to bring out.[39] Conway seemed hurt at what I said of the situation of the Ministers. I got up a second time, and satisfied him as to his own particular. It was on the whole a good day for me. Adieu, my dear Sir. I am ever yours. On reading this nonsense over, I suspect you had a good deal, if not most of it except the India debate before. You knew that Lord Lorne's peerage was in the

---

[38] Beckford on Dec. 9 moved for parliamentary inspection of the Company's charters, treaties, Bengal revenues, and accounts of expenditures. The opposition countered with a motion to adjourn and failed by 140 to 56.

[39] Burke had attacked the loose and irregular manner in which ministers conducted government business in the house, and satirized Chatham as an aloof and remote deity, "this Invisible Being before whom Thrones, Dominations, Princedoms, Virtues, Powers, all veil their faces with their wings." Laughter swept the house, and Augustus Hervey called Burke to order. Burke said to the Speaker: "Sir, I have often suffered under the persecution of order, but did not expect its lash while at my prayers. I venerate the great man, and speak of him accordingly."—Walpole, Horace, *Memoirs of the reign of King George the Third* 2: 288-289.

Duke of Bedford's budget. He had his Grace's and G. Grenville's leave to make a separate request. But it was neither their consent nor his request that I think carried it. A new link to Conway's chain.[40] Lord Beauchamp has not given us a vote yet. But as soon as his father got the Chamberlainship, he went to Sir T. Molyneux, Usher of the Black Road, and frightened him out of his wits by enquiring of him *whether he held his office by patent for life.* Does he degenerate?

23rd December

RICHARD BURKE TO O'HARA, December 27, 1766

My dear Sir,

You must certainly think that I begin to imagine my letters to be of no small importance to you, when I venture to force one of them on you without a frank. Ned is gone out of town to spend the recess at the Duke of Portland's with Lord Rockingham. Will and Jenny are gone for a few days to a friend's at Plaistow; little Dick is gone to domineer at his nurse's, and I am left at home to quiet the violence of the Doctor's temper by the mildness and quietism of my disposition. If you learn nothing else by my letter, you will at least know how your friends of this house are disposed of, and that people out of place can amuse themselves in the country as well as Ministers. Every thing is dead in town, all the Ministers being out of town; this is a bad style, I should not be sorry to have been able to mend it by leaving out the last *of town* and ending with *out,* but good Lord how long? Well patience must be the comfort. We are not I think here of a nature easily dejected, or at least not apt to lie very long under any dejection, and we are by no means without our satisfactions. To know that Ned is acting a free, manly, and honourable part is an happiness that none of us would part with, and tho' it brings no profit, yet we ought not to complain whilst it brings a just reputation. He told you that he got some credit for his last performance on the East India business, and now that his back is turned (for otherwise I dared not have done it) I will tell you that I believe no man ever got so much credit, by any single effort.

---

[40] John Campbell, Marquess of Lorne in the Scottish peerage, was made a British peer; he was a son of the Duke of Argyle and General Conway's brother-in-law.

The town rang with it, and have not yet done with it; believe
me, even I was tired almost with hearing of it everywhere and
from every creature. Whether he has not before deserved more,
I will not take upon me to determine, but this hit more exactly;
and you may be assured that there was not (notwithstanding
Mr. Hervey's order) the least personality in it; except fine
general and pointed satire can be called personal. It had its
effect. Conway disclaimed the servility ascribed to the nominal
Ministry, but disclaimed the Ministry also; called himself a
passenger in the ship; said he did not pretend to be a Minister. Ned replied in (as I hear) a most elegant manner, and
with very flattering, tho' just compliments to him. Townshend
declared himself no Minister; everybody knew his situation;
how disagreeable it was to him and how he was forced into
it, and out of a much more pleasing one. Not a man chose to
answer a word of his argument, nor to reply to an article of
his charge. Will you forgive me, my dear Sir, for taking up your
time thus, when there is not any thing else either of a public
or private nature (at least not within my knowledge) that
could afford you a moment's amusement. If Dr. Nugent has
any thing, I leave him an equal share of the paper.

[In Nugent's hand]

Dick's having told you that we are all well, leaves me but
little to add. All our common friends, that I can now remember, are well too. Your (particular) *friend* I have not heard
a word of, time out of mind. Your saying nothing of Charles'
leg makes me hope it is forgot both by you and himself. Our
old peer goes on for the winter stoutly enough,[41] and all his
are in good plight. Dick is now happily left me, to moderate,
he tells you, my exorbitancies. His piano and my forte make
good harmony enough; which, with the usual gambols of a
dark Christmas, serve to pass away the tediousness of our long
nights, and if possible make us forget the absence of our friends.
But to be serious, for the time they are to be from us, we may
possibly meet once or twice in the twenty-four hours, and be
content for the rest, if we find one another well. Adieu my
dear Sir. If I had any thing to tell worth telling, you should
assuredly have it.

27th December

---

[41] Baron Tyrawley.

VIII. The Follies of Chatham and Townshend

[During the Christmas recess Burke not only visited the Duke of Portland in company with Lord Rockingham, but accompanied the latter to Wentworth Woodhouse and to Sir George Savile's seat at Rufford Abbey.[1] The visits marked his further advance towards the inner circle of the "High" Whigs, and cemented more firmly his attachment to Rockingham. Hence he became ardently enlisted in the cause of building a coherent and principled party under the leadership of the Marquess. The chore of the party in the House of Commons was formed by Lord John Cavendish and his brothers, William Dowdeswell, Sir George Savile, Sir William Meredith, Sir Charles Saunders, Admiral Keppel, and Burke.

What had been inchoate in 1765 now took on body and form, and out of experience certain principles were drawn that would ultimately find classic expression in the party manifesto of 1770: Burke's *Thoughts on the Cause of the Present Discontents*. As an opposition corps in 1767, the party stood for the following: strict maintenance of the constitution as settled by the Revolution; supremacy of the British legislature throughout the empire, but an expedient abstention from taxing the colonies; dissent from the views of George Grenville on American affairs; defense of the East India Company against legislative aggressions; opposition to the influence of Lord Bute and the King's mother, the Princess Augusta; refusal to take office except *en corps* and on terms that would reserve all influence in the royal closet to the responsible ministers.

As Burke was being entertained by the Whig grandees, and preparing for new opposition tactics in Parliament, his friend O'Hara was entertaining thoughts that were not in harmony with the principles of the Rockingham Whigs.]

O'HARA TO BURKE, January 2, 1767

January 2d 1767

My dear Sir,

Tho' I am much hurried, I won't lose a post, but write while your last is fresh in my mind. I received it last night, and it was a comfort to me, for I was alone, and just returned from leaving Charles at Boyle on his way to Oxford. That I accompany you all is certain, and perhaps with near as much earnest-

---

[1] Wentworth-Fitzwilliam MSS, Rockingham to Dowdeswell, Jan. 8, 1767.

ness as any member of the fireside. What you say of modern opposition is all true. 'Tis just a place to show one's value in, unproductive of public good or reformation. I have had some late opportunities of information, which your letters had prepared my mind to receive as fast as it fell. The day after I wrote last to you, I knew C[onway] was to stay in with the approbation of all his connections. I knew his Grace's proposals were *inadmissable;* and I ken the Northern Earl [2] was to find a party, and the English to plan the measures. The Duke of Bedford goes further than you seem to think. Measures as well as places are his objects. He will not join in support blind-folded. The Grenvillian views are different. A friend of yours, if I mistake not, still keeps his *entrées libres* to the closet.[3] 'Tis not in the nature of things that there can be an union of such parties. All however will at times play their parts, and expose measures. 'Tis this which must do the business; a majority within doors is not to be thought of. The excuse for displacing must arise from a public disapprobation of measures, when the time comes; the Butians will then grow languid, and majorities sink. You know all that play. But the question is, who will then be sought for? I say the weakest batch and the fairest characters; the first for private reasons, the last to hold out to the public. Of this happening I have no doubt. If Lord R[ockingham] comes within this description, he will know his tenure before he enters. It can be but the same as his Earlship's.[4] For I look upon that point as gained, with wonderful patience and perseverance; but gained it is, and cannot be lost, but by some capital blunder in measures such as will raise a ferment. The Prince of the Norse is no more;[5] that party is divided and broke. Is the ghost to walk after the dissolution of the body? The scandal falls upon the first deserters, those of them who take a new part will be judged by their measures. Thus the state of things appears to me. And I think you'll understand me. Whether I be right or not, you'll know. But if I be, one's road is plain, and no union of the several parts of opposition necessary. Your supplication in favour of public credit can do no hurt within, and must do good without. Will's friends were

---

[2] Bute.
[3] Rockingham.
[4] Chatham.
[5] The late Duke of Cumberland, architect of the Rockingham administration of 1765.

in the right, and I am very glad you got up a second time to explain yourself. I rejoice at the authentic proof you give me of Lord Beauchamp's legitimacy. I wish it were known; some other things are, thank God. 'Tis a shameful overdoing the thing. I wish you would send me a pamphlet on the legality of embargoes, the title I have forgot, but I read a good extract from it. I should have been very happy to have heard all this, but I am happy here, putting things in order for another time. I hope Augustus Hervey will retain his spirit till he comes amongst us. We have had substantials hitherto, but a Hervey will be the prettiest side dish for opposition. Adieu. I am interrupted, with much more to say.

[Burke now felt it necessary to correct certain of what he considered were misconceptions in O'Hara's mind on the subject of party politics and the character of Lord Rockingham's connection.]

BURKE TO O'HARA, January 15, 1767

My dear Sir,

I give you up for this winter; but I am glad you are so occupied as you seem to be. As to the rest, your correspondents may, among them, give you as good an account of public matters, as if you were in the midst of the bustle. I think you are a little mistaken in the situation and plan of politics of my friend. The entrée was asked last summer, to supply an omission, at a former time, of claiming a right he had, as being of the Bedchamber. It went no further; nor do I think it has been used ever since. You are undoubtedly right, that the *weak* party with the fair character would be chosen on a new change. But if you are right in your principle, are you not mistaken in the application? The party you allude to is by a good deal the strongest of any separated from Government, and their connection the closest. They certainly stand fairest in point of character; but that fairness which they have kept, and are determined still to keep, goes against their practicability; which is a quality you know and feel to be indispensable with, upon such an occasion; and the person now at the head of them, neither would, nor I am sure could, take a lead upon such terms as the Earl holds it on. He is not desirous to lead that way; and if he did, most assuredly he never would be followed; and indeed how could he? Is not the present court system built on the ruins of his, and where would you lay the foundation of his, but on the ruins of theirs? All these considerations satisfy me that their turn never can be the next, whilst any party, of not more strength, and more practicability, may be found; and it may very easily. I look therefore upon our cause, viewed on the side of power, to be, for some years at least, quite desperate; from the difficulty, not to say impossibility, of its coaliting with any body in or out of possession. As to Conway, if you hear that he stays in with the approbation of his *family* connections, your intelligence is certainly good. If with that of his old friendships and political connections (if he will own the latter idea) you are extremely misinformed. He holds his present office to their great grief and inexpressible detriment; and contrary to their unanimous sense. He has given them a dangerous blow indeed. Whether he will indemnify the public for the mischief he has done the party, I know not; but I greatly doubt it. The Great Guide, as he advanced in his project of contesting the right of the E[ast] I[ndia] Company (instead of bargaining with them for a part of it) grew sick, I fancy, of his success. I imagine he found that votes and majorities cannot always get money in every way, at every time, and in every quantity. The thing, on examination, however considerable, fell short of his magnificent idea. He grew discontented. He changed his plan; went off to the country; and left powers with *his* administration to *treat* with the Company. This intention was signified to the General Court;[6] and they empowered the Directors to treat, a fortnight ago. Yesterday the Court met by adjournment; the Directors reported that they had obeyed the order of the General Court; had offered to treat with the Ministry; but that nothing whatever was done. The truth is, the people in office, when they came to act, did not know what to propose; they had no settled scheme; or if they had any thing like one, they did not dare to propose it for fear it should not receive the sanction of the real Minister. He was as unfurnished as they; less open to information and at a distance of 100 miles;[7] so nothing was done. And thus they carry on business. What they will do in committee, or how they can at once carry on an adverse inquiry, and an amicable agreement, I do not very well understand. However, thus things are at present.

---

6 The proprietors.
7 Chatham was at Bath.

Little as I like opposition, I relish it much more than the support of such an administration; indeed I never could have brought myself to the support of so monstrous a plan of government from any principle of connection. At least, I deceive myself much, if I could. We meet tomorrow, and the Guide not yet in town. Will is still in; but how long so? The only difficulty is to separate without a quarrel; and that will be if possible. Adieu my dear friend. God prosper your plantations, and protect your enclosures, and make every thing about you full of growing! All the friends salute you. I take it for granted we shall see Charles as soon as he can let us have that pleasure.

15th January

O'HARA TO BURKE, February 7, 1767

Nymphsfield 7th February

My dear Sir,

Though you have in some degree rectified my mistake, you have not added to my satisfaction. The system which would have brought things soonest about, into the channel I wish them in, was uppermost in my thoughts; apropos to Conway, the letter from which I wrote, and wherein I said his conduct had been approved of by all his friends, was from Lord John [Cavendish]: pretty good authority one would have thought. Taking in that whole batch, the party is certainly the strongest, and certainly will prevail at last. But if Lord Chatham should tire of his business, as my paper says he does, before he shall have applied all the resources, and taken upon himself the unpopularity of the whole, he will not leave so clear a road for his successor. Were I in London, sharing in the agitation of that great world, and sitting six times a week by your fireside, I should not perhaps foresee the mighty difficulties in public business which I now do. To preserve the low manufactures by which the poor are maintained, with such immense wealth pouring in upon you annually, is what I don't conceive possible.[8] I wish we were indulged in a few, our people can live poorly. And I must tell you that your plan for the encouragement of the fishery has done much service this year; something gained by exported fish, and a plenty created in the Kingdom.

---

[8] O'Hara feared inflationary results from the Treasury's appropriating the Company's territorial revenues in Bengal.

But I am in some pain about the linen manufacture. If the demand should continue as slack next summer as it was the last, many will leave off the business. The flax seed having failed last year, we shall have none but foreign this spring. And the poor people's money goes for provisions; they won't be able to buy. The great profit on the business centers in London, and as we are totally cut off from all communication with the West Indies, it can't be otherwise. Then the English demand for provisions now renders stock a surer profit than tillage, and will therefore obtain amongst us. I am afraid our new Lord Lieutenant [9] will not be kept in good humour enough to serve us. You know we have the misfortune to be involved in your vortex. And you know enough of us to believe the most advantageous reports are not propagated of his Excellency's intentions. We are much afraid of Lord Chatham. Of all countries upon earth, 'tis hardest to decide upon one's party in this. Men there are none to follow, measures few. People are not enough blended together for common cause. A scheme of popularity is nonsense in Ireland; for the people don't know their own interest. To feed their faction is destruction to them. To serve Government, *cui bono?* Government has nothing left to give. Lord Hertford took the gleanings into his own family. I have of late turned these things over in my mind, and protest that I am apprehensive of being at last obliged to consult my conscience, do what little good I can, and cast my cap at emolument. A most unmanly part for a gentleman to be reduced to! God keep you from so disagreeable a dilemma. I wish I could look down upon you and see a good fight. If I can but catch the close of the session, when tricks begin, I shall be satisfied. But the papers put me out of hopes; they talk of your being up early, in order to which you must do a great deal in a very little time. I don't think of going till the latter end of April. And then it will be without any scheme of business or pleasure, but to see you all. Adieu.

BURKE TO O'HARA, February 28, 1767

My dear Sir,

I have been a poor correspondent for some time past. I wish I had the excuse of being usefully employed to others or to myself in excuse of my neglect. But there is nothing

---

[9] Lord Bristol, who presently resigned without going to Dublin.

unfriendly in my laziness. It is rather laxity than perverseness of disposition; at least I think so; and I trust you will think so. Why have I heard nothing from Charles? I suppose when he plans an expedition to London he will announce himself. I take it, after all your partial accounts of me, that we must soon be well acquainted, and I fancy our intimacy will not break off suddenly. I confess, as to his politics, I should not be sorry that he was initiated into the school of our party; his age will make him relish such doctrines, and will enable him to wait their effect; for if they have any it will not be sudden. Is not this odd language, and sounding like an unnatural despondency in us, who gained yesterday one of the completest victories, for the substance, for the manner, and for the time, that ever was known? Yesterday then, the Chancellor of the Exchequer [10] moved the land tax at 4 shillings in the pound. Dowdeswell (as had been pre-concerted) got up after him; and showing from the general state of the revenue that the landed interest might be relieved, and yet leave a large sum for the discharge of debt, moved to amend the question by substituting 3 shillings in the place of 4. A long debate ensued. On the division it was carried for the amendment by 206 against 188. The Ministry had called down all their forces. On our part, the majority of the Rockinghams, the whole Bedfords and Grenvilles, reinforced by the almost complete corps of Tories, came into the field.[11] Such a victory, on such a question, shows plainly enough into what a contemptible state Administration has fallen. At another time, twenty-four hours after the division another set of people would have been in possession of the closet—certainly nothing like it has been known in this century. But as things stand at present, it is matter rather of laughter and surprise, than any ground to reason or act upon. It discovers indeed the weakness of all administration, especially of this most foolish and contemptible system; but that is all. It is easy to overturn the Ministry; far from it to find one to succeed. Observe, that in this division the Bute party stood firm, and voted to a man with the Administration. Will Burke is out.[12] Conway has got David Hume for his secretary.[13] Will

[10] Charles Townshend.

[11] Of the conduct of the Rockinghams on this question, Horace Walpole wrote that "Edmund Burke alone had the honesty to stay away rather than support so pernicious a measure."—*Memoirs, op. cit.* 2: 298.

[12] Four years later Burke said of Will's resignation: "For me he gave up a respectable employment of a thousand pounds a year, with other very fair

feels easy in the freedom he has purchased at so good a price. But it is freedom. You are out, I believe, in the date of Lord J[ohn] C[avendish]'s letter. There was a time when it was true: afterwards it was much otherwise.

I know you will feel with us, for the unfortunate accident which has befallen poor Richard.[14] He broke his leg about eight days ago. Ever since he has been upon his back; but the symptoms are as good as they can be in so unhappy an affair. He bears it in general with his usual spirit and resolution. Adieu my dear Sir. God bless you.

Saturday 28th

BURKE TO O'HARA, March 7, 1767

My last letter left things in an odd situation. They continue so. Lord Chatham, the day of his coming to town,[15] saw nobody but Lord Bristol; who, I suppose, is his go-between at the closet. There were two Cabinet councils on Indian affairs; one the day before the *Guide* came to town, the other the day after; in both which Charles Townshend and General Conway differed from all the rest of the Cabinet. They held that the propositions made by the Directors were a good basis of a treaty; the rest were of opinion (as they were directed) that they ought wholly to be rejected.[16] Beckford moved yesterday that they should be laid before the House. The Chancellor and Secretary wished nothing more, but they fought shy; they said that the terms were not sufficiently clear; Lord Granby[17] declared them totally inadmissible; Sir Edward

pretensions. He gave up an employment which he filled with great honour to himself, and with great satisfaction to his principal in office . . . he resigned it to give an example and an encouragement to me,—not to grow fearful and languid in the course to which he had always advised me."—*Correspondence* 1: 317.

[13] The Scottish historian and philosopher, who had served as secretary to Conway's brother, Lord Hertford, at the Paris embassy in 1763.

[14] Burke's brother.

[15] March 2.

[16] The proposals were to pay 500,000 pounds, in return for an extension of the Company's charter to 1817, certain advantageous alterations of duties, parliamentary permission to strengthen the authority of the Company over its servants in India, and confirmation of its territorial revenues. The Directors proposed also that after paying all expenses and distributing profits to the shareholders, the Company divide its surplus revenues with the state.—Sutherland, *East India Company, op. cit.*, 159-160.

[17] The Commander-in-chief and a member of the cabinet council.

Hawke (out of the gallery) informed the House, that the Ministry were divided on the subject. Then Charles Townshend got up; he said his situation had put him under difficulties before, but that now he thought himself at liberty; he began with great spirit, reserved himself on the question of right and jurisdiction; but asserted strongly the preference of treaty to force. He agreed to the bringing in of papers. However he grew a little more shy and dubious towards the latter end. The day ended with nothing more than the conversation. Lord Chatham, before the day, exerted every nerve to get a new Chancellor of the Exchequer; or at least somebody who would make or support his adverse measures to the Company. But every body declined. His plan is dictated solely by the miserable situation of his private affairs, which makes employment necessary to him. He took it at first, subservient to my Lord Bute as to *persons;* and since it must be so, he will hold it (if he can) subservient to Townshend and Conway, as to measures; for I hear his *ton* now is, that since he differs from such able and knowing persons on the India point, he grows doubtful of his own opinion and submits the whole to the wisdom of Parliament. He puts the same face, and holds the same language, on the loss of the India question; but this was not until he despaired of getting any one to take the places of those two rebellious officers. Their plan is, not to resign. As to Lord Chatham, he must make some capital change in his system, or it won't do. Lord Bute seems serious at last in supporting him; but is at a loss for means. As to himself (as usual with him at such times) he is gone out of town. All the opposition parties are still asunder. Nothing but confusion. God send order out of it. Adieu. I am in some haste.

Saturday 7th March

O'HARA TO BURKE, March 12, 1767

March 12th

The misfortune which has befallen poor Richard does indeed excuse your not writing, had I a right to expect an excuse; but this is a most shocking one. I had a full account of the manner and occasion of his fall from my long friend Toby Burke,[18] by last post; and I owe the letter in a good measure

---

[18] Possibly Thibot Burke; see Wecter, *op. cit.*, 26, 30.

to the interest he takes in every thing that relates to the family.
'Tis a most melancholy event; I count upon a few words from
the Doctor now and then to let me know how he goes on. But
he himself was not well when he wrote. Yet his talking of going
to the country looks as if he thought there was nothing to fear
for Dick. I wish the account of your victory in the House had
been unalloyed, that I might rejoice. I readily conceive that
the approaching elections had a share in it,[19] and that 'tis by
no means decisive. But my entertainment is to see a dupe of
such magnitude,[20] deserting a faithful, an honourable, and an
effectual connection, for a by-closet road, in which everybody
else could foresee that he would lose his way towards the close of
the session. In such a dilemma, should he have failed in the E[ast]
I[ndia] business, he'll die of jaundice in three months, and yet
I agree with you, much remains to be done. The effect can't
be sudden, if I understand how things are, and I think I do.
The late victory may be *matter of laughter, rather than ground
to reason upon,* but whenever such ground is gained it will be
a serious day; and till it is, it would be absurd to list. I agree
with you; I was totally wrong in a former letter, my speculation was foolish, and contracted.[21] I had then no mind that
Will should leave the office; I now think he has done right.
I have just allowed that the late victory was of no moment; I
have allowed too much. But yet I think there will be another
juggle before things come right. How does *my friend*[22] vote
in these things?

I have just finished a pamphlet said to be wrote by Flood,[23]
entitled a *Letter to the Speaker.* From the meanness of the
style, the no-arrangement of the matter, and total want of spirit
and elegance, I should never have guessed Flood for its author.
And yet I remember him to have used some of the expressions
in private; however 'tis universally given to him. I hear Lord
Chatham has laid a plan for new-modelling this country; and
committed the execution to Lord Bristol; the present structure
to be pulled down to the ground, and a new one built on the

---

[19] Burke later stated that the administration intended to take a shilling off
the land tax in the next session, just before the election in 1768 of a new
Parliament, "and thus to bribe the freeholders of England with their own
money."—*Works* 2: 125.

[20] Chatham.   [21] *Supra,* Jan. 2, 1767.

[22] W. G. Hamilton.

[23] Henry Flood (1732-1791), a patriot leader in the Irish Parliament; friend
and occasional correspondent of Burke's.

same foundation. The pulling down I have no objection to; but the rebuilding I hope will be in other hands. I don't wish for the magnificent pile held out to our view. A neat little edifice with the conveniences of life would suit us better.

Charles meditates a visit to you, but it will not be till summer, and then I propose to go with him, taking him up at Oxford. He's reading about and about law, but has not got into law yet; the dry part he don't take to; close investigations are painful to his mind, as yet. But when it has got hold of a thing, it makes good use of it. I am soon to go to the County of Kerry to see Ponsonby before he goes to Bath; I shall set out for the Curragh on the 9th April, and so round. I must in the mean time plan my business for this long wished for visit to you. God bless you all, my dear Sir,

most truly yours,

Charles O'Hara

BURKE TO O'HARA, March 14, 1767

My dear Sir,

I am obliged to you for thinking of us in your retirement. I shall hardly believe that it will destroy your social qualities, or social affections. I heartily wish it may answer all the other good family purposes to which you have devoted it. I do not believe it will contradict these very ends, which have caused it. Would to God any thing from this bustle would tend to relieve its languor, or find matter to enrich its speculations! I wrote a couple of posts ago, and directed to Dublin. Your letter had no date of place; and from what you said, I suspected you wrote from Dublin. The Ponsonby you mentioned I took to be the Speaker; I am very sorry to find he was so much nearer a connection with you.[24] If he comes this way he will call to see us. You will make us acquainted! We proceed in Parliament *victoriously* but not *successfully*. Last Monday we divided on a mere question of adjournment. We were 147, they an 180.[25] The Friday before, the printing of the East India papers

---

[24] O'Hara had written on Feb. 20: "I am kept in some uneasiness by Mr. Ponsonby's illness; and I wait the event in some anxiety." The allusion is to his son-in-law.

[25] On Monday, March 9, a petition from the Directors of the East India Company against the printing of their papers had been presented. An opposition motion to rescind the order of the previous Friday for printing the papers, was met by Conway's motion to adjourn, which was carried in the division to which Burke alludes.

was carried on a motion of Beckford's, with but a little grumbling; for the House was so impatient and tumultuous, that no sort of argument could be heard. You know the impatience into which they sometimes fall. This acquiescence was represented as very ill of us. We moved on Monday to rescind the motion—Conway moved only to adjourn the debate until Wednesday. On this we divided. We were willing to show how many would act against the *system* of the Administration, totally independent of the question. This was futile; but futile as these merits were, I think they were rather with us. On Wednesday we came to the body of the question on the expunging the resolution of Friday. The Ministry feared, (what our best members thought might be the case) that we should beat them, and gave us the substance of the dispute; nothing but the charters and treaties being to be printed. Conway and Townshend have declared in favour of negotiation with the Company, and against all violence. Lord Chatham seems resolved to ruin the latter but can get nobody to fill his place. Lord Bute is steady to him; their connection is more declared than ever. The King has given Lord Chatham the fullest powers. He has thrown off his blankets, laid aside his crutches, quitted his litter, and is abroad, as well looking as ever I saw him. We are still divided. Things are in as odd a way as you can conceive; but we are steady to our principle and in our conduct; and if we succeed, well! If not, we are no ways disgraced. It will now be seen what the Crown will do, and yet it is by yielding they have held hitherto. Lord Chatham will find some way of quitting his ground of a claim of right on the Company, and will at length negotiate a treaty; and having thus got out of the immediate difficulty, will prorogue the Parliament, and trust to events in the summer. Adieu my dear Sir. We are all truly yours.

14th March

BURKE TO O'HARA, March 17, 1767

My dear Sir,

I hope the pacquets you expected brought you my two last. The time is a little critical; and you will naturally expect to hear from us pretty punctually.[26] Things still remain in

---

[26] O'Hara may have been speculating in East India shares at this time.

suspence. Lord Chatham saw the King last Thursday; and he says got the fullest assurances of support; and in consequence, the fullest power over things and persons. However, as to the first, it is not always royal power itself that can govern them; and as to the second, it is easier to destroy than to create; he could turn out Townshend who is grown more and more rebellious, but he cannot readily get one bold enough and able enough to assume his seat in such times as these. In the Indian affair he will I am satisfied get off his high ground, and take that method to which reason ought at first to have directed, but which necessity had at length compelled him to pursue, that of fair treaty and negotiation upon terms of mutual advantage. He has rejected the Directors' proposal even as a *basis*. Sulivan made one in the General Court yesterday.[27] It is believed that he countenances this proposition. That of the Directors was to give Government 500,000 advance. Sulivan gives eight to be raised by a power of enlarging their capital stock by borrowing that sum, at 250 per cent. The rest of the 2 millions acquired by that method, to go in discharge of the simple contract debts of the Company. In other respects, the Directors' proposal seems at least as good, and far less complex than Sulivan's. But Sulivan is Lord Shelburne's friend; and his making a proposal acceptable to Government is to lead the way for him into the Direction. All negotiation with the Bedford party is suspended by the dreadful accident which happened to Lord Tavistock.[28] He was thrown from his horse, and received a kick by which his skull was fractured. The first operation took out a piece of bone 2 inches long and about one broad. On this operation he recovered his speech and senses. This was thought sufficient, and indeed all that in his condition they could venture to explore. He grew a little more easy and light, but ill symptoms have appeared again which made new openings necessary. They have taken out two pieces more of his skull. There

---

[27] Lawrence Sulivan, long an outstanding figure in the Company, had been forced out of the direction by Robert Clive in 1764, and was seeking now to return to a position of authority. He proposed in the General Court a plan for giving 800,000 pounds to the government, plus the territorial revenues after paying a guaranteed 14 per cent dividend to the proprietors. To raise the 800,000 pounds he proposed to borrow the money at 250 per cent, with a preference in the subscription for the proprietors. The scheme was well designed to catch votes in the General Court, but likely to bankrupt the Company. It failed to win adoption.—Sutherland, *op. cit.*, 164-166.

[28] Francis Russell, Marquess of Tavistock and son and heir of the Duke of Bedford; he languished for about two weeks and died, aged twenty-seven.

are no great hopes for him. My friend Gataker with great credit
to his skill and care attends him. The whole town takes a share
in the concern of Bedford House. Your poor friend Richard
goes on as well as can be. They are to raise him tomorrow.

17th March   St. Paddy and sober.

BURKE TO O'HARA, March 28, 1767

We live in expectation of seeing Mr. and Mrs. Ponsonby.[29]
They will be your precursors; but I hope *Monsiegneur vient*
will not be often reiterated before we see him. Poor Dick gets
on apace. He is out of bed; and the leg promises well, even
as to its future looks; and that to a young unmarried man is a
consideration. Thank God we have now no other anxiety. As
to our politics, nothing is yet decided. Lord Chatham has not
seen Conway or Townshend, yet they stay in. The latter speaks
very loud hostilities—and certainly his coming out at this time
would be most advantageous. But an advantage depending
upon his firmness is precarious indeed. The Bedfords seem to
come a little nearer to us. It is something that black blood is
over between us; and that our people and they meet and talk
amicably. Something may come of it. But you easily see, from
the pretensions of Grenville, the nature of the House of Commons, and the consequence of the lead there, that our party
cannot easily arrange with them, whilst they hold Grenville
high; and we have no leader but Dowdeswell, who though
by far the best man of business in the Kingdom, and ready and
efficient in debate, is not perhaps quite strenuous and pugna-
cious enough for that purpose; the best in the world to aid and
support such an one as Conway or Townshend.[30] Your mind
will carry you to the rest. Never was any grief more general
than for Lord Tavistock. The whole family almost ruined in
their health by it. I congratulate you heartily on Will, who is
beginning to be most active in the House.[31] His speech some
days since was far the best in the debate; well marked, forcible,
ingenious, and with a decent (and no more than decent) acrimony to those he answered. He will be an immense accession

---

[29] O'Hara's daughter and son-in-law.
[30] To win over either of these, but preferably Conway, was a tactical objective of the Rockinghams.
[31] Will Burke.

to the party; and you will, without regard to the party, rejoice in his success. We go on with the E[ast] I[ndia] enquiry.[32] We are now examining *viva voce* evidence. Adieu and believe us all as much yours as any people in the world.

28th March

BURKE TO O'HARA, March 30, 31, 1767

My dear Sir,

I have just come in from a long insignificant day in the House of Commons. Your letter met me at my return, and paid me for the *ennui* of our evidence. It is not post night; but our friends are at cards, and I cannot employ half an hour better than in writing to you. The first thing I must do is expostulate with you on some of your notions.[33] Good God! How do you think it possible, that I could take on with such an administration, in the conduct of such measures, as the present? If a little rectitude did not prevent it, surely the least particle of pride and spirit would never suffer one to engage under a person who is incapable of forming any rational plan, and is above communicating even his reveries to those who are to realize and put them into execution. He does not appear even at the Cabinet councils of his own creating. His Secretary of State and Chancellor of the Exchequer never see his face. In this great matter of the East India Company, not one in the House knows what the plan or design of administration is. Most people believe, that they have never conceived any thing like one. All they do is to run a blind muck at the Company's right to their acquisitions, without knowing the practicability or regarding the justice of the measure. Beckford, and Lord Clare,[34] (the first a confidential, the last a desperate instrument) conduct (if it can be called conducting) the whole. I do assure you from my heart, that I look with as much horror at the spirit,

---

[32] A general parliamentary inquiry into the affairs of the Company had been opened on March 20.

[33] O'Hara's letter which provoked Burke has not been found, but another (March 27) was now on its way. In it O'Hara said: "You have been right from the beginning. Will was right. I wish my friend Conway had! If honour is not clear-sighted enough to hold its course at setting out, it does mischief afterwards."

[34] Robert Nugent, now head of the Board of Trade, had been created Viscount Clare in the Irish peerage late in 1766.

as I do with contempt at the manner of this proceeding. We are to set ourselves up as judges upon a point of law, to decide between the subject and the Crown a matter of property of the greatest concern and magnitude without the least colour of right; at once judge and party! I cannot now enter into this subject, but be assured, from the best consideration I can give it, it is one of the blindest and one of the most wicked designs which ever yet entered into the heart of man.[35] Do you know, that they rejected all treaty with the Company; declared their first scheme of propositions *inadmissible,* without explanation or discussion; although it will be utterly impossible for the whole strength of Parliament to get any thing from that country, not only without the *acquiescence,* but without the *concurrence* of the Company. I wrote thus far last night, and it looks as if I were very angry with the Ministry. At times I am; but I am not so furious as you may think. I am not so angry as not sometimes to laugh a little. For some days indeed I have been somewhat ill; but it has not made me too peevish. With regard to the popularity you apprehend their system will gain by lowering taxes, depend upon it they have no such thought; the party they mean to relieve is of another kind, and in another situation; and it is not popularity they seek to acquire by the use they propose to make of this money. You know there are other necessities besides those of the subject. Townshend and Conway, complaining and complained of, proscribed by the invisible Minister, and called out by every motive of spirit and resentment, still hold their places. This is not of any great advantage to the character of Conway, (the other has none to lose) but is very disadvantageous to us in our present treaty.[36] But our leader is steady, and nothing will remove him from the clear walk he has taken.[37] Poor Richard sits by me. He has got down to us. The leg promises to be straight and shapely. Adieu my dear Sir. God bless you. If your retreat don't sink your spirit, what have you to lament in it? Our bustle I am sure is not worthy of your regret. We have indeed reason to be sorry that you are so long kept away from us.

31st March

---

[35] Presently, however, ministry accepted the principle of negotiation with the Company.
[36] Probably with the Bedfords; Conway could have brought much strength to the Rockinghams.
[37] Rockingham.

[As ministers negotiated with directors for a financial settlement between the Treasury and the East India Company, the parliamentary inquiry into the affairs of the Company, which had been opened on March 20, proceeded. Since it served no other purpose than to ventilate the lack of discipline and corruption among the Company's servants, Burke and the Rockinghams were eager to stop it, and toward this end they sought alliance with the Bedford faction. But their strategy was frustrated by the sudden introduction of an American question arising from Massachusetts' failure to comply correctly with the request of Parliament for adequate indemnification of the persons who had suffered in attempting to enforce the Stamp Act. The Duke of Bedford on April 10 tried to force the ministers to adopt a stern line of conduct against Massachusetts. But they, who were preparing certain American measures of their own, refused to be goaded by the opposition; most of the peers who followed Rockingham's lead rallied on this question to the support of the administration.]

Burke to O'Hara, April 18, 1767

My dear Sir,

We have now a little recess; and I assure you I enjoy it very perfectly.[38] Not that we have had business to take up the whole mind of a person of any activity, but there has been always something or other which drew me into a number of small vortices of affairs in which I have been in a sort of whirl for some weeks past. I do not know whether you understand me or not. I am perhaps not very clear in my own meaning. But be the cause what it will, I am pleased to find myself master of a week's dissipation. All agreement between the parties seems further off than ever. Events have happened of late, which though not productive of ill blood amongst us, yet have helped to shove us a little further asunder. The Duke of Bedford's friends, with what discretion I will not affirm, got him to plunge into politics as a diversion from the grief occasioned by his late great loss. Accordingly it was announced that he should make a motion in the House of Lords of the greatest consequence. The purport of this motion was kept a profound secret, not only from the Administration, but from the lords of our party. At length out it came. It was to address the Crown to take into consideration the act of indemnity and compensation

---

[38] Easter recess, April 16-28.

lately passed in the Colony of Massachusetts Bay as highly derogating from his prerogative, etc. etc. and to act in support of his just rights and those of this country, in such a manner as should appear most fitting to his wisdom with the advice of council.[39] The address was cautiously worded, (I have only given you the substance) and they flattered themselves our people would come into it. Conway was reflected upon by some Lords in the debate, as having encouraged the colonists to this improper act, by some expressions in his letter transmitting an account of the repeal of the stamp duty. There was some difference of sentiments among the Rockinghams on this subject. The Duke of Newcastle went away. Lord Rockingham and the rest (with one or two exceptions) voted with the Ministry. They carried it 63 to 36. Lord R[ockingham] is of opinion, that if the parties had carried on this measure in concert they would have had a majority of one. But the Bedfords and Temples chose to be politic, and did not communicate. A motion in which they would agree might easily have been settled. For want of *simplicity* in the contrivance the effect was defeated. The Bedfords were vexed. Lord R[ockingham] did right unquestionably; but an impression was given which weakened the whole body. I make no doubt that it hurt our division when we endeavoured again last Tuesday to hustle this villainous E[ast] India enquiry out of the House.[40] Administration divided 213 to our 157. They triumph intolerably on this advantage. It is certainly a point gained to them. We sat to it until two o'clock. Adieu dear Sir. The bellman warns.

Saturday

BURKE TO O'HARA, May 5, 1767

My dear Sir,

It is a long time since I wrote to you, or, I think, heard from you. In that time some curious events have happened which affected me at the time, and which at the time might have entertained you. But a mighty tide rushes on; and washes away,

---

[39] The Massachusetts act had stated that the legislature acted of its own free will and not in obedience to parliamentary command, thus implying that Parliament had no right to prescribe legislation to Massachusetts.

[40] Sir William Meredith, of the Rockingham corps, on April 14 moved the dissolution of the committee on the affairs of the East India Company.

and brings forward such things, with such rapidity, that yesterday's thoughts and politics are as if they had never been. At present, I consider things not absolutely at, but certainly very near a crisis. Lord Chatham's health, understanding, and power are undermined. He cannot possibly stand long. But the ———— [41] is resolved to keep up the show of an administration until the end of a session; and then to attempt another administration (for its year) on the old Bute basis. Lord Egmont, some think will be the undertaker. But if he cannot get at least some two of the great corps with him, his undertaking will be ridiculous; if not all, it will be difficult. They have come to a temporary agreement with the E[ast] India Directors. The General Court meets tomorrow to confirm it upon their part. There will be some warm work in that body.[42] This day we were to have had the grand American budget of resolutions, regulations, and duties. The Chancellor of the Exchequer, who had raised much expectation on this subject, had a fall last night by which he was cut over the eye. Lord North was to move them in his place.[43] But Rigby got up and moved to postpone the committee on account of his health; the House readily gave way to it. I doubt whether Charles was much obliged to him for his kindness and candour. Whenever the day comes on it will be as singular an one as ever was seen. Are we to entertain hopes of seeing you; and when? You have heard of Lord Rockingham's astonishing success. He brought off 6000 clear; and got as much more or near the mark for his friends.[44] Adieu my dear friend. We are all well.

5th May

[Charles Townshend, on May 13, brought before the House of Commons a punitive proposal to restrain the functions of the New York legislature until the assembly of that colony complied fully

---

[41] The King.

[42] Against objections from both directors and ministers, a majority in the General court on May 6 voted for an increase from 10 to 12½ per cent, in the annual dividend. Immediately, a bill to prohibit the increase was introduced in Parliament. The victorious party (led by Sulivan) in the General Court petitioned against this bill, without success, but did succeed in altering the previous temporary agreement between ministry and the direction. Late in May the terms of a treaty between the Company and the Crown were settled and accepted on both sides; its principal feature provided for the Company to pay 400,000 pounds annually to the Treasury.

[43] Frederick North (1732-1792) at this time was Paymaster.

[44] On the Newmarket turf.

with the requirements of the parliamentary Mutiny Act of 1765. New York was the military headquarters for North America, and its assembly had repeatedly refused to obey to the letter an act which laid on it the obligation to make certain specified provisions for the king's troops. For nearly a year the Chatham administration had known of this situation, and although it had aroused great ministerial indignation nothing was done about it until Townshend seized the lead from Shelburne, the minister responsible in American affairs, and brought forward his proposal. New York was not the only colony then posed in resistance to the will of Parliament, but it was evident that Townshend intended to make an example of it for the warning and instruction of the others. He presented also a proposal for laying American port duties on certain British goods imported by the colonists, in order to raise a revenue for maintaining an American civil list.

Two days after this "grand American budget" was before the House of Commons, O'Hara, who had received Burke's letter of May 5 and sensed something of what ministers would propose, replied from Nymphsfield.]

O'HARA TO BURKE, May 15, 1767

Nymphsfield May 15th

My dear Sir,

You have been silent so long, that I concluded things were at a crisis, and your share in them too great for private correspondence. I had seen a letter the night before I left town from a very vocal person, which gave me a comprehensive but an inaccurate notion of the state of affairs; yours which I found at Boyle in my way hither makes in part the *ripieno* of it; and I got it just while my imagination was at work about you: it was welcome. You have gone through by this an affair of great moment, and in which your part was extremely nice—the American business. But then the Great Guide had as nice a part in proposing, as you could possibly have in opposing. What a monstrous stake this is, to leave parties to scramble for! And at a time when people may be found equal to the task, and to whom no opposition would be given. Your East Indian affair I do not understand, not having had any thing to read on the subject. Nor do I mention this by way of calling for an explanation; this I shall soon have *viva voce*. But it must raise a ferment. Of the American I comprehend more; of your dominion over their commerce; of your right to bind them to a connection with and dependence on the mother country; but beyond this, nothing. To extend one's ideas further, one must be in the secrets of Administration. And as for popularity, your manufactures can't go on without an exclusive commerce with them; and yet people not concerned in them, and loaded with taxes, will wish to transfer some part of the load. You see my brain's intoxicated with a little drink; I long to drink largely with you, and set it right again.

I hear Lord Bristol must come to Ireland. His indecision on this head was not to be admitted, where only it could be objected to. We shall fritter his nerves; but notwithstanding all you may hear to the contrary, we shall do his business. We are totally ignorant of business, and there is no man left amongst us to circulate a good political lie. The Speaker talks, insinuates, and sometimes affirms; but there is little more dependence on his words than on his promises. Besides, it is generally understood that he only wants to make terms. For my own part, I shall endeavour to do some good; but for a very odd reason, because I shall not know what else to do.

I went from Dublin to a ball at Castletown, where Dick Marly [45] and I talked you pretty well over. I understood you thoroughly from different accounts. Every body tells me what they hear of my friend Burke. Upon the whole I wish you joy. God prosper you is the hearty prayer of an Irish friend, and all of you down to little Dick inclusive.

[O'Hara was right in his judgment that ministerial proposals on the question of America at this time would place Burke and his party in a delicate and somewhat embarrassing situation. They took little part in the deliberations which led to Charles Townshend's measures' being enacted into law. In the midst of this legislative process, Burke wrote again to O'Hara and never even mentioned the events that were to stir a new crisis in America.]

BURKE TO O'HARA, June 4, 1767

My dear Sir,

This pacquet will carry you so many more and so much better accounts of those, for whose welfare you must be at this time particularly anxious, [46] than I can possibly give, that I shall say little of them except what regards my own feelings and

---

[45] Probably Richard Marlay, the later Bishop of Clonfert and Waterford.
[46] O'Hara's daughter and son-in-law, the James Ponsonbys.

opinions of them.   Mr. Ponsonby, my new acquaintance,
seems to be a man of good understanding and good temper;
and seems, I think, to know the value of the possession you have
given him.   I am really pleased with him, and I must thank
you for his acquaintance.   As to the young lady, she is every
thing which the daughter of such a mother could have promised; I will say nothing of the father—she has something of both
of you, but most of Lady Mary.   She is quick and observing;
and I am sure a very few years will put her exactly on the plat-
form of her mother.   No one could wish her higher.   I think
Ponsonby looks well.   I know not whether he has yet stated his
case to the Doctor.

I thank you for your letters;[47] and am likewise very thankful, though I confess not a little surprised, that you are at all
satisfied with mine.   If you understand any thing at all of what
is doing here, it must arise from your own correct knowledge
of the *carte du pais,* than from any information of mine.   We
have begun the session early; we have continued it long; and
we have done nothing.   Never so much labour, never so little
product.   The Ministry broken, divided, weak, and fluctuating,
without mutual confidence, united interest, or common consultation, still holds.   The Secretary of State and Chancellor of
the Exchequer vote (on questions of state and finance) in a
minority.[48]   No one placeman follows them; and yet they hold
their places.   Sometimes an inferior member of an inferior
board, sometimes a person belonging to no board at all, con-
ducts what used to be considered as the business of Government.   The great officers of the Crown amuse themselves and
the House, with jests on their own insignificance.   This is our
state in the House of Commons, where the Crown is all-power-
ful, and yet does nothing.   The complexion of the H[ouse] of
Lords is more adverse to Administration.   A stubborn body
of sixty-one holds together and cannot be beat down one lower
in several conflicts.   One question was just carried by the
Princes of the blood.   Two days ago on the Quebec question,
accidents gave the court a majority of eleven.[49]   But the minority lost none.   In the meantime, I am satisfied the Butes

---

[47] The letter of May 15 is the only one for this period that has been found.

[48] A striking instance of this state of affairs was given on May 26 when
Conway and Townshend voted with the opposition against the bill to limit the
East India Company's dividend.—Sutherland, *op. cit.,* 175.

[49] The Duke of Richmond on June 2 moved a censure of the ministry for
delaying the establishment of a civil government in Quebec.

will defend their last redoubt. They are pushed to it. The Duke of Grafton seems to have gone over to that set, body and soul; and to maintain his ground with firmness, not to say obstinacy. Such is the general situation. We have a week's recess. I see no speedy end to the session. If you come, come quickly. Will is in the country. Dick hobbles about. Adieu my dear Sir.

4th June

["Victorious at the Curragh, I am come to town, and I think in my way to you," wrote O'Hara from Dublin on June 16. "Ponsonby and his wife, of whom you make such kind mention, are, *in a degree,* what you say; Friend Edmund's genius fancied all the rest. She tells me you talk of going to Italy, if I read her hand right; for 'tis rather fair than legible. It will refresh you after all your fatigue, and for that reason I wish it. But how can you be out of the way, at such a time?"

Parliament did not rise until July 2, and Burke did not go to Italy. O'Hara visited the Burkes in the early part of the summer.]

IX. A New Order for Ireland

[O'Hara may have been in company with the Burkes when the Duke of Grafton, soon after Parliament rose, approached Rockingham with a proposal from the King. The Marquess was asked to negotiate with other opposition leaders and form a plan for coming into a reconstructed administration. Rockingham soon discovered, however, that he could not unite with the Bedfords because of their ties with George Grenville, and that the King who, according to Grafton, intended the Treasury for the Marquess, did not mean to allow him to form a new administration with his friends in command of all the principal offices. Hence the negotiations, in which Burke seems not to have played any part, broke down. Afterwards, some alterations were made in the ministry, the most important being the appointment of George, Viscount Townshend as Lord lieutenant of Ireland, in succession to Lord Bristol who had never taken up his duties at Dublin. General Henry Conway, while retaining the seals of a secretary of state, was given Lord Townshend's former place as Lieutenant-general of the Ordnance.

In the fall of 1767 Townshend would go to Dublin as a permanently residing viceroy and begin the making of a political system which resembled somewhat the system that the King, Lord Bute, Chatham, Grafton, and their supporters had formed in England. The new political situation was discussed in letters of O'Hara and William Burke in August and September.]

O'HARA TO BURKE, August 16, 1767

> Nymphsfield 16 August, but you may direct to Merrion Square.

My dear Edmund,

God grant this may find you at Parson's Green [1] tranquillizing by your own fire side. The Doctor may say what he will, but no man living wants it more than you do. I have just finished a letter to Conway; Burton is reported to be dead, and I have desired him to tell Lord Townshend that I wish to succeed him as Commissioner of the Revenue. Don't however imagine that I expect it, but I expect either to get it or be refused, and either will govern my conduct. I don't know Lord Town-

---

[1] Burke was living in a suburban house that belonged to Lord Rockingham, located southwest of Westminster.

shend enough to apply to him, and perhaps may not between this and Christmas, at which time I propose to see you. Is he rich? If not I shall pity his banker, for he'll be £10,000 out of pocket by next winter; his Excellency must reside to reimburse himself. Lord Bristol managed his affairs well; he timed his resignation well; tho' I should think—thought otherwise. What think you of the Ordnance and the first regiment worth his acceptance? [2] The circumstance was nice and delicate: but all's well than ends well. I hear of an express sent after the Marquess. You know the Rigbyans have a large correspondence with Ireland. I met their story everywhere and heightened with one passage which I did not expect, the ridicule of the Marquess's acting as if the Treasury had been offered to him when ———— [3] denied it. I was at last provoked to tell my story as I had heard it, and with all the success I could wish, for Rigby who had so often damned himself and friends for quarrelling with Lord Bute, was no longer considered as a man to break off for American measures. [4] The intemperance of the Duke of Richmond cost me trouble, but that also I got over. Notwithstanding my victory the circumstances of your party is extremely delicate. The more I think on't, the more confirmed I am in my opinion that the people must make the arrangement: the *vox populi* will decide the question. When you meet with Lord Besborough I wish you would find out what success he has with Lord Townshend, for I can't know till I see the Speaker. [5] He was to see him on Irish politics the day after he wrote to him. I think the plan must be residency and consequently the same with Lord Bristol's. I breakfasted with the Prim[ate] on my way home. He told me he had heard from you, but no news only that Lord Rockingham had gained great honour. He was to go next to Corke and not to return till the meeting of parliament, but this I don't believe. He wrote to Lord Bristol for the seal and had received a very sensible answer, but against his pretensions. God bless you all. Yours most truly.

---

[2] Reference is to Conway.

[3] The King. When Rockingham sought an audience with the King to explain that he could not come into office, George III "owned that he had never intended to give him the Treasury, but to keep the Duke of Grafton."—Walpole, *Memoirs* 3: 61. Rockingham was much offended.

[4] The Bedfords had given out that their negotiations with Rockingham failed because of disagreement over American policy.

[5] Speaker Ponsonby and Besborough were brothers.

WILLIAM BURKE TO O'HARA, *ca.* August 18, 1767[6]

Do not imagine that my taking folio paper arises from a sense of the abundance of my matter; for in fact I have nothing in the world else to say, than that we hope you are well, and to add in the schoolboy style, we being so at the present writing. We have not much fear that you will suspect us of forgetting you, yet we are not without reproach to ourselves, for never having enquired after you, since you left us; and I write now simply to put an end to our omissions, and to desire that we may soon hear from you, of you, and all about you, where you are, have been, and will be; London we earnestly hope will be the answer to the last query. As for us, Richard is bathing for his leg at Southampton, and it is not impossible that we may all go to him, and Ned may leave his wife there, as he himself threatens a tour to the north. He is just returned from a short one to the Duke of Richmond's.[7] He was much struck with the Sussex country, whose green and wooded hills afforded a new scene to him.

As to our politics, I know not in the world what to say of them; the waters have been troubled, and though no agitation now appears on the surface, yet they are not quiet or at rest. To say the truth, for as much as I can discern, no party among us seems satisfied with themselves, or their own conduct. It is objected to Lord Rockingham that he did not coalite with the Bedfords, and again that he did not accede to the Duke of Grafton or Conway; the two charges can't stand, and indeed the one is a fair answer to the other, for when two sets object, each, that a man does not join them, it is not improbable that neither of them were fit to be joined; but on the whole I think there is no man found so bold as to object one point of incorrectness to Lord R[ockingham], all the world do justice to the entire fairness, openness, and chastity of his conduct, during that very intricate negotiation, where foul play and treachery abounded; and where I suspect every party would not have been dissatisfied to have found the Marquess tripping. But he walked his own pace, neither allured nor frightened,

---

[6] Letter is undated, but O'Hara wrote on the back "Received 27th August 1767," and he received it at Nymphsfield, which was about nine days from London by post. A comparison with Burke's letter to Rockingham of August 18 indicates that it was written about the same time.—*Correspondence* 1: 138-144.

[7] Goodwood, near Chichester.

and though he did not accept power, he lost no honour. His character is I think strengthened, and confirmed; and if ever a change of political atoms should produce a new negotiation, I should expect to see that general deference to his honour, that would leave the game much to the disposal of his wisdom. There is not indeed much appearance of such an event; for Administration talks stout and has taken a form. Lord Townshend is your Viceroy, and avows his principle of dependence on Lord Bute, to whom alone he acknowledges an obligation for his new blushing honours; the Secretaryship was offered to Jenkinson [8] who refused it, and is given to Lord Frederick Campbell in compliment I suppose to General Conway,[9] who has himself accepted of Lord Townshend's place in the Ordnance. I saw him yesterday morning, and contrived to dissuade him from his intention of declining the profits, and I think he was convinced of the futility of such an *entre deux maneuvre;* but I believe he had gone too far to recede; and I am persuaded he will be as much abused and more ridiculed than if he had taken the profits fairly at once with the place.[10] This however manifests an intention at least of not continuing a minister, and without him I think the Duke of Grafton will not stay in the Treasury. He has certainly ambition enough for it, but he has invincible unaptness to discuss business with individuals, which is indispensably necessary to that situation, especially with a Chancellor of the Exchequer whom he can't rely upon. General Conway indeed professed to me that he thought himself entitled to secure his retreat in his own profession, adding that he still does not despair of seeing such an administration as he wished; but he did not specify what it was he did wish, nor did I enquire. I doubt not however that both he and the Duke have an eye to the Marquess; but they do not accustom themselves to look steadily so as to see their object distinctly. They will find themselves full of embarrassment; they have so tied themselves neck and neck and surrendered to Lord Bute, that they will scarce be able, though ever so willing, to do more

---

[8] Charles Jenkinson (1727-1808) had been secretary to Bute from 1761 to 1763; served under Grenville as Secretary of the Treasury, and was turned out by Rockingham; was given a seat on the Admiralty board by Chatham. He was the leading figure in the corps of influential men in minor positions who were known as "the Butes" and were attached closely to the court.

[9] Campbell was Conway's brother-in-law.

[10] Conway took the "profits" of the Ordnance, and gave up his salary as Secretary of State, surrendering that office too after the end of the year.

than quit their places; and in that case if Charles Townshend [11] is bold enough to undertake as Lord Bute's doer, the whole will professedly be under that Great Man; it is indeed already so to public conviction, but Bute himself is a coward. Charles Townshend has no real spirit to meet a parliament with, so that things may be at sixes and sevens, and in that case some little regard to a little decency, and much profession, may incline the Duke of Grafton; and a little memory of obligation to the Cavendish name, some attention to character, with a present picque to the Bedfords, and an old resentment to Grenville, may induce General Conway to avail himself of his access to the closet, and Lord Rockingham may be sent for. I understand too, that the Bedfords see the folly of their wisdom past, and as General Conway has disposed of himself to the military, they will be glad to catch at that loophole, and suppose no objection then to lie between.[12]

If this does not happen, the session will be a strange one, possibly idle and futile; yet I have hopes it may prove active and bold, though my politics are just this: that we will meet early; adjourn immediately for a time, which will be the season of negotiation, and that they will surrender and leave the new parliament to be formed by others. The dissolution won't be, or at least the elections can't be in the winter, but the new people will have the appointing of the sheriffs. Sure I suppose you to have great patience, but having no facts I was obliged to pretend to reason. We all beg to be remembered to our late visitors here, and to our friend Charles if he is with you.

Adieu—

William Burke

I forgot to mention that our Attorney General DeGrey [13] is your Chancellor. The consequent arrangement here is not declared, possibly not actually resolved, but it is supposed Norton will succeed him.[14]

---

[11] Within three weeks (September 4) Townshend was dead.

[12] The Bedfords had objected to Conway's having the lead in the House of Commons, desiring this for Grenville; Rockingham had desired Conway to lead.

[13] William DeGrey (1719-1781) had been Attorney General since August, 1766; he did not now become lord chancellor for Ireland, that post going to James Hewitt.

[14] Sir Fletcher Norton (1716-1789) had served as Attorney General and Solicitor General from 1761-1764; he was now Master of the Rolls.

O'HARA TO WILLIAM BURKE, September 8, 1767

Kildare 8 September

Thank you dear Will, for your folio. I am always fated to write to some of you from Kildare, and as I received yours but the night before I left home, I cannot defer my acknowledgement to a quieter time. In answer to your account of G[eneral] C[onway], I heard of his getting the Ordnance the morning after my arrival in Dublin. It was settled the day after the return of the express to Lord Townshend in Norfolk. His self-denial as to emolument is perhaps upon better grounds than you knew when you wrote; the first vacant regiment he shall apply for. The account came from a Scotch quarter. Much of your speculation seems rather suggested by your wishes. I can see no reason to imagine that Lord Bute will agree to any change which may transfer the management of the elections to other hands. That he wished for the Marquess is beyond doubt, but [that] he wishes for him single, at least unconnected, is as certain. That G[eneral] C[onway] will avail himself of the closet is probable, but he will do it for *this* purpose. The Duke of G[rafton] will also consent to accomodate himself to any plan which shall have the Thayne [15] for its object, but to no other. So much has been done by this last, that the undoing would make too great a bustle. The Marquess's reputation would bring honour to Administration; the other batches would bring only number. I don't think a plan upon this principle inadmissable. It might involve in its formation the means of power, and this be afterwards extended. Thus you have the cobweb which my imagination spun on the road, working on the facts which I brought with me. But indeed I may be prejudiced as well as you; if friendship may be supposed as strong as interest.

By what I can see, Lord Townshend comes to us with advantage over Lord Bristol. If the parable had run that the unclean spirit had gone out and left one less wicked than himself, the case of that man would be less bad than the first. Bristol got £18,000 from Ireland, and has not only not given a Lord Lieutenant's plate, but has not answered the letter of application. Think how we treat him here. Lord Townshend has supplied the omission. I am as yet a stranger to what our

---

[15] Bute.

leaders intend, but I intend to journalize the family. When events fill a sheet, it goes.

I left Charles at Nymphsfield working hard; we have agreed upon a course approaching to what Ned recommended, but not quite the thing. Will sailed for the Honduras in perfect health on the 15th June. God bless you all.

[Burke's "tour to the north," which included a visit to Rockingham at Wentworth Woodhouse in September, may help to explain the fact that there are no letters from him to O'Hara until late in October. Meanwhile Lord Townshend went to Ireland and opened the Parliament at Dublin, and on the same day O'Hara wrote an account of Irish politics to Burke.]

O'HARA TO BURKE, October 20, 1767

My dear Sir,

A letter at the opening of our session is a thing of course; you'll expect it, for we are part of the whole; though a very small part. I thought at first that Lord Townshend came to us as little likely to be supported on your side, as any Lord Lieutenant we ever had. The appearance was such, with regard at least to all the ostensible members of the Administration. But seeing his speech yesterday, which he is this day to make, I found three articles which are in themselves a very great support. A message from the King to Parliament to appoint judges to their offices and emoluments for life.[16] There is also a promise of cooperation on my Lord Lieutenant's part to encrease the number if we shall think fit. This not directly expressed, but is to be explained into it. The second, tho' I doubt its feasibility, popular—an engagement to leave our whole military establishment constantly here, for the defence of the Kingdom, provided we will pay 3000 men more out of the Kingdom. The third relates to an act of Parliament passed last session in England prohibiting the importation of cambrics, in which an option of free trade with England [sic.] for this commodity, upon condition that we prohibit the importation also. This indeed is not a power directly given to him. As to his

---

16 An objective of the Irish patriots. Townshend's strategy was to please the patriots and the country gentlemen, in order to turn them against the oligarchic "undertakers" hitherto dominant in the country, and thus to augment the power of the crown. His first concrete objective was to obtain an augmentation of the king's army in Ireland.

parliamentary support, Lord Besborough has settled that matter between his Excellency and the Speaker before his coming hither. *Per contra,* this same Speaker has so embarrassed himself with engagements to the public, and with private engagements to parties, that he will soon be so entangled as rather to want, than to give support. For instance, he is engaged to support Septennial with all his might. [17] This is public, and I know people mean to hurry it up to Council in three days, then to delay the committee of accounts and supplies till they hear its issue in England. 2ndly, Tisdall [18] is not yet arrived, so Hutchinson [19] takes the lead; but takes it with such reserve for his own popularity and humours, that we shall be lame in some part of our proceedings. 3rdly, there is a commissioner's place vacant. Tisdall won't go on when he does come unless Boyle [20] gets it; I have a promise, and yet Price,[21] Lord Hertford's nephew, will get it from us both. This same Lord Hertford is a wonderful fellow for getting without any considerations of decency, measures, or character. The giving it to Price will undo Lord Townshend, for the other is detested here, and every thing belonging to him. Thus circumstanced we shall meet in Parliament this day.

You, I believe, despairing of peace, prepare for battle; I can as yet only wish you joy of Pilgrim's victory at Newmarket.[22] I have heard of the Duke of Bedford's speaking very handsomely of Lord Rockingham lately, and to a person who he did not imagine would proclaim it. This tells well for the alliance, but removes my favourite object to a greater distance. For you must absolutely conquer, and then there will be no occasion for terms to make room for so large a batch. Has Will been busy at India House lately? How do the whole fire side? You shall hear from time to time how our farce goes on. Adieu my dear Sir,

Ch. O'Hara

---

[17] The great goal of the patriots at this time.

[18] Philip Tisdall (1703-1777) was Attorney General.

[19] John Hely Hutchinson (1724-1794) , the Prime Serjeant, was a friend and occasional correspondent of Burke's.

[20] Not identified.

[21] Francis Price, whose seat for Lisborne was at the disposal of Lord Hertford.

[22] The victory of one of Rockingham's horses.

Burke to O'Hara, October 27, 1767

My dear Sir,

I was not more pleased with your kind and seasonable letter, than ashamed of myself, when I recollected how ill I have acted my part in the correspondence for some time past. But the truth is, I have been tossed a good deal up and down in the world. I spent some time at Wentworth. From thence I went westward to Manchester, Liverpool and Lancaster. At the last of these places, I got great encouragement to offer myself a candidate at the general election. I am satisfied I might carry a seat there; but some reasons induced me for that time to decline it.[23] In short, in these excursions, (something of business, something of compliment, something of pleasure) I spent the summer; and found on my return other people employed to as little purpose as myself. I am obliged to you most heartily for your short, but faithful and lively sketch of your political history. Supported, or even appointed, by all or any of the ostensible ministers, Lord T[ownshend] certainly is not. Instructed by them he is not—according to the common opinion. I should think, that very possibly various parts of his system came from various quarters detached, and without any communication; and that he has patched and pieced them together himself. If I were to guess, I would give his judges to Lord Camden, and his army to General Conway; I have heard that the latter had from time to time spoken of this project as desirable and feasible. But all this is conjecture; for from whence should I have intelligence? We get every day to greater and greater distance from the Ministry. General Conway has acted as the knowing ones foretold, and as I was very loath to believe he would. His family get every thing. Price I heard some time ago was the commissioner. I believe it very truly reported. In giving you the judges for life, government loses I think but little; and you do not get a great deal. The increase of the number will or will not be much desired, as the seats are or are not given to interests on your side of the water. Septennial parliament is your idol; how is the Castle as to that? As to what you

---

[23] Rockingham wrote to Burke on Oct. 6: "Your visit at Lancaster has alarmed a friend of ours who has great weight there, as he has got into an engagement with the old representative, from thinking there would be no stir there."—Wentworth-Fitzwilliam MSS. The old representative was Sir Francis Reynolds.

say of cambrics I do not remember any restraint laid upon the import hither of Irish cambric which might, upon the condition you mention, be taken off. I did not indeed attend the manufacturing of that law; but I did attend, and diligently, the resolutions in the committee. I remember I opposed (not the principle) but the quantum of duty laid on several articles of foreign manufacture, which I thought intemperately and rashly laid on. The Irish agent for the Linen Board attended the whole, and did not think the regulations then made detrimental to Ireland—on the contrary he strenuously solicited them, and seemed not wonderfully pleased with me for not going his lengths on the subject, and was rather, I think, impertinent. I will however cast my eye on the act. You will laugh at the *Public Advertiser* today; who, upon a presumption of my being the author of a very lively libel on their council for instructing the Lord Lieutenant or not instructing him— has abused me in a fine strain.[24] Let us hear from you as soon as you can; and may I beg of you to enclose me your public accounts whenever they are delivered. I mean particularly the accounts of the [   ] and other revenue and the general abstract of the establishments etc. I wish however the whole. Adieu my dearest Sir, and believe me ever yours,

E. Burke

27 October. 1767

What will be said here to your augmenting your army without asking any questions of Parliament here—But go on—and prosper.

BURKE TO O'HARA, November 12, 1767

Q. Anne Street   Nov. 12. 1767

My dear Sir,

I am not more obliged to you for your most friendly letters,[25] than for that truly indulgent excuse you have made for me of my worse frailties; one indeed so bad, that it merits to rank even with my faults; but be it frailty or be it fault, I will try

---

[24] A satirical sketch, allegedly by the unknown Junius.—Woodfall, G., *Junius* 2: 482-492, London, Rivington, 1812.

[25] A letter dated Oct. 22 is the only one of O'Hara's that has been found; it contains nothing to explain Burke's remarks, or to warrant inclusion here.

whether I can show that I am not the worse on account of forebearance. The situation of your Lord Lieutenant is, to be sure, critical enough, but on the whole not worse, I should think, on comparing your account with my own observation, than that of all his predecessors at this time of the year. This is the Equinox of your political climate, and these are the *rigs* (as the sailers call them) that happen, especially in the Irish Channel, at that season. There is generally a flush of good humour to welcome your Lord Lieutenant; then some ill humour to bring him into his trammels; and at last a wonderful deal of kindness and flattery to send him away in a proper temper for a kind representation in the closet, and for the obtaining all the jobs, of which we all, mutually on both sides of the water, stand so much in need. The account you give me of ———— [26] is just what I expected in every respect. But what tricks of the Newcastle folks are those that you allude to? I remember none, except telling lies of all kinds, and hurting me to the best of their power with my principal.[27] In other respects, I had very few transactions with them.

You express a wish almost like an expectation, that some union may take place between us and Conway. If we liked to get into the shabby situation in which he stands, I think we might tomorrow; but we are not at present in that disposition. As to him, I am at present far from thinking *him,* or what is the same thing, those who guide him, favourable to us. I hear and I am satisfied it is true, that he offered the vacant half of the Pay Office to Lord Edgecumbe, who has refused it. What shall we say to the friendly disposition of that man, who would not stir an hand to save a place of 1200 a year to Lord Edgecumbe, when saving him would save the party; and yet would offer him 3000 when his acceptance must be a stroke of the utmost ill consequence to them, and even lead to their ruin? I cannot explain all this into anything that is right. He has given up the emoluments of Secretary of State, and confined himself to those of General of the Ordnance. This is certain; and it looks like a preliminary to the resignation of the office itself, whenever it shall suit the convenience of our enemies that he should resign it. In the meantime it looks like a confession that his staying there is not over handsome. How all

---

[26] Space left blank in original Ms.

[27] The allusion perhaps was to Newcastle's warning Rockingham in 1765, that Burke was a Roman Catholic.

will end I know not. All my reasonings, and all my auguries lead to ill; to exclude our party from the least present or future success; and this view does not arise from ill spirits, for I am in the best; nor can it make any change I think in Will's conduct or in mine, for it was not the prospect of success that made us adopt it. I fear much that your Lord Lieutenant will play you a trick in the end; however, attend him and ply him. Do you ever see Dennis? A friend of mine got him the Secretary's protection; who has made him a chaplain and promised to provide for him. Since then Dennis has not written a single word to me, though I wrote twice to him. I begin to fear he has not got my letters; and may neglect to pay his court. You are kind about the accounts. Pray send them as soon as you can. You remember you promised me a copy of the state of your trade for two years which was laid before Parliament. May I also put you in mind of this?

Rigby's going over at this time gives me matter of speculation for this side of the water as well as for yours.[28] What can be his motive for absenting himself at the beginning of the session, and does this look like the furious attack which he threatens?

You don't tell me what part Flood takes and how he goes on. Here we have nothing but the certainty (as they say) of Price being your commissioner, and Jenkinson our half-pay-master. Adieu my dearest Sir—all of us jointly and severally most cordially yours.

We quit this house in a few days and remove to Charles Street, St. James Square. The Doctor continues in this house.[29]

BURKE TO O'HARA, November 27, 1767

My dear Sir,

We have opened our session, and with more extraordinary circumstances than perhaps ever happened in so short a space of time. During the summer the Bedfords had frequently

[28] Rigby, Master of the Rolls in Ireland, may have been exerting his influence against the bill for septennial parliaments.

[29] "Our friends live now in Charles Street St. James's Square where they have a good deal more elbow room, and are much more convenient to Saint Stephen's Chapel, where they attend daily, and very devoutly. I, an old cat, stick by the old tenement in Queen Anne Street. We see one another every day, and are just the same sort of people you always knew us; always of the same mind with respect to you, and one another."—Nugent to O'Hara, Nov. 26.

complained that our managements with regard to the Ministry at large, and the friendly intercourse we kept up with some of them, made it very difficult to judge of our intentions, and of course very unsafe to go into any close connection with us. We never (except in one instance) courted such connections. However, as the party had been abandoned by General Conway, it was necessary to give such a proof of our spirit and firmness as might induce in all other parties a confidence in our temper. It might indeed, from the violence of the Bedfords in all their conversations, have been expected, that they would have taken a lead in the attack. But in reality Dowdeswell led it, and took a very proper and decisive part, by proposing an amendment to the address of no other importance than that it obliquely attacked the Ministry for their neglect of some national concerns, and that it was an amendment. I supported him, was equally decisive, and managed very little either measures or persons.[30] Wedderburn (an *individuum vagum*) spoke on the same side with great spirit and ingenuity.[31] From the Bedfords, not a word—from Grenville not a syllable. We did not divide. When this question was disposed of, Grenville made a general attack (pretty much on our grounds) upon the speech; and at the latter end he stepped out of his way to fall on us, and on the idea of our holding heterodox opinions relative to America, excommunicated our whole party. The Bedfords looked glum; held their tongues; and so the day passed over. I wished to answer on the spot; but a friend of mine restrained me; he thought it best first to consult the heads of the party; and he thought right. The next day a resolution was taken to demand an explicit answer from the Bedfords concerning the conduct of G[eorge] G[renville], and on their declining to explain themselves properly, to separate ourselves from them entirely. We found that the cause of this attack was a report of Lord Rockingham's having at Newmarket expressed great hostility to the house of Grenville; and notwithstanding the entreaties of Rigby, George Grenville could not be prevented from this method of showing his resentment. We went down to the house, and in our turn, in

---

[30] The first of Burke's speeches to be preserved in print, although the accuracy of the text may well be doubted.—*Parliamentary history* 16: 386-392; Woodfall, *Junius* 2: 498-509.

[31] Alexander Wedderburn (1733-1805), a Scotch member soon to form the habit of acting with Grenville.

the strongest terms renounced him and all his works. We are since, to the great triumph of the Ministry, quite loose.

You may possibly hear of my speech on the second day, and as possibly may hear something in it misrepresented. If you should, you will set the matter right; if not you will be silent about it. Rigby took occasion to speak of Ireland, and of an attempt to augment the army there, and aimed at raising some apprehension in the House upon that subject. Conway replied, that there *was* such an intention; that an army was so far from a matter of uneasiness to the gentlemen of Ireland, that they liked it; that the augmentation probably would not be opposed there, and that he thought it desirable and necessary; because the country was, in a great degree, R[oman] Catholic, and therefore a rotten part of the British dominions. After I had spoke my mind about N[orth] America, I spoke to the subject of an army *in general;* expressed my own particular liking for it; considered it as interwoven with the Irish constitution; and admitted the truth of Mr. C[onway]'s observation on the temper of gentlemen of that country with regard to that object; but that this general liking had no relation to the *quantum* of the army; that liking an army, and liking new taxes were different things; and that I did apprehend many would dissent from the augmentation. As to the rottenness of the country—if it was rotten, I attributed it to the ill policy of Government towards the body of the subjects there. That it would well become them, to look into the state of that Kingdom; especially on account of a late black and detestable proceeding there, which reflected infinitely either on the justice or the policy of English government in ruining and putting to death many for carrying on a rebellion at the instigation of France, while the throne assured us we were in the most profound peace with that nation.[32] I laid this heavy on the ministries (without regard to any) at these periods; I was not answered; and the thing dropped. This I thought right to tell you, lest some lies should be circulated, as it is likely there may on so proper a subject for slander.[33]

How will your bar relish Hewitt? [34] He never practised in

---

[32] *Supra,* letter of May 24, 1766.

[33] Exactly the kind of occasion that started rumors of Burke's being a Catholic.

[34] James Hewitt (1709-1789), a King's Bench judge, now appointed Lord Chancellor of Ireland, to the disappointment of many who expected an Irishman to be named.

a court of equity. Tommy Townshend[35] is joint **Paymaster,**
Jenkinson a lord of the Treasury; and either Lord Beauchamp
or Rider will go into the vacant Admiralty. Adieu, when more
happens you shall hear from us.

Charles Street, St. James's Square

27 Nov. 1767

BURKE TO O'HARA, December 11, 1767

My dear Sir,

As first in importance, I will speak to you first on your
Newmarket business;[36] I am sure it is first in importance to
me, as it will prove a means of bringing you over. I am then
to tell you from Lord R[ockingham] that if you do him the
favour of sending your horse to his stable, the best care will be
taken of him. If you choose to have him tried with Lord
R[ockingham]'s young horses, to know whether he be good
for any thing, he will be tried—but if you are previously satisfied
of his performance, and do not choose any further experiments,
Lord R. assures you, that Singleton will never steal a trial. So
you will send, whenever it is convenient to you.

How you were deceived in the spirit of Conway and the
spirit of the Bedfords—or rather how soon have you forgot all
you must have known of both! A negotiation has been going
on between Bedford house and the Administration, now for a
week past; and, as I was told yesterday, was just brought to a
conclusion; however, I hear today, there is some hitch in it.
Conway stays in, as a Scotch warming pan, to keep the bed
comfortable for those who hate and despise him. He wants
but the completion of this business to finish and round his
character. If it comes to any thing or to nothing, I will take the
first opportunity of acquainting you with the event. This day
all your supply bills passed the Council, as they have passed
your House, *nem. con.* The Septennial has not yet come before

---

[35] Thomas Townshend (1723-1800) was a good friend of Burke's and had
previously acted with the Rockinghams; a junior Treasury lord under Rockingham, he had continued with Grafton.

[36] "I have a horse to run in a sweepstake at Newmarket next October. I
wish Lord Rockingham would let me send him to his stable; a stable of honour
is an immense consequence on such occasions."—O'Hara to Burke, Dec. 2, 1767.

them; I suppose they wait for Lord Northington, who I am told is ill.[37]

I forgot to mention to you, that the Bedfords and Grenvilles are on this occasion all to pieces. Lord Temple is gone to the country despairing of the commonwealth. Grenville has not been in the House for some days; but I hear his *ton* is to take the matter quietly, and to wait events; and in this, I apprehend, he is right. As to our corps, which are the *enfants perdus* of politics, we stay just where we were; keeping a distance from all others, shunning, and shunned by them. If we must be dupes, thank God, it is to our rectitude, and not to our politics, or if you like better, to our roguery; and I assure you both Will and I feel inexpressible comfort in finding ourselves among a set of men willing to go on all together on a plan of clear consistent conduct. For myself I really have no hopes. Everybody congratulated me on coming into the House of Commons, as being in the certain road of a great and speedy fortune; and when I began to be heard with some little attention, every one of my friends was sanguine. But in truth I never was so myself. I came into Parliament not at all as a place of preferment but of refuge; I was pushed into it; and I must have been a member, and that too with some eclat, or be a little worse than nothing; such were the attempts made to ruin me when I first began to meddle in business. But I considered my situation on the side of fortune as very precarious. I looked on myself, with this new duty on me, as a man devoted; and thinking in this manner, nothing has happened that I did not expect, and was not well prepared for. Therefore my dear Sir, cheer up; nothing very much amiss can happen [to] us, whilst it pleases God that we keep our health, our good humour, and our inward peace; none of which is yet gone from us. I write, and blot in some sort of confusion—being just risen from an heavy dinner and in some hurry—Adieu and believe me most sincerely and affectionately yours.

E. Burke

Charles Street   S. J. Square   11 December.

Conway and I were like to fall into some heat in the House a few days ago; but it led to nothing.

---

[37] The Lord President of the Council.

I do not know what share Administration had in your tea project.[38] None at all, I suspect. They have given notice of an intention here to limit the Company's dividend for some further term. They have leave to bring in a bill for explaining and amending the Act of the 10th of King William,[39] in order to increase the army of the Irish establishment. So you may soon hear of that matter—I don't much like, and think I will oppose, it.

[The "hitch" in the negotiations between ministry and the Bedford corps was owing, in part at least, to the latter's disapproval of the bill for establishing septennial parliaments in Ireland. That bill had just come over, with the approval of the Dublin Castle administration, for consideration by the Privy Council; the Irish Parliament, under patriot and popular pressure, was resolved that the enactment of the revenue laws for the next two years should be contingent upon the British crown's acceptance of the bill to limit the duration of parliaments. Since the administration intended to accept the measure, the Bedfords raised their demands for places. On December 18 the bargain was finally struck. Weymouth, Gower, Sandwich, and Rigby were given offices of sufficient importance to enable them to exert an influence on government measures and dispose of a large share of the patronage. In making this treaty, the Bedfords abandoned their old ally, George Grenville.

As a result of the ministerial alterations, General Conway in January gave way to Lord Weymouth as northern secretary of state. Lord Hillsborough, a king's man, about the same time was made a third secretary of state with charge over the colonies, which meant a great reduction of the weight of Shelburne in cabinet council. Thus little now remained of the administration Chatham had formed. He still held the privy seal, although he had vanished from the scene of politics, and Lord Camden was still Lord Chancellor, but the original Chathamite character of the administration was gone. Grafton as First Lord of the Treasury was little more than the titular head of the ministry. Lord North, a king's man and Chancellor of the Exchequer, led the House of Commons. An opposition riven by the Rockingham-Grenville antagonism faced a ministry formed on no other principle than the distribution of places.

As the new arrangement was forming, the Burkes prepared to

---

[38] "We have lowered the duties upon teas to 4d for black, and 6d upon green. I opposed it a long time and made some impression. I suspect it to be an English measure."—O'Hara's of Dec. 2.

[39] An act authorizing the king to maintain 12,000 soldiers, but not more, on the Irish establishment.

welcome O'Hara to the fireside. "I shall sail on Thursday and see you for a week," wrote O'Hara on December 19. He probably had returned to Ireland when Burke next sent him a letter.]

BURKE TO O'HARA, February 1, 1768

My dear Sir,

I hope you are by this safe and snug in Merrion Square. God give you peace and happiness there and everywhere. Your Act for limitation of parliaments has passed, as I just now hear; only made octennial instead of septennial. Sir Robert Rich is dead. A good regiment and an excellent government disposed of.[40] We have got rid of the East India question in our house. We battled it for about 6 hours on our own numbers and debaters. We divided but 41. Wedderburn (but I look on him as a separate person) was with us and did good service, but almost every man of the Bedfords and Grenvilles sneaked off.[41] However, no man ever got such a drubbing as Lord North. He was ill defended by the Butes who had brought, or rather forced him into the scrape. God bless you. Ever yours

E. B.

O'HARA TO BURKE, February 9, 1768

My dear Sir,

Yesterday served us for a birthday; and to complete our joy the bill for limiting the duration of Parliament arrived, with a clause for the dissolution of this.[42] Your administration corresponds with our folly. To throw us into our own pit was fair, but to enact a dissolution on the 24 of June, lays our government open to every popular measure that can be devised to catch an interest in future elections. But I take it for granted that something more is intended. The militia bill which comes in tomorrow will I think defeat the intended augmentation. Hutchinson, the Speaker and Shannon continue united, and

---

[40] The King immediately gave Rich's regiment to Conway.

[41] A bill to continue the restraint on the dividend paid by the East India Company.

[42] The Privy Council in approving the bill to limit the duration of an Irish Parliament altered the term from seven to eight years, and inserted a clause for the early dissolution of the house elected in 1761. Members, who disliked the very principle of this act, were enraged at the prospective dissolution.

determined to drive Government into their own measures.[43]
They could not have succeeded two days ago. But the additional
clause has discontented so many, and renders popularity of
such consequence that you will hear things from us as well
worth your notice as from America. I hear you hit Lord North
very hard, such was the phrase. The desertion of the Bedfords
from him looks as if a desire of change had begun to operate;
and particularly as the Butes did not support. And yet, I don't
know how to hope it. *Au bout du conte,* all parts of the British
Dominions are in a good state, and there is a watchful and
laborious administration to superintend the business of so great
an empire. I wonder Conway don't bring in his bill [to amend]
the 10th of William 3rd.

I can't find Dennis, so have wrote to him at Paris. I told
the Primate he would have a letter from the Duke of Northumberland. It will certainly do when it comes.[44] God bless
you all. Adieu

Ch. O'Hara

O'HARA TO BURKE, February 16, 1768

My dear Sir,

Our affairs have taken a turn not unexpected by me; but
yet such, as have much entertained the public. The Speaker,
Lord Shannon,[45] the Attorney General and Prime Serjeant
have in conjunction carried on an opposition here this whole
session. Their demands were given in early, and very exorbitant they were; they have however persevered and fought stoutly
for them. These people you know were never much loved.
Government gave them power, as their means of a temporary
expedient. Lord Townshend tired of soliciting them, took to
his natural course of life, very remote from business of any
sort. Their being sent for to the Castle ceased. They opposed
more angrily for this reason. The country gentlemen began
by canvassing the absurdity of being led into opposition for
the purposes of other men. They supported Government and

---

[43] Chiefs of the oligarchy of "undertakers" whose power Townshend's
strategy aimed at breaking.

[44] O'Hara expected to sit for Armagh in the new Parliament and had
solicited the Duke of Northumberland's influence with Primate Robinson, who
owed his see to the former Lord lieutenant. O'Hara confided to Burke on
Feb. 11, "I come in for Armagh, but am ordered not to say so."

[45] Richard Boyle (1728-1807), second Earl of Shannon, son-in-law of Speaker
Ponsonby.

have actually defeated the opposition. Pery at their instigation had sat in a committee for enquiring into [the] state of the military establishment. The report censured many things, but the Speaker relapsed into his constitutional timidity, and instead of angry resolutions, Pery moved a very humble address to his Majesty, submitting all matters in the report to his consideration. Thus has our Fabius conquered, not with the painful generalship of the first, but by eating, drinking, sleeping, riding out, and following his own road, which led away from all business and negotiation; I must indeed add, warm and effectual acknowledgements to and of the people who had supported him. But notwithstanding this flourishing state of things, we shall have frequent fights to the end of the session.

Were I to speculate upon these events, and their consequences, I should say that the Speaker will tire of the bustle, and look for an honourable retreat. What his confederates will then do, deserves not much consideration. But if I were to extend my speculation to all the probable consequences of the Octennial Act, you would have too long a letter to read. Lord Annaly [46] spoke against it fully, and tolerably well. His protest I have not read, but 'tis well spoken of. It has put us in a strange ferment.

Mr. Sheart of the County of Tyrone desired I would mention him to you as a suitor to Sir George Savile for his interest in the County of Tyrone.[47] 'Tis not a matter however in which I take any great concern.

I have got a very neat abstract of our revenues ready, but the whole in detail will take time, as people are continually sending for the books. Remember the East India abstract for me, I shall want the gross sums. I hear of your sitting very late; what are you about? They talk of Grenville's going into place. My love to the fireside, adieu

Chs. O'Hara

BURKE TO O'HARA, February 20, 1768

My dear Sir,

I thank you for your accounts of Octennial, my friend Dennis, and other curious public and private matters which

---

[46] John Gore (1718-1784), Baron Annaly in the Irish peerage, Chief Justice of the King's Bench in Ireland.

[47] Savile owned large estates in Ireland.

made the subject of your two last letters. The madness of the Government here which passed the Octennial Act is to be equalled only by the frenzy of your country which desired it, and the tameness of this country which bore it. I consider that act as a virtual repeal of one of the most essential parts of the Poynings Law;[48] and I think it will necessarily draw on a change in other parts; and indeed many material alterations in the state of your country, as it stands by itself, and as it is related to England. However, you have your day of joy, and your drunken bout for the present.

The explanation of the Act of King William is passed; no one directly opposed in the House of Commons but myself. The temper of the House was this; that they would cheerfully have voted the King a power of keeping 40,000 men more, provided any others than themselves was to find the supply. They opened it on two grounds: its necessity towards reforming the arrangement of the army for the purpose of a more convenient rotation; and then the propriety of providing a defence for Ireland, which from all circumstances internal and external they stated to be in great danger. Here we had, slightly from Conway, but much at large from Lord Beauchamp, the Whiteboys, the foreign regimentals, the French money and all that miserable stuff. This was on the second reading. It had been agreed, on account of Grenville's absence, (who sent word that he had some objections to the preamble of the Act) to defer all debate on the principle of the bill until the third reading. However, these two gentlemen took the line I have mentioned above, though they knew they could not be answered. When the bill came to the third reading, I spoke to it very fully and I believe for an hour together. My chief grounds were, the danger and impropriety of leaving the execution of an arrangement, which took in the military establishment throughout the whole British Empire, and which was argued as of absolute necessity, to the direction of the Parliament of Ireland; the false representation which had been made of the state of the Irish army; (for it was false, glaringly so) the

---

[48] The fundamental law of British supremacy in Ireland, enacted in 1494, and sometimes called the Statute of Drogheda. It provided that no parliament could be summoned in Ireland except under the great seal of England, and that no act of the Parliament of Ireland could be valid without the consent of the English Privy Council. It took its name from Sir Edward Poynings (1459-1512), Lord Deputy for Ireland under Henry VII.

absurdity of the stories on which the danger of that country had been presumed, and the ill policy of encouraging Administration to make it a government measure for Ireland to augment its debt in time of peace. Lord Beauchamp and General Conway answered me. The former was pleasant in his voice, language and manner; in argument, as you might expect. He was mightily cried up by all the ministerial people as a prodigy of genius. Thus ended the Irish army so far as related to us. It was but just attended, and very little regarded, people seeming to be indifferent enough about the good or ill success of the measure.[49]

You refined rather too much in your speculations upon what I told you of the complexion of parties on the last East India day. It was in truth no more than what is the natural consequence of the imbecility, disunion, and want of mutual confidence and concord, which prevail in the Ministry. However, they go on; and I think are sufficiently supported. Last Wednesday Sir G[eorge] Savile made a motion of which he had given notice some days before. It was to amend etc. the Act of the 2d of King James the First; and to extend the principle of prescription and limitation of claims, which prevail between subject and subject, to the Crown. It was agreed to open and to debate the matter upon general grounds, unless the adversary forced us to an application of particular grievances. Sir G. Savile, in one of the most elegant performances I ever heard, entirely confined himself to this plan; so did Sir Anth[ony] Abdy[50] who seconded. The ministers were imprudent enough to urge the non-existence of such grievances, as a reason for rejecting the bill; and this was done in so insolent a manner that out it came at last—I mean Sir James Lowther's grant.[51] It was managed with address by Yorke, who stated it rather as an example than as an accusation, at the end of a train of vexatious proceedings which have arisen for want of some limitation to the claims of the Crown. The ministerial people attempted some sort of defence, but so weak, trivial, inconsistent, and indeed childish and absurd, that they sunk

---

[49] No other report of this debate has been found.

[50] Sir Anthony Abdy, Bart. (d. 1775) usually acted with the Rockinghams.

[51] Sir James Lowther (1736-1802), son-in-law to Lord Bute, having discovered a flaw in the Duke of Portland's title to certain long-held properties in Cumberland county, applied to the Treasury in 1767 and obtained a lease of them.

far below what either friends or enemies expected from them. Paint as you please to your imagination the figure that they made, either for the merits of their conduct, or their address and dexterity in defending it; lower yourself to it as much as you please, you will never sink to the true pitch. Upon my serious word, it passes all conception. In a state suitable to such a defence, against a most strenuous attack they continued for from about half an hour after three to half an hour after eleven. So long the debate lasted. The numbers on the division were, for the motion 114—against it 134. About 6 of our people had fallen ill, or rambled for want of whipping in, or, you see, we should have run them very hard. Conway had the decency to absent himself. The temper of the House was such, that I have not the least doubt of our carrying our point next Parliament; they will scarcely venture, I think, to contest it.[52]

I rejoice to find that your seat is secure. Let us hear from you as often as you can. I look upon our business as pretty much over for the year. Adieu, and God bless you.

20th February

As well as I can recollect, the speakers in the debate were

for the motion	against the motion
Sir G. Savile	Lord North
Sir Anth[ony] Abdy	Lord Clare
Sir W. Meredith	Lord Barrington [53]
Mr. Dowdeswell	Mr. Jenkinson
Mr. Grenville	Mr. Beckford
Mr. Yorke	Mr. Price Campbell [54]
Lord J. Cavendish	Mr. Rigby
Mr. E. Burke	Mr. Stanley [55]
Mr. J. Pitt [56]	Mr. Dyson [57]
Mr. Fred. Montagu [58]	

[52] Burke was right; the Nullum Tempus Act, securing landowners against all dormant claims of the crown after an undisputed possession of sixty years, was passed in the first session of the next Parliament.

[53] William Wildman Shute (1717-1793), second Viscount Barrington in the Irish peerage, was Secretary at War and an obedient king's man.

[54] Price Campbell, a Scottish member, was a Treasury commissioner.

[55] Hans Stanley (1720?-1780), Governor of the Isle of Wight and Cofferer of the Household.

[56] James Pitt, a Dorsetshire member.

[57] Jeremiah Dyson (1722-1776) held a seat on the Board of Trade, from which Rockingham in 1766 tried without success to remove him; an active and industrious king's man.

[58] Frederick Montagu (1734-1800), a political intimate of Rockingham's.

(Sir Fletcher Norton spoke
for the bill though he defended
the legality of grant) He went
away without voting
Mr. Seymour
Lord Palmerston [59]

Conway absent
Attorney General absent

for the motion—114
against—   134

The division was on the question *that the order of the day be read.* They did not give a flat negative to the bill. They were in much confusion; and seemed to have changed their plan of defence more than once in the debate.

[O'Hara on March 3 sent news that his seat in the next Parliament of Ireland was not assured: "When the Primate told me he would bring me in for Armagh, for one, being engaged for t'other seat to the Attorney General in case he should not be chosen for the College, he added, unless the Duke of Northumberland made a point of it. I gave the Duke an account of it, and had this day a very civil and friendly answer, but full of concern: in short he has pressingly recommended Sir G[eorge] Macartney."

Northumberland's letter (February 22) is among the Annaghmore Manuscripts. He regretted his inability to comply with O'Hara's wishes, stating that he was under such engagements "to a person and family with whom I am particularly connected as oblige me to take the liberty of applying to the Lord Primate upon the subject of the ensuing election." Hence Sir George Macartney was to come in from Armagh; he was Lord Bute's son-in-law. Presently he replaced Lord Frederick Campbell as chief secretary in Ireland.

Meanwhile, the British Parliament having been dissolved (March 11), Burke was plunged into election politics. He was chosen again through Lord Verney's influence at Wendover.]

---

[59] Henry Temple (1739-1802), second Viscount Palmerston in the Irish peerage; father of the famous nineteenth-century statesman.

X. "Wilkes and Liberty"

[The parliamentary election of 1768 was the occasion for John Wilkes's sensational re-entry into the scene of politics. Four years before, he had been expelled from the House of Commons for writing a seditious libel, and after a flight to the continent had been sentenced to outlawry for the crime of blasphemy. Now he returned to seek the king's pardon and to stand for Parliament. The pardon was not given, but crown authorities made no move to arrest him. He entered the contest for a seat for London, but too late to make an effective campaign; hence he failed. But in the election in Middlesex county he was triumphantly chosen. A gifted demagogue, full of daring and insolence towards the ministers of the day, he reawakened the fury of the metropolitan mob against Lord Bute and set off a series of riotous demonstrations for "Wilkes and Liberty."]

BURKE TO O'HARA, *ca.*, April 1, 1768

I think it is a good while since I heard from you; and perhaps it is still longer since I wrote; but I believe there has been a stagnation of such matter as would prove interesting to either of us; I mean, the real inside of business. That Wilkes has been chosen for Middlesex is an event which, from the dull state of the public, and the oblivion into which he had fallen, I confess I did not at all expect. But at a time when the people are unfastened from all their usual moorings, as they are at a general election, nothing ought to occur as a matter of surprise. The hatred of Lord Bute never was stronger among the people; and this was a time to signalize it. Besides the crowd always want to draw themselves from abstract principles to personal attachments; and since the fall of Lord Chatham, there has been no hero of the mob but Wilkes. The surprise aided him; Government had not time to take measures; and they are indeed too disunited to take any that can be effectual. There must be a change, I think, before winter; but I still persist in the opinion I have long had, that no probable change will be advantageous to us.

Lord Rockingham is just come from Newmarket; he has himself been upon the whole successful there. He had no room in his stable just at the time when Hirpinus arrived but he has had full as good care taken of him. It happened that he was not in order to be entered for anything; for your servant, instead of being deficient, was rather over-careful of him. So that Lord R. says, he is just now fat as a stallion, and as wild as a colt; and of course it will be some time before he is in running order. In other respects he will be properly treated.

I am just going off for Italy; I mean in eight or ten days. Write to me as usual; and I shall be rather more than less happy. Adieu, my dear Sir, most truly yours

E. B.

[Burke did not go to Italy, but instead negotiated the purchase of a six-hundred-acre estate, Gregories Manor at Beaconsfield in Buckinghamshire.[1] He and his family were moving themselves to the home where he was to live for the rest of his life, when O'Hara, ignorant of this important business, wrote in reply to the previous letter.]

O'HARA TO BURKE, April 19, 1768

Dublin 19 April

My dear Sir,

I should have concluded by your going abroad, that no part of the new changes was designed for your quarter. I am glad on't, for I think the bustle is approaching, without which I never looked for a thorough change. If things for Great Britain and its other appendages are conducted as for this Kingdom, I should fear the clearing out would become Augean labour. The augmentation of our forces is to be proposed on this very day (this occasions my sending it) but in consequence of orders so positive, with so little power of accomodating the measure to the circumstances of the country, that I should rather think Lord Shelburne meant to defeat, than to promote it, if I could work out a solution by any system of politics.[2]

---

[1] "On the close of the last Parliament, I had thoughts, amounting almost to a settled resolution, of passing the summer in Italy. . . . But I have been diverted in another way. We have purchased a pretty house and estate, the adjusting of which has kept me in England this summer."—Burke to James Barry, July 19, 1768. Prior, *Life of Burke*, 2nd ed., 1: 178, 1826.

[2] Shelburne had taken over this business from Conway, and apparently objected to Townshend's purchasing support by the usual methods of corruption. Many members hesitated to vote for increased expense on the eve of an election,

Lord Townshend is an unfortunate man, to have come to us at such a time, and under the direction of such councils. He has wasted a monstrous deal of money, is now retired to the country to save, which he will not have much time to do, unless the measure of this day succeeds beyond my expectation. If this should find you in England, pray tell me what they mean. The K[ing] seems fond of augmenting the forces on this establishment, and yet I have not the least doubt, but Lord Shelburne wishes to prevent it.

Bob Fitzgerald [3] tells me that he left you in some uncertainty about your jaunt to Italy, that you expect business on the 10th of May, which you may chuse to wait for.[4] All my speculations then may be wrong.

None of those we call the King's Servants seem more disposed to support Government than they were two months ago; except the Prime Serjeant. With him I have conversed much of late; he wishes to support Government but no means of doing so are held out to him.[5] I must trouble you to direct the enclosed to Singleton at Newmarket. You have embarked in this business, and must go through with it. My service to everybody, yours most truly

Chs. O'Hara

[O'Hara's fear that the Irish Parliament would not accept Lord Townshend's proposal for augmenting the army by three thousand men proved well grounded. In spite of all the Lord lieutenant's efforts and struggles against the "undertakers," the bill was beaten. O'Hara voted for it.]

O'HARA TO WILLIAM BURKE, May 10, 1768

Dublin. May 10

My dear Sir,

I think Ned is gone for Italy, and I rejoice at it. But as I wish to hear of you all, some of you must write to me. Never

---

and some patriots feared the additional troops were destined for the coercion of America. Townshend preferred to delay the augmentation bill until a new Parliament had been chosen and rendered manageable, but Shelburne would have no delay.

[3] Possibly Robert Fitzgerald, a magistrate of Kerry and a member of the Irish House of Commons.

[4] The new Parliament would be opened on that day.

[5] Hutchinson evidently was ready to be bought, but had no offers.

was a time in which my curiosity ran higher, for instructions so earnest have been given for opposition here,[6] and within this fortnight, that I suspect your session may be some days longer than was expected. In consequence of these instructions we have had for two days the longest sittings I ever knew. An augmentation of the army agreeable to Mr. Conway's act was the subject. The expence called £36,000 a year, and not more than £60,000 to enable his Majesty to keep 12,000 men always here, but no security that that number should be kept here. We are running into debt for our present establishment; and I do confess that if we were able to pay more men out of the Kingdom, we could not bear the remittances. All this is true, but with a better managed revenue, the expence might well be born at home; and I think twelve thousand would always have been kept here. We have the intention of the English Parliament expressed in the act. We have the King's promise, except in cases of rebellion or invasion, and lastly the impossibility of making the remittances to them abroad. I thought we might have ventured, but the instructions mentioned in the beginning of this letter decided the day, by a majority of four. 'Tis thought this proceeding will have some consequence with regard to the Speaker and his friends. And 'tis thought not impossible but that it may be mentioned in your House, but this I don't conceive unless it be that no part of his Majesty's dominions should remain in good humour.[7] Wilkes I hope will take our part. It certainly was an odd division, to see victorious opposition composed of the King's servants and people in employment. But so it was; the Country Gentlemen formed the Government party. Our Lord Lieutenant has certainly no reason to boast of his support from Administration.[8] He thinks they neglect him; I think they have only forgot him and Ireland.

One newspaper brought Dick into Parliament, is it so?[9] Give me an account of the whole family, and believe me, my dear Will, most truly yours

Chs. O'Hara

---

[6] Presumably, instructions to members from those who disposed of their seats.

[7] The American colonies were now in reaction against the Townshend revenue and customs acts.

[8] In England.

[9] It was not so.

[On the day O'Hara wrote the previous letter, the new British Parliament was opened, in the midst of great metropolitan riots provoked by the supporters of Wilkes. A few weeks before, he had surrendered himself to the King's Bench court where he was denied bail and ordered to prison to await trial for libel and blasphemy. When Parliament convened the houses were surrounded by mobs shouting for "Wilkes and liberty." Other mobs attempted to deliver Wilkes and carry him to the House of Commons. Troops were called out and some blood was shed in the "massacre of St. George's Fields." During a short session (ending June 21) in which little but routine business was transacted, Burke urged a searching inquiry into the causes of these disorders.]

BURKE TO O'HARA, June 9, 1768

I have that abominable custom of running up a long arrear, not so much from hatred of paying, as from the general spirit of procrastination, which very unluckily attends me in at least a good half of all my business. I am really ashamed to find that I cannot very precisely remember when I wrote to you; but I am very sure, (for I have good tokens to remember your letters by) that in the interval of my silence, I have heard several times from you. However, don't be very angry with me; I had never less to say. If the world seemed to be very busy with Wilkes and Liberty and many fine things, one part of the matters, at least, was not your business nor mine. The plan of our party was, I think, wise and proper; not to provoke Administration into any violent measure upon this subject; nor be the means of stirring questions which we had not the strength to support, and which could not be lost without leaving the constitution worse than we found it. It could be no service to Wilkes to take him out of the hands of the *law*, and to drive him under the talons of *power;* besides we had not the least desire of taking up that gentleman's cause as personally favourable to him; he is not ours; and if he were, is little to be trusted. He is a lively agreeable man, but of no prudence and no principles. Had they attempted to attack him, as I do not think they could have done it without great oppression, we must have defended him, and were resolved to do it; but still as the cause, not the person. They did not omit to make this attack, from any want of ill will, but from the disunion which prevails among them; and which is greater than any one, who did not know of what discordant materials they are made up, and how discordantly those materials are put together, could believe. But in my opinion, they are strong from this weakness; no man adheres to another, but every man cleaves to his place; and so they all look to the common center, none to the circumference; and this centripetal force is as great in politics as in nature. I confess I think they may and will hold; if one may risk any prediction at such a time. Our people are almost all gone into the country; but we keep our union and our spirits, and are increased in numbers very considerably. They have managed their affairs in Ireland gloriously. Here Government is only disgraced; with you it is disgraced and defeated. My solicitude for Ireland is growing rather less anxious than it was. I endeavour to remove it from my mind as much as I can. My strongest remaining wish is about you; and I shall not be easy until I hear in what manner you have secured your seat. When that business is over we may hope to see you. We are in the direct road between Oxford and London. We have purchased an house, rather superb for us, and about 600 acres of land just by Beaconsfield where we now are, and where we shall be most happy to see you. The Doctor is come to see us, and to spend a day or two, and is yours as usual. So we are all. And this is my only news at the close of a session from whose activity you had so much expectation. But as it was difficult to get or keep our people in town so deep in the summer, the defensive was thought the better scheme. Adieu my dear friend. Make us happy by informing us that all is right as to the election; next by telling us so in person. Adieu.

Gregories near Beaconsfield,

June 9. 1768

[While waiting for further news from O'Hara, Burke appears to have been visited by his friend's son and to have advised him in his studies.]

O'HARA TO BURKE, July 9, 1768

Dublin 9th July

My dear Sir,

Thank you for your reception of Charles, and for your advice to him about reading. He mentioned it to me, as if you had made an impression. Here I am in expectation of the

College election on which mine depends.[10] 'Tis as certain as
such an election can be, but if the Attorney General should
lose it, he takes my place at Armagh. But I approach to moral
certainty. Lord Frederick Campbell insists upon being elected
for Irishtown, so I can't come in there, and yet I have reason
to believe he won't return. He ought not I am sure.[11] Lord
Townshend is retired to Leixlip, retired indeed. He will
quickly save his running out. You say you have withdrawn
your thoughts from Ireland. So far you are a minister. If
the same style of administration extends over all the British
dominions what will become of us! We get a kick now and
then, but 'tis not even a kick of reproof; mere unmeaning
provocation. The only considerable event in which Government has been of late concerned, was an accident, melancholy
in itself, which happened in Capel Street at a show of wild
beasts. A pretty young lad, an only son, went too near a tiger;
the beast seized him and killed him in an instant. The Lord
Mayor and Aldermen assembled to know what was to be done
with the tiger. The case was perplexing, and nothing decided.
It was proposed to send to my Lord Lieutenant. His Excellency
was also puzzled, the Law Servants of the Crown are all in
opposition; he had nobody to consult, but he ordered a guard.
I had the curiosity upon hearing this to go to the place this
morning, and I actually found a guard upon the tiger. This
may furnish a new argument for an augmentation of the army,
and some new arguments we must have.[12] The Speaker says we
shall have 94 new Members, which will take some time to
discipline. Lord Frederick must return to us, and soon.

Lord Charlemont is at last married.[13] There was a sentimental flirtation for a long time. He has lived a good deal at

---

[10] The contest for the Trinity College seat.

[11] Campbell, as Chief Secretary, bore some responsibility for the loss of the
augmentation bill, which was a serious and unusual defeat for an administration
to suffer.

[12] The editor is indebted to Father Aubrey Gwynn, S.J., of Dublin, for
drawing his attention to the following notice in the *Freeman's Journal* for
July 12-16 "By *order* of the GOVERNMENT on Saturday last, the *Wild Beast*
(which by *Permission of the Right Hon. the* LORD MAYOR was exhibited in
Capel Street Theatre, and in the Entertainment killed a young Gentleman)
was tried by *his Peers* for the Murder, and suffered death by *military* Execution."

[13] James Caulfield (1728-1799), created first Earl of Charlemont in the
Irish peerage in 1763, was the chief patron of the patriot party, and a friend
and admirer of Burke, although they differed politically. On July 2 he married
Mary Hickman.—*Charlemont Manuscripts* 1: 286-289.

Marino, she near it. He was building a dairy, she gave material directions as to inside contrivances. He talked of retirement, she doted on it. Yet he wished for some living creature in his room, even a rat. She sighed, and wished to be that rat. The sentiment pleased him, and matrimony ensued. You won't doubt this, when you are told that Miss Macartney vouches every tittle of it.

I shall see you before the end of the summer, put on my wisest face, and talk my best to make amends for all this nonsense. I only wanted to provoke you to an answer, and to tell you that I am most truly yours

C. OH.

[Soon after writing the above letter, O'Hara found himself a victim of the opposition's contest against Lord Townshend. Philip Tisdall, having won the College contest, insisted on being returned also for the constituency that Primate Robinson seems to have half-promised to O'Hara, who now appeared to be eliminated from the Parliament.]

O'HARA TO BURKE, July 26, 1768

Dublin 26 July

My dear Sir,

I am just setting out for Nymphsfield; I shall return to the Curragh on the 13th of September and in a week after set out for England. I shall hear at Oxford in my way where you are, and certainly look for you. I have just finished a letter to my friend Mr. Singleton, a correspondence that I am indebted to you for.[14]

Before I tell you of any other election, I shall mention my own circumstances. The Attorney General carried his election for Trinity College by a clear majority; the Provost's behaviour as returning officer allowed to be as fair as any thing of that sort ever was. But the animosity between him and Clements [15] is inveterate, and this last intends, or says so, to petition, for an opportunity of abusing the Provost. The Attorney [General] upon this applied to the Primate, to be returned for Armagh also. He represented that it would be an odd thing for the Attorney General to be returned but for one place, and to have

---

[14] *Supra,* Burke's of Dec. 11, 1767.
[15] Robert Clements.

a petition against him for that; and this when he is in opposition to Government. So that at present, I am returned for no place. Bar accidents, it is of little moment to me, for as our Parliament will meet before Christmas for the augmentation, I shall not be here at the opening of the session.[16] The augmentation will not be lost by my absence, for as it is a determined resolution in England to have it introduced as it was before, not to be recommended but required, the majority of people here are as determined not to submit. The whole of the matter would be easily agreed to; the difference is about the mode. In this and in other detached instances, we perceive a disposition to form a system for this country; but we find that none is as yet formed. Lord Townshend lives at Leixlip, and is literally his own Minister, Lord Frederick [Campbell] in England, Jackson[17] just gone; Lords Annaly, Tyrone[18] and Mr. Malone[19] at their elections; so that he has not even an adviser. Appropos to this circumstance, I put him in mind the other day that Louis Quatorze's genius would never have been discovered, if Cardinal Mazarin had lived.

Our people certainly did not foresee the effect of the Octennial law when they pressed it, nor English administration when they returned it to us. It will have cost the first £300,000 moderately speaking;[20] and has transferred so much power from the representatives to the constituents, as must necessarily disturb the proceedings of Parliament. We shall have many new Members; the Speaker talks of 90, I am sure of 70; the changes rather adverse to Administration. If connections hold, augmentation will be beat by 30. So much for Parliament. The effect of the Octennial upon the morals of the lower class of people is terrible, and the dissipation is such, that our manufactures will decline every day. The Duke of Leinster is quiet at Carton,[21] within a visiting distance, but not in the neighbourhood of Leixlip. The Speaker on the other side not more distant, nor better disposed. So that our principal people live not in greater harmony than yours. This is as much a

---

[16] But Shelburne left office in October, and the Irish Parliament's opening did not take place until a year later.

[17] Richard Jackson.

[18] George de la Poer Beresford (1735-1800), second Earl of Tyrone.

[19] Edmund Malone (1704-1774), a judge of the Irish court of common pleas.

[20] Election expenses.

[21] James Fitzgerald (1722-1773), twentieth Earl of Kildare, created Duke of Leinster in 1766; his ancestral seat was at Carton in County Kildare.

time for curiosity and speculation as ever I lived in, and I take care of my health in hopes of seeing the event. You will see it of course, and I doubt not will have a share in it; upon which much of my curiosity and my warmest wishes will attend. I am, my dear Sir, most truly yours,

C. OH.

BURKE TO O'HARA, September 1, 1768

My dear Sir,

Your letter to Dr. Nugent has given us some hope of seeing you here.[22] Take care not to disappoint us; in truth we should feel such a disappointment very much; for we have set our hearts a great deal on the pleasure we propose in having such a friend in a place more like our own than any we have had yet. Here you, who are a farmer as much by experience and skill, as I am by inclination, will go round with us and put us right in our original plan; for we have every thing to begin. I have ventured on pretty tolerable deep play at first, and have about 400 acres in tillage, grass, and spring woods in my own occupation. My hay is well saved, though at a smart expence. About half my corn is got in, or rather more. Three or four days of fair weather would set me to rights; but this we are not very likely to have. On the whole however, and considering rather the great concern of the public than my private adventure, there is a show of plenty, which is satisfactory after so much want, and so many disorders, and discontents in consequence of it.[23] Amidst this sort of cares and attention politics have almost slipped out of my mind. They would have done so entirely, if the Administration had not furnished us with very new and curious matter of speculation. You have heard, to be sure, how they affronted Sir J[effrey] Amherst by the manner of taking away his government and giving it to Lord Botetourt.[24] They thought their usual balsam of a pension would have salved all; but the wound was deep, and the

---

[22] Letter not found.

[23] A good harvest after several bad ones.

[24] Sir Jeffrey Amherst (1716-1797) had been Governor of Virginia without residing there. Hillsborough desiring a resident governor, it was suggested to Amherst that he either go to Virginia or give up the office for a pension; on his refusal, Lord Botetourt (Norborne Berkeley), a court favorite, was named governor. Amherst, who had great popularity in both England and America, felt injured, but accepted the pension.

patient more irritable than they expected. When he resigned his regiments, his income was reduced to very little. But he has stopped his buildings, dismissed his servants, and contracted all the scale of his living. They have made themselves as odious by this job, as they were contemptible for the other parts of their conduct. The affairs of America prosper ill in their hands. Lord Hillsborough has taken a step which has inflamed and united all that country.[25] In short they proceed wildly, by fits and starts, without order or system. They are made up of a set of people of opposite opinions and no principles; and they are steady to nothing but perpetual attempts to betray and disgrace one another. I met Lord Fred[erick] Campbell in the street about a week ago when I spent a day or two in town. You may easily imagine that our discourse was not very long or confidential. However he spoke as if there were no intention of meeting your Parliament this winter. In truth they must overturn every maxim of the policy of this country if they do.[26] But indeed considering their conduct in the Octennial and many other measures, I should not be surprised at any thing they could do in that way. They talk somewhat of our meeting in October; but I hardly think it probable. Charles is here, and well. So is your friend the Doctor. Adieu my dear friend.

Gregories Sept. 1

[From this time until May, 1769, there is a complete void in the correspondence of Burke and his family with O'Hara; not a letter has been found from either to the other. Indeed, Burke's letter above of September 1 is one of the very few of his letters that are known to be extant from the second half of the year 1768, which is the reason why this period, down at least to the opening of Parliament in November, has been ignored by all his biographers. In addition to the work of his newly acquired farm, it may be presumed that Burke at this time was writing his political pamphlet,

---

[25] Hillsborough in April had circularized the American governors with an order to prevent their assemblies from taking notice of the Massachusetts circular denouncing the constitutionality of the Townshend Revenue Act of 1767. Disorders in Boston had led early in the summer to the despatch of military and naval forces. Ministry appeared determined to uphold the authority of crown and parliament in North America.

[26] Constitutionally, parliamentary sessions were biennial in Ireland; the last session had been that for 1767-1768. No Parliament was held until October, 1769.

Observations on a Late Publication intituled "The State of the Nation," which was published early in 1769.

It is very unfortunate that we cannot illuminate the stormy and historic parliamentary session of 1768-1769 by means of Burke's letters to O'Hara. During it there were great debates on the affairs of America brought on by the ministry's efforts to break down colonial resistance to parliamentary taxation. Court, ministry, and Parliament plunged into a new conflict with Wilkes, which led to his expulsion, disqualification, and finally the seating, after four Middlesex elections, of the minority candidate, Col. Henry Lawes Luttrell, as a member of the House of Commons for that county. This raised a grave constitutional question touching the right of electors to choose their own members of Parliament. In all this Burke played a conspicuous part. These and other events produced a temporary union among all branches of the parliamentary opposition; the Rockingham party found themselves in alliance with George Grenville, and even with Chatham and Shelburne who both left the Grafton administration on the eve of Parliament's opening.

It is certain that O'Hara visited the Burkes, perhaps several times, during this long period, and that he joined Richard Burke in a speculation in East India Company shares. But we hear nothing of him until May 2, when he wrote to Richard: "I suppose you are all removed to Gregories, or about going there; I am making all the haste I can to go to you, but having forgot the day, I doubt whether I shall be time enough for the East India business. At all events, I told you my mind upon the subject, and once more commit myself to your protection."

On May 16, O'Hara wrote to Edmund, chiding him a little for his long silences: "When I tell you that I have wished to hear from you, do me the justice to impute it rather to the anxiety of a friend, than to political curiosity. . . . But I left Dick ill, and Will deeply embarked in East India business. I want to hear of both. The latter has so tumbled down that I am alarmed. . . . My small interest therein I committed to Dick. . . . I shall stay here [Dublin] long enough for an answer, and then to see you."

When Burke received this letter, he was at Gregories resting from the fatigues of his arduous parliamentary efforts. His mind appears to have been far from thoughts of the alarming decline in East India shares that had begun early in May, after a long rocketing boom. On May 26 news reached London that Hyder Ali had ravaged the Carnatic, and this set the stocks to plunging lower. Richard and William Burke were financially ruined, but five days later Edmund, in his Beaconsfield paradise twenty miles from London, appeared totally unaware of the disaster.]

Burke to O'Hara, May 31, 1769

My dear friend,

After some expectation of seeing you I received your letter, the only unwelcome one I ever had from you. I lose no time in answering it, since you have made my writing a sort of condition of your hastening your journey. We are now quite ready for you; serene and quiet at Gregories; still and calm as if debate, dissension, and the rage of party never had an existence. It is all done away; and I feel something, I suppose, like souls who have just escaped from the bustle of a tumultuous world into the regions of peace; and have left all the business and passions of feverish mortality behind them; and have lost almost the memory of that troublesome period of their existence. In reality I thank God I never was better in health, nor on the whole more easy in mind; not that all things, either public or private, are exactly as I wish. But I who am so eager and anxious about some things in the detail of life, never was so about the sum total; and I grow rather less than more so since I have cut so deep into life. This is not philosophy; but the effect of habit. My own endeavours have been of so little service to me in my life, I am so much the creature of Providence in every good event that has befallen me, that I have grown into a perfect resignation in every thing, but the virtue of that temper. Will and Dick are just gone to town; they love you as I do, and I think it a particular addition to our felicity, in our mutual friendship, that you have no objection to our association but are kind enough to be willing to fall in and make one among so odd a set of people. I reckon on having you and Charles for a great part of this summer.

Barré [27] and Tommy Townshend dined with me last Sunday. The latter is as usual eager and sanguine. Had there been fuel enough of matter to feed that man's fire, it would make a dreadful conflagration.[28] But there wants a sufficient staple in his mind. We have all broke up without any plan of action for the summer. Dispositions are favourable to a more formed and systematic opposition than has been yet, but as yet they

[27] Col. Isaac Barré (1726-1802) was associated with the Chatham-Shelburne party.

[28] Townshend had resigned the Pay Office the previous fall and gone into opposition.

are only dispositions.[29] You probably hear that there is a perfect coalition between us and Grenville; but there is nothing more than good humour towards one another, and a determination to act with joint forces against this new, usurped, and most dangerous power of the House of Commons, in electing their own Members. King [30] yesterday got a letter from Charles; he talks of coming before you. For God's sake don't delay long after him. Adieu my dear Sir. God bless you.

Gregories 31 May 1769.

[The next day Burke's "perfect resignation" was put to a hard test. He knew that financial catastrophe had struck the "fireside," and was shocked almost out of a clear memory.]

EDMUND AND RICHARD BURKE TO O'HARA, June 1, 1769

My dear friend,

I cannot be easy from the letter which I wrote to you a day or two ago; and the flattering impression it must naturally have left upon your mind. I wrote indeed in much security, and in the greatest tranquillity of heart that can be conceived; not at all apprehending the ruin of our situation in the light I now see and feel it but too distinctly. I am heartily sorry you should have any share in the loss. If you proposed to come here, as I flatter myself you did, for any pleasure you proposed in our company, this motive can subsist no longer. If your own affairs make a visit to London necessary, we are so circumstanced, that the sight of a friend will be a real cordial. It is all that is now left. You may easily guess the cause.

Charles Street. June 1. 1769

It is unnecessary to tell you that we need not make the matter worse by publication. I have only let Jack Ridge know of it. And with a recommendation to secrecy.

[on the reverse side and in the hand of Richard Burke]

I need add nothing to what you will find on the other side

---

[29] All who voted against the seating of the minority candidate, Luttrell, on May 9, had dined together at the close of the session, in demonstration against the ministry.

[30] A friend of Burke's son Richard.

in regard to ourselves. As to you, at the last settlement you stood indebted for £250 or thereabouts; this was occasioned by a fall so considerable, that we unfortunately thought it could fall no lower, and acted upon that supposition for you and for ourselves. However you can I apprehend suffer no more than the sum I have mentioned; possibly (for I do not yet rightly understand it) nothing at all. I cannot explain this in a letter. Let me join with Ned in recommending the most perfect secrecy.

[If O'Hara lost only 250 pounds he could not have been heavily involved in the market collapse. How much the Burkes lost does not appear, but it probably was a very substantial sum. The letters to O'Hara over the next two years reveal them in straitened circumstances, and the purchase arrangements for Gregories Manor had not yet been completed.]

XI. "The Interposition of the Body of the People"

[During the summer and fall of 1769, an extraordinary political agitation spread wide over England. Started in the metropolitan region by the partisans of Wilkes, it was taken up by all parties in the parliamentary opposition and it culminated in a mass of petitions to the King which centered upon one appeal: to dissolve the House of Commons that had violated the rights of the Middlesex county electors. The issue was clear and concrete, exactly what was needed to arouse the people and consolidate the opposition. Burke took an active part in promoting the petitions, urged Lord Rockingham to seize the lead and make the issue his own, and at the behest of his chief began at this time to write the famous party pamphlet, *Thoughts on the Cause of the Present Discontents*, which was published in 1770. Therein he analyzed the malign effects of a corrupt court influence on the House of Commons, and called for and justified "the interposition of the body of the people" as the only means for restoring the honor and independence of the representative part of the constitution.

O'Hara appears to have been with the Burkes in the early part of this historic period, for he was on his way back to Ireland when he wrote the following letter.]

O'HARA TO BURKE, August 20, 1769

Manchester August 20.

My dear Edmund,

I left you much against my inclination, and yet I stayed almost too long for my purpose of finding Mr. Conway at Park Place.[1] He was to have gone the morning after I got there, but stayed out of complaisance, and still more, came with me hither, but this I impute to the Bridgewater Navigation.[2] We called upon the Duke of Graf[ton] and stayed the night with him; met the Provost at Northampton, fresh from Woburn.[3] Conversation is always productive of something, and ours might be long, were we together. But I shall now only tell you, what you must, you ought at least to have known before; that the Gang and

---

[1] Near Twyford in Oxfordshire.
[2] The Bridgewater Canal, first cross-country canal in England, then in process of construction.
[3] The Duke of Bedford's.

the Thane are to pieces, in consequence of which Sir G[eorge]
Mac[artney] will not go to Spain, and yet was so afraid of
Ireland, that the Provost was forced to leave him behind.[4]
Advice is pleasanter, to the giver at least, than narration. I will
then proceed to express my earnest wishes, that you may not
use one argument with Lord R[ockingham] relative to a certain
measure now depending. Let him shape his course, and mind
your farm.

I shall long more than ever to hear from you; and wish to
get to Ireland for this reason, as well as to exert myself in the
business you mentioned to me.[5]

I delivered your letter to Mr. Hyde; who is very sensible,
and very obliging. He dined with us today, and in the course
of our conversation about America, and the means of reconciling them to us, he dropped it out from his heart, that till their
friends were ministers again they never would trust us. Think
how I was entertained with this doctrine. This however is
only to friends.

Adieu my dear Edmund, compliments to Mrs. Burke etc. etc.

Chs. O'Hara

[O'Hara's advice against Burke's using an argument with Rockingham probably was related to the slowness of the Marquess to
throw his support to the petitioning movement which Burke was
eager to promote and exploit for the good of the party. Letters
exchanged by Burke and Rockingham during this summer show
that the latter was unwilling to act until a strong opinion for a
petition had arisen among the Yorkshire gentry, and that Burke was
attempting to prod him.[6]]

BURKE TO O'HARA, August 28, 1769

My dear Charles,

We have had stormy weather; and it has been so very violent, that we were not without some uneasy sensations concern-

---

[4] Sir George Macartney (1737-1806), who had served as minister to Prussia
and Russia, had been appointed to succeed Lord Frederick Campbell as chief
secretary in Ireland. He was married to a daughter of Lord Bute. In spite of
political differences, he was a warm friend of both Edmund and William Burke.

[5] To raise money on certain properties held by Burke in Ireland, as appears
from subsequent letters.

[6] *Correspondence* 1: 168-185; also Wentworth-Fitzwilliam MSS, Rockingham
to Burke, June 29, July 17, September 1, 3.

ing your safety; concluding that about the time of these tempests you must have been at sea. We shall not be altogether free from apprehensions until we hear from you. Most heartily we thank you for your letter from Manchester. There is a great spirit all over the northern part of the Kingdom, which if improved, supported, and rightly directed, could not fail of being infinitely useful. But God has given different spirits to different men. The profligate and inconsiderate are bold, adventurous, and pushing; honest men slow, backward and irresolute. In order to do evil in the end, the dashers take noble steps; pretend good; and sometimes do it. The others are so fearful of doing ill, that they very frequently fall short of doing the good that is in their power. The world is thus constituted; and it is not just to murmur at the course of human nature and affairs. Considerations of this kind, you may be assured, will hinder me from pushing the business you hint at with any improper importunity; indeed with any importunity at all. This resolution has been in a great measure formed upon your former opinion. In what you wrote last you were reserved. But the matter is of so interesting a nature that when you are at leisure, and can do it safely, I shall be obliged to you for being more explicit. I wish to know it indeed from curiosity principally, not much for the direction of my conduct, for the line I have chalked out for myself is so very simple, that a child cannot go astray in it.

I had two days ago a letter from Mr. Dowdeswell in which he tells me that he proposes to go into Yorkshire some time in the next month, and wishes me to go along with him.[7] I was in doubt for some time, whether in my present state of mind I should go with him; I could be of little use, and I should meet wherewithal to fret me. However I resolved to go, upon considerations *supra totam materiam*. I shall, I hope, return very early in October—but do not, by any means, delay to write until then; and direct to me here. It gives me great comfort to hear from you. Though in general we are easy enough, I bless God, we have our moments of dejection; and we want all kinds of friendly and lenient support.

You asked me whether I would wait until you could raise

---

[7] Dowdeswell energetically supported the petitioning movement. While visiting Burke, he wrote to Rockingham on Aug. 5: "Yorkshire should set the example; if it is too late for that good office, it should confirm by its concurrence."—Dowdeswell MSS, W. H. Clements Lib., Univ. of Mich.

the whole money, or take it in pieces as I could get it. Our
exigencies have decided that question. So that I shall be infinitely obliged to you if you can, as soon after Michaelmas
as possible, (I could wish before) get a thousand pound or
seven hundred at least upon Gifford's security. Ridge knows
all the circumstances; you have yourself some idea of them.[8]

The Duke of Grafton dined the other day at Lord Temple's.
I make no doubt that on the side of his Grace there are some
political views. The late intercourse began with a civility on his
part; and all things considered a very extraordinary one. A man
at Buckingham who had some place died. The D. of G. un-
asked sent word to Lord T. that as the disposal of that employment was necessary for keeping up Lord T.'s interest in that
town, it should wait his recommendation. Lord Temple accepted the proffered kindness, and his man was put in. Adieu
my dear friend. Mrs. Burke and Will and all of us are most
cordially yours.

August 28. 1769

I agree with you that the Gang and the Butes have quarrelled—but what then? They must reconcile. If the plan of
the Butes be, as I imagine it is, to have those who will do all
kind of desperate and dirty work for them, how can they fit
themselves better? And as to the Gang, though they will
squabble and fight while any thing is to be got, they will not
once more be mad enough to risk the main chance.

O'HARA TO BURKE, September 26, 1769

Dublin 26 September

My dear Edmund,

General Conway's having been with me this fortnight has
occasioned a much longer silence than I intended to have been
guilty of. Visits, going to see places, dining out, and company
at home left me no leisure for such a correspondent as you.
He sailed this morning, most heartily tired. Lord T[ownshend]
was not in town when he arrived. At first his [Conway's] *accueil*
was most gracious, but I doubt whether his departure will give
the least pain, and particularly as Hutchinson dined with him

---

[8] Burke seems to have been trying to cash some sort of mortgage bond.

twice or thrice. He took much pains to bring Hutchinson over to an augmentation of the army, but in vain.[9] Yet I have not the least doubt that the report will be otherwise. You know we have a little Gang here, and in another sense that we have a little Lord Lieutenant, and little men are for the most part governed by impressions on their fears, and on their jealousy. Never did things promise in this country so fair for opposition in yours. The Duke of Leinster, Lord Shannon and Ponsonby stand firm, and their numbers are certainly a majority. I am inclined to think they will keep together; but an union of three is always a precarious tenure. The finances of this Kingdom are in a bad condition, such as can not well support additional expences. Yet such is human nature that notwithstanding all I have said, you will suppose it every day possible that a people without any real, without even a semblance of virtue, should yet bargain themselves into measures diametrically contrary to their present declarations.

I find the Gang is victorious, very contrary to my expectation; Sir George Macartney will probably arrive this evening.

I read of you at Aylesbury, when I thought you were in Yorkshire. William tells me, or rather what he says implies, that you are at Gregories. In Yorkshire they are going to petition without you. I would rather have you promote this measure at the first place than the last. Junius on the Duke of B[edford] has outdone his own outdoings.[10]

Ridge is again disappointed as to the whole, so I shall try immediately to get such part as you mentioned remitted. I lately saw you, and yet I long to see you again. Adieu my dear Edmund,

Chs. O'Hara

---

[9] O'Hara and John Hely Hutchinson were playing some sort of game. The previous summer O'Hara had solicited the Prime Serjeant's support for Townshend's proposed increase of the army, and Hutchinson had given a confidential declaration in favor of it. He said too: "I am also desirous to go on with Government . . . unconnected with any party, which I have done uniformly throughout his Majesty's reign till my military Master deny'd me my rank & reduced me to a subaltern." Toward the end of 1768, when Sir George Macartney was named chief secretary, O'Hara hoped that so good a friend of Burke's would give him what he was seeking, namely, a place as a commissioner of the revenue. Hutchinson did not yet know Macartney, but hoped to make use of O'Hara's prospective influence with him. He told O'Hara: ". . . if he makes you a commissioner of the revenue, I shall think myself more indebted to him that I have ever yet been to any person in his station."—Annaghmore MSS, Hutchinson to O'Hara, Aug. 4, Dec. 11, 1768.

[10] The 23rd letter, Sept. 19, 1769. Woodfall, *op. cit.* 1: 231-248.

[Burke probably was in Yorkshire when O'Hara wrote the letter above. After the Buckinghamshire meeting at Aylesbury, where a petition was adopted, Burke had set out on September 19 for Wentworth, whither Rockingham had summoned him in order to have his political counsel prior to the York county freeholders' meeting on September 27, when the most sagacious and statesman-like of all the petitions was adopted. On this day, but before the meeting, Burke wrote an account to O'Hara.]

BURKE TO O'HARA, September 27, 1769

My dear Sir,

What shall I say to you in excuse for my long delay in answering no fewer than I believe three of your most friendly letters? [11] The best of the matter is, that you are not a wonderfully exacting creditor. Indeed you are possessed of a virtue, of all others the most necessary for one's own ease, and the satisfaction of every one about them, in a world composed of men and events like those of ours; I mean indulgence and compliance. However the more excellent and necessary this virtue is, the less one ought to abuse it. Enough of my own ill part; now let me thank you for the good one that you have taken for me. Your activity is not more kind than necessary. The whole money if possible, even with a little delay; because, (among other reasons) if it should be made the gross security for the sum that shall be advanced, there is no hope of getting any of the rest by piecemeal, until the whole decree is executed; and when that may be I know not; very probably not until a time very inconvenient to my present circumstances, which are likely to be pretty much the same until a long day indeed.

I am now at Lord Rockingham's. I left Buckinghamshire about a week ago; after having done my part in the petition which was going forward there.[12] Our meeting was not a bad

---

[11] None has been found.

[12] For Burke's account of the Bucks meeting at Aylesbury on Sept. 14, see his letter to Rockingham in *Correspondence* 1: 191-194. William Burke, writing to O'Hara on Oct. 1, thus described Edmund on this occasion: "Among others Ned spoke, but with great modesty, declaring that the smallness of his property and the shortness of his time in the County made it a reluctant thing for him to speak, but, as was said by the men of sense (for the others were undistinguishing praise) he adapted himself to his audience. The fact is that everybody till he spoke was heard, well indeed, but patiently, but when he had done there was a thunder, and I who had kept myself in the crowd heard the fellows say, 'damn it, he has explained it,' and they all understood their grievances quite plain."

one; though there is no inconsiderable Court and a very considerable Tory interest in that County. Lord Temple was very active amongst us. He brought G[eorge] G[renville]'s eldest son with him, and answered for his brother's approbation of our proceedings. This was indeed in the Inn after dinner; not in the Town Hall, to which, I suppose upon some point of delicacy about peerage, he did not come. This delicacy, if there had been any ground for it, ought to have run through the whole proceeding; and it would have had more decorum, and more weight too, for G. G. to have answered for the Earls his brothers, than one of them for him. However, though I saw well enough the politic motives which influenced this style of proceeding, I took no notice of it. It was our business to show no distrust or uneasiness, whilst we were carrying on a measure so necessary to the public, with our joint forces. But I could not help being inwardly affected with the extreme difference between the spirit of that political school, and the party with which we act. We are diffident, scrupulous, timid, and slow in coming to a resolution; but when once we are engaged, we are not only much in earnest and very direct in our proceeding, but sufficiently bold and active in our conduct. As for our allies, their manner is quite different; they resolve early and with boldness; but in the prosecution of business, they are never fair and direct; they have a thousand underplots and oblique views; one of them always reserves himself while another acts; and they frequently dissipate and lose their public object tho' they have the art sooner or later of securing their private and real ends. I have lately seen enough both of the one and the other. You know how much I felt from the slowness and irresolution of some of our best friends. Even to this moment, there are some of them who cannot be prevailed upon to take that lead which is natural to their situation, and necessary to their consequence.[13] But in the main, things are flowing into the right channel; and will go, I hope, down an easy declivity for the future. On my coming here I found the petition determined on and prepared; a very manly and proper piece; and I think much the best of any which has yet appeared; and there is a spirit in the County fully adequate to the support

---

[13] He must have had the Duke of Richmond particularly in mind. Instead of taking the lead in Sussex, that peer went to Paris at this time, considering the whole movement hopeless.—Wentworth-Fitzwilliam MSS, Richmond to Burke, Sept. 2, 1769.

of it. The meeting, which is held this day, must be very great
in point of number, and still more considerable from the
opulence both landed and commercial of those who compose
it. Lord Rockingham does not think it right to be at the meeting; and on the whole I am satisfied he has reason. The day
before I departed from the south, I saw my old friend William
O'Hara.[14] He is come over for his health. He is as thin as
a whipping post; but otherwise seemed tolerably well and in
spirits. I don't know whether he has been yet at Gregories.
Adieu my very dear friend—and believe me ever yours.

E. Burke

Wentworth, Sept. 27. 1769

BURKE TO O'HARA, October 24, 1769 [15]

My dear friend,

Your attention to my affairs is in the usual strain of your
affection and steadiness; and the frequency of your letters is
an act of kindness, full as necessary, and far more grateful to
me, than your care of my business.[16] I informed you of the
dispositions of our friends in Yorkshire as they stood at the
time I wrote. What happened in consequence of them is not
related much amiss in the news paper. It is enough to tell you,
that the meeting and the procedure at York were what we could
wish, with regard to temper, to spirit and to the number and
consequence of the people assembled. A considerable number
of the clergy were there: men of weight and character; and I
was glad of it, because some people were willing to cast a stain
of profaneness upon our conduct, for our supposed patronage
of Wilkes. The Dean of York had been confined with the
rheumatism, but the petition called him out of his bed; he is
not only the first ecclesiastical commoner in that County, but
has a very large landed property in it, I believe to the amount
of four or five thousand pounds a year. It is agreed that Sir
G. Savile never spoke with more ability or address than he
did at that meeting. He began with lamenting the distressful
delicacy of his situation, on one hand as a member of Parlia-

---

[14] O'Hara's son.

[15] Completed on this date, but begun some days earlier.

[16] Presumably his attempts to raise money; no letters by O'Hara since that
of Sept. 26 have been found.

ment, bound by the major vote of the assembly to which he belonged, and on the other as a trustee for the County of York, obliged to account for his conduct to those by whom he had been chosen. He spoke with so much feeling upon this subject as to draw tears from the eyes of several gentlemen; and you may easily conceive the effect of the topics which might naturally occur upon such an occasion, touched upon by one, who, the whole meeting was sure, could speak nothing but what came from his heart. He then went through a narrative of the proceedings in the House of Commons relative to this business, from the beginning to the final confirmation of Col. Luttrell's seat upon the minority. He ended by telling them that *judgment* was given; that a *final* and *conclusive* judgment was given; that it was given by a lawful court, by a court altogether *competent* to the purpose; the *only* one which was competent; a court from which there lay *no appeal*—"When the twelve judges of England gave judgment in favour of ship money, their judgment was conclusive to bind the subject on the point of law; they were a court competent to the declaration which they had made; if any one desires to know what remedy remains in such a case,—let him enquire of Hampden!" Wedderburn I am told did wonders; and was *Whiggissimus,* in all his applications of history and arguments from law. None of the old Tories were at the meeting; but most of the young ones were there, and very sanguine and earnest for the petition. Such is the state of that party in most places.

You are in a glorious situation, God bless you, in Ireland. You have a Lord Lieutenant that knows how to keep up the dignity of Government. His Grace of Grafton does as much for it here to the full, with this difference; that with the mobbish meanness of your Government you have something cheerful, something convivial, something that *looks like* good humour. Here with the same want of dignity and decorum, we have an harsh, unsocial, gloomy austerity of manner, that makes our domination not only contemptible, but disgustful and odious.

I am returned hither but a few days—Baretti was attacked by a parcel of rogues and thieves in the street; and in the scuffle he killed one and wounded another with his penknife.[17]

---

[17] Joseph Baretti (d. 1789), the Piedmontese gentleman of letters who appears frequently in Boswell's *Life of Johnson;* his trial was on Oct. 20.

Hitherto the proceeding has been favourable enough. He takes his trial on Friday, and we go again to town in order to appear to his character. Until this affair is well over, none of us can be at our ease. I was so unlucky as to be absent when Will O'Hara was here. But all our people are charmed with him. You are fortunate in your children; a great and important point of happiness! A good father, like you, deserves it.

(later)

You say you long to see us again. Come then—the place longs for you, I assure you. While I was in town I forgot to send off this letter. Poor Baretti is honourably acquitted; and my hands are cleared of that business, as my mind is of the anxiety about it. I have heard a report which makes me uneasy; that our friend Mrs. Vesey's dead. I am much concerned at this account, and wish you would contradict it in your next, if happily it should not be true.[18] Our politics here have been in something like a stagnation; the Ministers have been out of town; but the coldness of the weather, not the urgency of business, has at length driven most of them to town. Lord Chatham has certainly recovered his health astonishingly;[19] he continues to speak very *vituperously* of the ministerial measures; and if the winter does not bring on a return of his former pains and weakness, will very probably talk in the same strain in their hearing. The Chancellor is considered as in open opposition. They are determined I believe to turn him out.[20] Wilmot is [in] their eye for the seals in his place.[21] But they must bribe him stiffly, to persuade him from his calm labour and secure anchorage, into so stormy a sea as this, where the waves run mountain high. What you tell me of our friend vexes me a little; his style of disqualification would surely be very proper if properly managed, and used to proper persons; but when a man speaks official and ostensible language where plainness and confidence are expected—it is in truth a desire of no more serious conversation upon business.[22] What you tell me of Conway's almost persuading Hutch[inson] to a consent to the augmentation is very extraordinary—what then,

---

[18] Mrs. Agmondisham Vesey did not die until 1791.

[19] Chatham returned to political activity in July, 1769.

[20] Camden did not go out until January, 1770.

[21] Sir John Eardley Wilmot (1709-1792) had succeeded Camden as chief justice of the Court of Common Pleas in 1766.

[22] Allusion is to Sir George Macartney, as appears subsequently.

is Hutchinson so very young, as after two years' opposition, to be *talked* into a liking of a measure the pro and con of which he must know ten times better than his persuader? Conway might think this—*credat Judeus Apella non ego.*[23] By the way, now I speak of him, I hear he is candidate for a military government of 600 pound a year just now vacant. How can it be refused to him? Give me the disinterested man for getting every thing. Adieu. God bless you. Oh! I had like to forget a choice story of a countryman of ours, one Patrick Murphy, who was tried the other day for a murder; but they have bungled the indictment and he is safe. He was one of the Spittalfiels rioters. On pursuing him he took refuge in a bed—they asked him how he came to be abed in the day time—O, I was very sick—Well, but why in your clothes?—Can any thing show more how sick I was, than that I was obliged to go to bed in my clothes!—But wherefore this belt with two case of pistols and a blunderbus stuck in it?—Faith, if you must have the truth of it, a very clever man gave it to me as a charm against the toothache. At that session Baron Smythe was very zealous against riots and rioters—and squinted at the popular Sheriff Townshend; the heat began in the court and was taken up again at the dinner. Sharp words passed between them; and people attributed Smythe's illness, which kept him from the Old Bailey the next day, to vexation.[24]

24 October. Gregories

I need say nothing to you of the necessity of hastening the money.

[In the meantime, the Irish Parliament had been opened on October 17, and Lord Townshend found himself confronted again by a Commons unwilling to bend to his will. O'Hara had not yet obtained a seat, but arrangements were in course for him to come in for the place he had sought the previous year, Armagh.]

O'HARA TO BURKE, November 4, 1769

4th November. Dublin

Thank you, my dear Edmund, for a long letter. Sir George S[avile] has the best right of any man in your House to act

[23] Horace, *Satires*, 1.5.100.

[24] Sir Sidney Stafford Smythe (d. 1778) was a puisne baron of the Exchequer, and James Townshend, alderman of London and sheriff of Middlesex, was a partisan of Wilkes, at this time.

John Hampden, as far as he did. I am told the Rockinghams and Grenvilles make common cause in all measures, and I hear from his relations that the Duke of Richmond can't hold out long. Sir George M[acartney] tells me that all accounts of Lord Camden's indisposition to serve are without foundation and that all things go well. I wish all things to go well as much as he does, but not with the same people. You tell me a friend of mine has asked for a government worth £600 a year. I hope so, 'tis sensible, for he's entitled to it. I have two or three more friends that I wish would run into port, for the weather promises to be very tempestuous. But when I wish them safe, I mean with the whole squadron; not without them. When I told you Mr. Conway had almost converted Hutchinson to an augmentation of the army, it was by stating such terms as were honourable to their supporters; and advantageous for this Kingdom. It went however no farther than conversation. What they mean to do with us in this respect, I know not: nor do they, by any thing I hear. Their obstinacy and absurdity well warrants my saying so, but in the trials of strength which they have hitherto made, they have been outnumbered: and entirely for want of management. I think they will continue to be outnumbered through the whole course of the session. The very little firmness of which the Speaker is capable has been roused by the state of things in England; and confirmed by the treatment he has received here. I told you of my first conversation with Sir George M[acartney]. I considered [it] as a denial of confidence, and you have construed it in the same way. But it was on the contrary thoroughly confidential; 'tis really the plan, to commit him in advice as seldom as possible; to obey orders, and to get for himself, and his old friends, the best things he can. I asked him yesterday when he would do any thing for Dennis; he told me he had £200 a year for him in his pocket. Lady Louise Conolly has applied to Lord T[ownshend] for Dick Marlay, and with success; I believe for a deanery. And Sir George got Marlay's for Dennis. He has also another old friend in tow: Poer the lawyer, and for something considerable, but this is a profound secret. Lord T[ownshend] is firm as a rock to his old plan of mismanagement. He cultivates no encrease of numbers, even those who served him last session share but little in his favours. His modes of business come entirely from the Gang; their friends here are his.[25] The modes harsh, and unaccomodating, no retreat held out to Ponsonby and his friends; rather an absolute prohibition. Were I to speculate upon these circumstances, I might perhaps derive them from a division still subsisting, however concealed, in your Administration and which marriage has not healed.[26] For however impeccable you may suppose a man to be, yet some one of the many things proper might be supposed to happen sometimes, if there was no plan laid down to the contrary. Some people suppose that a vigorous opposition was wished for, as it will authorize a good deal of turning out. The first will certainly happen, and the latter may. I don't at all dislike my not coming in till tomorrow sennight. The questions hitherto have had nothing in themselves decisive, but just to show numbers. But I hear Lord Kildare will introduce business of more moment.[27] He is growing very popular, and has firmness for Parliamentary business. The poor Speaker and Lord Shannon, now connected with him, will be much disappointed when they separate from him, for, if I mistake not, many of their forces will stay behind. I must conclude for this post, as company is just come in to me.

[Burke had not yet received the above letter, when he wrote the following, which throws light on the extreme difficulty he lay under to complete the purchase of Gregories Manor.]

BURKE TO O'HARA, November 12, 1769

Charles has had two or three letters from you; so that we are at ease about your health; but still a good deal in the dark about your seat; a point on which we cannot be indifferent; for though we have looked upon it as a thing almost certain, yet where politicians are concerned, I never find myself quite on shore until the matter is actually finished. Will, who is just come from town, tells me that a question has been lost by the Castle, and that the majority against it was 13. Labilliere is indeed the authority, and he knows nothing of the question, but that it was not the augmentation. Charles tells me from you, that the opposition upon your side did not intend to make their stand upon that point; but would try their strength

---

[25] Lord Weymouth, who had succeeded Shelburne late in 1768, now had Irish affairs in his charge; he was of the Bedford party.
[26] Macartney's marriage to Jane Stuart, daughter of Bute.
[27] William Robert Fitzgerald (1749-1804), son of the Duke of Leinster.

upon an election. Possibly this may be the case, because (if they are in earnest) the folly of it is beyond all conception. Is it not a fine composition for the Castle, if it finds itself weak, to be able to carry the measures which are to give it strength and reputation, which is strength, at the expence of the loss of a single friend at an election question? Of what use are our friends in Parliament but to carry such questions? If they can be carried by the enemies' consent, I think Lord Townshend as foolish as they are if he gives himself a moment's concern about their majority. I imagine them silly enough to think, that because Sir Robert Walpole resigned upon a question of election, that others will be justified in the same manner. They forget, that the body, which carried that election, far from let him carry his capital measures; would hardly give him leave to carry away his head. Pray let me hear something of your politics; what is doing in Parliament; how my friend Sir George [Macartney] exerts himself there; and how he stands with your *Monde*. One has an odd feel for a person one regards, listed in an adverse corps. I wish his system as ill as possible; but that he may make a decent figure in it.

Now my dear Charles, I have spoke to you about Irish politics, which concern me but little; permit me to touch on my own affairs, which concern me a great deal. To make out this purchase money, I can raise ten thousand pound upon mortgage, but no more. I want towards 24 to complete the transaction. God knows how much I want money for other occasions, which press me sorely; but still to get one business tolerably off my hands would be a great deal. Therefore, as I find Gifford's estate to be advertised for sale, would it be possible to get even 2000 pound upon our demand of it? If possible by any means, my dear friend, endeavour in the first place to get that; if not, why the thousand; but in the last case, speed will be as necessary as large supply in the other. I will make no apology for the great trouble I give you. But you very well know how I stand.[28] To add to our strange and

---

[28] When Burke contracted to buy Gregories Manor he told Richard Shackleton: "I have made a push, with all I could collect of my own, and the aid of my friends, to cast a little root in this country."—*Correspondence* 1: 154. But in the midst of title and mortgage complications, William and Richard suffered their heavy losses by speculation, with the result that Edmund had great difficulty in carrying through the purchase. Sir Charles Saunders lent him 3,600 pounds on mortgage, and 10,000 pounds were similarly obtained from Caroline Williams. Will Burke in 1769 borrowed 6,000 pounds from Lord Verney and this

unfortunate situation, Dick is ordered out by the Treasury.[29] Judge what a softener that is. Adieu, adieu.

Nov. 12. 1769

O'HARA TO BURKE, November 22, 1769

My dear Edmund,

You are the most zealous for opposition everywhere, with too much tenderness and too much virtue to turn it to your own advantage. The account you heard was true, and last night we were beat in three questions, by 19, by 21, and the last by 23—the subject the money bill sent over from Council as a cause for calling a Parliament. The usual motion that it should receive a second reading tomorrow morning; the second, that it be rejected—the third resolved because it did not take rise in our house. Will this satisfy you? I felt for Sir George. His scrapes were many, called often to order, and at last a general *cry to the bar*.[30] He was so ministerially mysterious with me at first, that I have in great part shunned his confidence since, tho' in some measure offered. The truth is, he has much art, and no capacity. But we live in intimacy, I told him much of your good wishes for him. But don't look for a defeat in the question of augmenting the army. That's mine, you know how. And that we shall carry tomorrow. But as for pensions etc. Government must take care of them.[31] I have ventured

---

probably went into the buying of Gregories. Not until July, 1771, were the mortgages negotiated and the purchase transaction completed.—Wecter, *op. cit.*, 32-38.

[29] Richard was ordered to return to his post as collector of customs in Grenada, but he did not go until the following spring. Burke told Rockingham about this time that Richard's leg "is not yet in a condition, as his surgeons tell me, and as he feels, to conflict with that climate. If he goes, he goes I fear to his death."—*Correspondence* 1: 200.

[30] Heretofore a money bill originating in the Privy Council had been the formal cause or occasion for summoning an Irish Parliament, but now this was challenged, "because it did not take its rise in the House of Commons." The Irish Parliament was attempting to assert a privilege of the English Parliament.

[31] That O'Hara, who had not got the commissionership he sought, had applied for a pension in return for his service to Lord Townshend, is evident from a letter the Lord lieutenant wrote to him on March 2, 1769: "I find by Mr. Jackson you have not yet received an answer to the Letter you wrote me with respect to the Pension you wish upon this Establishment. I should do wrong were I to flatter you with any Expectations of my being able to propose What you desire to His Majesty. Prior Engagements to recommend some persons here, when His Majesty's Affairs will admit of it, forbid me this Satisfaction."— Annaghmore MSS.

in these times to act without your orders. I went to my old friend Harward who loves you. I told him you wanted two thousand pounds to complete your purchase money, thinkin' he might have that sum, and told him the case, and that Ridge and I would be security. He sent immediately for Croker, and offered to join us. Whether it be his own money or not I can't say, but he told me this morning, he thinks he shall get it. He sent yesterday for Ridge to know the circumstances of the mortgage. I hope to give you good news on Friday, that your money is ready, that we have carried augmentation, that we have been beat on pensions etc.

I lament Dick's going most sincerely. Yours most truly

C. OH.

22 Nov.

[It is evident that some hitch developed to prevent O'Hara from sending "good news on Friday."]

O'HARA TO BURKE, November 30, 1769

November 30th

My dear Edmund,

Tho' the election of Roscommon in which Mr. Croker is employed on his son's account, Mr. Crofton's, prevents my having any thing to say to you on your own business, yet I will not omit acknowledging the receipt of the pamphlet; I have however wrote to Ridge, who was to look out for Croker, and from whom, I believe you will hear by tonight's post. Our little sphere of politics furnishes more matter, but much more difficulty in the description, for folly is so equally diffused through every part of the system, that one knows not which to prefer as the subject of a letter. Augmentation closed the scene of complaisance.[32] Pery was the ostensible conductor of it, I believe upon principle, or upon English engagement, for all his proceedings since have tended to the distress of Government. The great bodies formed against Government are obliged to throw away the scabbard. There is on one side an invincible

---

[32] Townshend succeeded in winning approval, by a majority of more than three to one, of a bill to increase the Irish army from 12,000 to 15,235 men. To obtain this he had incurred many and costly political obligations, which now would have to be met.

aversion, and on the other a spirit of determined defence. We partake amply of your confusions, but not of your tumult. Reports of a war abroad promise a suspension of hostilities at home; and I think will favour the Chatham party.[33] They say here, and the authority is good, you make common cause with them in all things. Yours most truly

C. OH.

[Unfortunately, there is a complete void in the correspondence of Burke and O'Hara from the late fall of 1769 to the late spring of 1770, which was one of the most important periods in Burke's parliamentary career. A united opposition attacked the ministry when the Houses convened in January, and forced a breakdown of the Grafton administration. The King, resolutely rejecting the petitions for a dissolution, met the crisis by placing Lord North at the head of a reconstructed ministry supinely obedient to the court; and afterwards the eccentric conduct of Lord Chatham and the extremist tactics of metropolitan radicals caused the Rockinghams to draw away from them. Hence the united opposition fell apart. In April Burke's *Thoughts on the Cause of the Present Discontents* marked the separate and high aristocratic policy of the Rockingham corps. Carrying Grenville with them, they chose rather to attack ministerial mismanagement of America, than to pursue the cause for which so many petitions had been addressed to the King.

One reason for this void in the correspondence must be that O'Hara spent part of the time in England with the Burkes, having been relieved of his parliamentary duties by Lord Townshend's proroguing of the Irish Parliament on December 26. It did not meet again for fourteen months. Townshend's action was of historical importance. Having obtained his primary object, the military augmentation, he chose to regard as dangerously unconstitutional the Parliament's rejection of the money bill originated in the Privy Council, and used this as a pretext for suspending the deliberations of a House dominated by his political enemies. His conduct was the subject of a debate in the British House of Commons on May 3, 1770. There Burke denounced the augmentation, which O'Hara had supported, and denied that the Irish Parliament had acted unconstitutionally; rather had the members "followed the great constitutional law of Parliament, which empowered them to reject a bill for any reason they might think proper. . . . It was a tricking measure to receive the supply, to thank them for it, to put

---

[33] Rumors of war arose from the French conquest of Corsica, and French aid to the Ottoman Turks in their current war with Russia.

the money into their pockets, and then prorogue." Burke feared the same trickery might be practised on the Parliament of Great Britain.[34]

Six days later, on May 9, Burke, acting for his party and in concert with Grenville, reviewed and arraigned the conduct of ministry in North America since 1767, and proposed eight resolutions of censure upon the administration. Lord North, however, easily mobilized the house against this opposition maneuver.

It is evident from the following letter that O'Hara had returned to Ireland about a month before this "American day." It is evident too that he now had well-founded expectations of receiving the reward for his support of Lord Townshend: a government job. However much the two friends had differed in their Irish politics, they were at one in hoping for that reward.]

O'HARA TO BURKE, May 10, 1770

Maryborough 10th May

My dear Edmund,

I have been a month in Ireland without writing to you; a very unusual thing. I waited for some time to see Ridge; and might just as well have not waited, for Ireland is singularly circumstanced as to money transactions. I wanted three hundred guineas to take with me to the Curragh, and my last resort was to Sir Hen[ry] Cavendish, who would not lend them to me, upon a draft accepted by Birch. Even the Treasury is reduced. The bankers ruin us. I was surprised to hear from Hutchinson, that even the law stands still for want of money.

My pamphlet, and all the rest came safe. No work of yours was ever so greedily read, nor so much applauded.[35] Few understand it; but 'tis the fashion to like it. I myself, tho' well acquainted with it before I left London, found infinite pleasure in reading it. Everything that I disliked in it is omitted, and one passage also, which I much liked. Its effect must be great in London, where people are used to reason upon subjects of that kind. Never was a man so enraptured as Hutchinson;

---

[34] Wright, J., *Sir Henry Cavendish's debates of the House of Commons during the thirteenth Parliament of Great Britain* 1: 559-560, London, Longmans, 1939.

[35] Published April 23; a copy with O'Hara's name inscribed on it is at Annaghmore.

it was his subject for a whole evening. He goes soon to Spa, and will spend a few days in London, in his way. Mrs. Hutchinson has been ill. But he could be of no use here, either to himself or Government, being but little, if at all in confidence. We too have our interior cabinet; wherein the old law counselors have no share. Sir George's pretended variance with Lord Townshend is now understood; he has avoided much solicitation by the appearance of it, and has much more leisure for the cabinet. Waite [36] and the Provost, sometimes, are the only people consulted. Nine new Privy Councillors were sworn in last Monday, and six struck out, of which Sir William Mayne was one. This the Duke of Leinster resents so much, that he insists upon his name being struck out. His letter is gone over by his own desire, and I dare say will be complied with. *C'est l'esprit du temps.* None have been yet displaced in the lower revenue employments, but they expect it; and indeed we have gone too far to stop.[37] The commission for the Board of Accounts is not yet come over.[38] I shall be absent about a month and much will be done in that time. I sat for two hours with Sir George [Macartney], we talked much of you. He had read the pamphlet, treated it as merely ideal, but commended it upon the whole. He still labours to do for Poer, but I did not mention Ridge. Apropos, in enumerating the cabinet, I should have mentioned our friend Dennis. Sir George thinks of sitting down again upon his own estate, till times grow quiet. He thinks them troublesome in England, and looks for quiet in Ireland. He and I differ much in opinion. Leland who enquires much for you, is writing a history of Ireland. I have talked to him on the subject, and I think his materials scanty. But he has sent two volumes to the press, to James I inclusive.[39] The Provost represents the whole Gang; and from their letters,

[36] Thomas Waite, later attorney general.

[37] Townshend was driving out the opposition men, to reward his own supporters.

[38] The Lord lieutenant had sought authority to create a new government office, the Board of Accounts, on which O'Hara had been promised a place. It was created in 1771, and according to Lord Charlemont it consisted of "five commissioners, all of whom were members of the House of Commons, and many of them actually purchased from opposition by the present appointment. Against this measure, as unconstitutional in its circumstance as in its spirit, a long protest was signed by nineteen peers."—*Charlemont Manuscripts* 1: 31.

[39] Dr. Thomas Leland's *History of Ireland* was published in 1773. He sought Burke's help in his work.—Leland to Burke, March 22, 1770, *Correspondence* 1: 221-224.

I should understand you have no chance. Con[way] fares rather worse than you do.

Dick, I suppose, is near leaving you; present my love to him. I am not without hopes that you'll have him soon recalled for a good exchange. I have no interest in this, for you know we never agreed.

I am now upon my road to the County of Kerry to see my daughter, where I never have been. If we could spend two or three days together on the banks of Killarney, they might perhaps be as pleasant as that we spent in the Dagle.[40] I long to see Mrs. Burke, and all of you, tho' contrary to a sort of resolution I made. If ever I go again to England, it will be so to see you. Adieu.

Burke to O'Hara, May 21, 1770

My dear friend,

I proposed not to write to you until my mind should be a little disengaged. But I find if I wait for that state of things, I must adjourn my letter to a very long day. I could wish indeed to give you only a share of my satisfactions, or my hopes, but the communion of friendship requires that we should pledge one another in the cup of bitterness as well as that of sweetness. Your poor friend Mrs. B[urke] has been a long time and still is very weak and low; lately, and I hope I may with truth say, *lately*, she has been in great danger; but the goodness of Providence aiding her father's constant attention, has given her some ease, and us some cheerful hopes for these two days past; though she is still very low and feeble; and far enough from being able to quit her bed.[41] Just at this time Richard is on the very point of going to the West Indies; and it adds not a little to his and to our affliction, that his sister is in such a state, that we cannot risque his taking leave of her; any agitation whatsoever, much more so great a one, being a great deal too much for her mind in its present state. As to the rest we are all thank God very well.

Our session from which many sanguine people expected so much ended just as I thought it would. You see the King's

---

[40] Probably the Dargle Glen, a wooded vale in Wicklow, where the two friends may have gone on holiday sometime in the early 1760's.

[41] Burke is writing of his wife.

speech says little of the past, and nothing at all of the future. Having no plan of conduct but the chapter of accidents; and no wishes, but to hold their employments as long and as lucratively as they can, they commit themselves for nothing. As to our firmness, which they commend, it has showed itself in persisting in our old errors; and our moderation, which they commend along with it, has shown itself in hearing with patience, not to say with tameness, every kind of insult for our perseverance. However, most certain it is that Parliament has reaped the usual benefit of low prudence and low spirit; and is still a living dog. The Ministers have in some late debates commended this Parliament for an unusual degree of independence. Undoubtedly no House of Commons was ever less in dread of an administration. They see plainly, that they are totally out of a condition to punish; and that their fund of reward is almost too large for the claimants; so that they are not afraid every now and then to contradict the leaders; and they know that the ordinary services will entitle them to a full share of emoluments. This is the case in all general questions, (such as Grenville's bill) [42] but when the question is such as may involve the fortune of the Ministry, or affect their interest in any degree, they support them with the utmost ardour and resolution. The majority does not act as subject to the Ministry, but as a sort of an *ally* which has a strong and common interest. For my own part, you know I had always a most contemptible opinion of the effect of an opposition in Parliament. The whole must be done without doors. I therefore pleaded hard for an early secession; which could not have failed of a considerable operation. We had a better and fairer ground for it upon a constitutional point, than they had in Sir Robert Walpole's time upon the Convention, which was a mere matter of state; and I think the numbers, the character, and the consequence of the seceders, as well as their probable constancy in adhering to any resolution taken in concert, would have been much superior to the former secession, which however did produce great effects. [43] I was overruled in this. We

---

[42] A law transferring the decision of disputed parliamentary elections from the whole House to a committee of fifteen, of whom thirteen were elected by ballot and the remaining two chosen by rival candidates. Committee members were bound to examine witnesses upon oath and sworn to decide according to the evidence.

[43] Reference is to Walpole's convention with Spain in 1738, in an effort to avoid the war of "Jenkins' ear."

have not indeed been quite idle (some in opposition have not)
in playing the popular engines; but the great calamity of the
time is, that those who could play them with the most temper,
skill, and energy, have a great reluctance to meddling with
them at all; and those who do undertake them are to say the
truth by no means our wisest, or perhaps our best men. So
that it is hard to say on the whole, whether the common cause
of opposition has gained or lost most, by what has been endeavoured on the part of the people. As to the Ministers they
are as weak and divided as when you left them. The band of
King's men are better supported than ever; they are the sole
object of the reign. As to your friends the Bedfords, they are
hated by them as formerly; and they know it. They are con-
scious that they are only kept in until another set can be got;
and you may depend upon it, that there is not one body of
the outs which would not be infinitely preferred to them. But
at present the K's friends have no other choice. We ended
the session by a motion of mine in the House of Commons,
(or rather a string of motions) which you have seen in the
votes, relative to the ministerial proceedings in America; and
by a similar set, by the Duke of Richmond, in the House of
Lords. Neither of us lost credit by our manner of opening and
supporting our propositions.[44] Lord Rockingham, I am told,
for I was not in the house, spoke very much at large, and with
great ability on this, and with great dexterity, so as not to give
the least offence to the opposite sentiments of some of the
allies. He has spoken so often this session, that he may be said
to be now among the regular speakers—a matter of infinite consequence to himself and to all of us. It was obvious, that if
he could conquer the difficulty of public utterance, he would
show more substantial and extensive understanding of business
than any of them. However the session has ended with as little
plan upon our side, as upon that of the Ministry. The City
of London is at work again, but they have so mismanaged their
last business, that they will find their example not so much
followed as they might expect. The King will give his answer
to their last remonstrance next Monday.[45] After saying so much

---

[44] Burke's speech and motions may be read in *Cavendish's debates, op. cit.,*
2: 14-37. He forced a division on only one of his motions, and lost by 79 to 199.
The Lords' majority against Richmond was sixty to twenty-six.

[45] The King on March 14 had rejected one "remonstrance" from the London
radicals; another, drafted by "the Lord Mayor, Alderman, and Commons of

of the general state of things, you will expect I should say a word of myself. I must say, that the session ended well for me, I thank God. I have no doubt that a plan had been formed, by general calumny of every kind, as well as by personal attacks in Parliament, to reduce my little consideration to none at all. So it has happened, that (notwithstanding I find any thing which goes through the Irish channel is very unfavourably reported for me) the malice of my enemies has not overpowered me; on the contrary it has been of service to me. The American day did me no discredit; and the Pamphlet, which contains our creed, has been received by the public beyond my expectations. The courtiers admit it to be a piece of gentlemanly hostility. The fiercest enemies it has yet met with are in the republican faction.[46]

Now my dear friend, last but not least, I wish to know of yourself and your own business, which I learn has been at least delayed. My fears on hearing this, have carried me farther; and considering the wonderful instability of every thing, I am not without apprehensions of its total failure. Do, as soon as you can, make us easy in this particular; it will be a comfort to us in the midst of our own vexations to find that any thing has happened, or is likely to happen well to you.[47]

I am in the last degree of distress for money. What delays have been thrown in the way of Gifford's business? I beg you will talk to Ridge and see whether any contrivance can be made for a present supply of 1200 or 1500 £. Forgive all this trouble. Mrs. Burke is this moment I learn so much better as to wish

the City of London, in Common Council assembled," was presented to the King on May 23, asking him to dissolve the House that had expelled Wilkes and seated Luttrell, and to summon "a full, free, and unmutilated parliament, legally chosen in all its members." The remonstrance appealed also for "the removal of evil ministers, and the total extinction of that fatal influence which has caused such a national discontent." The King rejected the remonstrance.— Woodfall, *Junius* 2: 111-113.

[46] The opinion of "the republican faction" may be seen in Catherine Graham Macaulay's *Observations on a pamphlet entitled, Thoughts on the cause of the present discontents,* London, Dilly, 1770. Attacking Burke's aristocratic politics, she said: "We cannot help wondering at the corruptness of the heart, and deception of the head of the same writer, who, whilst he emphatically sets forth the tyranny growing from a trust too long continued to parliaments, yet absolutely declaims against the quick return of power into the people's hands."

[47] Reference is to the prospective creation of the new board on which O'Hara was to have a place.

to eat; the first symptom of appetite which she has shown. The Doctor is constantly with her. Adieu my dear friend. God bless you.

Gregories 21 May 1770

Lord Chatham is without doubt the penman of the last remonstrance. It is not indecent or improper.

XII. Recreations and Reflections in the Summer of 1770

[O'Hara seems not to have received Burke's letter at the end of the stormy session of 1770, when he wrote next, during his visit in southwest Ireland.]

O'HARA TO BURKE, May 31, 1770

Crotto in Kerry, 31st May

My dear Edmund,

'Tis a long time since I have heard from you, tho' I sometimes hear of you. I had an account of the American business, which I like much; and from a man not at all prejudiced in your favour. I also heard of Mrs. Burke's recovery, before I heard of her illness: to my great satisfaction. They write me word from Dublin that there must be a change of the Ministry. But I see nothing in the papers that looks like it. If the Parliament had sat, they might have wished it to save Lord Hillsborough.[1] But in the present state of things, I should suppose the report arises from most people's thinking that a change ought to be made. I find by letters from England to friends of the Gang, that they wish for the Government if a change must take place, that Lord M[ansfield] and others, who none of you like, are for your party. My ideas in this remote corner, I mean Ireland, are just what they were when I saw you last. I should look with concern, yet with temper, from the shore, if you were safe landed. Your firmness and perseverance have often been the object of my wonder, but I do not wish to be put to further trial. Our system goes on slowly, from the little leisure your Ministers have had; but it goes on, and I think will extend to changes of all the revenue employments which are now in the hands of opposition members. In the meantime pamphlets come out upon constitutional subjects; some few see clearer than they did, and understand their grounds better. The Speaker's party grows so thin that I doubt whether he

---

[1] The main target of criticism from those who laid the disorders in America to ministerial mismanagement.

would be an object in case of a change. The Duke of Leinster
[is] much stronger than perhaps a new Chief Governor would
like to have him.[2] I hear a report that Sir G. Mac[artney] is
to get a pension of £1000 a year. A new Board of Accounts
is preparing, and I am in the County of Kerry thoroughly
assured in the integrity of my Lord Lieutenant. I came yesterday from the Lake of Killarney, upon which I spent four entire
days. I often wished for you, and often thought of our tête à
tête to the Dagle. You would have been very busy with your
glass, particularly in examining the wonderful vegetation of
plants, in rock, without any earth at all or water. You see
sometimes the whole root like network upon a rock without
a crevice or fibre to get in; and this ten feet from earth, and
as many from water. There are in a garden upon the borders
of the lake two apple trees, which grow out of the joints of
monstrous rocks; but joints so small, that we could not force
the point of a knife into. The stems, thickening immediately
upon the surface are enabled to support large heads, which
bear prodigiously. Ewe, holly, and arbutus grow spontaneously
on every rock; but not in so wonderful a way as the apple trees.
But here we must stop, to establish a superiority over every
other place; for every part is equalled or outdone by others
we have seen: yet the vastness and variety of objects, approaching to rivalship with any others singly taken, form a most glorious scene. I am told you excelled not long ago in describing
the right and wrong side of a country gentleman's character.
Let me tell you a little of my Lord Kenmare whose works
appear upon the face of the earth.[3] Observing the country
within three miles of the town, neatly dressed, and enclosed, I
asked with surprise, how that should happen in so remote and
wild a corner. I was told by the encouragement his Lordship
gives to his tenants. They have found lime to be the best
manure; and upon this, he gives bounties in proportion to the
quantities sold; so that every tenant has what quantities he
pleases; and in every situation, for the bounties are propor-
tioned to the distances. If a tenant of good character and industry does too much, or is otherwise unfortunate, he is sure

---

[2] Leinster was the only man of great influence who had opposed to the end
the augmentation of the Irish army.

[3] Thomas Browne (1726-1795), fourth Viscount Kenmare in the Irish
peerage, who was to become an active leader in the effort to repeal or modify
the anti-Catholic penal code of Ireland.

of adequate assistance: so they go on boldly. The town is neatly built for such a place, and encreasing fast, the streets full of people, that look wholesome and well fed. He gives bounties on the sale of provisions there; and thereby keeps up an agreeable plenty; and this has encouraged in some degree the linen manufacture. There's a neat new church; which raised my curiosity, as Lord Ken[mare] is a Roman Catholic; but I am told he makes no distinction; every man of good character was welcome, and should have proper places for worship in their own way. There is a man placed to take care of the woods; he has a great extent of mountain, and by way of rent, is to plant so many acres annually, to add to the beauty of the place. Thus much for a specimen of his character. I have much more to say; but 'tis full time to release you. I shall only add that his estate is now £10,000 a year, and by the good he does, will soon grow to £20,000. Yet this man has a baud wife, and an only son who is blind. Vid[e] Panglos[s] in Candid[e] for the solution—Adieu.

WILLIAM BURKE TO O'HARA, June 15, 1770

The last words of your last to Ned gave us an hope that the resolution of looking no more this way was broken;[4] and it is not in words of course that I say, its being so is of real comfort and satisfaction to me; for I know not how, you are the repository of all our views, and hopes, and fears, of our passions and our feelings, of all that's good, or evil in us, and a strange mass you hold, but whatever the contents may be, you are the casket, and valuable therefore, you will not dare deny. We have had little satisfaction since you left us. Poor Mrs. Burke has continued to almost this day alarmingly ill; her father is still with her in the country, and we hope she is in a promising way, but our best expectations even, are but of very slow and gradual reestablishment. Our poor Richard leaves us the day after tomorrow. Ned holds up his heart amazingly, I should almost dread a calm and quiet; he braves the storm, I should dread that in a calm he would not find the use of the rudder. With all the anxiety and none of the blame of our misfortunes, he sustains himself, and gives the example of manly firmness; and I do sometimes hope that patience and perseverance will

---

[4] Refers to a letter that is missing.

accomplish peace. As to himself and his personal situation, do not think me blinded; I love him as my mistress almost, but I see the wrong either in his conduct, or towards his fortunes, with that eye of curiosity that a mother sometimes discerns the slips of her child, which escape the common visitant. Take my word for it then, that he stands higher now in public estimation, than he ever did. Somehow envy and malice had linked and all the winter there was a set run at him. The two opportunities strangely forced on him, to speak of himself, and doing it with dignity and modesty, wonderfully conciliated and restored the affections of people;[5] the Pamphlet developing with such art the whole Court system, and yet attacking none of the persons expressly, was matter of applause to all parties. The indifferent people found in it what was the object of the parties; the opponents thought they had an escape in their own persons. Then too the last thing done in the House was his American discussion; all the world was gone into the country, and business over. The *hot* winter furor revived for a moment, and the expectations were very great, the House very full. He spoke very long, his motions palpably led to impeachments, but full of personal civilities, and I may say, the utmost expectations were fully answered—and he certainly stands higher than ever he did in his life—I had almost said the highest of any man in the country. You know that I felt with you the kind of odium that was gaining ground; I am sure if you were here now you would with me think it buried in the Red Sea.[6]

June 15th 1770

Your Charles is just come in, and dines with us. If I were to choose a son for you in the universe (as I certainly would not take little Dick from Ned) I should fix on Charles; I need not say he has good sense, for I think he has more liking for us, than a fellow who had not some could have.

Leland says something of a feature added to the Pamphlet, and seems to suppose it not all Neds.[7] What the devil would

---

[5] These occasions not certainly identified.

[6] Burke was accused of being Junius, a Roman Catholic, and a fortune-hunter in politics and the stock exchange. Much of the nature of this odium may be apprehended from the long letter written (probably to his former friend, Dr. William Markham, Bishop of Chester) in defense of his character and conduct.—*Correspondence* 1: 276-338.

[7] "C. O'Hara, in a conversation in Mount Gallagher, naturally asked me if I had received and read the 'Thoughts' etc. My answer was accompanied with

he be at? A great part of this I wish Jack Ridge saw, and a great part of what I write to him I wish you saw; and if jointly you could manage 1500 or £2000 to be sent to us, it would be a wonderful *ease* to us. Ned thanks you for your politics—I need not say, this is not seen by him. Adieu and God preserve you long to friends who value and esteem you.

BURKE TO O'HARA, June 20, 1770

You need not doubt of the pleasure I should have had in being of your party on the Lake of Killarney. Killarney with all its beauties would not have been necessary, to make a party with you a pleasant one to me. It must have been pleasant to you, who have a taste for improvements in a country, and in mankind, to see the judicious and humane plans of my Lord Kenmare. He was always a public spirited man. I have seen him once or twice; and he seemed to me to have a great deal of well cultivated good sense.[8] But he is a papist. And you know that such a man can not and ought not to be endured in your country, no more than the honest anabaptist at Lisbon. I remember they were going to fall upon him as well as upon others on the treasonable plot of the White Boys. *Mais cultivons notre jardin*—in spite of blind sons, disagreeable wives, party rage, ignorance, and bigotry. If we wait until these evils cease to be the lot of the best as well as the worst men, we shall have no cabbages. By the way, my field cabbages promise tolerably, though I am as yet far from sure that I have got the right sort. The horse hoe, for all sorts of garden crops that you bring into the field, is a glorious thing; and cabbages, beans etc. will be

---

a criticism I shall not repeat, qualified, however, with one remark; that, in my opinion, the business of a House of Commons had some little effect on the style of our friend, for that, in a few places, the phraseology was not as elegant as usual. I was directed to ascribe this to the very extensive communication of the work, and the author's admitting some insertions from other hands; and it provoked me, I confess, that when he accepted the thoughts of other people, he should not take the trouble of giving them his own colouring."—Dr. Thomas Leland to Burke, June 11.—*Correspondence* 1: 225. Leland was probably right in his criticism; it is at any rate very clear, from the published and unpublished correspondence of Burke and Rockingham, that the Marquess, William Dowdeswell, Sir George Savile, and the Duke of Portland all made suggestions or criticisms or contributions to the party pamphlet. The date of Leland's letter suggests that Will Burke wrote his postscript later than June 15.

[8] It was to Kenmare that Burke in 1782 would address his famous *Letter to a Peer of Ireland on the Penal Laws against the Irish Catholics.—Works* 6: 271-296.

infinitely benefitted by this practice; besides the advantage of preparing a [churning] clear and vigorous fallow for the grain which ought to succeed to them. I would not be positive, but I fear the idea of carrying the horse hoeing method to much greater lengths is little better than an ingenious amusement. From my experiences of this year I shall not venture to sow vetches late, and on poor ground. Otherwise my opinion of their profit is no way altered, both with regard to the advantage of cuttings for fodder, and of the service they do the ground towards further culture. But I see they require that the land should be in pretty good heart. You know I tried deep plowing on a miserable bad bit of clover lay which produced little or nothing last year. The soil is pretty deep and loamy, notwithstanding the failure of the grass. I went to ten or twelve inches in the ground. It is the most promising piece of my wheat; equal at least to a piece which had been well dunged after vetches, and superior to another clover lay on the same sort of soil, which had not been plowed so deep, though that also had been well dunged. But in writing to you, as well as in discourse, I am apt to ramble. Indeed I have little else to talk about. For news upon which I can depend, I have none; and as to my speculations, I have already told you all I thought, in a very long letter I wrote to you immediately after my coming to the country. I directed to your house in Merrion Street, imaging it would be sent to you into whatever part of the country you might have gone. I am glad your good nature had no share in the exercise of our minds. You heard of Mrs. Burke's illness and recovery together. This was her first illness of which she quickly recovered; but she came hither too early for her strength, and made too bold an use of it. So that she relapsed and continued miserably ill until within a few days; so that she and we all have passed many uneasy hours. She is now however, though very low in strength, I thank God in as fair a way as can be wished. Poor Dick is gone —the weather extremely stormy ever since. We are in the hands of Providence for every thing.

There is a report, I do not know how much credit it deserves, that Lord North thinks of retiring on an anticipated peerage, and pension, and that Lord Gower is to be first Lord of the Treasury in the new arrangement.[9] The Bedfords think

---

[9] Gower was then Lord President of the Council.

the Bute people absolutely dependent on them and prescribe
their terms accordingly. This has been long my Lord Gower's
object. But I cannot think that all the rest of the Gang can
be wonderfully desirous of his obtaining it. If Lord North
goes away I take it for granted that Elliot will have the lead
of the House—though it is likely enough that he will be averse
to the trouble. So will Conway. I hardly think they will put
up Jenkinson or Dyson or Barrington—not but that the pack
will indifferently be halloed by the whipper in, or stable boy,
or kennel sweeper, as by the oldest and most reputable hunts-
men. As to your Irish politics, you know they are confined
to one point, so far as I take a concern in them, your own
affair. I am not sanguine. When it is done, I shall believe
it out of danger.[10] Is it possible that the Privy Councillers
were removed in the insulting manner that I heard of? The
Doctor, Jane, Will—all heartily yours. We see Charles sometimes, not as often as we would. I expected him yesterday;
but these violent rains have kept him away. O speak to Ridge.
He has not answered my letter. Consult together on my lease.[11]
Adieu my very dear friend.

Gregories June 20. 1770

[in the hand of Dr. Nugent]
     The Doctor just adds a word to recall to your remembrance
an old man who long loved you, and often wishes to see you.
While our affairs here were so very doubtful I really could not
write to you, else you certainly should have had some of my
little tattle a great while ago. Mrs. Burke was in a sort of
disagreeable balance a great while. That balance is now turned,
though she is not able to walk yet. I have great pleasure in
hearing that Mr. and Mrs. Ponsonby, and (you will give me
leave to add) your little grandson, are well. May you live
as long and as happily as I wish you. Now I think on't I
began in the third person and end in the first. God bless you.

BURKE TO O'HARA, August 9, 1770 [12]

My dear friend,

     I am afraid we have been, every one of us, in your debt. We
shall always be so, I fear, in every thing but real affection, in

---

[10] O'Hara's prospective job, for which he seemed now to be in the greatest need.
[11] Still the business of raising money in Ireland.
[12] Begun on Aug. 5, as the contents indicate.

which I trust the account will ever be equally balanced between us. The uniform life I have led for some time, the likeness of one day to another, and the absence of all pursuits, has made us I believe hardly think any thing worth troubling a friend with, who is too distant to mind the little daily occurrence that rises and perishes with the hour, and to which nothing but the vicinity can give any interest. My silence, and the silence of all of us arose I think from this cause. I confess my dear friend, that I have read some of your late letters with concern; you are not in spirits; disappointments, some on your account, many on account of your friends, have somewhat sunk you; and you seem to have retired a little disgusted as well as fatigued.[13] Indeed there is nothing in public affairs to give a man consolation for private disappointments. No man of reflection or feeling can, I think, look at them with satisfaction; though the evils are now rather working in their causes, than experienced in all their bitter consequences. I do not wonder at your uneasiness; but my dear friend, all resources but in our minds and in Providence are vain and fallacious; and the sense of their being so, will I hope lead us to that temper of mind, which can alone afford us real tranquillity; and it will give it to us, if we seek it in good earnest. Now I have this Sunday evening preached my sermon, which has at least the merit of being a short one. Tomorrow I go to town to see Hely Hutchinson, who I find has left his name at my house in town. The newspaper today says he is Chief Justice. If this be true I suppose it is accompanied with a peerage to the family.[14] If he retires in this way I think he does wisely. For the sort of drudgery which is done by a parliamentary leader in Ireland is not pleasing, I think, at any time of life; nor very reputable at a time when life rather verges towards decline. He has lately been civil to me in my law suit, and I am otherwise (partly for your sake) inclined to behave to him with every attention. I shall ask him in what posture your affair is. I am firmly of opinion, that you ought not to let it rest on their own sense of propriety; but to continue, while any life remains in it, to press it by letter, by personal application, and by every way consistent with prudence and dignity.

The other day we lost my colleague Sir Robert Dowling; or rather acquired an opportunity of regaining the borough;

---

[13] No letters have been found to show what was troubling O'Hara.
[14] The report was not true.

which Lord Verney formerly lost by our own egregious neglects. Things are now in better order; and I trust there can be no further danger; he proposes to put Bullock in, upon whose Carmarthen business we had so unprosperous a fight in the House of Commons.[15] As to politics we have none. Every thing is sullen and quiet. I do not know whether the apparent ministers triumph or not. They may last some time, for the interior managers have nothing to fear from them; and they are in that thorough state of weakness and dissension that answers fully the purposes of their appointment. *Viribus ipsa suis ruit,*[16] may be the motto of all former administrations during this reign. I should think they must feel a little perplexed and mortified by the two late verdicts on their prosecution of Junius. I should feel better pleased if there were a little more consistency in the proceedings of juries, when they determine on libellous matter. To give damages to George Onslow, for some words spoke at a county meeting concerning his conduct in Parliament; and not to find a man guilty of the most egregious insults on the King—is the most astonishing conduct that can be conceived. The greatest objection to the opinion of a jury on matters of law and which I have never yet heard used, is the extreme difficulty if not impossibility of bringing it to any thing of previous certainty and consistency.[17] Charles is well—though it is some time since we have seen him. We shall take a turn to Birmingham together I think this summer. Mrs. Burke thank God is now recovering her strength very fast, and desires as all here do to be most heartily remembered to you. Adieu my dear friend. Heaven preserve you.

August 9. 1770

---

[15] Dowling had obtained one of the two Wendover seats in 1768, when his predecessor, Richard Cavendish, had taken office as chancellor of the diocese of Durham. Joseph Bullock was now elected to the vacancy.

[16] Horace, *Epodes,* 16.2 (suis et ipsa Roma viribus ruit).

[17] H. S. Woodfall, publisher of the *Public Advertiser,* was prosecuted by the crown for printing Junius's letter No. 35 (Dec. 19, 1769), which was alleged to be a seditious libel upon the King. Lord Mansfield, reserving to the court the determination of what constituted seditious libel, had instructed the jury to confine itself to the facts of printing and publication. The jury returned a verdict of "guilty of printing and publishing only." The trial took place on June 13, 1770.

XIII. Juries and Printers

[There seems to have been little communication between the Burkes and O'Hara in the late summer and early fall of 1770; and for the whole parliamentary session that opened in November the extant exchanges are few. They tell us something of the war scare that arose when it was learned that Spanish troops had expelled a British garrison from the Falkland islands. But more conspicuous in the letters from December to the following summer are the great controverted question of the rights of juries, raised by Lord Mansfield in the Woodfall case, and the question of the rights of printers, which was raised by Parliament's attempt to prevent the reporting of its debates in the newspapers. When the following was written, it was widely expected that a new war with Spain, and perhaps with France, was imminent.]

WILLIAM BURKE TO O'HARA, December 8, 1770

We have received your letters to Ned and myself, and I put yours into the penny post.[1] Ned, his wife, boy, the Doctor, poor absent Richard, and myself are all well. Having said this, I am not clear that I have not exhausted the whole epistolary matter; and yet, among other things that are odd and unaccountable I scarce know any thing more so, than our long silence. Ned did indeed begin a letter long since, the paper is grown into Rigby's definition of a record,—old, rusty, mouldy, illegible stuff. I too have forty times resolved to write, nay I thought I had business, for on the first rumour of a war, my friend and namesake occurred to me; the crisis of his life is now, so that it was very material to leave no stone unturned to push him forward.[2] Well, while I was meditating on this, the war might have been over and a new peace left him a lieutenant for life; well, he comes over himself, and makes me sick about delicacies and moderations and not troubling Mr. C[onway] too much; strange whims indeed for his father; and then what I had omitted to do from love and regard and good humour, rage and indignation drove me to do in an hurry. I was determined to drag you over on the instant as the only feasible hope of getting a ship for Will. And yet I have never

---

[1] A letter to Edmund of Nov. 23 is of too little interest for inclusion.
[2] Lieutenant William O'Hara.

said a word to you about it, and—consequently you are still at that damned Nymphsfield in Sligo. Well I have had time to cool—and in sober sadness let me beg you to leave off the nonsense of delicacy toward C[onway]. I know him as well as you; he must not be drove, you are right, but he must be *attended*. The notion of putting William in an Admiral's ship, recommended by Hawke upon C[onway]'s recommendation, is (take my word for it) just releasing Hawke from present *importunity* and unprofitably wasting Will's time. The Admiral (be he who he may) will feel that Hawke will probably not be at the head of the Admiralty, at the end of his voyage; and as to his respect to Conway, make what you can of it. I tell you plainly you must be at C[onway]'s elbow to take care that William shall be in the promotion of captains at home—this will not be, if you are not here. Lose therefore no time, come over immediately.

I say nothing of our love of you, and our desire to see you, but your own essential business requires your presence here. Do not laugh at this coming from me; I really know this business, and state it fairly.

As to politics. The Ministry wished, at least it was thought so, to feel the pulse of opposition as to peace or war; in short, they feared the war to be unavoidable, and wished to throw the blame of the measure on the outcries of party; but there is no cry for war, nor yet a call for peace. They are charged, and all our motions tend to it, with shameful neglect of the public safety; and I need not tell you that we carry nothing, nor have we had much business, and yet the Ministry are not on the *qui vive;* there is something rotten among themselves. Lord Chatham alluded last Wednesday to Lord Mansfield's doctrines in some late charges to the juries; Lord M. stood on the old law, and universal opinion of past and present judges.[3] Lord Camden denied the universality of that opinion, and pledged himself to give his own opinion fully and plainly when the business should come before the House. Lord Mansfield gave notice yesterday in the House that he will himself bring it on next Monday, how or in what manner he did not explain.

On Thursday Glynn moved for an enquiry into the conduct

---

[3] *Supra*, Burke's letter of August 9, 1770, n. 17.

of the courts in criminal proceedings.[4] He kept aloof from all
personalities, his second Oliver,[5] not so, but named Mansfield;
Mawby [6] named Smythe and Townshend alluded to other
matters—Ned for the enquiry, but quite clear of any thing like
personality. On the contrary, he defended in some sort the
conduct of Mansfield as founded on precedent and great
authority.[7]

In a word, Ned has I think got great favour with the House;
I think you'll understand me and be glad when I tell you, that
he is in that temper not to lose it.

We hear from Richard; he is well, and we have hopes that
his going out may have a very considerable benefit; we must
see you to explain more—God bless and send you to us. I have
not seen Charles or Will for some days. I consider them as I
shall I hope my own children; I love them, and think each
what he should be; if I descanted on Charles I might seem to
despise Will, if on Will I should seem to be wanting in love
for Charles, whereas I heartily love and esteem both. Adieu.

BURKE TO O'HARA, December 31, 1770

My dear Sir,

My long arrear of correspondence I must throw upon your
mercy. You have been an indulgent creditor, just as you are
kind and friendly in every other respect. Our first scene of
this third act of our seven years piece is concluded;[8] our fiddles
are playing, and we are here snug in the green room, to prepare

---

[4] John Glynn (1722-1779), member for Middlesex and partisan of Wilkes,
moved on Dec. 6 "that a committee should be appointed to enquire into the
administration of criminal justice, and the proceedings of the judges in Westminster Hall, particularly in cases relating to the liberty of the Press, and the
constitutional power and duty of juries."—*Cavendish's debates* 2: 126.

[5] Richard Oliver, a London alderman and friend of Wilkes.

[6] Sir Joseph Mawbey, Bart. (d. 1798) desired an inquiry into the conduct
of Sir Sidney Stafford Smythe, who had reduced a charge from murder to man-
slaughter after a jury had returned a verdict of guilty in a trial at Guilford.

[7] Burke had refused to criticize the courts, saying he had "the best opinion"
of them and denying that Mansfield had introduced "new doctrines" into the
law; but he believed that indiscreet and indiscriminate prosecutions for libel
had raised a serious situation which justified Glynn's motion.—*Cavendish's
debates* 2: 135-138. See also Burke's speech of Nov. 27, in which he denounced
Junius's libel upon the King and declared: "Libels have conquered the law.
The liberty of the press runs into licentiousness; and that licentiousness is too
strong for the Government."—*Ibid.*, 105-119.

[8] Parliament had risen for the Christmas recess on Dec. 21.

ourselves by a little leisure, laughing, and chat, to walk out
again with grave faces and solemn speeches upon the old stage.
Here we have your Charles, Dyer,[9] Dodwell, and Amy Burke,
and we pass our Christmas as like our ancestors as possible; not
indeed with quite so much jollity; but with that oblivion of
the past, and that blindness to the future, which to some persons, in some situations, must stand in the place of philosophy.
Are you preparing to meet again, in order to submit after the
stripes you have received, as Irishmen and men of spirit ought
to do?[10] Are you going to mob your merry Lord Lieutenant
and his melancholy country; and amidst broken banks, ruined
credit, stagnated circulation, declining trade, and decaying
revenues, to provide largely for the honour and security of your
portion of the British Empire, in the military peace which we
are likely to have (for any thing I can see to the contrary) for
years to come? I really think the circumstances you meet in
are very whimsical, without being at all over pleasant. As to
us, it is not easy to conceive into what a total indifference we
are sunk; and in this twilight condition, neither peace nor war,
we desire no glimmering of light; have neither hope nor fear;
neither wish peace nor apprehend war; but go on just as we are
bid, just as if all that was transacted belonged totally to another
people, and that we had no kind of interest in it.[11] This strange
insensibility has not only benumbed the House; but it has
stupified the nation too; and that in so extreme a degree, that
nobody I dare say remembers anything like it; nor has history
recorded a parallel case; every nation in the world, I believe,
and in every period of time being full of eagerness and movement, and agitated with an infinite variety of speculations, on
the approach or threatening of wars of much less consequence
than this. Lord Weymouth resigned the other day. Whatever
the true motive may have been, a difference in Council relative
to the present measures, and an avoidance of responsibility
upon them, has been assigned as the reason. This, one would
think, ought to have alarmed. Sandwich takes the seals; and
in three days a word is not spoken about it.[12] This I only

---

[9] Samuel Dyer (1725-1772), a man of letters.

[10] The Irish Parliament was opened on Feb. 26, 1771.

[11] The danger of war was receding; negotiations, begun at Madrid, were
concluded at London on Jan. 22. Spain restored Port Egmont to the British.

[12] Weymouth, the southern Secretary, had urged a bolder policy than his
colleagues were willing to approve. Sandwich, a month later, gave way to Halifax, and became first lord of the Admiralty.

mention to give you some taste of the general unconcern of the public; they will continue in it until they feel some blow. We ended with a silly dispute, at least attempted on the part of the minority, with the Lords; they behaved, for the *manner,* as if they had been quite frantic; but the design was politic enough—to clear both the houses at once, and to reconcile it to the people, by showing that no regard was shown to the members of either.[13] Our push for angry votes against the Lords had at least this good consequence, that we shamed the majority of our house from shutting out their constituents, upon the principle of a pretended retaliation on the Peers, when we could be persuaded to take no other step in vindication of our dignity. We have again opened the gallery. This is rather good for us; though to tell you the truth, for my own part, I would rather trust to the prejudiced narrative of the majority for what I say, than give an opportunity to the newspapers to publish such monstrous things as they do, for speeches of mine, which must if they are credited, give people without doors a most contemptible opinion of me. I never read any thing so abominable. G[eorge] Onslow speaks better and far more sensibly; what is most vexatious, when they are nearest to what I said, it is the worst; for when they write what they think fit, they don't mistake their own meaning; but I never knew them in one instance, when they remembered any thing of mine, that they did not totally misconceive the drift of it, and render it utterly ridiculous. You will excuse me for dwelling thus long on such a subject. I am really vexed at it. My friends have been of opinion, that I did not disgrace myself this session, but there is not a part of the world in which I must not, on these speeches, pass for one of the foolishest fellows in the House. My dear friend, I do not write to inform you of any thing; I have no news. Lord Rockingham is at Bath

---

[13] The standing order of the House of Lords that strangers must be excluded on the demand of any peer was invoked by Lord Gower on Dec. 10 during a speech by the Duke of Manchester, an opposition lord, on the defenses at Gibraltar. Visiting commoners were rudely turned out. Whereupon George Onslow, a Treasury placeman, moved in the Commons to retaliate upon the Lords by moving the exclusion of strangers. His motion was directed less against the peers as a body than against certain opposition lords who had gone out from their own house in protest against its conduct and were present as spectators in the House of Commons. Burke opposed Onslow's motion as "a part of a plan to make the two houses strangers to one another, and the people strangers to both." The house deliberated for four days upon modes of retaliation upon the peers, but approved none of them.—*Cavendish's debates* 2: 148-172.

on account of Lady R's illness which has been very dangerous. How like you the conduct of Lord G[eorge] Germain? It has quite set him up.[14] All here are yours. Dodwell desires me to tell you, that he is *after enquiring* for you. Adieu, my dear friend, believe me unalterably yours.

December 31. 1770. Last day of the year; how will the next decade end, or where shall we be?

[There are no extant pieces of the Burke end of the correspondence until the latter part of March. But two letters from O'Hara, in the meanwhile, tell something of the Irish scene, where Lord Townshend opened the Parliament on February 26 and completed his rout of the opposition, with the cynical but interested support of O'Hara.]

O'Hara to Burke, February 17, 1771

Dublin   Clare street   17 February

My dear Edmund,

I have often designed to write to you of late, but changing houses has been attended with some trouble. Our political system [is] too unsettled for description; and some disorders in my own private affairs, have also kept my mind unsettled. But for this last, writing to you would be my surest remedy. We are to meet for the dispatch of business on the 26th and yet we are told that there is no business to do; that Government has nothing to ask; that we are only called together to revive temporary statutes near expiring; and to include among these the Revenue act, if it can be brought about. The first *parole* given was, that in case of an overpowering opposition we were to be dissolved. This however was found to cut both ways. The ignominy of the condition revolted many; and the electors began to hope for a new election, and consequently to favour such points as might occasion a dissolution. This therefore has been recalled. As far as I can judge of the opposition, they will be moderate, and more likely for that reason to gain a little ground upon old Poynings. Violence might alarm, and revive us from that langour, which at present favours

---

[14] Lord George [Sackville] Germain fought a duel with George Johnstone in Hyde Park on Dec. 18; his cool courage and honorable conduct did much to wipe away the disgrace of his court martial in 1760.

them. Our Chief Governor has played a game too long, which for a short period seldom fails of good success. Holding out things, for a time, creates a following, but as expectation agitates, so it tires, and is for the most part succeeded by languor. Upon the whole, I think we shall rub through. Some little majority we have, and I hope we shall make a proper use of it. But the political state of this country changes fast, as some others do; but tho' the purpose be the same in all, yet the means should be different. In old times country gentlemen came to town, and eat and drank with George Stone, old Shannon, and Ponsonby. They drank success to the Administration for the time being; and they voted as they drank. These are laid aside for the present, in order to break the large following of two or three people; and Government plies at present with smaller craft.

Upon hearing by the last pacquet of the division on the clause in the Nullum Tempus bill, I comforted myself that a good cause would still triumph amongst you.[15] But the account just arrived of the division on the address upon the convention, staggers me.[16]

I have just received a letter from Charles, by which I find he was in London on the 15th. I hoped he was in his road to Ireland where I want him for a little time. I should guess he had not received either of the two last letters I wrote to him; but I suppose he since has, and therefore is not up in London. The letters were directed under cover to you and Will. If he has not received them, I beg you'll write him a note to say that I want him here, at this time, and that he should come immediately. Will told me in his last letter that Richard was well abroad, and that his going might be attended with good consequences. I should be glad to hear this repeated.

Ireland begins to recover, but slowly. Government feels the decay of trade, in the diminution of the revenue. By the first part of my letter, you see I am not an opposition member; and yet I really do not conceive how we can go on. The papers

---

[15] Sir William Meredith on Feb. 11 moved for leave to bring in a bill to modify the Nullum Tempus Act of 1769, in order to facilitate the Duke of Portland's defense against the claims of Sir James Lowther. Leave was given by 152 to 123, although later the bill was thrown out.

[16] The House of Commons on Feb. 13 approved overwhelmingly an address of thanks for the convention with Spain ending the Falkland Islands dispute.

say the Duke of Richmond has refused us. Lord Suffolk, I hear, certainly did.[17] Such is the contempt we are fallen into, that not one of our chiefs, and but the lowest of the puisne judges can be prevailed on to go circuit. Even most of the lawyers amongst the King's Council have refused. For in these hard times, many have been decorated with silk gowns, who, in quiet, would hardly ever have got a fee. Yet Ridge has not yet got this feather. Your friend the Knight [18] tells me he is frightened about Dennis, who gave up a living to accommodate Government but has not himself been accommodated with another. The Knight has neither the confidence nor the influence, which formerly belonged to his office, and tells me he is determined to leave us, as soon as this session is over. Should this happen, my guess is, we shan't have another while our present Chief Governor remains.

Now my dear Edmund, I leave you to something of more moment. Assure Mrs. Burke of my sincere regard; and I congratulate Dick with all my heart on a black eye. Adieu.

O'HARA TO BURKE, March 11, 1771

Dublin 11 March 1771

My dear Edmund,

Last packet brought me a letter from you, and another from Will, and I long for a third, to tell me that my old friend the Doctor is quite recovered.[19] On the other hand, I long as much to be able to tell you that I have got the money for you on Loyd's mortgage. Ridge has been about among the moneyed people. He has offered himself, Charles, and me security along with the mortgage. In any other time it would raise much more. But here it has not yet had any effect. We are in a sad way; but will work hard, and the sum is not large. James Fortescue asked me today if I could give him a week's credit for twenty guineas. He told me he had sent to all the banks, and to all the moneyed people for £100, and could not get it. Yet this man has unquestionable securities by him for sixty

---

[17] Henry Howard, twelfth Earl of Suffolk; with the death of George Grenville in Dec., 1770, he moved toward the court, and became a secretary of state in June, 1771.

[18] Sir George Macartney.

[19] These letters have not been found.

thousand pounds, and 4 or 5000£ a year at his own disposal. Our politics here are in a strange state and much unexpected. Government with large engagements, and great application had got a majority of twenty-five. Yet we were not able in a week to carry even the address to the King. The anxiety of mind was too much for Mr. Ponsonby. He sunk under it and Lord Betty,[20] to procure him ease, seized the opportunity of prevailing upon him to resign. He did, by a strange letter, without notice to any of his confederates.[21] Pery succeeds, upon promises to be a good boy. The opposition has dispersed, and left an open field to Government. This will in time introduce the system of our eldest sister; little men will be brought in to obey implicitly, and country gentlemen will form a corps of opposition. But places will be created, and those which have left us be brought back. Ponsonby has had a strange fall. A fortnight before our meeting he refused monstrous offers. I now think that all parts of the British Empire have conformed; and Administration has gained in this reign, what I used to think no ministers would dare to think of, and must remain so, till people are roused by some external blow. Sad remedy! The cure will be hardly worth it.

Charles stays here to be called to the bar, and will then return. He has not much application, except to works of taste. I have just got over a Norfolk farmer; when I sent for him I had no hopes of seeing you soon; you remember the only condition upon which I proposed to return. But as I may possibly be called over upon my son William's account, I have given him up to Mr. Ponsonby.[22] I shall write soon to Will. In the meantime assure Mrs. Burke of my most sincere regard, and believe me truly yours,

C. OH.

---

[20] Townshend.

[21] The Commons voted an address which thanked the King for continuing Lord Townshend in his government. Ponsonby wrote a spirited letter to the House, stating that as the Lord lieutenant had passed a censure upon the Commons at the end of the previous session he could not convey such a message to him lest this imply a relinquishment of the point for which the House had then contended. He requested his colleagues to elect another speaker. Ponsonby had been Speaker since 1756; his resignation and the election of Edmund Sexton Pery signalized the decisive triumph of Townshend over the pre-Octennial oligarchy.

[22] O'Hara's son-in-law.

[Burke's next extant letter to O'Hara was written in haste at a moment of great public excitement in London. During February and March the House of Commons opened a prosecution of certain London printers for publishing parliamentary speeches, in violation of a 1728 resolution prohibiting such publication. The prosecution had been provoked by numerous libellous distortions and misrepresentations. The magistrates of London, instigated by Wilkes who was now an alderman, obstructed the arrest of the printers; as a result, Brass Crosby, the Lord Mayor, and Alderman Richard Oliver, both members of Parliament, were on March 27 committed to the Tower for breach of parliamentary privilege.]

BURKE TO O'HARA, March 28, 1771

Thursday evening. March 28. 1771

My dear friend,

I have a deal to say to you, which I *reserve* for an hour's leisure at *my* Curragh solitude, to which I go with a full appetite tomorrow. We have had heavy, heavy work; Carlton House has kicked up one of its annual disturbances, in order to render the Ministry odious to the public, and subservient to themselves.[23] Our City people have played their part with a vengeance in the work; and it has required our utmost address to manage matters so, as not to abandon privilege, or to have it abased to an engine of tyranny; an abuse of which it is always susceptible, and now above all other times. The Lord Mayor is in the Tower; the City united and inflamed; the Ministry have got a ballotted Committee to sit during the holidays.[24] But of this a little more at large hereafter. Your proceedings strange! Your old Speaker! Your new Speaker! Pery made Speaker by the Court, acknowledging it; his throne erected on Poynings law! Strange things indeed! Ponsonby's resignation was I take it for granted foolish. But it is the universal opinion here that the letter was full of propriety and dignity. I shall answer your question of order as soon as I can. A thousand thanks for your friendly solicitude and attention about the money. Ridge has all my powers. I wish that you would drive the business of the assessment of the

---

[23] Carlton House was the residence of the King's mother; Burke regarded this establishment as the center of a powerful hidden influence.

[24] To consider the resistance to the orders of the House, and the means for overcoming it.

mortgage forward as fast as you can. It will give me material aid at present. You tell me nothing of your board; and I am uneasy about it. It is now late; I am come from the Thatched House.[25] Lady Rockingham is somewhat better; your old friend marvellously recovered.[26] I really had almost lost hopes; but he is, thank God, got through surprisingly. Adieu for a day or two. God bless you. My hasty love to Charles.

> Yours ever,
>
>   Edm. Burke

Mrs. Burke, Dyer, Will, and King with the boy are gone down before me.

[Four days later, while at Beaconsfield for the Easter recess, Burke sent O'Hara a fairly full account of the more important proceedings of the session.]

BURKE TO O'HARA, April 2, 1771

My dear friend,

I never found a little retirement more convenient or more comfortable to me. We have had a good deal of business; but it was a business ten times more tiresome from its kind, than its quantity. It is exceedingly disgustful to be obliged to act a part in affairs that are not commenced, nor can possibly be concluded, upon any ideas of your own, or of those in whom you have any confidence. The late proceedings against the City Magistrates has produced some heat. It is indeed a ferment too considerable to be overlooked, much less to be stirred up, by a wise government. The appearance of inflammation is however far greater than the reality. The people of the City have habituated themselves to *play* with violent measures. The most extraordinary proceedings on their part rather serve to show their petulance and indignation, than any solid or determined hostility to the Court. A Mayor of London sent to the Tower in his year of office, would at any other time have been a very dangerous symptom. It is now no indifferent one; but not what it would have been formerly. The Ministers bring on such things they know not how; being propelled

---

[25] A tavern in St. James street, much frequented by opposition members.
[26] Dr. Nugent.

forward by powers that they neither see nor understand. Lord
North has hardly the *vis inertia* to characterise him in the
series of agents; so far is he from approaching to any thing
like freedom of will or action. But a little ambition, much
want, few choices to make, and no opinions, keep him where
he is, as long as the disposers of the drama think proper; and
that will be longer than is generally imagined. If Lord North
is held to them by his necessities, necessities, though of another
kind, oblige the Court to cling to him. Lord Gower I know
flatters himself with a speedy succession to his office; but I can
hardly persuade myself that the King's friends wish it; and
I doubt much whether the Bedfords are more desirous of that
change; though their indifference to Lord North, and the
languid part they have taken during the whole session are very
remarkable. That set is no longer powerful; except that they
derive some relative importance from the insignificance of
Lord North and the other parts of the exterior Government.
Such was the apparent condition of Administration when the
two Onslows officiously brought two printers before the House
for a breach of privilege in printing speeches.[27] They were
much surprised to find an opposition to what they imagined
would have passed as a thing of course. However, the opposition within doors was of little consequence, compared to that
which was prepared for them in the City; where Wilkes and
that set of people were resolved to take the first opportunity
of falling out with the House of Commons. The printers were
encouraged to disobey our orders. The Ministers perceived
that they were brought into difficulties. The Onslows were
frighted out of their little wits, and severely reprimanded by
Lord North. It seemed resolved to continue the proclamation
but for a short time; and to let the affair and the session expire
together. This I know was their resolution. But to my utter
amazement when I thought that their hands were as full as
they could hold of the first business, and that they appeared

---

[27] Col. George Onslow had started parliamentary action against the printers
by carrying a resolution, Feb. 8, ordering two of them to appear at the bar of
the House. He was strongly supported by Mr. George Onslow, a Treasury lord.
Burke opposed on prudential grounds, saying: "It is impossible the liberty of
the press can exist, without the probability of its falling into licentiousness;
but, there is a corrective. If any thing having a libellous tendency should appear, do not make war against all publication of your proceedings; fix your
hand upon the particular libel." For the debate, see *Cavendish's debates* **2:**
257-260.

to have seen and to have shrunk from the danger, of a sudden
the Onslows appeared again on the stage, and moved for the
attendance of no less than six printers more. The former proceeding was ill attended, and apparently disgustful to every
body. The majority went into it, not from liking, but as not
knowing how to get rid of a complaint of breach of privilege.
But the second exhibition was attended in quite another
manner. Some members proposed to harrass them out with
questions of adjournment on every printer as he was ordered
to attend as well with divisions on every question and in every
stage of the business. This produced no less than 23 divisions
in one night.[28] Had the business been of any other than of
such a trifling, importunate, and yet insidious nature, this
method would have been uncandid, and indeed almost in all
respects intolerable. It brought out the secret of the whole
proceeding. Stuart Mackenzie, Ellis, Dyson, Jenkinson, Martin,[29] Elliot, Stanley, Lord Strange,[30] (I am not sure) Rice; [31]
all the King's friends, and most of the office men attended
through the whole of so vexatious and tiresome a controversy;
though the minority was not sometimes above 7 or eight; and
never above thirty had attended from the beginning of the
day. The House sat till near five. They were not much earlier
up on the second day, when the printers appeared; for these
printers, to diversify the scene, did appear. Partly from some
information I have had, much more from circumstances that
cannot lie, I am satisfied that the Cabal, when they found that
the printers' business was likely to be very troublesome to the
Ministers, and likely to carry the City leaders to extremities,
hurried it on with vehemence in order to make the House of
Commons an instrument for humbling the City; being frustrate
of their purpose at the time of the remonstrance, by the
timidity of the Ministers and the critical situation of the time.
I have dwelt longer perhaps than I ought on this business

---

[28] March 12-13. The next day the business was resumed and there were
thirteen more divisions before the Onslow motion was approved. Burke took
a leading part, strongly defending publication of parliamentary debates and the
unusual tactics of the opposition. Prosecution of printers was so discredited
that they were let off with a slight reprimand.—*Ibid.*, 377-400.

[29] Samuel Martin was Treasurer to the Dowager Princess.

[30] James Smith Stanley, Lord Strange (1717-1771), was Chancellor of the
Duchy of Lancaster.

[31] George Rice, Treasurer of the Chambers and a lord commissioner of
trade.

The newspapers, with a tolerable accuracy, have given a detail of the proceedings; I thought it necessary to say something of the spirit of them. As to our party, weighing as well as we could the circumstances; difficulties on both sides; enemies before and behind; a corps conscientious, and therefore a little timid, we have acted as well as could be expected. Lord R[ockingham] thought it right, (and sure on the whole it was right) to pay a visit to the Tower.[32] He is in perfect health; but not quite so active as usual, on account of Lady Rockingham's indisposition, which is tedious, distressing, and every now and then not without danger. I am sorry to tell you that the opposition is as much divided and deranged as the Ministry; and nothing can be in a more distracted state than they stand at present. Lord Chatham from the beginning of the session has been playing fast and loose; on the Jury Bill he and his friends thought proper to show themselves in a sort of systematic hostility. Charles has I dare say, given you a full account of a transaction, vexatious, though not unexpected by us; disgraceful to opposition, and matter of no small triumph to the courtiers; who saw (I believe a thing without parallel) the whole debate, a hot and a long one, carried on as if they were in the boxes of the opera.[33] Since that time we have held no conversation with Lord Chatham. We have had no declaration of enmity either. But the matter rests in a kind of sullen discontent on both sides. It would have, I dare say, broken out into something of more éclat by this, if we had not been hurried into action by other events, which have covered our mutual jealousy from the public. However it does not require a great deal of attention or sagacity to discover their perpetual

---

[32] A public demonstration of disapproval of the arrest of the London magistrates. Rockingham was accompanied by the Duke of Manchester, Earl Fitzwilliam, the Duke of Portland, Dowdeswell, Sir Charles Saunders, Admiral Keppel, Burke, Sir William Baker and Joseph Martin.—Albemarle, *Memoirs of the Marquess of Rockingham* 2: 208-209, London, Richard Bentley, 1852.

[33] Dowdeswell on March 7 moved for leave to bring in a bill to settle the disputed question of the rights of juries in libel cases. A Rockingham party proposal, the bill would have made juries "competent to all intents and purposes, in law and in right, to try every part of the matter laid or charged in said indictment or information." The Chatham-Shelburne corps opposed the bill as being unnecessary and favored a declaratory act affirming that juries had ever had the right which the Dowdeswell bill would give them; this faction appeared more desirous of vindicating the legal opinion of Lord Camden against that of Mansfield, than of determining the point at issue. Dowdeswell's effort was met by a motion to adjourn that was carried by 218 to 72.—*Cavendish's debates* 2: 353-377. Burke's speech on this bill is given in *Works* 10: 109-128.

492   BURKE AND O'HARA

endeavour to disconcert or disgrace us, even where it is most our common interest to act together. I could tell you many little anecdotes of the Chatham pride and policy, and of the Shelburne cunning, that would be truly entertaining. Add to this that from the beginning of the session, Meredith has quitted our party, and forms, with Phipps, a little light squadron of his own.[34] Your Pery seems to me the person whom he most resembles in his present style of acting. All these things render us, Ministers and opposition, perhaps the most discordant and perplexed system that ever existed. As to your proceedings in Ireland, I begin to feel every day less and less any interest in them; I thank God it is so; for otherwise, I should have uneasiness on what side soever I looked. For God's sake, has your Lord Lieutenant done any thing about the board; or has he quite abandoned the idea of it? [35]

I wish, if Ridge be not returned, that you would write to him about that mortgage. I am infinitely obliged to you for your trouble. You know how necessary that trouble is, especially at this time.

All here are well and as usual yours. The Doctor is well too. Remember us to Charles. My dear friend adieu.

Beaconsfield April 2. 1771

O'HARA TO BURKE, July 11, 1771

Nymphsfield near Boyle   11th of July 1771

My dear Edmund,

Our correspondence, on my part at least, has suffered an unusual interruption. *Pour vous dire la verité, mon esprit ne possedoit pas son assiette.* I had much business, and of a disagreeable kind: which it always is, when its object is to settle a perplexed state of money matters. Parliament with all its doings was unpleasant to me. Part of its proceedings I did not like, nor even the intrigues for my job, which accompanied it. To deal with the caprice, rather than the principle of man, is unpleasant; and yet, one never cares to lose one's ground.

---

[34] Capt. Constantine Phipps, R. N. (d. 1792) made the motion to adjourn which disposed of the Dowdeswell bill, and was supported by Meredith, who had for more than five years acted with Rockingham's friends. Soon afterwards, Meredith accepted office and became a supporter of Lord North.

[35] The projected Board of Accounts.

Of your situation I had nothing, till lately, to say, which I liked. And to write to you, without touching upon your situation, or my own, would have been a difficult undertaking. Charles tells me a piece of news, for the papers told another story, which I rejoice at. I mean the American agency which you have accepted of. It is a mark of the approbation of a people, and therefore more welcome than any favour from a single man. It leaves you free to your own pursuits, both in politics and farming. The first indeed I have long despaired of; the last must do well, as everything will do, when the whole is left entirely to yourself. I have no doubt of your being, at this time, the best farmer in England. I shall find no great difficulty in being the first here. But in order to compass it, I must part with every man whom I employed in it formerly. I find the mixed arrangements somewhere chosen for greater objects will not do for a farmer. Is it possible that what the papers impute to Malagrida should be true? I recollect some things which lead to that opinion, but yet it makes him so extraordinary a character that I can't thoroughly assent to it on news paper authority. I have laughed, tho' alone, at Wilkes being chosen sheriff. 'Tis a most ridiculous event, but a severe blow to a certain system.[36] 'Tis however established in every part of the British dominions. Ireland is ready to receive it, and much is done towards it. Residence alone was always sufficient to do the business, as far as 'tis done. But to substitute another arrangement, requires a regular cast of mind. Such is, and long has been, in agitation. 'Tis the work of Lord Townshend singly, without consultation or the advice of any man in Ireland. It is also without opposition from any man that approaches him, except the Chancellor.[37] His turn is to disapprove of every thing proposed, and I believe to raise as many difficulties as he can; not here only, but by his letters to England. What it proceeds from—natural perverseness, a desire of being the confidential Minister of this country, or the old leaven of his Chatham and Camden connection, I can't say,

---

[36] Wilkes had become estranged from some of his allies, who were patronized by Shelburne. The rival forces clashed in the shrievalty election in London in June, 1771, but Wilkes and his colleague, Frederick Bull, were elected.— Bleackley, Horace, *Life of John Wilkes*, 256-266, London, John Lane, 1917. It was Wilkes who, some years before, had given to Shelburne the sobriquet of Malagrida, from the Portuguese Jesuit of that name.

[37] James Hewitt was still lord chancellor.

but the fact is so. Lord Townshend protracts, from perplexity, and when he calls for help, where in the nature of things he should find it, meets with opposition and new embarrassment. Happy for him neither the Attorney [General] nor the Prime Serjeant love the Chancellor. And their superiority in business and in law bears heavy on him: and chagrin him so much in removing one difficulty, that they leave him in humour to raise a hundred others when they are not by, which is always the case. 'Tis absolute necessity occasions their being sent for. Your friend the Knight has not the least influence. There has been a strong jealousy of him; not of his abilities, but his connexion. So far did it go, that he was disposed to leave him, and communicated his intention to his wife's father.[38] Mark the event, it shows much of the character of the man. He wrote a letter to Lord Townshend about some trifling matters, a pair of colours or leave of absence for some ensign. The implication was obvious: "I should not trouble you, if my son-in-law had any share of that influence which belongs to his office." He [Townshend] came directly to see Lady Jane, told her of the letter, called upon the Knight, was unusually cordial. In two days he [Macartney] put on the mask of Minister, grew mysterious, and talked of staying. But this is confidential: for the letter is denied. He always enquires about you with affection. While he was absolutely unministered I was much in his confidence. He found me a safe repository; his manner is engaging, and I liked his society; for in that situation, candour was his interest. How it will be when I return to town, I know not; for tho' I was there on the day of the letter, I saw him not afterwards; its effect I had from Hutch.

'Tis an odd thing that I should owe Will a letter, but so it is, and a letter which gave me great pleasure, as it informed me that he had settled his Dutch transaction.[39] Present my love to him.

What I have said of the Chancellor and Lord T[ownshend] involves my particular case. All the difficulties the first had raised were obviated when I left town. What has occurred since, I know not. 'Tis hard upon me, not to be able to say when I shall see you. I must wait for some determination of this business. You know my regard for Mrs. Burke and the Doctor,— say for me what I ought to say. And believe me most truly yours.

[38] That is, Macartney communicated to Lord Bute.
[39] The letter is missing.

XIV. Politicians as Farmers

[The summer of 1771 found Burke disgusted with politics, but full of ideas about turnip husbandry and zeal to instruct O'Hara in the arts of farming.]

BURKE TO O'HARA, August 1, 1771

1 August 1771

My dear friend,

I was censuring myself for my silence and preparing amendment, when I received your letter. I am heartily mortified, but not in the least degree surprised at your disappointment, between a puzzling Chancellor and a giddy Viceroy. God send you well through your difficulties; when ours are to end God knows; we must depend on Him, and wait His will with patience.

I am just returned from a little tour into Sussex. I went down with very worthy men and agreeable companions, Sir Charles Saunders and Admiral Keppel. We stayed a week at the Duke of Richmond's, where, long as I have known his Grace, I had still more reason to esteem the integrity and goodness of his heart. His brother has got into difficulties by being too like himself, very full of rectitude, zealous against abuses, a little teazing in his disposition, and of little management with the world. The officers commanding in the several garrisons and posts in Minorca had been in the practice of compelling the soldiery to buy their wine of them, which they sold at an exorbitant profit. Lord G[eorge Lennox] [1] remonstrated against this, and got engaged in a quarrel with the Governor (that worthy man Jack Mostyn). [2] The Governor after some correspondence insolently told him he desired to hear no more from him, Lord G., upon the subject, on which Lord G. freely, but naturally and excusably replied, that if his duty had not compelled him he never would have had, nor

---

[1] Lord George Lennox (1737-1805), fourth son of the second Duke of Richmond, was a brigadier general and a member of Parliament; he had been aide-de-camp to the Duke of Cumberland.

[2] John Mostyn (1710-1779), a favorite of George III, had been made Governor of Minorca in 1768.

did he wish to have, any correspondence with him. This letter
Mostyn highly resented. Some friends interposed, and prevailed on Lord George to write a letter to the Governor in
which he disclaims any intention of behaving disrespectfully
to any person the King appointed to command in that Island.
As this letter conveyed no personal compliment to the Governor
but went solely to the office, Mostyn affected to consider it as
an aggravation of the first offence, and appointed a court
martial instituted as improperly as possible, to try Lord George
for his disrespect to a superior officer, though it was contained
only in a private letter drawn on by the General's own most
improper letter, and did not seem either in substance or manner in the nature of a military offence destructive of subordination, which can be the only ground for bringing such matters
before a court martial. The court confining itself to the letter,
and without calling for the rest of the correspondence, pass
sentence on Lord G. that he should write an apologetic letter
confessing his fault, which should be afterwards published in
orders. The sentence was changed here to a verbal apology,
without any notice in orders. However the Duke of R[ichmond]
thinks that his brother is not only blameless but meritorious;
that he ought not to submit to the sentence, but rather to resign
his regiment, and that he will take care that he shall not be a
loser by that resignation. The Duke's letter is handsome and
full of spirit. His military friends however think differently
from his Grace and are of opinion, that as the sentence is now
altered, Lord George may submit to it without the least deroga-
tion from his honour. The matter is now before Lord G. for
his determination.[3] I think they will at length drive every man
of character out of all service civil and military. What say you
to Wilkes's triumph over the Court and his own revolted officers
in conjunction? I confess I am ready to do justice to the good
management of the courtiers in this instance, though they have
failed in their attempt. The treacherous patriots of the
Malagrida faction, in order to receive the same justice, must,
along with their failure, be charged with the most ridiculously
perfect mixture of folly and knavery that can be conceived.
They thought that they had some popularity of their own; and
having fought successfully for Wilkes, they flattered themselves
that they could defeat the general under whose auspices they

---

[3] He did not resign, but became a major-general in 1772.

had conquered heretofore. They fought however only the battle of the Court. The Court managed their dissension with good policy. They put up the two senior alderman, as if they rather stood for the regularity of succession and the rights of office, than for any party object.[4] They came in just at the nick when every body in Mercutio's style were ready to cry "curse on both your houses," and they managed their time, so well chosen, in so proper a manner that they showed they had at least a powerful if not a victorious party in the City. In effect the contest was between them and Wilkes; the Shelburne people had no share except in the shame.[5] If Robinson's letter, as the Devil seldom fails of tricking those he loves best, had not unluckily for them been misdirected, and the cloven foot appeared too soon, I think they might have carried their points; and Wilkes, there defeated, would have sunk forever.[6] Our few but steady friends in the City acted a prudent resolute part. The Sheriffs Martin and Baker, who you know are of our corps, and as worthy men as any in the world, conducted themselves so as to keep up the credit of their connection at the height; and playing no sort of trick themselves, they escaped not only unhurt but much benefitted by all the tricks that had been attempted on them, both by the true courtiers, and the false patriots.[7] These small games of politics amuse us a little in this entire stagnation of the greater. The country is dead. No spirit of any kind remains; and for the present to take any offensive steps against the Court would be rather to serve than to hurt them. You compliment me on my farming. It comes a little unluckily in a year when I think I fail more than usual. Hay is next to nothing. All wheat sewed late, and on a clover lay, has been bad all over this county. The spring crops are pretty good; I do think I know pretty well what to do; but to make an effectual farmer something else is requisite besides skill and diligence. Of this I can assure you. As to your idea of changing your people on your farm, I say, if they are materially dishonest you are much in the right; if not you are better [to] retain your present unskilful managers, and by a little

---

[4] Aldermen Plumb and Kirkman.

[5] Shelburne backed Richard Oliver, who ran a poor fifth in the voting.

[6] A letter written June 25 by John Robinson, secretary to Lord North, to a certain Benjamin Smith, urging support of Plumb and Kirkman, miscarried to another Smith, who published it with an affidavit attesting its authenticity.—Woodfall, *Junius* 2: 253.

[7] The Rockinghams were not involved in the contest.

discipline, bring them to your point: this is far preferable to
the introduction of strangers, who are a long time before they
know the true genius of the farm; and when they do, may
possibly do you more mischief by dishonesty and want of attachment than they can serve you by a little more of merely practical
skill. A good gardener would make the best bailiff in all things
that do not regard cattle. They are usually more enlightened
than ordinary husbandmen; they soon attain any thing in the
farming way; and I look upon the introduction of the improved
turnip husbandry to be desperate in any other hands. Now that
I speak of turnip husbandry I must tell you that it is an expensive process; but it is by far the best in every respect; not
flattering yourself however that the turnips *as a crop* will ever
pay you; it is the advantage they bring in cleanness, sweetness,
and plenty of the succeeding crops, for which alone they are
to be valued. To prevent fallows from being entirely unproductive and to encrease the stock of cattle; these are the
desiderata which turnips answer. However, these are for your
consideration in another year. It is now too late. Prepare a
good fallow for them at Michaelmas, and give it two or three
plowings, the more the better; this winter and part of the succeeding summer will put your land in good order for turnips;
when you set seriously about it, I will trouble you with more
upon the subject. For the present God prosper your farming
and politics. We may see better days, but we must be content
with those we have. Things come by fits: now after a long
drought we have a deluge of rain. I do not know whether
the rainy season of our lives be over or not. Adieu, adieu. All
here are yours. The Doctor was with us; he is gone away again.
A slight fit of the gout has been a kind of physician to him.[8]

O'HARA TO BURKE, August 30, 1771

Nymphsfield 30 August 1771

My dear Edmund,

If men in describing their own happiness and pleasure were
to speak from a fair canvass of their lives, they would find
themselves limited to family society, and a few private friendships. All the rest is so mixed with, and turns so much on

---

[8] The gout was believed preventive of worse maladies.

anxious pains, that 'tis hardly to be called happiness, even when successful. And yet such pursuits are right, they are the manly occupations of the human mind. From this preface, I might well proceed to give you the details of Lord T[ownshend]'s budget, which lay before the K[ing] when the last letters came away, having first received Lord North's approbation. There I am, but do not know for what. When I get to town, you shall know the particulars. My reflection there arises from no political disappointment: I apprehend none. As a farmer, indeed I have some, but to these a speculative farmer is always resigned; and mixes with his religious motives a certain portion of vanity, which always tells him he grows wiser, even by his dearest bought experience. I now for instance learn, that I can make my cold barren clay too rich for wheat. Mine lies all flat upon the ground, and a deluge of rain falls upon it. I find that I must not think of natural grass for hay. One can never be certain in this country, but by early mowths. I find that field cabbage won't do here in a wet season. The caterpillar destroys it. I find that fallowing won't make my land rich enough for turnips. Such is the state of this season's experience. I am very wise to be sure; but undone as a farmer. I set my gardener and some of his men to hoe my turnips. They are used to weed them with hand in the garden. But armed with Norfolk hoes, they have torn up two thirds of my crop. They were thin before, and they are really a melancholy sight now. I don't understand why you call turnips an expensive crop. They have always paid me the rent of my land, and the labour. But my ground is so claiy, that I apprehend the carts will do a great mischief in drawing them off. I have hitherto always fed them upon the ground, which Mr. Young does not approve of.[9] I have this season burned a bit of turf bog and set cabbage in the ashes, without any tillage. They will be of enormous size, without hoeing. But the discovery is useless, for no carriage can get to them in winter. I had formerly sowed rye in such ground, so prepared, and had fine crops. We have such a rage for improving bog, that Ireland will want fuel in twenty years. Bog is already valuable in this County. Now that I have got so far into farming, let me ask whether you hear of their running more into stock, than they did a few years ago in England.

---

[9] Arthur Young (1741-1820), the famous agriculturist, traveler, and economist; a friend and correspondent of Burke. For their exchange of letters about this time, see Correspondence 1: 257-265.

The riots in times of supposed scarcity and with-holding the bounty may have occasioned it. But our graziers complain heavily of want of price. There is no demand, but for home consumption. The importation of German yarn into England has also made our poor poorer. Irish yarn brings but one half of what it did two years ago. These two articles make vent very backward.

My papers last night announce something like a change in Ministers, on your side.[10] And my letters from Dublin speak of a total change of men in Ireland. With us, they may do what they please. And England is too rich, and too busy, to attend to any little innovations which creep into their political constitution. Wilkes and the City may divert themselves, but it will go no further. Malagrida's late stroke will not redound much to his honour. But he treats them as they deserve. I rejoice that your friends were out of the scrape. But their situation was delicate. The fair character of your party is now its sole dependence. Opposition is vain, as matters are circumstanced. When a call comes for men of principle and ability, your farm may be less attended to, than it now is. But the occasion of such a call depends more, if I mistake not, upon the enemies of Great Britain than its friends.

When you write next, tell me of old Dick, and young Dick, for Charles who never omits to mention you all, is now out of town. I am glad the Doctor has got the gout. I trust in God we shall meet once more. The next session will keep me in Ireland till Christmas at least. Adieu

C. OH.

BURKE TO O'HARA, September 10, 1771

My dear friend,

I received your letter this day with that satisfaction which I always feel in receiving good accounts of your health, and of your remembrance of this house. Every part of it is interested in your welfare and your regards. I am rejoiced that there is one good thing in a budget which is transmitted from our governors to yours. You see I am pleased, without knowing dis-

---

[10] Only a rumor, probably started by a report that Lord Camden had paid a visit to the Duke of Grafton, who in June had re-entered the ministry as Lord Privy Seal.—Wentworth-Fitzwilliam MSS, Rockingham to Burke, Aug. 30.

tinctly the object, but as things are circumstanced, most anxiously as I wish you the best you can wish to yourself, I would have both yourself and all of us feel a satisfaction in anything that is tolerably decent and gentlemanlike, and anything else I think they will hardly offer, after all that has passed. I hope it will be something that may heal the wounds which the agriculture of the proprietor but too often gives to the estate. Soame Jenyns used to tell a story of the difference between an estate of a thousand a year, received in regular quarterly payments from the salary of an office, and the returns of a landed property of the same nominal value; one tenant bringing an excuse; another a bill for repairs instead of rent, etc. etc., and this contrast he supported with great humour in the stating; and he has shown himself very serious in the ground of it, by a most marked attachment to the said office all his life.[11] I hope you will find a good board a more certain return than a field of turnips. If you find them to pay in the year, I suspect it rises rather from the imperfect manner in which you state your accounts, than from the produce; which cannot be more advantageous to you than to us, and must be very little less expensive in the culture. If your land be as you describe it, universally a stiff clay, you must use admirable husbandry indeed to get good crops of turnips from it; they love a rich, but it must be rather a light and dry soil, in which they resemble the potato. You complain that in hoeing, your people have cut away two thirds of your crop. To be sure; for what else did they hoe? If your turnips came up as they ought to have done, you might very well spare that proportion, and find by an inverse arithmetic that one third is more than two thirds; and this upon much better and sounder principles than our House of Commons proceeded upon in the Middlesex election. I am not sure that sometimes, for the immediate profit of the crop, a field of turnips unhoed may not be nearly as valuable as one well hoed; but there is an end or very nearly so of the advantage. The sheep feed on the field is something; but far from being the greatest benefit. Possibly Young may be right in his opinion of the preferance of turnips drawn and consumed in the barnyard. Where there is a vast quantity of straw, and a great attention to the making of dung, perhaps the home consumption may be best. Where this is not the case, the

---

[11] Soame Jenyns (1704-1787) had sat on the Board of Trade since 1753.

feed in the field (well divided by hurdles moved as the sheep consume) is infinitely the more profitable practice. You will find it is the barley and clover that ought to follow that crop. That turnips have failed, is a calamity very common at all times. It is the general misfortune of this year. I have three pieces of fallow laid out for that crop. One of eight acres has done pretty well; one of ten is three parts in four destroyed by the fly; one of five is totally destroyed; not a green thing upon it. Though the turnips have been sowed four times, the fly has as often ruined them. This is the grand enemy; and it is impossible to find any way of guarding against his ravages when the season favours him. The same must be said of the caterpillar with regard to cabbages. A crop will now and then be lost in that way. However turnips and cabbages, with all their casualty, and the expence attending them, are really worth the cultivation; but in your stiff cold clay that cultivation will be more difficult; a complete fallow, with five good ploughings and as many harrowings—all this will not be too much for clay; and it must be well dunged into the bargain. You apprehend it was owing to a cultivation and manure overdone, that your wheat is laid. That is impossible. The lodging is accident of the season; but surely the clay you describe can never be too rich for wheat. Clay is the natural soil for wheat; but it must be a clay well ploughed and well dressed. Send for your cabbages into your bog; the *trotters* will be able to get at it, and it is worth man's carriage; by your describing it as so large at present, it will not hold the winter; it will burst and rot; so consume it before the end of next month. Mine are backward; none till the beginning of January; some not till the end of April. I am now busy in building a windmill; I think it will pay its charges. These occupations, if they do not totally banish from my mind, they suspend many cares, sorrows, and anxieties. They are my dearest pleasures; they would be so in a state of the greatest prosperity; and they have something soothing to a mind that is sore, and sick of many griefs. I do not know how, but they bring one nearer, and by a gradual slope down to our natural repose; and our grave is thus gently prepared for us, like one of the trenches into which we throw our grain in the hope of resurrection. All the rest is vanity; some vanities are more sprightly than others; but it is not in our power to make our *choice* of follies; and it is well perhaps that it is out of our power. Politics, one of the worst of them, I almost as completely forgot as if I never had any share in them; and most assuredly if the thing were to do again I never should meddle with them. Either the thing itself is something wrong; or the time is unfavourable; or I am not made for the thing, or for the time. Adieu, my dearest friend. I am well; marvellously so, I thank God. King is gone [on] a marine tour, in the course of which he has met your William, and they have been very happy together. Charles sometimes calls upon us, and he seems not to dislike his father's old friends. I am flattered with the attention of this most excellent young man.

Beaconsfield   September 10. 1771

XV. While Opposition Slept

[The fall and winter of 1771-1772 found Burke and his party in the political doldrums. Opposition to the administration headed by Lord North seemed futile; the Rockingham corps therefore became less active and dwindled in numbers. O'Hara was lodged at last as a placeman: a commissioner of the new Board of Accounts in Ireland. If politics afforded no satisfactions to the Burke family, they were not without cause for rejoicing: Richard Burke returned on furlough to England in October, with prospects for great wealth from the West Indies. He reached Ireland first and O'Hara was able to receive him and give him a letter (October 14) to carry to his brother: "Never was surprise so great or so agreeable as mine at seeing the bearer of this letter, in perfect health. I wish you joy of him. He is the same Dick, the same enthusiast in honour, and consistency; as honest, and as wrong as ever he was in his life. Don't wait for the event, but let me know your opinion of the business which has brought him over."

Richard Burke's "business" was the purchase of a large tract of land from the Red Caribbs on the island of St. Vincent. Governor Melville of Grenada refused to admit the legality of this purchase, and Richard went home to secure his claim through appeal to higher authority. If successful, he expected to realize a large fortune.[1] Unfortunately, no letter from Edmund in response to O'Hara's request for an opinion on this matter has been found.]

BURKE TO O'HARA, November 18, 1771

My dear friend,

I am not now going to write, of my own special grace and mere motion (I wish you had such a letter, from a proper hand, for a proper object) but by order of an old and sincere friend of yours who is just recovered from a dangerous illness; and one of the first things he has done is to direct me to tell you of his recovery, which is going on prosperously. It is your friend Dr. Nugent. He has had a fever which to a younger man, and in other circumstances, would be of no alarming nature; but to the wrong side of seventy, these strokes are always dangerous.

---

[1] Wecter, *op. cit.*, 57-59.

He got it, by rising at night in a sweat to attend his sister Mrs. Augier in her last illness. That poor woman's death while he was himself so ill, was an additional shock which he could ill bear. However, it has pleased God that for this time he has weathered it; and is, I trust, for this turn, out of danger. I do assure you, real good men are scarce. A father, a friend, and a physician in one would be an heavy loss to those who have other things to console them; guess how we must be affected with it! With regard to me, I have only to put you in mind of Macbeth, where towards the end of the play he says, "The Thanes fly from me." Oh! I have such things to tell you, whenever I can do it with leisure and privacy enough—you could scarce believe it, acquainted as you are with the meanness and servility of the world. However, let it keep cold. I cannot *unwrite* what I have said, and I begin to be sorry that I have raised a curiosity that it is not in my power yet to satisfy. But really Will and your humble servant, in the first instance, and the rest of this house in the second, have been much surprised and mortified.[2]

The Cumberland match is too stale a piece of news to entertain you with.[3] Indeed the newspapers had this intelligence, as soon as I had it; and I have heard no circumstance that they did not contain. It is certain that the Court is extremely vexed; and not a little puzzled in what manner they should act. They talk of an act of Parliament to prevent such matches in future. To rescind the present is even in contemplation. This last measure would be full of violence; and if any issue should arise from the marriage would create more disagreeable difficulties than the match itself, supposing it legal, and that it was suffered to proceed to all its consequences. The utmost which could happen is, that the issue (by the female of no very popular subject's family) might sit on the throne of England; and that if any accident should happen to the K[ing] and the Duke of Gloucester, the Duke of Cumberland,

---

[2] Burke was being scurrilously abused by writers in the pay of the government; Lord Mansfield had spoken ill of him; his old friend William Markham, Bishop of Chester, had attacked his character and also that of Richard and William. The most dangerous allegation against him was of being Junius.— *Correspondence* 1: 270-338.

[3] It had become public knowledge that the King's brother, Henry Frederick, Duke of Cumberland (1745-1790), without royal consent had married Anne Luttrell Horton, sister of Col. Henry Lawes Luttrell and daughter of Simon Luttrell, first Baron Irnham, who was reputed to be a dissolute man.

much probably under the influence of Lord Irnham, would preside in the regency. On the other hand supposing, indeed what is not very probable, but what is possible enough, that the question of the right of succession might come on the collateral of the present royal branch? The Duke of G[loucester]'s marriage and issue—how is that to be? Is that marriage too to be annulled? [4] To be annulled, it must be first acknowledged. Here are two violences instead of one; and who can say that in some future time, on the possible failure of the King's children, people may not incline rather to think of rehabilitating the issue of these marriages, than of calling a remoter kindred to the succession—and here may be a most fatal controversy. I really am at a loss what opinion to form on it. With regard to the preventive law, I am much for it; if I did not see infinite, and I should fear unsurmountible difficulties in the manufacture of such a law. It is possible we may hear something of their plan before next session.

I read with surprise of the pompous funeral of Dr. Lucas. By the account one would take it for the funeral of a prince. Was his family in a condition to afford this piece of vanity—or was it a kind of *Caesar's* funeral made by the opposition to keep alive the spirits of the *populace?* What is your Government, if Government at all it be, doing? Their scheme seems to me the destruction of the grants.[5] Never certainly was there more abuse in any practice—but a reformation might, and I think would, unless conducted with care and sobriety, greatly retard the improvement of *your* country—I was going to say *our*—but I have not much more interest in it, than that it furnishes some matter of reproach against me to the Scotch writers in pay of the Ministry, without any one in that country thinking himself concerned in supporting me. It is bad to be loaded with the local prejudices against a country without getting anything by those in favour of it. Tell me some good news of yourself if you can. Adieu, and believe me your very real and affectionate friend.

Beaconsfield Nov. 18. 1771

---

[4] Gloucester, the King's eldest brother, had been for several years secretly married to Maria Walpole, Countess of Waldegrave.

[5] A system, begun in 1753, of granting funds for public works and internal improvement. This now was threatened by an impoverished treasury, a swollen public debt, and an enlarged pension list.

Opposition with us is fast asleep. If that ugly fall that happened to Sir George Savile had been what it was first reported, one might well say that he was dead. What an irreparable loss Lord Rockingham and this nation would have had! The fact is he is much better. I have not yet heard anything of it from Lord R.

[The following letter suggests that O'Hara replied to Burke's letter above, but no reply has been found.]

BURKE TO O'HARA, December 18, 1771

My last left some uneasiness upon your mind. Indeed mine was in no very pleasant state when I wrote that letter. Just now it is impossible to explain the cause of it. When we meet it will furnish ample matter for an evening's conversation. A dead calm has followed all that perturbation. Let your curiosity sleep upon it, as my feelings have done for some days past. The matter is all over. The majority which has been mustered against the Castle was rather beyond my expectation.[6] But the little use which has been made of it, is just what I should have guessed, from the strange state of anarchy into which parties have got upon both sides of the water. Your patriots seem to be frighted with their own victory. The resolution about Dyson's pension was surely too much or too little. If they only meant a slur, they ought to have made quite another sort of resolution; but to vote, that they would not grant a supply for that pension, and then to grant not only the usual supplies, but a large loan into the bargain, was surely a little inconsistent. The point the most censurable in the giving that pension was the breach of promise on the part of Government; a resolution hitting that mark would have been well directed.[7] It seems to be now at random. Parliament on their part have made a resolution which they have contradicted almost in the very breath in which they came to it. They followed it with no resolution of menace to those who should pay it. So that their

[6] Jeremiah Dyson in 1770 had been granted a pension on the Irish establishment of 1,000 pounds a year for his life and the life of his sons. Late in November, 1771, the Irish House of Commons passed a resolution condemning this pension, by a vote of 105 to 93.—*Journal* 15: 150-151, 154.
[7] Lord lieutenant the Earl of Northumberland in 1763 had promised in the king's name that no more pensions of this kind would be granted on the Irish establishment.

resolution will remain on the journals; and Dyson will continue to receive the pension with that incumbrance. However, I ought not to be so ready in censuring a parliamentary measure at this distance from the scene of action. Perhaps they could bring up their troops to face this; and no more. It scarcely ever happens, that leaders can compass the whole of what they intend, even with a sort of majority at their back. Who is this Sir W[illiam] Mayne who does everything in your House? Is it the foolish Scotchman that we knew here? People here suspect, that the Bloomsbury Gang have had some share in raising the disturbance upon your side, in order in the tumble to make room for Lord Weymouth. Be it as it may, I rather think the Court will continue Lord Townshend if Lord Townshend will continue for them. It costs nothing to the people who direct all, to have Government disgraced, provided those who are employed in it are humbled; if I do not greatly mistake, their wish is to see ministers of all sorts subsisting in defiance of public opinion. If it distresses them for a moment, they trust, not unwisely, to the chapter of accidents and the dissension of their enemies for their deliverance; in the meantime their great ruling principle of weakness in all the springs of government, but one, is confirmed and extended. Your simile of the coach going on with the driver in the dirt, is very exact and clever.

The Doctor is here; and desires his love to you. He is gathering up strength very fast. Mrs. Burke wishes you to remember her. William and Richard are in town. Your Charles we expect in the holidays. Are we to hope for your coming in this recess? Ridge talked of coming to us for a few days; but I now almost despair of him. If he should be in town will you be so good to tell him that we are much disappointed in not seeing him; let us at least hear from him. Adieu. We shall remember you in our Christmas compotations.

Beaconsfield December 18. 1771

King, and Richard the lesser, desire their love.

[No letters from either of our correspondents to the other during the next five months have been found, but Burke's appeal to O'Hara to prompt John Ridge to write proved effective. Ridge's letter not only helps to bridge the gap in the principal correspondence, but throws light on Burke's Irish connections and continued efforts to raise money in Ireland.]

RIDGE TO BURKE, January 28, 1772

My dear Burke,

Tho' I have a great deal to say to you, I can't at this time accomplish it. This is but a line about business. I have hopes that Loyd will pay his mortgage money without much delay. He is to be in Town immediately, and intends to raise the money here if he has not already done it in the country. His attorney told me so this day. You know I have not the mortgage deed or other papers relative to that business. I wish you would find some method of sending them to me without loss of time, and a proper letter of attorney to receive the money and to reconvey. There is a young gentleman, Mr. Stacpole, who is a particular friend of mine, whom you may hear of at the Grecian Coffee House; and if he ben't immediately coming to Ireland, he probably knows some body that is, and will (I dare say) be glad to assist you in finding some safe hand to send the deed by. I fear this business of Gifford's will be tedious, and that our demands will be lessened in some particulars (especially Will's) if we shall be obliged to go into a new account, which there is some reason to apprehend. As to Sir Duke's engaging to pay you by installments,—you'll see by the enclosed state of his fortune that he is not able to do it. Nor can any means be found to satisfy your demands but a sale of part of the estate. We long since had a receiver of his rents appointed by order of the court; but the prior family incumbrances must be paid their interest, and the court would allow something decent for the support of Sir Duke and his family; all which together would leave little more than would keep down the interest of the debts for payment of which the bill was originally brought. This being the situation of his fortune, he seems to be at last convinced that it is his interest to cooperate with us, and to push, as well as we, for a sale of a part of the estate for payment of the debts, and in consequence of this we have consented not to put him upon the mercy of the court for a subsistence out of the estate; so long as we find him not only not obstructing our proceedings, but actually aiding us. There have been however some very adverse and cross answers put in to our last amended bill by the children of Sir Duke who are minors, and who set up family settlements against us. But this was before Sir Duke perceived the folly of his own conduct; and we shall I think find land enough unsettled to pay us every shilling. But it is wonderful how these deeds and settlements escaped the attention of your father and brother especially as they were registered. You already know my sentiments about Howard, which I have not yet had any reason to alter. He is very fond of writing letters, and unfortunately he wrote two to me from his house in the country about this suit of Gifford's which tho' I answered in civiller terms than ever I did any other correspondent, he complained of a want of respect to him in my manner of writing. He is an extraordinary scab that takes all the abuse and ridicule which is thrown out against him in newspapers and pamphlets, as high compliment; and my compliments he takes as abuse. What makes him consider the attacks upon him in the public papers as compliments, is because they are printed in the common character. "I know (he says) it is not irony because it is not in italics; assure yourself the writer is quite in earnest. No italics! No italics!" [8] As this is a letter of business, I'll mention it all at once and have done with it for a while. There is a Captain Terry here who has a mind to gavel the estate with your ward, or rather to get some provision, £700 in money and £50 a year during his life, out of it. His terms tho' reasonable, I fear it will be very difficult to come into, as the boy is so young and can't be tied down I believe, even by the act of his guardian, tho' manifestly in this case, for the minor's benefit. Nor on the other hand can the Captain being a Papist alienate his estate or his right without good and valuable consideration in money really paid; nor for any consideration to his nephew who is a Papist. [9] That Neagle who pretends to have some right to your County of Cork interest plagued me here last summer, till out of charity and as from myself, and on a promise that he would never be troublesome again, I gave him a new suit of cloaths, hat, wig, shoes and some money to carry him back again to the County of Cork, but he has lately commenced a correspondence with me; that is, he has wrote to me, but I have not answered him, nor do I mean to do it. There is another disagreeable business which probably, unless your privilege protects you, you will soon receive a subpoena in. You and I are trustees in your

[8] Probably Gorges Edmund Howard (1715-1786), a solicitor and land agent who published legal writings and some tragedies.

[9] The editor is indebted to Mr. Basil O'Connell, Dublin genealogist, for the information that Burke was guardian of John Joseph Therry (1766-1853), the son of his cousin, Elizabeth Nagle. The Captain named above has not been identified.

sister's marriage articles, by which Pat French's father was to settle £2000 in money or farms upon him. After the father died, and I believe when you were last in Ireland, he told me more than once or gave me to understand, that ample value had been given him for the £2000—but as this value consisted principally in leases, and as lands for near three years past have rather decreased in value, or as he does not make that advantageous use of them which others might, he now wants to throw these farms off his hands and to oblige his father's executors to pay him £2000 in specie, which it is not I believe in their power to do without grossly wronging his brothers and sisters. And he is urging me to issue an execution on the judgment confessed by his father as security for the performance of the articles—which if I do, the consequence will be to have a bill filed against you and me, a circumstance not very pleasing to a person of my profession. But this should not weigh with me, were I not pretty well assured that no wrong has been done him. The farms should be estimated at the value they were of, when he first got them, and no casual rise or fall since that time ought to have any effect. However I will look narrowly into the affair and see what is to be done for him,—in the meantime I thought it not amiss to apprise you of it, as it is likely he may write to you about it.

It was my intention to have run over to you at Christmas, and to have been happy for three weeks or a month. But a thousand things prevented me, a thousand tormenting things with which I shan't plague you. This poor woman is recovering; but a perfect recovery I don't expect till the return of the fine season. I am not sure but I will make an effort to see you before the end of February—but shall be glad to hear from Richard, how his business stands, as soon as he conveniently can. Poor Mrs. Augier! I fear her death affected the Doctor too much in spite of his good sense. All your letters I received, and the long and satisfactory one, last August I believe.[10] This fellow here is repenting "that he gave *that rascal Dennis* so much" and the Primate and other prelates are angry with him for wearing a *purple* coat, which it seems they consider as an episcopal colour. Leland is angry at it too.

Adieu. You shall soon have a history from me—

J. R.

28 January 1772

---

[10] None of these letters has been found.

[Two letters from Will Burke to O'Hara and one to Ridge, in February-March, also help to bridge the gap at this time. They provide many glimpses of Edmund's conduct in the parliamentary session of 1772, and carry on the stream of political commentary.]

WILL BURKE TO O'HARA, February 2, 1772

We have had the hardest frost for about three days, followed by great rains and much snow, so that it has made the oddest medley of weather you can conceive; which if you are not very curious about, I can't help it; but our politicians are all agaze, and there is nothing to speak or write about but the weather. Yet in this dearth of matter you would have had a dozen letters from me, if writing and resolving to write had been the same thing.

Richard last night took away your letter of congratulations upon his eating beef at Lincoln's Inn, with an intent to give you a banging, and so to his hands I leave you, only professing that I agree totally with you, that a very and very few years would make him considerable here, if this was his intended scene of action.[11]

The bill that stands in the first instance in Richard's way is so complete with absurdity, that we have even hopes that they cannot pass it; whether when it is defeated he is the nearer to his mark, time must tell. It is however something to remove one obstacle, and I rather feel that the doing so may in itself lead to success. So far it seems out of doubt that they are themselves ashamed of the bill, which was referred to Jackson, as Solicitor to the Board of Trade, before Christmas, and he has not *reported* yet,—a pretty tolerable proof that they are in no hurry for their report.[12]

I hope your Governor will have done you all the good he was capable of in as short a time as he could. We are ourselves,

---

[11] Richard Burke, although thirty-eight, began to prepare himself for a legal career.

[12] An act of the St. Vincent's council annulling all purchases of lands from the natives had been referred to the Board of Trade for consideration on Dec. 10, 1771. Richard Burke filed a caveat against it. Edmund, whose duties as agent for the New York Assembly now carried him often to the Board of Trade, was on very friendly terms with the Secretary and Solicitor, John Pownall and Richard Jackson. This may have been a reason for Will Burke's optimistic hope that the act would be reported for disallowance.—*Journal of the Commissioners for Trade and Plantations from January 1768 to December 1775*, 269, London, H. M. Stat. Office, 1937.

thank God, very well, and so is Charles. Ned is removed to the house Dr. Markham once lived in, near the abbey.[13] It is convenient for the House of Commons, airy in itself and very roomy; Mrs. B[urke] has her two rooms, and Ned his study all upon the one floor. Richard is in lodgings.

I suppose the total silence of all parts of opposition, a thing not heard of even when opposition scarce existed, could not but surprise you. It happened however from no previous concert of parties; ours had among themselves determined to take no part unless the course of things particularly called upon them.

The Speech, one of the silliest and worst wrote that ever was uttered, gave room for everything, if it had been thought proper to look for occasions; but it called for nothing, and we rested mere spectators. Others looked to us to begin, possibly meaning to traverse us whatever line we might take; our silence kept them dumb; no one creature spoke but the mover and seconder, and the address passed. The Ministers laughed but it was from the teeth not the heart. The same silence has prevailed; Ned has not once opened his lips.

There has indeed been no business except the addition of 9000 seamen, a mere job of the Admiralty; the Admirals Saunders and Keppel showed the extravagance of it as a peace establishment, and its insufficiency as a war establishment. The Ministry argued it as neither for war nor peace, for both and for neither. Dowdeswell exposed the folly and imprudence of a pretense of their saving, that they had last year robbed the country of a shilling land tax to throw away this year upon a needless augmentation of the navy, and foolishly boasting they did it without increasing the debt. Lord North said it was only for this year, and yet avowed that his M[ajesty]'s profession of the pacific dispositions of his neighbours was founded.

Sir George Savile cloaked his argument in a story where the logic was enlivened by wit. A physician, says he, comes to town and tells me my friend such an one is perfectly, perfectly recovered, as well as ever he was in his life. "Oh bless me I am very glad of it, then he hunts and amuses himself and goes on as he used to do before his illness—we shall have him in town." No sir, no, no, by no means no, says the Doctor, I have ordered a bleed and a blister.—"Oh you think then, I

---

[13] A house called Broad Sanctuary.

suppose, bleedings at certain seasons and a perpetual blister may be good for his constitution?" No, says the Doctor, I don't mean at all a continued blister, I tell you he is as well as ever he was in his life, nothing ails, and I have now just for the moment ordered him a blister. Sir George being very puzzled declared he could not comprehend what such a physician meant, but he could not help concluding that there was some understanding between the Doctor and the Apothecary.

This gave a momentary life to the House. Cornwall [14] expressed an earnestness and vehemence that at another time would have kindled a debate. Dowdeswell at another season would have made the country gentlemen ashamed in a time of peace to throw away a million upon an useless military augmentation; but the Admirals while they condemned the measure, disclaimed all thought of offering to name a number of their own; so that men saw no division was intended and ran away to dinner. The country gentlemen not willing to contradict the Court, and afraid to have it said they supported the measure, absented themselves; so that it was an heavy day, and the question passed without a division.

Sir W. Meredith, who has not accomplished his bargain, and his lieutenant Cap[tain] Phipps, who has got his family job but probably wishes some personal situation, were very much and very naturally mortified at this deadness, for it does not quicken their bargain. The same may be said, possibly without injustice, of Lord Chatham, Lord Temple, and Lord Shelburne, and all the gang that wished to make the Rockinghams their stalking horse, to take the surer aim at office and emolument; who vilified and disparaged them, while they affected to act with them, and who in common with the Court laboured to destroy that character and reputation they never so much as wished to deserve. These now, in common with the Court, are half confounded at the sight of the Rockinghams lying on their arms.

Sir W. Meredith has given notice that next Thursday he brings in the petition against the subscription to the 39 Articles.[15] I am far from saying what may happen when

---

[14] Charles Wolfran Cornwall (1735-1789), brother-in-law to Charles Jenkinson, but at this time an opposition man.

[15] A petition from certain clergymen and others, chiefly of the legal and medical professions, praying to be relieved from strict doctrinal adherence to the Church of England, without loss of membership.

religion begins to warm the people, but the nearer this affair comes to its trial, the less eager people seem to be about it; it is at present in the hands of some of the clergy; the Dissenters seem to keep aloof. Sir W. Meredith, I heard was very warm, but his notice of the day was full of quiet, and I suspect he has not yet determined which side to be violent upon. But tho' this should for the moment blow over, the seed is sown, man's faculties are roused, and religion is unfortunately the object of their attention.

Seymour too has given notice that he will bring in a bill to take away the Nullum Tempus from the Church. The poor Church has not as many friends as she had, in the beginning of the century. The Bishops I find are vexed and alarmed, but the Crown that has lost its own prerogative, will probably not be very earnest to preserve this right to the Church.

The Speech you see announces the East India affair; how far they mean to seize and plunder I don't know, but if once the Crown has India the forms of a Parliament will be but the security of an irresistible tyranny.[16]

With all this, the news writers brave both houses and this unresisted majority acquiesce.

The story you see in the papers from Denmark is founded; the Queen is in custody, and possibly the King little better; for those who have ventured for the King, for that nation's honour, or for their own ambition to go these lengths, will hardly leave themselves exposed to the weakness of a Prince who was afraid to vindicate his own honour, and from weakness may in a moment be made the instrument of their destruction.[17]

I understand the King was much affected, and I find people from the worthiness of their own natures inclined enough to suppose the Queen of Denmark a spirit of light and an injured innocent, but I do not believe the Court has given the word.

---

[16] The speech (Jan. 21) rather hinted than announced: "The concerns of this country are so various and extensive as to require the most vigilant and active attention, and some of them, as well from remoteness of place as from other circumstances, are so peculiarly liable to abuses and exposed to danger, that the interposition of the legislature for their protection may become necessary.—*Parliamentary history* 16: 233.

[17] Queen Matilda, wife of Christian VII of Denmark, was a sister of George III. Accused of being the paramour of the Minister Struensee, she was the victim of a palace revolution against that statesman. Matilda took refuge in Hanover.

The Dowager is in a very bad way.[18] It is well for you that I don't write often, but I dine today with the Speaker,[19] and that I suppose has put it into my head to be troublesome; and I shall write this morning to Ridge, but not without much uneasiness, for we expected to have seen him and have not heard a word from him. Adieu.

Luttrell has done nothing; I understand that the state of parties has not encouraged him—his answer to people is, "I can say neither yes nor no." [20]

Once more, adieu.

Feb. 2. 1772

Mem. How could you be idle enough to suspect that we could have any expectations of that empty fool, whom you mention as hoping to get a seat in Parliament here? [21] Possibly he may, but be assured that I am persuaded that they who expect ability or worth in him will be liable to every disappointment that a fool and a knave can bring them.

WILL BURKE TO O'HARA, March 13, 1772

March 13, 1772

I have begun with my postscript, and told you what I imagine, from the best information I could get, was the state of Mr. O'Hara's piece.[22] I now thank you for your late letters; if any even but a whisper that does not seem calculated for a Midas's ears, reaches me relative to intentions towards your side of the water, you shall certainly be immediately apprised of it.[23] At present there does not appear the least, I won't say uneasiness, but the least attention about Ireland. Banks's voyage to the unknown parts of the globe proceeds under the sanction

---

[18] Augusta, the King's mother, died on Feb. 8, 1772.

[19] Sir Fletcher Norton.

[20] "What turn your politics will take in England I don't know. But don't be surprised if the Middlesex member should appear in opposition, armed with secrets of a great and dangerous nature."—O'Hara to E. Burke, Dec. 28, 1771.

[21] Not identified.

[22] The "postscript" is lost, but it is certain that "Mr. O'Hara's piece" was a musical and dramatic production by Charles O'Hara's brother, Kean O'Hara.—O'Hara to W. Burke, Feb. 22, 1771.

[23] "If you should hear any whisper of a Lord Lieutenant for us, name him to me, for a change is probably not remote."—O'Hara to W. Burke, March 5, 1771.

of Government;[24] but if he should happen with all his crew
to be drowned, and lost, I apprehend there would be about as
much anxiety in Government, and as much attention towards
the cause of his failure, as there is towards Ireland and Lord
Townshend.

As to our English politics, the Ministry are incumbered
with the greatness of their majority. In the case of Charles
Fox you see the cup ran over. They will not however probably
let good liquor be lost; they will lick it up while it lies on the
ground, before it mixes with the great waters of opposition.[25]

This Royal Marriage Bill does not appear to be much to
the relish of our visible governors.[26] The Lord Chancellor it
seems has owned the brat, but we have heard of men proud
of owning children they could never get;[27] this is thought rather
to be Mansfield's getting. It will almost to a certainty live, yet
it is confoundedly ricketty and ill-shaped; its nurses and friends
are in perpetual alarms about it.

Upon the message we as well as the Lords addressed and
promised; we proceeded no further till the Lords passed the
Bill; for the whole course of it they kept their doors closed.
Lord Chatham remained in the country—Lord Rockingham
managed the whole opposition to it, with great dexterity, and
spoke in every stage with clearness, perspicuity and address.
It came to us last week; the printing of it was moved by Seymour, and refused by 190. The searching of the Lords' journals
was agreed to without a debate; the committee for searching
reported protest and all. At the 2nd reading Dowdeswell,
grounded on the journals of the Lords then on our table,
moved—that the proposition in the K[ing]'s message asserting
that the care and approbation of *all* the *marriages* of the
R[oyal] F[amily] belonged to the Crown, is not agreeable to

---

[24] Sir Joseph Banks (1743-1820), explorer and naturalist, visited Iceland
in 1772.

[25] Charles Fox (1749-1806) had been made a junior lord of the Admiralty
in 1770; he now resigned to oppose the Royal Marriage bill, but a little later
came back into administration as a junior lord of the Treasury.

[26] A bill to forbid all descendants of George II (save those born of princesses
married into foreign houses) from marrying without the king's assent signified
under the Great Seal, until after they were twenty-five years old; after which
they could marry lawfully only by giving twelve months notice to the Privy
Council, and not incurring the disapprobation of parliament.

[27] Henry Bathurst, Lord Apsley (1714-1794) had been made Lord Chancellor in 1771.

the law of the land, nor warranted by the opinion of the judges.

The Ministry made but a poor figure in endeavouring to show this prerogative to have been always in the Crown. Wedderburn went through English history to prove that the Kings of England had often had distant relations for whom they found good matches.[28] Dunning answered him with but little management. Sir Gilbert Elliot proved the prerogative from the practices of the patriarchs, from the rules of the Roman law, from the rights of the feudal system, from the courts and from the doctrine of the Star Chamber.

It was eleven o'clock, and people began to be weary and sleepy, but Edmund had the good fortune to awaken and re- fresh them; all sides of the House did justice to the force of his argument conveyed in the most brilliant exposition of wit. He lamented that Sir Robert Filmer [29] should not be a witness to see his clumsy misshaped principles dressed and adorned in the decorations of Elliot's eloquence, etc. etc. etc.—you'll mind my et ceteras, as Lord Coke does Middleton's, who you know says there is much more in that lawyer's *re* often, than in all that is expressed by his text. He congratulated Elliot's dex- terity in grounding the common law of England on the patri- archal age, which expired in the establishment of civil society; or in the Roman law, which never had existence here; or in the feudal system, which is abolished; or in the doctrines of the Star Chamber, which are exploded etc. etc. etc. He buried the patriarchs, the Roman law, the feudal law, and the Star Chamber in one grave, and crushed them all with the weight etc. etc. of the common and statute law etc. etc. He did not forget a wise distinction of Wedderburn's that this was not the prerogative of the Crown but the prerogative of the people.

It has in short happened to him this session, that the last speech has been said to be the best he ever made. There is not in fact that load of envy, which seemed formerly so busy to crush him; the course of business this session has not as be- fore excited those storms of animosity. His real sentiments have led him to support the cause where the interest and passions of others were engaged. On the clerical petition the

---

[28] Wedderburn had become Solicitor General in 1771.

[29] Sir Robert Filmer (d. 1653), author of the *Patriarcha,* a political treatise in support of divine right monarchy.

petitioners had no ground of offence given nor any taken by them while the Church men felt an obligation, and indeed perhaps there never was so noble an exertion of learning and wisdom adapted to a national assembly.[30]

In the Church nullum tempus, though he did not run the length of Church prejudice, he was measured, wise and temperate, as well as learned to a vast depth and extent.[31]

In the answer to Elliot and Wedderburn, he thought it too late in the night to go into a law argument, but the wit with which *il a bouleversé* their arguments was felt by all parties.

On Wednesday when the Royal Marriage Bill came on, Charles Fox opened the debate against the Speaker's leaving the chair; our people thought it more advisable to make the stand in the committee; and to fight for amendments, where we shall probably catch stray consciences. The Shelburnes and Meredith of course were of another opinion. Ned took no part in this debate, but after midnight Sir William Meredith in the flimsy insolence of his nature, complained of Lord John Cavendish and Dowdeswell as not taking a fair manly open honest part—that their letting it into the committee while they profess to detest the bill, was like marrying and taking to their arms a diseased prostitute, in order to reclaim her. An attack upon his friends and his party was no indifferent thing to Edmund. He took his seat—he valued himself on his integrity, his fairness, his openness of conduct, yet was satisfied to stand second in these respects to Lord John and Dowdeswell. He would not take a strumpet in his arms, but before he turned her adrift in the street, he would endeavour to persuade her to the asylum. He showed the propriety of making the stand in the committee. He disclaimed all right of attacking those who professed the same intention with him, though they took a different route—he went to Church, but the Baptist, Anabaptist, the Seekers (Sawbridge and those people were near him) they were all Protestant and his brethren, and he complained of none. Meredith was mounted on a fine stately steed;

---

[30] Burke was with the majority of 217 to 71 that rejected the petition for the relief of certain persons from the subscription to the strict creed of the Church. For his speech on Feb. 6, see *Works* 10: 2-21.

[31] On Feb. 17 a motion was made for leave to bring in a bill to quiet the possessions of the subject against dormant claims of the Church. Burke supported the motion, which was negatived by 117 to 141. His speech is given in *Works* 10: 142-146.

he was a poor man content to walk afoot, but could wish that while they travelled the same road, the man on the fine steed would not bespatter him. He had been 7 years in opposition, might possibly continue so 7 more. He had a long way to go. He could let slip a little momentary popularity, and catch it at his leisure another day. Those who had a short journey to make, intending to go but a stage or two, might cry out, "come on, come on, you do not go fast enough." They were right. They had but a little way to go, but he who was prepared to go a long journey must go at his own pace. He had observed in his barn that when a gentleman took up the flail, he could in 1/2 an hour do as much as the poor thresher would do in an hour, and the reason was plain; the gentleman meant to work but 1/2 an hour, the thresher was to work all day. Every allusion was understood by everybody, but if the wit was poignant, the good humour of the manner added to its force.[32] All parts of the Ministry as well as the opposition had the same plaudit. Sir William felt not a little of what his worthless malignity deserves to suffer. He would have explained, that it was time to part since they travelled a dirty road and only meant to bespatter others, i.e., the Administration. The House cried out that no such thing was said. When he said it was time to part, Ned with great good humour bowed his head and cried, "goodbye to you." So that this had one good effect. It let the world see that we disown Sir William and puts it less in his power to betray us; and it is certainly his treachery not his wisdom that could hurt any party.

It is certainly true that Edmund has this session not made himself common in their eyes; he has spoke so seldom that appetite is far from satiated; but still you are much mistaken, if you suppose him idle and unemployed; *sic notus Ulysses?* Sir William Hamilton has applied to Parliament to buy his collections; Edmund was applied to to support the proposition.[33] He did so on very liberal manly principles. Banks's voyage too is in part to be at public expence, and Ned is applied to to justify the measure, which he thinks reasonable and proper. And he gives that gloss and colour, which the continual attention of the Ministers to job and pitiful dealing, renders them

---

[32] No other account of this speech has been preserved.

[33] Sir William Hamilton (1730-1803), archeologist and diplomat, sold a collection of Greek antiquities to the British Museum in 1772.

incapable of, and for want of which things of real utility, which in spite of their teeth fall in their way, might fail of success.

There is too a sort of report that the King does not wish the bill in its full extent, and there are now and then appearances of some crack; whether it is simply in the partition walls or reaches to the foundations, time must show.

If Charles is with you, remember us very cordially to him. We flatter ourselves that we may consider him as one of our little inner circle. Tell him his friend Hampden [34] has spoke, and very well on the Marriage bill.

Poor Richard has had a severe and alarming illness, but is getting well—his business, we hope well of. Pray give our love to Ridge, as this is a sort of history of Ned, shamefully too long for you alone, share it with Ridge, who will I am sure without regret take his part in it. Tell him we are not a little chagrinned in his not having been able to fullfil his purpose. Adieu.

WILL BURKE TO RIDGE, March 24, 1772

My dear Ridge,

Before you broke your last silence, I really felt an alarm at not hearing from you. I thank God I found my fears ill grounded, and I will not allow them to get up again; but there are other and better motives than fear that make us wish to hear from you, so prithee from time to time let us know something about you. And by the bye it is now a good while since under cover to Sir G[eorge] M[acartney] I forwarded Lloyd's mortgage to you, and neither from him nor you do I know whether they got safe. Their loss would be no small inconvenience.[35]

Idle folks have some advantage over you men of business, and I experience it. At present, I am waiting at Lord Rockingham's, till the doctors come down; he has been alarmingly ill, but at present no danger is apprehended, tho' he still keeps his bed. I seize the moment to write you.

I left Edmund and his good woman at breakfast; she has got a cold, and swelled face. He is a good deal jaded, by the attendance of the Royal Marriage Bill. It is to be read the 3rd

---

[34] Probably Thomas Hampden, member for Lewes in Sussex.
[35] *Supra*, Ridge's of Jan. 28, 1772.

time today. It was reported with its amendments yesterday, and we divided 132 to 150 on an amendment of Rose Fuller's, to limit it to the King's life and three years after it. Eight of our people returning from dinner were locked out, and had we pressed an attendance we should have carried it, as many of their country gentlemen are weary of the business, and fairly came over to us. I will keep my letter open to let you know the division today; they will stir heaven and hell on the Ministerial side to have all their people. Had Lord Rockingham been well, I really believe it might have been possible to beat them.

(later)

People came in, I left off and went to the House; the debate I cannot call it, for the Ministerial people literally speaking did not utter a word. Lord North simply said he was ready to hear, but did not think himself bound to speak, so that about 6 o'clock we divided 115 to 158. They have therefore carried their bill; for the amendments, tho' disgraceful to the Chancellor and those who affected to say that nothing should be changed, are of no great importance.[36]

I wrote some time ago to Ch[arles] O['Hara], and through him, at you. You two are the only people whom I conceive interested in us, so that whichever my letters are addressed to I really write to both. I mentioned to him that that load of envy that was ready to assist the malice of the world, to overwhelm our Edmund, has been a little ashamed to show its face this session. He stands perhaps, to an incredible degree (considering the height he held in spite of all the ill nature and ill passions of mankind) higher in the opinion and esteem of parties than he ever before attained. The fact is, that the course of things has given his exertions fairer play in the passions and prejudices of others; but that we must accept; it is not worth our while to dispute whether he had not before done full as great things; the present moment is always better than the past, and that present being granted, we need not dispute about the past. It has over and over again been said that the last night speech was the best he ever made. But the last Wednesday's speech was I agree the most affecting speech that in my judgment I believe any house of Parliament ever felt.

On the praemunire question he ran a most noble parallel

---

[36] The third reading was on March 24; which fact dates the letter.

between the pretended prerogative, and the intended law, showing that the prerogative supported by all the power of the Star Chamber was mercy and clemency in comparison to the law we were going to pass.[37] He asked who could have framed this clause, "unions to the peace and comfort of domestic happiness," and finished it with, "He had no children." I do assure you the House was at once in an uproar and dead silent. They beat with their feet as well as their voices, and yet in such a manner afraid to interrupt, that made a one uniform sound that did not interrupt. Tom Pitt, in speaking of it to Lord Temple, said that he was ashamed to find himself in tears, till observing those round him, he perceived them in the same condition.[38] I do assure you, I trembled, and till then I had not conceived what eloquence could do—I have never been so affected. This language from me would be foolish to any other than to you or Ch[arles] O['Hara]; to either of you it needs no apology.

In today's debate Ned took no part. Lord Rock[ingham]'s illness was very unlucky; for it is not impossible but his health might have defeated the bill.

They say Lord North is to have the blue ribband in reward for his achievements—of having a majority, for as to reasoning, he has not even attempted it in the course of the whole session.[39]

Adieu—all here love you—God be with you and yours.

BURKE TO O'HARA, June 1, 1772

My dear friend,

I will not waste a great deal of this late letter in apologies for my silence. You will not attribute it to a wrong cause. If you did, you could no longer be uneasy about it. We have stagnated in a political calm for upwards of three months. We had a few equinoctial squalls about the change of the session; but it ends as it began in a sort of drowsy calm; a stillness without repose; a sort of troubled sleep; much uneasiness and no movement. This is the picture of the Cabinet and the Court; of the House of Lords and House of Commons; of

[37] All who celebrated or assisted at a marriage in violation of the act were made subject to the penalties of *praemunire,* a statutory offense to the damage of the authority of the crown.
[38] Thomas Pitt (1737-1793), a nephew of Chatham.
[39] North was presently made a knight of the Garter.

Ministry and Opposition. Ali are discontented, but the discontents are so general and so balanced, that there is not an effort from any part. I have rather found this state of things unanimated than very offensive; I have turned myself to matters of police and interior economy; in which I take some pains; but on the whole have passed the session with less labour, less contest, and less of an adverse struggle than ever I passed so much time since I came into Parliament; and so, please God, will end my seventh session; although Colonel Luttrell threatens to carry away the remainder of it in a whirlwind. He brought down a mob of upwards of a thousand joiners and cabinet makers the other day to the House with a petition against some of the ministers of the inferior courts who used their character as a pretence for dealing in French furniture. This was indeed shabby in them; but not stuff for much parliamentary bustle. Luttrell attacked Lord Holderness; and after praising the decency and sobriety of his mob, was not however sure that repeated provocations might not alter their dispositions, so as to endanger the safety of the Prince of Wales, who was often in an house that was no better than a magazine of smuggled goods.[40] He afterwards went to the door, and harangued the mob most magnificently. What think you of Luttrell's bearding the Ministry with a mob without doors and a popular declamation within? On Wednesday he proposes to move an address for vacating his seat; there was a moment in the session when such a motion with good management might have done some execution; but now it is our friend Harward's *amen-shot*. Do you know Lord Harcourt with any intimacy, who they say is destined to succeed Lord Townshend?[41] Your Lord Lieutenant has accepted the Ordnance. Neither communication, nor apology to Conway; from whom this appointment takes eight hundred pounds a year, and all the consequence of his office. He certainly intends to resign. What is mortifying, the courtiers affect not to believe that he has any such intention.[42] They say Sir George Macartney is to continue secretary to the *Lieutenancy*, for neither formerly nor now is he properly secretary to the *Lord Lieutenant*. He

[40] Robert Darcy (1718-1778), fourth Earl of Holderness, was Governor of the Prince of Wales.

[41] Harcourt, ambassador to France since 1768, presently was made lord lieutenant of Ireland.

[42] Since Lord Granby's resignation in 1770, there had been no master-general of the ordnance. With that office went the command of the Blue Guards

will now have a very calm and even-tempered man to deal with. Have you settled the salary which your *rank* at your Board requires? I should be sorry that you had this point to negotiate with the successor. I am to tell you that in all probability the St. Vincent's act against the Caribee purchases will be given up.[43] This is some step. Adieu my dear friend! The Doctor, Madame, Will, Richard, all are sincerely yours. Let us hear from you and remember us to our excellent Charles. I owe Jack Ridge a letter. I will soon write.

June 1st 1772

[At the end of the session of "stillness without repose," Burke returned to his farming; and to his agricultural interests he now was adding horses, an interest most necessary to complete his becoming a Buckinghamshire squire. Wrote O'Hara to him on July 4: "Charles came laughing into my room this morning, to tell me of an extraordinary turn you have taken. King is his correspondent, and I believe his Yorkshire blood suggests the undertaking. You intend to breed for the turf; and for that purpose, you have made some reversionary bargain for Charles's brown mare. I did not laterally think that mare wholesome enough for a brood mare, but she's well bred, and what I objected to, may not descend. But if the rage should continue, allow me to give you one, large and fine, got by my stallion Pickpocket. . . . Never did I foresee that I should have occasion to give *you* the pedigree of a brood mare. She is now in foal to my Sejanus, as good a sire as you can get in England."

As O'Hara was preparing to send over the mare, Burke was paying a visit to the Duke of Richmond at Goodwood in Sussex, and from there he replied.]

BURKE TO O'HARA, July 30, 1772

My dear friend,

I was just setting out from London for this place when I received your letter. My taste for breeding, which has but just laid hold of me, does not deserve a name so noble as that of *rage;* it is as yet only a *folly* and but a little one. To what size this infantine folly may grow if well nourished and trained I

regiment, and this had devolved on Conway as lieutenant-general; but now it was taken from him and given to Townshend, who became master-general. Conway did resign, but soon accepted the governorship of the Isle of Jersey.

[43] The Board of Trade on June 24 recommended "the disallowance of an Act of the island of St. Vincent relative to the Charibb purchases."—*Journal of Commissioners, op. cit.,* 310.

know not, but as I begin my breeding upon your mares, the genius of that stable may grow upon me; at present I am almost as little engaged in eagerness as in knowledge; but both may increase together, however rarely zeal and knowledge may be companions in this or in any other particular. Charles's mare has contracted a very noble alliance. How far the breed will answer in performance the extreme beauty of the sire, time is to show; but any thing more beautiful of the *Houyhnhum* race I never beheld. Gregory talks of sending his two horses to his estate in Ireland. I accept your mare with thanks, and will dispatch a trusty person to meet her at Smith's [in Chester] who will I hope conduct her to me with safety.

As to your farming it is almost impossible that you should not derive some advantage from it; pleasure you certainly will have of the best kind. Stick particularly to the potatoes. To do them in drills, is beyond all doubt the most productive and the cheapest method; and prepares the land the most properly for wheat; but to turn it to good advantage you must dung liberally and hoe vigorously, not only with the horse hoe but with the hand hoe in the rows. It is not easy to exterminate grass and keep the land clean in Ireland. In my own judgment I prefer potatoes to turnips for all purposes of cattle, to say nothing of men; and if the former is properly pursued you will not have a great deal of reason to regret the latter. Not that I think them at all rivals; both may and ought to be pursued. These crops that keep cattle in the winter and require perpetual stirring are the mainsprings of all agriculture, uniting the fertilizing manure of the old to the vigorous culture of the new husbandry. Besides it will be vain to look for the artificial grasses in any perfection without such fertilizing, and such cleansing, and those I think of the greatest importance; let me add, that when land is to be laid down with the *natural* grass seeds, this previous method is perhaps the most necessary of all. However, if potatoes or turnips must be neglected, I am clearly for abandoning the turnips, as by far the most precarious; the most expensive; and the least productive crop of the two.[44] I speak this always on a supposition that you have not dung sufficient for both. I am sensible, that when we talk of advising any practice in Ireland we ought to have an eye to the mode and course of agriculture there. You commonly

---

[44] *Cf.* his opinion on turnips the previous year in letter of Sept. 10, 1771.

let a great part of your farms lie for many years to grass; and you then plant potatoes or sow corn upon the lays, liming or dunging as you have means, without any idea of keeping the land true to a regular succession of fallows, crops, and grasses. Here our land is entirely in courses, grass or tillage for ever. Both methods have something right and something wrong. But upon the whole I hold the English method of tillage to be preferable. Therefore I will suppose that you mean to continue some of your land which you till at present, in a course of tillage. On that principle I will take any piece, neither the richest nor most exhausted, and give it a good dressing of dung and lime and turning both lightly in, as soon as they are spread, about the end of autumn. Early in spring I would give it a good ploughing and harrowing; the harrowing once at least, if not twice, and then as soon as the frosts are over, dibble in the sets of potatoes in rows about 30 inches asunder. As soon as they appear distinctly in the rows, I would give the field a good harrowing to clear off the weeds and open the ground; which harrowing I would repeat when they got to be two or three inches high, if the weather permitted that operation. Then I would pass a stout swing plough between the rows, about one way and about another in order to throw the earth to the plants on each side. For this a double moulded plough would be best; but with a little more labour any plough without wheels will do. At the time of this ploughing the rows ought to be carefully hand howed; and wherever the potatoes have failed, to turn the earth to those that remain. A little before the potatoes begin to knit, that is when they are in full flower, this ploughing and hoeing ought to be repeated, which with working over the field with an hoe afterward will be sufficient. This will make the land sweet and yield a good crop of potatoes; at least with as little expence as the common method in Ireland of trenching on a *lay*, which lay I would always (or generally) keep for oats or wheat on one ploughing. The potatoes, being sowed early may be out of the ground at or before Michaelmas; at farthest at old Michaelmas. Then the ground sweet and mellow may be ploughed up and sowed with wheat; and early in the spring, the usual quantity of good clover ought to be sown upon it, and rolled with a wooden roller, if the weather be dry. The autumn following, after the wheat is off, you will have a good feeding; and let your ground lie the next year in clover to be twice mowed, the first time for the hay, the second for seed. Then manure your lay lightly, and you may have at your pleasure a wheat or potato crop again at your pleasure and without in the least forcing your land; but the potatoes are best, on account of the winter fallow, and the summer hoeings; but you will find it clean enough and in proper order even for wheat on one ploughing. This you see is variable according to discretion, in every part of it. But I am sure the principle is right. With regard to the pease and beans, if they are not well hand and horse hoed, the rows about 16 or 18 inches asunder, it is better [to] have nothing to do with these crops. They are very uncertain, and they leave the land intolerably foul. But with proper manuring, harrowing, and hoeing they prepare ground for wheat as well as potatoes, and the process for them is exactly the same. When they are ripe the course here is to pluck up the pease haulm (the pease along with it) with hooks made for the purpose and to let them dry in little round bundles; then to carry them away and stack them, and after threshing to put the *haulm* into cribs in the farmyard for your dry cattle or young oxen. They will eat a good deal of it, if it be well saved; and it agrees with them. As to beans, the usual methods are either to mow them with a scythe or to pluck them up by the roots and to set them in bundles cone fashion, to dry. If these be got in tolerably dry, after threshing, horses will eat a great deal of them. There is nothing they like better than the bean straw made up green as hay after the pods have been pulled for market, and they fatten on that alone; but this cannot be done where you have no such market. However some will always be consumed, the rest will rot and litter the yard for dung. When you get up your beans, lose no time in ploughing; you may go on between the bundles and plough one part of the field while the beans are drying on the other. I have seen some curious farming since I left home. I am now tired but I will give you another letter on it. The Duke of Richmond's is admirable and very near ordinary practice. He never uses the horse hoe; but he never raises potatoes or beans. My dear friend, adieu and give you peace in your retirement. I wish I had a little in mine.

Goodwood July 30th

My love to Charles. I return homeward tomorrow to my wheat harvest.

XVI. The Crown and the East India Company

[Burke had always been deeply interested in the affairs of the East India Company, but never more so than during the summer, fall, and winter of 1772-1773, when the Company's financial exigencies and administrative scandals laid it open to new attack by the crown and Parliament. Sometime in the early summer of 1772 the Directors decided to send a commission of supervisors to India, to inquire into abuses and reform the Company's administration in Bengal. Burke was approached with a proposal to head this commission, and he was considering it when he visited the Duke of Richmond late in July. Will Burke alluded to this business in the following letter, which was begun while Edmund was at Goodwood and finished after his return.]

WILL BURKE TO O'HARA *ca.* July 31-August 1, 1772

My dear Sir,

It is a long time since I wrote to you, and as I am no farmer nor have as yet determined to keep running horses, and as there are no politics showing, what in the name of wonder can I say to you, unless I tell you that Joe King was monstrously afraid Ned might be too late in his acceptance. But take his own words—"no faith horse, no time, old O'Hara is a jockey, and will fob you off for next year, and save the foal for himself." I leave you Yorkshire and horse men to settle this account, for I assured Joe I would let you know it, so if you send a whip with the mare, his shoulders I think deserve it.

We have had moments of pretty strong hopes of the St. Vincent's business, but hopes are like a summer day, that has its clouds and showers; the prospect has however never been lost, and having (we think without doubt) defeated their damned law, we are not without expectation of concluding the business before winter.[1]

I yesterday met my friend Will, who is very well, and tho' he is as lean as Cassius, I don't believe he has a grain of spleen or malice about him.

---

[1] He can hardly have been aware that Hillsborough, although approving disallowance of the St. Vincent's act invalidating Richard's purpose, at the same time favored a new act that would not less effectively blast Richard's hopes.— Wecter, *op. cit.*, 62.

My friend Almon tells me for certain, that Lord Hillsborough is going out, but in perfect good humour. But on a point of honour about an Ohio grant, wherein he stood single in opinion; he retires, it is Almon's intelligence.[2]

We are not without uneasiness about Dyer. He has this fortnight past been troubled with a disorder that prevents his swallowing; he now lives barely on broths, and not always without difficulty in taking that; our good man has thought it serious enough to call in Heberdon. There is great worth in the man, and so very far on the other side of ostentation, as to be wanting in doing himself justice; perhaps so far as to want the incitements that are possibly needful towards giving wisdom and virtue themselves their effect. We hope however he will get well.

Edmund is on a tour and at present at the Duke of Richmond's. I don't know whether I ought to mention it even to you, for as he will not (I think) accept, I don't know whether it is fair to mention it; to the world one would not, to a friend one may, and to you, who will naturally be interested in all that concerns your friends—you will not be sorry to know that Ned has since he left town had an offer to go out at the head of the Supervision to India. The profit will be very great, the credit, if they really do any good, will be considerable to those concerned; yet I rather think on the whole he will decline it. It is not so much the subject fit for a letter; we shall I hope one day or other meet, and explain. Ned is you know never eager towards his own profit, but I on the whole coincide with him, and think him right to decline.

There is a sort of talk that Hillsborough or North must go out, but North's doing so is of no more consequence than Hillsborough's.

*   *   *

Ned returned to us last night, earlier than I had expected by a good deal, but it was necessary to give his answer, which he did not choose to do till he had talked it over with R. B. and me, and the result is he declines it.[3] Adieu.

---

[2] Hillsborough resigned shortly afterwards and the Earl of Dartmouth became secretary of state for the colonies.

[3] Writing to O'Hara later in August, Will Burke said the offer to head the commission was made to Burke "with all the circumstances that could make it honourable and advantageous. He was at the Duke of Richmond's when he received it, and to him he mentioned it, and had a long discussion on the subject. He came to town, and Richard and he and I debated it among ourselves—we

Joe King has wrote to you about the mare, a Yorkshire youth shall meet her at Chester.

O'HARA TO BURKE, September 11, 1772

Nymphsfield 11th of September 1772

My dear Edmund,

I have just come in from a variety of farm business and sit down to thank my teacher.[4] I neither mean to compliment you, nor to flatter you, when I say that you have recovered my mind from the confusion which Mr. Young had thrown me into. You have given me the principle of the new husbandry, fertilizing and cleansing the ground, which was all I wanted. Young gives us such a variety of practice, of utensils, and of calculation, without explaining why any one is better than another, that I have for some time thrown him aside. But upon the whole, I was led to think, and your letter confirms me in the opinion, that the land of Ireland is in general richer than that of England. If after a crop of potatoes horse-hoed and hand-hoed as you prescribe, I was to sow wheat, it would all lodge, and never be worth cutting. I find it rather too rich for barley, tho' sown very early. If the season be at all wet, it lodges. But neither my turnips, potatoes, nor cabbages have been half hoed, hardly at all. I have taken a little more care this season, and shall try barley and clover on my potato ground. I am this day cutting very good wheat, which grew upon ground ten years under oats, without any manure, only a winter fallowing and four ploughings. I am now in a way of trying the course regularly, and shall be able to give you an accurate account of the effect. I am in daily expectation of an English

chose so to do without calling in any of political friends, as if we all thought it right no other opinion ought to prevail against us in such a point; and if it was not to be accepted there was more dignity to himself, and more justice to them to do it without their interference." Burke told the Duke of Richmond: "As I trotted towards town yesterday, I turned over in my mind the subject of our last conversation. I set it in every light I could possibly place it, and after the best deliberation in my power, I came to a resolution not to accept the offer which was made to me. My family friends, whom I met in town, have employed their thoughts on the same subjects, and on talking the matter pretty largely, concurred in the same opinion. I shall therefore call on Sir George Colebrooke tomorrow, and give him my final answer."—*Correspondence* 1: 339-340. It is clear that Burke wrote this letter to Richmond on or about Aug. 1, not in October, as the editors of the *Correspondence* stated.

[4] *Supra*, Burke's of July 30.

farmer from whose diligence I hope to be released in some degree from the close attendance I now give it. I have embarked largely in it, not for amusement only, but to turn a very considerable desmesne to some profit, which has been hitherto a large expence to me. I went on in a sort of career which prevented my feeling it; but in so doing economy becomes at last necessary. But a desire of further instruction is by no means the only reason of my writing to you. Your refusal of an employment of great magnitude, added to some random accounts in the papers, give room to suspect that some general change was expected. A partial change was certainly wished for; but offers of this kind have been before made, and as often refused. But tho' no actual good arises from such, they yet give consequence to a party. And that at least I wish you. The papers say that General Conway has agreed to remain Lieutenant General of the Ordnance. This will be very contrary to what I expected, from late letters. You have certainly seen Sir Geo[rge] Mac[artney] and heard much about us. He writes to Hutchinson, but says he knows nothing; rejoices at his escape from a very critical situation, and talks of private life. Pity 'tis that he can't bring himself to a little candour, that he can't assume an air of truth; for he is capable of friendship, and certainly has parts; his errors are in his judgment. I am convinced in my own mind that his object is a post of consideration in this country, and a principal part in the management of our affairs; and I grow confirmed in this opinion by Lord Harcourt's resolving that his Secretary shall not be in Parliament. The English Ministry give themselves much trouble about us, to very little purpose; they aim at carrying some great point here, from ignorance of the circumstances of this poor Kingdom. 'Tis unable to do any thing for them, and all their attempts must end in their own disgrace. Lord Townshend proposes to stay till Lord Harcourt arrives, which will be a new scene. He talks indeed of remaining some time after his arrival, in a private capacity: he says till all his engagements are performed. But Lord Harcourt is to share with him in conferring the favours. The obligation is to be to him principally.

Scarcely had I finished the foregoing side when Will's letter arrived which will save you the trouble of answering many questions.[5] Had I been with you when the consultation was

---

[5] The letter of late August, *supra*, n. 3.

held upon the offer made you I certainly should not have differed from my brethren. Tho' nothing can be thoroughly explained by letter, particularly of this nature, yet I see enough to make me rejoice that you did not accept. Yet Charles, to whom I communicate most things, and with great safety, wishes much that he could go in some way to make money. He is not content to make money slowly at the bar to clear the estate, nor does he seem to think of marriage as probable means, but amuses himself with the other idea, and desires, tho' you don't go, that I will tell you so; but that in the mean time he sticks to the bar. He talks of going soon to England, and will therefore see you before I shall. I will not suffer myself to despair of Mr. Dyer, tho' my old friend [6] from well grounded hopes in the variety of his sources is generally late in giving over; because it would lead me to a melancholy subject. I laterally knew him well, and in part, his value.

I have just read over Hutchinson's letter again, and I find I mistook him about Sir George, who was in the North of Ireland when he wrote, going, not gone to your side. But you will soon see him, and if you have a spark of curiosity about Ireland, he can give you as full information as any Secretary that ever went from us. He took a great deal of pains, and improved much as a Minister in every thing but gaining the confidence of those with whom he was necessarily connected. I knew as much of him as any body, and upon my own account have but one thing to object to him, that he never would write a letter for me in favour of my son William, to recommend him for promotion. I knew he could do it effectively; he let me see that he could. His friendships are very strong, where he loves; but where he esteems only they are cold. Ridge whom I often mentioned to him, was a strong instance of this. In reading that part of Will's letter which expresses some apprehension for the last, I had the pleasure of knowing that he might be with you on the very day, or the next at farthest; I knew the cause of his delay, and had an account of its being removed. He is a most valuable man. [7]

I have not heard a word of the grey mare more since her

---

[6] Dr. Nugent.

[7] John Ridge. Will had written: "We have been for some days in expectation of our old friend Ridge, and from the late winds not without anxiety."

arrival in Dublin, but suppose her at Chester, or on the road
to Beaconsfield, where I wish myself most devoutly.[8] Adieu.

BURKE TO O'HARA, September 30, 1772

Wednesday. 30 September, 1772

My dear friend,

There is no expressing the loss we have all had in the death
of poor Dyer. We can ill spare a man of that importance to
every business, and every satisfaction of our lives. I believe
he has not left his equal on earth in every particular that can
make a man useful or amiable. He was the most correct and
critical scholar I ever knew, not only in the ancient erudition,
but in the English, French, and Italian and even in German.
He was deep in geometry, and natural philosophy; they who
were good judges thought no man understood music better.
It is singular, that many people had long been acquainted with
him without taking him for anything else than an easy companion. He was the only person I ever met with, who was
totally free from vanity in any one of the shapes that it puts on.
None was ever more simple or open; I have seen him for
years, at all hours and in all humours, and never discovered
the least escape of that kind. I do not know that I ought
to consider it as one of his virtues, the little display he
made of his extraordinary parts of learning; but if that be a
fault, as in him I rather think it was, it is the only fault I
could ever discover in him. He had a tender heart, and a serene
quiet temper, which do not always meet together; but when
they do, they form the best preparation for virtue which our
nature is able to furnish. With a character the furthest removed that can be imagined from faction, he was a real friend
to sober liberty, and neither liked arbitrary government, nor
any of the measures that lead to it. You could yourself in part
perceive the sweetness and equality of his temper; but very

---

[8] O'Hara had written to Burke on Aug. 23: "This day, as good a brood
mare, if I may judge by a year-old daughter of hers, as any in England, set out
for Dublin. I waited to hear of an approaching opportunity of shipping her
for Chester, which I am told there will be very soon. I have wrote to Smith to
fetch her from Park Gate, and to keep her till you send for her. I told you she
is in foal, and by what horse. If Lord Rockingham will put the product into a
sweep stake, I shall beg leave to go fifty with him."

few, except this family, know how warm his affections were.[9] But we have lost him, and must submit to Providence in this, and many other instances; for we are getting fast to that period in which we must be lost to our friends or they to us; and there is no refuge for us but in submission or indifference; however it has still pleased God to leave us some consolations, and of the best sort.

Ridge is not yet arrived; you begin I see to know one another and that is enough to bring on the rest. Our political acquaintance of the Castle, (I call him acquaintance, because no man is my friend who is not so to those I love) arrived in London a few days ago. I have not yet seen him.[10] I shall hear much from him upon Irish affairs; but I shall hear nothing of them as they are, or even as he thinks they are. I shall indeed know what opinions he wishes to circulate, and that's all. I never was the least in his confidence; though he has expressed much regard both to Will and me; and perhaps is obliged in some particulars to William. The parade of political communication he may as well omit as I am ill enough qualified for such circulation and full as little disposed to it. I wish tolerably well to Ireland as to its general interests. The parties which have, or aim at having the management of them, and indeed the whole chart of the country begin to wear out of my memory, and are, I suppose, much changed since I knew them. But I have little desire to renew my acquaintance in that quarter. I see the plan there is to be of the same nature with the scheme here, that of drawing away every thing from the natural powers and interests of the country to private influence and Court cabal. Here they have succeeded perfectly; but at the small expence of all the credit and all the energy of Government. Your parties have struggled hard, so have we; but you too will give way at last; and their system will be established, without indeed much approbation, but with a perfect acquiescence of the people. [11] The Court measures have in the detail been often odious, and always foolish; but when the

---

[9] Writing to O'Hara on Oct. 22, Will Burke said of Samuel Dyer: "He was of our bosom consultation, and as secret as the grave that holds him now. We must not look to replace him."

[10] Sir George Macartney.

[11] ". . . the system which we have often talked of, is established in all its parts; and I have as little doubt of its duration, as I had of the completion when I last saw you, till some sudden brush from abroad shall occasion a consternation."—O'Hara to Burke, Oct. 20.

question came upon the professed system of the Court, it has always had favour in the eyes of the vulgar: for it looks somewhat like anarchy—just like Swift's brothers Peter and Jack; though their schemes were different, their passions, and not a few of their notions were alike. Rags, says he, have at a distance a sort of fluttering appearance like finery; so that the tawdry beau and the shabby blackguard were frequently mistaken for one another. You scarcely can conceive how nearly the Court and the mob approach one another in their sentiments; only that in the one it is design, in the other folly. However, between both, those I wish best to and think best of, are excluded from Government, and disabled in opposition. It is not always politic to speak the worst one thinks; but to you I am no politician. Without some extraordinary change, then I am satisfied that the Court may assume as uncontrolled a power in this country as the King of Sweden has done in his,[12] without running any risks, or meeting any more opposition, than is just convenient to give their measures the sort of countenance that things receive from the supposition of their having been fairly debated. I know that this has been said ever since the Crown has got its great influence in Parliament. But it was not said truly, while the people preferred one man to another; it was not said truly, while a new Ministry supposed a new Parliament; it was not said truly, whilst it required art, address, and influence to secure a majority. Whether or no things were prepared for this in the last reign, I cannot justly say; but this sort of power was then either not fully discovered, or nobody chose to venture upon it. I don't know how I came to run on so much about politics. Don't imagine from this that my thought or conversation takes that turn. Indeed they do not—you can conceive nothing more concentrated within ourselves and our own concerns, than we are, every one of us, in this house.

If I had leisure to lay open to you the true state of things relatively to the East India Company and to my own situation, you would not I think censure me for declining to accept the offer of the Supervision.[13] The affairs of the Company are at

---

[12] Gustavus III established a royal absolutism (Aug. 19, 1772) by military coup d'etat.

[13] O'Hara replied Oct. 20: "I am one of the last men in the world that could wish you absent for three or four years. Besides, you are not the sort of man to do a little in any business you set about. You have the sort of mind that

once flourishing, and in the greatest confusion and the greatest danger—just like the affairs of this country. Our parliamentary proceedings have added to the confusion, and our subsequent neglects have completed it. In this situation what is to be expected for a young man of an ingenuous nature and delicate principles, in the profession of the law, and in India? As yet there is nothing deserving to be called law in that country. An attempt was made last year (a very lame attempt) to form a plan for courts of justice; but it failed, and since that time no steps have been taken to substitute anything else in the place of it. There is therefore no juridical establishment in which our Charles could have an employment, nor courts in which to all appearance he could hope to exert his abilities with credit and advantage. Whenever any light appears he shall know it; but in the mean time he ought carefully to keep his thoughts to himself. I think it impossible but that, by degrees and by force of a systematic resolution, he must arrive at eminence in his own country. He will certainly whenever he can reconcile his mind to the profession.

Now from the East Indies let us come to their antipodes. Your Sligo mare is safely arrived, and she looks in all respects the highbred thing she is. I am almost ashamed to commend her, my judgment is so little; but I really think her the finest of her species I ever saw. Cadina, your other mare, has rather a better head, but in all other respects is inferior. What is her name? Or do you never give names to those who have never done anything to deserve them; to those that never have been in training? Your lady is sadly wild; she will not submit to a collar; she is truly in a state of that savage nature which you are sometimes so much in love with. Now give me leave to explain a matter concerning farming in which you mistook me. I spoke high things of the Duke of Richmond's farm, and I spoke but the truth. In saying that he did not drill and horse-hoe, I did not mean to insinuate that he did not make clean fallows for his wheat; and hoe his turnips; but this is by the hand, and in the common method. Suffer me now,—I speak of common

would have embraced the whole of the Company's situation at once. You would attempt the cure of all its disorders; possibly without success, and yet with such entire attention to their interests that you would never think of the usual means of enriching yourself, or have spurned them if you did. 'Tis unlucky for the Company that you refused, but happy for yourself and family. England is the scene for you."

and of curious methods of agriculture,—to mention what I
think was idle in the Dublin Society. They give their premium
for *drilled turnips*. Their object ought to be general, practical,
and not ingenious and speculative agriculture. This method of
drilling turnip-seed, if ever it ought at all to be used, (which
is very doubtful) falls only within the province of gentlemen,
and men who have time and fortune to command. I suppose
that in all England there are not an hundred acres of drilled
turnips. There are at least 500,000 of broadcast and hand-
hoed. Therefore I wish you would give your premium for
broad-cast and hand hoed; and leave the other method to those
who make experiments; for all the drill culture is expensive
in the instruments, nice in the management, and requires to
be pursued with an accuracy, care and charge that few are equal
to. I must add, that if you wish to encourage the turnip husbandry you must give large premiums, or what is better, progressive premiums according to the number of acres hoed. For
this branch of husbandry is extremely expensive and precarious; and its whole effect in profit depends upon its having its
proper place in a judicious course of crops—for it is in agriculture as in poetry, *series juncturaque pollet* [14]—otherwise the
turnip husbandry had better be let alone. The potato is far
better. You tell me, that if you gave your potatoes good tillage
and good hoeing you would have the succeeding wheat crop
lodged and in bad order. If you know this by experience, I
have nothing further to say. But if only from the information
of others, or from a singular instance of one such lodged crop,
then I do venture to say that it must be a mistake. For on that
principle a good fallow must be prejudicial to a wheat crop, a
thing impossible; and what does potato-drilling with good
ploughing and hoeing between do, but imitate (as well as it
can) a clean summer's fallow? Do not believe any such; but
whether your land be light or heavy, that kind of culture must
be good for your potatoes; and good too, and indeed better, for
your succeeding crop of wheat. That wheat follows potatoes to
advantage is well known, and for a long time, especially in
Ireland. The grand point in any of the hoeing crops is to prepare for the artificial grasses: the greatest improvement in
husbandry. But I shall sometime or other say more to you on
this subject.

------

[14] Horace, *Ars Poetica*, 240.

* * *

When I wrote this I came to town. I saw Sir George, who spoke handsomely of you. I saw the Primate who did the same, both of you and Charles. The latter considered your additional salary as settled; the former spoke of it as a thing he wished, but not probable. Nobody that I converse with knows anything of Lord Harcourt's views, or designs. The talk was that Mr. Blaquiere was not to be in Parliament.[15] The Primate tells me he does not relish that idea. In the new scheme it is absurd for the Lord Lieutenant, for the Secretary himself I think comfortable. Adieu my dear friend.

E. B.

[From October, 1772, to March, 1773, there is another large gap in the correspondence. A letter from O'Hara to Will Burke on November 8 hinted an intention to go over to England in February, but there is no evidence that he went. During these months Burke's attention was chiefly taken up by the bill which was carried through Parliament to place the East India Company under a great degree of crown control. He opposed the bill vehemently, but in vain. In January he went to France to place his son in residence there, and early in March he returned to England. His letter to O'Hara which now follows indicates that he had long neglected his old friend.]

BURKE TO O'HARA, March 26, 1773

My dear friend,

I am half afraid you have forgot my hand. I am indeed very, very faulty. But I am sure my heart never went from you for two days since I saw you. A thousand things made me think of you and wish for you whilst I stayed in France. I could have wished too to have remained there longer; for there is much to see, much to learn, and something to enjoy. The thing was new to me; and the pledge I have left there made it interesting. I am come to a scene here no way pleasing. We are in an odd situation. The India business, which has subverted the little sense of mankind, has so distracted our party, that the idea of opposition to the Ministry is ridiculous, on that, or on any thing else. This is the leading object, which gives tone and character to the rest. It is to be our business all this

---

[15] Sir John Blaquiere (1732-1812), the newly named chief secretary for Ireland; he had been previously Lord Harcourt's secretary to the legation at Paris.

session, all the next, and I suspect forever. The Dissenters' affair diversified the scene a little, and gave me an opportunity of saying something which was not against the universal feeling of the House.[16] In other respects we have nothing to do unless we make business for ourselves.

I left Dick and King[17] extremely pleased with their situation. They have good air, good company, and good protection. I think too, they have good humour and good hearts. The first is the best ingredient to be happy; the second is the means of rendering it worth any one's while to wish or to make us so.

There is some factious internal ferment in the Ministry; but whether this movement will bring on the dissolution of its frame, or work an improvement in its constitution, is more than I can guess; but I suspect that the struggle has been for some time pretty violent. People speculate, or rather did some time ago speculate, very much upon these appearances; however I can never persuade myself that they can make any great changes in the present system of things without risquing that system which by several years' labour they have been endeavouring to perfect, and which I have observed they always grow more fond of in proportion to the mischief it does to the public, and even to its own contrivers. There will be no essential change. It is possible that the Shelburnes will be taken in; they work hard at the Court. Townshend disavowed to Lord Hertford the remonstrance he presented; after going about the town, and condemning it as violent and indecent.[18] See where the patrons of moderation and decency are to be found! Whether after this the Court will reward them for their pious labours is yet to be seen; indeed I neither much know or care.

Your mare has given me a fine foal; and has laid in another (I hope) at Lord Abingdon's. She returned to me sadly wounded, by a stake I believe near her udder. But she is recovering; the foal takes very kindly to other diet than milk;

---

[16] Sir Henry Houghton on March 7 moved for leave to bring in a bill to lift certain disabilities from the Dissenters. Burke supported the motion by a speech which is given in *Works* 10: 22-40.

[17] Heretofore, the King who accompanied Richard Burke to France has been identified as Thomas, but the present documents make clear that he was Joe King.

[18] James Townshend, Lord Mayor of London, was a follower of Shelburne and a bitter enemy of Wilkes. Early in March he was compelled to present a Wilkite remonstrance to the crown; doing this, he whispered to Lord Chamberlain Hertford that he was "only acting officially."

but if she continues long out of order I will give the foal a cow. Charles's breed goes on prosperously. This account I give of his mare. The account I have of his setting himself seriously to the profession gives me greater joy than all the annals of Newmarket could afford me.[19] He *must* be considerable; and that profession is so important, that I always rejoice when I find an honest man like to be leading in it. But he must be patient, and suffer some years to go over in the first part of the progress; afterwards it is rapid; and honours and wealth come when wealth and honours are most wanted, in the decline of life. Youth is so abundant in its own pure, native, genuine riches, in its charming possessions, and its charming hopes, that it stands in little need of these exterior props and plasterings to support and decorate it. Adieu. All here are yours. May our young people have all, and be all that they ought, and let our decline be easy, if it please God. Adieu

March 26. 1773

Let me have the pedigree of the mare, and who the sire of the foal is. Let me have too, if you please, the pedigree of Charles's mare. I intend to call the young lady foal Atalanta as she was got near the Atlantic Ocean.

[O'Hara had not received the above letter from Burke when he wrote the following.]

O'HARA TO BURKE, April 3, 1773

Nymphsfield, 3rd April 1773

My dear Edmund,

Since your return from your travels, I have had no sort of correspondence with you. I often hear of you, and every time a packet arrives I pay my tribute of thanks to those worthy printers who nobly persevered in printing the debates of your House. They have left off giving us the speeches, and content themselves with the subject and the characters of the speakers. In this I can rely on them; in their former undertaking I could

---

[19] "Your friend Charles attends the courts and reads with much nonchalance, but when he has a little business to do, he grows earnest." O'Hara to W. Burke, March 4, 1773.

not. Their account of the part you took on the petition of the Dissenters set me much at my ease for a week. I now want to hear more of you. Tho' I have lost much of my recollection of your motives, I can respect your conduct, and rejoice at it. 'Tis at least giving fair play to the best human heart, and the best principles. 'Tis an ample experiment, how far they may prevail in such an age. I think, from what I remember of England, their effect can't be great for public service. Quiet times befriend not genius and abilities, no more than they do liberty. The spirit of a mixed government is party and bustle. I begin however to think that you have, on one side, played part of your game very ill in lowering the reputation of Parliament. 'Tis taken up by others, and amongst you, you have raised a cry against it almost general, for not doing what is impossible, lowering the price of provisions.

I think physicians, when they forsee a change in chronic disorders, prepare to make the turn as favourable as they can. If I be wrong in this, my old friend must excuse me to you. But if I am [not] right in the practice of the faculty, I am certainly so in the allusion. Sawbridge [20] and Wilkes are able doctors; but their remedies are not a panacea. I find America begins to stir again. Ireland is almost undone, and people grow so sensible that a serious attention must be given to public business next session, that opposition will breathe a different spirit from what it has hitherto done. Our Lord Lieutenant pays great court to all the country party, with such a total neglect of all those who supported Government, as to go beyond giving offense; 'tis laughed at. Even the Law Servants of the Crown, who used to be little ministers amongst us, have not yet been called into the closet. On the contrary, they are given to understand that their aid is expected in Parliament, but they are not to be ministers. Everybody in employment has received intimation that they are amply provided for. Lord Harcourt sees none of them upon business. His excellency is Minister, and Col. Blaquiere is to lead in the House of Commons. They call upon clerks in office for information and with these only do they converse on business. I should have excepted the Chancellor; I believe he is in confidence. I don't complain of the circumstance; 'tis rather amusing, and I particularly like

[20] Alderman John Sawbridge (d. 1795), the persistent advocate of annually-elected Parliaments; brother of Mrs. Catherine Graham Macaulay, Burke's severe critic.

it at this time, as it gives us a fairer prospect of being able to put things to right, if possible, than we otherwise could have had. But can you tell me, my dear Edmund, why your Ministers give themselves so much trouble about us? They carried at all times every point they had a mind to carry. They encreased our military establishment; they load us with pensions as much as they pleased. They gave all our great employments to English; and yet we drank the bumper to the glorious memory of William the 3rd and continued still the King's humourous lieutenants. What do they desire more! 'Tis not enough for some people to get good things, they must get them in their own way.

Tho' I am as fond of this place as a man can be of a place without a house,[21] passionately fond of farming, which is now my principal avocation from the ways of the world, I must yet leave it next week for Dublin. I have returned no visits here these two years, which makes my retreat absolutely recluse. I am either about my farm, or at some book from morning to night. I grow knowing in both. Charles is gone circuit, and seems fond of the profession. My principal errand to Dublin is to prepare for England.[22] Mrs. Ponsonby [23] has taken it into her head that she shall never see me more, and wishes too earnestly for my company to be refused, from thence to England. Yours most truly.

O'

[A strong party in Parliament, not content with enacting a law to place the East India Company under a large measure of crown control, attempted to carry a criminal impeachment against the greatest of the Company's servants and founder of its territorial empire, Robert Clive. This dramatic case dominated the attention of Parliament and the public in the month of May.]

BURKE TO O'HARA, May 22, 1773

I hope you got my last, in which I gave you a short account of the spirit of the proceedings against the nabobs, on the

---

[21] Probably Nymphsfield was undergoing repairs.

[22] But on May 24 O'Hara wrote: "I can't see you as soon as I wish; there is something in the way of office to be done; something else in the way of money."

[23] His daughter.

report of the select committee.[24] This morning we finished the questions on Lord Clive at 5 o'clock. Lord North, who from the commencement of this business blew hot and cold, and veered round the whole thirty-two points of the compass of uncertainty and indecision, and would have gone through two and thirty hundred, if the same compass had contained them, met the natural and just reward of that sort of conduct, and was beat by 155 to 95. General Burgoyne, after giving notice of a motion of the harshest censure against Lord Clive, had considerably reduced it; however the motion still contained a description of his acquisitions, as being made under military influence; and the act of making them was charged as being contrary to his trust, and as of evil example to the servants of the public.[25] By the former part, the acquisitions came within the words of the resolution which gave them to the state; by the latter he became liable to criminal process. By two motions (both carried) for amendments, Burgoyne's proposition was reduced to a simple stating of the fact that my Lord Clive had received presents. These amendments were moved by Hans Stanley and Rose Fuller; both, you know, ministerial men.[26] Lord Clive made a short and spirited speech and left us about ten. The debate continued with great vivacity until five. Lord North took a sanguine part against Lord Clive on this last day, when it was too late to affect Clive or to save his own credit. He let his sheep wander in the Commons in the morning, and he could not get them together to the fold at night. He is not a good shepherd and the flock has not regard to his voice; because he is an hireling, and the sheep are not his own. The Bedfords continued to the last, furious; the Shelburnes kept up the same temper without remission. As far as I can con-

---

[24] Burke's "last" has not been found. Presumably he had given an account of the proceedings on the report of a select committee named the previous year to inquire into the East India Company. As a result of this report, General John Burgoyne on May 10 had moved and carried several resolutions to provide a foundation for the impeachment of Clive.—*Parliamentary history* 17: 856.

[25] On May 19 Burgoyne moved, "That the right hon. Robert Lord Clive . . . in consequence of the powers vested in him in India, had illegally acquired the sum of 234,000£ to the dishonour and detriment of the state."—*Ibid.*, 872.

[26] Stanley on May 21 moved to amend Burgoyne's resolution to the mere statement that Clive had acquired the stated sum by means of influence and the powers with which he was entrusted. Rose Fuller would have watered down the charge still more, but the Stanley amendment was passed as stated. Burgoyne then moved that Clive had abused his power "to the evil example of the servants of the public," and to this the House agreed.

jecture from appearances, the Butes set the Bedfords on Lord North; and when they had made them oppose Lord North, by not joining with them, and by joining with them, they left them both in the lurch. Stuart Mackenzie was very brisk at first. The last day he was absent. When Wedderburn saw that we had carried things by a triumphant majority, he moved a fresh resolution expressive of the services Lord Clive had done to the public.[27] It went without difficulty. Lord Clive has thus come out of the fiery trial, much brighter than he went into it; and not only not condemned, but actually approved by Parliament. His reputation too for ability stands higher than ever. Wedderburn conducted the whole ably. Lord G[eorge] Germain did extremely well on this last day and Thurlow and Barré were the best in support of the charge. I had formerly quitted Indian affairs—but my friends wished me to take a part, and I spoke just at four in the morning; though I had taken no refreshment since the preceding morning, my spirits were tolerable.

The King has appointed three commissioners, the Archbishop of Canterbury, the Chancellor, and the Bishop of London, to examine into the legality of the Duke of Gloucester's marriage. The Duke has demanded it on account of doubts raised at Court upon that subject. There may be some fracas. When you get any news from us communicate it with our love to Ridge and your Charles. Adieu my dear friend. All here are yours.

Speakers for the amendments		against
Stanley	Mr. E. Burke	Lord North
R. Fuller	Mr. T. Townshend	Dyson
Wedderburn	Mr. Byng	Thurlow
Sir R. Sutton	Hotham	Cornwallis
Seymour	Lord Barrington ! ! !	Popham
J. Grenville, Jr.	Norton. son to the	Ch. Fox
Dowdeswell	Speaker	Johnstone
Sr. Ch. Saunders		F. Vane
Lord Pigot		Hopkins
Genl. Carnack		W. Ellis
Genl. Conway		Burgoyne
Lord G. Germain		Meredith
Lord Fred. Campbell		
Sir G. Elliot		

[27] "That Robert Lord Clive did, at the same time, render great and meritorious service to this country."

O'HARA TO BURKE, June 3, 1773

Dublin 3rd June 1773

My dear Edmund,

I am to thank you for a clear account of as extraordinary a day as ever happened in Parliament. All your conjectures must be admitted, or the whole remains unaccountable; but another account of it from one of the Gang puts it beyond doubt. That body of men will not be readily pacified. I don't know which is most divided at this time, the Ministry or the opposition. You are as little in favour with the Court as the Bedfords with the Butes. Our Chief does not seem to think it will occasion any change of administration. I am sorry he does think so, for he's well informed. And yet upon the whole, I am more cheerful than I was; the event gives me more pleasure than any thing in English politics, without one consideration, should do. Our merchants reckon themselves much obliged to you for the part you have lately taken in favour of our linen trade.[28] To defeat Lord North on this subject would save this country from ruin. It would at least get me my rents, of which at present I can't get a farthing.

Our Secretary goes over immediately to lay our circumstances before the Ministers, with plans of taxation and every other material for a new arrangement of things amongst us. The late Government party is absolutely proscribed, but the neglect of them is so marked that I incline to impute it to policy. There has been a way of taking people in to disgrace them, not unknown on your side of the water since the year 1760. And something extraordinary, too heavy for a weak majority, is probably intended. Subjects for consultation can't long remain secret: you'll hear of them in their circulation. They will serve you for amusement, and may be of consequence to me.

I forgot to answer a question in one of your letters, viz., whether I get them regularly. I dare say I do, and unopened: which is a circumstance not belonging to the time. Yet I can't be persuaded they grow honest, rather indolent in their roguery.

---

[28] The Irish linen trade was severely depressed, because of the competition of continental linens in the English market. On March 17 Lord Frederick Campbell moved for a committee to consider this subject. There is no record of Burke's part in this, but probably he supported the Irish interest in the committee.—*Parliamentary history* 17: 796-799.

I have a notion the Bishop of Chester [29] has had some hand in our present system of politics, in favour of Flood. He certainly has stirred, and not improbably adopted his ideas. He is a good man and a powerful advocate at this time.

Here Ridge came in upon me in high spirits. He had heard that you revived a very drousy tired House at four o'clock in the morning; and cracks his jokes, and wants to know how many lacs of rupees Clive gave the Rockinghams. I refer him to Will for an answer.

There was a meeting of the wise ones this morning to consult about ways and means to encrease the revenue, and to raise a very large sum of money to pay off the Treasury debt; of which I hope to hear something, and therefore laid by this letter till evening. But I have been out, yet saw nobody to inform me. My enquiries would have been about the men, not the measures. For the Primate and Prime Serjeant are the only people amongst them in tolerable temper. I believe they have totally left the Provost out. So the Bedfords on this side of the water are in disgrace, and the Butes flourish. My love to the whole family. Adieu.

BURKE TO O'HARA, August 20, 1773

My dear friend,

Among my many arrears of all kinds I owe you a great deal on account of correspondence. I hope however you will believe me that the balance in matter of affection and real esteem is pretty equally balanced between us. An universal deadness has fallen upon all things; and my mind has got a blow from the same petrific mace. Want of any pleasing hopes, want of object, want of pursuit, inaction without repose, has thrown me into such a troubled sort of sleep for a long time past that I grow forgetful of the offices of friendship; because, in truth, I grow, as I wish to grow, forgetful of myself; and in that oblivion, find that heavy sort of comfort, which, to those who see only what is outward, may pass for tranquillity. My temper is not naturally sanguine; and my time of life is too cold to grow any thing visionary, or that belongs to the soil and climate of fairy land. However, though now and then sorrowful, I am no ways penitent. I trust I am so in some degree, for my

---

[29] William Markham (1719-1807), at one time a close friend of Burke's, but no longer.

private offences—but I am as sure as I can be of any thing in the world, that my public conduct, and that of those I act with (abating for human infirmity and indiscretion) has been entirely right both in action and intention. I ought not to be disappointed to find rectitude and success at a very great distance asunder. It would be ridiculous to murmur at not meeting what it would be ridiculous to expect to meet. If all were to do over again (omitting certain over-earnestness) it would be done exactly in the same manner. Your last letter [30] seems to think something mysterious in my conduct in the last session, as you hear I had voted with Lord North. This was merely a newspaper mistake or misrepresentation. Several of the ministerial people voted the same way our friends did in the business of Lord Clive; but Lord North voted against him, and was beat. The conduct of the whole nabob affair was weakness itself. It was pleasant to see the same house that voted down the East India Company out of envy to the opulence of their servants, when they had both before them, continue to persecute the master and let the servants escape. For my own part I thought their proceedings with regard to both parties, illegal, unjust, and impolitic, and as they pursued it, to the last degree weak and inconsistent. Will Burke, who has little reason to love or esteem Lord Clive, entered with warmth into the sentiments I felt, on the mere motives of public spirit, and took a strong part for him. What do you think of the man himself, who when he had just, and with infinite difficulty, escaped the injustice of a parliamentary inquisition, egged on the Ministry to the same injustice towards his masters and benefactors, and as it were to insult those by whose exertion he had been saved from present ruin.[31] Servility, certain situations and dispositions make very tolerable. But outrageous, daring, rampant servility is something shocking and unnatural; it is however common enough in the world, though not in the degree in which this man showed it.

I do not know how I have come to wander into this discourse; it arose, I believe, from my having mentioned the report of my voting with Lord North. I suspect I have in the session told you what I thought of this business once before; but as Lord Halifax said to the fatigued toad-eater that told him he had heard his story before—"Why then you shall have it again."

Your affairs will shortly draw to a crisis. Flood, I find, has

---

[30] Not found.   [31] Clive voted for the East India regulating act.

been in London, but incognito. I have not seen him nor have several other of his friends. I suppose that the state of his negotiations requires this privacy. Blaquiere wants a power of charging some new duties upon English malt liquors, in order to support the excise as well as the brewing trade in Ireland. If he can prevail on the Ministry to consent to this he imagines the popularity of such an act will enable Lord Harcourt to get well through the session—otherwise I am told they despair of it. I fancy the Treasury will not readily come into that proposition. However, if the landed interest can be quieted, the brewers are a body not sufficiently numerous to give much trouble to government. They may more easily carry that than any thing else which tends to lay a restraint upon the trade of England, but even such a restraint, though not unreasonable in the present state of things, will be full of difficulties.

My brother's affair has been heard before the Treasury; counsel supported it, and witnesses were examined. The Treasury seemed to be convinced that his offers were advantageous to the Crown; but still the spirit of indecision and the return of Sir William Young [32] will wholly defeat him, I am afraid. For that man is active, specious, and plausible, and does not want friends in the Treasury. In order to divert a pursuit from his own very great misconduct he will move heaven and earth to turn their thoughts against this purchase.[33]

We expect Jack Ridge over very soon. O, if we could expect you too! but that until the Christmas recess is impossible. Remember us most cordially to Charles, who takes to his profession in a manner to give me the best hopes and the most real satisfaction. Our lads in France were well when we last heard from them. I had a very tolerable French letter from Richard. The Doctor is well—so are Will and Dick and Madame. Adieu my dearest friend.

Beaconsfield August 20. 1773

---

[32] Lieutenant governor of Dominica.

[33] During 1772 British forces fought a small war against the natives of St. Vincent, and the government wished to reward the victorious commander, General Sir Richard Monckton. Charles Fox, a friend of the Burkes and now a junior lord of the Treasury, undertook to help them secure Richard's lands by proposing to Lord North that they be granted to Monckton on the understanding that he would sell them to Richard Burke for 10,000 pounds. The Burkes preferred to pay the Treasury directly, but North proceeded to grant the lands to Monckton without binding him to sell for Richard's price; and this the general refused to do, as the lands were worth more.—Wentworth-Fitzwilliam MSS, Burke to Rockingham, Sept. 21, 1773, partly transcribed and published in Magnus, Sir Philip, *Edmund Burke,* 338-342, London, John Murray, 1939.

XVII. Ireland and Absentee Landlords

[It came to the ears of Lord Rockingham in the early fall of 1773 that the North ministry was prepared to approve, in the Privy Council, the heavy taxation in Ireland of the rent rolls of all landlords who did not reside in that country. Irish state revenues were seriously deficient, and it was the intention of the Harcourt-Blaquiere administration to approve such a tax bill, which had long been a favorite scheme of the Irish patriots. Henry Flood was to sponsor the measure, and Dublin Castle was to acquiesce in it, with the assent of the British cabinet.

Rockingham was one of the great landlords who would suffer from an absentee tax. So was Sir George Savile. Indeed a large part of the income of the leading men in the Whig party was drawn from their Irish estates. The Marquess was aroused; he saw such a tax scheme not only as unjust discrimination against landlords who chose to maintain their residence in England, but as a threat to Anglo-Irish community. Hence he mobilized his friends to bring all possible pressure upon the Irish Parliament to defeat the tax, and in the event of failure in Dublin, to fight it in the English Privy Council. Burke took a leading part in this campaign, furnishing his friends in the Irish Parliament with arguments against the tax.[1] The bill had not yet been defeated when he wrote the following to O'Hara.]

BURKE TO O'HARA, November 19, 1773

My dear friend,

You are now the busy and I the idle man. I am sauntering in town along with Will and the rest of us; and Jack Ridge, that has brought us to London, makes our stay in it pleasant to us. We do not complain of the emptiness of the town though it is thinner than I think is quite usual at this time of the year. The universal poverty very much recommends the country life, and paints a raw and weeping November in more engaging colours than the gaudiest pencil of the pastoral poets ever decked the blooming month of May. This insolent poverty, which is as bold as death, and as irresistible, has dared

---

[1] For Burke's arguments see his letter to Sir Charles Bingham, Oct. 30, 1773, in *Works* 9: 134-147.

even to pollute the seat of majesty itself. The current rumour here is, that our first business at the meeting will be the discharge of the Civil List debts. People think them very great, and the scheme of paying them quite certain. Our premier meets, every now and then, some little marks of discountenance, which are attributed to his desire of adjourning this critical business to a new Parliament. Those who are not in a situation of responsibility with regard to the measure will naturally urge it on. They will make themselves acceptable at Court upon the credit of forwarding that, of which another is to bear the whole weight of the public odium. There are in the world an innumerable multitude of bold counsellors, and who are bold upon this principle. About foreign affairs we are absolutely asleep, though his Prussian Majesty, God bless him, does all in his power to awaken us. In the City there are some little faint remains of life, which only shows itself by the distempers it feeds. Wilkes assaulted by the Court, and trimmed by the treachery of the Shelburne party, still maintains his ground. He is on his part as imprudent as his enemies of all sorts could wish; but with his success, I do not know what part of his conduct, after all, one can venture to call by the name of imprudence.[2] It may perhaps be rather some unusual and eccentric kind of wisdom. All the rest of the Kingdom is quite stupefied; except a small part which you have awakened by the scheme of an absentee tax. You know the steps that have been taken in this business, by the circular letter and correspondence; which by being sent to all the absentees, have undoubtedly found their way to Ireland through more channels than one. Could any one believe it possible, even among all the dreary visions of this raving (but not inspired) age we live in, that such a project should be entertained among the ways and means of English Government? Proposed by an English Secretary—to an English Lord Lieutenant—adopted, and what is more, avowed by an English First Lord of the Treasury—*stante Jove*

[2] Wilkes about this time was elected Lord Mayor of London. Earlier in the month Burke attended a dinner in the city where Wilkes was present, and related to Rockingham: "As to Wilkes, I cannot be persuaded but that in the end he will jest and buffoon himself out of his consequence. His petulance and levity are something beyond what is credible. I sat near him and he was ridiculing and abusing his adherents without any management, and in the hearing of several people. I hinted to him jestingly that his friends, by being such, were too respectable not to be treated with a little decorum. O, he says, I never laugh at my *friends*, but these are only my *followers!*"—Wentworth-Fitzwilliam MSS, Burke to Rockingham, Nov. 7, 1773.

et urbe Roma! [3] I hear the pleasant end of it may be, that it will be smothered in the filthy slime and mud of that very popularity to which it owed its equivocal generation. Sir Charles Bingham has written me two long and friendly letters on the subject.[4] It is amazing with what spirit and activity Lord Rockingham exerted himself on the occasion. Malagrida disapproved the measure, as you may easily judge—but he acted too in the manner you may easily judge.[5]

I find you have given up the Excise Board; but that the members are properly secured. If so, I wish you had rather been with the falling than the standing establishment. Good lord, what a proceeding has the whole of this been! When Lord Northington found that Lord Camden immediately after he had taken the seals had given up a great point of law and politics that he had strenuously insisted on, Old Sarcasms sent him a verbal message by an officer of his court to the following tenour—"Go tell your master that if he begins his office by giving up his measures, I shall see his arse and his mace in the kennel within a fortnight, by God." It is said that Flood did not complete his bargain while he was here; and that your Irish Ministry was not more fortunate in any other negotiation; [that] the old hacks are neither (as I hear) bridled or saddled; that there is nothing in the rack and manger for them; and that none else are taken into the stable; but that, however, things though they have a very disconcerted have not as yet a very angry appearance. When there is any thing worth knowing you will let us know it. When otherwise you will at least let us hear from you that you are well, and then I assure you I care very little what news comes from your side of the water. Ridge tells me that you are wonderfully well. He says things too of Charles that please but don't surprise us. Your oldest friend (we are all now old friends) William, Richard, Madame and our new part of the family truly yours. My dear friend, believe me from the bottom of my heart ever so.

Nov. 19. 1773

[3] Horace, *Odes,* 3.15.12.

[4] "You have furnished me with arguments, that I had not yet heard any person make use of, and have put this extraordinary attempt into the proper light.—Wentworth-Fitzwilliam MSS, Bingham to Burke, Nov. 7, 1773.

[5] Shelburne, whose Irish rent roll exceeded that of any other absentee landlord, at first welcomed and then refused to support Rockingham's campaign against the tax, probably because Chatham thought it a proper revenue measure for Ireland.

[postscript by Will Burke]

minus 4 days

Ridge is here and that is a point of satisfaction pure and unmixed. Shall I tell you a foolish thing? I waited for months to begin a letter to you with "Ridge is here, and"—well Ridge is here and that is a certain good; the *and* is today within the grasp, and then a thousand miles distant, and then hopeful, then desperate.[6] At this moment I know not what to say of it, but let what will be, we are yours. Remember us to Charles and William.

[The absentee tax had been lost in the Irish Parliament by the time Burke wrote his next extant letter.]

BURKE TO O'HARA, December 11, 1773

My dear friend,

I have not received any thing for a very long time with so much real satisfaction as your last letter.[7] It was excellent in what it gave; and it was better in what it promised. Oh! come over, if possibly you can, and let us walk one Christmas more in the pavement of our hall by the glimmering lamplight; and try whether we can delude the cares of this life a little longer— a little longer. The coming of our dear friend Ridge was a real cordial; but you know the consequence of taking cordials—we only long for you the more on his account. So let us see you again. I am told you are better than ever—we are not worse—I think we have carried great health quite through. This is no mean blessing; and I hope we are not unthankful for it.

I thank you for your political map of Ireland. I am sure it is as true as the ablest survey and the best observations can make it. You have measured with your chain on the earth and you have not neglected to take observations of the higher bodies. I think I see that confusion and all the effects of it. I return in the very middle of the scene, your description is so very lively. I quite agree with you, that they are bringing both countries to a perfect state of uniformity. I assure you if they can effect this, your government, (I won't say your business;

---

[6] Probably refers to Richard's St. Vincent's business.
[7] Not found.

for you will have none) will go on very smoothly. I really once
thought that abilities were of some use in the management of
public affairs; and that where they were wanting, great and
uncommon industry and attention were absolutely necessary
to fill the void. However I am seriously undeceived. For when
I think on the hard struggles, and often very unsuccessful ones,
that the great men in history have gone through, merely to
keep government on its ordinary basis, without either extending or contracting its powers; and on the other side, when I
consider the perfect ease with which the present people, not
only with very moderate abilities, but with little or no exertion
of the abilities they have, carry on administration with the most
perfect success and perfect tranquillity, I am strongly inclined
to believe that parts and industry, however they may serve the
public in the long run, are inconvenient to the present quiet
and security of the holders of power. If these people had been
as calm as they have been indolent, I should not wonder that
little enterprise should meet with but few difficulties. But
they have been driven, every now and then, to the most critical
attempts. In many of these attempts they have been foiled.
But it is in their defeat that their strength is discovered. They
lose nothing; not even credit; because the only credit they
have any occasion for is an opinion of stability. I am often
amazed how they go on. They neither spread the sail, nor ply
the oar—however they tide it over. What say you to the whole
proceeding on the Absentee Bill? I don't mean with regard
to the merits of the measure—because I don't know your
opinion—but to the conduct of it, both in England and Ireland.
They have got Flood—but with his assistance they have not
been able to carry the measure on which the treaty was
grounded, and the popularity of his change was to be ensured.
His bridge cracked as soon as the arch was turned.[8] Is it possible, is it even now possible, that you have such speeches in
the Irish House of Commons as we read in the papers? "Let
nobody vote for *complaisance.*" "The misfortunes of Ireland
not owing *solely* to the late Lord Lieutenant"—together with
the King of Prussia and the review at Portsmouth and a long
etc. etc. etc. Well I turn from these follies to call you by all
sorts of prayers and incantations to us, *votis omnibusque, at*

---

[8] The patriot leader was negotiating to abandon opposition and come into
government with the passing of the popular absentee tax, which had failed.
Not until the fall of 1775 did he close his bargain with administration.

precibus, vocamus. Jack Ridge joins us in these prayers—all here do sincerely love you and your Charles.

December 11. 1773

Have you got my last letter?

O'HARA TO BURKE, December 18, 1773

18th December 1773

I have two of my dear Edmund's letters before me to answer, an unusual circumstance. The first I received just as a letter of mine to you went off. Politics are now so well, and so universally understood, that no room is left for speculation and conjecture and are therefore of no further use, either for conversation or correspondence. New incidents may furnish examples, but the theory is, and will, for its period, remain the same. Your India Bill and our Absentee Tax, however different in appearance and relation, are yet from the same shop; in which the craft work much harder than you seem to think. The plan is uniform, and the labour of the execution is softened by regularity and method. I was against the tax from the first mention of it, to its burial. My objections reached to more remote consequences than could be introduced in debate, and were indeed too delicate for a man in the service of the Crown to utter. But they had their effect in confidential communication. You repeat some passages of certain speeches; they are justly reported, so accurately that I suspect they were sent to the press: some speeches, I know, have been. There is now in a course of arrangement a new order for the Staff, which gives great offense to the military. A large addition is made to the emolument of a few, but with great diminution of dignity, and not a little of liberty. I dare say 'tis known in London. Mr. Keppel,[9] who was appointed to a command-in-chief, must have it; which makes me think a copy unnecessary to send you. Our Administration perseveres in rejection of all advice from people here and therefore nothing is communicated. The Prime Serjeant is the Minister of the House of Commons, but his information is incidental only, and progressive, never full and given at once. The Chancellor is the only

---

[9] William Keppel (d. 1782), brother of the third Earl of Albemarle.

Minister, his connexion solely with Lord Chatham and Lord
Camden; and Flood returned to us with letters of marque from
the same shop. Think of this master broom, and tell me
whether English Administration be so simplified, as you describe it. When the Absentee Tax was opposed in England
by those whose interest was to be affected by it, Lord Shelburne
did not join with them, and for this reason: because Lord Chatham approved the measure. When it was defeated here after
a long discussion, and an account of it transmitted to Lord
North, this last was then released from his engagement. So
that Flood's bringing it on again, was so critical to Lord Harcourt, that had it been carried, he would have thought himself
obliged to withdraw from the Government of this country as
soon as he could—and therefore exerted himself against it with
all his might; the effect was answerable. For Lord Townshend's
irregular administration, like the hussars of an army, broke
all parties here, tho' unable to form an effectual one for his
own use. But its effects are now felt, and much to the ease of
the present Government. One thing however will some time
or other happen; the reconciling of strong forces of men to
the measures of the times, restores a reunion amongst themselves; they will again grow powerful, and if the present spirit
should last, another ministerial exertion will be necessary to
pull them down. So that I think (with regard to the reigning
system) we are rather retrograde than advancing. Flood's situation isn't enigmatical, and I am not sure that some measures
against the legality of the Chancellor of the Exchequer's patent,
now in embryo, may not facilitate his pursuit of that object.[10]
Some steps in relation to the Master of the Rolls' patent will
very soon be taken, but with reserving to Rigby for life.[11]

I can't give you a better view of the secrecy of our present
Administration than by stating to you, that the new stamp duty
is to be under our care as Commissioners of Accounts, that yet
neither I, nor any of my brethren, have ever been spoke to on
the subject.[12] Nor shall we, until the arrangement is completed.
This actually prevents all intrigue, but substitutes much dissatisfaction in its place; of which however I have no share,
having made my mind to the times, growing daily less anxious

---

[10] This patent was held by William Gerard Hamilton.
[11] He had held this sinecure since 1759.
[12] A stamp tax had been laid on various legal and business documents.—
Statutes at Large . . . in Ireland 10: 366-379.

about my political interests, and much less curious about state affairs. One thing indeed, tho' of the political kind, troubles me: that by means of these stamps, I am prevented from spending this Christmas with you, for 'tis not possible I can go till this business is settled. The bill will be here tomorrow, and I must watch the arrangement which is to follow it. But my fixed resolution is, to go as soon as ever I can. Charles who is almost as much yours as I am, enquires constantly for Ridge, and when he will return. He says, to get at his books; but I believe rather to tease him for advice.

I told you years ago that the linen manufactury of this Kingdom was upon the decline. 'Tis now sunk to a very low ebb, and if something ben't done for us next session, it will fall away to nothing. But I fear you are somewhat upon the decline in Great Britain also. Your commercial credit has received a wound which must affect your manufactures. The acquisition of Danzic to Prussia must be some loss;[13] much has happened against England since we parted, nothing for it. Thus things appear to me, but at too great a distance to see clearly. I long for those lamplight walks you invite me to; and I would not at this time of life accept of any business which may keep me longer from them, if it were not necessary to my affairs. I want to change what I have for something in the law line for Charles. I am still young enough to scheme, because I am perfectly well, and forget, perhaps too much, that I grow old. You have been idle in the literary way of late. Have you nothing in the stocks? Is such a candle to be hid under a bushel? I designed this for a longer letter, but the money bills are come and I am called to the House at half an hour past eight. Adieu, my dear friend, my compliments to the family.

BURKE TO O'HARA, December 22, 1773

My dear Sir,

I wrote to you just at leaving town; since we came hither we have been flattering ourselves every hour that we might possibly see you, and make a good Christmas of it, before you went to your school and I to mine. I see they have added a new department to your Board; I trust this additional employment

---

[13] The first partition of Poland, arranged by the 1772 Treaty of Reichenbach.

will not be a means of detaining you; or if it should, that they may make it up to you in salary. I really do not see how they can think of encumbering you with a new duty without some compensation. For if they can make you a commissioner of stamps, an office which will not be without business, it will be a tacit admission that either your first employment was nearly useless, or your first salary very inadequate, when they lay a complete new establishment upon your shoulders without any consideration for it. However that may be, I cannot help treating you like a great man in office solely because I know you will not treat me like one. Your board of stamps will in all likelihood have occasion for a solicitor. If you are not already engaged in promise, or by a just claim of preference to any friend of your own, I wish to recommend one of mine. I mean Mr. Kiernan, an attorney who lives in Tishamble street; one for whose judgment, fidelity, and diligence I can thoroughly answer. I confess I am under obligations to him, and would serve him if I could.

I saw your name in the late majority on the Absentee Tax. The Parliament of Ireland have I think done themselves much credit. I believe no man rejoiced more who saved the ten per cent on his estate than the Ministry did here when the Parliament refused to send them that coal of fire which they could neither know how to cast away or to hold. Most of the Cabinet here were utterly unacquainted with the design; they railed at it open-mouthed. If it had come hither there would certainly have been some work; but you saved us the trouble and the sport. However I may judge by some conversations, and by the stir the Court hirelings have made in the news paper when it was so evidently the wish and interest of most of the Ministers to let the matter drop, the attempt will be revived another time. I suspect it came from the Sanctum Sanctorum. It must indeed be either very deep design or very consummate folly that first gave rise to it—possibly a little of both.

We have our old friend the Doctor with us. The rest are gone to town for a day or two. Would you but come in upon us! Adieu, we all salute you. You have no friends that love you better. Our regards of the best and warmest sort to Charles and William—and to Mrs. Ponsonby if in town.

Beaconsfield December 22. 1773

[postscript by Dr. Nugent]

My dear Sir,

The post was pretty near going off when Edmund brought me the above to say something for myself in the remnant he had left me. I have many pardons to ask that I had not long since acknowledged the pleasure of your last very agreeable and friendly letter. Your account of the Antiquarian Society, and certain steps taken to promote it gave me real satisfaction. I doubt your learned historian looks several ways at once; and that he squints towards preferment as devoutly as he can.[14] He has too many *Epithets* and perhaps too few dates. I have not read it through, so may be too hasty in my opinion. I am however not sorry that he has declined the foreign correspondence, as I imagine he would not be glad to make too many discoveries. I cannot say that I am at present as well as you or I could wish. I have a heavy cold which I hope to get the better of in time. Hitherto I have been really well for a youngish man of 76; but whether sick or well or young or old I have a memory which still serves me to remember you and your early friendship with a certain feeling that can never quit me. I assure you it will much shorten my cold to see you here in a little time. Our worthy friend Mr. Ridge is now in town though to be here in a day or two. How long his stay may be in England I cannot tell as yet.

[The Burkes passed the Christmas holidays without sight of O'Hara, and early in the new year received news from him that he had been ill; but his letter has not been found. It seems to have been directed to Dr. Nugent and to have solicited his medical advice.]

BURKE TO O'HARA, January 6, 1774

My dear friend,

The Doctor got your letter this day. He is in that state, in which such a letter cannot fail of doing him good. I mean such a letter, with such sentiments, and from such a friend. It was the whole composition of *all* the ingredients in the royal medicine of this Mithridates which produced the salutary effect.

---

[14] Possibly, Dr. Thomas Leland. O'Hara's letter to Nugent is not found.

He has indeed been so ill as to alarm us a little; but his recovery has been regular, steady and uninterrupted. He intended to write himself but I insisted, that he should not do
it now; but reserve it to his full strength; which I now think
a very few days will restore to him. He seems to have had a
mixture of gout in his complaints; and a sort of soreness in
a great toe seems to have gone a good way towards his recovery.

Having left him, I bless God, in so good a way, I now set
at discharging his commission relative to your *late* complaints;
I hope I speak of a thing that remains only in your memory.
You mention, that you had taken a purgative medicine for
the bleeding piles. He desires me to tell you, that, though
he will not assert that in such a case no medicine at all ought
ever to be taken, (as he can imagine circumstances in which
remedies would be very proper) yet he lays it down, as general as a rule can well be, that when nature makes that sort
of a push, and gets rid of its own grievances in its own way,
any kind of attempt which interferes with it, even by way of
assistance, much less of counteraction, may be of extreme
danger, and rarely can be productive of any good consequences.
He therefore wishes you not to consider a visit of such piles
as a distemper, but as a physician, that keeps off gout in some
complaints. This, (with the temperaments, which reason and
judgment gives to all general rules) is his direction to you;
and from which he wishes you not to deviate but upon the
soundest advice.

I heartily thank you for your letters to myself. If the Parliament of Ireland rejects the alterations made here, in the heads
of the bill, which they substitute in the place of that they reject, they will do something manly, and which will bring the
privilege they claim to an issue.[15] When they rejected last
session an altered money bill, and afterwards adopted the
alterations, they did wisely, considering it as a thing that might
not occur again, and in which they might temporize in order
to prevent too much discussion on a subject, which, for the
good of both sides, ought to sleep forever. But when they
not only continue the practice, but grow upon you in the use
of it, then temporizing is submission; and your rejecting their

---

15 The Irish House of Commons held that the "heads" of money bills sent
over for approval by the English Privy Council ought not to be changed on
being returned. O'Hara on Dec. 24 had written: "Tell me why four of our five
money bills have been altered."

bill, in order to save your honour together with their amendments, is only a more circuitous, inconvenient, and expensive way of admitting their right and answering their intentions. It is at best a sort of *protest* on your part—and a protest against an act voluntary on the part of the doer can have an effect but *once*. If a man acts under *compulsion,* his protest *toties quoties* is good and saves his right; not because the right is saved merely by the protest; but that the protest is a record of *violence,* which violence is in reality what saves the right, and not the formality of the protesting. But where it is in a man's choice, whether he should do a certain act or not, he may do it under protest for *once* without losing his right, because the singularity of some special occasion may be a reason for suspending his privilege without any intention of abandoning it. But *frequent voluntary* compliances *annul* the protest and *affirm* the demand—for what is a constant compliance with an *adverse claim* but a dereliction of the right of opposing it? These are my poor opinions of acts of protestation. If you proceed in the way that will be recommended to you, the whole of your privilege (however founded) will amount to this; that when Attorney or Solicitor Generals alter your money bills, they must pass twice through the forms; and that is the most perfect admission of the right claimed on the part of the Council, and at the same time the most inconvenient manner of exercising it for all the parties concerned.

I *knew* of Lord Chatham's *quasi*-approbation of the absentee tax, and *suspected* that Flood had concerted the affair with him here. But as far as it is safe to affirm any thing of the Grand Ex-Jesuit, he knew nothing at all of it until Lord Besborough informed him of the design.[16] He was first all fire and flame against it; but he refused to agree to the application to Ministers as too tame a measure. Then he heard from Lord Chatham, who had his *doubts* that the scheme might be a good one. Then he declined all cooperation—he called the measure of writing to Lord North violent and indecent,[17] in his discourse with courtiers—when he met with patriots, it was

---

[16] Shelburne.

[17] Rockingham, the Duke of Devonshire, Lord Milton and the Earl of Upper Ossory had addressed a letter, Oct. 16, to North stating that it was publicly reported that the absentee tax was being encouraged by the British administration, and denouncing it in the strongest language.—Albemarle, *op. cit.,* 2: 277-278.

cold and languid. In short, in a few days he took no less than six different turns in this business, which tended infinitely to raise him in the esteem of all that had an opportunity of observing the beautiful harmony and consistency of his proceedings. What system on the whole this discovers, I know not. I am persuaded that, whatever share Lord Chatham or Lord Camden are permitted to have through the Chancellor in the affairs of Ireland, they have little or none here. As to Flood, he has observed that no small consequence is to be derived from a supposed connexion with the old man of the mountain.[18] You may repeat his opinions just as you please. He never disavows you until he gets something by doing it; and nothing is lost by an attachment to him; for he lets you take what part suits best your own interest until he calls upon you; which he never does, but when the cards are, or he thinks they are, quite at his own packing. In the mean time a man in Ireland is always helped by being thought the representative here of some great and weighty party in this Kingdom. It is a fine thing to be admitted a partaker of the mysterious solemnity of every thing that approaches the great oracle. Adieu! I am not initiated into those mysteries, nor in the greater mysteries of the Court. I am as old Homer says, amongst those who have heard a sort of report, but *know* nothing. All salute you and yours most affectionately. God bless you.

January 6th. 1774

---

[18] Chatham.

XVIII. America and Bristol

[For the momentous parliamentary session of 1774, when the coercion acts against Massachusetts were passed and the grand American crisis precipitated, there is unfortunately a total void in the surviving correspondence of Edmund Burke with Charles O'Hara. This void continues through the year until it is broken by Burke in November with a letter telling of his election to Parliament from Bristol. From the manner of that letter, it may be concluded that it was not a renewal of a long-broken correspondence. Probably these men wrote many times to one another during those ten months, but the letters have not come to light.

There are, however, several letters from William Burke to O'Hara which provide many glimpses of Edmund and the "fireside" in this period. They help to bridge the great gap in the main correspondence.]

WILLIAM BURKE TO O'HARA, May 6, 1774

May 6. 1774

I do not on the whole imagine that procrastination is among my characteristic vices; for in fact I don't feel that indulgence for it in others, that one bears to the faults one finds oneself apt to fall into. But perhaps a man is in most danger of sinning deeply, when he falls into those offences he has least practised, like the old Quaker here happening after fifty to get into a bawdy house, stayed there three weeks, and run up a bill of £1500. If some of my friends delay their letter duties a month or two, they take up again as a thing in the way of business; this delay is a vice they are used to; they fall into and out of it, as a thing of course, while my delay operates in me [as] an actual inaptitude. I really found a sort of moral impossibility of writing to you; I was obliged to create to my own fancy some *novus ordo rerum*, as the necessary instigation to my taking up my pen again. This I fancy Ridge has informed you of, but as I fixt the arrival of some fortunate event among us, as the source and spring of this renovation of correspondence, you who are apt to reason with some logical sort of conjecture in your expectation of events, have not I believe entertained any sanguine hopes of hearing from me soon; and the truth is that inured to disappointments and crosses, they are almost become my natural element. When I can't succeed in an object today, I have actually learnt a faculty to put off my vexation and disappointment till tomorrow, and strange as it may seem, sad disappointment, with me at least, has strengthened hope, and makes me look for things unreasonable to be expected; but this indeed I am encouraged to do, from such very and most extremely fortunate incidents that befall in the very midst of ill fortune, that I trust I may still see the end of grief and may live *traducere leniter aevum*. One thing I feel and thank Providence for—these fortunate events keep up and fortify the mind, and tend to preserve a correctness and some dignity in; for that man who falls into misfortune and does not find his heart corrupted and degraded, finds wherof to thank his God most justly; and such instances I have seen in the unfortunate, as have terrified me more I had almost said than my own misfortunes.[1]

I am sure that when I took up my pen, I had no thought of writing in this kind; my falling into this sort of language will perhaps show you more than any *eclaircissement* I could make to you, how much in reality I am unfit to write to you at all.

From the message I sent you by Ridge, a letter from me will as I said raise your expectation of fortunate events, and yet there is no change public or private that concerns immediately ourselves, to rejoice you. Had indeed our dear Ridge actually succeeded in his object, I would have accounted it a full and just cause for my renovation of correspondence with you, and I do trust that by following it up both on your side and ours we may effect the objects we have in view for him; and any thing to his credit or fortunes cannot surely be to us other than a fortunate event of great satisfaction.[2] Tell him we showed his letter to Sir G.—who was much pleased and will not fail to acquaint his friend of the attention that has been paid to his recommendation, and which of course lends to the further recommendation.

I do not however mean this to go to you without acquainting you with a very fortunate event, and which in fact was the occasion of my writing today.

---

[1] The cause or causes of this rather maudlin melancholy were probably related to the bleak political outlook for the Rockingham party and Richard Burke's failure to vindicate his St. Vincent's claim.

[2] Ridge was seeking the "silk gown" of a king's counsel.

Our Joe King has got the care of the education of the young Marquess of Blandford. He has £200 a year, a servant, and a pair of horses, till he is provided for; two or three years will certainly give him a dignity in the Church, and in fact there is no dignity that is not fairly within his hopes in time; *en attendant,* he is in a most respectable situation, with a very good income. You will very readily conceive how deeply we are interested in this event; the worthiness of King must naturally make us, who know him, rejoice in his good fortune; but besides and independent of that, it takes a load off us, for the perhaps most unsatisfactory circumstance that attends an unsuccessful party is their disability to serve their friends. If their own fortunes or their own ambition are unadvanced, they may find their recompence within themselves, but your friends can't judge of your motives, nor will probably admire your wisdom, when your conduct runs so diametrically opposite to their interest. I say this merely as a general reasoning, seriously unapplicable to our Joe, who is the most disinterested creature that lives; and would have loved Edmund and his boy, tho' he had been for life condemned to a curacy. But his worthiness makes his good fortune but an additional satisfaction to us, as you may easily imagine. The thing has been in agitation ever since his return from France. Our little Richard has some reputation, and surely it is an high satisfaction that the first effects of a man's reputation should effect such an essential service to a friend, to whom he owed so much. Joe who would have been contented, aye and happy too, upon a curacy, you may imagine if you please, to have been quite at his ease and unanxious about this; but, if such is your imagination, you never were more out in your life; he was as busy as a hen with one chick, and it required a little of the housewife's care that the chick should not be over laid and crushed by carefulness. But the thing is now done, and Joe is pretty much at ease; nor would he be obliged to me for insinuating that he ever was anxious or uneasy; for you must know that my friend is persuaded that the *savoir faire,* and a knowledge of the world, is his forte. Now I rather take him to be a most worthy, disinterested, honest, simple character, but who had great good fortune to have had a person of little Richard's experience to have taken care of him while he was abroad. But I assure you Joe differs very much with me in this opinion; not but I believe at bottom, that he defers a great deal to his friend Richard too.

Well then! You see I have not stayed in vain; a fortunate event has arrived, to justify my writing to you. Repay me in kind, and let me know that our friend Ridge has a silk gown. My last to him mentioned the exact state of R[ichard] B[urke]'s affair, so I need not mention it.

I believe if I could fairly tear the first sheet without interrupting the sense, I should do it; for if I remembered, it has a melancholy air, and that is an air one ought not to communicate. It is only in my own room that I admit it to myself. But if I broke off, by destroying that, God knows when I should write, whereas one letter will produce another, and now you will hear often enough.

The House is now busied in giving a constitution to Canada, or rather they are saving themselves the trouble of framing one, by establishing a council there which they make absolute and uncontrollable.[3] This seems to alarm the people at home a little; it makes more noise a great deal than the *annihilation* of Boston did; but still they carry it swimmingly. North is never at ease when he is a little pushed, and he seems now vexed and ill at ease.

There was a talk of dissolution this summer, but I have I think pretty good reason to suppose it will not be.

Poor Dowd[eswell] is very ill; his death will I seriously think prove of bad consequence; and to add to that, he is a man of intrinsic worth.[4]

Lord Chatham has shewn himself, with no reasonable expectations that they would pay for seeing him, and he has gone home again. Whatever views Shelburne had, they [were] in the news paper phrase, premature. He and his are in furious opposition. Lord G[eorge] G[ermain] has I fancy been humbugged; I don't find he gets any thing, and yet he has been made to disgrace himself with opposition; at least I think he has.

The people in power here affect to say that the old ministry in France will continue; whether their hopes or their information say this I can't determine.[5]

---

[3] The Quebec Act. Reference to this proves that this letter was not completed until near the end of May.

[4] Dowdeswell was mortally ill, but did not die until the next year.

[5] Louis XV died on May 10, and soon afterward the Duc d'Aiguillon was replaced by the Comte de Vergennes as minister for foreign affairs.

Remember us all most cordially to Charles; the accounts Ridge gave us of him were very and very satisfactory. If Charles continues his application, it cannot fail making him very considerable in his country. The respect our young Richard has for Charles has been a very useful instrument to me, and I shall continue to make use of him; but I believe Charles will do me the justice to believe that I have stronger motive for his honour and prosperity, than his mere example, tho' to our Richard. The Doctor is very stout, and we are all thank God well. Let us soon know that you are so.

WILLIAM BURKE TO O'HARA, September 2, 1774

I don't know where this is to find you. I would give something that it pursued you to London, where we have a deal to say to you. If we had you now, in Verdict Lane, showing you the marked trees, you would be soon enabled to make Charles perfect master of the whole doctrine of lord and tenant's right to trees growing outside of hedges; and you would in a moment see what a cursed vexation it must have been to have lost the pretty oaks, and to have that pretty private lane of communication adjudged a public road; you would see what future law suits, squabbles, and vexations it would be productive of, and you would have congratulated our Edmund in avoiding all this mischief, by a jury of gentlemen after a view. But to show you what a good thing success is, and how much wise men should cultivate and pursue it, he is actually become popular in his County from and by succeeding in his cause. *in medias res rapit ac quasi notat*, is I think a rule of writing, and was I suppose my motive for taking you a walk through this pretty lane of Ned's, which you are to know the lord of the manor wantonly attempted to take as part of his waste, and was defeated with such shame that he left the assizes with his blinds all drawn up, and has not shown himself since. To say the truth, Ned throughout the whole conducted himself so quietly, modestly, and prudently, that he deserved all the praise he got for his gentlemanly carriage, but it was his success more than any possible merit that gained him the respect of the County. You who know Ned will not wonder how little he wished to carry a cause to be tried against an old family of the County. He is a stranger

and an Irishman; you need not be told the feelings the man
had; he has costs against his adversary.[6] And independent of
the satisfaction of the lane above a mile long being more de-
cisively his own, than without a decision it could have been,
it has really been of great service to him.

People say they did not know him, as indeed I believe there
is not in the world a man less understood. A good-humoured
booby squire speaking of us both to some women of our
acquaintance allowed me willingly enough all the idle merit
of companiability, but "by G— that t'other Burke man," says
he, "I should not like to drink a bottle with him at all." The
women did Ned justice and assured him as the truth is, that
the poor fellow was as idle and good humoured as a fool—
but no; that could not be, "it was impossible that a man like
that, always in a fruitless violent opposition, always crossed,
should not at last, whatever he might be first, grow peevish and
ill natured." I allow my squire's whim was somewhat above
the level of squire understandings, but the truth is that not
the merit but the success of your conduct is what insures the
approbation of mankind; a man is a traitor or a patriot by the
event, not by his motive. My squire however begged Ned's
acceptance of the stewardship of Aylesbury Races for next
year, so there at last you see Edmund is in office! And has
actually touched the people's money! To be sure there are
other offices that Ned is full as fit for; and to say the truth,
he blushed as if a bribe had been offered him, but Murragh
O'Brien [7] was near him and kicked his shins till he made him
accept it; and in fact Ned never will (I'll swear) take any
thing in whatever shape it comes, if some one that he is sure
loves him, does not kick his shins into it; not but I think at
present his shins don't seem to be in much danger. And yet
things are so oddly situated, that I should not be surprised at
what I do not expect, and I am sure when we went to the races,
we as little expected this little country gentleman glory, as
we do a change of ministry; and believe me it was the little
long lane that he succeeded in, that made him steward of the
races. My God, if Ned was in office, how he would be be-

6 "I have scarcely been from home an hour since I saw your Lordship;
except at the assizes of Buckingham, where I was obliged to go on a troublesome matter of litigation, which is now over. . . ."—Burke to Rockingham,
Sept. 16, 1774, *Correspondence* 1: 470.
7 Murrough O'Brien (1731-1808), later Earl of Inchiquin.

praised! If it pleases God to bring him there, without sacrifice of friends or opinions, good!—if not, I won't break his shins. If my own avarice or what else inclined me to it, I feel that *reverentia puero;* I stand in awe of young Richard. We have taken no little pains to make him an honest public man as well as a fair private man, and we must not destroy our own work, which with the blessing of God we have succeeded in, for there is nothing *turpe* or *populari quicquam* about the young man.

For my own part, I have a feel of a sort of ease and good humour about me, that has an air of prosperity; full of perplexity and difficulties, I proceed as if I had an hope to get through them all. If you cross the water you will certainly bring us some good in bringing yourself, but my mind divines you'll be the witness of some other good to us, and I long with more than usual concern for the performance of your promise. I wrote yesterday a long letter to Ridge; when you have taken wind after going through this, if you are not tired, I refer you to him about his business too, which I wish you to conn over together.

Apropos of races I should have told you that Ned has 3 fine colts all born easily, one from Calna and one from your mare, both by Julius Caesar, I think; and one from a mare Gregory gave young Richard, and don't know the sire; but they have all three the strangles, and that most terribly; Cadena's colt will lose an eye and the mare herself has it too, which we fear will hurt her foal that she carries. Young Richard too has a present of a very beautiful horse from Fenton, very quiet and tractable tho' not cut. It was a sort of good omen that Joe King arrived almost at the instant with the horse; dinner was not half over before Joe was on his back, and round the park in full speed; to show his horsemanship, in he came full gallop into the court yard, not choosing to draw up till he came to the very door, and up the steps he went, nor did he break his own neck, or hurt the horse. By the bye this to your namesake, you may assure him that his friend is not to be changed by time or climate; he is the same good fellow and giddy pate he always was; this however is only among friends. He is well liked and very justly; at his new situation he has great success with the boy, who is fond of him as all boys and all men, all women must be. He stayed with us but one night, and had all the spirit that a school boy broke loose runs wild with. One is vastly delighted to see it, but still afraid the heathen will tumble over the banisters, or drown himself, or set the house afire; but mum—I shall offend young Charles, but assure him that this is a language I use to no man alive but you, and as Goldsmith said to Lord Ossory, when he assured his lordship that all lords were and must be fools, I only mention it to you and I am sure you won't tell any body. Apropos to Cadena, pray send me her great pedigree vouched properly; Joe has promised to write to you for it, any time these 2 years, so pray send it to me, for Zouch [8] has a *regular shed book*. Tell Charles we love him, and wish him to grow up in love of us, as we grow old in loving him. Adieu. The Doctor is poorly. I am alone in town.

[At the end of September, 1774, the King dissolved the now six-year-old House of Commons. Both Edmund and William Burke were confronted with the problem of how to come into the new Parliament, for which elections were held during October and November. Lord Verney was unable or unwilling to provide again for Edmund at Wendover, and for some reason Will could no longer stand for Great Bedwin. Edmund momentarily considered entering the contest for the City of Westminster, but saw that he could not succeed and accepted Rockingham's invitation to be returned from the Wentworth family borough of Malton in Yorkshire. Then came the summons to contest for the Bristol representation. The voting at Bristol was still in course and undecided, when Will, who had stood for Haselmere in Surrey, wrote the following letter.]

WILLIAM BURKE TO O'HARA, October 22, 1774

Well! You shall not want a few words. Westminster grew into perplexity and confusion; I can only tell you of it, that our old and valuable friend Lord Besborough was in no sort wanting in that uniform good nature and friendly intentions that we have always found in him, but the thing grew too wild for Edmund to meddle. He went up to the north where he was returned for Malton. He was hurried by expresses from Bristol, where with every possible circumstance of honour and respect they had put him up. His brother and he are there now, and in all human probability will carry it.

---

[8] Served Burke as a kind of secretary.

For myself, I have stood a contest at Haselmere against 2 Court members, Molineux and Burrel. I did not expect to be returned; my hopes all along were in a petition, and I trust my seat is safe and the borough mine in perpetuity.[9] All these things are conclusions, which you must accept, and wait for quiet for the how and the why—I am from morn to night among the Bristol voters in all the beer houses in town.[10]

Just before my hurry I got a letter from Ridge; I expected to hear again from him, and I need not say that I am always ready to do as he wishes. It is impossible for me just now to answer his letter and I know he will feel it so. God send him success in any thing. All here are yours.

[postscript by Dr. Nugent]

You see my dear Sir a whole *Iliad* in William's nutshell. The hows and whys you are to have from the same quarters as soon as our people can fetch a little breath. So William promises, and he is, you know, a very pleasing correspondent. As to me, I think it will not displease you to have it under my hand that I am very well, and that I love you without re- serve, and ever shall. I won't say how much I long to see you in London. Adieu my dear Sir,

　　　ever yours

　　　　　　　　　　　Christopher Nugent

October the 22d 1774

[At the conclusion of his hard-fought and historic election at Bristol, Burke hastened to report the results to O'Hara.]

BURKE TO O'HARA, November 2, 1774

Cruger [11]	3565	Burke	2707
Brickdale [12]	2456	Clare [13]	283
	Majority for Burke 251		

---

[9] Will Burke's petition failed, and he never re-entered the House of Commons.

[10] Rounding up Bristol freeholders in London and Westminster and urging them to go to Bristol to vote for Edmund.

[11] Henry Cruger (1739-1827).

[12] Sir Mathew Brickdale, the 'old Tory' candidate, had sat for Bristol for nearly twenty years.

[13] Robert Nugent, Lord Clare, a government candidate, retired early from the contest, which provided the occasion for Burke's candidacy to be started.

Return tomorrow at 10

My dear Sir,

At the confused ending of all the confusion of the stormiest contested election we have had since the dissolution of the late Parliament, you will not wonder if I am not very full or very precise. I only wish you to know, that we have rest at last, and thank God victory. The poll closed with a majority of ———.[14] It lasted a month. My absence, in the beginning, had like to be fatal; but it was balanced by the incredible activity of the best and most spirited friends that ever man had; the faces of any of whom I never saw until this election. The defeated party threatens a petition; but I do not think they can succeed on the ground they take. Richard is with me. Without him I do not know what I could have done. He desires to be remembered affectionately to your Charles, and to William if he is with you; as I do most cordially. Communicate this to Ridge. I think it will give him pleasure. You know that W. Burke lost his return at Haslemere; but he is advised, that he is next to certain on his petition. God send it. I am persuaded he is on very good ground. Adieu my dear friend. You shall have a more full account at greater leisure.

Bristol November 2d.

WILLIAM BURKE TO O'HARA, early December, 1774

Grosvenor Square

I must tell you at once, that I take the opportunity of waiting Lord Rockingham's coming down, or else in the sort of faith you profess concerning me you might imagine that I had just taken possession of some great house here. But so it is, that I continue what you left me, my nature rather inured to the clime, than the country itself much changed; which is, I think one of the benefits that one of Milton's heroes *aux enfers* promises to himself and his friends, by their being content to be unfortunate; and so far I think the Devil was wise. I have sometimes at a bad inn met a very bad bed, and I never got to rest till I had resolved to lie quiet; the kicking and

---

[14] Since the poll did not close until Nov. 3, Burke left this space vacant; instead of filling it the next day, he wrote the final results across the top of his page.

sprawling never softened the bed, but on the contrary increased the knots and bumps that made the uneasiness. Now having given you this recipe for a tolerable good night's rest in a bad bed or two, that you may find in your journey from Holyhead, let me tell you that we don't at all relish a sort of report we hear, that you have put off your hour further than your letter to me seems to imply; there is that trembling on the beam, here, that I seem to want your midnight intelligence of what is saying and doing. We heard before that you were to change your office, and keep the only good it had, and I need not say we are most cordially pleased with it, and we accord no less in the good sense of pushing Charles in his profession.[15] I find he applies very seriously to it, and doing so, it is not in the nature of things that he should not rise in it; and whatever your interest or industry can do, to make the first stage more comfortable or more in the line of being marked and seen, is all right.

My petition stands for the 28th March, and I have really good grounds to think I shall succeed. Ned's for the 3 February. The objection does not stand simply on the admission after the *teste*,[16] tho' that is part, but it is also objected that the fees of admittance were paid for them; nor, were he driven to a new election, which is the utmost object of the petition, have we any possibility in our notion of things, that he should not be vastly at the very head of a poll, in the case of a new contest.

As to your damned Ireland, it is a sort of thing I no way understand, but shall always in the natural fondness one has for anecdotes, be glad to hear of, as I shall like to hear of any incident that befell Caesar or Pompey.

As to affairs, North sings small; the Bedfords affect to laugh, and Rigby is full of humanity; Wilkes sits quiet, and the courtiers affect to say he really behaves very well.[17] Ned is in vogue; the extreme good sense in his manner of steering

---

[15] O'Hara's "last" is not found; probably he told of giving up his board and receiving the income of 500 pounds per annum as a pension during pleasure. —*Journal of Irish House of Commons* 18: 120. What had been done for his son Charles, does not appear.

[16] The clause in the election writ expressing the date of its issue. In the Bristol election many new freeholders were admitted to the franchise after the issue of the writ; on this ground Brickdale petitioned against Burke's return, but without success.

[17] The new Parliament was opened Nov. 29; Wilkes, returned from Middlesex, took his seat without opposition.

between extremes, (which is the nasty virtue of our scoundrel times) of his accomodating himself to being all things to all men, has made him very fashionable; and his running in the *teeth* of the popular nonsense, upon his political and truly philosophical grounds, has gained him great respect, because he did what every man of common sense and common honesty wished to have done, but which he alone could do in the conclusive way he did.[18] It is utterly impossible to pursue the system of violence to America; it is as impossible that a change of measures by the authors of the violent measures can be effectual. There is a talk of Gower [as] 1st Lord of the Treasury and Jenkinson Chancellor of the Exchequer; there is a talk too of Chatham, and I rather incline to suspect the latter, but can say nothing positively or reasonably. We are all well, and shall spend some days at Beaconsfield. Pray remember us all cordially to Charles—where is Will, can you do nothing for him? I write a line to J[ohn] R[idge] tomorrow. Adieu, ever yours

WB

[On January 10, 1775, Burke's speech on American taxation of the previous April 19, in which he had pleaded with the House of Commons to repeal the fatal tea tax and restore the old order in Anglo-American relations, appeared as a pamphlet. A copy was sent to O'Hara, who returned the following commentary.]

O'Hara to Burke, January 23, 1775

Dublin 23d January. 1775

My dear Edmund,

I have read your speech more than once, compared your different arguments, deduced the conduct of each administration from the character you have drawn of each chief. I know the times, much of the men; yet all parts of my jumbled recollection arranged themselves anew in my mind; it became an office of old records new swept and put in order; I felt comfort in recollection, and pursued your inferences to conviction. So I felt, and so I believe the House felt when you spoke it; but

---

[18] Burke spoke Nov. 20 on the address, warning against precipitate declarations or inconsiderate actions in the American crisis. His notes for this speech are given in *Correspondence* 4: 464-469.

now it comes like a prophecy illumined by accomplishment. What I think more of your powers, I won't say. Still less should I tell you what Ridge and Charles say. For my part, there is one capital objection to it; an inflexibility in the cause of truth which can never make its way to preferment, till times grow *too* great. You have hung a millstone about the present leader's neck; but others there are in plenty.

It is not printed here, but is in the press. Its effect amongst us will be far beyond your conception; the general declaration of *legislative supremacy* had before made an impression. Now I tremble and doubt.

I wrote with brevity because I hope soon to converse. Yet I am so oddly circumstanced, that I can't say when. I work at present for double pay, and should therefore work double tides. But by the notice received I shall not be at liberty this month. Most truly yours

C. O'H.

XIX. Arms Against America

[The British Parliament had not yet taken the fateful step of approving the proclamation of rebellion in Massachusetts, when O'Hara heard news of a most alarming nature—Irish troops ordered to make ready to go to America.]

O'HARA TO BURKE, January 25, 1775

25 January 1775

My dear Edmund,

Desire Will or Richard to unriddle me this. An order is come to us for three Regiments of Infantry, and one of Dragoons to be ready to embark at Cork for America, and to take their horses with them. A Regiment of Dragoons with their horses to cross the Atlantic! What does this mean? The petition of the West India merchants is all vanity and vexation of spirits. But upon the whole, this article may be new to you.

I find you have spoken to Sir John Blaquiere for our friend.[1] You could not apply to a better person, for I'll be his security as a man of honour, if he gives you hopes. At least, such is my present opinion of him.

The news papers say Lord Rockingham and some of his friends were at the Council, but as I can't reconcile this to the Regiment of Dragoons, I shall conclude most truly yours,

Chs. O'Hara

[In the weeks that followed, Burke fought to arrest the drift to war, making his supreme effort on March 22 in his speech on conciliation with the colonies, while Will contested in parliamentary committee for the Haslemere seat. About this time, they were visited by young William O'Hara.]

WILLIAM BURKE TO O'HARA, *ca.* April 7, 1775

My dear Sir,

My namesake that is lately come among us resembles you in so many respects that if we had begun to forget you, or

---

[1] John Ridge.

could have slackened in our regard for you, he would have brought you full to our memories and made us again love you with all our hearts. He has told you that he is destined for the Mediterranean, and goes out with a Captain, a particular friend of mine; you must stir heaven and earth to get him recommended to the present Admiral there, though I fear all won't do for this time. I must however confess that I am myself and not friend William the true subject of this letter; I can't endure that you are anxious about Haslemere, and silence would make you conclude it lost; now we have on the contrary hopes, even to the expectation of success, but the holydays coming on, I have not thought it advisable to controvert an adjournment of the case to the 28th April.

We have had a ten days hearing already; they have almost gone through their defence and little more than our reply remains. That is in the hands of Bearcroft, who will now come fully prepared to it.

Be so good to forward this to Ridge, for I know he is on the circuit. Ned has seen Mr. Ponsonby, who was very polite, but we don't immediately expect much. Poor Sir Anth[ony] Abdy is dead, and is succeeded in the management of the Devonshire affairs by a Mr. Hotham, with whom I think Edmund is on the very best of terms; this is all that at present we can say relatively to our friend Ridge.

Edmund's plan of conciliation put him I think on an higher form than I believe any man has ever stood. He immediately withdrew, and has never once debated the American questions since; he is pressed by friends, and foes I almost said, to print it. I took such notes; and some remembered such parts that he may do it, and I think will.

Remember us to Charles. We are all well, and all yours.

BURKE TO O'HARA, April 26, 1775

My dear friend,

A young gentleman of the Marine walked in to us some weeks ago, so very like you, that I could not help loving him. A few minutes ago he walked in again, and has got your letter. Having the wisdom to make the best of all events, when it is only a friend who is concerned, I must say, that since a good command cannot reconcile him by the rank to any local destination, it is something to him, that he is going to an agreeable part of the world, and that he is to be stationed in the Mediterranean. He is really a very fine young fellow; and has the most engaging temper I ever knew.

When Lord North opened the fishery business, he expressed himself in an open and liberal manner; his argument went to a large consideration of the Irish trade; but when I desired him to have his motion amended to his argument, and to add the word *trade,* he drew himself immediately into his shell; refused the amendment, and declared that he only proposed some little matters.[2] In truth the affair I mentioned was very little indeed, no more than to suffer the sugars brought from the West Indies for Irish consumption to be landed originally in Ireland.[3] What Conolly proposed in a very supplicatory tone about the woolens of Ireland was of greater magnitude; but he would listen to neither.[4] I knew that some of the Irish here think great matters will be done for the *herring* fishery; but I rather think, that they will go no further than to put you on a par with America in the whale fishery; a thing that I think cannot be of sixpenny worth of advantage to you. In that I heartily agree with you. Something of this kind is a bonus for Lord G. Germain for his services to Ministry on some critical occasions; not that he will be content with this; but it is to reconcile Ireland to the promotion of his friend Irwin.[5] I am for one heartily reconciled to it—he is a good humoured well behaved man, and will do his duty very decently.

---

[2] Parliament having forbidden the Atlantic fisheries to the Americans, it became necessary to encourage British and Irish fishing ventures. North on April 11 moved for the House to go into committee on this subject. Burke thanked North for his friendly disposition toward Ireland, but "however desirous he [Burke] might be to promote any scheme for the advantage of Ireland, he would be much better pleased that the benefits thus held out should never be realized, than that Ireland should profit at the expence of a country which was, if possible, more oppressed than herself." Burke offered an amendment to include trade and commerce with fisheries, but North would not accept it.— Almon, J., *The parliamentary register* 1: 428-430, London, Almon, 1775.

[3] O'Hara had advocated this in 1766, *supra,* his letter of March 10, 1766.

[4] Thomas Conolly (1738-1803), an Irish privy councillor and brother-in-law to the Duke of Richmond, pleaded for a generous opening of the trade of the empire to Ireland. He "drew a very melancholy picture of the present state of Ireland, and recapitulated many instances of the eminent loyalty of that country, and of the repeated proofs she had given . . . of her readiness to contribute, much beyond her ability, to the common support."—Almon, *op cit.,* 430.

[5] Sir John Irwin (1728-1788), Major General, now appointed commander-in-chief of land forces in Ireland.

You tell us you will take a ride with us. Oh, don't disappoint us—there are few things in the world I long for more. We are all in the same sentiment. Adieu, embrace Charles for us and believe me ever my dear friend yours.

E. B.

April 26. 1775

O'HARA TO BURKE, May 3, 1775

Dublin 3rd May 1775

Dear Edmund,

I was rejoiced once more to see your hand. But don't mistake this as a claim, for I never desire to hear from you when you have any thing else to do. My likeness in some things does me honour, but is too like me in others. But if even his nose procures your attention, I am flattered. He has been unlucky in my having been so long detained here, and the more so as he has been in a good measure the cause of it. He would have been sometime a captain if I could have gone. The Mediterranean will be pleasant, but it will also be expensive. I now wait for the return of Sir John Blaquiere, but do not expect him while the Parliament sits. I find the resolutions which relate to Ireland were taken up in the House of Lords on the 27th, the day after the date of your letter. They seemed to me rather aimed at America, than for the service of Ireland, except the bounty on imported flax-seed, and an allowance to import lumber and sugars directly to Ireland. The first will do something towards paying the advanced price which flax-seed must bear under the non-importation clause, and the latter will save a month's freight upon every ship so loaded. But lumber was permitted before, which their lordships did not know. The whole merit of these measures Sir John Blaquiere takes entirely to himself; not a word of Irwin, nor of Lord G. Germain. But let the praise light where it may, the delusion operated, and country gentlemen will think we have gained a great deal. The ignorance of our people hurts us more than their venality. I don't think we could benefit by any commercial advantages you could give us, and this from the poverty of our merchants. They are unable to trade upon their own bottom; what little they do, is by commission. Our home demands for our woolens is as much as our manufacturers can supply; and our wool is scarcely sufficient for it. The number of our sheep is lessened by one half within these twenty years, and for a reason inexorably true; that if people have no market for their surplus, they will never grow enough of any commodity. I know but one point in which their indulgence would be of advantage to us; and that is, to extend their bounty upon exported linens to those sent from hence to foreign markets. In short we are too poor to benefit by any advantage you can hold out to us; unless you shape it so as to make it worth while of the English to employ their money here. But the present object seems to be merely with a view to keep Ireland in good humour, while America is in ferment; not to plan any thing for our real advantage. And we are so foolish, that very few *douceurs* will do it. 'Tis a strange time. I grieve for our friend Samuel Johnson; how fallen from what he was; upon former occasions I used to delight in his fervid style, where the swell was raised by the breath of honesty and of truth.[6] But he's now so low, a Saracen's head for the sign of a ginshop. I remember some such. Think of him in partnership with Dean Tucker.[7] Beaumont and Fletcher, Johnson and Tucker. But enough of this till we get on horseback at Beaconsfield. I wish you had said something of Haslemere, your silence bodes no good; and yet I have a confidence in Will Burke; his efforts are so vigorous in whatever he undertakes. Ridge dines with me today, somehow or other you'll all be mentioned: you may even suppose that we shall drink your healths. Adieu

Ch. O'H.

I trouble you with another letter to William.[8]

---

[6] Dr. Johnson, a severe critic of the Americans, had just published his *Taxation no Tyranny; an Answer to the Resolutions and Address of the American Congress.* "That this pamphlet was written at the desire of those who were then in power, I have no doubt."—Boswell, James, *Life of Dr. Johnson* 1: 526, Everyman's Library ed.

[7] The Rev. Josiah Tucker (1712-1799), Dean of Gloucester Cathedral and well known economist. While a Bristol rector he had opposed Burke's election from that city. Holding the opinion that the colonies were useless, yet constitutionally subservient to the mother country, he made a public attack on Burke in *A Letter to Edmund Burke, Esq., Member for the City of Bristol, and Agent for the Colony of New York.*

[8] His son.

O'HARA TO WILLIAM BURKE, May 22, 1775

Dublin 22d May 1775

My dear Will,

I did not care to write to you after so disagreeable an event as the loss of your election. You could have no attention to my correspondence, nor was my own humour fit for it. But by your last to Ridge which he sent me today, I perceive your mind is returned to its own *ton,* and such a sort of mind it is, that if it fails in one thing, it will succeed in another. The hopes you give Ridge from Sir J. Blaquiere I join in, but Ponsonby is of all men breathing the most unperforming promiser, and the most futile fellow. Sir John may have many faults as a minister, but has few as a friend. The Chancellor meant well to our friend, but he has not the influence which he ought to have.

I thought there was great propriety in Edmund's silence after the rejection of his advice, at least with regard to America, but I find by the papers, that New York has brought him on again.[9] You talked of his speech on that day being made public. I wish it were, but can't hear that it is.[10] The dilemma is important and yet unpleasant, for if he was right, England must be for a time undone; if he should have been wrong, they will not hereafter allow him to be a prophet, whatever encomium they may give to his argument and elocution.

Your friend Charles has had some little success at the bar, or partiality has turned some small matters to his reputation. His opportunities have not been many; I suppose people thought of him as I used to do, and therefore did not employ him, for I had doubts about him as a public speaker. But talents lie dormant till occasion calls them forth.

You mention Sir J. Blaquiere's intention to return soon. When he does I shall be at liberty, which I ardently long for. I ought not, but you are in fault, for I long to see you. Mercantile correspondence states the probability of a Spanish War so plausibly that they have frightened all Ireland. And the mockery of the House of Commons in pretending to give us some new advantages, and all ending in the whale fishery, is

---

[9] Presentation on May 15 of the remonstrance of the New York Assembly.

[10] The speech-pamphlet on *Conciliation with the Colonies* was published early in June.

equally disgustful.[11] Irwin is much liked here, and will continue a great fav'rite. Your bustle is now almost over, and I
shall hope to find you quiet at Gregories. Adieu my dear Will.

Chs. O'Hara

[Parliament was prorogued on May 25, a few days before the
arrival of news of the beginning of military hostilities in America.
Burke was one of the first to hear it because a correspondent of his
at Bristol had arrived there on a ship from America which had over-
taken the vessel carrying official intelligence. Immediately he sent
an account to O'Hara, which probably was on its way to Dublin
before British ministers knew what had happened at Concord. The
following letter must, therefore, be one of the first descriptions to
be written in England of "the shot heard round the world." Because a week was the usual time for a letter to go from the London
region to Ireland, and because O'Hara received Burke's letter on
June 4, it is evident that it could not have been written later than
May 28.]

Burke to O'Hara, *ca.* May 28, 1775

My dear friend,

I rejoice with you that Charles is beginning to appear in
the eyes of the world, what his particular friends have long
known him. It is certain that he must *do;* and then he will be
in a situation to *command* what others must *solicit;* and solicit
perhaps in vain. This gives me great pleasure. It does something towards consoling me for other bitter disappointments.
Will's loss of his election was not only vexatious, but the more
mortifying for being so wholly unexpected; very much so by
me, and by every body else. But we must endure, if not stoutly,
at least patiently. Otherwise we throw away this world; possibly too the next; which is the larger stake.

All our prospects of American reconciliation are, I fear,
over. Blood has been shed. The sluice is opened. Where,
when, or how it will be stopped, God only knows. A detachment was sent to destroy a magazine which the Americans were

---

[11] Late in April Parliament passed an act to give bounties to Irish as well
as English ships in the whale fisheries. The Irish were permitted also to export
hooks, lines and various implements for fishing, as well as clothing and
accoutrements to Irish soldiers serving with the king's forces overseas.

forming at a village called Concord. It proceeded with secrecy and dispatch. But the Americans were alert and conveyed their stores, all to four pieces of cannon and some flour, to a more distant town called Worcester. The country was not embodied; but they rose, without concert, order, or officers, and fell upon the troops on their return. Lord Percy was sent out to sustain the first party, which without his assistance would most certainly never have returned. He too would have been defeated, if it had not been for two pieces of artillery which he had the precaution to take, and which were well served. The troops behaved well, and retreated thirteen miles in pretty good order; it was a fatiguing day for them. Their loss did not exceed 70 killed; and probably about the same number wounded. The Provincials harrassed them the whole way. Their loss was thirty-nine. During the time of this strange irregular engagement, which continued almost the whole of the day of the 19th of April, expresses were sent to every part of America with astonishing rapidity, and the whole Northern part of the Continent was immediately under arms. So that, by the 28th of the same month upwards of twenty thousand men were assembled in the Towns of Cambridge, Roxbury, Watertown, and other villages in the neighbourhood of Boston; who have blocked up all the avenues to that place. There is one principal camp of 2,000 men; there are three or four smaller. The rest are cantoned in all the adjacent country, wherever they can find any sort of roof to cover them. My informant, who is a sober, intelligent man, was at the head-quarters of their army on the twenty-seventh. He says, that they are at least as numerous as I have told you they were; they were then in a good deal of disorder; but that their officers were active in making proper dispositions. A Mr. Bribble is the commander-in-chief.[12] They have much confidence in him, as he has served a good deal, and with reputation. But he was very ill when my man came away; and a Mr. Ward commanded in his place.[13] Ward has great popularity, and is a steady, sensible, and temperate man; but without much military experience. However they have under him several officers of

---

[12] Probably Jedediah Preble.
[13] General Artemus Ward (1727-1800), who as a major-general remained second in command to Washington, after the latter was appointed by the Congress.

competent skill; and Col. Patman [14] from Connecticutt, who
has a considerable military character, joined them before the
27th. He marched from Connecticutt at the head of 6,000 men,
with great diligence, on the first news of hostilities; but he
told my informant that he had left them at about 25 miles distance, fearing that he could not obtain subsistence for them,
if he marched further. But he proceeded to the head quarters
of the Massachusetts Army in order to assist with his advice.
He was much disposed to an immediate attack on General
Gage; but Ward and the rest were unwilling to expose the
people of Boston to the carnage which might ensue; and Gage,
looking on that people as hostages in his hands, will not suffer
one of them to go out.[15] In this strange situation things were
on the 29th of last month. The news of this breach raised the
people wherever it arrived. At New York (as I am told in
letters from Bristol) the populace broke open the provincial
stores and began to arm; they likewise unloaded two vessels
going with provisions to the King's troops. Everything was
everywhere in a confusion not to be described. The Ministers
have had as yet no account. It is odd, that they should have
their advice sent by a merchantman, and a bad sailor; for my
Bristol correspondent's captain passed by their advice schooner.
Adieu my dear friend, we do most passionately long to see you.
Remember us to Ridge and Charles.

All the inhabitants of the seaport towns in the Massachusetts are leaving their habitations and retiring into the
country. The populous town of Marblehead was almost a
desert.

O'HARA TO BURKE, June 5, 18, 1775

Dublin 5th June 1775

Your letter, my dear Edmund, which I received last night,
contained much matter of melancholy importance, and the
more alarming, as there must have been every week, since the
Massachusetts Army cantoned about Boston, skirmishes of
different kinds, till either the avenues to the town were cleared,

---

[14] Recognizably, Israel Putnam.

[15] Thomas Gage (1721-1787), Commander-in-chief of the king's forces in
America, who in 1774 had been made Captain-General of the Province of
Massachusetts Bay.

or the regulars retired; by this time the battle's lost or won in that quarter, but if the rest should unite, it will render the attempt so ridiculously wild, that the only refuge of your Ministers from the hatred of the people, will be to their mockery and laughter. But I believe they will be apter to laugh on this side of the water, than on yours; for here we sympathize more or less with the Americans; we are in water colours, what they are in fresco. The language of your ministerlings have made us what we are; for till Jenkinson & company told us we were slaves, we never knew it; and might have gone on in the same happy ignorance. The same game is played in one place as in the other, and from you we learn to understand our share. Ridge breakfasted with me this morning; when three such fellows (take Charles in) without any superior, get together, those great affairs are discussed with freedom, but not without prejudice, for where you have the most distant concern, we must submit to the imputation.

This letter bears another date than it ought to do; I thought to have finished it before I left town; but finding it thus far advanced at my return, I proceed upon my first feelings. I shall say no more of Haslemere, but bury the recollection of it in hopes of better fortunes; for I agree with Pope, "all chance direction which we cannot see." [16]

Tho' the last accounts from America came too quick to give hopes of further particulars immediately after, yet on this 18th day of June, we should certainly have heard more if the intercourse of correspondence were not more closely watched than it had been before. I pray for peace amongst them, and upon conditions held forth to them by people they can trust. And indeed one can only pray for it; for difficulties occur which exceed all human means. To go no higher, there is a great name amongst you cooperating at present, but with views so different from yours that you can never coalesce, and who is always to be had; who to use his own terms, when a friend of yours was mentioned for the Treasury, treated it as farcically ideal, that it would excite the laughter even of the little village of Hayes. This will always be a man, of whom the most persevering spirit upon earth may avail itself. [17] The subject grows

---

[16] The correct line is, "All chance, direction, which thou canst not see."— *Essay on man.*

[17] Lord Chatham.

too delicate to say more upon, but I shall not be out of all relation to it, when I say that nothing could be better that the
publication of your last conciliatory speech. I shall set about
another reading of it as soon as I have finished this letter. You
have suggested one idea to me, and for which you are therefore answerable, that taxation is not comprised within the term
Legislative Supremacy; I am sure it is not; but I am sure of
it as Doctor Halley was of the longitude, that it must be discovered some time or other, tho' he himself despaired of the
investigation. Four hundred years ago it might have been
proved; when representatives ventured not to tax without
consulting their constituents; it was then the grant of the body
of the people; but now it is against order to receive even a
petition against a tax proposed in Parliament. Yet I am still
sure of my point. I confess the proof of this proposition is no part
of your plan; tho' I have taken the idea from it: which perhaps
I may make you answerable for, when I get you a'horseback.

Nothing puzzles me so much as the surprising demand for
every produce both of Great Britain and Ireland; and the
greatest part for America. Our manufacturers are all employed,
and demands upon them for more than they can furnish. This
you shall also account for. When I began this letter, I counted
upon setting out about this time for England, but Eyre French
who married my niece is reduced to the last stage by a para-
lytic stroke. The circumstances of the family makes it necessary that I should stay to put their affairs in a little order before I go. No man ever detested a *sejour* so much as I do this
place. Besides *la maladie, non pas du pays, mais d'Angleterre
me tourmente la rage.* 'Tis in effect to see you and one more,
for I doubt whether I shall go to London; at most it will be
but for three or four days, to walk about and see new things.
You may think it too late for me to change my course of life;
it actually is so; and yet, if my health lasts, I am determined
to wander out the remainder of it. As relish for a practical
intercourse with mankind lessens, a retreat to observation may
not be unpleasant. I wish I had thought of it earlier, that I
might be better prepared for it, than I now am. A country
retirement for life is a dead repose, a temporary grave, for a
man of the world. And I have generally suspected fallen
Ministers of affectation, who have pretended to like it. I remember a letter of Sir Robert Walpole's in the year 1743 much

commended by his friends; he praised his pastures because they did not flatter,—a laboured composition, a make-believe that he was happy. The truth was that he would have liked them better if they could have flattered, for he had no taste for them; but as they could not, he soon grew dropsical and died. The late Lord Stair had a more liberal mind; when John Duke of Argyle went to Scotland to recruit for opposition, he found my Lord at his farm of Newtesser; after commending its beauties, he wished that he himself had early adopted that taste, for it was the only happy life; to which my Lord replied, "I wish your Grace had been a farmer, for then I never should have been one,"—alluding to their old competition. You'll observe that Gregories does not come at all in question; a periodical retreat and avocation from business is delightfully useful. It strengthens the digestion of the mind for the load that lies upon it; and invigorates it for honest purposes. Yet no man living wants it less than you do, tho' no man enjoys it more. Perhaps the rest of your friends are less acquainted with your real character than I am. Do they know that of all the busy men upon earth, you the busiest have the least ambition? Do they know that of all the opponents Government has, you are perhaps the only one who would not do evil that good may come of it? Do they know upon the whole, that you are much a better man to bring honour and credit to a party, than to conduct its intrigue? And yet these are the ruling features of your character. I am persuaded that the Ministry might have bid you defiance if they would have taken your advice as to measures; and equally so, that you are the last body they will recur to, when the time of danger comes. I think this prediction will soon be verified. And yet, they are very stout, and talk of pushing things with vigour, but this rather from the *parole* given, than their own feelings. I have some reason to believe that our Chief will not remain here if the great man should be sent to. The name of the Marquess does not yet appear so formidable. My own opinion is that my friend Sir John [Blaquiere] stays to watch this event. Nothing relative to Ridge will be done till he comes over. Yet I think he stops the passage, so that nobody can get in before him. In reality there is no man that ought to be considered in competition with him, who has not already got forward. And yet, one is not to count too much upon this.

When favoritism prevails, men, like water dogs, are often chosen for their deformity. I have an animal of this sort, now at my feet, that I am very fond of.

Charles calls often to me for some account of young Richard, as King has left off writing to him: and he's an idle fellow for it. Besides his last letter to him was on business, of a kind in which I am much interested. I long to be after seeing you, you know the dialect, that I may learn to conclude when I write to you. For actually I don't know how to leave off. I have not said one word on Irish affairs; no thanks returned for the majority of the British Parliament in granting us a bounty upon ships fitted out for the whale fishery. What end could such mockery answer to Administration, or even to the Government of this Kingdom? A child of yours, now fourteen years old, begins however to flourish.[18] The fishery upon our coasts, after much pains and various plans of encouragement, begins to make a figure. The capital of our merchants is so small, that we find it very difficult to spirit them up to a new enterprise. I have been obliged to recur to the Dublin Society, where I have more influence, and less variety of interests to struggle with, than in Parliament. Besides our Treasury is bankrupt. The Establishment is £126,000 a year too great for the revenue, so that in the next session we shall have a new debt to provide for of £252,000 with some new expenses necessarily to be incurred, amounting to £100,000 more. There is nothing in this circumstance to invite a Lord Lieutenant to stay longer amongst us. Yet bad as things are, if a change was to take place, and some friend of yours was appointed to this department, all would be found within remedy, provided Administration on your side of the water would favour the system. The object at present is, to create the necessity for a land tax, which without an equivalent, will not succeed. Adieu my dear Edmund,

C OH

BURKE TO O'HARA, July 26, 1775

My dear friend,

I am caught in my roothouse by a shower of rain, and very luckily I find the instruments of writing; and they tell me, or something else tells me, that I cannot employ them better

---

[18] *Supra*, O'Hara to Burke, July 4, 1763, n. 19.

than in acknowledging the receipt of your letter and in pressing you to make good the most acceptable part of it. We really long inexpressibly to see you. We have amusements enough; real comfort and satisfactions very few. The sight of such a friend as you, though for no more than the short interval between this and the meeting of your Parliament (possibly of ours too) would make our leisure a real repose; and would enable us to look business in the face with a little more spirit, when the disagreeable and hopeless hour of business arrives. You see we are actually engaged in a civil war, and with little, very little hopes of any peace; and in my poor opinion with full cause to despair of any that shall restore the ancient confidence and harmony of the parts of this empire. For one I am sure I have laboured as much as any body to procure it; and upon the only terms of honour and safety I know of, that is, to give them our own constitution or what is most substantial in it. How could you imagine that I had in my thoughts anything of the theoretical separation of a power of taxing from legislation? I have no opinion about it. Those things depend on conventions real or understood, upon practice, accident, the humour or genius of those who govern or are governed, and may be, as they are, modified to infinity. No bounds ever were set to the parliamentary power over the Colonies; for how could that have been but by *special convention?* No such convention ever has been; but the reason and nature of things, and the growth of the Colonies ought to have taught Parliament to have set bounds to the exercise of its own power. I never ask what government may do in *theory,* except *theory* be the *object;* when one talks of *practice* they must act according to the circumstances. If you think it worth while to read that speech over again you will find that principle to be the key of it.

You will see by the *Gazette,* that there has been another, but a more regular, and far more bloody engagement. Two such victories, as Mrs. B. observes after Pyrrhus, would ruin General Gage. He has lost in killed and wounded, a thousand men; and got nothing in the world, but a security from some batteries which those he calls rebels were erecting against him. It was only a successful sally of a besieged garrison.[19] Pray—

---

[19] Bunker Hill, June 17-18.

Pray come to us. All here are yours and not less Charles's the younger.

July 26. 1775

Why don't we hear from Jack Ridge?

[O'Hara never again saw England. About this time an illness struck him which six months later proved fatal.]

O'Hara to Burke, August 4, 1775

Dublin 4th August 1775

My dear Edmund,

I have had your letter from the root house, at least I received it four days ago. But Ridge got immediate possession of it, and I have not been able to get in back from him, tho' I have daily wished to exert what little strength is returned to me, on a full answer to it. When I wrote last, I had little doubt of being with you about the middle of last month, but an attack so sudden and so violent suspended my thoughts of any journey to be made in this world. My old friend the Doctor knows my circumstances; I wrote to him early, and since my approach to convalescence. When I shall be able to leave Ireland is uncertain, but my first proof of perfect recovery shall be a visit to you. There are few things upon earth I long for so much as to see you, and I am satisfied that nothing would contribute so much to the recovery of my health; but yet it can't be for some time. A greater degree of recovery will be absolutely necessary before I can stir from home. Besides some remaining complaints, I am still very weak.

I did not make myself understood, in what I said about taxation as distinct from other legislative powers, when you supposed I imputed the doctrine to you. I know your argument turns wholly upon the policy, not the right. But having some opinion of that kind myself, and as you had said nothing against it, nor was it your purpose, I thought it possible, and from your manner of treating the subject not improbable, that you might have thought so too. Tho' your arguments could not prevail for preserving the English Empire, they must bring you in time the reputation you deserve; but more it will not do; for I believe there never was a more determined spirit of perseverance in any measure. What the Ministers say and write, I hear sometimes; but never yet a word which promises the least remission of the present pursuit. Nothing surprises me so much as the tranquillity of the merchants of London, and of the trade of England in general. Are there no thinking men that look with horror on what has passed, and on what is to come? None such come over to us; the universal language is that America must be conquered.

I remember Flood was once your acquaintance, when he had not so great a part to act as he assumes at present. You know a Vice-Treasurer's place has been vacated for him, and from your intimacy with Charles Fox you must know the terms.[20] Flood has always declared that he would take no employment that should be procured by laying an additional load upon this Establishment, and has actually refused; and was firm to his purpose on Thursday night; I believe is still, but I have no authority for saying so. I should have told you that the treaty was carried on without ever consulting him, upon a principle that he could not refuse. If his virtue should hold out, he will be a great character amongst us. But it will be very distressful to Government. The only event likely to give them much uneasiness, the revenue business, tho' in strange disorder, will be left to a successor. And by the time of change, there will probably be other Ministers, about whose success in this or any other department the present set will not be very anxious.

I take it for granted that you are all well, because you say nothing to the contrary. And 'tis not yet a time to hear good tidings. I must have patience as well as you, for I am as much interested, if I may believe my own feelings. Most truly yours,

C OH

O'HARA TO BURKE, August 9, 1775

My dear Edmund,   9th August 1775

My head is not quite clear enough for writing; but yet contrary to every other correspondence it relieves my spirits

---

[20] Fox in 1774 had inherited the rich sinecure of clerk of the pells; he soon sold it for 30,000 pounds and a pension on the Irish establishment of 1,700 pounds per annum for a period of thirty-one years. The pells office was conferred on Jenkinson, who vacated the vice-treasurership, which now was offered to Flood. The Irish administration deemed it of great importance at this time to win over the patriot leader.

to write to you. Your letter to Charles would call upon me for thanks, if true affection were to be returned by thanks.[21] I shall say nothing of my state of health, for that is quite in the possession of my old friend, whose letters are of great use to me, even at this distance.

I received your plan of the last fight, which we laugh at here; well knowing that 'tis a false representation.[22] We are however preparing with great spirit. Everything looks like perseverance, *coute que coute*. The American Army by this time twelve month will be upon paper 26 or 27,000 men;[23] which, if they resist, the enthusiasm for liberty must be strong indeed. What has already happened is little less than incredible. When such a man as Dr. Warren takes up arms, and the command of a redoubt, who can remain inactive?[24] Mad as I think the measure on your side, there is yet one piece of management for which I give Ministers great credit. Their contriving to keep the trade so far open that I believe our exports to that part of the world are equal to what they were; and how 'tis done I neither conceive, nor can any man in trade inform me. But this it is which keeps all quiet in England. The sanction of Parliament for all the Ministers can do against America secures them and with the tranquillity among the manufacturers will keep all quiet, and steady while they last; the same men and the same measures. And so far does this idea go, that we are promised Lord Weymouth for our next Lord Lieutenant.[25] In recruiting our army for America, I find 'tis determined to keep clear of the Protestant Counties; which need not be explained to you. But if either Gibraltar or Mahon be taken, while garrisoned by Hanoverians, what an uproar it will make.

I shall go to the country in four or five days, hoping for a quicker recovery there. My mind, upon which much depends, will be less hurried there.

Ridge has heard much of you of late, and I through him, from a Mr. Goold who has lately been with you. I was glad to hear that you are not to be kept up after eleven by any

---

[21] Letter to Charles is not found.

[22] Not found.

[23] The army to subjugate America.

[24] Dr. Joseph Warren (1741-1775), physician and soldier, who fell at Bunker Hill.

[25] Harcourt remained until succeeded by Buckingham in 1777.

company. He told me one thing more, which has comforted us in a point we had almost given over, the St. Vincent business. For my part, I should not in my ignorance be sorry that it hung over for one session more. New men might do better than old friends. Assure Mrs. Burke of my most sincere regard. Yours most truly,

Chs. O'Hara

BURKE TO O'HARA, August 17, 1775

My dear friend,

I rejoice most sincerely, along with the rest of your real friends here, in the letters which I received from you and from our other Charles.[26] It gave me unfeigned satisfaction to see the hand firm, and the head clear. I think the heart is beyond the power of any disorder. The Doctor has wrote every thing which may tend to your perfect recovery. He is here now, and I am sure will not contradict me in the piece of advice I shall add to his prescriptions, which is, to hurry yourself in mind and body as little as possible. Fair and softly my dear friend; your recovery will be early enough provided it be sufficiently perfect.

You will be surprised that a time like this I should have consented to be steward at an horse race and dancing assembly. It would be shameful indeed, if it were accepted in this moment, or done for no better end than the diversion. But I undertook this office such as it is, a little before the general election, and in prospect of that event in order to serve some little county purposes to my friends; and having once accepted I could not refuse to act.[27] I am this moment returned, after having spent three days of diversion with as little entertainment as possible; and with more expence than I liked or could well afford. But it is over, and I *am again* returned to my farming, and to not the pleasantest reflections on the aspect of public affairs. I found the paper which I send to you when I came hither. It contains some things very striking, others very affecting; though on the whole not so well penned, as some of the American performances which we have lately had. This I see is the last which ever will be addressed to this country.

---

[26] Charles's letter is not found.
[27] *Supra*, W. Burke to O'Hara, Sept. 2, 1774.

Our madness passes all conception. Theirs too in some particulars is extraordinary. They have attempted to discredit
and disable the only friends they have in this country; and
they place all their reliance on a man, who refused to put himself into a responsible situation to serve them; and when he
came into power himself, if he did not actually produce at
least made one of the Administration who laid the tax which is
the fatal cause of all this mischief; and indeed never did them
a single service, that I can recollect, in the whole course of his
life.[28] That life is now in effect over. It is, I believe impossible
he should recover. Times are such that I cannot give a guess
whether his death would be serviceable or mischievous. He
was such a man, that his existence, in health and understanding, never could be neutral to this country. The present temper
of the nation is quite without example. Not a single man is
to be found in any situation, or in any party, who approves
of the measures of Ministry, as conceived or conducted with
the smallest degree of common sense. At the same time, scarcely
one can be found who will take a step towards putting our
affairs in a better condition by endeavouring a change of hands
or an alteration of counsels. The despair that has seized upon
some, and the listlessness that has fallen upon almost all, is
surprising; and resembles more the effect of some supernatural
cause, stupifying and disabling the powers of a people destined
to destruction, than anything I could have imagined. The
people seem to have completely forgot the resources of a free
government for rectifying public mismanagements and mistakes.

You seem to think our manufactures find as free a way into
America as formerly, and that our Ministers deserve some credit
for having by their dexterity procured this accommodation to
trade. If they have given out such a report, it is a very strange
attempt to delude the people. You may depend upon it that
from the day of the non-importation agreement not a single
article of goods has been shipped to the Colonies from any
port in Great Britain, one instance alone excepted. The transports which conveyed the last reinforcements to Boston took
on board about 200 tons of nails, a large parcel of stockings,
and some other goods. The Port of Boston, which was shut
up by act of Parliament, was the only port of America into
which any goods could enter from Great Britain. There, con-

---

[28] Chatham.

trary to our law and their agreement, I take it for granted they were admitted; and as far as the consumption of that unfortunate town can extend they will be sold. Whatever loss is sustained, the Treasury I suppose must make good. The Dutch upon the non-importation agreement sent large orders for American goods on speculation. But they soon stopped; and I am persuaded will be losers. All these poor resources could not hinder the trade from suffering extremely by the loss of a full seventh of the whole, if the peace between Russia and the Turk,[29] and the settlement, bad as that settlement is, of Poland, had not opened a most astonishing market for almost every article of produce, which used to be exported to the Colonies. Add to this, that the military preparations do, of themselves, put life into many branches of trade; and the transport service has given the shipping abundant employment. Another circumstance, which is very honourable to the Americans, has done them great mischief, and prevented commerce from feeling the blow which the Americans intended. They were injudicious enough not to make their non-exportation keep pace with their non-importation. They have paid at least a million of their debts without sending a single new order. Our ports have been filled with their corn ships, and they have sent a plentiful supply of tobacco, without which revenue and mercantile credit, particularly in Scotland, would have suffered an heavy blow. The large supplies sent to the West Indies from the Continent have preserved to us that vast traffic. All these resources, without any act of Ministry, except their military preparation, have kept up the ball of business, and will keep it for some time longer. When it falls—

The spirit of America is incredible. Who do you think the Mr. Mifflin, Aid-de-Camp to Washington, is? A very grave and staunch Quaker, of large fortune and much consequence.[30] What think you of that political enthusiasm, which is able to overpower so much religious fanaticism? Washington himself is a man of good military experience, prudent and cautious, and who yet stakes a fortune of 5000 a year. God knows they are very inferior in all human resources. But a remote and

---

[29] Treaty of Kutschuk-Kainardje, June 15, 1774, had ended a six-year war between Russia and the Ottoman Empire.

[30] Thomas Mifflin (1744-1800), a member of the Congress who with a major's rank accompanied Washington to Cambridge. The Quakers for this expelled him from their meeting.

difficult country, and such a spirit as now animates them, may do strange things. Our victories can only complete our ruin. I have much to say to you on the part Ireland has acted in this business—but I have tired you, and it is late. Adieu my dear friend—God give you health and peace of mind, and the fortune long to survive these calamities. All here most cordially salute the Charles's.

Thursday. August 17. 1775

O'Hara to Burke, August 28, 1775

My dear Edmund,   Nymphsfield 28th August 1775

Yesterday's post brought me your welcome letter, for which I thank you. I am enough recovered to find the same pleasure in writing you I ever did. Nor does it at all disturb that tranquillity which you so anxiously recommend to me; yet I write with feeling when I write to you, a feeling however without perturbation; 'tis rather calm than exercise of the mind. The air of this place was always wholesome, and my gradual recovery is a further proof of it. I take no remedies, because none are ordered for me, but I have written a peremptory demand for something to restore my stomach. I sometimes do things contrary to general rules, when appetite suggests them. For instance, I breakfasted this morning upon toast and butter and three cups of tea. Strong desire will sometimes make things wholesome, which are not so in themselves. I have seen a longing woman drink two bottles of champagne in a very short time, and they did her good. Upon the whole I have very little doubt of a thorough recovery from the effects of my late illness; I don't propose to dance at your Stewardship's assembly, but in a walk or a ride, I hope to keep you company again. Somebody diverted me lately, with an account of your taking them on a walk a little before dinner, and leading them a round of seven or eight miles. I believe it was Pery. They say in Dublin that he was very solicitous when in London to get into Hamilton's place; I can't believe it.

From what you say, and other accounts, I should fancy the Great Man's career is at an end. I have paid my tribute of admiration to his character for many years; but he should have

been to England as the Ark of the Covenant, never to
have been exposed but in the greatest and most imminent
perils from foreign powers. Domestic business was too small a
detail for him; he must act from genius and enterprise, or he
could not act to any good purpose. He was fond of the character of a public man, and boasted that he had divested himself of all private friendships and connexions, and certain it
is that his moral character had totally merged in his political.
He never had common honesty since I have known his story.
He was in himself however a great body of opposition; the
eyes of mankind were fixed upon him, and yet such was his
arrogance, and such his duplicity, that they always knew he
was to be had, whenever they should think it worth while to
call upon him to make his own arrangements, in which they
could always introduce whom they pleased, while he trusted
to his great name for the government of the whole. He is, if
gone, the greatest loss the Court could have suffered. America
solely looked up to him; and yet no man in England would
sooner have dared at a proposal to let loose 30 or 40,000
foreign troops amongst them. By what I can find, Lord Shelburne is their next fav'rite. The repeal of the Stamp Act is
forgot: or perhaps the Declaratory Act is remembered, and
not understood. Certain it is, that they have not for some time
distinguished their true friends. But that game seems to me
to grow desperate every day. A man must have a nearer view
of things than I can have, to decide whether it would be worth
while to play the remainder of the game: whether any honourable means of compromise be yet left. And woe be to them
in whose hands the game shall be lost! What effect this great
event may have I can't say, but as yet, you are not *en odeur de
sainteté* with the Grenvilles; and as little so with his R. H.'s
party. Your own numbers are diminished; and yet you still
remain the first. But there will be more nicety requisite when
the day comes, than there would have seven years ago. I am
obliged to you for your commercial account; the subject had
so puzzled me, that I kept on my enquiries even while I was
ill, and had received some of the information you give me.
They are lucky Ministers, and Ireland has shared in the good
fortune, for our foreign demands have all continued. Further
than effects of this sort, Ireland has no concern with any
part of the known world. Even England has so managed our

interests, that we have little concern with her welfare. For instance in the present case, will our trade with America be less in case she succeeds than it is at present? Will she be stricter in her enumerations? Our people are so heterogeneously classed, we are no nation; our internal weakness is such, that they have rendered us as incapable of giving aid, as we were before of resistance. We can venture upon no trade of our own, but trust to commissions from other countries: our freedom is but courtesy. But when they are so wild as at present, with regard to their own interests, we can't blame them with regard to ours.

I have gone further, upon unknown ground, than I generally presume to do. [From] the variety of people from England of rank to know, and of curiosity to enquire, often interested, who come over here from time to time (for 'tis now the fashion) from letters etc., I have been led to the opinions which make a great part of this letter. But they are such as I have no reliance on; but rather trust them to your indulgence, than suppose them worth your consideration. For one must be allowed to talk sometimes idle, where one's wishes are warmly concerned. Adieu my dear friend.

XX. "A Species of Turpitude Not Decent to Name"

[O'Hara's illness and Burke's preoccupation with the political business of arousing opposition to further military measures against America may help to explain why no letters seem to have been written by either man to the other during the next two months. It is evident, however, that O'Hara's son, Charles, kept the Burkes informed of the state of his father's health.

Fortunately, this gap is not a total void. Two letters from John Ridge help somewhat to fill it. They were addressed to the collective "fireside," and are of considerable historical interest since they provide a view of the Dublin scene just before and at the opening of one of the most critical sessions of the Irish Parliament. How far Great Britain would carry on the war in America depended a good deal upon the extent to which the crown could employ the Irish army, and this in turn depended on the conduct of the Irish parliament. Ridge's letters illuminate some of the trends and motives then discernible.]

RIDGE TO THE BURKES, September 25, 1775

My dear friends,

There is nobody more sensible of the disadvantages of procrastination, nor any one more frequently and incorrigibly guilty of it than I am. For a good many months have I been intending to write to you *tomorrow*. And even now the indolence of my nature suggests that I had better do some business, which presses me, and let this alone for the present because it may be done at any time. No! No! I am determined not to suffer on my part a stagnation in our correspondence any longer. Alas, the determination has heretofore been made and broken by me, a thousand and one times at least; and as sure as is the operation of any other natural cause, will again be broke. Would you believe that the letters inclosed with this, or under another cover, to Jack Nugent,[1] might with as much ease and convenience to me, and much more decent and friendly attention to him, have been sent to him so long ago as last May; and were intended to be sent by every pacquet that sailed from that time to this? Having given you this sweet

---

[1] Probably Dr. Nugent's son.

599

picture of myself, let me beg in return that Edmund and Richard (who have not wrote to me for an age) will furnish me with theirs, not drawn by Sir Joshua but by their own masterly pencils. I have no call upon William, having some sketches of him in the Rembrandt style.

At this dead season when almost every body is out of town, I am at a loss how to fill this paper. Politics we have none, public at least, except Flood's squeamish coyness relative to the office of a Vice Treasurer. He promised in Parliament that he would never take any place that would load the establishment; which the pension to Fox in lieu of the Pells to Jenkinson does. But his friends are of opinion, that the establishment being already loaded with that pension, and the Vice Treasurership being now absolutely vacant, he may as well take as let it go to another.[2] As his friends are of this way of thinking, it is to be hoped his sentiments are not utterly averse from theirs, and that his virgin modesty will soon give way. In the mean time Hutchinson would rather see your dog Chuff a Vice Treasurer; or even Ponsonby, who would be glad to have it, and to leave the chair to Pery unless he could have both—tho' it is possible Mr. Ponsonby may have neither. Do you know that Flood from being a most sublime orator, is become a most sublime poet? A Pindar? He lately printed at London for the use of his friends, an ode to Fame, and a translation of the first Pythian odes of Pindar, both, in my mind as hard as iron; and the last probably intended to show Lord Chatham that he translates better than Chatham's cousin, West.[3] It is said and probably not without some foundation that repeal of the Octennial Law will be moved for in our Parliament this session, and the same set tho' elected but for eight years, to continue to sit *sine die.* All the Protestants as far as I can see, especially the Presbyterians, except a few who have connexions in the army at Boston and a few military geniuses (such as Lord Bellamont) [4] are here with us, friends to the American cause. The Roman Catholics who receive no favour, no quarter, from their fellow subjects of a different persuasion, and are indebted only

---

[2] Flood presently accepted office and abandoned opposition.

[3] Gilbert West (1703-1756), a relative of Chatham's on the Temple-Grenville side, published a translation of the *Odes of Pindar* in 1749.

[4] Charles, fifth Lord Coote (1738-1800), created Earl of Bellamont in 1767; a son-in-law of the first Duke of Leinster, and bitter enemy of the former Viceroy, Townshend, with whom he fought a duel in 1773.

to government for some lenity in the execution of the laws again them, and who have no liberty like the American Dissenters at stake—are ready to give their beggarly assistance to government. For my part I can't see on what principle a man of any other denomination in this Kingdom who is a native of any property, can be unfriendly to a people who think they are fighting the cause of liberty, and ultimately perhaps the cause of Ireland herself. It does not appear to me, (possibly from my own dimness of sight) that the Colonists give due credit for the redress in some respects actually given, and in all, endeavoured to be given them, by a certain party for several years past in Parliament—but devolve the whole of their past obligations, and future hopes upon Lord Chatham, to whom in reality they owe nothing, but for the moonshine of some empty inoperative speeches. If this be true—if it be true, that the body of the landed interest in England love liberty so much as to keep it *all* to themselves, and not suffer it to breathe freely but within the four seas—which Burgoyne's letter to Lee I think intimated,[5] and which the supineness of the people at home whilst those abroad are butchering one another without remorse, seems to prove—I say if these things are so, to what purpose in the world, consistent with prudence to himself or his family, should our Edmund, who has already said all that was to be spoken in favour of the Americans, and predicted all that was to be foretold concerning them, render himself obnoxious by taking a more active part for the future in their favour, than other honest spirited but moderate men bending a little to the temper of the times, will do? Parliamentary privilege protects freedom of debate in the house; but even there is very unavailing. People who go determined before they hear, "will not listen to the voice of the charmer, charm he never so sweetly."[6] Out of the house, political debate if published has no protection but from the liberty of the press, which is but a feeble fence against Prerogative, abbetted by Parliament and countenanced by a majority of the people whether landed

---

[5] When Burgoyne arrived at Boston, in May, Charles Lee addressed to him a letter implying that he was acting against his better judgment. Burgoyne, replying on July 8, justified his conduct, maintained that it was his duty to defend the constitution and authority of the king, and proposed a meeting with Lee for "such explanations as might tend in their consequence to peace." This letter found its way into the newspapers.

[6] Psalms LVIII, 4, 5. (very loosely rendered).

or .commercial, abroad, who consider themselves as parties interested against the Colonists, and in such a cause become a dangerous jury. And after all—Lord Chatham with the parade of a crutch, blanket, and the bubble of inflated expression, shall gain as much estimation with the Americans, as the man who with the deepest and most cogent reasoning, vindicates their right to a participation of the British constitution.

Jenkinson was here for some time, and is now making what may be called a voyage royal round the Kingdom.[7] Young Hutchinson, the Provost's son, went with him as aid-de-camp, or if you please, as bear leader to him. The people of fortune wherever he goes are gorging him with all the good things earth, air, and water afford, in order to impress this inquisitive observer with a just idea of the poverty of this Kingdom, in hopes he and Rigby may be the more moderate in the tax they have in contemplation for it, should they succeed, or whether they do or not, against the Americans. He has, says Dean Barnard,[8] "something very well about him"—"His heart (says Leland) is in the right place"—meaning I suppose such a place as his own. It is no wonder that our obsequious friend, who makes the profoundest reverence even to the empty coach of a great man, should speak favourably of Lord Bute's favorite, when every ecclesiastic in the three kingdoms would probably join Doctor Pomposo and the Dean of Derry in the same cry. Sir John Blaquiere is here; I have not seen him. Why? Because Scott[9] will not let me, without himself to introduce me, and yet will not introduce me.

I intended long since, but forgot to mention to you, that Jephson[10] from some misinformation imagined that Edmund said something in the House of Commons, to prejudice his play. I asked Tighe,[11] who lately came from England, about it. He said that on the contrary Ned did it great honour. Whether it was that people here knew less of the poetry or more of the poet than in England, but the play did not succeed with us. Perhaps you did not know that Jephson is cousin

---

[7] Charles Jenkinson at this time held no public office except that of clerk of the pells.

[8] Thomas Barnard, Dean of Derry.

[9] John Scott (1739-1798), an influential placeman and later attorney general.

[10] Robert Jephson (1736-1803), playwright.

[11] Edward Tighe, who had been a colleague of O'Hara's at the Board of Accounts.

german to Murrough O'Brien. As I mention Murrough, I was sorry he did not come to Dublin when last in Ireland. Lord Frederick Cavendish [12] I saw here—I wish I could see yourselves and Sir Joshua. Charles O'Hara old, and young, is at the country. The father had a dangerous illness this summer, and is not yet quite free, probably never will, from the consequences of it. However I would compound to be sure of him as he is, during my life.

John Burke lately sent to me, to know whether Mr. Edmund Burke had wrote to me to represent him as godfather to Burke's son. I answered that Mr. Burke had not wrote to me, probably presuming me to be on circuit, but that I was ready to stand for him, without waiting for any letter from him. And accordingly I have performed that service, and all the requisites so far as five guineas (full enough for a volunteer proxy) went. Doyle was my brother gossip. The fight between Doyle and Hutchinson on the continent, will be of use to the Provost, so far as to save him from much abuse.[13] The young man acquitted himself extremely well. His father showed me a letter he had from Major Laviere, the *second,* giving a very honourable account of that business. Tho' the Provost did not say so, he wished I should mention it to Ned, which I do in good time. There is on board the ship called *Recovery,* which probably may be in London before this, a hamper of cyder consisting only of 22 jars such as seltzer water is kept in, directed to the Broad Sanctuary. There is so little of it, that it was not worth sending, except as a curiosity, being I believe the very best kind that is made in Ireland. I had it from George Gould of Cork, who gave me hopes of getting such a quantity as might be worth sending, but could not. The broker's receipt is inclosed.

I do not love to put Edmund or William upon asking any thing for any body. And yet when I am applied to by a man who is the husband of a very near and very amiable relation of mine, and who as an attorney is the best friend I have in the line of my profession, I can't refuse to try at least, to do him a service in his. It is Denis O'Brien who wants to be

---

[12] Brother of Lord John and Lord George Cavendish.

[13] John Hely Hutchinson in 1774 had succeeded Francis Andrews as Provost of Trinity College, which was then an important political office. Hutchinson's son, Richard, fought the duel mentioned above.

appointed law agent to Lord Milton[14] in the room of Lane, with whom his Lordship has quarrelled. Lane was very able in that business, but not more than O'Brien, who certainly will not disgrace your recommendation; and knows I believe every acre of Lord Milton's extensive possessions in this Kingdom. Lord Milton has not yet named any one to succeed Lane. I gave O'Brien less than no hopes—but I write because I ought not omit any thing in my power to serve him. Therefore excuse me. Kitty desires her love to you all. Her nerves have lately had a violent attack upon them from a cold. But she is now very well. She was very glad to hear from young Gold that the little bird was still alive when he was at Beaconsfield. A propos—I hear you call it *Butler's Court* [15]—pray why so? Unless it be so called in Doomsday Book, I am hurt at its having any other name, than that by which it was called fifty years ago in the *Vitruvius Brittanicus*. Will you favour me with the derivation of this *old* name, or *new* misnomer. Yours always.

J. R.

At sitting down to write I thought I should not get through a sheet but have found so much of nothing to say, that I can't finish Jack Nugent's business till tomorrow.

A letter from you directed here, will find me tho' I should go to Loughrea for some little time. Kitty's illness kept me hitherto in town.

Stephen's Green West　Dublin　25 September 75.

RIDGE TO THE BURKES, October 11, 1775

11 October Dublin

My dear friends,

Late on Wednesday night, after returning from the house, I have only time to tell you that a Manchester address to the King echoing back the second paragraph of the speech, has

---

[14] Joseph Damer, Viscount Milton in the Irish peerage.
[15] The manor house at Gregories.

been on the last division carried by 90 to 54.[16] Ponsonby spoke exceedingly sensibly and well—Conolly on the same side said a great many strong things—and Hussey, who is now called *Burgh* was truly able and eloquent.[17] These and many besides, argued on the impropriety of entering at all into the American business, or calling it *rebellion,* if it was to make any part of the address. There was a good deal of talk, but nothing like argument on the other side. But the disciplined regulars of government were too numerous for the Provincials. Flood was absent; kept away, it is said, by indisposition. It is probable he mayn't be able to go abroad, till the Vice Treasurership shall be disposed of in some way or other. Hutchinson refused to support administration with respect to the American part of the address, and tho' in the house, neither spoke, nor voted— and the Attorney General was worse than languid. The Prime Serjeant (Dennis) [18] said, he wished America had not been introduced into the address, but since it was, it could not be left out without casting an implied imputation on the measures of Government. That if the British Parliament's taxing America could in some sort infer a similar right in them to tax Ireland, the arguments used by the opponents to this part of the address would be unanswerable. But that this was disclaimed (as indeed it was for the present purpose) by the servants of government in the house. In short I thought he was speaking booty. The Provost's backwardness is ascribed by his enemies, to discontent at not getting the Vice Treasurership, and leaving the Provostship to Flood or any body else. I rather think he considered the cause of the Colonists, the cause of Ireland. In the Lords' house, the minority was but six, who protested against that part of their address relative to America, but entered no reasons in support of their protest.

---

[16] Harcourt, in his speech opening the parliament Oct. 10, requested that while the King's government was "disturbed by a Rebellion existing in a Part of His American Dominions, you will be ready to shew your inviolable Attachment to His Person and Government in the Assertion of His just Rights, and in the Support of His legal Authority." A motion was made for a loyal address containing a promise of exactly what was asked. An amendment calling for "an amicable Termination" of the trouble in America was defeated, 90 to 49; a second amendment to strike out all words signifying approval of the forceful proceedings in America was rejected, 90 to 50; and a motion to adjourn before adopting the address was defeated, 82 to 39.—*Journal of the House of Commons . . . Ireland* 17: 14-15.

[17] Walter Hussey Burgh (1742-1783).

[18] James Dennis, later Lord Tracton.

Lord Irnham said Lord Harcourt was not of sufficient magnitude to be Chief Governor of this Kingdom. The address in the Commons was moved by that quondam incorruptible patriot Sir Charles Bingham. It is said he has given his 2 seats at Castle Bar for the next Parliament to Lord North; in exchange for his seat in the English house, an Irish peerage etc.[19] He will lose the County of Mayo by it. I lately wrote a long letter to you. . . . [20]

[A few days after Parliament was opened in the fall of 1775, Will Burke, at Edmund's request, sent to their ailing friend a general account of the political situation.]

WILLIAM BURKE TO O'HARA, *ca.* November 7, 1775

My dear Sir,

You will easily believe that the state of your health has been matter of no small concern here among us; your and our Charles has been very kind to us, in making us easy when he could, and always in apprising our best man as well as best physician, of your state. Poor man, he is now himself afflicted by this ugly cold that runs about, and no attack upon him can be without uneasiness to us.[21]

If I might ever pretend a merit in a letter to you, I must not now claim it, for it is by Edmund's express injunction that I do what, in truth, I know he has not time to do today; and I believe, in this odd state of things, I verily believe he excessively wished to do, to endeavour to give you some account of the political situation of things here. As to men and things with you, they are too wild and extravagant to be spoken of in sober prose. I don't know what one might think of their conduct, if one was left to one's own discretion; but from their apologies, and we have seen them in more instances than one, we must conclude them altogether inexcusable. I am sure if they are right, our Edmund is very wrong and does not deserve to be left at large; which however, notwithstanding rumours, he enjoys the benefit of, in spite of the most con-

---

[19] Bingham presently became Earl of Lucan.

[20] The rest of the letter is missing.

[21] O'Hara on Oct. 30 had written by his son's hand to Dr. Nugent, telling of an "increase in my disorder." Nugent died on Nov. 12.

temptuous treatment he has given the addresses and proclamations; things meant perhaps to encourage friends and deter foes, but whose base ground and absurd superstructure makes their framers a little ashamed when they are confronted by men able and not afraid to avow a cause founded in justice and truth. I suppose you have seen the Protest, and Lord Thanet's name to it;[22] and it will strike you as a strange thing that Burgoyne should have cited him as an approver of the measures against America. Today Edmund meant to have made his motion; which he had last week announced, for a conciliation; a question upon a Scotch petition accidentally came on, and he did not choose to begin his business at 8 o'clock, so he put it off till Monday. Charles Fox's return too not being ready, made him the more willing to postpone it. I suppose you know that Charles's carelessness in the arrangement of his pension exposed him to doubts upon the legality of his seat; it was adjusted by his vacating for the Chiltern Hundred, leaving the other question open and undecided, and making the vacancy for the Hundred involving in it all the causes of vacating.[23] Ned's object is by act of Parliament to repeal the obnoxious acts, and replace things as nearly as they ought to be to 1763. I don't believe I shall be able to give you any idea of the Tuesday's debate, for not a creature was admitted today, while Ned's question was expected. The line the Duke of Grafton took the first day of the session you have heard; he has uniformly and manfully opposed them ever since. His friends have resigned, and he is succeeded by Lord Dartmouth who is succeeded by Lord George Germain.[24]

Lord Rochford [25] has retired upon a pension of £2000 per annum and the blue ribband, and is succeeded by Lord

---

[22] The protest of a group of peers, including Sackville Tufton, eighth Earl of Thanet, against the address of the lords in support of the ministry.

[23] Lord North had written to Blaquiere on Sept. 19: "I suppose you have heard of Mr. Fox's difficulty about his pension. . . . In truth I believe he is utterly disqualified from sitting in parliament by his acceptance of the pension. This you will keep secret, for, though I fear it will be known, it ought not to be known by you or me."—Lecky, W. E. H., *History of England in the eighteenth century* 4: 426, London, Longmans, Green & Co., 1882. The pension, which had been authorized on Aug. 22, was now surrendered. See pension lists in *Journal of the House of Commons . . . Ireland* 17: 120; 18: 80.

[24] Grafton resigned the privy seal, which was given to Dartmouth, who was succeeded by Germain as Secretary of State for the Colonies.

[25] William Henry Nassau Zuylestein (1717-1781), fourth Earl of Rochford, had held the seals for the southern department since Dec., 1770.

Weymouth, who must have been somehow urgently pressed to
take an office of business, as it is called, and which in truth does
require a man some times to be up by 2 or 3 o'clock. Lord
Ashburnham succeeds him as Groom of the Stole and Lord
Pelham [26] him in the Wardrobe, and is himself succeeded in
the office of Justice in Eyre by Lord Lyttelton. This wretched
man has divided with and against, against and with Administration, in the American questions. He is wise to accept their
offer, for his voice did not gain him a salute from any man in
opposition when he voted with them; but their wisdom in
buying him is not great.[27] But I suppose they meant to save
appearances by leaving nothing empty. Germain American
Minister and Weymouth *malgre lui* Secretary of State does
not look like the system that is to stand, and yet it may; but
these things may make the wavering wander, and the weak
go astray. Then too Lyttelton more than cost them in shame
what he brings in his talking, and I would not affect, among
all the dirt one sees, to say they could be hurt by the shame of
any associate in the House except Lyttelton; and I do assure,
bad and profligate as the times are, men are ashamed of him.
Men are not afraid of showing their contempt of one who will
not resent it, so that the very baseness of the times assists the
world in their disrespect of this one bad fellow.

There is no explaining to you the contempt that the address and proclamation are treated with in both Houses, and
withal their arrangements the Ministry show no heart; and it
is yet to be seen how this *divisum imperium* of 1st Lord of
the Treasury and Secretary of State will accord, or how this
new Colony War Minister will be received in the House. The
very bringing him there implies a doubt of North's firmness;
indeed his pro and con declarations don't leave a doubt.
Whether the exertions of Germain will answer and make up
their doubts, time will show, and tho' I don't know that time
will effect any right change, I do believe time will teach them
that their madness is impracticable. It is on Monday next
Edmund brings on his motion, unless a sort of wish that the

---

[26] Thomas Pelham (1728-1801), Baron Pelham of Stanmer.

[27] Thomas, second Baron Lyttelton (1744-1779) was known as "the wicked
Lord Lyttelton." He was the only son of Lord George Lyttelton, and "his
character was uncommonly odious and profligate, and his life a grievous
mortification to his father."—Walpole, *Memoirs* 3: 146.

new Colony Secretary Germain should be present to oppose him, induces him to postpone it, for another week.[28]

I heartily hope that your spirits are good enough to go through this long and idle sketch of our confusions. My best regards attend Charles, and that of all the house are with me—Adieu.

O'HARA TO WILLIAM BURKE, November 18, 1775

My dear Will,

Your letter was welcome, and tho' Edmund should have made you write it, the obligation is not less pleasant for his share in it. I wonder how either of you can find time to write, for I believe you have little more leisure than he has.

The new arrangement was not new to us here; we had all but Lord Lyttelton a week before it transpired in London. What a strange thing for Lord George Germain at sixty years of age to embark in such an undertaking! But as his resolution is not to hold it longer than he retains his power over the other offices, I think he'll soon retire. Edmund was quite right in putting off his motion till his Lordship could attend. But I was before, and shall be again much surprised at their not calling upon Edmund to state to the House his reasons for believing that the Americans would be satisfied in case the acts since 1763 were all repealed. 'Tis upon the whole a troublesome piece of business, and will be the cause of shedding some blood at home as well as abroad.

Never was so strange a piece of work as the plot. Great matters were expected from it. They have all failed, and even the ridicule of the thing has died away.[29] The Duke of Grafton

---

[28] Not until Thursday, Nov. 16 (the first day Germain appeared in the house) did Burke ask leave to bring in a bill "for composing the present troubles, and quieting the minds of his majesty's subjects in America." He proposed to repeal all acts offensive to the Americans, renounce parliamentary taxation of them, recognize the American Congress, and pardon all Americans who had taken part in the rebellion. The house divided against Burke, 210 to 105.— *Parliamentary history* 18: 963-994.

[29] The alleged plot by pro-Americans to seize the King at the opening of Parliament. The only man arrested was a Mr. Sayer, a banker, who was soon released. In his letter of Oct. 30 to Dr. Nugent, O'Hara said he had read in a newspaper that Burke had visited Sayer in the Tower; and he feared such conduct would be dangerous and discreditable to Burke, who "has got much too high in the world to turn visits of that kind to any purpose."

has acted sensibly, Lord Rochford more so. The last I believe will come to us. I shall send your letter presently to Ridge, who between the influenza and business can't come near me. He does indeed labour hard. I could not have hoped that my old friend should escape an epidemic cold, who has one of course almost every winter, but I trust in God he has got over it by this time. He has been of great service to me in my illness; for tho' his advice and Doctor Quin's have little differed, yet my confidence in the first added to the effect of recipe. 'Tis very odd he should have known that ice would agree with my stomach; 'tis the thing in the world I long for most, but can't get. Upon the whole my recovery advances so uniformly, that I hope to see you as soon as the weather will allow an invalid to travel. Our little parliamentary business is almost over, not much in profit, still less to the honour of this country.[30] Meanness and corruption are as rife as the influenza. Charles joins in compliments to you all. Adieu.

WILLIAM BURKE TO O'HARA, December 17, 1775

My dear Sir,

I have time but for a word—our Saturday's *Gazette* [31] announced Carleton's march somewhat pompously as out of doubt to defeat the rebel invaders before St. John's, who the Gazette assured us could not stand as want of provision and desertions had already distressed them.[32] So! Great the danger of talking nonsense and lies of a Saturday night—the Sunday morning brought accounts from Gov. Tryon to the Government that Chamblix fort was taken the end of October, that on the 2nd of November Carleton was repulsed by a detachment of Montgomery's called the Green Mountain Boys. Carleton has lost but about twenty killed and fifty prisoners. Carleton is certainly a brave man and this loss as a positive loss could not have made him retreat, but whatever the relative loss was, he

---

[30] The principal business was authorizing the crown to send 4,000 troops from Ireland to other parts of the empire, at the expense of the British government. The house of commons agreed to this on Nov. 27 by 103 to 58.—*Journal* 17: 205, 208.

[31] *The London Gazette*, Dec. 16, which establishes the date of the letter.

[32] Sir Guy Carleton (1724-1808), Governor General of Quebec, attempted to defend Montreal against the advance of the American forces under Brigadier General Richard Montgomery; Montreal fell to them in mid-November.

felt it, and retreated, and St. John's surrendered the 3rd of November, 6000 prisoners of war,[33] with cannon, etc. etc. etc. The capitulation granted carries an air of the gentleman about it, that does honour to Montgomery, who is an Irishman.[34] The *London Evening [Post]* which will probably have the packets, shall doubtless go to you tomorrow night. In the mean time take this sketch. Thanks to our dear Charles for his last, and for every thing he does. Adieu. Poor Richard Sr. has an heavy cold. The rest are well. The young one came to us this instant. Send this to Ridge unless all Irishmen are so devoted to slavery as to be shocked at the generous start of a noble nation.

[A short note written on almost the last day of the fateful year of 1775 appears to be the last letter O'Hara wrote to any one of the Burkes.]

O'HARA TO EDMUND BURKE, December 29, 1775

Dublin 29 December 1775

My dear Edmund,

It was formerly your disposition to be civil to your Irish acquaintances when you met them in London. And I just mean this to let you know that the Provost sailed this morning, and will stay but a few days in London. You will hear of him at the St. James's Coffee House: and finding him quickly, will look as if the magnitude of the event has published it. He goes over on an appeal, but without any aversion to a little political intrigue: and Ireland is at present a subject of importance, if they should dissolve the Parliament next month; a thing solicited by Pery to obtain the chair in a new one, and so drop most of the bills gone over, and going. It may make some entertaining confusion, with the 4,000 from our establishment, and the introduction of 4,000 foreign troops etc. etc. The Provost will explain all to you. My compliments to Mrs. Burke, most truly yours,

C OH

---

[33] The number was 600, not 6,000.

[34] Montgomery was born in Ireland and served with Wolfe's army at the capture of Quebec in 1759; his brother Alexander Montgomery was at this time a member of the Irish Parliament.

[If O'Hara's information provided Burke with any grounds for hoping that some sort of opposition concert might be formed with the politically powerful Provost of Trinity College, who had not yet given his support to the Irish Government's cooperation with Great Britain against America, such grounds quickly dissolved.]

BURKE TO O'HARA, January 7, 1776

My dear friend,

A letter from you, written with a good firm hand, in spirits, and without a word concerning your health, makes me as happy as anything could do, except your making one among us in this snowy season, round our fire of old wood. My friendships, and with them all my satisfactions, are narrowing and concentering very fast. The few which remain grow infinitely the more important.

I thank you heartily for your advice about Hutchinson. It was conceived with your usual judgment and sagacity. I followed it punctually; beginning with a letter to him and announcing a visit. It was taken with all possible kindness, which is expressed in a letter I received from him this morning. He tells me he is come over on a lawsuit of his own; whether his own as Provost, or as Controller of Strangford, or as plain Hely Hutchinson, or in which of his characters public or private, I know not. But a man who has a great many things that are valuable, has a great many parts on which he may be attacked. When I heard of his arrival I rather thought he intended to enlarge his possessions by political negotiation, than to protect any of his old acquisitions by law. He was squeamish at the beginning of the session; but he begins I hear to be a little mended in his appetite since. How comes it? How does he arrange with Flood? If they did not love one another as opponents, they will love still less as friends and colleagues. These are a sort of pigs that do not credit the old proverb of "love by *pigging*." As to your general politics in Ireland, they are so sublimely profound, there is such a grandeur of meanness in them, that they pass my expression and indeed my comprehension. Passiveness and servility seem to be natural companions just as violence and tyranny. Our conduct to America, though wicked and foolish, yet is natural wickedness and folly; yours is a species of turpitude not decent to name. Your conduct has this aggravation in it, that you had a part assigned you by Providence to act, that rarely, if ever, happens to a nation, rarely indeed to mankind; you were in the situation, in which you might act as the guardian angels of the whole Empire; and without hazard, or danger, or scarcely trouble, have appeared in mediatorial character of the utmost dignity and benevolence; and with all certainty, at once have secured your own liberties and given peace to our general country. I know, that things have often hung in so even a balance (and they so hung until very lately) that the least movement on the part of Ireland would have decided in favour of peace. I say I know it; and speak from certain observation, and not loose conjecture. Indeed a refusal on your part to be active in the war or to approve it would have been sufficient. Things are run so near, that without the four thousand men you so handsomely take from defence to lend to oppression, the war would in all human probability expire from want of fuel to feed it. What surprises me the most, is the language of your minority. If Mr. Hussey's speech is rightly represented in the news paper, he stated himself as in a difficult dilemma—either to do a wrong thing, or offend a nation too strong for you to contend with. If that be the case, you never can exercise your own rights without fear of offence. But the time chosen for this terror is very extraordinary—a time, in my opinion, when the weakness of this country, in point of power and of intellect to guide it, is more truly an object of pity. I remember that Ireland was capable of making a troublesome, petulant, and obstinate opposition to England, when in the zenith of her power, and that too for things of doubtful right and certain insignificance; but she is now afraid not to be active; and to ruin herself in endeavours fundamentally to destroy everything like liberty in the dependencies of this Kingdom, in a conjuncture wherein our malice and strength are so totally disproportionate to each other. You will forgive me for speaking so freely of the place where we were born; but I must give myself a little vent. It is not often that I do it, or with such warmth.

As to America—what will happen to her God knows. She is acting a part of the utmost magnanimity under every disadvantage, (except the distance of her enemy) that can be imagined. I think their constancy will be proof against the burning of their towns and ships, and the barbarous waste which the Ministry meditate on their sea coast. It is not the fault of that Ministry, that at this hour the slaves are not cutting the throats of their masters, the savages massacring all on their frontier, and the Russian Tartars making their usual devastation of all our hopeful plantations.[35] I look on that people as alienated for ever—let the event of the war be what it may. The greatest difficulty the provincials labour under is the want of gunpowder. Habituated as they have always been to supplies from abroad of everything, they have not been as diligent in establishing manufactures of military stores as their situation necessarily requires. In the meantime Ministry goes on just as before. Lord George Germain's coming in rather heartens them in the course they meant before to pursue than produces any alteration either in the *resolution* to hostility or to the mode of it. They had resolved before he came in on a divided and piratical war.[36] They persevere in it. Before he came in, they would make any submission, never so base, to the Americans, provided they would trust this Ministry enough to accept their humiliation; they would still do it. His being brought in rather shows the plan than makes it. He has scarcely said anything in the House since he got the seals. He is remarkably reserved. Some of the pifflemen have let fly at him, in such a manner, that the soberer part of us scarcely knew how to look whilst it was going on.

There is scarcely anything in history that exceeds the march of Arnold into Canada and his passing the River St. Lawrence in defiance of so many armed vessels.[37] This is the person that our wise *Gazette* qualifies with the contemptuous appellation of *one* Arnold. Indeed they are in the right, they have *few* such.

The people begin somewhat to feel the loss of America, and the charge at which they lose it. But those who used to be most troublesome and loquacious, the merchants, are very well

---

[35] The government was attempting to hire Russian soldiers for use in America.—W. Eden to Lord G. Germain, Oct. 21, 1775, Hist. MSS. Com., *Report on the manuscripts of Mrs. Stopford-Sackville* **2**: 12, London, H. M. Stat. Office, 1910.

[36] To conciliate some colonists and distress others: a strategy of negotiation and war which Burke in his speech of Nov. 16 called "a mixture of war and treaty," and to which he could see no end, but in the ruin of the empire.

[37] Benedict Arnold's expedition through the Maine wilderness to Quebec; he crossed the St. Lawrence on Nov. 13, and then joined Montgomery for the attack on the city.

satisfied, whatever the manufacturers suffer. The immense number of transports taken up, and all the charges of a war, supply to the most powerful of them most abundantly the loss of trade. Besides the West Indies being now to be supplied wholly from Europe has opened a new channel of trade which keeps many busy and in heart. The suffering of the West India planters, who have already several of their articles enhanced cent per cent is their gain.

My dear friend, adieu. Salute our Ridge and our Charles. All of us that are left are yours most cordially.

January 7. 1775

Charles wished to see what I said on my motion.[38] I have made several memoranda since I came down, as well as while the thing was most fresh. But till the session is over I cannot do it completely. I rather think it was my best in that way of proposition.

[The above letter may have been the last that went from Burke to Charles O'Hara, who died in Dublin on February 3 and was buried in St. Anne's churchyard.

Death, which had claimed Dr. Nugent the previous November, would carry off John Ridge in March, 1776. The next year Will Burke, despairing of politics and a profitable career in England, went out to India in hopes of acquiring the fortune that Richard had failed to gain in the West Indies. The fireside group, along with the British empire, was disintegrating. Privately and publicly, Edmund Burke's life was in a major transition.

Burke-O'Hara family links were not, however, completely broken. At Annaghmore there are several letters written by Burke to Charles O'Hara the younger in the 1780's, which reveal an affectionate contact. Together they stood in some sort of trustee or guardian relationship to certain young people named Ridge, children or grandchildren of their deceased friend. The younger Charles O'Hara entered the Irish House of Commons in 1780, and after the union of 1800 was a member of the British Parliament until his death in 1822. When Burke's son, Richard, went to Ireland in 1791 to act as secretary and agent for the Irish Catholics who were seeking removal of their civil and political disabilities, Charles O'Hara gave active and sympathetic support to that effort in the Parliament.]

---

[38] Probably, that of Nov. 16.

References for Part I

ABBOTT, W. C. 1929. New York in the American Revolution. New York, Scribner.

ALBEMARLE, GEORGE THOMAS, EARL OF. 1852. Memoirs of the Marquess of Rockingham and his Contemporaries, 2 v. London, Richard Bentley.

ALEXANDER, E. P. 1939. A revolutionary conservative, James Duane of New York. New York, Columbia Univ. Press.

Annaghmore MSS. Letters of Edmund, William, and Richard Burke to Charles O'Hara, owned by Mr. D. F. O'Hara.

The Annual Register. 1758-1767. London, Dodsley.

APPLETON, MARGUERITE. 1933. The agents of the New England colonies in the revolutionary period. *New Eng. Quart.* **6:** 371-387.

BASYE, ARTHUR H. 1926. The Lords Commissioners of Trade and Plantations, 1748-1782. New Haven, Yale Univ. Press.

BECKER, CARL. 1909. History of political parties in the province of New York, 1760-1776. Madison, *Bull. Univ. of Wis.* **286.**

BOND, BEVERLY. 1930. The colonial agent as a popular representative. *Pol. Sci. Quart.* **35:** 372-392.

Board of Trade. Journal of the Commissioners for Trade and Plantations from January, 1768 to December, 1775. 1937. London, H. M. Stationery Office.

BORAN, MOTHER M. CONSILIA. 1954. William Dowdeswell and the Rockingham Whigs. New York, Fordham Univ. Dissertation.

BURKE. 1815-1827. Works of the right honourable Edmund Burke. 16 v. London, Rivington.

————— 1816. Speeches of the right honourable Edmund Burke in the House of Commons and in Westminster Hall. London, Longmans, Hurst.

BURKE, WILLIAM, and EDMUND BURKE. 1757. European settlements in America. 2 v. London, Dodsley.

BURNS, JAMES J. 1935. The colonial agents of New England. Washington, Catholic Univ. Dissertation.

CHALMERS. George Chalmers MSS, New York Public Library.

CLARKE, M. P. 1911. The Board of Trade at work. *Amer. Hist. Rev.* **17:** 17-43.

COBBETT, WILLIAM, and J. WRIGHT. 1806-1820. Parliamentary history of England. 36 v. London, Hansard.

COLDEN, CADWALLADER. 1877-1878. Colden letter-books. 2 v. *N. Y. Hist. Soc. Coll.*

————— 1918-1937. Letters and papers of Cadwallader Colden. 9 v. New York, *N. Y. Hist. Soc. Coll.*

Commerce of Rhode Island. 1914. 2 v. Boston, *Mass. Hist. Soc. Coll.* 7th ser. **9.**

COPELAND, THOMAS W. 1939. Burke and Dodsley's Annual Register. *Pub. Mod. Lang. Asso.* **54:** 223-245.

————— 1949. Our eminent Friend, Edmund Burke. New Haven, Yale Univ. Press.

————— 1952. Burke's first patron. *History Today* **6:** 394-399.

Dartmouth. Manuscripts of the Earl of Dartmouth. 1887. Hist. MSS. Comm. 11th Rep. App. Pt. V. London, H. M. Stationery Office.
——— 1895. Manuscripts of the Earl of Dartmouth. Hist. MSS. Comm. 14th Rep. App. Pt. X. London, H. M. Stationery Office.

Delancey. William H. Delancey Papers. Library of Museum of City of New York.

Dickerson, Oliver M. 1951. The Navigation Acts and the American Revolution. Philadelphia, Univ. of Penna. Press.

Dictionary of American Biography. 1928-1937. 22 v. New York, Scribners.

Dictionary of National Biography. 1908-1909. London, Oxford U. Press.

Dowdeswell. William Dowdeswell MSS. W. L. Clements Library, Ann Arbor.

Duane. James Duane MSS. Library of N. Y. Historical Society.

Evans, Charles. 1941-1942. American bibliography. 12 v. N. Y., Peter Smith.

Fitzwilliam, Charles William, Earl, and Sir Richard Bourke, eds. 1844. Correspondence of the right honourable Edmund Burke. 4 v. London, Rivington.

Fitzmaurice, Lord Edmond. 1875-1876. Life of William, Earl of Shelburne. 2 v. London, Macmillan.

Flick, Alexander C. 1901. Loyalism in New York during the American Revolution. N. Y., Columbia Univ. Press.

Fortescue, Sir John, ed. 1927-1928. Correspondence of King George the Third from 1760 to December 1783. 6 v. London, Macmillan.

Freiberg, Malcolm. 1948. William Bollan, agent of Massachusetts. *More Books, Bull. of Boston Pub. Lib.* 23: 43-54, 90-100, 135-146, 168-182, 212-220.

Gipson, Lawrence Henry. 1936. The British Empire in North America before the American Revolution 1. 8 v. Caldwell, Caxton—N. Y., Knopf (1936-1954).

Grant, W. L. and James Munro, eds. 1908-1912. Acts of the Privy Council, colonial series. 6 v. London, Wyman & Sons.

Guttridge, George H. 1934. The American correspondence of a Bristol Merchant 1766-1776. Berkeley, Univ. of Calif. Press.
——— 1942. English Whiggism and the American Revolution. Berkeley, Univ. of Calif. Press.

Hamm, M. A. 1902. Famous families of New York. 2 v. N. Y. Putnam.

Hardwicke MSS. 35424. British Museum.

House of Commons Journals 30, 31, 34.

Hutchinson, John Hely. 1891. Letters and papers: Donoughmore MSS. Hist. MSS. Comm. 12th Rep. App. Pt. IX.

Johnson, Sir William. 1921-1939. Papers of Sir William Johnson. 9 v. Albany, N. Y. Division of Archives and History.

Jones, Thomas. 1879. History of New York during the revolutionary era. 2 v. N. Y., N. Y. Historical Society.

Lee, Charles. 1871-1874. Letters and papers of General Charles Lee. 4 v. N. Y. *N. Y. Hist. Soc. Coll.*

Lilly, Edward P. 1936. The colonial agents of New York and New Jersey. Washington, Catholic Univ. Press.

Lossing, B. J. 1873. Life and Times of Philip Schuyler. 2 v. N. Y., Sheldon.

Livingston, E. B. 1910. The Livingstons of Livingston Manor. N. Y., Knickerbocker Press.

Macaulay, Catherine Graham. 1770. Observations on a pamphlet, entitled Thoughts on the cause of the present discontents. London, Dilly.

MACKNIGHT, THOMAS. 1858-1860. Life and times of Edmund Burke. 3 v. London, Chapman & Hall.

MILLER, JOHN C. 1943. Origins of the American Revolution. Boston, Little, Brown & Co.

MURRAY, ROBERT H. 1931. Edmund Burke, a biography. Oxford Univ. Press.

New York, colony of. 1764-1766. Journal of the votes and proceedings of the general assembly of the colony of New York from 1691 to 1765. 2 v. N. Y., Hugh Gaine.

———— Journal of votes and proceedings, Oct. 27, 1768-Jan. 2, 1769; April 4-May 17, 1769; Nov. 21, 1769-Jan. 27, 1770; Dec. 11, 1770-March 4, 1771; Jan. 7, 1772-March 24, 1772; Jan. 5, 1773-March 8, 1773; Jan. 6, 1774-March 19, 1774; Jan. 10-April 3, 1775. N. Y., Hugh Gaine.

———— 1861. Journal of the legislative council of the colony of New York 2. 2 v. Albany.

———— 1894. The colonial laws of New York from the year 1664 to the revolution. 5 v. Albany, J. B. Lyon.

New York Gazette and Weekly Postboy.

New York Journal

Newcastle papers. Add. MSS 32974. British Museum.

O'CALLAGHAN, E. B., ed. 1849-1851. Documentary history of the state of New York. 4 v. Albany, Weed, Parsons & Co.

————1856-1887. Documents relative to the colonial history of the state of New York. 15 v. Albany, Weed, Parsons & Co.

———— 1866. Calendar of historical manuscripts in the office of the Secretary of State. 2 v. Albany, Weed, Parsons & Co.

PARES, RICHARD. 1953. King George III and the politicians. Oxford, Clarendon Press.

PENSON, LILLIAN M. 1924. The colonial agents in the British West Indies. London, Univ. of London Press.

PRIOR, SIR JAMES. 1878. Life of the right honourable Edmund Burke. 5th ed., London, G. Bell.

RITCHESON, C. R. 1952. The elder Pitt and an American department. *Amer. Hist. Rev.* 57: 376-383.

———— 1954. British politics and the American revolution. Norman, Univ. of Okla. Press.

Rivington's New York Gazetteer.

RYERSON, EGERTON. 1880. The loyalists of America. 2 v. Toronto, Briggs.

SABINE, LORENZO. 1864. Biographical sketches of loyalists in the American Revolution. 2 v. Boston, Little, Brown.

SCHLESINGER, A. N. 1918. The colonial merchants and the American revolution. N. Y., Col. Univ. Press.

SCHUYLER. Letters and papers of General Philip Schuyler. N. Y. Public Library.

SMITH, WILLIAM. MS. Diary. N. Y. Public Library.

SMITH, W. J., ed. 1852-1853. Grenville Papers: being the correspondence of Richard Grenville, Earl Temple, K. G., and the right honourable George Grenville, their friends and contemporaries. 4 v. London, J. Murray.

SMYTH, ALBERT HENRY. 1905-1907. The writings of Benjamin Franklin. 10 v. N. Y., Macmillan.

SPARKS, JARED. 1832. The life of Gouverneur Morris. 3 v. Boston, Gray & Bowman

SPECTOR, MARGARET M. 1940. The American Department of the British Government, 1768-1782. N. Y., Columbia Univ. Press.

STEBBINS, CALVIN. 1903. Edmund Burke, his services as agent to the province of New York. *Proc. Amer. Ant. Soc.* (n.s.) **9:** 88-101.

STEVENS, JOHN AUSTIN. 1865. Letter of Mr. John Austin Stevens, Jr., Secretary of the Chamber of Commerce of the state of New York, accompanying the portrait of Mr. John Cruger, first president of the Chamber, on its organization in 1768. *Pamphlet Publications*, N. Y. Chamber of Commerce.

STORY, D. A. 1931. The Delanceys. London, T. Nelson & Sons.

SUTHERLAND, LUCY S. 1932. Edmund Burke and the first Rockingham administration. *Eng. Hist. Rev.* **47:** 46-72.

———— 1952. The East India Company in eighteenth-century politics. Oxford, Clarendon Press.

TANNER, E. P. 1901. Colonial agencies in England during the eighteenth century. *Pol. Sci. Quart.* **14:** 22-48.

TAYLOR, W. S., and J. H. PRINGLE. 1838-1840. Correspondence of William Pitt, Earl of Chatham. 4 v. London, J. Murray.

TINKER, C. B., ed. 1924. The letters of James Boswell. 2 v. Oxford, Clarendon Press.

TOWNSHEND, CHARLES. MS. letters to Dr. Richard Brocklesby and unidentified other persons. W. L. Clements Library, Ann Arbor.

Trumbull Papers. 1885. Boston, *Mass. Hist. Coll.,* 5th series 9.

VAN DOREN, CARL. 1947. Letters and papers of Benjamin Franklin and Richard Jackson. Philadelphia, *Amer. Philos. Soc. Memoirs* 24.

VAN SCHAAK, H. C. 1852. Life of Peter Van Schaak. N. Y., Appleton.

———— 1859. Henry Cruger, the colleague of Edmund Burke in the British Parliament. N. Y., C. Benjamin Richardson.

WALPOLE, HORACE. 1894. Memoirs of the Reign of George III. (G. F. R. Barker, ed.) 4 v. N. Y., Putnam.

———— 1910. Last journals of Horace Walpole during the reign of George III. (A. F. Stewart, ed.) 2 v. London, Richard Bentley.

WEARE, G. E. 1894. Edmund Burke's connection with Bristol. Bristol, William Bennett.

WECTER, DIXON. 1939. Edmund Burke and his kinsmen. Boulder, *Univ. of Colo. Studies.*

———— 1939-1940. Burke, Franklin, and Samuel Petrie. *Hunt. Lib. Quart.* **3:** 315-338.

Wentworth-Fitzwilliam MSS. Sheffield Central Library.

WERTENBAKER, T. J. 1948. Father Knickerbocker rebels: New York city during the Revolution. N. Y., Scribner.

WOLFF, MABEL W. 1933. The colonial agency of Pennsylvania, 1712-1757. Philadelphia, privately printed Bryn Mawr dissertation.

WRIGHT, J., ed. 1839. Sir Henry Cavendish's debates of the House of Commons in the year 1774 on the bill for making more effectual provision for the government of the province of Quebec. London, Longmans.

———— 1841. Sir Henry Cavendish's debates of the House of Commons during the thirteenth Parliament of Great Britain. 2 v. London, Longmans.

YOSHIPE, HARRY. 1936. The Delancey estate. *New York History* **7:** 167-169.

INDEX